FINANCIAL ACCOUNTING

FINANCIAL ACCOUNTING
Concepts and Uses

SECOND EDITION

Rudolph W. Schattke
Howard G. Jensen

University of Colorado

Allyn and Bacon, Inc.
Boston · London · Sydney · Toronto

Copyright © 1978 by Allyn and Bacon, Inc.

Copyright © 1974 by Allyn and Bacon, Inc., 470 Atlantic Avenue, Boston, Massachusetts 02210. All rights reserved. Printed in the United States of America. No part of the material protected by this copyright notice may be reproduced or utilized in any form or by any means, electronic or mechanical, including photocopying, recording, or by any information storage and retrieval system, without written permission from the copyright owner.

Library of Congress Cataloging in Publication Data

Schattke, Rudolph Walter.
   Financial accounting.

   Includes bibliographical references and index.
   1. Accounting. I. Jensen, Howard G., joint author.
II. Title.
HF5635.S3122   1978   657   77-20284
ISBN 0-205-05901-5

Second printing . . . December, 1978

Contents

Preface ix

PART I — THE FRAMEWORK OF FINANCIAL ACCOUNTING   1

1 Accounting in Modern Society   3

The Evolution of Accounting / The Role of Accounting Today / People in Accounting / Accounting and Bookkeeping / Purposes of the Business Enterprise / Forms of Business Enterprise / Introduction to Financial Accounting / Objectives of Financial Statements / Summary

2 The Statement of Financial Position   29

The Accounting Equation / Assets / Measurement of Assets / Liabilities / Owners' Equity / Statement of Financial Position Classifications / Balance Sheet—Content and Preparation / Some Important Concepts for Accounting / Asset Valuation and Income Determination / Summary

3 The Income Statement and the Statement of Changes in Financial Position   60

The Income Statement / The Statement of Retained Earnings / The Statement of Changes in Financial Position / Summary of Concepts of Financial Accounting / Summary

PART II — PROCESSING ACCOUNTING DATA   91

4 The Accounting Cycle: The Recording Process   93

Outputs / Inputs / Processing / Accounting Transactions / Ledgers / Journals / Posting / Trial Balance / Preparation of the Financial Statements / Merchandising Transactions / Accounting for Purchases of Merchandise / Summary

Contents

5 Adjusting Entries: Completion of the Accounting Cycle 124

Accrued Expenses / Accrued Revenues / Unearned Revenues, or Collections in Advance / Prepaid Expenses / Depreciation, Amortization, and Depletion / Bad Debts / Merchandise Inventory / Statement Preparation / The Closing Process / Alternative Procedure / Post-closing Trial Balance / The Accounting Cycle / Summary / Appendix: The Worksheet

6 Processing Accounting Data 167

Information Needs / Source Documents: Inputs of the Data Processing System / Processing Data Manually / Journals / Subsidiary Ledgers / Limitations of Manual Data Processing / Electronic Data Processing (EDP) / Summary

PART III MEASUREMENT OF ASSETS, LIABILITIES, AND INCOME 201

7 Asset Valuation Concepts, Cash and Short-Term Receivables, and Revenues 203

Asset Valuation Concepts / Types of Assets / Cash / Accounts Receivable / Notes Receivable / Revenue Realization / Sales Controls / Summary / Appendix: Bank Reconciliations

8 Investments 239

Temporary Investments / Long-Term Investments / Summary / Appendix: Present Value

9 Inventories and Cost of Goods Sold Expense 271

Definitions and Objectives / Items Included in Inventory / Cost of Inventory / Determination of Inventory Costs and Cost of Goods Sold / Costing Methods / Adjustments of Inventory Cost / Market Valuations / Inventory Errors / Control and Safeguarding of Inventory / Summary / Appendix: Perpetual Inventory Records

10 Property, Plant, and Equipment and Other Long-Lived Assets; Depreciation 303

Types of Long-Term Unexpired Costs / Measuring Cost / Subsequent Treatment of Unexpired Costs / Natural Resources / Property, Plant, and Equipment / Intangibles / Disposition of Long-Term Unexpired Costs / Long-Term Asset Problems / Presentation in Financial Statements / Summary

11 Liabilities 340

Short-Term Liabilities / Long-Term Liabilities / Other Liabilities / Summary

PART IV OWNERS' EQUITY 373

12 Stockholders' Equity 375

Rights of Stockholders / Classes of Capital Stock / Par Value and No-Par Value Stock / Accounting for the Issuance of Capital Stock / Subsequent Operations of Corporations / Comprehensive Stockholders' Equity Illustration / Summary

13 Consolidated Financial Statements and Business Combinations 405

Parent-Subsidiary Relationship / Criteria for Consolidated Statements / Consolidated Balance Sheet / Consolidated Income Statement / Limitations of Consolidated Statements / Business Combinations—Purchase Versus Pooling / Summary

14 Sole Proprietorships and Partnerships 429

Sole Proprietorships / Partnerships / Admission of New Partners / Dissolution of a Partnership / Converting a Partnership to a Corporation / Theoretical Issues / Partnership Form Versus Corporate Form / Summary

PART V ACCOUNTING THEORY AND ANALYSIS 451

15 Accounting and Changing Prices

Limitations of Historical Cost Valuation / General and Specific Price Changes / Alternative Valuation Approaches / General Price-Level Accounting / Summary

16 Accounting Theory: Importance, Development, and Prospects 484

Interested Parties: Needs and Pressures / Historical Development of Accounting Principles and Standards / Where Are We Now? / Where Are We Going? / Purposes and Objectives of Accounting / Financial Accounting Theory in Perspective / Summary of Financial Accounting Theory / Summary

17 **The Statement of Changes in Financial Position**   517

Resources, or Funds / Uses of the Statement of Changes / Resources Provided and Applied / Preparing the Statement of Changes / Complications in Preparing Statements of Changes / Summary / Appendix: The Statement of Cash Flows

18 **Analysis of Financial Statements**   549

Investors' Decisions / Analysis of Operating Results / Use and Quality of Assets / Analysis with a Creditor Emphasis / The Composite Picture / Beyond Financial Analysis / Overall Critique of Financial Analysis / Summary

APPENDIX A
Glossary   580

APPENDIX B
Solutions to Selected Problems   591

APPENDIX C
Present Value Tables   630

Index   633

Preface

Our intent in writing this book is not only to present traditional accounting but also to expose students to ideas, stimulate thought and discussion, and give students some insights into the excitement to be found in accounting today. The book reflects our belief that accounting produces information that is vital to the economic decisions of managers and investors and that such information is used most effectively by those who understood accounting measurements and their shortcomings.

ORGANIZATION

This book, organized into five parts, starts with a panoramic view of accounting, progresses to a consideration of accounting's detailed structure, and returns to a broad perspective of accounting. A three-chapter introduction to financial statements is given in Part I, "The Framework of Financial Accounting." Chapter 1 stresses the role and objectives of financial accounting, giving examples that help the beginning student appreciate the accountant's approach to measuring income and financial position. Chapter 2 discusses the statement of financial position, and chapter 3 covers the income statement and the statement of changes in financial position. Concepts underlying the statements are emphasized. Part I includes consideration of the effects of important economic events, so the student gains a realistic picture of accounting at an early stage. We believe that the emphasis on the end products of the financial accounting process provides a rationale for students beginning their study of accounting and prevents students from confusing *accounting* with *bookkeeping*. It is also an appropriate approach for the student who will be a user of accounting information rather than a professional accountant.

Chapters 4 and 5 of Part II ("Processing Accounting Data") contain a concise treatment of the accounting cycle. The accounting cycle is meaningful at this point because students are already aware of the objectives of accounting and the end product of accounting entries. Entries for both service and merchandising enterprises are introduced. The discussion of the recording of merchandise inventory in chapter 5 has been revised and improved for this edition. Chapter 5 also includes a brief appendix on the use of the worksheet. Special journals and subsidiary ledgers are explained and illustrated in chapter 6. In response to suggestions of users of the first edition, who felt that a full chapter on the computer was not warranted in an introductory text, materials on computerized accounting are included as part of chapter 6. This chapter can be treated briefly or omitted when there is limited time or a desire to avoid this aspect of the recording process.

Part III, "Measurement of Assets, Liabilities and Income," includes some noteworthy changes. Chapter 7 covers asset valuation concepts and cash and receivables, chapter 8 is devoted to investments, both temporary and long-term. The discussion of temporary investments emphasizes the short-term instruments commonly used by business firms, including U.S. Treasury Bills and certificates of deposit. The discussion of equity investments includes the equity method and recent official pronouncements by the Accounting Principles Board and the Financial Accounting Standards Board. An appendix to chapter 8 gives a brief exposition of present value. Chapters 9 and 10 cover short-term and long-term unexpired costs. Inventories and cost of goods sold expense are presented in chapter 9, followed by property, plant, and equipment; intangibles; and depreciation in chapter 10. Finally, short-term and long-term liabilities are covered in chapter 11. Throughout Part III the emphasis is on the relationship of assets and liabilities to revenues and expenses. The problems presented by inflation are succinctly covered. This edition includes expanded coverage of present value in connection with receivables, investments, and liabilities.

In Part IV, owners' equity is treated. Chapter 12, "Stockholders' Equity," includes basic coverage of the nature of equity ownership and related accounting issues and a concise treatment of earnings per share. The EPS coverage is a new feature of this edition. (EPS is also picked up in chapter 18, "Analysis of Financial Statements.") Chapter 13, "Consolidated Financial Statements and Business Combinations," and chapter 14, "Sole Proprietorships and Partnerships," conclude Part IV. Chapters 13 and 14 can be omitted if there are time constraints.

The text ends with Part V, "Accounting Theory and Analysis." Chapter 15, "Accounting and Changing Prices," is a new chapter. It is an elementary but thoroughly up-to-date discussion of current proposals for dealing with specific and general price changes. The usefulness of the different approaches is stressed. Chapter 16, on accounting theory, emphasizes the environment of accounting and the influences of authoritative bodies such as the Financial Accounting Standards Board on accounting. The statement of changes in financial position is covered in chapter 17. Cash flow statements have been included in an appendix to the chapter rather than in the main body of the chapter. Chapter 18, "Analysis of

Financial Statements," includes a discussion of analysis in a time of rapid price changes. The purpose of Part V is to help students integrate their understanding of accounting. Chapter 18 can be omitted when time constraints exist.

New to this edition, at the end of the book, are three appendices. Appendix A is a glossary of important terms in financial accounting. Appendix B consists of solutions to selected problems. These solutions can be used by students to check their understanding of material presented in the chapters. Appendix C is a set of interest tables.

Each chapter of the book is followed by a list of important terms covered in the chapter. Discussion questions, short exercises that emphasize particular points, and problems are included at the end of each chapter. Care has been taken to assure that the problems are closely linked with the chapter materials to help the student develop a clear understanding of how concepts are applied. Many chapters include one or more case problems that require a thoughtful approach to lifelike situations.

The real value of a textbook is determined by its impact on the student. We are confident that a student who completes this book will have a good understanding of the purposes and objectives of accounting and an appreciation of accounting as a tool of investors and management in a time of change. Students who continue their studies in accounting will find that this volume provides a sound basis for their future accounting studies. All users can be assured of exposure to some of the *why* of accounting rather than just the *how* of accounting. The companion volume, *Managerial Accounting: Concepts* and *Uses*, can be used to complete coverage of basic accounting.

USE OF THE TEXT

This text is designed for use in a one-semester or two-quarter course in financial accounting. The text is designed to give instructors maximum flexibility in selecting financial accounting topics that fit the emphasis the instructors find most desirable within their particular time constraints. The chapters are arranged in the order favored by the authors. Some changes in that order are feasible. For example, chapter 17 could follow chapter 3 to introduce a complete consideration of the statement of changes in financial position early in the course. Chapter 15 could be brought in before chapter 7 to focus early attention on the problems of changing prices. Chapter 16 could be covered before chapter 4 if an early emphasis on accounting theory and the environment of accounting is desired. For a course with serious time limitations, all or parts of chapters 6, 13, 14, 15, 16, and 18 could be omitted without disturbing the sequence

Preface

of development. Several sample sequences are given in the instructors manual.

PRESSURE FOR CHANGE IN ACCOUNTING

As a consequence of the complex interactions of economic expansion, recession, and inflation, the adequacy of traditional accounting measurements has been questioned, and some changes have been made in accounting. The present outlook is for more change at an accelerated rate.

The current pressures for further change in accounting pose problems for text writers. How do we deal with changes that seem imminent? How do we deal with changes that have occurred but which may be highly technical in their application? We have tried to solve these problems by basing this revision on the broad underlying objectives and concepts that still form the foundation of accounting. Since we do not consider this foundation to be inviolate, our approach to the concepts is both expository and critical. We want to make students aware of how economic forces may affect accounting concepts. We also want to help them recognize the shortcomings of accounting measurements that ignore economic realities. After presenting and critically evaluating the underlying concepts of present accounting practice, we discuss alternatives to those practices. Accounting changes that have occurred are covered in an introductory fashion, without getting hopelessly bogged down in a morass of accounting technicalities.

ACKNOWLEDGMENTS

We are grateful to our professors, colleagues, and students for their influence in shaping this book. We thank the users of the previous edition for their helpful comments and criticisms. The help and encouragement of our editors, Larry Atkins, Mary Johnson, and John Peters, we gratefully acknowledge. All of these individuals have helped us improve the book.

At various stages in the development of the second edition, a number of dedicated teachers and scholars provided their advice and criticisms. We wish to mention their names and thank them for their comments. The shortcomings, errors, and omissions, which we trust are well hidden, are our own responsibility. Larry P. Bailey, Temple University; Keith Burdick, University of Wyoming; Rosita Chen, California State University at San Francisco; Louis S. Corsini, Boston College; Neil Dale, Mt. Hood Community College; Dale F. Falcinelli, Lafayette College; Sharron R. Hoffmans,

University of Texas at El Paso; Thomas E. King, University of Iowa; Daryl Lindsay, University of Minnesota; Frederick L. Neumann, University of Illinois at Urbana-Champaign; Charles R. Purdy, University of Minnesota; Philip P. Robbins, State University College at Oneonta; Timothy L. Ross, Bowling Green State University; D. Gerald Searfoss, Arizona State University; John R. Simon, Northern Illinois University; Mary J. Swanson, Bowling Green State University; Anita I. Tyra, Bellevue Community College; Anna M. Wagoner, Oregon State University; Thomas Weirich, Central Michigan University.

PART I

The Framework of Financial Accounting

1

Accounting in Modern Society

Accounting plays an important role in today's society. It provides information vital to economic decisions. These decisions range from (1) individual choices about an immediate course of action to (2) business judgments that determine the future profitability of a company to (3) economic policy determinations by Congress that affect the well-being of each one of us.

Accounting is defined as the activity of providing quantitative information, mainly financial in nature, that is intended to be useful in making economic decisions. The information supplied by accounting deals with an area of life that is important to almost every person and organization. In fact, many individuals and organizations find present-day accounting information indispensable. Large organizations cannot operate without it; accounting information is a necessary communicating device among various parts of the organization. For example, the J. C. Penney Company needs accounting information on results of each store's operations in order to gauge the progress of each store, the effectiveness of advertising campaigns and company policies on a local level, and the efficiency of store managers. In addition, results from all stores must be totaled to provide information on total company operations. There is no way in which management can monitor the far-flung operations of the company personally.

In society as a whole, accounting information becomes more significant as our lives become more complex and more interactive. For example, more and more often in their attempts to deal with inflation, unemployment, energy crises, and all the other economic problems that beset us, Congress and the president have been using accounting information about companies and the economy as a whole. Thus, accounting data on retail sales and inventory fluctuations are used in deciding on appropriate

Accounting Defined

policies to stimulate a lagging economy, and data on oil company profits were a center of attention during the 1974–75 oil crisis. This increased use of accounting information is natural, because people and organizations must know more about what is happening in the economic sphere when their destinies are inextricably bound up with those of other individuals and organizations.

As an information gathering and disseminating device, accounting is in a strategic position in the modern world. The complexities of the changing world in which we operate make accounting a challenging field. Accounting is also a dynamic field, one which is constantly developing in a search for greater usefulness. This means that accountants cannot be satisfied with the status quo. They must continually adapt their work to the demands of society, or else they risk obsolescence.

To be able to appreciate the need for change and improvement in accounting, we must understand the nature of accounting information as it exists now. Accounting data produced today are being used effectively by individuals, businesses, and other organizations. The nature and content of current accounting information are discussed extensively in this book. This provides a foundation for appreciating the strengths and weaknesses of today's accounting methods and using accounting information intelligently.

Accounting embraces a wide spectrum of activity, ranging from routine record keeping to highly complex analysis. In this chapter we describe accounting and its role in our society. Toward the end of the chapter we look at the business enterprise and introduce financial accounting for business. This focus on financial accounting continues throughout the book.

THE EVOLUTION OF ACCOUNTING

Today, accounting information is a well-established feature of economic life. The present influential position of accounting is the result of a long, fascinating evolutionary process. It is useful to touch upon some of the highlights of that evolution.

Development to the 1930s

Accounting records have existed since ancient times. Simple accounting records are among the oldest written records of mankind. Simple records were sufficient for the simple economic interactions of ancient times, but the development of trade and the accompanying increased complexity of economic interactions led to the development of more sophisticated systems of accounting records. In the fourteenth and fifteenth centuries, as

Europe emerged from the Dark Ages and trade became more widespread, the need for accounting information that would tell merchants about the profitability of trading ventures led to formal systems of accounting. The structure of modern accounting emerged in the fifteenth century. The first known treatise on accounting, published in 1494, was written by an Italian mathematician and Franciscan monk, Fr. Luca Pacioli.

Pacioli

The accounting described by Pacioli proved to be surprisingly durable. Its simple structure remains the foundation of the complex accounting systems we know today. The accounting of Pacioli's time could be relatively simple because business enterprises were small and localized. The merchant-owner was close to the operations of the business and could check the accounting records whenever he chose. There was no need for the periodic accounting reports that characterize accounting information today.

Over the centuries since Pacioli, economic life has changed significantly. Beginning in the late nineteenth century, the single-owner enterprise gave way to the business corporation as the dominant factor in economic enterprise. The corporation is a legal entity, organized under the laws of a state, that has the ability to assemble large amounts of capital from investors. A single corporation may be huge and complex and have thousands of stockholders who have invested their capital funds in the enterprise. In many cases, those who invest in the corporation are far removed from its actual operations.

Rise of the corporation

The rise of the corporation to a position of dominance led to some far-reaching developments. Individuals generally needed financial information about companies in which they had invested or in which they were interested in investing. Generally, they wanted information about the profits of the company, since they made investments to earn a profit. And they wanted information about the ability of the company to pay its debts as they became due and thus have a continuing economic existence. Lending institutions such as banks needed accounting information about the security of the loans they were asked to make.

Lenders had a marked influence on the development of accounting. They demanded considerable accounting information, and companies generally provided it voluntarily. Investors, particularly the average investor, were less fortunate. Until the early 1930s the kind of accounting information made available to the typical investor was a matter of company discretion. Most companies attempted to provide useful data, but too often the information was fragmentary, and in many cases, no accounting information was given at all. Critics of the corporation denounced companies for their failure to give investors sufficient information to make rational investment decisions.[1]

---

1. See William Z. Ripley, *Main Street and Wall Street*, for a fascinating account of corporate conduct in the early twentieth century. (Lawrence: Scholars' Book Co.: 1972, originally published 1926.)

Accountants themselves were under continual pressure by lenders and the investment community to develop reliable and consistent financial information. The public accounting profession, composed of certified public accountants (CPAs), in particular, was enjoined to articulate consistent accounting principles that would be a guide to reliable and consistent financial measurements. Movements in developing accounting principles begun in the early years of the twentieth century were accelerated in the 1930s.

Developments from the 1930s to the Present

Congress passed the Securities Act of 1933 and the Securities Exchange Act of 1934 "to provide full and fair disclosure of the character of securities sold in interstate and foreign commerce...." The laws provide that the companies covered by the act (principally large corporations) must file annual reports with the Securities and Exchange Commission (SEC) and a registration statement covering securities to be offered for sale. The reports and statements must include financial information audited by an independent public accountant. The SEC, given authority to prescribe the detailed standards for the required financial information, asked the CPA profession to develop the standards. The CPA profession responded with well organized efforts designed to produce standards that would help accountants to develop reliable and consistent information.

In 1936 the American Institute of CPAs,[2] the national organization of CPAs, established a Committee on Accounting Procedure. This committee began publishing Accounting Research Bulletins in 1939. Each bulletin covered a particular accounting information problem and recommended a procedure for dealing with it. A successor organization, the Accounting Principles Board (APB), was formed in 1959 by the AICPA to hasten the progress toward a consistent set of generally accepted accounting principles. The board issued thirty-one APB Opinions and four Statements during its lifetime. CPAs had to follow pronouncements of the board. The pronouncements also were supported by the SEC and the stock exchanges and were followed by all large companies.

APB

In 1972, the APB was replaced by the Financial Accounting Standards Board (FASB), an independent, full-time board financed by contributions from business and from the accounting profession. From time to time, the board issues Statements of Financial Accounting Standards that deal with urgent accounting problems. These statements have the same support and authority that APB pronouncements enjoyed. The FASB has also given consideration to the broad conceptual framework underlying

FASB

---

2. Prior to 1957 the organization was named the American Institute of Accountants.

accounting. It remains to be seen whether the board will be successful in its efforts to develop consistent and useful accounting standards.

THE ROLE OF ACCOUNTING TODAY

Over the years, many people have been influential in shaping accounting. They include accountants, bankers, investors, company managers, and even members of Congress. Billions of dollars are spent each year to develop useful accounting information. *Useful to whom? To persons who make economic decisions about their own affairs or about the affairs of organizations in which they have an interest.* Probably, these statements about the usefulness of accounting information make little sense to the person beginning the study of accounting. Some examples may be helpful.

EXAMPLE 1-1

Gordon Lawson is considering purchase of a used car. He finds a 1965 Dodge that he can buy for $340. Insurance and licenses will cost $140 for the first half year. He has $100 cash but can only apply $80 of that to the car because he must retain some money for food. He can borrow the other $400 from the bank but must repay the total amount in two months. Since Gordon only makes $170 per month, he decides not to buy the car.

Example 1-1 illustrates the use of accounting information in a personal decision. No special accounting skills were needed to gather the economic information about Gordon's money and income. The accounting information was gathered by Gordon himself. Most people keep their own accounting records for most of their day-to-day needs and even for preparing their own income tax returns. Most personal financial decisions can be made on the basis of simple information such as bank balances and personal income figures. A person who has a complex financial problem probably will seek competent assistance.

This book does not cover personal accounting; rather, it focuses on the accounting needs of organizations, particularly those of the business enterprise. We are still concerned with people, but in their roles as owners, investors, creditors, or managers of an enterprise. Accounting information about a business firm usually cannot be produced by an untrained person. Even the business manager may lack the expert knowledge necessary to produce the information needed to manage the enterprise. Consider Example 1-2.

EXAMPLE 1-2

The Berry Electronic Company has been in business for a year. Don Berry, the president and principal owner, is pleased with the steady flow of customers into the store. He presumes that his first year of business was profit-

Example 1-2 (Cont.)

able. But he is shocked to discover that the cash in the bank is down to $100. Berry is extremely disappointed because he started the business with $6,000 in the bank. He wonders how the company could lose so much, because business seems to be so good. He asks a friend, Fred Furness, who is a CPA, whether the business is losing money and whether the business is going broke. Furness asks for all of the company's financial records for the year. In two days, Furness brings back the following reports.

BERRY ELECTRONIC COMPANY
Income Statement
for the Year Ended December 31, Year 1

Sales to customers		$85,200
Less cost of goods sold expense		44,700
Gross margin on goods sold		$40,500
Less operating expenses:		
Salaries of president and employee	$19,000	
Rent of building and equipment	6,000	
Advertising expense	6,000	
Utilities and telephone	1,800	
Supplies used	500	
Insurance and taxes	800	
Accounting fees	200	
Other expenses	200	
		34,500
Operating income		$ 6,000
Less income taxes		1,600
Net income		$ 4,400

BERRY ELECTRONIC COMPANY
Statement of Financial Position
December 31, Year 1

Assets		Equities	
		Liabilities:	
Cash	$ 100	Accounts payable	$ 3,000
Accounts receivable	2,500	Total liabilities	$ 3,000
Merchandise inventory	10,800		
Total assets	$13,400	Owners' equity:	
		Capital stock	$ 6,000
		Retained earnings	4,400
		Total owners' equity	$10,400
		Total liabilities and owners' equity	$13,400

Furness gives Mr. Berry the financial reports and confers with Berry about them. "You asked me whether your business was losing money and whether it was going broke. You also were concerned that your cash had fallen from $6,000 to $100. I used the data in your financial records to prepare two reports: the income statement for the year and the statement of financial position at year end. The income statement shows a net income for the year of $4,400, not a loss as you thought. Net income is much more than simply the change in cash during the year. Revenue includes all the sales you made, including sales to credit customers. You will notice that customers who bought from you during the year still owe you $2,500 (accounts receivable). Expenses include all of the costs you incurred to carry on your business. You will notice that some of the merchandise you bought during the year is still in your business as an asset. This merchandise inventory will not become an expense until it is sold next year. Furthermore, some of the assets and services acquired during the year have not been paid for. These debts to suppliers are the accounts payable. The primary reason for the cash decrease is the substantial investment in merchandise inventory on hand at the end of the year. Even though you still owe $3,000 to suppliers (accounts payable), a substantial amount of money had to be spent for merchandise; therefore, the money is not available in your bank account.

"The statement of financial position shows that the company is not going broke. The company has adequate assets to meet its liabilities. Of course, you probably should not let your cash balance get as low as $100.

"Overall, I'd say that your business is doing well. You as manager are getting a salary of $12,000. In addition, you make a profit of $4,400. Is that enough to warrant your staying in business? Here you must consider what you would earn with the money you might receive if you sold out and how much you could earn working for someone else."

Owner-managers

Example 1-2 illustrates accounting information that might be used by an owner-manager. Numerous small businesses are managed by their owners, who employ their own accountants or hire outside experts, such as a CPA, to help them get accounting information about their companies. The accounting information they prepare ought to help the owner-managers make decisions. The questions that Berry raised are examples of questions that may be answered with the help of accounting information. Of course, many factors enter into decisions, so we cannot expect accounting information alone to provide definitive answers. But we can expect the information to be an important, useful input in most economic decisions.

(The student beginning to study accounting probably finds the accounting information in Example 1-2 difficult to understand. That is to be expected. The statements shown, though simple, are not closely related to one's everyday experiences. Preparing financial statements of the type illustrated requires specialized knowledge and skills, which CPAs and other accountants acquire through training in a college accounting program and through experience. The purpose of this text is to give the student an introductory level of understanding of the accounting information found in financial statements.)

Investors

Owner-managers, such as Berry, are close to the day-by-day operation of their business and can get the accounting information they need directly from an accountant. But most owners and investors in corporations are far removed from the business firm in which they have an interest. Therefore, corporations send their stockholders and other interested persons annual and quarterly financial reports similar to, but more complex than, the reports of the Berry Electronic Company (Example 1-2). These financial reports are used extensively in economic decision making.

Internal management

Accounting information is also useful to those who manage business enterprises. The manager of a small enterprise may find that reports similar to those in Example 1-2 will suffice for his needs. Generally, such reports will be made on a monthly or a quarterly basis. In many businesses, it will be helpful for the accountant to produce income statements on the different departments of the small business. Larger enterprises generally will require much more accounting information because of the complexity of their organization and because of their many activities. One large metal and minerals company has 23 mines and 11 metal refineries. Such a company would want accounting information on each mine and each refinery, including the costs of mining and refining and, if feasible, the profit of each mine and refinery.

Government and nonprofit organizations

Governmental organizations and other nonprofit organizations also use accounting information. Legislative bodies and governing boards require information on what it costs to produce the various services being rendered by the organization in order to determine how much money should be budgeted for the organization. Managers within these organizations need accounting information that tells them how effective and efficient they are in carrying out their objectives.

Management accounting and government accounting are both important, but they are beyond the scope of an introductory textbook. They are covered in more advanced accounting texts. Our text is limited to *financial accounting*, which is accounting devoted largely to developing accounting information for owners, investors, and creditors.

Social role

While owners, investors, and others use accounting information to make their own decisions, accounting information has a social role as well. Generally, society wants its resources directed into the most efficient uses. In the private sector (that occupied by business firms), accounting information about profits of individual companies helps direct resources into the most efficient companies. The classical justification for a profits system is that, on the whole, profits are made by providing people with the goods and services they want, at prices they can afford, with an appropriate level of efficiency. If an enterprise produces things people do not want or prices its output too high or is inefficient, it will not earn a profit. Profitable enterprises are generally those that are useful to society, and profitable enterprises can and should attract resources.

Aggregate profits (total profits earned by all companies) in the economy help Congress and government policy makers establish policies and pass legislation concerning income taxes, economic growth, environmental protection, and other matters affecting citizens and business enterprises. Thus, accountants' measurements of profit are an element in policy decisions that have important effects on all of us.

PEOPLE IN ACCOUNTING

We estimate that in 1978 there are over 1,000,000 accountants in the United States, about 1 percent of the total work force. The areas of specialization are given in Table 1-1.

TABLE 1-1. Areas of Specialization of Accountants in 1978

Area of Specialization	Number	Percent
Public accounting	310,000	29
Business, industry and other employments	610,000	58
Government	140,000	13
Totals	1,060,000	100

Figures are the authors' projections of 1970 census figures, using the 1950–70 compound annual growth rate of 3.3%.

Public Accountants

Both *certified public accountants* and other accountants offer their professional services to the public. The work of CPAs will be described because CPAs are, by virtue of their training and credentials, generally recognized as professionals. A CPA firm offers professional service to the public in auditing, taxation, and (in many firms) management advisory services. The work of the CPA in public practice is called public accounting.

CPAs

Auditing consists of reviewing a client's financial reports for conformance with generally accepted accounting principles, the general rules that accountants (through bodies such as the FASB) have developed over the years to guide them in preparing the financial reports. The auditor also reviews the accounting system to make sure that it produces accurate financial reports and provides reasonable safeguards against fraud. In most states, only a CPA is permitted to practice as an auditor.

The auditor

In *taxation* work, the CPA advises clients on tax policy questions and helps clients to prepare their tax returns. *Management advisory services* include advice on accounting system and computer system design and special studies in such areas as product costs and profitability, inventory management, and long-term investment problems.

A person becomes a CPA after passing a three-day comprehensive examination covering accounting, auditing, and business law, and after fulfilling certain education and experience requirements. The education and experience requirements vary from state to state. Generally, a bachelor's degree is required, and the experience must be in public accounting. Many CPAs are employed elsewhere than in public accounting.

Becoming a CPA

TABLE 1-2. Areas of Employment of Certified Public Accountants in 1978

Area of Employment	Number	Percent
Public accounting	112,000	62
Business and industry	56,000	31
Government	7,000	4
Education	5,000	3
Totals	180,000	100

The author's projection is based on a 1975 estimate.

We estimate that in 1978 there are about 180,000 CPAs employed in the areas described in Table 1-2.

Many CPAs have responsible jobs in business and government. Some typical business positions include controller (the chief accounting officer), treasurer, and income tax specialist. In government, a CPA may head the division of accounting or be, for example, an internal auditor or a budget analyst. In many colleges and universities, a graduate degree (such as a doctorate) and a CPA certificate are an effective combination for college teaching.

Accountants in Business and Industry

There are many accounting opportunities in business firms. Two major areas of accounting can be identified. *Financial accounting,* the focus of this book, concentrates on the general-purpose financial reports covering the whole enterprise. These reports are directed primarily to owners, investors, creditors, and other outside persons or organizations with some interest in the company.

Management accounting is concerned with the financial information necessary for the internal management of the firm. Management accounting is a broad field that includes determination of the cost and profitability of the company's products, budgeting or profit planning, preparation of performance reports showing the results of different divisions or departments of the business, and cost and benefit analysis to help management resolve special problems such as whether to manufacture or buy a special part.

Other important accounting areas in a business firm include the following: (1) *taxation accounting,* which is concerned with determining income tax policies and preparing the company's income tax returns and other tax reports; (2) *accounting systems and data processing,* which covers the development of accounting systems, the means by which accounting reports and other outputs are produced, and the use of the computer in accounting systems; (3) *internal auditing,* which involves the testing of accounting operations to see whether they conform with the system requirements and, in some companies, the testing of company operations against standards of effectiveness.

Accountants in business and industry need careful training, usually in a college or university. Although many private accountants are CPAs, a CPA certificate is not needed in business and industry. The accent is on proficiency and imagination in the area in which the accountant works. Many people find that accounting jobs in business are an excellent stepping-stone to higher management responsibilities. Many chief executive officers of large companies have an accounting background.

Accountants in Government

Accounting in government has been influenced mainly by the legal requirement that expenditures must not exceed the amounts appropriated by legislative bodies. At present, considerable progress is being made toward bringing management accounting into government. One stimulus towards that end is the recent movement calling for greater accountability in governmental use of societal resources.

All governmental agencies—federal, state, and local—have accounting staffs. Some governmental organizations concentrate on accounting. The Securities and Exchange Commission, a regulatory agency, requires companies that sell their stocks and bonds in interstate commerce to file information reports, many of which are in the form of accounting statements. The SEC, in cooperation with the CPA profession, has developed standards for these accounting statements. The Internal Revenue Service is concerned with the income tax returns of all taxpayers, including large corporations. The General Accounting Office is the audit arm of Congress. The GAO does financial audits and operational audits (audits to determine the effectiveness of governmental programs). The Cost Accounting Standards Board (CASB) is responsible for developing cost accounting standards for companies undertaking large defense contracts. State governments have auditing organizations similar to the GAO and have large accounting staffs to help manage the large amounts of money expended.

Agencies

ACCOUNTING AND BOOKKEEPING

Routine record keeping or *bookkeeping* is sometimes equated with accounting. Bookkeeping is the activity of recording the raw data of accounting, the data that describe the numerous financial events known as transactions. It is vital that these data be quickly and accurately recorded. If the bookkeeping is done haphazardly, the accounting uses of the data will be adversely affected, and the accuracy and the reliability of the accounting reports will be suspect.

Notwithstanding the importance of bookkeeping, accounting is not the same as bookkeeping. Accounting uses the data that emerge from bookkeeping activities to prepare the financial reports that are used for numerous management and investor purposes. Accounting is a technical, professional activity that requires judgment in measurement and communication and that normally requires college training. Bookkeeping provides the input to the accounting activities and is only a part of the total accounting picture.

PURPOSES OF THE BUSINESS ENTERPRISE

A business firm exists to provide goods and/or services for customers and to give a return, or profit, to its owners. There must be a need for the product or service and a potential for profit. It would be fruitless indeed to organize a business if there was no potential demand for its products. Furthermore, investors would not be willing to invest their resources unless there was a potential for profit, because they have alternative investment opportunities that offer a return.

Income (profit)

The importance of income (profit) must be underscored. Income is a complex concept that will be discussed more fully later in this book.[3] For now, we can say that the resources a profitable enterprise receives from its customers in exchange for goods and services are more than the money, materials, and other resources it uses up in producing the goods and services. The excess, expressed in money terms, is income (or profit) and belongs to the firm's owners.

Income is essential to healthy business existence. Without income, a business cannot grow. The unprofitable business cannot retain income to invest in economic resources such as new plants and equipment. The unprofitable business has trouble getting new money resources from investors, since investors expect to receive a return from their investment. The business community views income as the single most important measure of business success. Small wonder, then, that the measurement of income of past periods and the estimation of future income are the most important activities in accounting.

Financial position

Another important objective of the business enterprise is to maintain a strong *financial position*. To survive, a company must be able to pay its debts as they come due. A measure of financial position is found in the relationship of a company's assets to its liabilities.

---

[3] The term *income* is always used to mean *net income* when we discuss business enterprise operations in this text. Gross inflows as a result of operations are called *revenues* rather than *income*.

Accounting provides information about income and financial position in the *income statement*, the *statement of financial position*, and the related *statement of changes in financial position*. All three statements will be covered in this book. The student will learn what concepts underlie each statement, how the statements are constructed, and how to interpret or use the statements.

FORMS OF BUSINESS ENTERPRISE

Businesses have a legal existence that is determined by their form of ownership. A business may be organized as a *sole proprietorship*, a *partnership*, or a *corporation*.

Sole Proprietorship. A sole proprietorship is the simplest form of business. A single owner invests money and other assets in the business. Legally, the owner and the business are viewed as inseparable. The owner risks not only his investment in the company but his other assets as well. While the law does not separate the owner from the business, accounting does. By viewing a business as separate from its owners, an accountant can report on the financial results of that business, showing interested parties the progress being made.

Partnership. The partnership is like the proprietorship except that a partnership involves more than one owner. Each partner has a vote in making decisions. A contractual relationship is established among the partners, and this has important accounting implications. The contract, or partnership agreement, determines such things as profit shares, limitations on withdrawals from the firm, and freedom of the partners to sell or otherwise dispose of their ownership interest. If the partners change, a new contract must be made.

Corporation. The most important form of business enterprise in the United States is the corporation. A corporation is an artificial person created by law. Consequently, persons desiring to form a corporation must first secure a charter from the state. Then investors contribute money and other resources to the corporation in exchange for ownership shares called capital stock. An individual owner (or stockholder) has a claim against corporation assets and earnings in proportion to the number of shares of capital stock owned. Legally and for accounting purposes, the corporation is separate from its owners (or stockholders). The stockholders can change without affecting its existence. Stockholders usually have limited liability; they risk only their investment in the enterprise. Stockholders elect members of a board of directors who in turn select the chief executive of the company. The board of directors determine the

Part I   The Framework of Financial Accounting

general policies of the corporation and are responsible to the stockholders. The corporation president (chief executive) is responsible to the board of directors for the effective operation of the company.

Most of this book assumes the corporate form of enterprise. However, most accounting for corporations is also applicable to the other forms of enterprise. The differences are found primarily in accounting for the ownership interest. These differences are highlighted in chapters 12 and 14.

INTRODUCTION TO FINANCIAL ACCOUNTING

Accounting has been called the "language of business." This term is appropriate because world phenomena are described and explained through language. The phenomena of interest to financial accounting are shown in Figure 1-1. The figure indicates that the primary concern of financial accounting is with the economic *resources* and *obligations* of the business

FIGURE 1-1

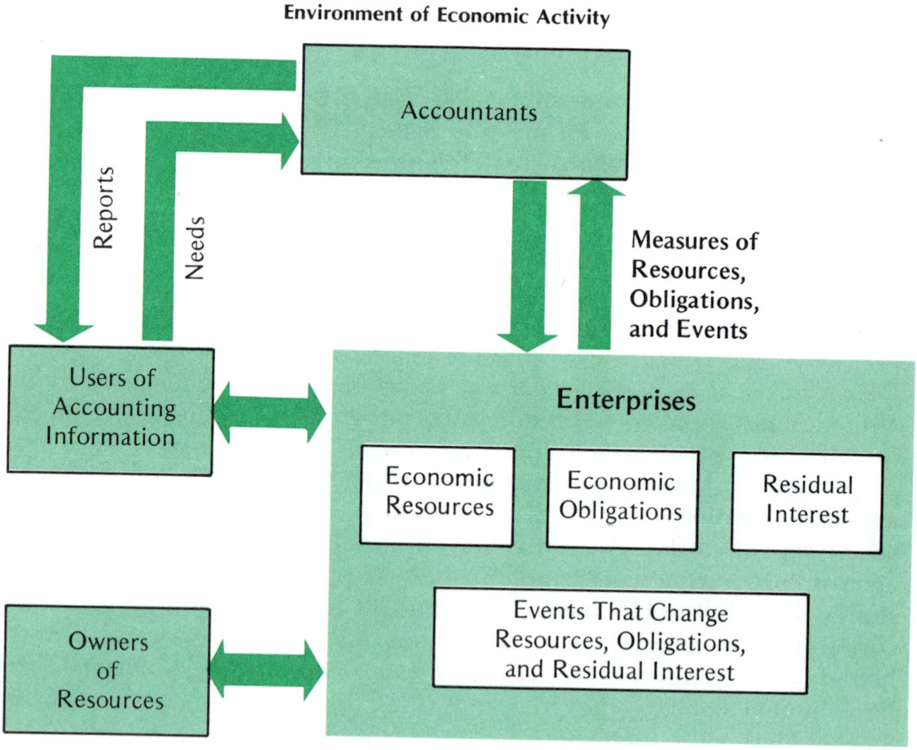

Environment of Economic Activity

- Accountants
- Reports / Needs
- Measures of Resources, Obligations, and Events
- Users of Accounting Information
- Enterprises
  - Economic Resources
  - Economic Obligations
  - Residual Interest
  - Events That Change Resources, Obligations, and Residual Interest
- Owners of Resources

enterprise and with the *economic events that change those resources* and *obligations*. The figure also indicates that financial accounting is concerned with communicating information about enterprises to interested parties, who will use the information as a basis for decisions. A series of interactions is indicated in the diagram. The nature of enterprises affects the outlook of accountants, and the way in which accountants interpret and measure enterprise activities affects the enterprise. The needs of the users affect accountants, and the type of information provided by accountants conditions the users. Decisions of the users affect enterprise operations, and the operations affect the income, position, and power of the users. Owners of resources are hired and paid by enterprises, and some of the owners are also users of accounting information.

Communication

Concentrating on the business enterprise, we note that a business firm's many valuable resources include physical plant and other material goods, cash and various claims to cash, and right to use the valuable services of the people who work for the firm. These economic resources are the scarce means available for carrying on economic activity. Accounting presently is concerned only with the resources that can be measured in dollars; those resources are called *assets*.

Resources and assets

An enterprise has many obligations, including its debts and its broader obligations to society (such as protection of the environment). Accounting is concerned with the obligations that can be measured and that represent a present obligation to pay out money in the future or to provide services in the future. Those obligations are called *liabilities*. Accounting is also interested in *owners' equity*, the difference between assets and liabilities.

Obligations and liabilities

Owners' equity

Owners' equity represents the owners' interest in the business. It is a residual interest, being the excess of assets over liabilities. Substantively, owners' equity results from owners' investment of assets in the firm and from company income (earnings) retained in the business. According to law, the income of the business becomes a part of the owners' equity. In a corporation the owners' investment is evidenced by shares of capital stock, and amounts of income accumulated in the business are called *retained earnings*, or retained income, and are added to the capital stock in computing total owners' equity. Owners' equity differs from liabilities because the enterprise is not obliged to repay the owners. The owners are the ultimate risk-takers, who may see their interest in the business increase or shrink, depending upon the success of the enterprise.

Retained earnings

The *events that change resources and obligations* cover a wide range and include investments in, and withdrawals from, the enterprise by owners; exchanges in which productive resources (including services) are acquired; productive activities; exchanges with customers in which products or services are sold; inflation or deflation; and changes in prices of resources held or obligations incurred. These economic events lead to income or loss and affect the assets, liabilities, and owners' equity of the enterprise.

Events

Part I   The Framework of Financial Accounting

FINANCIAL REPORTS

Financial accounting is concerned with general purpose reports on financial position and the results of operations. These reports are directed primarily to owners, investors, creditors, and other outside persons or organizations that have some interest in the enterprise. The three basic reports are the following:

Basic accounting statements

1. The *statement of financial position*, or the *balance sheet*, reports on the status of the assets, liabilities, and owners' equity of the enterprise at a point of time, usually the end of an *accounting period*.
2. The *income statement* covers the income-directed activities of the firm and shows items such as sales and business expenses (resources used) *during* the accounting period. The income statement shows the income or loss made by the enterprise.
3. The *statement of changes in financial position*, or the *funds statement*, reports the flow of funds into the business *from all sources* and the *uses* to which the funds were applied. Usually, company funds are defined as cash plus other liquid and short-term assets, less the short-term liabilities.

Measurement

Measurement is emphasized in accounting. Resources, obligations, and events are proper subjects of accounting only if they can be measured in dollars. Thus, some important resources and obligations are presently excluded from accounting reports. For example, the value of the human resources employed in the enterprise are excluded from the statement of financial position, as is the firm's social obligation to safeguard the environment.

Forces leading to change

It should be noted, however, that accounting presently is in a state of flux. Forces at work in the economy and in society are causing accountants to question their present approach. Inflation and a growing concern among many influential persons for greater accountability from corporations and from governmental organizations are two factors causing great excitement in the accounting world. The literature of accounting includes frequent suggestions for changing accounting so that it can more adequately fulfill its responsibilities to society. It is too early to predict what changes will be made in accounting in response to these forces. Some of the problems and suggested changes in accounting will be discussed in chapter 15 and also when we cover the topics of inventories and depreciation in chapters 9 and 10.

The financial reports we know today have evolved over many years. Fifty years ago financial reports were sketchy documents characterized more by their omissions than by what they included. Since then, business enterprises and their accountants have responded to the influences of the investment community and the Securities and Exchange Commission by improving reports. Today we have relatively informative reports. Progress has been slow, and some persons have suggested that one important reason for the glacier-like progress is the lack of specific objectives to guide accounting improvement. In recent years, the CPA profession and the academic community have begun to develop objectives of financial statements that can guide and speed future improvement of accounting. As yet, no definitive set of objectives exists. But if we consider some of the more important suggested objectives, we should be able to better appreciate and judge the adequacy of current financial reports.

OBJECTIVES OF FINANCIAL STATEMENTS

It is generally agreed that the basic purpose of financial reports is to provide information useful for making economic decisions. The information appropriate for decisions depends on the needs of the decision makers or users. There are several different groups of accounting information users. Investors (including stockholders), creditors, management, employees, government, and the general public all are interested in accounting information. At present, the information needs of each group are not known precisely. Because we do not know the specific needs of the different users, we usually make assumptions about information that should be useful. One assumption is that investors and creditors are the primary parties served by financial reports. Another assumption is that investor and creditor groups have common needs; they require information about enterprise income and enterprise financial position. Other interested parties are assumed to share the need for this type of information to at least some extent. These assumptions are fairly reasonable, for information provided on the basis of these assumptions appears to be useful to a large number of financial statement users. Much work remains to be done, however, in identifying user needs and providing information that will meet those needs more effectively.

Basic purpose

Assumptions

The objectives of accounting are directed toward satisfying the assumed needs of users of financial statements. One set of objectives of accounting deals specifically with the kind of information about progress and position that should be presented. In a broad economic sense, the information should aid in an efficient allocation of resources. On an individual level, the information should aid in fulfilling individual objectives such as wealth maximization and security. It is hoped that accounting information can aid in both areas and that effective individual decisions will be consistent with efficient resource allocation.

To be useful, accounting information must reflect the economic environment of the enterprise accurately. There must be a minimum of distortion and a variety of helpful interpretations. When events in the environment affect an enterprise, the events should be reflected promptly and accurately in accounting reports. Accordingly, the objectives of financial accounting relating to the environment are to provide reliable information about the following:

Environmental objectives

19

Part I   The Framework of Financial Accounting

1. Economic resources and obligations—the bases of the assets and liabilities reflected in accounting
2. Changes in economic resources and obligations from income-directed activities—the basis of the events reported in the income statement
3. Other events that change resources and obligations—these include events such as financing and investing activities that are reflected in the statement of changes in financial position and other statements of change
4. Aspects of the environment that cannot be measured in dollars, that are related to accounting measures, and that may provide useful information to decision makers

These objectives are not very specific, but they do indicate the concern accounting has with things that happen in the world. *Only if accounting deals effectively with the environment will the information it provides be useful.*

Cash flows

The FASB has emphasized the interest that investors and creditors have in cash flows in the form of dividends, interest, and payment at maturity of securities and loans. The FASB emphasizes that economic resources are sources of future cash inflows and that economic obligations are causes of future cash outflows. Furthermore, changes in resources and obligations from earnings and other activities are helpful in assessing a company's ability to pay cash dividends, interest, and obligations when they come due. Thus, it is appropriate that information specified in objectives (1) to (4) be provided by financial accounting.

The FASB focuses on cash flows because it is rational for investors and creditors to emphasize cash flows in their decisions. Investors want dividends or interest and also want to be able to sell their securities at a good price. Creditors want to collect interest and want to collect the amount owed to them at maturity. The prospective cash flows are affected by the enterprise's ability to generate cash through its earning and financing activities. Prospective cash flows are also affected by the way investors and creditors perceive the enterprise's cash generating ability, because that perception will affect the market price of the enterprise's securities.[4]

Qualitative objectives

Accountants have agreed on a number of qualities that accounting information should possess. A discussion of these qualitative objectives follows.

Relevance

If accounting is to be useful to those making economic decisions, it must provide information that is relevant—information that bears upon the

---

4. Financial Accounting Standards Board, *Tentative Conclusions on Objectives of Financial Statements of Business Enterprises,* Dec. 2, 1976, pp. 4–5.

decisions for which it is used. This obvious fact has some important implications for accounting. Setting relevance as an objective faces accountants with responsibilities that they have often ignored in the past. It raises a series of questions at every stage of the accounting process. Will this information be useful? Is it the most relevant information that can be presented? Does it meet user needs? Should other information be added to insure full relevance?

It is difficult to assess the relevance of financial statements. Some persons believe that income figures should be given for major segments of the enterprise, not just in total. Some feel that a wider use of current market values (as opposed to the usual historical cost) is necessary to get a better picture of financial strength. One thing is clear: a great deal more research into the problem of relevance is required before accountants can present statements that are fully relevant to the needs of different users.

Understandability

Accounting information must be understandable to users. This objective places a communication burden on accountants. It means that they cannot provide highly technical information that gives no consideration to the user's ability to understand. The users have some responsibility as well, however, for they must be at least somewhat familiar with the economic activities of enterprises and must have some understanding of financial accounting. The FASB suggests that financial statements should be understandable "to those who have a reasonable understanding of business and economic activities and financial accounting. . . ."[5]

The understandability of the published financial statements of large corporations obviously varies with the knowledge of the user. If the statements are considered from the viewpoint of the average reader, they are perhaps somewhat obscure. They contain technical terminology, and the notes that accompany almost all published statements are often difficult to follow. And yet, our criticism is blunted by the recognition that the operations of large corporations are immensely complicated and thus are difficult to convey in a set of simple statements.

Verifiability

Accounting information should be verifiable. That is, independent measurers using the same measurement methods should be able to substantially duplicate the information. Verifiability is important because the usefulness of information is enhanced if it is reliable, and reliability depends in part on verifiability. No measures can be completely free of

Reliability

---
5. Ibid., p. 3.

subjective elements, because human agents and human reasoning are involved in the measurement process. If information is testable by others and can be corroborated, however, it meets the scientific standard of verifiability, or objectivity.

Generally, financial statements meet this criterion fairly well. Data in the statements are based primarily on exchanges with other entities and therefore can be easily corroborated. The statements do contain some estimates, but for the most part they rely on prices determined in exchanges.

Verifiability has been heavily emphasized in financial accounting. This emphasis is an important reason for the approach accountants take to recognition and measurement of assets and liabilities and owners' equity and of economic events that change them. At times, the emphasis on verifiability has even entailed some sacrifice of relevance. That is, some relevant information has not been presented because it is not verifiable. It is hoped that this situation will change in the future.

Neutrality

Financial accounting information should not be slanted to the needs of particular users; rather it should serve common needs of users. This objective is based on a presumption that users do have common needs that can be served by financial accounting information. But some needs of users differ, and accounting should avoid biasing the information in order to meet the special needs of one group. The CPA auditor's opinion on financial statements attests to the fair presentation of the statements and to their basic neutrality.

Timeliness

Financial accounting information should be communicated early enough to be useful in decisions. This objective is simply the accounting application of the old saying that there is nothing as stale as last week's newspaper. If financial accounting information is to be useful, it must be timely. This means that a degree of verifiability or some other objective may have to be sacrificed occasionally to make the information available early.

Most published financial statements are issued within two months after the end of the company's accounting period and thus are fairly timely. Most large corporations also provide quarterly reports of their operations to interested parties.

Comparability

Financial accounting information should be comparable both between enterprises and between years for the same enterprise. The primary basis of comparability is consistent application of accounting principles and procedures from period to period and a relative degree of uniformity of principles and procedures between enterprises. If the number of acceptable alternative practices that are available is minimized, comparability is facilitated. Consistency in form and content is also important. If accounting information is comparable, conclusions concerning relative financial strengths and weaknesses and relative success are more likely to be valid.

Consistency

At first glance it would seem that adherence to the ideal of comparability would effectively stop progress in accounting and reporting. Accountants could not use a new and better way of reporting if it was inconsistent with previous treatments, because it would destroy comparability. However, accountants have generally agreed that a change can be made *as long as the effect of the change is clearly disclosed.* This disclosure allows the user of information to make his own adjustment of trends. At the same time, the practice of disclosing changes gives assurance that information without a disclosure contains no variations from previous practices.

Changes in reporting

The objective of comparability applies to financial statements in two ways. First, the statements for a given year should be comparable to statements of other years for the same company. Most published financial statements meet this test because each statement includes amounts for at least two years. The reader can assume that there were no changes in methods that would inhibit comparability. Any changes that did occur would be explained in the notes to the statement. Second, the statements should be comparable to those of other companies. Thus, General Motors' statements should be comparable to those of Ford, Chrysler, and American Motors and to those of other manufacturing companies. The statements of companies are not always completely comparable, however, because of differences in the accounting methods the companies use. These differences may cause considerable differences in net income and in the amounts of assets and liabilities. Lack of comparability because of differences in accounting methods is a serious problem in financial accounting today. Because the differences do exist, it is desirable that companies disclose the particular methods they have chosen in accounting for important areas of operations.

Completeness

Financial accounting information should be complete and should not selectively omit information. This objective indicates *how much* information should be presented. Financial accounting should present all information about resources and obligations and changes in them that conforms to the first six qualitative objectives.

Full Disclosure

Full disclosure has long been considered a vital aspect of reporting financial accounting information. Full disclosure means disclosure of all the important facts—all the facts that might affect the decisions of an informed user of the statements. Full disclosure is related to, and derived from, a number of other objectives of financial accounting, particularly relevance, neutrality, completeness, and understandability. The requirement of full disclosure in financial statements is influenced by several factors. Many leaders in business enterprises have a highly developed sense of social responsibility. They feel responsible to users of their financial information and often take the initiative in fully disclosing all facts. Outside interests also influence disclosure in company reports. If a company is listed on a stock exchange, the exchange often sets standards for published reports. The United States Securities and Exchange Commission (SEC) also sets standards of disclosure for reports filed with it. Most large corporations are affected by these requirements. At times, other regulatory agencies of the government prescribe the content of financial reports issued by companies under their jurisdiction. Creditors often demand full information before granting credit. Finally, most large companies are audited by CPAs, who advocate full disclosure. The record of disclosure of American business is quite good, as a result, although there are enough lapses so that those who are concerned with the problem cannot rest on their laurels.

Influences on disclosure

ACHIEVING THE OBJECTIVES OF FINANCIAL ACCOUNTING

Present-day financial accounting does not meet all of its objectives. They are achieved to some extent, but there is much room for improvement. For example, some economic resources of an enterprise, such as human resources and internally developed technology, are not included in financial statements. Also, some events that affect enterprises, such as price changes on assets held by an enterprise, are not generally reflected in statements. The accounting statements at times also lack relevance and understandability, are not comparable to those of other enterprises, and are not as timely and complete as they should be. The existence of imperfections in financial accounting is a problem for students, because to obtain a complete understanding of the capabilities of financial accounting the students must have a firm grasp of its limitations. The gap between ideal and actual also provides excitement and dynamism, because the field of accounting is changing rapidly and there is lively controversy about the direction in which it should go.

Another factor causing some difficulties is the lack of agreement on objectives in the accounting profession. The profession is currently concerned about the direction it should take; accordingly, objectives are receiving considerable attention. In 1973 a committee of the American Institute of CPAs published a report entitled *Objectives of Financial Statements*, which explores issues further. The objectives proposed by this committee emphasize cash flows, predictions, and current values. The committee's suggestions have been warmly debated in the profession. Out of this debate we may be able to arrive at agreement on what objectives should be.

Despite difficulties in defining and achieving the objectives of financial accounting, the objectives listed above are still helpful. It appears that the accounting profession is moving toward objectives that will put more direct emphasis on cash flows, but the tentative conclusions reached by the FASB also emphasize economic resources and obligations, earnings, and qualitative objectives similar to those we described.[6] Thus the objectives listed above are useful—they set the tone for financial accounting and define in some important respects the way in which accountants should approach their task of dealing with the economic environment. They are useful to some extent in evaluating and improving financial accounting information. And finally, they allow a user who is aware of the objectives of financial accounting to better interpret financial accounting information.

SUMMARY

Accounting encompasses a wide variety of activities ranging from routine bookkeeping to report preparation that requires professional knowledge and skill. Accounting has evolved over the centuries in response to the needs of owners, investors, and others for information useful in making economic decisions. Today, probably over a million people are involved in accounting work, in businesses, in governments, in nonprofit organizations, and in the CPA profession. The CPA offers professional service to the public, and entrance into the profession is governed by the laws of the individual states.

While accounting is important in all organizations, this book concentrates on financial accounting for business enterprises. Financial accounting is concerned with the information found in the statement of financial position, the income statement, and the statement of changes in financial position. Other important areas of accounting, such as management accounting, auditing, and governmental accounting, are not considered in this text.

The accounting profession is working to develop objectives to guide

---

6. Ibid., pp. 4–7.

the future improvement of financial accounting. There is general agreement that the basic purpose of accounting is to provide information that is useful in making economic decisions. This basic purpose is supported by a series of more detailed objectives. Some objectives relate to the kind of information about progress and position that should be presented. They specify that reliable information about economic resources and obligations and the events that change resources and obligations should be presented. Another set of objectives specifies the qualities that accounting information should have. These are relevance, understandability, verifiability, neutrality, timeliness, comparability, and completeness. An objective such as relevance raises many questions that must be answered before it can serve as a useful guide to accountants.

IMPORTANT TERMS

Accounting
Corporation
Securities and Exchange Commission (SEC)
Accounting Principles Board (APB)
Financial Accounting Standards Board (FASB)
Income statement
Statement of financial position
Financial accounting
CPA
Auditing
Management accounting
Business enterprise
Sole Proprietorship
Partnership
Resources
Obligations
Assets
Liabilities
Owners' equity
Retained earnings
Relevance
Understandability
Verifiability
Neutrality
Timeliness
Comparability
Completeness
Full disclosure

QUESTIONS

1-1. What is the purpose of accounting? How does financial accounting attempt to accomplish this purpose?

1-2. Why do you suppose accounting records are among humanity's earliest written records?

1-3. It is said that accounting developed rapidly as trade developed and expanded. How would you explain that co-development?

1-4. Why is profit, or income, an important objective of business enterprises?

1-5. Would the need for accounting disappear if the profit motive were replaced by some other business objective?

1-6. What is meant by financial position? Why is a strong financial position important in a business enterprise?

1-7. What is a CPA? How does one become a CPA?

1-8. How does a corporation differ from a partnership?

1-9. What is the principal accounting job in an industrial company? What accounting functions are normally found in a large manufacturing company?

1-10. Some governmental agencies have unique accounting responsibilities. Describe the unique accounting functions of the Securities and Exchange Commission; of the General Accounting Office.

1-11. What are the types of accounting work generally found in large CPA firms?

1-12. Define *resources*. What resources does accounting deal with?

1-13. Define *obligations*. What obligations does accounting deal with?

1-14. Define *owners' equity*.

1-15. How does owners' equity differ from liabilities?

1-16. How do obligations differ from liabilities?

1-17. Define *income* in your own words.

1-18. If financial accounting has evolved over several centuries in response to the demands of developing business, why is it now necessary to develop some objectives for financial accounting?

1-19. Why is *relevance* the most important qualitative objective of accounting information? What is difficult about achieving relevance?

1-20. What is meant by *verifiability*?

1-21. What is meant by *full disclosure*? What dangers do you see in this concept?

1-22. Consult a published financial report of some company. (Your instructor or the library may have some for your use). Do you think this company is following good practices of disclosure? What additional information would have been beneficial?

EXERCISES

1-23. *Library project.* Look up the financial reports of a large corporation. Identify three or four resources reported by the company; identify three or four obligations reported by the company.

1-24. *Statement preparation.* Using the illustrations in the text, prepare a statement of financial position for the Amos Tailoring Company as of December 31, Year 1. The accounting records of the company show the following data as of December 31, Year 1.

Part I The Framework of Financial Accounting

Cash on hand and in bank	$ 6,700
Amounts owed by customers	10,700
Sewing machines and other equipment	25,000
Accounts payable	2,500
Notes payable	3,000
Capital stock	20,000
Retained earnings	16,900

1-25. *Statement preparation.* Prepare a statement of financial position for the Bedrock Cleaning Company as of December 31, Year 1. The following data are available:

	December 31, Year 1
Cash	$ 250
Cleaning supplies	800
Prepaid rent on store	150
Accounts payable	1,500
Cleaning equipment	6,500
Capital stock	5,000
Retained earnings (to be determined)	?

(Solution in Appendix B.)

2

The Statement of Financial Position

Financial accounting is the branch of accounting that provides a chronological record (or history) of the assets, liabilities, and owners' equity of a business enterprise and of the events (or transactions) that change assets, liabilities, and owners' equity. The results of the financial accounting process are found in the financial statements. The assets, liabilities, and owners' equity of a business enterprise are reported in the statement of financial position, which is discussed in this chapter. The income statement and the statement of changes in financial position are covered in chapter 3.

Financial accounting defined

All parties concerned with a business enterprise are interested in its financial position, which is portrayed by the *balance sheet*, or *statement of financial position* (the names are used interchangeably). The balance sheet indicates the assets owned by the enterprise and the claims against those assets, and purports to give a picture of the position of the enterprise at one particular time. The statement complements the statements of changes—the income statement and the statement of changes in financial position—which portray company progress over a period of time. The balance sheet is like a still picture that freezes motion at a point in time, while the statements of changes are like motion pictures that show action over a period of time.

The financial reports published by large companies include much more than the three financial statements proper. Several pages of explanatory notes are usually included. The notes explain the accounting policies followed, attempt to clarify difficult items, and disclose information about enterprise commitments that will create future liabilities,

Notes

about contingencies (things that *might* take place that would require future payments), and about other financial matters that pertain to the company at the time the financial statements are prepared. The notes are an integral part of the financial statements and should be considered with the balance sheet to get an adequate picture of financial position. We do not cover notes to statements in this text, except for selected illustrations.

THE ACCOUNTING EQUATION

Assets and claims

The statement of financial position shows the assets of the enterprise and the claims against these assets. The assets are claimed by various parties. If the parties are outside interests (creditors), the claims are called liabilities. Claims of the owners are called owners' equity. Sometimes the claims of both creditors and owners are called equities. This is proper, since an equity is "any right or claim to assets." However, since the term *equities* is not widely used in accounting to refer to all claims against assets, we will generally use the term *liabilities and owners' equity*.

On a statement of financial position, assets will be equal to claims against the assets. The equality occurs because in our society all valuable property is owned, or is at least subject to some ownership claims. For example, a home costing $100,000 may have a $60,000 mortgage. The home "owner" has an ownership claim of only $40,000. If a homeowner's only asset is his home, the facts about the home can be portrayed as follows:

Homeowner's Balance Sheet

Asset		Claims against Asset	
Home	$100,000	Mortgage payable	$ 60,000
		Homeowner's equity	40,000
	$100,000		$100,000

In this situation the homeowner's claim is the difference between the cost of the home and the amount owed on the home. Both the liability and the owner's claim can be related to the specific asset.

In a business enterprise, specific assets usually cannot be related to specific claims. Enterprise assets change continually, making it impossible to trace claims to specific assets. With some exceptions, claims against assets are general claims against *total* enterprise assets. If a creditor has an explicit legal right against a specific asset (for example, a bank loan may be secured by a mortgage on a specific piece of property), that fact can be indicated in a note to the financial statements.

The relationship of enterprise assets to claims can be expressed in an equation:

$$\text{Assets} = \text{Claims against Assets (or Equities)}$$

This equation states that the dollar amount of assets is equal to the dollar amount of claims against total assets (or equities). The equation is usually stated as follows:

$$\text{Assets} = \text{Liabilities} + \text{Owners' Equity}$$

Basic accounting equation

This equation, termed the *basic accounting equation*, is the basis for using the term *balance sheet* as another name for the statement of financial position. The total of the assets must equal the total of the liabilities plus owners' equity. The two totals must *balance*. In a corporation, the owners' equity is often called stockholders' equity, and the right-hand side of the equation is listed as Liabilities plus Stockholders' Equity.

The accounting equation gives the accountant an effective framework for recording the events that change a company's financial position. Example 2-1 will illustrate.

EXAMPLE 2-1

On August 1, Marcella and Sam Adams form a company for the purpose of operating a women's clothing store. The Adamses receive shares of capital stock in exchange for their investment of $50,000. The Adams Company balance sheet on August 1 shows the following:

ADAMS COMPANY
Balance Sheet, August 1

Assets		Liabilities and Stockholders' Equity	
Cash	$50,000	Stockholders' equity:*	
		Capital stock	$50,000

* The assets of $50,000 are claimed in total by the owners, since there are no liabilities.

On August 5, the Adams Company borrows $30,000 from Marcella's brother on a 5-year, 8% note for the purpose of buying store property. This increases the company's assets by $30,000 and the company's liabilities by $30,000. The balance sheet on August 5 shows the following:

ADAMS COMPANY
Balance Sheet, August 5

Assets		Liabilities and Stockholders' Equity	
Cash	$80,000	Liabilities:	
		5-year, 8% note payable	$30,000
		Stockholders' equity:	
		Capital stock	50,000
Total assets	$80,000	Total liabilities and stockholders' equity	$80,000

Transactions

In Example 2-1, we showed two events. The first event was the initial investment in the new company by the Adamses. The second event was the borrowing of $30,000 by the company. These events are called *transactions*. We can observe here that any transaction will maintain the equality condition: Assets = liabilities + owners' equity. The dollar amounts may change, but the equality must be maintained. We recognize that this merely follows the mathematical rule that a change to one side of an equation must be equalled by the same change on the other side.

Example 2-2 illustrates another type of change.

EXAMPLE 2-2

On August 6, the Adams Company purchases a parcel of land on which a store building will be erected. The purchase is made for $18,000 cash. This transaction has the following effects on the accounting equation:

- Asset cash is reduced by $18,000.
- Asset land is increased by $18,000.
- Neither liabilities nor owners' equity is affected.

The Adams Company balance sheet on August 6th is as follows:

ADAMS COMPANY
Balance Sheet, August 6

Assets		Liabilities and Stockholders' Equity	
Cash	$62,000	Liabilities:	
Land	18,000	5-year, 8% note payable	$30,000
		Stockholders' equity:	
		Capital stock	50,000
Total assets	$80,000	Total liabilities and stockholders' equity	$80,000

The transaction in Example 2-2 affected only the assets side of the equation, while maintaining the condition of equality. The change effected by the transaction was in the composition of the assets. Cash of $18,000 was converted to property assets of $18,000. Total assets remained unchanged.

The accounting equation is the basis of modern double-entry accounting. The term *double-entry* simply means that the transaction has a dual, or two-way, effect. A transaction will affect both sides of the equation by the same amount in the same direction or it will affect only one side by both an increase and a decrease. More explicitly, a transaction will do one of the following:

1. Increase both sides of the equation by the same amount
2. Decrease both sides of the equation by the same amount
3. Increase and decrease the same side of the equation by the same amount

Example 2-1 illustrated the first type of transaction, and Example

2-2 illustrated the third type. Example 2-3 will illustrate the second type of transaction.

EXAMPLE 2-3

Marcella Adams, the president of the Adams Company, decides that the company needs only $52,000 cash instead of $62,000. The company pays $10,000 on August 7 to reduce the note payable to $20,000. The balance sheet on August 7 is as follows:

ADAMS COMPANY
Balance Sheet, August 7

Assets		Liabilities and Stockholders' Equity	
Cash	$52,000	Liabilities:	
Land	18,000	5-year, 8% note payable	$20,000
		Stockholders' equity:	
		Capital stock	50,000
		Total liabilities and	
Total assets	$70,000	stockholders' equity	$70,000

The formal accounting process based on the accounting equation will be covered in detail in chapters 4 through 7. Now we turn to a discussion of assets, liabilities, and owners' equity. Our objective is to further develop understanding of these important accounting concepts.

ASSETS

Assets defined

In accounting, assets are based on economic resources (discussed in chapter 1). That is, *assets are properties and rights owned by an enterprise that have monetary value and are of present or future benefit to the enterprise.* Assets include actual *physical properties* (such as product inventories, land, buildings, and machinery) and *intangible rights* (such as cash, accounts receivable from customers, and patents).

Properties and rights are listed as assets of an enterprise only if the company owns them. Thus, some resources used by the company are excluded from the balance sheet. For example, competence of company personnel may be an important factor in company success, especially where scientific research is important in company operations or where employees must be highly trained. However, since the company does not own the employees, this resource is not shown as an asset.

Assets also must have monetary value. This requirement excludes items that have no value and items for which a monetary value cannot be computed. A good reputation built up by years of good service to customers may be of great value to an enterprise. However, it is very difficult to set a dollar value on this feature; therefore, it is usually excluded from a balance sheet. An exception occurs when a value on a company's reputation is set through a transaction in which the company is sold by one party to another. For example, when a company sells its business intact to another company, the price paid includes an amount for the company's name and reputation. When this asset does appear on a balance sheet, it is called *goodwill*. It represents an intangible right to the benefits of the name and reputation purchased by the acquiring company.

To say that assets must be of present or future benefit to the enterprise means that assets must be useful to the enterprise. This usefulness may take the form of services that will flow from the asset (such as transportation services from a truck) or of purchasing power that resides in the asset (as in the case of cash). An item that has no present benefit and is not expected to be of benefit in the future is not an economic resource and on that basis should be excluded from assets. In cases where there is doubt about future benefit, accountants usually exclude the items from assets.

Perhaps the most important principle that determines what resources are recognized as assets is that *transactions between an enterprise and other parties usually are necessary before resources can be recognized as assets and measured and recorded by the enterprise.* Accountants use transactions as the signals for recognition of asset values. Accountants are unwilling to record resources as assets unless a transaction has occurred, even though the resources may have clear future benefits. This emphasis on transactions is part of the accountant's search for data that can be measured objectively. The emphasis is also reflected in the types of changes in assets that are recognized. These are discussed in chapter 3.

MEASUREMENT OF ASSETS

Assets are expressed in dollars and cents on balance sheets. Therefore, some sort of valuation of the assets is necessary. What valuation is appropriate for assets? Presumably, the appropriate valuation would indicate the value of the assets to the enterprise. But *value* is a very subjective concept; for, like beauty, value often lies in the eye of the beholder. What one person values highly, another may consider worthless.

Cost Valuation

Cost

The accountant's measurement, or valuation, of enterprise assets is generally based on their *cost*, a price determined in the transaction in which each asset is acquired. Cost is defined as the sacrifice incurred in economic activities. In accounting, the amount of the sacrifice is determined at the time the asset is acquired. The result is that assets are initially recorded according to their transaction price.

It is important to recognize that in accounting, *once an asset valuation has been established through a transaction, the valuation usually continues to be based on the transaction until another transaction takes place or the asset is used up or becomes worthless.* This means that changes in market values for assets are generally ignored in present generally accepted accounting procedures.

Cost principle

The valuation, or measurement, of specific assets is related to the purpose for which the asset is held. Some assets are important because of the purchasing power they represent. Cash represents immediate purchasing power. A business needs to hold a cash balance to take care of daily expenditures. Claims to cash, which will be converted to cash within a short period of time, are also important because of the purchasing power they embody. Most businesses grant credit to their customers and thus possess accounts and notes receivable that will be converted to cash within a short time. Cash and claims to cash are measured at their cash value, generally based on the amount of the asset as established in a transaction.

Some assets are held for future sale. These assets are called merchandise inventory (in retailing and wholesaling companies) or finished goods inventory (in manufacturing companies). Merchandise is acquired by purchases, and finished goods are produced in manufacturing operations. Even though it is the intention of the company to sell these assets, they are generally measured at their cost. Why cost instead of selling price? The principal reason for using cost rather than selling price is that the cost has been established in past market transactions, while the selling price will not be assured until there is a future sales transaction.

Many enterprise assets are acquired for future use or future serviceability. An example is a raw material inventory that is to be used in the manufacture of salable products. Another example is a cash register that is to be used in connection with the collection of cash from customers. Clearly, there is no intention to sell these assets. Consequently, they are measured on the basis of their cost to the company.

The term *unexpired cost* is frequently used to describe those assets that are measured on the basis of their cost. This term is favored by many accountants because it focuses on the importance of cost in measuring assets and also suggests that the assets will be used up (or expire) in the future. Basically, almost all cost-based assets are used up or sold (in the case of product inventories) in the operations of the business. As assets are used or sold, their costs become expense. The term *unexpired cost* emphasizes the close relationship between the balance sheet and the income statement.

The accountant's emphasis on cost measurements is based in part on two related assumptions of accounting and in part on a qualitative objective of accounting.

The first assumption is that the business firm is a *going concern*. The business firm is expected to continue operating indefinitely into the future. There is no present intention to voluntarily close down the business. Nor

Going concern

is it expected that the business will be forced to close its doors because it cannot pay its creditors. If a business is expected to continue operating indefinitely, then it may not be appropriate to show the assets held for use at their selling price. The intention is to continue using them and not to sell them.

Stable unit of measurement

The second assumption is that the dollar is a stable measurement standard. This is known as the *stable unit of measurement* assumption. It assumes that prices are essentially unchanging, or that changes in prices are not significant. If this assumption is valid, then cost as a basis for asset measurement is valid. At present, this assumption is open to serious question. It is clear that there has been substantial price inflation. This problem will be discussed in chapter 15.

The accounting objective that measurements be verifiable is another reason for using cost. Cost is an objective measure that can be verified by an independent, qualified person, since it is the result of an exchange price arrived at in an arm's-length transaction between the buyer and the seller. The cost recorded at the time an asset is acquired is often called *historical cost* to emphasize that it is an amount established in the transaction in which the asset was originally recorded.

Problems with Cost Valuation

Valuation at cost is objective and verifiable, and it does indicate the enterprise resources invested in an asset at the time of the transaction. But because market values change, a value at one point of time, such as historical cost, only rarely indicates current market value. In a time of rapid changes, the gap between historical costs and current values will be great. Problems with historical cost become more pronounced the longer assets are held. Supplies bought a week ago have a cost that is very close to their current market value, and this cost will have little chance to get out of date before the supplies are used up. But a building purchased in 1940 and still in use today has a historical cost that is completely out of date.

Economists criticize historical cost valuation because it is not meaningful in many cases. They prefer a valuation based on market value, or *discounted future cash flows*. But current market values may be no better than historical costs as a valuation basis for assets. There is no guarantee, for instance, that the sum of the market values of the individual assets of a company will indicate the value of company resources as a whole. The complex whole may be more valuable than the sum of the values of its parts. The difference between the value of the whole and the sum of the values of its assets is further magnified because some valuable aspects of an enterprise are not included in the definition of assets (for example, trained personnel). Furthermore, it has been argued that an enterprise may find current market values irrelevant if it intends to continue to operate as a business. If it cannot sell some of its assets and still operate, then the selling prices of these assets are irrelevant.

There is much discussion in accounting about asset valuation, and increasing numbers of accountants question the validity of historical cost valuation. However, most accountants still believe that the objectivity and verifiability of historical cost valuation generally outweigh its drawbacks. Therefore, although historical cost is an oversimplified approach to asset valuation, it is the method generally used under current accounting principles.

LIABILITIES

Claims against an enterprise by outside parties are called liabilities. *Liabilities are economic obligations of an enterprise that result from past or current transactions or events and require settlement in the future.* Payment with cash is the most common method of discharging liabilities. Rendering service is another way of settling some liabilities. For example, when a company has been paid by a customer or client for services that it has not yet rendered, the company has a liability to the customer or client. This liability will be settled by performing the services for the customer or client.

Liabilities defined

Accounting principles dictate that liabilities usually arise from transactions. A transaction usually involves an exchange or other type of interaction with another enterprise or individual. For example, a company may purchase an asset on credit. This transaction results in both an addition to assets and the creation of a liability—the obligation to pay for the asset. Similarly, when a lawyer renders services to the company, a liability arises—the company is obligated to pay for the services. The lawyer's part in the transaction in this case would be the current, ongoing rendering of service to the company.

In some cases, however, liabilities are recorded on the basis of other occurrences and events, such as lawsuits and natural events (floods or fire, for example). In general, *accounting principles provide that liabilities should be recognized whenever there is a clear and measurable obligation on the part of an enterprise.* The test of liability recognition is thus not as stringent as the test for asset recognition. Accountants generally are more concerned with recording all possible obligations than with recording all possible resources.

Liability recognition

Liabilities often are the counterpart of assets and services provided to the company. If an employee works for an enterprise, the service he renders is balanced by an obligation on the part of the company to pay for those services. When an asset is contributed by outside parties, an obligation to pay for the asset also appears. Only in a few cases do liabilities appear without assets or services also appearing. Taxes, which arise from legal requirements, are an example. In the case of taxes, the services rendered by the particular governmental body involved are usually not related to the amount of taxes paid.

Some liabilities payable in the future are related to transactions that have already taken place. Examples include the following:

- Guarantee obligations payable in the future and arising out of current sales
- Pension obligations arising out of employee services rendered in the current period

These liabilities are examples of the complex, ongoing transactions and events that exist in many large companies, affecting enterprise obligations.

OWNERS' EQUITY

Owners' equity defined

Liabilities are outside claims. *Claims of the owners of an enterprise are called owners' equity.* (In a corporation they are called stockholders' equity.) Liabilities must be paid; they involve a legal obligation. Owners' equity differs from liabilities in that the owners usually have a continuing interest in the business and do not expect their claims to be paid. In addition, owners' claims rank behind creditors' claims. That is, the owners are residual equity holders; they bear the ultimate risk of the enterprise, and claims of creditors must be satisfied before claims of owners. Of course, in return for bearing risk, the owners claim any net income (and suffer any losses) that the company earns.

If an enterprise earns net income, the result is a net increase in enterprise assets. These net assets are claimed by the owners. If the income is withdrawn by the owners (as dividends, for example), their claim is reduced. Fewer assets are left in the business for the owners to claim. If the owners leave the net income in the enterprise, their ownership claim will be increased by the amount of that income.

In a corporation, the owners' equity is usually divided into two portions—capital invested by the owners and income left in the enterprise by the owners. These amounts are called *contributed capital* and *retained earnings*. They will be discussed more fully later in the chapter.

Owners' equity in partnerships and individual proprietorships is discussed extensively in chapter 14.

STATEMENT OF FINANCIAL POSITION CLASSIFICATIONS

A mere listing of assets on the one hand, and liabilities and owners' equity on the other, does not lead to a full understanding of an enterprise's

The Statement of Financial Position

TABLE 2-1. Commonly Used Balance Sheet Classifications

Assets	*Liabilities*
Current assets	Current liabilities
Investments	Long-term liabilities
Property, plant, and equipment	
Intangible assets	*Stockholders'*
Other assets*	*Equity*
	Contributed capital
	Retained earnings

*This classification is used occasionally for items that do not fit conveniently into other categories.

financial position. Balance sheets, therefore, have a number of categories into which assets, liabilities, and owners' equity are classified. These categories have evolved over many years and are fairly well standardized. Table 2-1 gives a representative list of classifications.

An illustrative balance sheet that uses these classifications is given in Example 2-4. Our discussion below refers to this balance sheet.

The heading of the statement identifies the company, the name of the statement, and the date of the statement. It is common practice to present the balance sheet of the previous year in order to provide a comparison. A balance sheet presented this way is known as a *comparative* balance sheet.

The Bolle Supply Company balance sheet follows the *report form*. That is the name given the format in which assets are given before liabilities and owners' equity. The equality of the accounting equation is still maintained.

Classification of Assets

Current Assets. Cash and the assets to be converted to cash or used up in the near future are shown first in a balance sheet. These liquid assets are called *current assets*. Current assets are defined as cash and other assets that are reasonably expected to be realized in cash or sold or consumed during the normal operating cycle of the business or a year, whichever is longer. A normal operating cycle covers the following series of transactions:

$$\text{Cash} \rightarrow \text{Inventory} \rightarrow \text{Receivables} \rightarrow \text{Cash}$$

It covers the time it normally takes to buy goods, sell them, and collect the receivables from the sale.

EXAMPLE 2-4

BOLLE SUPPLY COMPANY
Statement of Financial Position
December 31, Year 2 and Year 1

Assets		December 31 Year 2		December 31 Year 1
Current assets:				
Cash			$ 20,000	$ 18,000
Accounts receivable	$ 74,500		$ 68,100	
Less allowance for doubtful accounts	7,300	67,200	6,800	61,300
Merchandise inventory, at cost		75,000		67,000
Prepaid expense		4,000		4,000
Total current assets		$166,200		$150,300
Investments:				
Stock of the Burgess Wholesale Company (at cost which approximates market)		$ 67,000		$ 42,000
Property, plant, and equipment:				
Land		$ 32,000		$ 32,000
Building	$128,000		$128,000	
Less accumulated depreciation	51,000	77,000	44,000	84,000
Store and office equipment	$ 50,000		$ 50,000	
Less accumulated depreciation	18,000	32,000	10,000	40,000
Total property, plant, and equipment		$141,000		$156,000
Intangible assets:				
Goodwill		$ 20,000		$ 24,000
Total assets		$394,200		$372,300
Liabilities and Stockholders' Equity				
Current liabilities:				
Accounts payable		$ 43,600		$ 40,600
Notes payable		6,000		10,000
Income taxes payable		14,000		12,500
Accrued interest payable		600		800
Accrued wages and other expenses payable		2,000		2,200
Total current liabilities		$ 66,200		$ 66,100
Long-term liabilities:				
8% note payable, due in Year 5		$ 48,000		$ 48,000
Total liabilities		$114,200		$114,100
Stockholders' equity:				
Contributed capital:				
Common stock, $5 par	$ 60,000		$ 60,000	
Amounts paid in excess of par	180,000		180,000	
Total contributed capital		$240,000		$240,000
Retained earnings		40,000		18,200
Total stockholders' equity		$280,000		$258,200
Total liabilities and stockholders' equity		$394,200		$372,300

Cash, the most liquid asset, is shown first. Cash includes the money kept on the premises and the money kept in banks. *Accounts receivable* are amounts owed to a company by its customers. A deduction is made from accounts receivable in the form of the *allowance for doubtful accounts* (or allowance for uncollectibles). The allowance is an estimate of the amount of receivables that will not be collected. The Bolle Supply Company estimates that of the $74,500 owed to it by its customers, $7,300 will not be collected. Thus, the expected cash value of accounts receivable is $67,200.

Merchandise inventory consists of the products that a company holds for sale. The Bolle Supply Company has $75,000 of inventory on December 31 of Year 2. The $75,000 is the *cost* of the inventory. The last item in current assets is *prepaid expense*. This includes amounts paid for such things as supplies that will be used up in the near future and insurance premiums that will provide insurance protection in the future.

Investments. The investments section of the balance sheet includes relatively long-term investments of money in stocks and other securities issued by other companies. Sometimes a company will invest in real estate properties with an eye to future use of the property. The purpose of stock or other security investments is usually to control another company or to assist another company financially. The Bolle Supply Company holds stock in a wholesale company, perhaps to have some influence in the management of that company. Note that the investment increased substantially in Year 2.

Property, Plant, and Equipment. Property, plant, and equipment are tangible (physical) long-lived assets that are used in business activities. *Land* is the property on which the building rests. Land is considered to be permanent and normally does not lose any value as a building site over time. *Buildings* and *equipment* decrease in value over time from physical causes, such as aging and wear and tear from use, and from economic causes, such as obsolescence. Accordingly, the cost of buildings and equipment are gradually written off to recognize this decrease. The cost written off during an accounting period is called *depreciation* and is an expense of doing business. The *accumulated depreciation* is the cumulative amount of cost written off since the assets were acquired. Both the cost of the assets and the accumulated depreciation are shown on the balance sheet. The cost of the assets less the accumulated depreciation is called the unexpired cost, *book value*, or *net book value*. The net book value means the value according to the accounting records. It is not intended to represent the current value of the assets. This fact should be remembered when interpreting the figures given on the balance sheet.

Intangible Assets. Intangible assets are relatively long-lived assets that have no physical existence. Their value is dependent on the rights and benefits that the owner derives from them. Many manufacturing companies own *patents* that give them exclusive rights to use the processes involved for seventeen years. The Bolle Supply Company has the intangible *goodwill*, which means that in the acquisition of another company, Bolle paid an amount for factors such as customer loyalty and business location, which make the company more valuable than the sum of its other assets. Goodwill usually has a limited life; hence, it is written off over its expected life. In the case of the Bolle Supply Company, the goodwill had an unexpired cost of $24,000 at the end of Year 1. This value was reduced to $20,000 at the end of Year 2. This means that Bolle is writing goodwill off at the rate of $4,000 per year, in accordance with the estimated number of years over which benefits are expected.

Intangible assets are written off over their useful life. According to current rules, intangibles must be written off over no more than forty years. The cost written off during a period is usually deducted directly from the cost of the intangible asset (no separate deduction like the accumulated depreciation is used).

Classification of Liabilities

Current Liabilities. Current liabilities are obligations due within the normal operating cycle of the business or within a year, whichever is longer. They will generally be paid from the current assets. They are shown at the amount owed as of the balance sheet date. *Accounts payable* are amounts owed to general creditors, usually as the result of purchasing merchandise or services on account. *Notes payable* usually arise from bank loans and are evidenced by promissory notes signed by the borrower. *Income taxes payable* is the amount owed to federal, state, and local governments for income taxes. The interest owed on notes is included in *accrued interest payable*, which also includes any interest owed on long-term debt of the company. *Accrued wages and other expense payable* include amounts owed to employees for work they have performed but for which they have not been paid. Also included would be property taxes owed at year-end and amounts owed for electricity, telephone, and other utility services.

Long-term Liabilities. These are obligations of a company that come due a year or more hence. The Bolle Supply Company has an 8% note payable that will come due in Year 5. The 8% refers to the interest charge on the loan. The interest owed on the $48,000 loan and unpaid at December 31 is included in the current liability item called accrued interest payable.

Classification of Stockholders' Equity

Contributed Capital. Contributed capital consists of amounts invested and donated to a corporation by its owners and others. It includes dollar amounts assigned to shares of stock issued by the company to its owners. It also includes other categories of owners' contributions, such as amounts contributed in excess of par value. In the Bolle Supply Company, the shares of stock were assigned a par value of $5.00 each. In addition to the total par value of $60,000, Bolle shareholders contributed a total of $180,000 in excess of par.

Retained Earnings. Retained earnings are amounts of company income reinvested in the company. As of December 31, in Year 2, the Bolle Supply Company has reinvested a total of $40,000 of its income.

Interpreting the Classified Balance Sheet

Having considered the standard categories of assets, liabilities, and owners' equity, we now ask, What information can be derived from a classified balance sheet? More specifically, what can the balance sheet of the Bolle Supply Company tell us about the company. We might be tempted to skip all of the detail on the assets side and go to the bottom of the balance sheet to see the total assets figure, and we may mistakenly conclude that the company is worth whatever that figure shows. Unfortunately, the total assets amount conveys very little about the company other than a rough idea of size. The total assets figure does not give us the worth of the company because it excludes many important resources that cannot readily be measured in dollars, and it combines cash and near-cash values with unexpired cost figures. Many of the cost figures may be substantially out of date.

It is the detail on the balance sheet that is most useful. The classifications of items on the balance sheet help us gain valuable information about the company. Let us turn back to Example 2-4 to see what information we can derive from the balance sheet.

The current assets, along with the current liabilities, inform us of the short-run ability of the company to pay obligations as they become due. Current assets and current liabilities are related in that current assets are used to pay current liabilities. The excess of current assets over current liabilities, termed *working capital*, and the ratio of current assets to current liabilities, termed the *current ratio*, are commonly used indicators of the short-run financial strength of a company. The Bolle Supply Company has working capital of $100,000 and a current ratio of 2.5 on December 31 of Year 2, compared with working capital of $84,200 and a current ratio of 2.3 a year earlier. Both of these measures suggest a fairly strong current position, and both indicate improvement in the past year.

Current ratio

Within the current assets we find a clearer indicator of immediate debt-paying ability in the cash and near-cash assets. Near-cash assets are those that can be quickly converted to cash. On December 31, Year 2, the Bolle Supply Company has $20,000 in cash and expects to collect

$67,200 from its customers in the near future. These cash and near-cash assets of $87,200 are substantially greater than the current liabilities of $66,200, indicating that the company should have no difficulty in meeting its short-term obligations.

The investments category shows that Bolle Supply Company has invested in the stock of the Burgess Wholesale Company and has increased its investment over the year from $42,000 to $67,000. Capital stock investments of this kind are usually intended to give the investing company some long-range benefit, perhaps some assurance of a steady source of supply for merchandise.

The property, plant, and equipment category discloses the kinds of long-lived tangible assets the company is using in its operations. The comparative balance sheet shows that Bolle Supply Company has had no new investment in this type of asset over the past year. The decrease in the unexpired cost (or book value) is due to depreciation for the year. It is important to recognize that the figures shown are not current-value figures, but unexpired cost.

Bolle Supply Company has one intangible asset, goodwill, arising from the acquisition of another business sometime in the past. The change in the goodwill figure reflects the write-off of $4,000 during the year.

The current liabilities have already been discussed. The long-term liability of $48,000 is not due for several years and hence is of no immediate concern except for the annual interest requirement. Stockholders' equity shows that the owners have contributed $240,000 in invested capital and have (through action of the corporation's board of directors) plowed back earnings of $40,000. It is interesting to note that the company's owners have supplied about 71% of the company's total assets and creditors about 29%. This would be interpreted by most business analysts as a conservative approach to financing the enterprise.

BALANCE SHEET—CONTENT AND PREPARATION

To illustrate the content and preparation of the balance sheet and also to indicate the effect of transactions on the balance sheet, we now consider Example 2.5.

EXAMPLE 2-5

Fred Roller begins the Roller Trucking Company late in Year 1. He invests $7,000 of his savings in the new company on December 15, Year 1, and receives 700 shares of stock in the company in return. At this point the balance sheet appears as follows:

ROLLER TRUCKING COMPANY
Statement of Financial Position
December 15, Year 1

Assets		Stockholders' Equity	
Cash	$7,000	Capital stock (700 shares)	$7,000

Before the end of the year, Fred leases a garage and two trucks by signing one-year leases on the garage and on the trucks. The leases cover the entire Year 2. The terms of both leases require that the last month's rent be paid when the lease is signed and that each month's rent be paid by the fifth of that month. The monthly rents are $1,000 for the garage and $1,500 for the two trucks. Using credit, Fred also purchases $2,000 of supplies to be used in the business. Fred's wife, Edna, is hired to be office manager at a salary of $800 per month; Fred and an employee, Samuel Harvest, are to operate the trucks. Fred is to earn a salary of $1,000 per month, while Harvest is to be paid $800 per month. Salaries begin in January, Year 2. The Roller Trucking Company statement of financial position for December 31, Year 1, reflects the initial activities of Fred Roller in starting the company. Note that the hiring of employees is not reflected because no work has been done at year end.

ROLLER TRUCKING COMPANY
Statement of Financial Position
December 31, Year 1

Assets		Liabilities	
Current assets:		Current liabilities:	
Cash	$4,500	Accounts payable	$2,000
Truck supplies on hand	2,000	Stockholders' Equity	
Prepaid rent:			
Garage	1,000	Capital stock	
Trucks	1,500	(700 shares)	7,000
Total assets	$9,000	Total equities	$9,000

The *prepaid rent* is for one month's rent on the garage and the trucks, in accordance with the terms of the leases. These are assets because the amount shown represents the right of Roller Trucking Company to occupy and use the garage and the trucks for one month. This is a valuable right that the company has paid for.

Turning to the liabilities, *accounts payable* is the amount owed to suppliers as a result of the purchase of supplies on credit. Owners' equity consists of 700 shares of *capital stock*. That is, the ownership interest is represented by 700 shares, all owned by Fred Roller.

Assets, liabilities, and owners' equity are changed by economic events. The economic events recognized in accounting are called *transactions*. *External transactions* are events that involve the enterprise and some

Effects of transactions

other person or organization. *Internal transactions* are events or conditions that are recognized within the firm. An example of an external transaction is the sale of merchandise to a customer. An example of an internal transaction is the use of supplies inventory in the operation of the business.

The effect of a few transactions on the balance sheet is illustrated in Example 2-6, which returns to the Roller Trucking Company.

EXAMPLE 2-6

On January 2, Year 2, the Roller Trucking Company is almost ready to begin operations. There are some important matters that Fred Roller feels should be taken care of on January 2 before he begins to operate. Fred's brother, Gordon, wants to join the company, so Fred permits him to buy 500 shares of capital stock for $5,000 cash. Capital stock now consists of 1,200 shares. Part of the deal is that Fred hire Gordon's son, Delbert, as a truck driver at a monthly salary of $550. A third truck is needed, and on January 2 Fred buys a new truck for $12,000. After borrowing $9,000 from the bank on a three-year, 10% note payable, Fred pays the truck dealer $12,000 in cash. Under the terms of the note, the principal of $9,000 will be paid on January 2, Year 5, and interest will be paid on each January 2. Thus, on January 2, Year 3, the payment due will be $900 interest (10% of $9,000 for one year). On January 2, Fred purchases some stationery and other office supplies costing $300 and a typewriter costing $600, both for cash. Operations are scheduled to commence on January 3.

Example 2-6 reveals five events. One event, the act of hiring Fred's nephew as a truck driver, while important, has no immediate effect on financial position and is not recognized as an accounting transaction. When Delbert performs his services, the company will then owe him the agreed salary and a transaction will then be recorded. Example 2-7 shows the effects of each of the other events on financial position.

This extended example shows that the balance sheet continues to balance—that is, that assets continue to be equalled by claims against assets after each transaction. When an enterprise has many transactions, it is useful to keep track of the effects of transactions in separate statements. These statements, with particular emphasis on the income statement, are discussed in chapter 3.

EXAMPLE 2-7

ROLLER TRUCKING COMPANY
Effects of Transactions on Financial Position

Transaction 1: Gordon Roller invests $5,000 cash in the business.

Effects
- Increases asset cash by $5,000.
- Increases owners' equity by $5,000.

Balance Sheet after Transaction 1

Assets		Liabilities	
Current assets:		Current liabilities:	
Cash	$ 9,500	Accounts payable	$ 2,000
Truck supplies inventory	2,000		
Prepaid rent:		*Stockholders' Equity*	
Garage	1,000		
Trucks	1,500	Capital stock	
		(1,200 shares)	12,000
Total assets	$14,000	Total equities	$14,000

Transaction 2: Roller Trucking Company borrows $9,000 from the bank.

Effects
- Increases asset cash by $9,000.
- Increases liability three-year, 10% note payable by $9,000.

Balance Sheet after Transaction 2

Assets		Liabilities	
Current assets:		Current liabilities:	
Cash	$18,500	Accounts payable	$ 2,000
Truck supplies inventory	2,000	Long-term liability:	
Prepaid rent:		Three-year, 10%	
Garage	1,000	note payable	9,000
Trucks	1,500	Total liabilities	$11,000
Total assets	$23,000		
		Stockholders' Equity	
		Capital stock	
		(1,200 shares)	12,000
		Total equities	$23,000

(Continued)

Part I   The Framework of Financial Accounting

Example 2-7 (Cont.)

Transaction 3: Roller Trucking Company purchases truck for $12,000 cash.

Effects
- Increases asset trucks by $12,000.
- Decreases asset cash by $12,000.

Balance Sheet after Transaction 3

Assets		Liabilities	
Current assets:		Current liabilities:	
Cash	$ 6,500	Accounts payable	$ 2,000
Truck supplies inventory	2,000	Long-term liability:	
Prepaid rent:		Three-year, 10%	
Garage	1,000	note payable	9,000
Trucks	1,500	Total liabilities	$11,000
Total current assets	$11,000		
Plant and Equipment:		Stockholders' Equity	
Trucks	12,000		
Total assets	$23,000	Capital stock	
		(1,200 shares)	12,000
		Total equities	$23,000

Transaction 4: Roller Trucking Company purchases office supplies costing $300 and equipment costing $600, paying cash.

Effects
- Increases asset office supplies inventory by $300.
- Increases asset office equipment by $600.
- Decreases asset cash by $900.

Balance Sheet after Transaction 4

Assets		Liabilities	
Current assets:		Current liabilities:	
Cash	$ 5,600	Accounts payable	$ 2,000
Truck supplies inventory	2,000	Long-term liability:	
Office supplies inventory	300	Three-year, 10%	
Prepaid rent:		note payable	9,000
Garage	1,000	Total liabilities	$11,000
Trucks	1,500		
Total current assets	$10,400	Stockholders' Equity	
Plant and Equipment:			
Trucks	$12,000	Capital stock	
Office equipment	600	(1,200 shares)	12,000
Total plant and equipment	$12,600	Total equities	$23,000
Total assets	$23,000		

The Statement of Financial Position Chapter 2

SOME IMPORTANT CONCEPTS FOR ACCOUNTING

At this point we consider some of the concepts that influence the balance sheet. Three of the concepts have already been discussed and illustrated. The fourth one is new but has already been illustrated in this chapter.

Going Concern Assumption. Accountants assume that the business enterprise has an indefinite future life. Therefore, assets such as machines, supplies, and buildings used in the business need not be measured on the basis of their selling price, since there is no intention of selling them.

Stable Unit of Measurement Assumption. Accountants assume that prices are unchanging or that changes in prices are not significant. Hence, cost as the basis for measuring assets is warranted. This assumption worked fairly well until the late 1960s because price increases were modest. Since the late 1960s, prices have risen dramatically. This fact has caused accountants and other interested parties, such as the SEC, to reexamine this assumption and to consider seriously the use of current values in addition to historical costs for asset measurements. This problem will be discussed in chapter 15.

Cost Principle. In accounting, assets are measured on the basis of the cost incurred when the assets were originally acquired by the enterprise. This original valuation continues to be used until another transaction takes place or the asset is used up or becomes worthless. Valuation at cost is based on both of the assumptions above. An important aspect of this principle is that cost is measured objectively, since it is based on a price determined in a market transaction. Thus, cost is relatively free from subjective elements.

Entity Assumption. The entity assumption states that economic activities of entities can be separated from those of their owners. This allows us to view the enterprise as being completely separate from its owners. In the Roller Trucking Company example, all of the assets and liabilities are those of the trucking business. The Roller brothers, who are the owners, are represented in the owners' equity section of the balance sheet. The owners may well have many more personal assets and liabilities, but these are not brought into the accounting for the business they own. The entity assumption permits exclusive concentration on the activities of the trucking company. Thus the owners and the creditors and other interested parties can get information that pertains only to the trucking enterprise, and it is easier to see whether the trucking enterprise is a worthwhile economic activity.

ASSET VALUATION AND INCOME DETERMINATION

Exchange price

Asset valuations are crucial in determining enterprise income as well as enterprise position. *When costs are first incurred, an asset is recorded at the exchange price, which is the historical cost of the item.* The recorded cost of the asset may subsequently be embodied in new forms as a result of business operations. For example, raw materials may become part of a finished product as a result of manufacturing activities. In this stage, the historical cost of the original asset is reassigned to a new asset. Valuation thus continues at historical cost.

Subsequently, the asset is used up or leaves the enterprise, and the asset value becomes an expense of operations. What valuation should be used for the expense? It seems logical and appropriate that the value placed on the asset before it expires should also be the value placed on the expense after the asset expires. The amount of the expense is therefore dependent on the asset valuation.

Thus we can see that asset valuation and income determination are interrelated. We also can see that the statement of financial position and the income statement are related. Many assets on the statement of financial position are expenses held in suspension, awaiting some future matching with revenues. Also, the valuation used for the statement of financial position is generally the basis for the subsequent charge to expense when the asset is used up in operations.

SUMMARY

The financial position of an enterprise is portrayed by the statement of financial position and the notes to the financial statements. The balance sheet (another name for statement of financial position) indicates the assets, liabilities, and owners' equity of the enterprise as of a certain date. The fact that total assets are claimed in total by creditors and owners permits us to say that:

$$\text{Assets} = \text{Liabilities} + \text{Owners' Equity}$$

This is the basic accounting equation, the basis for double-entry accounting.

Grouping the assets, liabilities, and owners' equity into standardized categories makes the balance sheet more useful. The usual classifications for assets are current assets; investments; property, plant, and equipment; and intangible assets. For liabilities, the classifications are current and long-term. Owners' equity is divided into contributed capital and retained earnings. The classified balance sheet provides information about the company's debt-paying ability, the kinds of resources employed in the company, the long-term debt obligations, and the composition of financing. It is important to remember that the balance sheet cannot indicate the company's present worth. Assets cannot include all of the company's resources, nor can liabilities show all of the company's obligations. Further, many assets are based on cost figures that are considerably out of date.

Accounting statements, including the balance sheet, are based on concepts that have evolved over many years. Most of the concepts have proved durable and useful, but the stable unit of measurement assumption is undergoing examination now because of inflation. Problems caused by inflation and accounting alternatives for dealing with it are discussed in chapter 15.

IMPORTANT TERMS

Financial accounting
Accounting equation
Assets
Cost principle (historical cost)
Unexpired cost
Going concern assumption
Stable unit assumption
Liabilities
Owners' equity
Current assets
Operating cycle
Investments
Tangible assets

Property, plant, and equipment
Net book-value
Intangible assets
Current liabilities
Long-term liabilities
Stockholders' equity
Contributed capital
Paid-in capital
Retained earnings
Current ratio
Working capital
Entity assumption

QUESTIONS

2-1. What is *financial position*? How does the accountant define financial position?

2-2. Define *asset* in your own words. *Liability. Owners' equity.*

2-3. Some assets are measured at their cash value, while others are measured on the basis of their cost. Why not measure all assets at their cash value?

2-4. What is the merit of a classified statement of financial position?

2-5. What is the basis of the term *balance sheet*?

2-6. What is the accounting equation? Explain its role in the accounting process.

2-7. What determines whether an asset is a *current asset*? Give three examples of current assets.

2-8. What is *cost valuation?* How is valuation at cost related to *objective measurements?* To the *going concern assumption?*

2-9. What is the *operating cycle?* Why is this concept important to financial accounting?

2-10. One of the assumptions of accounting is *stable measuring unit.* Explain what this means and discuss its validity in today's economy.

2-11. What is *unexpired cost?*

2-12. What is the *entity assumption?*

EXERCISES

2-13. *Resources and assets.* Which of the following resources would appear as assets on a company's balance sheet?

- Cash in bank
- Prepaid rent on a leased building
- The estimated value of the company's location
- The estimated value of the company's human resources
- Land owned by the company
- Merchandise inventory

For those you decided would be included as assets, give the basis for the dollar amount of the asset. For those you decided to exclude, give your reason.

2-14. *Current assets.* A large baking company includes the following in its balance sheet:

- Cash
- Ovens, machinery, and equipment
- U.S. Government securities
- Wrapping materials and supplies
- Construction in progress
- Prepaid expenses
- Raw materials
- Common stock

Which of the above would you include in current assets? How would you classify those items you did not include?

2-15. *Current liabilities.* Which of the following are probably current liabilities?

- Marketable securities
- Salaries and wages expense
- Retained earnings
- Salaries and wages payable
- Long-term debt due within one year
- Federal and state income taxes payable
- Accounts payable
- Accrued vacation expense payable

2-16. *Assets.* List two or three different assets that are probably *unique* to the following types of companies.

  a. bank
  b. grocery supermarket
  c. petroleum company
  d. summer resort
  e. ski resort
  f. CPA firm
  g. automobile manufacturer

2-17. *Classification.* Classify each of the following according to current assets; investments; property, plant, and equipment; intangibles; other assets.

  · Cash
  · Trucks (in a trucking company)
  · Land (as a building site)
  · Marketable securities
  · Patents
  · Accounts receivable due in 90 days
  · Investment in the stock of another company
  · Goodwill

2-18. *Classification.* Classify each of the following according to current assets; investments; property, plant, and equipment; intangibles; other assets.

  · Short-term government securities
  · Postage stamps
  · Prepaid insurance
  · Land (held for future expansion)
  · Typewriters (held as merchandise)
  · Copyrights

2-19. *Classification.* Classify each of the following as current liabilities, long-term liabilities, or not a liability.

  · Cash in savings account
  · Wages payable to employees
  · Income taxes payable
  · Common stock, par value $2.50
  · Notes payable, due in five years
  · Current maturities of long-term debt

2-20. *Asset valuation.* How do you measure the following items for presentation on a statement of financial position?

  a. An inventory of 100 radios that have a retail selling price of $50 each. The radios cost the company $30 each when they were purchased over the past two months.
  b. Customers owe the company $15,000 for purchases the customers made from the company over the past two months. A credit expert has told you that in all probability, $1,200 of the $15,000 will not be collected.

2-21. *Statement preparation.* The Wilson Company, a corporation, began business early in Year 1. George and Ira Wilson started the business with an invest-

Part I   The Framework of Financial Accounting

ment of $25,000 cash between them. The company purchased merchandise on credit for $15,000. The credit terms are 30 days from date of purchase. The company also rented a store building in a good location on a one-year lease. The building's owner was paid $6,000 in cash for the first three months' rent. Prepare the company's statement of financial position as it would be immediately after the above transactions.

2-22. *Transactions and balance sheet.* The Dog Grooming Palace, Inc., was organized on March 28, Year 1. At that time 2,000 shares of $10 par stock were issued for $20,000. Subsequently, the following took place:

March 29   The company hired Jason Fleece as head groomer at $200 per week and Harry Taille as assistant at $150 per week. Employees will start work April 3.

April 1   The company rented facilities for the business at $400 per month. The first month's rent is paid, covering the remainder of April.

April 2   The company bought $3,000 of equipment for cash.

April 3   The company bought $1,200 of supplies on account from Baker Supply Co.

Required:

Prepare a balance sheet as of April 3. (Ignore any expiration of rent for April).

PROBLEMS

2-23. *Balance sheet.* The liabilities and owners' equity items below are from the balance sheet of an oil company. Prepare a classified liabilities and owners' equity side of the balance sheet. (Hint: current liabilities should total $123.6 million.)

	Millions December 31, Year 1
Retained earnings	$85.5
Taxes payable (other than income)	13.3
Mortgage notes payable	62.9
Other notes payable due in Year 9	2.6
Accrued liabilities	6.8
Additional paid-in capital	6.5
Accounts payable	51.5
Notes payable, short-term	46.5
Common stock, par value $1	7.1
Deferred federal income taxes payable	5.1
Long-term debt due within one year	2.6
Income taxes payable	2.9

(Solution in Appendix B.)

2-24. *Balance sheet.* The assets below are from the balance sheet of an oil company. Prepare the asset side of the company's balance sheet, properly classified. (Hint: current assets should total $140.0 million).

	Millions December 31, Year 1
Pipeline and storage terminals	$ 17.8
Inventories:	
Refined products	30.5
Crude oil	29.9
Materials and supplies	3.9
Cash	15.7
Trade receivables	27.1
Allowance for uncollectible accounts	1.5
Marketing properties and equipment	28.4
Allowance for depreciation, depletion,	
and amortization	85.0
Prepaid expenses	9.4
Refining and petrochemical properties	137.5
Production equipment	54.3
Recoverable income taxes	25.0
Investments and other assets	5.4

2-25. *Balance sheet.* A company reports the following on its balance sheet:

	Millions December 31	
	Year 2	Year 1
Property, plant, and equipment	$57.5	$55.1
Shareholders' equity	89.6	76.6
Current liabilities	42.5	27.2
Other assets	2.6	3.0
Other liabilities	11.6	12.3
Investments	1.4	.9
Current assets	96.7	73.2
Long-term debt	14.5	16.1

   a. What is the company's working capital on December 31, Year 2 and Year 1? What is its current ratio on the same dates? Has the company's working capital position improved or deteriorated? Explain.

   b. What are the company's total assets on December 31, Year 2 and Year 1? Total liabilities? Owners' Equity?

2-26. *Working capital.* From the following data, compute the working capital and the current ratio of Company Z on December 31, Year 1:

	Company Z December 31, Year 1
Cash	$ 3,200,000
Current maturities of long-term debt	2,000,000
Accounts payable	18,000,000
Accounts receivable	38,000,000
Allowance for doubtful accounts	1,200,000
Inventories of products	65,000,000
Income taxes payable	11,000,000
Notes payable, due in Year 2	5,000,000
Mortgage payable, due in Year 18	70,000,000
Investments in affiliated companies	3,000,000
Marketable securities	2,500,000

2-27. *Balance sheet.* Prepare a classified balance sheet as of December 31, Year 1, from the data below:

MANN COMPANY
December 31, Year 1

Cash	$ 8,000
Accounts payable	10,000
Capital stock, par value $5	12,000
Merchandise inventory	14,000
Office supplies inventory	2,000
Capital in excess of par	39,000
Equipment	24,000
Retained earnings	18,000
Accumulated depreciation on equipment	8,000
Notes payable, due June, Year 2	4,000
Building	45,000
Accounts receivable	18,000
Accumulated depreciation on building	19,000
Allowance for uncollectible accounts	1,000

(Solution in Appendix B.)

2-28. *Balance sheet.* Prepare a classified balance sheet for the Bakers' Bakery, Inc., as of December 31, Year 1. The information is given below:

	December 31, Year 1
Cash	$ 22,650
Accounts payable	29,870
U.S. Government securities, at cost which approximates market	25,580
Inventories at cost:	
Finished products	8,360
Wrapping materials and supplies	8,570
Raw materials	14,940
Accrued federal income tax payable	4,780
8% note payable, due in Year 6	17,110
Accrued wages payable	2,940
Prepaid expenses	1,100
Long-term debt due within one year	1,500
Land	11,240
Common stock, $3 par value	24,000
Buildings	54,200
Ovens, machinery, and equipment	115,420
Amounts paid in in excess of par	13,960
Delivery equipment	5,720
Retained earnings (to be determined)	?
Building construction in progress	6,650
Goodwill	3,010
Accumulated depreciation	90,910
Accounts receivable	25,580
Allowance for uncollectible accounts	1,210

2-29. *Balance sheet.* The bookkeeper of the Rush Wholesale Corporation, a small wholesale company, has given you an alphabetical listing of the company's assets, liabilities, and owners' equity. You ascertain that the amounts given are correct and that the list includes everything.

Accounts payable	$15,000	Merchandise inventory	$80,000
Accounts receivable	7,000	Mortgage payable, due	
Building (net)	70,000	on Dec. 31, 1999	40,000
Capital stock	90,000	Note payable, due	
Cash	8,000	Nov. 1, Year 2	15,000
Fixtures and equipment	30,000	Other payables	2,000
Income taxes payable	5,000	Prepaid insurance	3,000
Land	12,000	Retained earnings	43,000

The items above are amounts at December 31, Year 1. You are asked to prepare a statement of financial position, or balance sheet, as of December 31, Year 1.

2-30. *Statement of financial position.* You have been asked by Janis Dodge, the principal owner of a corporation known as the Fancy Duds Place, to assemble a balance sheet that she needs to give to her banker. Dodge has given you the following data, all of which pertains to December 31, Year 1.

a. Cash on hand	$ 100	g. Accounts payable	$1,800
b. Cash in bank	700	h. Value of store	
c. Merchandise inventory	4,500	employees	6,000
d. Accounts receivable	1,200	i. Note payable, due on	
e. Estimated uncollectible		June 30, Year 2	2,000
accounts receivable	200	j. Capital stock	4,000
f. Value of customer		k. Store equipment	2,000
goodwill	12,000		

You confirm that items *a, b, c, d, e, g, i, j,* and *k* are correct. You ask Dodge about items *f* and *h*, and also note that retained earnings is missing. Dodge tells you that *f* and *h* are her estimates of the value of an attractive location and the store's congenial salespeople. Customers have frequently remarked how attractive the store is and how convenient its location is. Furthermore, Dodge has observed that many new customers have bought merchandise simply because the sales people are so pleasant. She says she doesn't know anything about the retained earnings and hopes you can figure it out.

Required:
Prepare a statement of financial position for the Fancy Duds Place as of December 31, Year 1. (Hint: retained earnings is the missing figure in the equation:

Assets − Liabilities = Capital Stock + Retained Earnings)

2-31. *Transaction and balance sheet.* The Second Seed Company has the following balance sheet on December 18, year 1:

Part I The Framework of Financial Accounting

SECOND SEED COMPANY
Balance Sheet
December 18, Year 1

Assets		Liabilities	
Current assets:		Current liabilities:	
Cash	$ 26,000	Accounts payable	$ 26,000
Accounts receivable	12,000		
Merchandise inventory	20,000	Long-term liability:	
Total current assets	$ 58,000	Long-term notes	40,000
Plant and equipment:		Total liabilities	$ 66,000
Land	$ 15,000		
Buildings	60,000	Stockholders' Equity	
Less: accumulated depreciation	(10,000)	Capital stock	$ 40,000
Total plant and equipment	$65,000	Retained earnings	17,000
		Total stockholders' equity	$ 57,000
Total assets	$123,000	Total equities	$123,000

During December 19 and 20 the following transactions occurred:

December 19	The company bought $8,000 more inventory on credit.
December 19	The company paid $10,000 on long-term notes.
December 20	The company bought a delivery truck for $8,000, paying cash of $3,000 and giving a 60-day note for $5,000.
December 20	The company collected $4,000 of amounts owed by customers.

Required:

Prepare a balance sheet in good form after the above transactions on December 20.

2-32. *Changes in financial position.* The Gorki Company has the following statement of financial position immediately following its organization:

GORKI COMPANY
Statement of Financial Position
December 20, Year 1

Assets		Liabilities	
Cash in bank	$25,000	20-year, 10% mortgage payable	$30,000
Land	5,000		
Building	50,000		
	$80,000	Stockholders' Equity	
		Capital stock	50,000
			$80,000

The Gorki Company will begin manufacturing electronic products in January of Year 2. The company was started by M. Gorki, principal owner, and his wife, Lili. Together they own 100% of the stock. A local investor, Bertie "Short" Circut, sold Gorki the land and building and assumed the 20-year mortgage.

The following events occurred from December 21 through December 31, Year 1:

a. An engineer, Gordon Module, was hired to supervise production activities. He will be paid $18,000 per year plus a share of the profits, beginning in Year 2.

b. Various electronic parts and materials were purchased on credit, $8,000. The amount payable must be paid by January 15, Year 2.

c. Testing machines and other machines were purchased on the following terms: $5,000 cash and a 2-year, 12% note payable in the amount of $10,000. This note is due on December 29, Year 3.

d. George Woodrow, a carpenter, was paid $3,000 cash for his work in building some work stations and benches for assembling work. This amount covered materials as well as George's labor.

e. Five factory employees were hired to begin work in Year 2. They will be paid $4.00 per hour for a 40-hour week.

Required:

Prepare a statement of financial position as of December 31, Year 1, giving effect to all of the transactions above. If an event is not a transaction, explain why it is not.

3

The Income Statement and the Statement of Changes in Financial Position

Accountants provide financial information about business enterprises in three primary statements: the statement of financial position (balance sheet), the income statement (or earnings statement), and the statement of changes in financial position (or funds statement).[1] The three statements are interrelated. The financial position of an enterprise is portrayed by the balance sheet, or statement of financial position. The balance sheet indicates the assets owned by the enterprise and the claims against those assets. It gives a picture of the status, or position, of the enterprise at one particular time. The balance sheet complements the income statement and the funds statement, which show the changes that have taken place in position over a period of time. The statements of changes can be compared to motion pictures, which show action over a period of time; the balance sheet is like a still picture, which freezes motion at a point in time. The relationship between the statements of changes and the statement of financial position is illustrated in Figure 3-1. Income statements and other statements of changes are connecting links between balance sheets. Or, to look at it another way, balance sheets are momentary pauses in the flow of enterprise activities in order to take stock of the situation.

In this chapter, we discuss the nature and makeup of the income

---

1. In this text we shall use alternative titles at times to develop familiarity with the various names used for the statements.

The Income Statement and the Statement of Changes in Financial Position Chapter 3

Relationship between Statements of Changes and Statement of Financial Position FIGURE 3-1

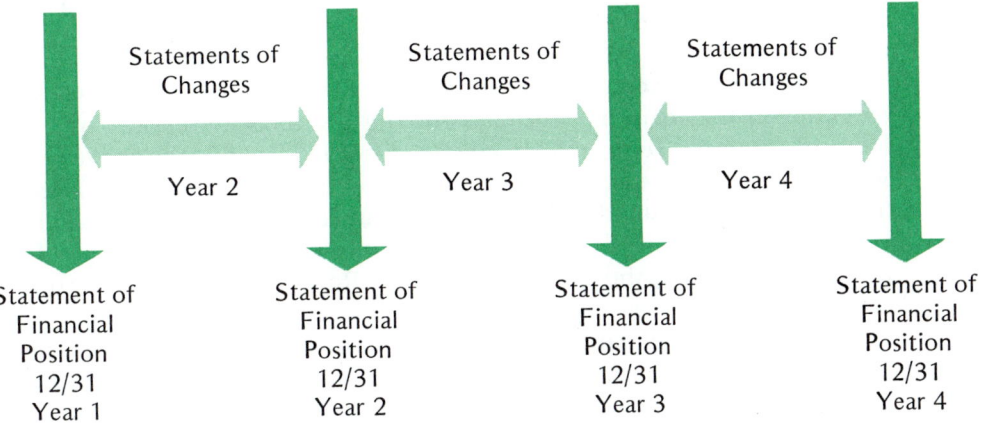

statement and the funds statement. The statement of retained earnings, a supporting statement, is also covered briefly. The chapter ends with a summary review of the fundamental concepts and principles of financial accounting.

THE INCOME STATEMENT

In financial accounting, particular attention is focused on enterprise progress. Accountants attempt to measure progress by determining the *net income* of the enterprise. The results of the measurement process are reported in the *income statement*.

Net Income

Accountants define *net income* as the difference between *revenues realized* during the accounting period and the *expenses recognized* in the accounting period. Accountants like this definition because both revenues and expenses have been defined so that reasonably objective measures of revenue and expense can be obtained.

Revenues

Revenues are the inflows of assets to an enterprise as a result of products and services transferred by the enterprise to its customers during a period of time. Revenues for

Revenues defined

61

Sources of revenue

many enterprises arise from sales of goods to customers. Other businesses earn revenues by rendering services or allowing others to use enterprise resources. Revenues can also result from disposing of resources other than products—for example, selling a building or investments. In each case, revenue involves an inflow of assets to the enterprise. The assets can be either in the form of cash paid for the products or services or in the form of amounts receivable from the customer (valid claims that will be settled by a later receipt of cash). Revenue occasionally appears as a reduction in liabilities instead of as an increase in assets. Revenues should not be confused with assets. Revenues are measures of the flow of assets for a period; they are not the assets themselves. Revenues do not appear on the balance sheet.

In a large enterprise, revenues can come from the sale of a large number of products, and possibly from the rendering of several kinds of services as well. For example, in 1977 the NCR Corporation, a large manufacturer of computers and related business equipment, reported sales of over a billion dollars, of which about two thirds was sales of equipment and one third was sales of services.

The revenue section of the income statement is generally simple. Generally, each major source of revenue should be reported, as illustrated in Example 3-1.

EXAMPLE 3-1

BILBO COMPUTER COMPANY
Revenue Section of the
Income Statement
for the Year Ended December 31

	Year 2	Year 1
Sales of products	$ 45,320	$ 38,780
Rentals	84,700	78,220
Sales of services	38,360	35,700
Total revenue	$168,380	$152,700

Realization Principle. The *realization principle* governs the recognition of revenue. It provides the answers to the questions of when revenue is to be recognized and how much is to be recognized. According to this principle, the earning process must be complete or virtually complete and an exchange must take place before revenue can be recognized. The amount to be recognized is determined in the exchange transaction. The practical test for this principle is the sale of goods or the performance of a service.

The realization principle is applicable to the vast majority of business operations, for in most enterprises the sale is the most important event in the total operations cycle. Goods are purchased or manufactured, stored, and then sold for cash or on credit terms, and then the agreed price is collected. The sale is the culmination of a series of activities, all of which point to the sale. After the sale is made, collection is highly probable because credit terms are usually honored by customers. A customer who doesn't pay his bill on time is in danger of getting a poor credit rating.

Exceptions in Revenue Recognition. Although the sale is the most important event in most situations, there are times when other events are more important than the sale.

Cash Basis and Installment. Where payment of bills is highly uncertain, as in some medical practices, the revenue is recognized upon the collection of cash, rather than at the time the service is rendered or the sale is made. When goods are sold under long drawn-out installment terms, a company may recognize revenue only as installment collections are made, particularly if ultimate collection is uncertain. In both these bases of revenue recognition the uncertainties of collection outweigh the importance of the sales transaction.

Production Method. In the production of commodities such as gold and silver, production is the most important activity. When production is complete, all that remains to be done is to sell the precious metal at the established market price. Sale is assured in every case. Many agricultural products have the same degree of certainty of sale. Hence, revenue may be recognized when the crop has been harvested. In the construction industry, contracts may require more than one year to complete. In this case, it is appropriate to recognize revenue on the basis of degree of completion. Production methods are used when production, rather than sale, is the most important event in the cycle of operations.

Expenses

Net income is determined by subtracting appropriate *expenses* from revenues. *Expenses are the outflows of assets or the increases in liabilities that take place in connection with products and services transferred by an enterprise to its customers during a period of time and in connection with other income-directed activities of the enterprise.* Expenses are the opposite of revenues. They are the negative aspect of the income measurement process, whereas revenues are the positive aspect. Expenses, like revenues, appear only on the income statement; they are never found on the balance sheet. Only the results of asset outflows and liability increases appear on the balance sheet. Expenses include the following:

Expenses defined

1. The cost of the assets or services that are sold. This is called *cost of goods sold expense* or *cost of sales.*

Types of expenses

Part I   The Framework of Financial Accounting

2. The cost of directly purchased services used in the production of revenues. Salaries expense is an example.
3. The cost of assets used in the production of revenues. Examples are cost of supplies (which are physically consumed) and depreciation of machinery (where the machines age and wear out).
4. Taxes of various kinds, such as income taxes and social security taxes.
5. Losses in assets because of normal occurrences, such as the estimated loss from uncollectible accounts.

Cost and expense

Expense Recognition. The fundamental idea of expense is that an asset is used up. For every expense, a cost (a sacrifice) must be incurred at some point. That is, for every dollar of expense, there must be a dollar of cash outlay. The cash outlay may have occurred in some past accounting period, it may occur in the present accounting period, or it may be expected to occur in some future accounting period. The timing of the cash outlay need not coincide with the timing of the expense. The problem of expense recognition lies in determining when costs become expenses. This is the central problem of accounting. The specific problems of expense recognition associated with particular types of cost will be discussed in detail when those costs are discussed in future chapters. At this point we want to indicate the three general principles of expense recognition.

Direct matching

1. *Direct Matching Principle. Some costs are recognized as expenses on the basis of a direct association (matching) with specific revenues.* A cause-and-effect relationship can be established between revenues and certain costs. For example, when a product is sold, the cost of the unit sold becomes an expense that is directly related to the sales revenue. Any commission or cost of delivery to customers also can be related directly to the revenue.

Direct matching is most highly developed in the field of cost accounting. Traditionally, the major activity in cost accounting has been the computation of the cost of products. During production, costs of materials, labor, and other elements used in production are accumulated and related in some way to units of product. When the products are sold, the product costs can be related directly to the sales revenue. Production often involves continuous and very complicated processes, however, and computing the precise correlation between particular efforts and particular results is often quite difficult.

Because many costs cannot be related directly to specific revenues, two additional recognition principles are necessary.

Cost allocation

2. *Cost Allocation Principle. Some costs are recognized as expenses on the basis of a systematic and rational allocation wherein the cost is allocated to the period or periods benefitted by the cost.*

The cost allocation principle provides a basis for relating costs to accounting periods when they cannot be related to specific revenue. If an asset provides benefits for several periods, its cost is allocated as an expense to those periods. If it provides benefits to only one period, it is recorded as an expense in that period. A pattern of benefits is determined, and the allocation is then based on this pattern. Assumptions must usually be made, because a pattern of benefits can seldom be conclusively demonstrated. Examples of allocations over several periods are depreciation of buildings and allocation of the cost of a three-year insurance policy. Examples of allocations to a single period are store rent for a month and office salaries earned in a period.

Relating expenses to periods rather than to specific revenues does not deny the importance of the particular activity or function involved; it merely indicates the lack of any satisfactory basis of direct association with revenue. As measurement techniques are developed, some expenses now related to periods may be related on a direct basis. But so many assumptions would be involved in some cases that the resulting income figure might not be valid.

3. *Immediate Recognition Principle. Some costs are recognized as expenses in the current accounting period because there is no discernible future benefit associated with those costs.* — *Immediate recognition*

There are many costs that cannot be associated with particular revenue and whose benefits cannot be systematically associated with a number of periods. Executive salaries are good examples. Presumably, the largest benefit of the year's salary is for the current year, but there probably are future benefits from the work the executive is doing this year. But the whole salary is considered an expense of the current year because the future benefits are too difficult to measure.

Kinds of Expenses. An expense is often called an expired cost, for an asset has been consumed or used or a liability has been created (leading to a future decrease in assets). Many expenses are associated with an enterprise's income-directed activities and contribute to the production of revenue either directly or indirectly. Expenses may also occur as the result of accidental events such as fires, theft, and storms. These expenses, recognized under the third expense principle above, are called *losses*. The — *Losses* disposition of certain assets through sale or retirement may also result in what are commonly called losses. For example, a machine carried on the records at $10,000 may be sold for $2,000 because it is no longer efficient in operation. The difference of $8,000 would be recognized as a loss on sale of assets. The loss is actually the difference between the asset inflow (revenue) of $2,000 and the asset reduction (expense) of $10,000. For unusual transactions such as this, the net amount is usually all that is reported. Significant losses that are unusual and non-recurring are shown in — *Extraordinary items* the income statement in a special section entitled "Extraordinary Items."[2]

---

2. Gains arising from similar events are also treated as extraordinary items.

The expense part of the income statement is more complicated than is the revenue section. There are many different expenses, and they are reported in a variety of ways. An approach often used in annual reports is shown in Example 3-2.

EXAMPLE 3-2

BIBLO COMPUTER COMPANY
Expense Section of the
Income Statement
for the Year Ended December 31

	Year 2	Year 1
	(in thousands)	
Expenses:		
Cost of products sold	$ 14,270	$ 12,420
Cost of rentals and services	33,265	29,530
Selling, general and administration	37,400	36,200
Research and development	8,560	7,400
Interest on debt	1,100	1,800
Income taxes	45,100	40,200
Total expenses	$139,695	$127,550

Stages of Cost

Keeping track of costs is a complicated accounting task. Some of the complexities can be seen by looking at three typical stages of cost.

Cost Incurrence. Cost incurrence is the stage of initial entry of costs into the enterprise. In this stage, the costs are assets of the enterprise—that is, items of value that will be used in subsequent operations. An obvious example is an inventory of merchandise bought by a company. The merchandise is purchased for subsequent sale by the company. The sale usually does not occur immediately after purchase; thus there is a period during which the items are held. These items are obviously assets to the company. The purchase of a delivery truck is another example of cost incurrence.

Cost Transformation. Some costs that are in the form of assets do not become expenses directly; first they are changed into new asset forms by the company's operations. For example, raw materials used in manufacturing do not become expenses when they are put into production. Instead, their costs are added to the manufacturing costs, such as labor and overhead, to become work in process inventory (goods being worked on, in the process of manufacture), and then an item of finished goods inventory. Both of these inventories are valuable to the company and are shown as assets. When the finished goods are sold, the material cost finally becomes an expense as part of the cost of goods sold expense.

In accounting we assume that the material cost becomes embodied in the latter asset stages (work in process and finished goods inventory), and the cost is accounted for as if it were transformed into new asset forms. This holds true for labor and overhead as well as for materials. When production employees work on changing raw materials into a finished product, it is assumed that their wages also become embodied in the product (the labor cost is transformed into products almost at the moment of cost incurrence). The labor and the supporting overhead costs are essential in producing the finished item; therefore, the assumption of embodiment is reasonable. Thus, material, labor, and overhead costs are transformed into work in process and finally into finished products.

Some costs never go through this type of transformation. A delivery truck, for instance, goes directly from the asset stage into expense (depreciation), with no intermediate steps. In fact, cost transformations are usually confined to items that are associated directly with revenue. Items related to periods of time generally do not go through transformation.

Cost Expiration. The final stage of costs in an enterprise is *cost expiration*. At this stage, a cost stops being an asset and becomes an expense. For example, consider the delivery truck described above. There is no question but that the truck is an asset when the cost is first incurred; what is not as readily apparent is that the truck gradually becomes an expense. As the truck is used, it wears out and the cost expires. This cost expiration, called *depreciation*, is an expense to the company. As another example, when the item of finished goods inventory mentioned above is sold to a customer, the cost is transferred into an expense category called *cost of goods sold expense*. Figure 3-2 illustrates the process.

Not all costs go through the three stages in the illustration. Some costs, such as merchandise inventory, pass through only the cost incurrence

Three Stages of Costs

FIGURE 3-2

Cost Incurrence → Cost Transformation → Cost Expiration

Purchase of Materials, Labor, and Overhead → Work-in-Process Inventory → Finished Goods Inventory → Cost of Goods Sold Expense

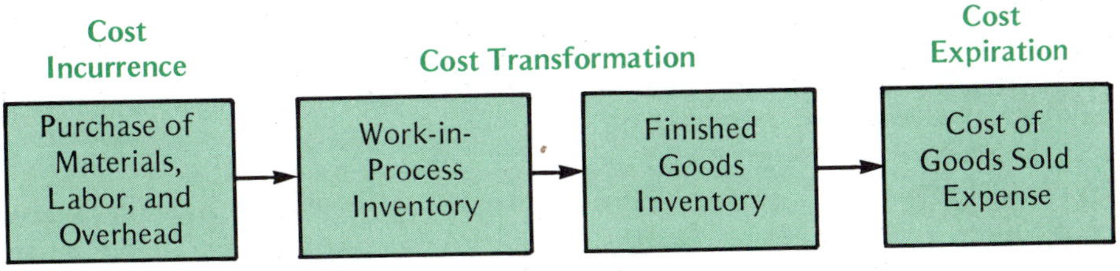

Part I The Framework of Financial Accounting

FIGURE 3-3

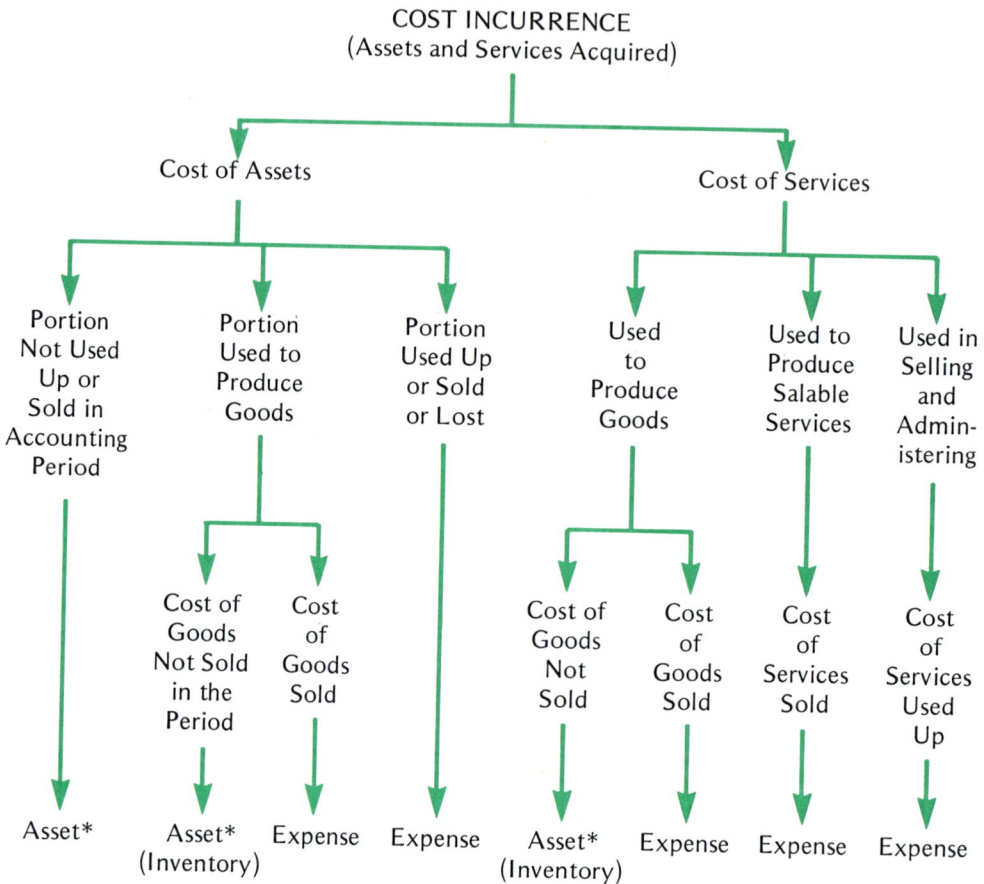

*Becomes an expense in future period(s)

and cost expiration stages. Some costs, such as office salaries, income taxes, and delivery expenses, expire when incurred; there is almost no asset stage at all. When office salaries are incurred, they become an expense.

Figure 3-3 illustrates and summarizes the flow of costs through the enterprise, with eventual classification as either an asset or an expense.

The Accrual Basis of Accounting

In the discussion of revenue and expense, the phrases *cash received* (in the recognition of revenue) and *cash paid* (in the recognition of expense) have been avoided. The emphasis has been broader than cash receipts and cash payments in order to encompass the complete income earning process. Revenues are recognized when realized, and expenses are recognized when incurred.

Payment is not synonymous with incurrence, for some expenses may be paid for after they have been incurred. The important point with respect to incurrence of expense is the benefit received by the enterprise; it is not necessary that the expense be paid for. Rent may be owed for a period and be unpaid—the expense has still been incurred. If salaries have been earned by employees by working during a certain period, the expense has been incurred, regardless of whether the salaries have been paid.

What are the tests of incurrence? Usually they involve the receipt of assets to which the company has title. For items that are immediate cost expirations, the test is the rendering of service to the company or the creation of a new claim against the company. No one test is available for recording expenses incurred; instead accountants develop a "feel" for what is appropriate, based on their experience, their understanding of accounting principles, and their knowledge of what should be reflected on financial statements.

In some cases, an expense may be incurred on the basis of estimates because of the requirements of proper matching. An example is the expense connected with guarantees on products sold. Revenues from sale of products is recognized in accordance with realization rules. All expenses connected with the revenues should be associated with them in the period of sale. Therefore, even though customers may not make any claims under the guarantees until a later period, the expense is often estimated and recorded in the period of sale.

Thus, expenses may be incurred when assets are used by a company, when services are received, when a new claim against the company arises, and when an expense needs to be recorded for proper matching. *Recording expenses when they are incurred rather than just when they are paid for and recording revenues when they are earned rather than when they are collected is called accrual accounting.* It is contrasted to *cash basis accounting*, in which events are not recorded until cash changes hands.

Accrual accounting

The Classified Income Statement

In an income statement a careful classification of revenue and expense can be helpful to the user. A commonly used classification is associated with the *multiple-step income statement* (see Table 3-1 on page 70). The term *multiple-step* means that several subtotals are obtained before final net income.

A much simpler classification is employed by many companies in their *single-step income statements*. All revenues and income are listed and

TABLE 3-1. Income Statement Classification

Major Classification	Items Included	Examples
Revenue	Major sources of revenue	Sale of products
		Sale of services
	Revenue deductions and adjustments	Sales returns
Cost of goods sold	Costs incurred to acquire or manufacture goods that have been sold	All elements of the cost of products sold
Operating expense	Selling expense	Sales commissions
	Administrative expense	Office salaries
Other revenues and expenses	Revenues and expenses from financing and minor activities	Interest expense
		Interest income
		Rental income
Income tax	Taxes levied against enterprise income	Federal income tax
		State and local income taxes
Extraordinary items	Significant, non-recurring gains and losses (net of tax effect)	Fire loss

totaled. Then all expenses, including income taxes, are listed. The total of expense is then deducted from revenues to derive net income. Extraordinary items are usually handled as in Table 3-1, as a special item at the bottom before arriving at net income.

We now turn to a discussion of each of the classifications on the multiple-step income statement.

Revenue. *Revenue* from the primary operations of the business enterprise is the starting point of the income statement. In many businesses important adjustments of the total revenue are recognized. These adjustments include sales returns and allowances and sales discounts given to customers for early payment of their bills. These adjustments may be shown parenthetically rather than as separate totals in the income statement.

Cost of Goods Sold Expense. *Cost of goods sold expense* is a major expense in companies that sell products. It does not appear on the statements of a company that sells services. The size of cost of goods sold expense and its direct relationship to sales are enough to warrant separate disclosure of this item. Some detail of cost of goods sold is often provided. This detail traces the flow of costs through the business. The cost of goods purchased (net of any returns and allowances) during a period and freight on goods purchased, called "freight in," are added to the cost of goods on hand at

Pictorial Representation of Flow of Costs to Cost of Goods Sold FIGURE 3-4

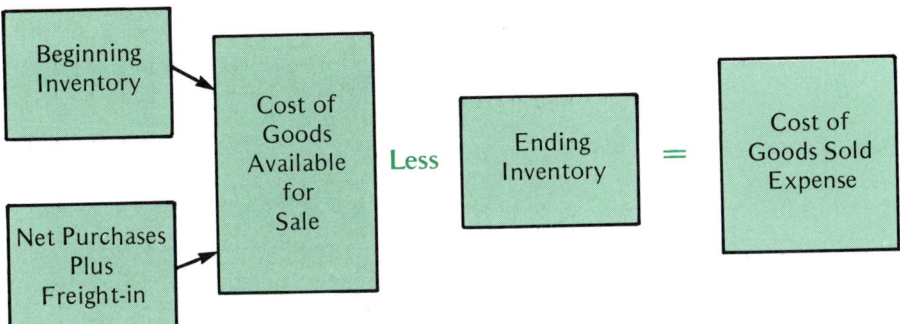

the beginning of the period (beginning inventory), forming a pool of cost of goods that could be sold during the period. This pool of costs is called *cost of goods available for sale*. The goods left at the end of the period are subtracted to arrive at the *cost of goods sold*. (See Figure 3-4). Purchase returns or allowances or discounts are deducted from purchases as adjustments of the total purchases. This is consistent with the treatment of revenue adjustments described above.

Cost of goods sold expense involves a complicated computation in manufacturing enterprises, where the cost of goods sold figure is the end product of the cost accounting activities. Internal management is usually given a detailed report of the manufacturing activities. Reports to investors generally do not carry this detail. A cost of goods sold section in a manufacturing company's report to investors might have one figure, or it might present a short schedule such as the one in Example 3-3.

EXAMPLE 3-3

BURRIS MANUFACTURING COMPANY
Partial Income Statement
for Year 1

Sales		$782,000
Cost of goods sold:		
Beginning inventory of finished goods	$ 42,000	
Cost of goods manufactured during the year	416,000	
Cost of goods available for sale	$458,000	
Less: Ending inventory of finished goods	51,000	
Cost of goods sold expense		407,000
Gross margin		$375,000

Management is provided with a detailed report on the elements of cost that make up the cost of goods manufactured. They include material, labor, and overhead costs.

Operating Expense. The *operating expense* category includes all expenses of the actual operations of the business other than cost of goods sold expense. These expenses are connected with sales, administration, and some of the more general supporting functions in the enterprise. Most of the expenses in this category are matched on a period basis.

Other Revenues and Expenses. *Other revenues and expenses* include revenues and expenses that are not part of the main operating activities. Financial revenues and expenses, such as interest earned and interest expense, often are shown in this category. A company that manufactures products would not necessarily have any interest expense. This expense occurs because of the way the business is financed, not the way it is operated. If a company obtains incidental revenues from sideline activities, such as renting part of the store building or selling display counters, these revenues are shown among the incidental items.

Income Tax. *Federal and state income tax expense* is usually shown as a separate item on the income statement. Most other taxes, such as property taxes and employment taxes, are shown among the operating expenses. Corporate income taxes are deductions from revenues, just like other expenses, but they are unique in two ways:

1. Income taxes are assessed only if a company has a net taxable income. Other expenses are *determinants of* income; income taxes are *determined by* income.
2. Income taxes generally have been substantial, averaging close to 50% of income before taxes for large companies in the United States. They have a considerable effect on business decisions and planning.

If the business is a partnership or sole proprietorship, no income taxes are levied against the business. Instead, the owners pay personal income taxes on their share of the business income.

Extraordinary Items. *Extraordinary items are large items of gain or loss that, because of their unusual nature and because of their infrequency of occurrence, cannot be combined with other revenues and expenses without distorting the income statement.* Suppose a company loses $200,000 because of flood damage in a year when its operations net only $345,000. The flood loss would be an extraordinary item. A possible treatment is illustrated in Example 3-4. Note that the total amount of the flood loss, $380,000, is reduced by the amount of income tax reduction related to the loss, $180,000. The net loss to the company is only $200,000 because the government in effect bears part of the loss. Sometimes an extraordinary item is shown *net of tax*. In this example, that would involve showing just the $200,000 net loss, labeled "net of taxes."

EXAMPLE 3-4

FLAVIUS CORPORATION
Partial Income Statement
for the Year 1

Income before taxes		$700,000
Income taxes		355,000
Income before extraordinary items		345,000
Extraordinary item:		
Flood loss	$380,000	
Less tax reduction	180,000	
Net loss		200,000
Net Income		$145,000

An Income Statement Example

Example 3-5 (see page 74), the income statement for the Bolle Supply Company, illustrates many of the points discussed above. This statement is a classified multiple-step statement. The comparative information for two years gives useful information about trends in operations.

Bolle's primary source of revenue is sales of merchandise. *Gross sales* were $888,000 and customers' returns and allowances of $4,000 reduced revenue to $884,000 in Year 2. The return figure is an important indicator of customer satisfaction.

Expenses are divided into cost of goods sold, operating expenses, other revenues and expenses, and income tax. The detailed breakdown of the cost of goods sold tells the reader the components of cost of sales and the relative size of inventory.

Sales less cost of goods sold gives *gross margin*, the excess of revenue from goods over the cost of the goods. It reflects the quality of management's decisions on kinds of goods acquired, the prices set for those goods, and the selling efforts expended.

Operating expenses are divided functionally into *selling* expenses and *administrative* expenses. The expenses in the selling category are related to selling activities. Sales salaries are paid for the services of salespersons. Building depreciation reflects the cost of the use of the store building. Advertising expense is the cost of newspaper, radio, and other kinds of advertising. Store and selling supplies used is the cost of supplies used during the year to maintain the building and to service customers. Depreciation expense is the estimate of the cost of wear and tear, aging, and obsolescence on store equipment, such as cash registers.

EXAMPLE 3-5

BOLLE SUPPLY COMPANY
Income Statement
for the Years Ending December 31, Year 1 and Year 2

	Year 2		Year 1	
Gross revenue from sales		$888,000		$748,000
Less sales returns and allowances		4,000		3,000
Net sales		$884,000		$745,000
Cost of goods sold expense:				
Inventory, January 1	$ 67,000		$ 54,000	
Purchases of merchandise	510,000		440,000	
Freight on purchases	7,000		5,000	
Cost of merchandise available for sale	$584,000		$499,000	
Less inventory, December 31	75,000		67,000	
Cost of goods sold expense		509,000		432,000
Gross margin		$375,000		$313,000
Operating expenses:				
Selling expenses:				
Sales salaries	$ 94,000		$ 90,000	
Building depreciation	7,000		7,000	
Advertising expense	66,000		59,100	
Store and selling supplies used	11,000		10,200	
Depreciation of store equipment	5,000		4,000	
Total selling expenses	183,000		170,300	
Administrative expenses:				
Officer's salary	$ 26,000		$ 23,000	
Office salaries	53,000		50,000	
Utilities and telephone	14,000		12,000	
Depreciation of office equipment	3,000		3,000	
Office supplies used	5,000		4,100	
Insurance and property taxes	8,000		7,200	
Uncollectible accounts expense	7,300		6,800	
Accounting and legal fees	8,000		6,300	
Goodwill amortization	4,000		4,000	
Miscellaneous expenses	6,800		2,400	
Total administrative expenses	135,100		118,800	
Total operating expenses		318,100		289,100
Operating income		$ 56,900		$ 23,900
Other revenue and expense:				
Dividends received on investments	3,000		2,000	
Interest expense	(4,100)	(1,100)	(4,400)	(2,400)
Income before taxes		$ 55,800		$21,500
Less income taxes		22,000		7,200
Net income		$ 33,800		$ 14,300
Earnings per share		$ 2.82		$ 1.19

Many selling expenses cannot be directly matched with sales revenue. These expenses are recognized on the allocation principle or the immediate recognition principle.

Administrative expenses are those expenses incurred to administer and oversee all business activities. The officer's salary is for Mr. Bolle, who is the general manager of the business. Office salaries, utilities, telephone, depreciation of office equipment, office supplies used, and insurance and property taxes are expenses of running the business. The uncollectible accounts expense is the loss from accounts receivable that cannot be collected. It is related to the allowance for doubtful accounts on the statement of financial position. Accounting and legal fees were paid to a local CPA firm and a local law firm for professional services. Goodwill amortization is the cost of goodwill written off during the year. Miscellaneous expense covers all other administrative expenses. Administrative expenses are only indirectly related to sales revenue, but they are necessary for overall business operations.

Gross margin less operating expenses gives operating income. This is the income generated by the main-line activities of the business. The expense and revenue from financing and minor activities of the firm are deducted from, or added to, operating income. Dividends received on investments and interest expense appear in the example.

Income tax is usually shown separately. It is an expense that exists only if there is taxable income. Income tax is frequently described as one of the distributive shares of income. That is, government and owners share in the income of the corporate enterprise.

Earnings per share (EPS) are shown on most corporate income statements. For Bolle the amount in Year 2 is computed by dividing the $33,800 income by the 12,000 shares of stock outstanding (see Example 2-4). For shareholders, the EPS figure is a handy indicator of company progress.

Relationship of the Income Statement to the Balance Sheet

There is an intimate connection between the income statement and the balance sheet. This follows from the basic notion of income as an excess of revenue over expense. This excess belongs to the enterprise owners. Net assets can be defined as assets minus liabilities. Because revenue is an inflow of net assets, and expense is an outflow of net assets, net income is a net inflow of net assets and increases owners' equity. A net loss, which occurs when revenue is less than expense, has the opposite effect: a loss reduces net assets and reduces owners' equity.

Net assets

The fundamental relationships can be stated as follows, beginning with the basic accounting equation:

$$\text{Assets (A)} = \text{Liabilities (L)} + \text{Owners' Equity (OE)}$$
$$\therefore A - L = OE$$
$$\text{or Net Assets} = OE$$

Effect of revenue:

$$+ \text{Net Assets} = +OE$$

Effect of expenses:

$$- \text{Net Assets} = -OE$$

Therefore, effect of net income (revenue minus expenses) is:

$$+\text{Net Assets} = +OE$$

These relationships are stated in the form of simple equations. The relationships are nevertheless profound and deserve serious consideration.

Uses of Income Statement Information

The income statement is supposed to inform the reader about enterprise progress over time. Owners, creditors, potential investors, and others who are concerned with an enterprise are usually interested in its progress. Investors use reports of enterprise progress to assess the performance of a company and, to some extent, to help them predict future progress of the company. Creditors want this information because the company that is making progress probably can pay its bills promptly.

What is meant by progress? An enterprise that has made progress in a year is somehow better off at the end of the year than it was at the beginning of the year. But how should "better-offness" be measured? Most accountants and business managers would probably assess progress, being better off, in terms of growth in a company's wealth. A company's wealth may be reflected in its net assets:

$$\text{Net Assets} = \text{Assets} - \text{Liabilities}$$

It would appear that the income statement does reflect a company's growth in wealth, since income does increase net assets.

Before this statement is accepted outright and uncritically, one should recall that income is measured as follows:

$$\text{Income} = \text{Revenues Realized} - \text{Expenses (measured by reference to the historical cost principle)}$$

The restrictive realization test may not be the best measure of revenues earned. Similarly, historical costs may not be the most appropriate basis for measuring a company's expenses in a year. If individual prices are rising and if the general price level is rising, questions can be raised as to whether the historical cost approach really reflects the current cost of the resources consumed (expenses). In other words, the continued relevance of a previously incurred cost can be challenged.

In using income statements based on current accounting principles, the user must take into account the changing value of the dollar. Authoritative accounting bodies have given this subject considerable attention. Authoritative rule-making bodies for the CPA profession have suggested supplementary financial statements that reflect the changing general price level. The Securities and Exchange Commission, the regulatory agency responsible for establishing legal requirements for the statements of most large companies, requires that certain current expenses based on current replacement values be reported in the notes to the financial statements of large corporations. These problems and alternatives to historical cost statements will be fully discussed in chapter 15.

Investors and others are interested in the predictive value of income statements. But the income statement is a report of some past period, such as a year. Only insofar as the future replicates the past will the income statement be a sound basis for predicting future earnings. Predictions in the form of forecasted statements have been suggested as a way of dealing with this problem. Forecasted statements have been a controversial topic in recent accounting discussions.

Forecasts

THE STATEMENT OF RETAINED EARNINGS

The income or loss for a period changes the amount of owners' equity. In a corporation, the change is reflected in the part of stockholders' equity that is called *retained earnings*. Retained earnings may also be affected by items other than net income or loss, such as dividends (income distributions made to owners). A statement of retained earnings is usually included in financial statements to indicate the cause of any change in retained earnings. Example 3-6 shows a statement of retained earnings for the Bolle Supply Company.

EXAMPLE 3-6

BOLLE SUPPLY COMPANY
Statement of Retained Earnings
for the Years Ending December 31, Year 2 and Year 1

	Year 2	Year 1
Retained earnings balance, January	$18,200	$15,900
Net income for the year	33,800	14,300
	$52,000	$30,200
Dividends on common stock	12,000	12,000
Retained earnings balance, December 31	$40,000	$18,200

Part I   The Framework of Financial Accounting

THE STATEMENT OF CHANGES IN FINANCIAL POSITION

The statement of changes in financial position, or the funds statement, reports the inflow of working capital (funds) into the business and the outflow of working capital. You will recall that working capital is current assets minus current liabilities. The inflow of working capital is identified as to *source*, and the outflow is identified as to *use*. The statement of changes in financial position is a statement of changes in enterprise assets, liabilities, and owners' equity that is designed to help business managers, investors, and others answer questions such as the following:

- How did the company finance its expansion?
- What factors caused the deterioration or improvement in the current position of the company?
- What does this company usually do with its net income? How much is distributed to owners, and how much is plowed back into the business? And where is it plowed back?

The income statement and the statement of financial position do not provide complete answers to this type of question. The income statement reports the amount of the net income but does not indicate what has been done with it. The statement of retained earnings gives some information about the amount of net income that was distributed to owners but contains no information about the disposition of the income that was retained in the business. The statement of financial position tells about the amount of assets and liabilities in the enterprise but does not indicate what changes occurred or how they were financed.

The statement of changes in financial position is designed to show the financing and investing activities of the company. It shows the major sources of increases in an enterprise's working capital for a period, for example, net income, borrowing, owners' investments, and sale of assets other than products. It also shows how the enterprise used its working capital during the period (for example, in buying other assets, paying debts, and paying dividends).

The statement of changes in financial position indicates changes in the working capital from various causes during a period. The statement is concerned with changes in total working capital rather than with the composition of working capital. Thus, the statement would not report a shift in composition of working capital—for example, a shift from receivables to cash—but would report an increase in total current assets arising from a factor such as the issuance of additional capital stock. Example 3-7, the statement for the Bolle Supply Company, shows the main features of the statement of changes in financial position.

EXAMPLE 3-7

BOLLE SUPPLY COMPANY
Statement of Changes in Financial Position
for the Year Ending December 31, Year 2

Sources of working capital:		
From operations:		
Net income		$33,800
Add expenses not requiring the outlay of working capital:		
Depreciation expense, building		7,000
Depreciation expense, equipment		8,000
Goodwill amortization		4,000
Total working capital from operations		$52,800
Total sources of working capital		$52,800
Uses of working capital:		
Acquisition of investment in Burgess Company	$25,000	
Dividends	12,000	
Total uses of working capital		$37,000
Increase in working capital		$15,800

During the year, Bolle Supply Company generated working capital of $52,800 from its operations. The uses of working capital were the acquisition of an investment and dividends to stockholders. The overall result was an increase in working capital of $15,800. Working capital was $84,200 in Year 1 and $100,000 in Year 2 (see Example 2-4).

The statement of changes in financial position is discussed more fully in chapter 17. At this point only one explanatory comment will be made. Note that depreciation expense is added to the net income to arrive at the total working capital provided by operations. Depreciation expense and similar items, such as amortization of intangibles, are unlike many other expenses in that they do not result in any decrease in working capital. If salaries or cost of goods sold is recorded, the result is either a decrease in current assets (cash or inventory) or an increase in current liabilities (wages payable). The recording of depreciation, however, results in a decrease in the plant and equipment assets and has no effect on working capital. Depreciation and similar items are added to the net income to determine the total effect of revenues and expenses on working capital. The addition is made not because depreciation *provides* working capital, but because it does not *use up* working capital.

The information presented in the statement of changes in financial position is so important that the statement is considered one of the primary financial statements. All published reports should include this statement.

SUMMARY OF CONCEPTS OF FINANCIAL ACCOUNTING

It was stated in chapter 1 that the financial accounting statements are based on objectives, assumptions, and principles that have evolved over many years. The more important of these fundamentals have been identified and discussed in these first three chapters. Having discussed the three basic financial statements in some detail, it is appropriate here to summarize the important concepts. This summary should give the student a helpful reference point for the detailed study of financial accounting that follows in the remainder of the book.

Objectives

Objectives are intended to guide the development of financial accounting. Authoritative, definitive objectives do not exist as yet. A tentative set of objectives was discussed in chapter 2.

Basic Assumptions

Assumptions are common understandings about the environment of accounting upon which useful principles can be constructed. Frequently, assumptions are not stated but implied. Assumptions are generally not questioned unless substantial changes in the environment are experienced. The following are among the most important assumptions of accounting:

1. **Entity.** The accounting entity is the business enterprise, which is separate from its owners.
2. **Going concern.** The enterprise has an indefinite future existence in the absence of evidence to the contrary.
3. **Money measurement.** The activities and position of an enterprise can be measured meaningfully in terms of money.
4. **Stable measuring unit.** The dollar has the stability to qualify as a good measuring unit that allows comparability between accounting periods and between enterprises.
5. **Period.** Accounting measurements can be related meaningfully to relatively short time periods.

Principles

Principles are broad generalizations that are intended to guide accountants in recognizing and measuring economic events.

1. **Cost.** Exchange prices in enterprise transactions are used to measure resources acquired.
2. **Realization.** Revenue is recognized when it is realized; that is, when the earning process is virtually complete and there has been an exchange transaction.
3. **Direct matching.** Some costs are recognized as expenses on the basis of a direct association with specific revenue. The expense should be recognized in the accounting period in which the revenue is realized.
4. **Cost allocation.** Some costs are recognized as expenses on the basis of a systematic and rational allocation process wherein the cost is allocated to the several accounting periods benefitted by the cost.
5. **Immediate recognition.** Some expenses are recognized in the current accounting period because there is no discernible future benefit associated with the particular cost.
6. **Exception.** Accounting principles are not iron-clad. Exceptions to a general principle should be made when there is convincing evidence that more useful measurements will result.

The specific rules of accounting measurement, which translate principles into action, are not listed above. They will be considered when the specific measurements are discussed in the chapters ahead. We suggest that the student test each measurement with the objectives, assumptions, and principles in these first three chapters. Are they consistent? Have there been changes in the accounting environment (such as rapid inflation) that make other measurement approaches more realistic for fulfilling our basic objectives?

Validity of Current Assumptions and Principles

The objectives, assumptions, and principles discussed in these first three chapters have evolved over many years. They are valid when the economic and social environment is fairly stable—in the absence of deep economic depression and in the absence of substantial inflation. The concepts have served fairly well in times of moderate recession and moderate inflation.

When this country has experienced deep and lasting depression (as in the 1930s), exceptions to the principles have generally been permitted in order to derive more useful measurements. For example, in the 1930s many assets were written down sharply to reflect a more realistic situation.

We have not witnessed a similar departure from principles under inflation. Sharp but temporary inflationary pressures were experienced in the post–World War II years and in connection with the Korean conflict. Accounting authorities took the position that the inflations were not serious enough to depart from accounting principles. There was much heated discussion among accounting practitioners and accounting professors about whether some change was warranted, but no official actions were taken. Some minor changes were made within the boundaries of the generally accepted historical-cost accounting framework, but the basic framework was not altered.

Now we are experiencing a rapid inflation that has persisted since about 1968. Official cognizance has now been given the problem. The Financial Accounting Standards Board, the authoritative principle-formulating body of the accounting profession, has suggested that supplementary financial statements be issued that reflect the impact of inflation. The Securities and Exchange Commission requires that current replacement values of certain assets and expenses be shown in the notes to the statements of some companies. These actions do not change the basic framework of accounting, although they point the direction to possible future changes. In this text, we shall base our consideration of accounting measurements primarily on the currently accepted principles. Where appropriate, the price level and current value implications will be considered. The entire problem will be discussed in greater detail in chapter 15.

SUMMARY

The income statement, the statement of changes in financial position, and the retained earnings statement show the reader what is happening during the accounting periods between balance sheet dates. The income statement shows the revenue, expense, and extraordinary items of the accounting period. Revenues realized less expenses and losses recognized gives net income. Usually, revenue is recognized at the time of sale. Other bases for revenue recognition are sometimes used when unusual conditions prevail. Expense recognition offers more difficult problems than revenue realization. Some expenses are governed by the direct matching principle; others are governed by the cost allocation principle; and still others are recognized under the immediate recognition principle.

The income statement is frequently classified to give useful information about the earning process. One useful classification is found in the multiple-step income statement. A simpler form is used in the single-step income statement.

The income statement purports to measure enterprise progress. During periods of economic stability, the statement does an adequate job even though it focuses on the past rather than the future. Present inflationary pressures have caused the accounting profession to consider whether changes ought to be made in measurement processes to reflect inflation and current values.

Accrual accounting is followed in most businesses. In accrual accounting, costs are recorded as incurred (rather than when paid for) and revenues are recorded when realized (rather than when cash is received).

The statement of changes in financial position (or funds statement) shows the sources of working capital coming into the firm and the outflows of working capital for major company purposes. All of the changes in financial position are reported here. Therefore, the statement is considered an important complement to the income statement and the balance sheet.

The statement of retained earnings reports the effects of net income and dividends on earnings retained in the business.

The chapter closes with a summary review of concepts that have been discussed in the first three chapters. We raise the question whether these concepts are adequate for today's world. This question is a vital concern of those who are searching for valid approaches to measuring income and financial position. The student can be assured that these are exciting times for accounting and that those entering the profession now will have some influence in deciding upon the most appropriate way to change accounting.

IMPORTANT TERMS

Net income
Revenue
Realization principle
Cash basis
Production method
Expense
Direct matching principle
Cost allocation principle
Immediate recognition principle
Losses
Cost incurrence
Cost transformation

Cost expiration
Accrual basis
Multiple-step statement
Single-step statement
Cost of goods sold
Gross margin
Operating income
Extraordinary items
Net assets
Earnings per share
Funds

QUESTIONS

3-1. Define revenues. Give three examples of different sources of revenue.

3-2. What is the realization principle? Why is this principle considered to be central in the recognition of revenue?

3-3. If the realization principle is so important, why are exceptions sometimes made? Give two examples of enterprises in which an exception to the realization principle is made, and explain why the exception is made.

3-4. How would you define *expense?* Give four or five examples of expenses.

3-5. Explain the direct matching principle. Give two examples of expenses that are recognized under this principle.

3-6. Why is a cost allocation process necessary for some expenses? Give two examples of expenses that are recognized in this way.

3-7. What are extraordinary gains and extraordinary losses? Why are they shown on the income statement? Why must these items be clearly identified and segregated in the income statement?

3-8. What is the gross margin of an enterprise? the operating income? Explain the significance of each.

3-9. What are the advantages of the single-step income statement? the multiple-step income statement?

3-10. It has been said that the funds statement shows all of the changes in financial position. If that is true, why have an income statement, which shows only those changes related to income-directed activities?

EXERCISES

3-11. *Income statement.* Prepare a statement of income for the current year, using the following data taken from the financial records of the Burger Company:

Finished goods inventory, January 1	$ 42,000
Finished goods inventory, December 31	50,000
Sales to customers during the year	340,000
Cost of goods manufactured during the year	260,000
Salespersons' salaries	25,000
Other operating expenses	41,000
Income tax expense	8,000

3-12. *Stages of cost.* Identify each of the events listed below as (1) cost incurrence, (2) cost transformation, or (3) cost expiration. More than one stage of cost may be appropriate for some items.

    a. We purchased office supplies to replenish inventory.
    b. We purchased a new machine for use in our factory.
    c. We paid salaries to salespersons.
    d. We recognized that $200 of office supplies had been used up.
    e. We recognized depreciation expense for the period on factory machines.
    f. We took raw materials from the storeroom and used them in our manufacturing processes.
    g. We completed products in our factory and transferred them to our finished goods warehouse.
    h. We sold completed products and shipped them to customers.

3-13. *Income statement.* Prepare a multiple-step, classified income statement for the Kamen Company for the Year 1.

Supplies expense	$ 800	Sales	$28,000
Rent expense	3,000	Utilities expense	4,000
Delivery expense	2,000	Cost of goods sold	16,000
Income taxes expense	400	Interest expense	500

3-14. *Revenue.* What would you expect to be the *principal* revenue and *principal* expense of the following businesses?

    a. Men's clothing store
    b. Wholesale hardware company
    c. Automobile manufacturer
    d. Barber shop
    e. Laundry
    f. Railroad

3-15. *Statement of changes in financial position.* Indicate for each item below whether it is a *source* of working capital, a *use* of working capital, or *neither*.

    a. Acquisition of new production machinery
    b. In January one of our customers pays last year's bill
    c. Purchase of land for a building site
    d. Net income for the period
    e. Borrowing on a 5-year note payable
    f. Paying dividends to stockholders

3-16. *Revenue and cost of goods sold.* Prepare a partial income statement for the Year 1 (down to gross margin) from the following figures, which are given in millions.

Sales	$50.2	Sales returns	$ .8
Salespersons' salaries	3.5	Inventory, January 1	11.4
Inventory, December 31	15.2	Interest expense	3.0
Purchases of merchandise	39.3	Freight on purchases	.6

3-17. *Income statement events.* Show how each of the following events affects the basic accounting equation.

    a. Products are sold to customers on account.
    b. Products are sold to customers for cash.
    c. The cost of the products sold in *a* and *b* is recognized as an expense.
    d. Wages are paid to office employees.
    e. Wages are paid to factory employees who work directly on our production line.
    f. Depreciation expense on office equipment is recognized.
    g. A bill for newspaper advertising covering the past month is received.
    h. The cost of office supplies used during the period is recognized.
    i. An old machine is sold at a price below its net book value.

PROBLEMS

3-18. *Forms of the income statement.* From the following data, construct (a) a single-step income statement and (b) a multiple-step income statement. The data, for the year ended December 31, Year 1, pertains to the Crocker Company. Treat the gain on sale of land as an extraordinary item.

Cost of products sold	$325,000
Cost of services sold	182,000
Salesperson's salaries	32,000
Office salaries	5,000
Revenue from products sold	420,000
Revenue from services sold	280,000
Gain on sale of land (net of income tax)	120,000
Research and development expense	12,500
Interest expense	3,000
Income tax expense	53,000
Other operating expense	16,000

3-19. *Changes in financial position.* The Webber Laundry Company has the following balance sheet on December 31, Year 1:

WEBBER LAUNDRY COMPANY
Balance Sheet, December 31, Year 1

Assets			Liabilities		
Current assets:			Current liabilities:		
Cash	$10,000		Accounts payable		$ 5,000
Supplies inventory	3,000				
Prepaid rent	2,000		Stockholders' Equity		
Total current assets	$15,000				
Plant and equipment:			Capital stock, par value $2		$30,000
Laundry machinery and			Retained earnings		8,000
equipment	40,000		Total owners' equity		38,000
Accumulated depreciation	(12,000)				
Net plant and equipment		28,000	Total liabilities and		
Total assets		$43,000	stockholders' equity		$43,000

At the end of Year 2, the company accountant prepares the following statement of changes in financial position:

WEBBER LAUNDRY COMPANY
Statement of Changes in Financial Position
Year Ended December 31, Year 2

Sources of Funds:		
Net income	$5,200	
Add depreciation expense	8,000	
Funds from operations		$13,200
Borrowing on 10%, 10-year note		25,000
Total sources of funds		$38,200

Uses of Funds:	
Dividends to stockholders	$ 3,000
Purchase of laundry equipment	20,000
Total uses of funds	23,000
Increase in working capital	$15,200

Required: Prepare a balance sheet as of December 31, Year 2. You may assume that the cash balance at year end is $20,000, accounts payable are $7,000, supplies inventory amounts to $4,000, and prepaid rent is $1,000. Any remaining change in working capital is reflected in a new current asset, marketable securities.

3-20. *Financial statements.* Prepare a statement of financial position as of December 31, Year 2, and an income statement for the year ended December 31, Year 2, from the following items. An income statement item is for the entire year, whereas a balance sheet item is the value at December 31, Year 2. All items should be used. Net income should be $3.4 million; total assets should be $146.0 million.

PITTMAN COMPANY
Financial Statement Items
at December 31, Year 2,
or for Year Ended December 31, Year 2

	Millions
Accounts payable	$ 17.4
Accounts receivable	4.4
Accrued liabilities	10.5
Accumulated depreciation	22.8
Allowance for uncollectible accounts	.3
Cash on hand and in banks	5.5
Capital in excess of par	41.6
Common stock, $1 par value	4.3
Cost of goods sold expense	174.1
Current maturities of long-term debt	2.1
Income taxes expense	1.9
Income taxes payable	1.6
Interest expense	8.0
Inventories	89.5
Investment in subsidiary companies	11.3
Land and buildings	9.8
Long-term debt	25.9
Machinery and equipment	38.1
Notes payable due in Year 3	5.0
Notes receivable due in Year 5	3.8
Other assets	1.5
Prepaid expenses	5.2
Sales	256.0
Selling and administrative expenses	68.6
Retained earnings (includes the net income for Year 2)	37.6

Part I   The Framework of Financial Accounting

3-21. *Statement of changes in financial position.* Prepare a statement of changes in financial position from the following information that covers the year ended December 31, Year 1, for the Ammerson Company. Not all of the items should be used.

Net income for year (after deducting depreciation of $160,000)	$ 523,000
Acquisition of new production machinery	750,000
Cash received from customers during the year	6,830,000
Borrowed on a 5-year, 10% note	1,200,000
Dividends paid to stockholders	450,000
Additional shares of stock issued	2,500,000
Manufacturing plant purchased to support increased manufacturing activity	3,600,000

(Solution in Appendix B.)

3-22. *Statement of changes in financial position.* From the following items, you are asked to prepare a statement of changes in financial position for the year ended December 31, Year 4. Not all of the items should be used. There should be an increase in working capital for the year of $3.3 million.

	Millions
Increase in accounts receivable	$ 24.2
Issuance of long-term debt	4.2
Net income	38.4
Sale of plant assets	7.4
Sale of investments	13.9
Sale of capital stock	5.2
Short-term borrowing	50.2
Sales of products during year	645.9
Depreciation expense	24.2
Reduction in long-term debt	20.1
Dividends paid	12.9
Purchase of intangible assets	1.2
Purchase of plant assets	55.8

3-23. *Statement of changes in financial position.* Prepare a statement of changes in financial position for the Dark Oil Company from the following data covering the Year ended December 31, Year 1. Not all of the items should be used. There should be a decrease in working capital of $17.6 million.

	Millions
Net income	$ 7.0
Decrease in long-term debt	5.0
Depreciation and depletion	13.2
Additions to plant and property	59.0
Dividends paid	3.6
Increase in capital stock	25.2
Increase in cash	5.7
Income tax expense	3.0
Mineral properties written off	4.6

3-24. *Income statement.* From the following data, prepare an income statement in good form (multiple-step) for Year 1 for the Roper Company.

Commissions paid to salespersons	$ 3,200
Estimated loss on uncollectible accounts	1,300
Office supplies used	1,900
Sales to customers	138,000
Interest expense	800
Cost of goods sold expense	84,400
Depreciation expense	12,000
Utilities expense	2,400
Property taxes expense	2,100
Insurance expense	900
Loss from flood damage (net of taxes)	6,000
Salaries expense	20,000
Income tax expense	1,300

(Solution in Appendix B.)

PART II

Processing Accounting Data

4

The Accounting Cycle: The Recording Process

Financial accounting information is provided by the financial accounting process. This process takes *inputs*, manipulates (*processes*) them, and generates *outputs*. In this chapter we describe each of these aspects of the financial accounting process in turn, starting with the outputs, then considering inputs, and then concentrating particular attention on processing.

OUTPUTS

The most important outputs of the financial accounting process are the financial statements that were discussed in chapters 2 and 3. These statements provide interested parties with information about the position, results of operations, and financing and investing activities of an enterprise. The statements are prepared periodically (at least once a year, but often quarterly or monthly) and distributed to appropriate parties.

The financial accounting process also provides tax returns and other information required by law. A substantial amount of time and effort is required to prepare the multitude of forms that have to be filed with various levels of government. Some forms, like income tax returns, are compiled from basically the same information as the financial statements. Other forms, such as social security tax and unemployment compensation tax returns, require added sets of records.

Another important output of the financial accounting process is business documents, such as bills to customers of the enterprise, checks to employees and suppliers, and orders for goods and services needed by the enterprise. The process is set up in such a way that these documents are generated as part of the system.

Management accounting information can also be derived from the financial accounting process, either directly or by making suitable modifications. The financial accounting process usually provides the framework on which much of management accounting is based.

INPUTS

Source documents

Basically, the inputs of the financial accounting process are economic events that affect the enterprise. These events, called transactions, often find expression in business documents that enter the business. These documents are called *source documents*, because they are a source of information to the enterprise. Examples of source documents include invoices (bills) received from suppliers, checks received from customers, time cards filled out by employees, and receiving reports filled out by the receiving department when goods are received.

Source documents generally trigger the financial accounting process. They provide data that start the recording and processing activities. Therefore, the accuracy and validity of source documents are vital. For example, bills received from suppliers normally result in the issuance of checks to suppliers and the recording of costs or expenses on the financial statements. If the bills are incorrect and are admitted to the processing system, incorrect checks will be drawn and incorrect financial statements will be prepared. Because of effects like these, businesses generally exercise considerable effort to make sure that data on source documents are valid.

PROCESSING

We now turn to the third part of the financial accounting process: the processing phase itself. The entire process is shown in Figure 4-1.

FIGURE 4-1   **The Financial Accounting Process**

Inputs
Source Documents
Reflecting:
External Events
Internal Events

→ **Processing System** →

Outputs
Financial Statements
Legal Information
Business Documents

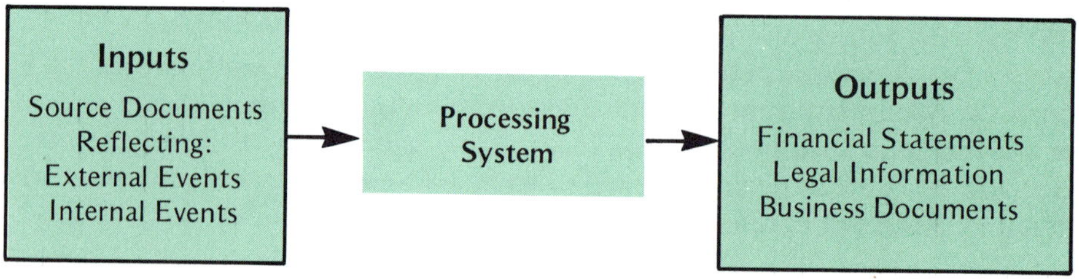

The processing phase is the stage in which inputs are collected, classified, recorded, and manipulated so that the outputs of the process can be produced. The processing phase is carried out according to a formal set of rules and procedures that we will examine in this chapter.

ACCOUNTING TRANSACTIONS

The data collected for financial statements are derived from financial accounting transactions, which are the raw data in the accounting processing system. *An accounting transaction is an economic event recognized in accounting that affects the amount, the nature, or the composition of a company's assets, liabilities, or owners' equities.* For example, an accounting transaction takes place when a company purchases merchandise from its suppliers. The firm obtains new assets in the form of merchandise. It also decreases (or uses) some of its asset cash or incurs a liability (accounts payable).

Transaction defined

External Events

Either external or internal events may give rise to accounting transactions. An external event usually involves the accounting entity and a second party outside the entity—for example, the purchase of merchandise from a supplier or the sale of merchandise to a customer. Many external events give rise to source documents when the events occur. For example, when a sale is made to a customer, the source documents generated might include (1) a sales order from a customer, (2) a shipping notice from the shipping department, (3) a freight bill, and eventually (4) a check from the customer. In addition, the company will prepare a sales invoice and send it to the customer. External events that qualify as transactions but do not involve a second party include floods, fires, and other acts of God. If asset values are changed by these events, the events are recognized in accounting.

Internal Events

Internal events giving rise to accounting transactions affect assets and equities but do not involve a party outside the business. The consumption of supplies is an example. When the supplies are purchased, they are an asset. As the supplies are used up during the period, they become an expense. The use of the supplies does not involve the action of any outside party. Internal events are not necessarily accompanied by documents from outside the enterprise. As a result, the enterprise itself has to make sure that the events are appropriately documented. For example, a trucking firm may require that drivers provide a daily report of miles driven and deliveries made.

Transactions and Accounting Principles

Influence of principles

The operation of a business consists of a continuous series of events. Some of these events give rise to financial accounting transactions that affect the assets, liabilities, and owners' equity of the firm. Other events do not give rise to accounting transactions. The basis for deciding which events are to be recognized as accounting transactions is the principles that are generally accepted in accounting. (Broad aspects of these principles have been referred to briefly in chapters 1 to 3.) These principles generally provide that:

1. Interactions with other parties are recognized (except for agreements that are unperformed by both parties).
2. Unfavorable effects of other events are often recognized.
3. Favorable effects of other events are not recognized until they are validated by an interaction with other parties.

The more detailed rules used to implement principles are the subject of this and later chapters and must be understood if one is to have a good grasp of accounting.

Types of Transactions

Accounting equation

Every accounting transaction maintains the basic equality of the accounting equation:

$$\text{Assets} = \text{Liabilities} + \text{Owners' Equity}$$

Since all properties or property rights have corresponding sources or claims, no transaction can arise that will disturb the equality of the accounting equation. Given this basic equation, with three different types of items, only nine possible types of transactions (or combinations of two or more of these nine basic types) can occur. Some of these nine types occur frequently, others infrequently. A summary of the nine possibilities appears in Table 4-1. The following are examples of each of the nine types of transactions:

1. Collect amounts owed by customers. Cash is increased and accounts receivable is decreased.
2. Borrow money from the bank on a note. Cash and notes payable are increased.
3. Owners invest cash for shares of common stock. Cash and common

TABLE 4-1. Summary of Types of Possible Accounting Transactions

	Assets	= Liabilities	+ Owners' Equity
1.	(+) (−)		
2.	(+)	(+)	
3.	(+)		(+)
4.	(−)	(−)	
5.	(−)		(−)
6.		(+)	(−)
7.		(+) (−)	
8.		(−)	(+)
9.			(+) (−)

Types of transactions

stock are increased. Another example is a sale on account to a customer. Accounts receivable is increased and retained earnings is increased by the revenue.

4. Pay an amount owed to a creditor. Cash and accounts payable are decreased.
5. Pay dividends. Cash and retained earnings are decreased. Another example is salary expense, where cash and retained earnings are decreased.
6. Receive an electric bill. Accounts payable is increased and retained earnings is decreased by the expense.
7. Send a creditor a note on account. Accounts payable is decreased and notes payable is increased.
8. This is a relatively uncommon type of event. An example is a conversion of long-term debt into shares of stock. This reduces bonds payable and increases common stock.
9. This is another uncommon type of event. An example is a stock dividend consisting of additional shares of stock. This increases common stock and decreases retained earnings.

These nine types cover all the possible transactions that can occur in accounting. It can be seen that every transaction maintains the equality of the basic accounting equation.

LEDGERS

The accounting equation provides the framework for processing transactions. We now consider two accounting records that are essential parts of the processing system, the *account* and the *journal*. In the discussion that follows, we shall see how the accounting equation governs the use of these two records.

Part II   Processing Accounting Data

Accounts

An account is a record of the transactions that affect a particular type of asset, liability, or owners' equity. Thus, an account is established for each type of asset, liability, and owners' equity. For example, the account for *cash* shows the effects of cash receipt transactions, cash disbursement transactions, and the resulting balance of cash. All the asset, liability, and owners' equity accounts together comprise the *ledger*.

In its simplest form, an account consists of the title of the item (for example, Cash), and two sides—one side for recording increases in the item and the other side for recording decreases in the item. This form, called a T account, is set up as follows:

Title of Item	
Left side (debit)	Right side (credit)

Debit and credit

The terms *debit* and *credit* are used in accounting to refer to the left side and the right side of an account, respectively. To debit an account means to record an amount on the left side of the account; to credit an account means to record an amount on the right side of the account. Debit is abbreviated Dr. (based on the Latin spelling of the word), and credit is abbreviated Cr. The balance of an account is the difference between the total debits and the total credits to that account. If the total of debits exceeds the total of credits, the account is said to have a *debit balance*. If credits exceed the debits, the account has a *credit balance*.

Following are the basic rules for recording increases and decreases in asset, liability, and owners' equity accounts:

Assets		Liabilities		Owners' Equity	
Increase side (debit)	Decrease side (credit)	Decrease side (debit)	Increase side (credit)	Decrease side (debit)	Increase side (credit)

The rationale for these rules is derived from the basic accounting equation, where assets are conventionally on the left (debit) side and liabilities and owners' equity are on the right (credit) side. Thus if assets increase, there should be more on the left (debit) side; if liabilities or owners' equity increase, there should be more on the right (credit) side. Decreases in accounting are recorded by placing amounts on the opposite side of an account rather than by direct subtraction.

Revenues, as increases in owners' equity, are increased by credits; expenses, as decreases in owners' equity, are increased by debits, as follows:

Revenues		Expenses	
Decrease side (debit)	Increase side (credit)	Increase side (debit)	Decrease side (credit)

It is important to note that the terms *debit* and *credit* refer only to the left side and right side of an account. The nature of the account determines whether a debit entry will increase or decrease its balance.

The basic rules for recording increases or decreases in the various types of accounts should be memorized. These rules are conventional; that is, they are a matter of agreement among accountants. The rules could be changed without changing the basic concepts of accounting. However, all accountants do use these rules, and there is no point in being innovative in this area. Following these rules provides a simple recording system with built-in checks and balances.

In accounting, *transactions are always recorded by entering equal debits and credits in the accounts for each transaction.* This method of recording transactions, known as *double-entry bookkeeping*, maintains the equality of the accounting equation, ensures that a complete analysis of each transaction has been made, and acts as a check on the numerical accuracy of the analysis. Since each transaction has equal debits and credits, it follows that all debit balances in accounts at any given time will equal all credit balances.

Double-entry bookkeeping

Examples of Transactions

Several examples will illustrate the analysis of transactions into debits and credits. Note the equality of the debits and credits in each transaction.

EXAMPLE 4-1

Transaction: A corporation is formed, and $20,000 of cash is received for stock issued to stockholders.
Analysis: The asset cash is increased. Debit cash for $20,000. The owner's equity account capital stock is increased. Credit capital stock for $20,000.

Cash		Capital Stock	
20,000			20,000

EXAMPLE 4-2

Transaction: A building is leased for $600 per month. The first four months' rent is paid in advance. The prepaid rent is an asset until it is used.
Analysis: The asset prepaid rent is increased. Debit prepaid rent $2,400. The asset cash is decreased. Credit cash $2,400.

Prepaid Rent		Cash	
2,400			2,400

EXAMPLE 4-3

Transaction: Office equipment is purchased on account for $2,200.
Analysis: The asset office equipment is increased. Debit office equipment $2,200.
The liability accounts payable is increased. Credit accounts payable $2,200.

Office Equipment		Accounts Payable	
2,200			2,200

EXAMPLE 4-4

Transaction: A payment of $1,000 is made on account.
Analysis: The liability accounts payable is decreased. Debit accounts payable $1,000.
The asset cash is decreased. Credit cash $1,000.

Accounts Payable		Cash	
1,000			1,000

Assume that the four transactions above occur in the same firm, the Acme Perfume Company. Hence, all four of the transactions are recorded in one set of ledger accounts (see Example 4-5). To help you trace the entries in that ledger to the transactions in Examples 4-1 through 4-4, we have identified each entry by the number of its corresponding example.

EXAMPLE 4-5

THE ACME PERFUME COMPANY LEDGER ACCOUNTS

Assets = Liabilities + Owners' Equity

	Cash				Accounts Payable		
(4-1)	20,000	(4-2)	2,400	(4-4)	1,000	(4-3)	2,200
		(4-4)	1,000				

	Office Equipment			Capital Stock	
(4-3)	2,200			(4-1)	20,000

	Prepaid Rent	
(4-2)	2,400	

Revenue and Expense Transactions

The above examples dealt with transactions involving asset, liability, and owners' equity changes. Within the same framework, we can also record transactions dealing with revenues and expenses, but a few words of explanation may be helpful before these types of transactions are illustrated.

The income statement presents revenue and expense data. Revenues and expenses increase or decrease a corporation's owners' equity through retained earnings. Separate accounts are used to record the details of individual revenues and expenses for preparing the income statement. These accounts reflect particular types of periodic changes in owners' equity. *Revenue accounts* record increases in owners' claims as assets are received from the sale of goods or services. *Expense accounts* record decreases in owners' claims as assets are used up or liabilities are incurred in operations.

Revenue accounts are increased by credits, since they are increases in owners' equity. On the other hand, expense accounts are increased by debits, since they reflect decreases in owners' equity. The basic accounting equation (assets = liabilities + owners' equity) can be expanded to include these accounts as follows:

Assets = Liabilities + Owners' Equity } Balance sheet accounts
$\underbrace{\phantom{\text{+ Revenues - Expenses}}}$
+ Revenues − Expenses } Income statement accounts

Expanded accounting equation

Revenue and expense accounts can be viewed as a subclass of retained earnings, with revenues on the right side (increasing retained earnings) and expenses on the left side (decreasing retained earnings). Revenue and expense accounts are referred to as nominal (or temporary) accounts, because they record the specific revenues and expenses of an enterprise for a given time period.

The rules of debits and credits, as expanded to include revenue and expense accounts, are as follows:

Debits

1. Increase assets
2. Decrease liabilities
3. Decrease capital stock
4. Decrease retained earnings
5. Decrease revenues
6. Increase expenses

Credits

1. Decrease assets
2. Increase liabilities

Part II Processing Accounting Data

3. Increase capital stock
4. Increase retained earnings
5. Increase revenues
6. Decrease expenses

Debit and credit framework   This framework of debits and credits may be more easily visualized as follows:

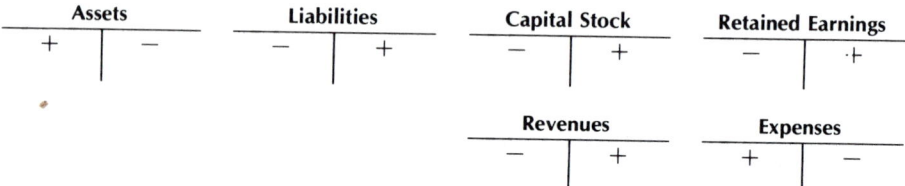

Some examples will illustrate the analysis of transactions affecting revenue and expense accounts. Notice the equality of the debits and credits in each transaction.

EXAMPLE 4-6

Transaction: A certified public accountant completes an audit for a client and receives $900 payment in cash.
Analysis: Cash is increased. Debit cash $900.
Revenue is increased. Credit auditing revenue $900.

```
         Cash                            Auditing Revenue
(4-6)    900                                       (4-6)    900
```

EXAMPLE 4-7

Transaction: The CPA pays $300 for the month's rent.
Analysis: Rent expense is increased. Debit rent expense $300. Cash is decreased. Credit cash $300.

```
      Rent Expense                          Cash
(4-7)    300                      (4-6)    900  | (4-7)    300
```

EXAMPLE 4-8

Transaction: Salaries of $500 are paid in cash to employees of the CPA.
Analysis: Salaries expense is increased. Debit salaries expense $500.
Cash is decreased. Credit cash $500.

```
     Salaries Expense                         Cash
(4-8)    500                      (4-6)    900  | (4-7)    300
                                                | (4-8)    500
```

Account Format

Although the T accounts used in the illustrations so far are adequate for analysis, a bookkeeping system uses more formal accounts. The ledger account generally provides for the accumulation of the following data for each account:

1. *Account title and number of account.* The title of the account indicates the type of asset, liability, or equity. The use of account numbers allows for efficient organization of ledger accounts. Through the numbering system, the accounts can be classified into various groups and subgroups (such as assets and current assets) and arranged in logical sequence. The recording process is facilitated with a numbering system, especially with machine accounting methods.
2. *Date and PR (or ref.) columns for each entry into the accounts.* The *PR* (posting reference), or *reference,* column indicates the source from which the information entered in the account is obtained. The use of this column will be explained later. There may be room for some explanatory comments in an account, also.
3. *Amount columns.* A ledger account must have at least two amount columns, one for increases and one for decreases. There may also be a third amount column for the *balance,* or net amount.

Figures 4-2 and 4-3 illustrate common forms of a single ledger account. The body of the ledger account in Figure 4-2 is divided into two parts, one for increases and one for decreases. Each part has separate columns for the date, explanation, PR, and amount. The ledger account in Figure 4-3 has separate columns for the amount of increases, the amount of decreases, and the balance of the account.

Ledger Account, Two-Column Form　　　　　　　　　　　　　FIGURE 4-2

Title							Acct. No.
Date	Explanation	PR	Debit	Date	Explanation	PR	Credit

Ledger Account, Three-Column Form　　　　　　　　　　　　FIGURE 4-3

Title					Acct. No.
Date	Explanation	PR	Debit	Credit	Balance

Part II   Processing Accounting Data

We do not have to be concerned with the exact format of a ledger account. The form will be fitted to the particular business situation. Where a computer is used, the accounts may be in the form of magnetic codes on magnetic tape. No matter what the form, the essentials are the same.

JOURNALS

Transactions were entered directly in the ledger accounts in the examples above. In an actual accounting situation, with hundreds of different ledger accounts and thousands of transactions, this procedure becomes unwieldy. For one thing, in making the entries directly in the ledger accounts the identity of the individual transaction is lost. Any one ledger account contains only part of a transaction. If the ledger contains hundreds of accounts (all on separate pages), relating individual debits and credits to one another becomes almost impossible.

A separate record of each transaction is needed. An accounting journal is used for this purpose. Each recording of an accounting transaction in a journal is called a *journal entry*. Each transaction is recorded (*entered*) in a journal before the amounts are transferred to the ledger accounts (*posted*). Thus, the journal is referred to as a book of original entry. It contains a permanent chronological listing of all transactions and an analysis of each transaction into debits and credits. Using a journal (in addition to the ledger) as a recording medium has several advantages:

Advantages of journal

1. The journal provides a complete chronological history of all transactions.
2. A complete picture of each transaction is provided in one place.
3. There is room in the journal for an explanation of the entry.
4. Use of the journal reduces the possibility of an error when transactions are first recorded.
5. More than one person may record transactions at the same time.

The General journal

We will now consider a particular type of journal, the *general journal*, which can be used to record all possible accounting transactions. At times, specialized journals are used for particular purposes. These other types of journals will be considered in chapter 6.

Example 4-9 lists transactions of the Mason Surveyor Service. The form for entering the transactions in a general journal is illustrated in Example 4-10. The form has been standardized in accounting practice and should be followed. The form and arrangement of account titles and amounts are important in interpreting transactions that have been journalized.

EXAMPLE 4-9

The Mason Surveyor Service begins operations on August 1. During August, the following events occur:

Aug. 1 $2,000 cash is received for 200 shares of common stock.
Cash is increased. Debit cash $2,000.
The owners' equity common stock is increased. Credit common stock $2,000.

Aug. 2 The firm rents office space and equipment for $300 per month, and three months' rent is paid in advance ($900) by issuing check number 1.
The asset prepaid rent is increased. Debit prepaid rent $900.
Cash is decreased. Credit cash $900.

Aug. 3 A secretary is hired at $500 a month and a surveyor at $900 a month.
No entry necessary until some services have been performed by employees.

Aug. 4 Supplies are purchased on account for $450 from Brown Co.
Supplies on hand are increased. Debit supplies on hand $450.
Accounts payable are increased. Credit accounts payable $450.

Aug. 20 Services are performed for a customer, Ajax Construction Co. Ajax is billed for $1,200.
Accounts receivable are increased. Debit accounts receivable $1,200.
Revenue is increased. Credit revenue from surveys $1,200.

Aug. 21 Services are performed for customers, and the customers pay cash of $1,300.
Cash is increased. Debit cash $1,300.
Revenue is increased. Credit revenue from surveys $1,300.

Aug. 22 Cash received on account from Ajax Construction Co. amounts to $900.
Cash is increased. Debit cash $900.
Accounts receivable are decreased. Credit accounts receivable $900.

Aug. 24 Payments of $250 are made on account to Brown Supply Co. by issuing check number 2.
Accounts payable are decreased. Debit accounts payable $250.
Cash is decreased. Credit cash $250.

Aug. 31 During the month, supplies costing $125 are used as indicated by a count of supplies still on hand.
Supplies expense is increased. Debit supplies expense $125.
Supplies on hand is decreased. Credit supplies on hand $125.

Aug. 31 One month of the prepaid rent on the office has expired at the end of the month.
Rent expense is increased. Debit rent expense $300.
Prepaid rent is decreased. Credit prepaid rent $300.

(Continued)

Example 4-9 (Cont.)

    Aug. 31   Salaries for the month, amounting to $1,400, are paid in cash to employees hired August 3. Checks 3 and 4 are issued. Salaries expense is increased. Debit salaries expense $1,400. Cash is decreased. Credit cash $1,400.

Journal procedure

The transactions in Example 4-9 are entered in a general journal as indicated in Example 4-10. Notice that the debit and credit *amounts* in each transaction are equal. The accounts to be debited are listed first; the accounts to be credited follow and are indented. There are separate columns for debit amounts and credit amounts. Under each entry is a detailed explanation of the entry. The explanation should be brief, but should contain all information essential to an understanding of the transaction. When an entry is self-explanatory, the explanation may be omitted, but it is better to err on the side of overkill than to omit information that might be useful later. The information in the PR column comes from the posting process described later in this chapter.

POSTING

Cross referencing

Posting is the process of transferring the debits and credits that have been entered in the journal to the ledger accounts. In order to post the debit to cash in the first entry in Example 4-10, for example, the bookkeeper locates the cash account in the ledger and enters $2,000 on the debit side. In the PR column of the ledger, the journal page number (page 1 in Example 4-10) will be entered, to show the source of the ledger entry. Then in the PR column of the journal, the account number of the cash account (account number 1) is entered. Thus, it is possible to tell from the journal whether an amount has been posted and to what account it has been posted. This system provides a convenient cross-reference between the ledger and the journal. The PR column in the ledger indicates the journal page on which an entry originates, and the PR column in the journal indicates the ledger account to which an item was posted (blank spaces indicate which items in the journal are yet to be posted.)

The steps in the posting process are illustrated in Example 4-11, using the three-column form. Note that the date, amount, and journal page are entered in the ledger and the ledger account number is entered in the journal. The posting reference in the ledger indicates the source of each posted amount; J1, for example, indicates page 1 of the journal. The posting reference in the journal indicates the number of the account to which the amount has been posted.

EXAMPLE 4-10

MASON SURVEYOR SERVICE
General Journal

Page 1

Date		Accounts	PR	Debit	Credit
Aug.	1	Cash	1	2,000	
		Common stock	20		2,000
		200 shares of common stock issued for cash			
	2	Prepaid rent	3	900	
		Cash	1		900
		Three months' rent paid in advance. Check No. 1.			
	4	Supplies on hand	4	450	
		Accounts payable	10		450
		Supplies purchased on account from Brown Supply Co.			
	20	Accounts receivable	2	1,200	
		Revenue from surveys	30		1,200
		Ajax Construction is billed for services performed			
	21	Cash	1	1,300	
		Revenue from surveys	30		1,300
		Cash received for services			
	22	Cash	1	900	
		Accounts receivable	2		900
		Collections received from Ajax Construction Co.			
	24	Accounts payable	10	250	
		Cash	1		250
		Payment on account to Brown Supply Co. Check No. 2.			
	31	Supplies expense	42	125	
		Supplies on hand	4		125
		Supplies used during month			
	31	Rent expense	41	300	
		Prepaid rent	3		300
		Rent expired—one month at $300			
	31	Salaries expense	40	1,400	
		Cash	1		1,400
		Salaries paid for month. Checks 3 and 4.			

EXAMPLE 4-11

Illustration of Posting Process

Journal

Page 1

Date	Account	PR	Debit	Credit
Aug. 1	Cash	1	2,000	
	Common stock	20		2,000
	200 shares of common stock issued for cash			

Ledger
Cash

Account No. 1

Date		PR	Debit	Credit	Balance
Aug. 1		J1	2,000		2,000

Ledger
Common Stock

Account No. 20

Date		PR	Debit	Credit	Balance
Aug. 1		J1		2,000	2,000

The ledger accounts for the Mason Surveyor Service, as they appear after posting the journal entries from Example 4-10, are shown in Example 4-12. Note that the accounts are arranged in the ledger in the order in which they appear in the financial statements, with assets first, then liabilities and owners' equity accounts, and finally revenue and expenses. Accounts are numbered so that each class of accounts is clearly indicated.

EXAMPLE 4-12

MASON SURVEYOR SERVICE LEDGER ACCOUNTS

Cash — Acct. No.1

Date		PR	Debit	Credit	Balance
Aug. 1		J1	2,000		2,000
2		J1		900	1,100
21		J1	1,300		2,400
22		J1	900		3,300
24		J1		250	3,050
31		J1		1,400	1,650

Accounts Receivable — Acct. No. 2

Date		PR	Debit	Credit	Balance
Aug. 20		J1	1,200		1,200
22		J1		900	300

Prepaid Rent — Acct. No. 3

Date		PR	Debit	Credit	Balance
Aug. 2		J1	900		900
31		J1		300	600

Supplies on Hand — Acct. No.4

Date		PR	Debit	Credit	Balance
Aug. 4		J1	450		450
31		J1		125	325

Accounts Payable — Acct. No. 10

Date		PR	Debit	Credit	Balance
Aug. 4		J1		450	450
24		J1	250		200

Common Stock — Acct. No. 20

Date		PR	Debit	Credit	Balance
Aug. 1		J1		2,000	2,000

Revenue from Surveys — Acct. No. 30

Date		PR	Debit	Credit	Balance
Aug. 20		J1		1,200	1,200
21		J1		1,300	2,500

Salaries Expense — Acct. No. 40

Date		PR	Debit	Credit	Balance
Aug. 31		J1	1,400		1,400

(Continued)

Example 4-12 (Cont.)

Rent Expense — Acct. No. 41

Date		PR	Debit	Credit	Balance
Aug. 31		J1	300		300

Supplies Expense — Acct. No. 42

Date		PR	Debit	Credit	Balance
Aug. 31		J1	125		125

TRIAL BALANCE

The equality of the accounting equation (*assets equal liabilities plus owners' equity*) can be shown by preparing a formal balance sheet. If the total assets are equal to the total liabilities plus owners' equity (including the increase in owners' equity because of the current period's income), the balance sheet is *in balance*. However, accountants may want to ascertain that the accounts are in balance before preparing a formal balance sheet. They can do this by listing all accounts with debit balances and all accounts with credit balances and comparing the two totals.[1] This list of all the accounts is a *trial balance*. A trial balance for the Mason Surveyor Service is shown in Example 4-13.

EXAMPLE 4-13

MASON SURVEYOR SERVICE
Trial Balance
August 31, Year 1

Account	Debit	Credit
Cash	$1,650	
Accounts receivable	300	
Prepaid rent	600	
Supplies on hand	325	
Accounts payable		$ 200
Common stock		2,000
Revenue from Surveys		2,500
Salaries expense	1,400	
Rent expense	300	
Supplies expense	125	
	$4,700	$4,700

---

1. A second method is to run an adding machine total of all account balances, putting all debits into the machine as additions and all credits as subtractions. The total should, of course, be zero.

The trial balance provides a partial check on the numerical accuracy of the accounts. It does *not* indicate that the accounts are correct, however. If a posting is made to a wrong account, if a complete entry is omitted in posting, if offsetting errors are made in posting or computing account balances, or if the original analysis of the transaction was in error (but the debits were equal to the credits) the trial balance will still "prove" the equality of the debits and credits. On the other hand, if the trial balance does not balance (if the debits do not equal the credits), then the trial balance shows that there is at least one error in the data collection process.

Value of trial balance

PREPARATION OF THE FINANCIAL STATEMENTS

The income statement, the statement of financial position, and the statement of retained earnings can be prepared from the data in the trial balance. The income statement is usually prepared first because the amount of net income (excess of revenues over expenses) is needed in preparing the other two statements. The statement of retained earnings is prepared second. It shows the effect of net income and distributions of income (dividends) on the stockholders' equity. Finally, the statement of financial position shows the assets, liabilities, and stockholders' equity at the end of the period. The statement of changes in financial position can also be prepared from this same basic data. Its preparation is discussed in chapter 17.

MERCHANDISING TRANSACTIONS

The Mason Surveyor Service example illustrated the accounting process for an enterprise that provide services to customers. We now turn to accounting for businesses that sell merchandise to customers. The same rules of debit and credit apply, but some additional problems arise in accounting for sales and purchases of merchandise.

Accounting for Sales of Merchandise

A merchandising firm obtains its primary revenue by selling goods to customers. The selling price must be high enough to cover the cost of the goods sold and all other expenses of the enterprise and, hopefully, to provide a profit for the owners.

When merchandise is sold for cash, the following type of journal entry is made:

Part II   Processing Accounting Data

	Debit	Credit
Cash	200	
Sales		200
Sale of merchandise for cash.		

In many retail businesses, one entry is made at the end of each day for total cash sales, using the cash register(s) total as the basis for the amount of the entry.

If sales are made on credit (that is, with the customer promising to pay at a later date), revenue is recorded and a receivable is set up as follows:

	Debit	Credit
Accounts receivable	150	
Sales		150
Sale of merchandise on credit; payment due in one month.		

Credit cards

If a customer uses a credit card to charge the sale, the entry to record the sale is essentially the same as the entry for a regular charge sale. If there is a need to distinguish credit card sales from regular charge sales, accounts such as credit card receivables and credit card sales may be used.

Returns and allowances

Most businesses allow customers to return goods that are unsatisfactory. It is also possible that customers may be allowed credit if goods are damaged in shipment or have defects that are serious enough to warrant return of the merchandise. Returns and allowances could be deducted directly from sales. However, the usual practice is to record them in a separate account so that information will be available on the total amount of revenue lost from these causes. Following is the entry to record a return or allowance:

	Debit	Credit
Sales returns and allowances	100	
Accounts receivable (or Cash)		100
Goods returned by Ajax Co.		

Cash is returned to the customers only if they do not owe any amounts to the company.

Discounts

Sometimes customers are offered a discount if they pay their accounts promptly. Availability of these discounts is expressed in credit terms such as 2/10, n/30. These terms mean that 2% may be deducted from the amount owed if payment is made within 10 days after the sale and that the net amount is due in any case in 30 days. If a $500 sale were made on Feb. 4 with terms of 2/10, n/30, the sale would be recorded as follows:

		Debit	Credit
Feb. 4	Accounts receivable	500	
	Sales		500

If the customer paid on February 12, the following entry would be made:

		Debit	Credit
Feb. 12	Cash	490	
	Sales discounts	10	
	Accounts receivable		500

Both the sales returns and allowances account and the sales discounts account are deducted from total sales on the income statement to arrive at the net revenue from sales.

ACCOUNTING FOR PURCHASES OF MERCHANDISE

Two basic approaches are used in accounting for costs of merchandise purchased for eventual sale to customers. One approach is the *perpetual inventory method*, in which an inventory account is kept perpetually up to date, with additions (goods purchased) being debited to the account and deductions (cost of goods sold to customers) being credited to the account at cost. This approach will be covered in chapter 9 and will not be illustrated at this point.

Many enterprises, including most retail businesses, do not use a perpetual inventory system. Instead, they determine the amount of inventory periodically by taking a count of the merchandise on hand. This type of approach is called the *periodic inventory method*. In a periodic inventory system, all purchases are recorded in a purchases account, any purchase returns or allowances are recorded in a separate account, and all freight costs on goods purchased are recorded in a freight-in or transportation-in account. No entry is made to record the cost of the goods sold at the time of sale. Instead, the total cost of all goods sold is determined at the end of the period, as indicated in chapter 5.

Periodic inventory method

When merchandise is purchased for cash, the following journal entry is made:

	Debit	Credit
Purchases	600	
Cash		600
Purchase of goods for cash.		

A purchase on credit, or *on account*, is recorded as follows:

	Debit	Credit
Purchases	1,300	
Accounts payable		1,300
Purchase of merchandise on credit; payment due in 30 days.		

The purchases account is used *only* for purchases of merchandise that is to be sold to customers. Purchases of supplies or equipment are debited to the supplies on hand or equipment accounts, never to the purchases account. The purchases account is essentially an expense account, which is increased by debits.

Freight paid on goods purchased is part of the total cost of acquiring the goods. Freight paid on a purchase is charged to a separate account called either freight-in or transportation-in. Freight-in should be distinguished from freight paid on goods sold to customers, which is a delivery expense and is part of operating expenses.

If goods are returned to a supplier for some reason or if an allowance is granted by a supplier because of damage or some other cause, the entry is as follows:

	Debit	Credit
Accounts payable	150	
Purchase returns and allowances		150
Allowance granted for goods damaged in purchase of Jan. 5.		

A separate account is used for returns and allowances so that information will be available about the dollar amount of purchases that caused problems during a period.

Credit terms may be available on purchases. Suppose that goods are purchased on February 12 with terms of 2/10, n/30. The following entry would be made:[2]

		Debit	Credit
Feb. 12	Purchases	3,000	
	Accounts payable		3,000
	Purchase from Jones Co.; terms 2/10, n/30.		

If payment is made within the 10 days, the entry would be as follows:

---

2. An alternative method of recording purchases at the net price is discussed in chapter 11.

		Debit	Credit
Feb. 21	Accounts payable	3,000	
	Purchase discounts		60
	Cash		2,940
	Paid Jones Co. within 10 days.		

If payment were made after the 10-day discount period, the full $3,000 would have to be paid.

At the time of sale of goods, a sale is recorded, but no other entries are made to record the cost of merchandise removed from inventory and sold to customers. Instead, cost of goods sold is computed at the end of the accounting period. This is facilitated by "taking an inventory," that is, by counting the ending inventory of merchandise on hand. The assumption is usually made that merchandise not on hand has been sold.

A trial balance for a merchandising concern at the end of an accounting period is illustrated in Example 4-14. Note the contrast between that trial balance and the trial balance for the Mason Surveyor Service illustrated previously.

EXAMPLE 4-14

ELWELL COMPANY
Trial Balance
December 31, Year 1

	Debit	Credit
Cash	$ 6,500	
Accounts receivable	15,000	
Inventory (beginning of year)	18,000	
Furniture and fixtures	8,000	
Accumulated depreciation—furniture and fixtures		$ 3,000
Accounts payable		7,000
Capital stock		20,000
Retained earnings		6,000
Sales		84,000
Sales returns and allowances	2,000	
Purchases	41,000	
Purchase discounts		800
Transportation in	3,400	
Salaries expense	16,000	
Depreciation expense	400	
Other expenses	10,500	
	$120,800	$120,800

To prepare an income statement and balance sheet from the information in Example 4-14, the ending inventory would have to be counted and entered in the records. The procedure for recording the ending inventory is explained in chapter 5.

SUMMARY

In this chapter the financial accounting recording process has been discussed and illustrated. Journals and ledgers are the two media used in the recording process. Journals are used to record specific accounting transactions in chronological order. Recording transactions initially in a journal provides a complete picture of each transaction in one place and reduces the possibility of error. The ledger shows the effects of transactions on the individual accounts. The ledger account balances provide the data presented in the financial statements.

After transactions for a period have been posted to the ledger, a trial balance is taken. Equality of debits and credits on the trial balance gives some evidence of mechanical accuracy.

Transactions were illustrated for both a service enterprise and a merchandising concern. A merchandising concern buys goods for resale and utilizes special accounts to record sale and purchase transactions.

In later chapters both journals and ledgers will be used. Generally, we will use the simplest form of records, because our emphasis is on analysis rather than record keeping. In fact, when we emphasize analysis of various types of transactions, we will seldom consider anything other than the journal entry. Ledger accounts will be used, on the other hand, when we are concerned with analyzing the effects of several transactions on particular accounts.

IMPORTANT TERMS

Transaction *Perpetual inventory*
Ledger *Periodic inventory*
Account *Purchases*
Journal *Credit terms*
Posting *Sales discounts*
Trial balance *Purchase discounts*

QUESTIONS

4-1. "At all times, total assets must equal total equities." Explain.

4-2. What is the reason for putting increases in assets on the debit side of asset accounts?

4-3. The net income for a period could be determined from the change in retained earnings during the period. Why do we bother to maintain revenue and expense accounts?

4-4. "If the sum of the total debits is equal to the sum of the total credits on the trial balance, no errors have been made." Do you agree? Why (or why not)?

4-5. Do the expenses of a period have any necessary relationship to the cash paid in that period? Explain.

4-6. Distinguish between a *trial balance* and a *balance sheet*.

4-7. What is the usefulness of the cross-references between the journal and the ledger?

4-8. Why is it desirable to establish a separate account for sales returns and allowances?

4-9. If a purchase of supplies is debited to the purchases account rather than the supplies on hand account, will the trial balance still balance? What will be the effect on the financial statements at the end of the period (assuming none of the supplies have been used up)?

4-10. It has been said that double-entry bookkeeping is a waste of time because everything is recorded twice. Discuss.

EXERCISES

4-11. *Account identification.* For each of the accounts listed below, state whether it is an asset, a liability, a revenue, or an expense. For each account, indicate whether it normally has a debit or a credit balance.
  a. Cash
  b. Office supplies on hand
  c. Notes payable
  d. Professional fees earned
  e. Interest on notes payable
  f. Office equipment
  g. Rent paid for office space
  h. Salaries of employees
  i. Notes receivable
  j. Interest on notes receivable

4-12. *Analysis of transactions.* Analyze the following transactions of Ace Laundry, indicating whether they increase or decrease assets, liabilities, owners' equity, revenues, and expenses.

Jan. 1	Owners invest $20,000 cash in the laundry business and receive shares of stock.
Jan. 2	Rent a building, paying $2,000 rent in advance for first two months.
Jan. 4	Buy laundry equipment on account from Bean Machine Co. for $18,000.
Jan. 5	Borrow $6,000 cash, giving a note to the Third National Bank.
Jan. 10	Collect $1,600 cash from customers for laundry services.
Jan. 11	Bill other customers $2,700 for services.
Jan. 12	Pay salaries of $1,300 to employees.
Jan. 15	Pay Bean Machine Co. $10,000 on account.
Jan. 20	Collect $1,000 from customers billed on January 11.
Jan. 31	One month's rent (see January 2) has been used up in January.

4-13. *Journalizing.* Refer to Exercise 4-12 and record each of the transactions in a general journal.

4-14. *Posting.* Refer to Exercise 4-13 and post each of the transactions to ledger accounts. Number the accounts and include cross references.

4-15. *Analysis of transactions, merchandise.* Analyze the following transactions of the Krueger Mercantile Company, indicating whether they increase or decrease assets, liabilities, owners' equity, revenues, or expenses. The company has been operating for several years.

Oct. 2	Purchase merchandise on account from Apex Co. for $3,000, terms 2/10, n/30.
Oct. 4	Sell merchandise to Sanders Co. for cash $4,200.
Oct. 6	Purchase equipment for cash from Huizinger Co., $6,000.
Oct. 7	Sell merchandise to Beverly Co. on account, $4,000, terms 2/10, n/30.
Oct. 9	Pay for purchase of October 2.
Oct. 15	Pay salaries of $2,600.
Oct. 16	Beverly Co. returns some damaged goods and is allowed $500 credit.
Oct. 20	Receive a check from Beverly Co. in full payment of amount owed.

4-16. *Journalizing.* Refer to Exercise 4-15 and record each of the transactions in a general journal.

4-17. *Posting.* Refer to Exercise 4-16 and post each of the transactions to ledger accounts. Number the accounts and include cross references.

4-18. *Trial balance.* The following balances are in accounts of Dexter Co. on June 30. Arrange them in a trial balance.

Cash	$ 8,000	Salaries	2,700
Sales	26,000	Purchases	13,200
Supplies on hand	600	Inventory	11,000
Accounts payable	4,000	Capital stock	10,000
Accounts receivable	5,000	Retained earnings	2,100
Rent expense	1,600		

4-19. *Analysis to determine transactions.* As a result of five transactions during February, the first month of business, Neumann Medical Company has the trial balance below. Indicate what the five transactions were by recording them in general journal form. You may assume that supplies were bought on account.

Trial Balance

	Debit	Credit
Cash	$ 7,400	
Accounts receivable	6,000	
Accounts payable		$ 500
Capital stock		10,000
Salaries expense	2,100	
Revenue from medical services		6,000
Supplies expense	1,000	
	$16,500	$16,500

PROBLEMS

4-20. *Journalizing transactions.* The Sharpshooters, a firm of real estate brokers, had the following transactions during June. Prepare journal entries to record these transactions.
  a. Arranged the sale of an apartment building owned by a client. The commission for making the sale was $12,000, but this amount will not be received until July 20.
  b. Paid $300 salary to a salesperson for time worked during June.
  c. Collected cash of $1,500 from an account receivable. The receivable originated in April from services rendered in selling a client's home.
  d. Borrowed $4,000 from the National Bank, to be repaid in three months.
  e. Purchased a typewriter for $300 cash.
  f. Collected $150 from a dentist to whom Sharpshooters rented part of its building. The amount represented rent for the month of June.
  g. Paid $2,000 plus $30 interest in settlement of a loan obtained three months earlier.
  h. Paid a garage $200 for automobile repair work performed in May and previously recorded as a liability.
  (Solution in Appendix B.)

4-21. *Journalizing transactions.* Prepare journal entries in good form for the following transactions:

May 1		Issued $60,000 capital stock in return for cash investment of stockholders.
May 4		Purchased office equipment for $15,000 cash.
May 5		Received $16,000 cash for services rendered to customers (use a fees earned account).
May 11		Purchased office supplies on account for $350. These supplies will last for several accounting periods.
May 15		Billed customers for services rendered, $4,000.
May 18		Paid for the office supplies acquired on May 11.
May 23		Received payment in full from clients billed on May 15.
May 25		Declared and paid a $2,000 cash dividend to stockholders.
May 29		Paid the salaries for the month, $2,300.
May 30		Recorded the use of office supplies, $145.

4-22. *Analysis of transactions.* On the first day of the month, Denver Grocer had assets totaling $80,000 and liabilities totaling $20,000. During the month, merchandise that had cost $22,000 was sold for $36,000, and operating expenses totaled $4,000. On the last day of the month, assets totaled $85,000 and liabilities totaled $16,000. Determine the amounts below.

  a. Owners' equity on the first day of the month.
  b. Revenue for the month
  c. Net income for the month
  d. Owners' equity on the last day of the month
  e. Increase in the owners' equity during the month
  (Solution in Appendix B.)

Part II Processing Accounting Data

4-23. *Journalizing, posting, and statement of financial position.* Jack and Jill decide to organize a water well drilling enterprise. The following transactions occur during December.
  1. Jack invests cash of $5,000, and Jill invests land and a building. The land cost Jill $1,000 in 1939, and the building was constructed in 1941 at a cost of $10,000. An independent appraiser estimates the land's current value at $3,000 and that of the building at $15,000. In return, Jack receives 50 shares of $100 par value capital stock, and Jill receives 180 shares.
  2. Office furniture and equipment are acquired on account for $3,000.
  3. Supplies are purchased for $2,000 cash.
  4. Well drilling equipment is purchased on an 8-month installment contract. The total cost is $8,000. A down payment of $2,000 is made immediately.
  5. A payment of $725 is made on the installment contract. The payment of $725 includes $125 interest.

Required:
  a. Prepare journal entries for the above transactions.
  b. Post the journal entries to ledger accounts.
  c. Prepare a statement of financial position for the J & J Drilling Enterprise on December 31.

4-24. *Journalizing merchandise transactions.* Record the following transactions of Becker Co. in journal form. The company has been operating for several years.

May 2	Sell merchandise to Tuck Co. on account for $8,000, terms 2/10, n/30.	
May 5	Buy merchandise from Bayle Co. for cash, $2,200.	
May 7	Return $300 of goods to Bayle because they were damaged. Bayle sends us a check.	
May 10	Collect amount due from Tuck Co.	
May 12	Buy merchandise on account from Lynn Co. for $5,000, terms 2/10, n/30.	
May 14	Pay freight of $300 on shipment from Lynn.	
May 17	Lynn bills us $200 more because of computational error made on the invoice.	
May 21	Pay Lynn the full amount owed.	
May 22	Collect $3,000 from Petrocelli Co. on a sale made in April.	
May 23	Purchase office supplies on account from Ford Office Supply, $600.	

(Solution in Appendix B.)

4-25. *Comprehensive problem.* The following transactions relate to Kerry Laundry for March of the current year.

Mar. 1	Sam Kerry invested $5,000 cash, a $4,000 truck, $3,000 land, and a $20,000 building in the laundry company in exchange for 320 shares of $100 par value stock.	
Mar. 2	Three employees were hired. Jim is to be paid $2.00 per hour; Jerry, $75 per week; and Jay, $400 per month.	
Mar. 3	Equipment costing $10,000 was acquired. Cash of $1,000 and a note for the balance was given.	

Mar. 4   Four months' rent was paid in advance, $1,600.
Mar. 15   Cash receipts for laundry services performed totaled $5,000.
Mar. 16   In addition to the cash received on March 15, customers were charged $8,000 for laundry services.
Mar. 20   Employees were paid $700.
Mar. 25   A dividend of $200 was declared and paid.
Mar. 31 $125 was owed to employees at the end of the month for salaries and wages.
Mar. 31   One-half of one percent of the building had depreciated.
Mar. 31   One months' rent paid for on March 4 was used up.

Required:

a. Journalize the above transactions for the laundry.
b. Post from your journal to "T" accounts.
c. Prepare a trial balance.
d. Prepare financial statements for the laundry.

4-26. *Analyzing statements to determine transactions.* Prepare journal entries for the month of January that might account for the changes occurring during the month, using the information for Cable Corporation below. Revenue from services is billed to customers on account. $600 of dividends were paid during January.

CABLE CORP.
Income Statement for January

Revenue from services		$6,000
Expenses:		
Rent	$ 600	
Taxes	300	
Supplies used	250	
Insurance expired	100	
Salaries	4,000	
Total expenses		5,250
Net income		$ 750

CABLE CORP.
Comparative Balance Sheets

	January 31	January 1
Assets:		
Cash	$2,100	$1,400
Accounts receivable	4,100	3,000
Unexpired insurance	300	400
Supplies on hand	550	800
Total assets	$7,050	$5,600
Liabilities and Stockholders' Equity:		
Liability—Taxes payable	$ 500	$ 200
Stockholders' Equity:		
Capital stock	5,000	4,000
Retained earnings	1,550	1,400
Total equities	$7,050	$5,600

(Solution in Appendix B.)

Part II   Processing Accounting Data

4-27. *Transactions from ledger.* A fire at the Blacomb Company burned the journal for April, the first month of operations, but fortunately the ledger was saved. Using the ledger below, reconstruct the journal entries that must have been made. Include an appropriate explanation for each entry.

Cash					1		Accounts Payable				10
4/1	30,000		4/2	1,400		4/6	1,000		4/2	11,000	
4/7	8,000		4/3	1,200		4/22	5,000				
4/25	4,000		4/15	800							
			4/20	6,000			Capital Stock				11
			4/22	5,000					4/1	30,000	
			4/30	800							

Accounts Receivable				2		Sales				20
4/17	7,000		4/25	4,000					4/7	8,000
									4/17	7,000

Supplies on Hand				3		Supplies Expense		23
4/3	1,200		4/30	700		4/30	700	

Purchases		21		Salaries Expense		24
4/2	11,000			4/15	800	
4/20	6,000			4/30	800	

Purchase Returns			22		Rent Expense		25
		4/6	1,000		4/2	1,400	

4-28. *Comprehensive problem, merchandising.* The Holzer Company has been operating for several years and has the following balances in its accounts on January 1 of the current year:

	Debit	Credit
Cash	12,000	
Accounts receivable	11,000	
Merchandise inventory	20,000	
Equipment	25,000	
Accumulated depreciation		3,600
Accounts payable		8,000
Notes payable		5,000
Capital stock		40,000
Retained earnings		11,400

The following transactions take place in January:

Jan. 2   Pay rent for January of $1,000.
Jan. 3   Sell merchandise to Rose Co. on account, $4,000, terms, 2/10, n/30.
Jan. 4   Pay $5,000 on account.

Jan. 5   Collect $7,000 on account from customers who owed money on January 1 (no discount is involved).
Jan. 7   Purchase merchandise on account from Perez Mercantile Co., $6,000, terms 2/10, n/30.
Jan. 8   Return 10% of the goods purchased on January 7 because they are defective.
Jan. 9   Pay freight of $300 on purchases of January 7.
Jan. 11 Collect amount owed by Rose Co. (see January 3).
Jan. 15 Pay salaries of $900.
Jan. 16 Purchase supplies on account from Beasley Supply Co. $600, terms, n/30.
Jan. 20 Pay Perez Mercantile Co. the amount owed.
Jan. 25 Cash sales amount to $22,000.
Jan. 26 Pay dividends of $1,000.
Jan. 27 Cash purchases of merchandise amount to $16,000.
Jan. 30 Pay the note payable plus interest of $30.
Jan. 31 Record depreciation for the month of $120.
Jan. 31 Of the supplies purchased on January 16, $400 has been used by January 31.

Required:
a. Record the above transactions in a general journal.
b. Set up 3-column accounts for each item in the list of accounts on January 1, placing in them the balances indicated. Post the transactions to the accounts, opening other accounts as needed.
c. Take a trial balance on January 31.
d. Prepare an income statement for January. The ending inventory on January 31 is $21,000.
e. Prepare a statement of retained earnings for January.
f. Prepare a balance sheet as of January 31. Use $21,000 for the inventory.

5

Adjusting Entries: Completion of the Accounting Cycle

Objectives

Some of the events that affect an enterprise occur gradually over a period of time. For example, supplies are consumed during the entire period, a portion of prepaid rent or prepaid insurance expires each day, interest income is earned (or interest expense incurred) throughout the entire period in which the money is loaned (or borrowed), salaries are earned by employees day by day, and a building depreciates over the time it is used. These events could be recorded each day as they occur, but this procedure is too expensive. Also, it is unnecessary. It is easier to enter the effect of these events periodically, sometimes in connection with the recording of an external event (for example, the periodic payment of salaries).

At the end of an accounting period, some events giving rise to accounting transactions will not yet have been recorded. Entries will be necessary to record those events. The necessary entries at the end of an accounting period are known as *adjusting entries*.

The objective of making adjustments at the end of an accounting period is to enhance the accuracy of the financial statements. On the income statement, adjustments are made in order to state revenues at the correct amount and to relate appropriate costs to the revenues. On the balance sheet, adjusting entries are made in order to include all appropriate assets and liabilities and to state them at correct amounts. The objectives of adjusting entries can be detailed as follows:

On the income statement:

1. Revenues
   a. Record all revenues that have been earned during the period.
   b. Exclude revenues that belong to other periods.
2. Expenses
   a. Record all cost expirations that have occurred during the period.
   b. Exclude from expenses any costs that relate to future periods.

On the balance sheet:

1. Assets
   a. Record any assets that exist at the balance sheet date but have not been recorded.
   b. Exclude from assets any costs that have already expired at the balance sheet date. Record other appropriate decreases in asset values.
2. Liabilities
   a. Record any liabilities that exist at the balance sheet date but have not been recorded.
   b. Exclude from liabilities any amounts that are not owed, or that do not represent an obligation, at the balance sheet date.

If these objectives are fulfilled, the books will be brought up to date, and the financial statements will be more accurate.

Most adjustments involve either the accruing of an item not yet recorded or the apportionment between accounting periods of an item already recorded on the books. For convenience, adjustments will be classified and discussed under the following headings:

1. Accrued Expenses
2. Accrued Revenues
3. Unearned Revenues, or Collections in Advance
4. Prepaid Expenses
5. Depreciation, Amortization, and Depletion
6. Bad Debts
7. Merchandise Inventory

Remembering the objectives of the adjustment process will help you to understand the accounting cycle and how adjustments relate to the end product of the accounting process, the financial statements.

ACCRUED EXPENSES

To accrue means to grow, to increase, to accumulate. An adjustment for accrued expenses is necessary whenever an expense has grown or accumulated during the period but has not been recorded at the end of the period. Salaries, utilities, interest, and taxes (both income and property) are expenses for which this type of adjustment may be necessary. The accrual of the expense also involves the gradual growth of a liability of equal amount. Accrued expenses are illustrated in Examples 5-1 and 5-2.

EXAMPLE 5-1

During Year 1, payments actually made to employees for salaries amounted to $255,000, and salary expense was debited and cash was credited for this amount. On December 31, Year 1, salaries amounting to $5,000 have been earned by the employees, but this amount will not be paid until the next pay date, which is January 4, Year 2. This $5,000 represents an expense of Year 1 and an obligation, or liability, owed to the employees on December 31, Year 1. To adjust the salary expense account so that its balance will show a salary expense of $260,000 for Year 1, and to recognize the $5,000 liability for salaries owed to employees on December 31, Year 1, the following adjustment will be made:

		Debit	Credit
Dec. 31	Salaries expense	5,000	
	Salaries payable		5,000
	Accrued salaries.		

After the adjustment has been posted, the salaries expense account and the salaries payable account will appear as follows:

Salaries Expense		
During Year 1	255,000	
Dec. 31 Adj.	5,000	

Salaries Payable		
	Dec. 31 Adj.	5,000

EXAMPLE 5-2

A firm issues a $5,000, 6%, 3-month note on November 1, Year 1. Since interest = principal × rate × time, the interest when the note is due will amount to

$$\$5{,}000 \times 6\% \times \frac{3}{12} = \$75$$

On December 31, Year 1, the interest that has accrued up to that date is

$$\$5{,}000 \times 6\% \times \frac{2}{12} = \$50$$

Hence, the adjusting entry on December 31, Year 1, is as follows:

	Debit	Credit
Dec. 31 Interest expense	50	
Interest payable		50

$$\$5{,}000 \times 6\% \times \frac{2}{12}$$

Note that interest rates are quoted in annual terms regardless of the term of the note.

Adjusting entries provide accurate figures for salaries expense and interest expense on the income statement, and they indicate the liabilities for salaries and interest owed on the balance sheet. Without the adjusting entries, both statements would be inaccurate.

For both Example 5-1 and Example 5-2, there will be a payment of the accrued liability in the next accounting period (Year 2). The salaries will be paid on the next pay date, and the interest will be paid when the note matures on February 1, Year 2. Let us examine the entries that will be made in each case.

On January 4, Year 2, the salaries are paid. The payment is for all salaries earned but unpaid up to January 4. Let us assume that this amounts to $6,000. The first $5,000 of this was recorded in Year 1; the other $1,000 covers the first two days of Year 2. The entry is as follows:

Year 2		Debit	Credit
Jan. 4	Salaries payable	5,000	
	Salaries expense	1,000	
	Cash		6,000
	Payment of salaries, including accrual of Dec. 31.		

Notice that the liability created in the earlier adjusting entry has now been paid. Also, the expense in Year 2 is only $1,000, even though $6,000 is paid. This is because $5,000 of the payment was for wages earned in Year 1.

Let us now turn to the interest on the note. On February 1, Year 2, the note and the total interest are paid. The entry is as follows:

Year 2		Debit	Credit
Feb. 1	Notes payable	5,000	
	Interest expense	25	
	Interest payable	50	
	Cash		5,075
	Payment of note and interest.		

The total payment of $5,075 is split into three parts—the payment of the face amount of the note ($5,000), the payment of the interest owed on December 31, Year 1 ($50), and the interest expense of $25. This $25 amount represents interest incurred in Year 2 from January 1 to the due date of the note, February 1. Again, notice that the liability created in the adjusting entry has been eliminated.

ACCRUED REVENUES

When revenue grows or accumulates during the period but has not been recorded, an adjustment is made to recognize the revenue and the related asset. The revenue is recognized because it has been earned during the period. The related asset is the form that the revenue takes.

For example, assume that a finance company lends a customer $2,400 at 5% interest for 3 months on December 1, Year 1. The following adjustment is made to show the asset (interest receivable) and the revenue (interest earned) on December 31:

		Debit	Credit
Dec. 31	Interest receivable	10	
	Interest earned		10
	($2,400 × 5% × 1/12)		

Failure to record the adjustment would understate the assets on the December 31 balance sheet and would understate the revenues on the income statement for Year 1.

When the loan is paid by the customer on March 1, Year 2, the following entry is made:

Year 2		Debit	Credit
March 1	Cash	2,430	
	Loans receivable		2,400
	Interest receivable		10
	Interest earned		20
	Cash received on note and interest.		

This entry eliminates the interest receivable that was recorded on December 31. The interest earned of $20 is the amount that belongs in Year 2 and represents interest revenue for the months of January and February, Year 2.

UNEARNED REVENUES, OR COLLECTIONS IN ADVANCE

In some instances, cash is collected prior to the rendering of the service or the earning of the revenue. Such collections can be credited to a liability account at the time the collection is made.

There is a liability because the firm owes the customers the goods or services for which they have paid, and the firm will continue to have an obligation until the goods are delivered or the services are rendered. The liability can be referred to as "unearned revenue," "deferred revenue," or "collections in advance." At the end of the accounting period, an adjustment is necessary to transfer to the revenue account the portion of the revenue collected that has been earned in the current accounting period.

Recorded originally as a liability

For example, assume that a company leases a portion of its warehouse to a customer for eight months beginning on October 1, Year 1, at a monthly rental of $200. The customer pays the entire $1,600 on October 1. The $1,600 represents revenue for eight months, to be apportioned $600 to Year 1, and $1,000 to Year 2. If, on October 1, a liability account is credited, the entry will be as follows:

		Debit	Credit
Oct. 1	Cash	1,600	
	Unearned rental income		1,600
	8 months rent received in advance.		

Then, on December 31, the following adjusting entry will be made:

Dec. 31	Unearned rental income	600	
	Rental income		600
	To record 3 months rent earned.		

After the adjusting entry has been posted, the two accounts will appear as follows:

Unearned Rental Income

| Dec. 31 Adj. | 600 | Oct. 1 | 1,600 |
| | | Bal. 1,000 | |

Rental Income

| | | Dec. 31 Adj. | 600 |

Recorded originally as a revenue

Instead of being recorded to a liability account, collections in advance can be credited to a revenue account when the collection is made. For example, when the company receives the $1,600 rent for the warehouse on October 1, it can credit rental income for the total as follows:

		Debit	Credit
Oct. 1	Cash	1,600	
	Rental income		1,600
	8 months' rent received.		

An adjusting entry on December 31 will still be required, but the adjustment will be to transfer from the rental income account to a liability ac-

129

count the portion that has not yet been earned ($1,000). The adjusting entry will be as follows:

Dec. 31   Rental income   1,000
                Unearned rental income   1,000
            To record 5 months of unearned rent.

After the adjusting entry has been posted, the two accounts will appear as follows:

Rental Income

Dec. 31 Adj.	1,000	Oct. 1	1,600
		Bal. 600	

Unearned Rental Income

		Dec. 31 Adj.	1,000

Note that in the two cases, given the same situation, the October 1 entries differ and the adjusting entries differ, but the result is the same (the rental income account shows a balance of $600 and the unearned rental income account shows a balance of $1,000).

To summarize, when receipts recorded as unearned revenue have been partially earned at the end of the accounting period, the portion earned should be transferred from the liability account to a revenue account so that only the unearned portion remains as a liability. If receipts that were recorded as revenue are unearned at the end of the accounting period, the unearned portion should be transferred from the revenue account to a liability account. Thus, when making adjustments for items that have been recorded previously, the first step is to determine what entry was originally made. Only then can one make the appropriate adjustment in light of the previous entry.

PREPAID EXPENSES

Many costs incurred by a business benefit more than one period. Costs of this nature are called *unexpired costs*. Included in this broad category are costs such as an item of plant and equipment, costs of merchandise, and prepayments, such as prepaid insurance or supplies. Although the adjusting entries for these different types of unexpired costs are basically the same, there are some differences. Hence, we will deal separately with each type of adjusting entry. In this section, we will discuss the third type, the prepayments, or prepaid expenses. (Apportionment of the cost of plant and equipment and apportionment of the costs of merchandise are discussed in later sections of this chapter.)

Costs incurred for prepayments, such as prepaid rent, prepaid insurance, or supplies, can be debited to an asset account when incurred. At the end of the accounting period, an adjustment is necessary to remove from each asset account the portion that has expired or been consumed. That portion is transferred to an expense account.

Recorded originally as an asset

Assume that a company purchased a total of $4,500 of supplies during the year, debiting them to the asset account supplies on hand. A physical count of the supplies at the end of the period reveals a balance on hand of $500. Therefore, $4,000 of supplies have been used (assuming none were lost or stolen). An adjusting entry is necessary at the end of the period to transfer $4,000 from the supplies on hand (asset) account to the supplies expense account.

		Debit	Credit
Dec. 31	Supplies expense	4,000	
	Supplies on hand		4,000
	To record supplies used.		

After the adjusting entry has been posted, the two accounts will appear as follows:

Supplies on Hand

During period	4,500	Dec. 31 Adj.	4,000
Bal. 500			

Supplies Expense

Dec. 31 Adj.	4,000		

Instead of debiting asset accounts, it is possible to record prepayments as debits to expense accounts when the payment is made. If the supplies were debited to the supplies expense account as they were purchased, then an adjustment would be necessary at the end of the period to transfer the $500 remaining on hand out of the expense account into an asset account.

Recorded originally as an expense

		Debit	Credit
Dec. 31	Supplies on hand	500	
	Supplies expense		500
	To record supplies on hand per physical count.		

In this case, after the adjusting entry had been posted, the two accounts would appear as follows:

	Supplies Expense		
During period	4,500	Dec. 31 Adj.	500
Bal. 4,000			

	Supplies on Hand	
Dec. 31 Adj.	500	

Note that in the two cases, given the same situation, the entries for acquisition of the supplies differ and the adjusting entries differ, but the results are the same. This emphasizes the necessity of analyzing the data to determine what entry was originally made.

In summary, when costs recorded as assets have been partially consumed at the end of the accounting period, the portion consumed should be transferred to an expense account so that only the unexpired portion of the costs remains in the asset account. When costs originally recorded as expenses are still partially prepaid, unexpired, or unconsumed at the end of an accounting period, the unexpired costs remaining should be transferred from the expense account to an asset account.

DEPRECIATION, AMORTIZATION, AND DEPLETION

Long-lived assets such as plant and equipment yield their services over a number of years. The costs of these assets expire as the enterprise uses their services or as time passes. The cost expiration is called *depreciation, depletion,* or *amortization,* depending on the nature of the asset. Assets that yield services through repetitive, physical use, such as machinery, are said to *depreciate*. Assets that yield service by literally being consumed, such as natural resources, are subject to *depletion*. And assets that yield services because of the exclusive rights or values they confer, such as intangible assets, are subject to *amortization*.

The process of recording the expiration of a long-lived asset is essentially the same as recording the expiration of any other cost; an asset is reduced and an expense is increased. Thus, the adjustment for recording the expiration of a long-lived asset debits an expense account—depreciation expense, amortization expense, or depletion expense, depending on the nature of the asset.

For a depreciable asset, the corresponding credit usually is made to a separate account called accumulated depreciation. This procedure is used because the amount of acquisition cost can be determined with reasonable certainty, whereas the portion expired involves an estimate. Also, using separate accounts gives a better indication of the amounts of physical assets in use. And the relationship between accumulated depreciation and the cost of the assets tells the user of the financial statements whether the assets as a whole are relatively new or old.

For an *amortizable asset* (an intangible asset) or a *depletable asset* (natural resources), the corresponding credit often is made directly to the asset account. At other times, an account for accumulated amortization or accumulated depletion is used.

Recording Depreciation

The periodic adjusting entry for depreciation involves a debit to a depreciation expense account and a credit to an accumulated depreciation account. To illustrate, assume that a company purchases equipment at a cost of $15,000 on which annual depreciation expense is $1,450. The expense is recorded as follows:

		Debit	Credit
Dec. 31	Depreciation expense—equipment	1,450	
	Accumulated depreciation—equipment		1,450
	Annual depreciation		

The depreciation expense account appears in the income statement, whereas the accumulated depreciation account appears in the balance sheet as a subtraction from the cost of the asset. The balance sheet at the end of each of the first two years of the equipment's life would show the following:

	End of Year 1	End of Year 2
Plant and equipment:		
Equipment	15,000	15,000
Less accumulated depreciation	1,450	2,900
Undepreciated cost	13,550	12,100

The $13,550 at the end of the first year and the $12,100 at the end of the second year are the net undepreciated cost of the asset. The net undepreciated cost, called the *book value* of the asset, is the portion of the asset's cost that is unexpired. The book value does not indicate the current market value of the asset.

Book value

Computing Depreciation

The amount of periodic depreciation depends on the cost of the fixed assets, their salvage value (if any), and their estimated useful life. To some extent, these three factors represent a matter of judgment.

Cost is the actual expenditure involved in acquiring a fixed asset and placing it in operating condition. Cost includes the purchase cost of the fixed asset, transportation costs, installation costs, and costs incurred in testing the asset and preparing it for use in the business. *Salvage value* is the estimated disposal value at the end of the useful life of the asset minus the estimated costs of its removal. *Useful life of an asset* is the period of time during which the asset will be of use to the particular business enterprise. The useful life of an asset can be estimated in terms of time or in terms of units of use. For example, the useful life of an automobile can be estimated in terms of years or in terms of miles.

When the acquisition cost of a fixed asset has been determined and the salvage value and the useful life have been estimated, the next problem is to determine how the cost of using the asset should be allocated to the accounting periods in its useful life. Cost can be allocated in a number of different ways (discussed in chapter 10), but at this point we will use the straight-line method of computing depreciation. Under this method, each accounting period receives the same dollar charge for asset services consumed. Assuming that we have an asset with an original cost of $10,000, an estimated salvage value of $2,000, and an estimated life of 5 years, the annual depreciation charge would be computed as follows:

$$\text{Depreciation per Year} = \frac{\text{Cost-Salvage}}{\text{Life}} = \frac{\$10{,}000 - \$2{,}000}{5}$$
$$= \$1{,}600 \text{ per Year.}$$

This $1,600 amount would be charged to depreciation expense and credited to the accumulated depreciation account in each year of the asset's life. A fuller discussion of depreciation can be found in chapter 10.

BAD DEBTS

When a company sells goods or services on account, an *account receivable* is created. Most businesses have found that these accounts receivable are not always fully collectible. The expense resulting from uncollectible accounts is called *bad debts expense* or *uncollectible accounts expense*. This expense should be recognized in the same accounting period as the original sale that produced the account. It is incorrect to burden a later period with the expense, even though the loss may be determined in this later period.

In order to recognize the bad debts expense in the current period and to evaluate the accounts receivable in terms of expected collectibility, an adjusting entry should be made at the end of each fiscal period. If, for example, it is estimated that $5,000 of the total sales of $500,000 during the year will be uncollectible, the following adjustment should be made:

		Debit	Credit
Dec. 31	Bad debts expense	5,000	
	Allowance for doubtful accounts		5,000
	To record estimated uncollectibles.		

The bad debts expense account, with its balance of $5,000, is included as one of the expenses on the income statement. The allowance for doubtful accounts represents a reduction in the amount of the asset accounts receivable. The credit is made to the allowance for doubtful accounts[1] rather than directly to the accounts receivable account because at the time the adjustment is made, it is not known which particular customers' accounts are uncollectible.

Using the data from the example above, the accounts receivable account and the allowance for doubtful accounts would appear on the balance sheet as follows:

Accounts receivable	$100,000	
Less allowance for doubtful accounts	5,000	$95,000

Note that the objectives of the adjustment for bad debts are twofold:

1. To show the accounts receivable (asset) on the balance sheet at the expected realizable value.
2. To achieve a matching of the bad debts expense against the sales revenue on the income statement.

A failure to make an adjustment for bad debts expense results in an overstatement of the accounts receivable on the balance sheet *and* an incorrect matching of expenses and revenues on the income statement.

The estimated amount of bad debts expense can be determined by using one of several different methods. These methods are discussed in chapter 7.

MERCHANDISE INVENTORY

The *merchandise inventory* of a firm is composed of the goods that are offered for sale to customers in the normal course of business. *Inventory cost* includes all costs of acquiring the merchandise, getting it to the firm's place

---

1. Accounts such as the allowance for doubtful accounts and accumulated depreciation, which are deducted from assets, are sometimes referred to as contra-asset accounts.

of business, and getting it ready for sale to customers. Inventory cost therefore includes such costs as the purchase price of the merchandise, freight charges, and costs of unloading and handling the merchandise.

The costs associated with units of merchandise that have been sold become the cost of goods sold expense on the income statement. The costs associated with unsold units of merchandise are recorded as ending inventory on the balance sheet. Essentially, there are two methods by which inventory costs can be accumulated and assigned to sold and unsold units of merchandise: the perpetual inventory method and the periodic inventory method.

Perpetual Inventory Method

Under the *perpetual inventory method,* all costs of merchandise purchased are recorded directly in an inventory account. The costs of the units sold are transferred from the inventory account to the cost of goods sold expense account at the time of sale. The balance of the inventory account therefore reflects the cost of merchandise remaining unsold. Physical counts of the merchandise on hand are made from time to time to verify the accuracy of the inventory records and to determine whether any merchandise has been lost or stolen. The perpetual inventory method is illustrated in chapter 9.

Periodic Inventory Method

Many companies use a periodic inventory system, in which all purchases, purchase returns and allowances, and purchase discounts are recorded in separate accounts and all freight costs are recorded in a freight-in or transportation-in account. The costs of all goods acquired during the period are accumulated in these accounts. At the end of the accounting period, the total of the net purchases (purchases less returns and allowances and purchase discounts) plus transportation-in is added to any inventory on hand at the beginning of the period to determine the total cost of merchandise available for sale. The ending inventory is determined by physically counting and costing all unsold units. This inventory figure is subtracted from the cost of merchandise available for sale to determine the cost of the merchandise actually sold.

The net income cannot be determined until the total cost of goods available for sale is apportioned to the cost of merchandise sold during the period and to the ending inventory. A physical count of merchandise on hand at the end of the accounting period is necessary to determine how much cost should be apportioned to inventory. The balance is then assigned to merchandise sold. The quantity of each item on hand is determined by the physical count. The unit cost of these items must then be determined from the purchase invoices. The number of units multiplied by the unit prices yields the figure for ending inventory. This amount is subtracted from the cost of goods available to determine the cost of goods sold.

At this point, let us review the major points in applying a periodic inventory method:

1. The beginning inventory, plus purchases and transportation-in, less purchase returns and allowances and purchase discounts, equals the total cost of goods available for sale.
2. The merchandise on hand at the end of the period must be physically counted and valued to determine the cost of the ending inventory.
3. The ending inventory is subtracted from the cost of goods available for sale to arrive at the cost of goods sold during the period.

After it has been counted, the ending inventory is entered on the records in the following two steps:

1. Clear the inventory account of the beginning inventory by crediting inventory and debiting the income summary account.
2. Record the ending inventory as a debit, with the offsetting credit going to the income summary account.

To illustrate, let us consider the trial balance of the Elwell Company (see Example 5-3). A physical count shows that the merchandise on hand at the end of the year amounts to $20,000.

EXAMPLE 5-3

ELWELL COMPANY
Trial Balance
December 31 Year 1

	Debit	Credit
Cash	$ 6,500	
Accounts receivable	15,000	
Inventory (beginning of year)	18,000	
Furniture and fixtures	8,000	
Accumulated depreciation—furniture and fixtures		$ 3,000
Accounts payable		7,000
Capital stock		20,000
Retained earnings		6,000
Sales		84,000
Sales returns and allowances	2,000	
Purchases	41,000	
Purchase discounts		800
Transportation-in	3,400	
Salaries expense	16,000	
Depreciation expense	400	
Other expense	10,500	
	$120,800	$120,800

Using the procedure suggested, the ending inventory could be recorded as follows:

			Debit	Credit
	(1)			
Dec. 31	Income summary		18,000	
	Inventory			18,000
	Close beginning inventory.			
	(2)			
Dec. 31	Inventory		20,000	
	Income summary			20,000
	Record ending inventory.			

The two entries above (1) remove the beginning inventory from the inventory account and charge it to expense and (2) set up the ending inventory as an asset. The income summary account used in the two entries for inventory is a temporary owners' equity account used at the end of an accounting period for this purpose and for the closing process, which is discussed later in this chapter. The debit to this account in the first entry indicates an increase in expenses, in this case the cost of goods sold expense, and the credit in the second entry indicates that total expenses (cost of goods sold expense) are reduced by those goods purchased during the period that are still on hand. Many methods are used in practice to record inventories under a periodic inventory system. The method illustrated is simple and effective. It accomplishes the recording of the ending inventory and the correct adjustments of the expenses for the period.[2]

STATEMENT PREPARATION

After all adjusting entries have been entered in the journal and posted to the ledgers, the financial statements can be prepared.[3] An income statement is prepared first, using the revenue and expense accounts in the ledger. Example 5-4 is an income statement for the Elwell Company. Note the inventory amounts in the cost of goods sold section.

The net income increases the retained earnings balance as indicated in the statement of retained earnings (see Example 5-5).

A balance sheet for Elwell can then be prepared (see Example 5-6).

---

2. A cost of goods sold account is sometimes used instead of the income summary account. In this case purchases and related accounts must also be transferred to the cost of goods sold account at the end of the period.

3. Another trial balance, called an *adjusted trial balance*, can be taken prior to statement preparation as another check on clerical accuracy.

EXAMPLE 5-4

ELWELL COMPANY
Income Statement
for Year 1

Sales			$84,000
Less sales returns and allowances			2,000
Net sales			82,000
Cost of goods sold:			
Beginning inventory		18,000	
Purchases	41,000		
Less purchase discounts	800	40,200	
Transportation-in		3,400	
Cost of merchandise available for sale		61,600	
Less ending inventory		20,000	
Cost of goods sold			41,600
Gross margin			40,400
Operating expenses:			
Salaries expense		16,000	
Depreciation expense		400	
Other expenses		10,500	26,900
Net income			$13,500

EXAMPLE 5-5

ELWELL COMPANY
Statement of Retained Earnings
for Year 1

Balance, January 1	$ 6,000
Add income for the year	13,500
Balance, December 31	$19,500

EXAMPLE 5-6

ELWELL COMPANY
Balance Sheet
as of December 31, Year 1

Assets			Liabilities and Stockholders' Equity		
Current assets:			Current liabilities:		
Cash		$ 6,500	Accounts payable		$ 7,000
Accounts receivable		15,000	Stockholders' equity:		
Inventory		20,000	Capital stock	$20,000	
Total current assets		$41,500	Retained earnings	19,500	39,500
Plant and equipment:			Total equities		$46,500
Furniture and fixtures	$8,000				
Less accumulated depreciation	3,000	5,000			
Total assets		$46,500			

Part II   Processing Accounting Data

After the statements have been prepared and submitted to management, the bookkeeping process can be completed.

THE CLOSING PROCESS

Nominal and real accounts

As stated in chapter 4, revenue and expense accounts are nominal, or temporary, owners' equity accounts. Balance sheet accounts, on the other hand, are often referred to as *real* accounts. The function of revenue and expense accounts is to record information about operating activities during a particular period of time, usually one year.

At the end of that period, the revenue and expense accounts are closed. The closing is a mechanical process that reduces the balances of revenue and expense accounts to zero so that the accounts can be used to record data for the next period. Closing also transfers the net income (the net difference between revenues and expenses) for the period to retained earnings. This process is called *closing the books.* The entries made during this process are called *closing entries.*

Income summary account

Closing entries transfer the balances of all revenue accounts and all expense accounts to retained earnings. Usually this transfer is accomplished through use of a summary account called *income summary.* Entries are made to transfer the balances of all income statement accounts to the income summary account and the balance of the income summary account (which is equal to the income or loss for the period) to the retained earnings account. Any income distribution accounts that have been used during the period are also closed at the end of the period. An example of an income distribution account is dividends paid to stockholders, which would be closed to retained earnings as part of the closing process. This account is not illustrated in this example or used in this text.

The income summary account is called a *clearing account;* it is used only at the end of each accounting period. After the closing entries are complete, the income summary account will not be used again until the end of the next accounting period.

The books are closed only at the end of the fiscal year. Financial statements may be prepared more often, but the mechanical process of closing the revenue and expense accounts is usually done only once a year.

Closing process illustrated

We will illustrate the closing process, using accounts based on the data given in chapter 4 for the Mason Surveyor Service. The revenue from surveys account has a credit balance of $2,500. The object of the closing process is to get rid of this balance. A debit of $2,500 will reduce the balance to zero. The offsetting credit goes to the income summary account. The following journal entry is made:

Adjusting Entries: Completion of the Accounting Cycle Chapter 5

			Debit	Credit
Aug. 31	(a) Revenue from surveys		2,500	
	Income summary			2,500
	To close the revenue account.			

The effect of this entry is to reduce the balance of the revenue account to zero and to transfer its balance to income summary. This entry is labeled (a) to facilitate identifying the transaction in the ledger accounts (Example 5-7 through 5-9).

EXAMPLE 5-7

Revenue from Surveys

		Debit	Credit	Balance
Aug. 20			1,200	1,200
21			1,300	2,500
31	(a)	2,500		0

Income Summary

		Debit	Credit	Balance
Aug. 31	(a)		2,500	2,500

All of the expense accounts have debit balances, which are closed by a credit entry. The offsetting debit is to income summary. This entry is labeled (b) to identify it in the ledger accounts in Examples 5-8 and 5-9.

			Debit	Credit
Aug. 31	(b) Income summary		1,825	
	Salaries expense			1,400
	Rent expense			300
	Supplies expense			125
	To close the expense accounts.			

EXAMPLE 5-8

Salaries Expense

		Debit	Credit	Balance
Aug 31		1,400		1,400
31	(b)		1,400	0

Rent Expense

		Debit	Credit	Balance
Aug 31		300		300
31	(b)		300	0

(Continued)

Example 5-8 (Cont.)

Supplies Expense

Aug 31			125			125
31	(b)				125	0

Income Summary

Aug 31	(a)				2,500	2,500
31	(b)			1,825		675

Now, all the revenue and expense accounts have zero balances, and the income summary account has a balance equal to the net income for the period ($2,500 − $1,825 = $675). The final step in the closing process is to transfer the balance of the income summary account to the retained earnings. Thus, a debit to income summary for $675 and a credit to retained earnings for $675 completes the closing process. This entry is labeled (c) to identify the transaction in the ledger accounts in Example 5-9.

			Debit	Credit
Aug 31	(c) Income summary		$675	
	Retained earnings			$675
	To close net income to retained earnings.			

EXAMPLE 5-9

Income Summary

			Debit	Credit	Balance
Aug 31	(a)			2,500	2,500
31	(b)		1,825		675
31	(c)		675		0

Retained Earnings

Aug 31	(c)			675	675

The closing process may be summarized in the following steps:

Steps in the closing process

1. Close all revenue accounts by debiting them for the amount of their balance, and credit the income summary account.
2. Close all expense accounts by crediting them for the amount of their balance, and debit the income summary account for the total.
3. Close the income summary account by debiting it (if there is a net income) or by crediting it (if there is a net loss) with the offsetting credit or debit to retained earnings.
4. Close income distribution accounts (e.g., dividends) by crediting them and debiting retained earnings (not illustrated in this example).

The closing process for a merchandising concern is basically the same as for a service enterprise and follows the four steps listed above. The closing entries for the Elwell Company (see trial balance in Example 5-3) would be as follows:

		Debit	Credit
Dec 31	Sales	84,000	
	Purchase discounts	800	
	Income summary		84,800
	Close income accounts with credit balances.		

		Debit	Credit
Dec 31	Income summary	73,300	
	Sales returns and allowances		2,000
	Purchases		41,000
	Transportation-in		3,400
	Salaries expense		16,000
	Depreciation expense		400
	Other expense		10,500
	Close income accounts with debit balances.		

The income summary account for the Elwell Company will already have two amounts in it, arising from the inventory entries we mentioned in the section entitled "Periodic Inventory Method." Example 5-10 shows the income summary account after the above entries have been posted.

EXAMPLE 5-10

Income Summary

Date		Debit	Credit	Balance
Dec 31	Beginning inventory	18,000		18,000 DR
31	Ending inventory		20,000	2,000 CR
31	Credit balances		84,800	86,800 CR
31	Debit balances	73,300		13,500 CR

A final entry would then be made to close the income summary account, as follows:

		Debit	Credit
Dec 31	Income summary	13,500	
	Retained earnings		13,500
	Close income summary.		

The $13,500 is the net income for the year, as indicated on the income statement prepared previously.

Part II   Processing Accounting Data

ALTERNATIVE PROCEDURE

Entries to close the beginning inventory and record the ending inventory are frequently combined with the normal closing entries at the end of the period. To illustrate this alternative procedure, let us again use the data in the illustration relating to the Elwell Company.

The revenue and expense accounts are closed in the usual manner to the income summary account. At the same time, the inventory account is credited for $18,000 to close the beginning inventory and debited for $20,000 to record the ending inventory.

		Debit	Credit
Dec. 31	Income summary	91,300	
	Inventory		18,000
	Sales returns and allowances		2,000
	Purchases		41,000
	Transportation-in		3,400
	Salaries expense		16,000
	Depreciation expense		400
	Other expenses		10,500
	Close expenses and beginning inventory.		
Dec. 31	Sales	84,000	
	Purchase discounts	800	
	Inventory	20,000	
	Income summary		104,800
	Close revenues and set up ending inventory.		

After these closing entries are posted, the income summary appears as in Example 5-11. Normally, compound entries are used to close the accounts; but to make it easy to follow this illustration, we have shown the amount of each account individually. Cost of goods sold is enclosed within the shaded area.

EXAMPLE 5-11

Income Summary

Sales returns	2,000	Sales	84,000	
Beginning inventory	18,000	Ending inventory	20,000	Cost of
Purchases	41,000			goods sold
Transportation-in	3,400	Purchase discounts	800	($41,600)
Depreciation	400			
Salaries expense	16,000			
Other expense	10,500			

The final entry closes the income summary account:

Dec. 31 Income summary	13,500	
Retained earnings		13,500
Close income summary		

POST-CLOSING TRIAL BALANCE

After closing entries have been posted to the accounts, all revenue and expense accounts will have zero balances. The only accounts with balances will be balance sheet accounts. As a final check on the accuracy of the bookkeeping process, it is often desirable to take a *post-closing trial balance* at this point. Example 5-12 is a post-closing trial balance for the Mason Surveyor Service.

EXAMPLE 5-12

THE MASON SURVEYOR SERVICE
Post-Closing Trial Balance

	Debit	Credit
Cash	$1,650	
Accounts receivable	300	
Prepaid rent	600	
Supplies on hand	325	
Accounts payable		$ 200
Common stock		2,000
Retained earnings		675
	$2,875	$2,875

Note that no revenue or expense accounts are listed and that a balance appears in the retained earnings account as a result of the posting process.

To complete the accounting process, accounts are totaled and ruled where necessary. If the three-column form of account is used, balances at the end of a period will automatically appear in accounts at the end of the period. In the two-column type of ledger account, however, balances must be computed by totaling each side and subtracting the smaller total from the larger. When an account has a zero balance, the two sides of the account are added and the totals are written on the same line. A double line is then drawn beneath the totals to indicate that the account is "closed." Most businesses use a three-column form of account.

THE ACCOUNTING CYCLE

Adjusting and closing entries are part of the accounting cycle, the process through which financial statements are prepared. The steps in the process (discussed in chapter 4 and here) are as follows:

1. Identify and analyze transactions.
2. Record transactions in the journal.
3. Post from the journal to the ledger accounts.
4. Take a trial balance at the end of the period.
5. Record adjusting entries in the journal.
6. Post adjusting entries to ledger accounts.
7. Take an adjusted trial balance (optional).
8. Prepare financial statements.
9. Record closing entries in the journal.
10. Post closing entries to ledger accounts and balance and rule accounts where necessary.

SUMMARY

Determining what adjustments are necessary to the accounts listed in the trial balance requires analytical ability on the part of an accountant who is familiar with the operations of the accounting system, the accounts used, and the interrelationships among the accounts. The need for adjusting entries arises from the periodic preparation of financial statements and the concept of matching costs incurred against benefits received. No underlying document automatically signals that an adjusting entry must be made. The accountant has to determine the appropriate entries from a study of the trial balance, a review of the accounting system, and an analysis of information from sources outside the records themselves. The accountant must look in the trial balance, for example, for prepayments, collections in advance, and depreciable assets. These accounts normally require adjustments. The accountant may examine notes receivable and notes payable to determine interest adjustments, examine insurance policies to determine what portion of prepaid insurance has expired and what portion is still prepaid, and review the physical count of the merchandise and supplies on hand to determine adjusting entries for cost of goods sold or supplies expense.

Recording of ending inventory and determination of cost of goods sold is an important function. If a periodic inventory system is used, the inventory must be counted and priced and then recorded by an adjusting entry or as part of the closing process. The beginning inventory must be removed from the assets and recorded as part of the expenses. In a perpetual inventory system, the inventory account is kept up to date and no adjustments are needed at the end of the period.

Adjusting entries will be encountered again in the remaining parts of this book. The reason is that adjusting entries are an integral part of the accountant's search for accuracy in statements of income and financial position. Thus it is important that the concepts and objectives behind adjusting entries be thoroughly understood and that some facility be developed in preparing adjustments.

The closing process is a mechanical process by which the accounting records are readied for transactions of the following period. All revenue and expense accounts are brought to a zero balance, and the net balances of these accounts are transferred to the income summary account and then to stockholders' equity (retained earnings).

IMPORTANT TERMS

Adjusting entries   *Closing process*
Accrued expense   *Nominal accounts*
Accrued revenue   *Real accounts*
Unearned revenue   *Income summary account*
Prepaid expense   *Worksheet*
Depreciation   *Accounting cycle*
Bad debts expense

APPENDIX 5-1: THE WORKSHEET

Adjusting entries must be completed before the financial statements can be prepared. If adjustments were omitted, some balances on the statements would be out of date and incorrect. Before adjustments are entered in the journal and posted to the ledger, a worksheet is often prepared.

The worksheet allows the accountant to prepare the financial statements before he or she goes through the bookkeeping process of recording and posting the adjusting and closing entries. Thus, statements are prepared at the earliest possible time in the accounting cycle. As a result, they are more likely to be timely and useful. A *worksheet* is simply a sheet of paper on which the accounting data are organized and arranged to facilitate the adjustment process and the preparation of the financial statements. It can be thought of as a rough draft of the final steps in the accounting cycle. The worksheet is useful to the accountant in completing the accounting process but does not replace any of the records (journals or ledgers) or financial statements.

On the worksheet, the ledger account balances are listed and adjustments for the period are recorded. The adjusted balances are then classified according to the financial statements on which they appear. Completion of the worksheet provides some assurance that all the details of the year-end accounting procedures have been brought together. The worksheet then serves as the source of data for the preparation of the formal financial statements and for the adjusting and closing entries that are entered in the journal and posted to the ledger.

The form and arrangement of the worksheet depend to some extent on the nature of the business and on the preferences of the individual accountant. One commonly used form is illustrated in Example 5-13 (see pages 150–151). The steps in its preparation are as follows:

1. *Set up the heading for the worksheet and the column headings.* The heading consists of the name of the company, the title of the schedule, and the period of time covered. In the body of the worksheet, a column is provided for account titles, and pairs of columns are provided for unadjusted trial balance, adjustments, income statement, statement of retained earnings, and balance sheet. Each pair of columns consists of a debit column and a credit column.
2. *List the account titles, and insert the account balances from the ledger in the first two amount columns of the worksheet.* Total these two columns to check on their accuracy. The unadjusted trial balance for Camera Corporation is entered in the first two columns in the illustration.
3. *Enter the year-end adjustments in the adjustments columns opposite the appropriate account titles.* If an account to be debited or credited in an adjustment does not appear in the trial balance, the title of the account is listed immediately below the trial balance totals. The debits and credits of each adjustment should be identified (coded) with a letter or number to facilitate reference to them. Total the two adjustments columns to be sure the debits equal the credits.

Data for adjustments for Camera Corporation are as follows:

a. Depreciation on the delivery equipment is 25% of cost.

	Debit	Credit
Depreciation expense—delivery equipment	5,000	
Accumulated depreciation—delivery equipment		5,000

b. Bad debts expense is estimated at 1% of net sales.

	Debit	Credit
Bad debts expense	2,900	
Allowance for doubtful accounts		2,900
1% × ($300,000 − $10,000)		

c. The balance of prepaid insurance on December 31 amounts to $2,500. The expired portion of the $4,000 balance in the prepaid insurance account, $1,500, is transferred to insurance expense.

	Debit	Credit
Insurance expense	1,500	
Prepaid insurance		1,500

d. On October 1, the company sublet a portion of its building for four months. The rent was collected in advance and credited to rent income. As of December 31, three months have been earned and one month is still unearned.

	Debit	Credit
Rent income	1,000	
Rent collected in advance		1,000

e. Accrued interest on the notes receivable amounts to $125.

	Debit	Credit
Interest receivable	125	
Interest income		125

f. Supplies on hand on December 31 amount to $1,500.

	Debit	Credit
Supplies used	4,500	
Supplies on hand		4,500
($6,000 − $1,500 = $4,500 used)		

g. Accrued sales salaries not paid amount to $700.

	Debit	Credit
Sales salaries	700	
Accrued sales salaries		700

h. The company uses the periodic inventory method. Merchandise inventory on December 31 amounts to $55,000. No adjustment is necessary if the closing procedure discussed in this chapter is followed.

These adjustments appear in the second pair of columns on the worksheet for Camera Corporation.

4. *After the adjustments are entered in the adjustments columns, compute the adjusted balance of each account and extend it to the appropriate column for the statement in which the balance should appear.* Debit balances are extended to debit columns, and credit balances are extended to credit columns. The balance is computed by combining the amount in the unadjusted trial balance with the amount, if any, in the adjustments columns. For example, the account allowance for doubtful accounts has a credit

Part II   Processing Accounting Data

EXAMPLE 5-13

CAMERA CORPORATION
Worksheet
For the Year Ended December 31

	Trial Balance		Adjustments	
	Dr.	Cr.	Dr.	Cr.
Cash	30000			
Accounts receivable	40000			
Allowance for doubtful accounts		500		b 2900
Notes receivable	23000			
Merchandise inventory	40000			
Prepaid insurance	4000			c 1500
Supplies on hand	6000			f 4500
Delivery Equipment	20000			
Accumulated depreciation on delivery equipment		5000		a 5000
Accounts payable		47000		
Capital stock		70000		
Retained earnings		24600		
Sales		300000		
Sales returns and allowances	10000			
Purchases	224000			
Purchase returns and allowances		3000		
Sales salaries	24000		g 700	
Office salaries	6100			
Advertising	10000			
Utilities expense	6000			
Rent expense	12000			
Interest income		1000		e 125
Rent income		4000	d 1000	
	455100	455100		
Depreciation expense—delivery equipment			a 5000	
Bad debts expense			b 2900	
Insurance expense			c 1500	
Interest receivable			e 125	
Supplies used			f 4500	
Rent collected in advance				d 1000
Accrued sales salaries				g 700
			15725	15725
Net income				
Retained earnings—end of year				

150

Adjusting Entries: Completion of the Accounting Cycle   **Chapter 5**

Income Statement		Retained Earnings		Balance Sheet	
Dr.	Cr.	Dr.	Cr.	Dr.	Cr.
				30000	
				40000	
					3400
				23000	
40000	55000			55000	
				2500	
				1500	
				20000	
					10000
					47000
					70000
			24600		
	300000				
10000					
224000					
	3000				
24700					
6100					
10000					
6000					
12000					
	1125				
	3000				
5000					
2900					
1500				125	
4500					1000
					700
346700	362125				
15425			15425		
362125	362125	0	40025		
		40025			40025
		40025	40025	172125	172125

151

balance of $500 in the trial balance columns. This $500, combined with the $2,900 credit appearing on the same line in the adjustments column, results in the adjusted credit balance of $3,400, which is extended to the balance sheet credit column. The prepaid insurance account is another example. This account has a debit balance of $4,000 in the trial balance column. This $4,000 debit amount, combined with the $1,500 credit appearing on the same line in the adjustments column, gives an adjusted debit balance of $2,500, which is extended to the balance sheet debit column. In a similar manner, all account balances are extended to the appropriate columns.

Inventory

The merchandise inventory for December 31 is placed directly into the income statement credit column and into the balance sheet debit column. One function of the income statement columns is to collect all of the accounts involved in determining the cost of goods sold. By entering the ending inventory in the income statement credit column, the accountant is, in effect, deducting it from the total of the beginning inventory, purchases, and freight-in (which are extended to the income statement debit column). The ending inventory is entered in the balance sheet debit column because it will appear on the balance sheet as an asset at the end of the year. Handling the inventory in this way maintains the equality of debits and credits.

5. *Total the income statement columns.* The difference between the debit column and the credit column is the net income or net loss for the period. If the credits exceed the debits, enter this difference in the income statement debit column and in the statement of retained earnings credit column. The caption *net income* is written in the column for account titles to identify this amount. If the debits exceed the credits in the income statement columns, the difference is the *net loss* for the period. This difference is entered in the income statement credit column as the balancing figure and in the retained earnings debit column. In the illustration, the net income for Camera Corporation amounts to $15,425.

6. *Total the retained earnings columns.* If the credits exceed the debits (the usual case), enter the difference as a debit in the retained earnings debit column and in the balance sheet credit column. This figure is the retained earnings at the end of the year. If the debits exceed the credits in the retained earnings columns, the difference is entered in the retained earnings credit column and in the balance sheet debit column. This difference is described as a retained earnings deficit. In the illustration, the retained earnings of Camera Corporation amount to $40,025.

7. *Total the balance sheet columns.* The totals should be equal. If they are equal, rule the various column totals.

The financial statements can be prepared directly from the data in the worksheet. It is only necessary to organize and classify the data in the proper form for each statement. After the financial statements have been prepared, it is not difficult to prepare the adjusting and closing entries from the worksheet. Data recorded in the adjustments column of the worksheet provide the information needed for the preparation of the formal adjusting entries in the journal. The adjusting entries can be taken directly from the worksheet, entered in the journal, and posted to the ledger accounts. (The adjusting entries were listed in Step 3.)

The closing entries also can be taken directly from the worksheet, entered in the journal, and posted to the ledger. The procedure would be as follows for Camera Corporation:

1. Each account in the credit column of the income statement on the worksheet is debited, and the income summary account is credited. This entry closes all of the nominal accounts that have credit balances and records the merchandise inventory on hand at the end of the period. The merchandise inventory has been entered on the worksheet as a credit in the income statement columns and as a debit in the balance sheet columns, but it has not been recorded in the journal or posted to the ledger. Thus, the merchandise inventory adjustment is made as a part of the closing process.

	Debit	Credit
Merchandise inventory	55,000	
Sales	300,000	
Purchase returns and allowances	3,000	
Interest income	1,125	
Rent income	3,000	
Income summary		362,125

2. Each account in the debit column of the income statement columns on the worksheet is credited, and income summary is debited for the total.

	Debit	Credit
Income summary	346,700	
Merchandise inventory		40,000
Sales returns and allowances		10,000
Purchases		224,000
Sales salaries		24,700
Office salaries		6,100
Advertising		10,000
Utilities expense		6,000
Rent expense		12,000
Depreciation expense—delivery equipment		5,000
Bad debts expense		2,900
Insurance expense		1,500
Supplies used		4,500

Notice that the beginning inventory is closed out as part of this entry.
3. The balance in the income summary account is transferred to retained earnings.

	Debit	Credit
Income summary	15,425	
Retained earnings		15,425

Cycle with Worksheet

The accounting cycle, as set forth in chapters 4 and 5 and modified here by use of a worksheet, can be summarized as follows:

1. Analyze transactions and enter them in the journal.
2. Post debits and credits from the journal to the ledger accounts.
3. Prepare a worksheet.
4. Prepare formal financial statements from the worksheet.
5. Using the worksheet as a guide, enter the adjusting entries and closing entries in the general journal.
6. Post the adjusting entries and the closing entries to the ledger accounts.
7. Balance and rule the ledger accounts and bring forward balances to start the next cycle.

QUESTIONS

5-1. Why should rent paid in advance be treated as an asset?

5-2. What are the steps in the *accounting cycle?*

5-3. Why is the adjustment for estimated bad debts made?

5-4. What is the difference between *revenues* and *cash receipts?* Give examples of items that are revenues of a given period but not receipts of that period. Give examples of items that are both revenues and receipts.

5-5. What is the difference between *expense* and *cash disbursement?* Give examples of items that are expenses of a given period but are not disbursements of that period. Give examples of items that are both expenses and disbursements.

5-6. Sam Spade, owner of Spade Construction Company, objected to allowing for estimated bad debt losses on the income statement. "I am extremely careful in extending credit. But even for the few accounts that do go bad, I don't think it's right to estimate the loss in advance. The income statement should state facts—not estimates." Comment on this statement.

5-7. Ordinarily, liabilities are items that require future payments. How then can you justify including items such as advances by customers and rent collected in advance as liabilities?

5-8. You have just presented the current year's financial statements, showing an income of $75,000, to the president of the company. The president states that they must be in error as the company has $25,000 less cash than it did last year. What explanation could you offer for this apparent discrepancy?

5-9. What is the function of closing entries?

5-10. After the books are closed, there are no accounts with balances. True or false? Why?

EXERCISES

5-11. *Adjustments.* Prepare the adjustments at December 31, Year 1, from the following trial balance data and transaction information:

Trial Balance Data

	Debit	Credit
Prepaid rent	$1,200	
Office supplies inventory	456	
Subscriptions received in advance		$3,125
Interest expense	172	

a. On May 1, Year 1, rent for one year was paid in advance, to extend to April 30, Year 2.
b. Inventory of office supplies at December 31, Year 1, was $200.
c. Of the subscriptions received in advance, $1,125 had not been earned at December 31, Year 1.
d. Forty-five dollars of interest on notes payable had accrued by December 31.

(Solution in Appendix B.)

5-12. *Adjustment for unearned rent.* On April 1, a landlord received rent of $1,500 for one year in advance and prepared the following journal entry:

	Debit	Credit
Cash	$1,500	
Rent received in advance		$1,500

a. What adjusting entry would the landlord make at December 31?
b. If the original entry had credited rent income, what adjusting entry would the landlord make at December 31?

5-13. *Entries for note receivable and interest.* On December 1, Year 1, the AB Corporation accepted a 6-month, 6% promissory note in settlement of John Brown's overdue account of $1,000. John Brown paid the total amount owed on the note and interest on the required date. On the books of the AB Corporation, show how the above transactions should be recorded in the journal in Year 1 and Year 2. (Include the December 31, Year 1, adjustment.)

5-14. *Adjustments.* Prepare adjusting entries on December 31 for the following items:
  a. A count of supplies reveals that $200 is still on hand. The supplies expense account was debited for all supplies purchased during the period.
  b. Employees are owed $1,720 for work during the last few days of December, for which they have not been paid.
  c. On December 1, the company paid $6,000 for a 3-month advertising campaign that began on that date. Advertising expense was debited.
  d. The beginning inventory was $37,000, and the ending inventory is $43,000.

5-15. *Adjustments.* The Hewlett Company adjusts and closes its books once a year on December 31. The trial balance of the company, on December 31 of the current year, includes the following account balances, among others:

	Debit	Credit
Interest revenue		$ 350
Unexpired insurance	$ 3,600	
Buildings	70,400	
Office salaries expense	13,200	
Investments in securities	10,000	
Rental income		2,600
Sales		210,000

Analysis discloses the following data. Prepare the adjusting journal entries at December 31.
  a. Interest earned on investments but not yet received amounts to $115 at December 31.
  b. The rental income is received in advance. As of December 31, $200 is still unearned until next year.
  c. The unexpired insurance account balance is the cost of a 2-year policy taken out April 1 of the current year.
  d. The salaries of the office staff earned but unpaid at December 31 amount to $750.

5-16. *Bad debts expense.* At the year-end, the allowance for bad debts account of the Ranso Co. had a credit balance of $150 just prior to the adjusting entry to provide for bad debts expense for the year.
  Required:
  a. Compute the bad debts expense, estimating that one-half of 1% of sales, totaling $175,000, will result in bad debts.
  b. Compute the balance of the allowance for doubtful accounts after the adjustment.

5-17. *Adjustments.* The popular monthly magazine *Sub-basement* began publication on July 1. At that time the business collected $1,000,000 on one-year subscriptions, $2,000,000 on two-year subscriptions, and $1,500,000 on three-year subscriptions.

All subscriptions began with the July issue. All amounts collected were credited to subscription revenue in July. Give any adjusting entry necessary on December 31, the end of the company's fiscal year.

5-18. *Adjustments and computation of income.* Selected account balances (before adjusting entries) for the Catalina Sales Company on December 31 of the current year are as follows:

Sales	$250,000
Cost of goods sold	140,000
Selling expenses	30,000
Administrative expenses	20,000
Prepaid rent	12,000
Office supplies on hand	6,000
Accrued salaries	0

Additional information:
1. On June 7, $12,000 rent for one year in advance (to June 1 of next year) was charged to prepaid rent.
2. During the year, selling supplies amounting to $15,000 were purchased and charged to selling expense. Of these, $3,000 were still on hand on December 31.
3. Office supplies purchased during the year, amounting to $6,000, were charged to office supplies on hand. As of December 31, all of these have been used.
4. Sales salaries are charged to selling expense as paid. Accrued salaries on December 31 amount to $700.

Required:
a. Compute the net income that will be reported if the adjustments are not taken into consideration.
b. Journalize the appropriate adjusting entries.
c. Compute the net income that will be reported if the adjustments are taken into consideration.

5-19. *Adjustments.* In analyzing the accounts of L. S. Stone on December 31, the end of an annual fiscal period, you have gathered the data listed below. What adjusting entry would be made for each item?
a. The unexpired insurance account shows a debit of $450, representing the cost of a 3-year fire insurance policy dated September 1 of the current year.
b. On November 1, rental income was credited for $600, representing income from a subrental for a 3-month period beginning on that date.
c. Purchase of advertising supplies for $400 during the year was recorded in the advertising expense account. On December 31, supplies of $60 are on hand.
d. On August 1, $750 was paid as rent for a 6-month period beginning on that date. The rent expense account was debited for this amount.

5-20. *Bad debts.* The following accounts, among others, appear in the ledger of the Morton Co. at December 31 of the current year:

	Debit	Credit
Accounts receivable	10,000	
Allowance for uncollectible accounts		80
Sales		72,000

Part II   Processing Accounting Data

Required:
a. In the past, uncollectible accounts have averaged 1% of sales. The company expects this relationship to hold in the coming year. This adjustment normally is made on December 31. Make the appropriate adjustment.
b. What is the amount of bad debts expense that will appear on the income statement for the current year?
c. What is the balance of the accounts receivable that will appear on the December 31 balance sheet? What is the balance of the allowance for uncollectible accounts that will appear on the balance sheet?

5-21. *Depreciation.* The Rockett Company purchased a machine on January 1, Year 1, at a price of $8,800. The company estimated the machine would have a useful life of five years and would have a $300 salvage value at the end of its useful life.

Required:
a. What is the estimated depreciation expense for Year 4?
b. What is the amount shown as accumulated depreciation on the balance sheet at December 31, Year 4?

5-22. *Omission of adjustment.* On July 1, Year 1, the proprietor of the Central Car Park received rentals in advance totaling $1,200 for the year to June 30, Year 2. These rentals were credited to the rental revenue account. He prepared financial statements at September 30, Year 1, and made no adjusting entry in respect to the above transaction.

Required:
a. Show the adjusting journal entry that should have been made September 30, Year 1.
b. State the effect that this non-adjustment had upon the accuracy of the financial statements on September 30, Year 1, and September 30, Year 2. If the accuracy of a statement is not affected, then explain why.

5-23. *Adjustments.* On July 1, Year 1, the Rollo Company paid 3 years' rent in the amount of $3,300 in advance for its warehouse properties. On July 1, Year 4, the lease was renewed in the amount of $4,800 for the next three years, all paid in advance. These payments have been debited to prepaid rent, and appropriate adjustments have been made at each December 31 through Year 3. Make the appropriate adjustment for December 31, Year 4.

5-24. *Adjustments.* Milo operates a typewriter repair service. On September 1, Year 1, he entered into a contract with a certain business to service its typewriters for a 2-year period for a stipulated fee paid in advance. The receipt was credited to an account entitled unearned service fees. This account was properly adjusted on December 31, Year 1. Before adjustment at the annual closing on December 31, Year 2, the account had a balance of $900.
Required:
a. Make the appropriate adjusting entry as of December 31, Year 2.
b. Give the total amount of the fee received on September 1, Year 1.

5-25. *Inventory adjustment.* The Bench Company had the following balances in selected accounts on December 31 of the current year:

	Debit	Credit
Inventory	16,000	
Sales		165,000
Sales returns	6,000	
Purchases	104,000	
Purchase returns		3,000
Advertising	11,000	
Freight in	2,000	

A count of inventory on hand on December 31 yields a figure of $22,000.

Required:
a. Prepare any adjustments necessary for inventories.
b. Prepare a schedule of cost of goods sold.
(Solution in Appendix B.)

5-26. *Closing entries.* In December of Year 1, the bookkeeper of the Suds Laundry eloped to Mexico with the daughter of Mr. Suds. Before leaving, however, he prepared a trial balance of the accounts appearing in the ledger. Unfortunately, no two-column paper was available, so he listed all the amounts in a single column.

SUDS LAUNDRY
Trial Balance
December 31, Year 1

Accounts payable	$ 2,000
Accounts receivable	5,000
Accrued salaries	1,000
Accumulated depreciation	15,000
Cash	5,000
Capital stock	6,000
Depreciation	1,000
Equipment	25,000
Insurance expired	200
Laundry revenue	20,000
Retained earnings	4,000
Salaries	6,000
Laundry supplies on hand	2,000
Laundry supplies used	3,000
Prepaid insurance	800
	$96,000

Required:
a. Prepare an appropriate trial balance.
b. Prepare closing entries for the laundry.
(Solution in Appendix B.)

Part II Processing Accounting Data

5-27. Working papers. Below is a list of items from the worksheet of a merchandising concern. To the right of the items, represented by parentheses, are the last four columns from the concern's worksheet. Indicate for each item the column or columns in which amounts will appear when the worksheet is completed. The first item is given as an example.

	Income Statement		Balance Sheet	
	Dr.	Cr.	Dr.	Cr.
Example: Accounts receivable	( )	( )	(X)	( )
1. Accumulated depreciation, equipment	( )	( )	( )	( )
2. Allowance for bad debts	( )	( )	( )	( )
3. Bad debts expense	( )	( )	( )	( )
4. Bond interest payable	( )	( )	( )	( )
5. Bonds payable	( )	( )	( )	( )
6. Common stock	( )	( )	( )	( )
7. Cost of goods sold	( )	( )	( )	( )
8. Depreciation of equipment	( )	( )	( )	( )
9. Expired insurance	( )	( )	( )	( )
10. Interest payable	( )	( )	( )	( )
11. Merchandise inventory (beginning)	( )	( )	( )	( )
12. Merchandise inventory (ending)	( )	( )	( )	( )
13. Office salaries	( )	( )	( )	( )
14. Repairs	( )	( )	( )	( )
15. Retained earnings	( )	( )	( )	( )
16. Sales salaries	( )	( )	( )	( )
17. Supplies on hand	( )	( )	( )	( )
18. Supplies used	( )	( )	( )	( )

PROBLEMS

5-28. Insurance adjustments. The unexpired insurance account has a balance of $6,000 on December 31, Year 2. An analysis of the insurance policies of this company shows the following:

	Total Premium	Date Policy Acquired	Term of Policy
Policy A	$1,800	Jan. 1, Year 1	2 years
Policy B	600	July 1, Year 1	1 year
Policy C	4,800	July 31, Year 2	2 years

Required:
- **a.** Prepare the adjusting entry required on December 31, Year 2. You may assume that proper adjustments were made on December 31, Year 1.
- **b.** Indicate the balance of unexpired cost that should remain in the unexpired insurance account at December 31, Year 2.

5-29. *Adjusting entries.* Prepare in journal form the adjusting entry necessary for each of the following independent cases. The company's fiscal year ends on December 31, Year 5.
- **a.** A two-year insurance policy was purchased on November 1, Year 5 and the premium of $3,600 for the policy was debited at that time to prepaid insurance.
- **b.** A two-year insurance policy was purchased on November 1, Year 5, and the premium of $3,000 for the policy was debited at that time to insurance expense.
- **c.** On October 1, Year 5, a 6%, 1-year note receivable for $1,000 was received from a customer. The principal and all interest is to be paid by the customer when the note matures.
- **d.** The count of office supplies on hand on December 31, Year 5, totaled $250. All office supplies are debited to office supplies expense when acquired. The office supplies expense account shows a balance of $1,275.
- **e.** On December 31, Year 5, the balance in the office equipment account was $10,000. No equipment had been acquired during the year, and all equipment has a 10-year life with $1,000 salvage value. Record the annual depreciation expense.
- **f.** The balance in the sales account is $50,000. The company's past experience indicated that 1% of the sales will prove to be uncollectible.
- **g.** Office space was rented to another company on November 1, Year 5, at a monthly rental of $150. The tenant paid one year's rent in advance on November 5, and the entire $1,800 was credited to rental income when received.
- **h.** Office space was rented to another company on October 1, Year 5, at a monthly rental of $200. The tenant paid one year's rent in advance on October 1, and the entire $2,400 was credited to unearned rental income when received.

5-30. *Adjusting entries.* Henderson Grocery Store adjusts its accounts, closes its books, and prepares financial statements on each December 31. By reference to the supplementary data and the partial trial balance shown below, make the normal year-end adjustments for Henderson Grocery Store. The entries should be keyed to the letter identifying each item of supplementary data.

Additional information:
- **a.** The balance in notes receivable is comprised of a 4-month, 6% note dated December 1.
- **b.** The balance in the unexpired insurance account is comprised of the premium on a 3-year fire insurance policy acquired on April 1, Year 1. The account was last adjusted as of December 31, Year 1.
- **c.** Depreciation on the building is computed at 3% per year.

Part II   Processing Accounting Data

    d. An inventory was taken and showed that $135 of supplies were on hand as of December 31, Year 2.
    e. On September 1, Year 2, the Allied Drug Chain rented a portion of the Henderson Grocery Store for the establishment of a Drug Department and paid $2,400 as 2 years' rent in advance.
    f. Salaries earned by Henderson's employees and unpaid on December 31, Year 2, amounted to $680.

Partial Trial Balance
December 31, Year 2

	Debit	Credit
Notes receivable	5,000	
Unexpired insurance	594	
Building	100,000	
Accumulated depreciation—building		4,500
Unearned rent income		2,400
Salary expense	10,000	
Supplies used	900	

(Solution in Appendix B.)

5-31. *Adjustments.* Shown below are some of the amounts from the trial balance of the XYZ Corporation after adjusting entries have been completed. List the amounts that would appear in the accounts *before* adjustments were completed.

	After Adjustments	
	Debit	Credit
Prepaid insurance	150	
Salaries expense	350	
Rent revenue collected in advance		400
Income tax expense	175	
Cash	1,770	
Equipment	1,200	
Interest revenue		50
Accrued salaries payable		20
Accrued interest receivable	50	
Depreciation expense	200	
Notes receivable	1,200	
Insurance expense	50	
Income tax payable		175
Sales revenue		1,800
Rent revenue		200
Cost of goods sold	1,200	
Retained income		500
Accumulated depreciation—equipment		1,000

5-32. *Accounting cycle—year-end entries.* The following unadjusted trial balance was prepared from the books of the A. B. Cee Corporation on December 31, Year 1:

Trial Balance

	Debit	Credit
Retained income		$ 20,000
Sales revenue		100,100
Accounts payable		9,300
Cash in bank	$ 2,125	
Equipment	56,000	
Operating expenses	22,400	
Equipment—accumulated depreciation		6,000
Merchandise inventory	20,000	
Bonds payable—5%		10,000
Purchases	60,000	
Common stock		40,000
Bond interest expense	375	
Allowance for uncollectible accounts		200
Temporary investments	10,000	
Accounts receivable—trade	14,700	
	$185,600	$185,600

Additional information:
1. Included in operating expenses is $300 for rent relating to Year 2.
2. Depreciation expense has not been recorded. The current year's depreciation is $3,600.
3. Three months' interest is owed on the bonds.
4. A total of $2,300 of supplies was purchased during the year and was charged to the operating expenses account. A count on December 31 shows $700 remain on hand.
5. Bad debt expense for this year is estimated to be $\frac{1}{2}$ of 1% of sales.
6. The ending inventory is $23,000.

Required:
a. Set up T accounts and place in them the balances from the unadjusted trial balance above.
b. Prepare, in journal form, adjustments as of December 31, Year 1.
c. Post the adjustments to the T accounts.
d. Prepare an income statement for the year and a balance sheet as of the end of the year.
e. Prepare closing entries in journal form.
f. Post the closing entries.
g. Prepare a post-closing trial balance.

5-33. *Worksheet.* Listed below are the accounts and the balance of each account for the XB Zee Company on December 31, Year 1. Enter the amounts in the first two columns of a worksheet and secure a trial balance. Then complete the worksheet using the additional information.

163

Accounts:

Accumulated depreciation—equipment	$ 48
Accounts payable	16
Accounts receivable	52
Cash	22
Equipment	80
Freight-in	16
Merchandise inventory	54
Prepaid insurance	10
Purchases	132
Purchase returns	9
Rent expense	22
Sales	312
Sales returns	16
Stores supplies expense	14
Wages expense	88
Capital stock	100
Retained earnings	21

Additional information:

a. Depreciation of equipment	$ 8
b. Expired insurance	6
c. Store supplies on hand	9
d. Accrued wages	9
e. Prepaid rent	4
f. Ending merchandise inventory	60

5-34. *Financial statements.* Using the worksheet prepared in Problem 5-33, prepare financial statements on December 31, Year 1, for the XB Zee Company.

5-35. *Adjusting and closing entries prepared from worksheet.* Using the worksheet prepared in Problem 5-33, journalize adjusting and closing entries on December 31, Year 1, for the XB Zee Company.

5-36. *Worksheet and preparation of financial statements.* The data from the trial balance of Wall Corporation, as of December 31, Year 2, the end of the company's fiscal year, are presented below. Unfortunately, the bookkeeper who prepared the trial balance didn't have any two-column paper, so all amounts are listed in one column. Prepare working papers for Wall Corporation.

WALL CORPORATION
Trial Balance
December 31, Year 2

Cash	$ 15,974
Accounts receivable	51,391
Allowance for doubtful accounts	2,011
Merchandise inventory—December 31, Year 1	28,000
Unexpired insurance	1,410
Delivery equipment	1,344
Accumulated depreciation—delivery equipment	671
Furniture and fixtures	21,136

Accumulated depreciation—furniture and fixtures	4,467
Accounts payable	10,692
Capital stock	70,000
Retained earnings	7,965
Sales	198,562
Sales returns and allowances	3,529
Sales discounts	2,416
Purchases	145,241
Purchase returns and allowances	1,642
Purchase discounts	415
Freight-in	2,919
Selling expenses	9,341
Delivery expenses	1,235
General and administrative expenses	12,401
Interest expense	88
	$592,850

Additional data:
1. Depreciation, delivery equipment—25% per annum (a delivery expense)
2. Depreciation, furniture and fixtures—12½% per annum (a selling expense)
3. An examination of the insurance policies reveals that the following policies were in effect throughout Year 2:

	Term	Original Premium
Furniture and equipment	4 years	$1,140
Delivery equipment	3 years	270
Merchandise	5 years	410
		$1,820

4. Accrued wages and salaries:

Salespersons	$280
Drivers	162
Office clerks	195
	$637

5. Supplies on hand on December 31 amounted to $200. Purchases of supplies have been charged to selling expenses.
6. Merchandise inventory: December 31, Year 2, $32,000.

CASE PROBLEM

5-37. *Case problem.* The Record Magazine Company has recently begun operations. During Year 1 the following events took place:

1. Sold 60,000 3-year subscriptions for $10 each. The entire amount was credited to revenue from subscriptions. Subscriptions began with the first issue on July 10, Year 1. The magazine comes out monthly.
2. Sold advertising for $450,000. Of this amount $310,000 was for ads appearing in Year 1 issues and $140,000 was for ads to appear in Year 2.
3. Entered into a printing contract with Excelsior Printing Company. The contract called for payments in advance of $80,000 per issue.
4. Paid $260,000 for art work on ads. Of this amount $68,000 applied to ads to appear in Year 2.
5. Various other operating transactions were also recorded (see trial balance).

RECORD MAGAZINE COMPANY
Trial Balance
December 31, Year 1

	Debit	Credit
Cash	$ 480,000	
Accounts receivable	50,000	
Accounts payable		$ 100,000
Capital stock		400,000
Subscription revenue		600,000
Ad revenue		450,000
Printing expense	560,000	
Artwork expense	260,000	
Other operating expenses	200,000	
	$1,550,000	$1,550,000

Required:

a. In what respects was Record's accounting deficient?
b. Prepare correcting entries for Record.
c. Prepare an income statement for Year 1 on the basis of the trial balance given.
d. Prepare a corrected income statement for Year 1.
e. Comment on your results in *c* and *d*.

6

Processing Accounting Data

The two-column journal introduced in chapter 4 is frequently called the general journal. This name is appropriate because any transaction or adjustment, however complex, can be recorded in this journal. Nevertheless, the two-column journal has a sharply restricted role in actual accounting work. No business firm or organization of any size could maintain an effective accounting system employing only a two-column journal. The reason is simple. Each debit and credit entry in a general journal requires a separate posting to the ledger. As the volume of transactions grows, the accounting work quickly expands beyond the capacity of the two-column journal system.

    Accountants and others concerned with accounting data have long recognized the problems posed by the simple-journal approach. Ingenious systems employing both simple and complex mechanical and electronic devices have been designed to cope with the problems. Among the different methods that have been devised are electronic data processing (EDP) and machine accounting.

    In this chapter we consider the information needs of an enterprise and the general features of a data processing system. We then examine the elements of manual data processing and its limitations. Finally, we deal briefly with EDP and accounting.

INFORMATION NEEDS

Business firms vary widely in their size and in the complexity of their operations. The magnitude and the difficulty of management's task tend to correspond with the size and complexity of the operations for which they are responsible. A common problem for all managers—whether in large or small organizations—is getting the information they need to plan, coordinate, oversee, and control the activities for which they are responsible.

The owner-managers of small firms have few problems in this area. They not only oversee the activities, but also perform most of the activities themselves. The problems of coordinating the work of their few employees are relatively simple. Direct and perceptive observation of activities, combined with study of the periodic financial statements that show the degree of financial success, is probably sufficient to give them the information they need.

Large firms have the same coordination problems as the small firm, but the difficulties are multiplied because the activities are distributed among many people. Direct observation may be impossible. Therefore, increased reliance must be placed on written information about the activities. The written information (or reports) are generated from facts (or data) that describe various facets of enterprise activities. The collection of data and the manipulation of these data to produce reports is known generally as *data processing*.

Data processing

To carry out their responsibilities, managers need information that is relevant and timely. For example, the manager of a department in a store needs to know what merchandise items require replenishment. A report showing only the items that need to be reordered is superior to one showing all the items stocked in the department. The manager can focus on the items that need attention and will not have his view cluttered by irrelevant data. The reports must be received in time for the manager to do something about the matter being reported. It is fruitless for a manager to concern himself today with a report on matters that should have been attended to weeks ago.

Relevant data

Timely information

The information needed by managers determines the kinds of data collected and the structure of the data processing system. Matching the data processing system to informational needs is the most challenging task facing the firm's accountant. This task is more complex than preparing the periodic financial statements. It demands an intimate knowledge of management's problems, as well as a knowledge of modern data processing equipment and its capabilities and the most effective means of communicating information. In brief, the accountant must become an information specialist.

Management needs and system

SOURCE DOCUMENTS: INPUTS OF THE DATA PROCESSING SYSTEM

The financial reports and related documents (such as bills or statements to customers, check payments to suppliers, and payroll checks for em-

Processing Accounting Data   Chapter 6

FIGURE 6-1

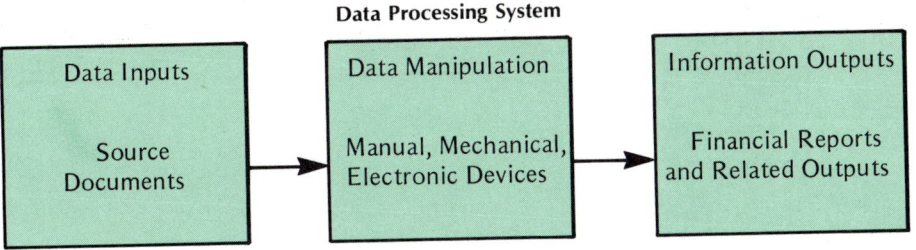

ployees) are the *outputs* of data processing. These outputs are generated by the data processing system on the basis of *inputs* into the system. These inputs, known as *source documents,* are the bases for the reports; hence, they are crucial in the operation of the data processing system. The accuracy of the documents determines the accuracy and reliability of the resulting financial reports.

Source documents

Typically, source documents are records of transactions. They provide the raw data that are inputs into the data processing system. The data are manipulated in various ways to generate the outputs of the system. These general relationships are charted in Figure 6-1.

Some examples of data processing system elements are given in Figure 6-2.

Accuracy is a prime requisite of source documents. Undiscovered errors in the data cause the results of further processing to be incorrect. Consequently, the dictum "do it right the first time" is heavily underscored in data processing. Great emphasis is placed on obtaining accurate data and on making sure that the data are put into the system accurately. For example, documents are designed to encourage accuracy in their use, and multiple copies of documents are used to avoid rewriting the data. Preprinted data are used to avoid errors in customer data. Much effort also goes into the verification of data on documents; for example, clerks in the sales department will verify the data given on orders transmitted by the salesperson.

Accuracy

Despite the efforts made to avoid errors, they do creep in, so it is important to know how to detect and correct them. Data can be tested to verify their accuracy. For example, an adding machine tape showing the total for the sales invoices being posted to customers' ledger accounts can be checked against the total of the debits posted to those accounts. If the two total figures are equal, there is a strong presumption that the data processing is error free. Similar checks can be used in more sophisticated computer processing.

PROCESSING DATA MANUALLY

In many systems, source documents bearing the raw data of transactions are not used directly as information. The data are manipulated, or op-

FIGURE 6-2   Examples of Data Processing Elements

DATA INPUTS

Examples:

1. Sales transactions on sales invoices
2. Cash received transactions on cash receipt forms
3. Purchase transactions on purchase invoices
4. Cash payment transactions on check stubs or vouchers
5. Employee time cards

DATA MANIPULATION

Examples:

1. Record transactions in journal
2. Record amount of sales invoices to customers' accounts
3. Record amount of purchase invoice in creditors' accounts
4. Record earnings of employees on employee earnings records

INFORMATION OUTPUTS

Examples:

1. General ledger trial balances
2. Income statement
3. Balance sheet
4. Customers' statements
5. Employee pay checks

erated upon, in various ways before meaningful information can be obtained. This manipulation is called *processing the data.* Before data on source documents can be processed, they must be put into the system in some way.

Humans as processors

Human beings are versatile data processors. For example, they can recognize an amazing variety of data forms. They can read a number whether it is in Arabic numerals, Roman numerals, or English words. Persons read documents and transfer the data to their memory units (that is, their brains). They may then extract the data and write them on some record. The persons may process the data still further by classifying them in some way and by adding them to similar data. Later the persons are able to produce reports by combining and recombining data, performing mathematical operations on the data, and writing the results.

For example, in processing sales data the accounting clerk begins with a stack of sales invoices on which the credit sales of the previous business day are recorded. The clerk then adds the several invoice amounts to get the total credit sales. This total is the basis for the journal entry:

	Debit	Credit
Accounts receivable	xx	
Sales		xx

The clerk then sorts the sales invoices by customer name. Sales to each customer are written on the customer's ledger card (the company's record of what the customer owes) and on the customer's statement, which will be mailed to the customer at the close of the month. Both of these records can be updated in the same operation by use of carbon paper. The total of the postings to customers' ledger cards should equal the total sales recorded in the journal. If the totals are in agreement, the clerk can proceed to the next step.

The next step may be simply to file the invoices by customer. In that case, data manipulation is at an end. But there are rich opportunities for obtaining important information through additional processing. For example, the invoices could be sorted by individual salespersons to get sales figures for each salesperson. The sales invoices could also be sorted by product classes to get information on which products are selling well and which are not. Of course, the quantity of additional data processing is limited by the inherent weaknesses of individuals: they are slow, and their work is subject to errors.

JOURNALS

Journals are used in most data processing systems, including computerized systems. *A journal is a chronological record of transactions. Each transaction is recorded on the basis of its debit and credit effects on general ledger accounts.* The date, source document number, and other pertinent identifiers are also recorded to provide a complete cross referencing of the transaction.

General Purpose Journals

The simplest journal is the two-column variety with which you are already familiar. For many businesses, the expansion of this simple journal into a multi-columnar general journal is adequate for basic accounting needs.

Multi-columnar journal

A multi-columnar general journal is a journal with a series of money columns devoted to particular ledger accounts. If there are a lot of transactions with customers, a set of columns for accounts receivable (debit and credit) is established. Similarly, columns for cash debit and credit, accounts payable debit and credit, sales credit, purchases debit, and other common events can be established. One pair of columns is reserved for all other transactions. When an entry is recorded, the appropriate columns are used. Posting can be simplified by posting totals of columns at the end of a period to the respective accounts indicated. In this way considerable time can be saved.

The multi-columnar general journal is admirably suited to the small organization. All accounting entries can be conveniently accommodated. The special columns provide for efficient summarizing of similar, repetitive transactions. The number of special columns incorporated can be expanded appreciably by using a double-page columnar journal.

Limitations

Usefulness of this journal is strictly related to the size of the organization and the volume of transactions. It is impossible to state the specific size at which the firm should shift to another system. As long as the system remains efficient, there is no need to change. But a change should be made when the growing business detects symptoms of inefficiency in the multi-columnar journal operation. Accounting work will tend to be slower than the business operations themselves. Bills to customers will be delayed. Financial statements will be late in coming out. These symptoms probably indicate that the business has outgrown the simple system and must seek other means for its accounting work. A system of special journals that facilitates division of accounting labor will appreciably increase the firm's capability for handling fairly large volumes of accounting data.

Specialized Journals

Specialized journals are designed to save time in the recording and posting of items that recur often in an accounting period. Repetitive transactions that occur during a period include the sale of merchandise, the purchase of merchandise, the collection of cash from customers, and the payment of cash to creditors. Accordingly, a typical enterprise might have a sales journal, a purchases journal, a cash receipts journal, a cash payments journal, and a general journal. Each journal is designed for a specific purpose: all sales of merchandise on account will be entered in the sales journal, all purchases of merchandise on account will be entered in the purchases journal, all cash receipts will be entered in the cash receipts journal, all cash payments will be entered in the cash payments journal, and all items that do not fit any place else will be entered in the general journal (the same journal you used previously).

Sales Journal. A business of almost any size will have many transactions involving sales during a period. One common transaction is the sale of merchandise on account, which is recorded by a debit to accounts receivable and a credit to sales revenue. If there are many sales on account, the bookkeeper can save time by setting up a specialized sales journal. The sales journal includes the same information as that recorded in a general journal entry for a sale on account, but with less work. The sales journal consists of a place for the date of the transaction, a place for the name of the customer, a place for the dollar amount of the sale, and, often, a place for the posting reference so that a cross reference is maintained between the journal and the ledger.

One common form of the sales journal is illustrated in Example 6-1. This journal has only one money column. Only one column is needed because every transaction that is entered in this sales journal consists of both a debit to accounts receivable and a credit to sales revenue. Because all the transactions are similar and because the same accounts are affected in every case, the journal contains one money column headed *accounts receivable debit and sales revenue credit,* instead of two columns

EXAMPLE 6-1

Sales Journal

Page 23

Date	Customer	Terms	PR	Accts. Rec. Dr. Sales Rev. Cr.
Jan. 2	Bill Adams			1,200
Jan. 2	John Doe			800
Jan. 31	Monthly total			12,300

headed *accounts receivable* and *sales revenue.* In order to enter a sale to a customer (John Doe) the accountant only has to write down the date, the name of the customer, and the dollar amount of the sale. The time involved in recording a whole series of transactions is minimized as compared

Part II Processing Accounting Data

to the time involved in entering these transactions day by day in the general journal.

Where it is desirable to keep track of sales by department or product category, a sales journal with several columns can be used. A sales credit column can be established for each important category.

Purchases Journal. The purchases journal is a counterpart of the sales journal except that purchases is debited and accounts payable is credited at the end of the period. An abbreviated example is shown in Example 6-2.

EXAMPLE 6-2

Purchases Journal

Page 12

Date	Creditor	Terms	PR	Accts. Pay. Cr. Purch. Dr.
Jan. 1	Brown Supply Co.	n/30		400
2	Copeland Co.	2/10, n/30		2,200
2	Murray Mercantile	1/10, n/30		700
Jan. 31	Monthly total			13,400

Cash Receipts Journal. The cash receipts journal has several money columns rather than just one because cash receipts in a typical business come from a variety of sources. Since the collection of cash on account is common, the cash receipts journal has an accounts receivable credit column. Since the sale of goods for cash is also a common transaction, the journal has a special column for sales credits. All the transactions in the cash receipts journal involve a debit to cash, so the journal has a cash debit column. A sales discount column is available for receipts on which a discount is allowed. Cash transactions that occur less frequently are handled in a sundry, or miscellaneous, credit column. At times, a sundry debit column might also be needed.

EXAMPLE 6-3

Cash Receipts Journal

Page 17

Date	Account Credited	PR	Cash Dr.	Sales Disc. Dr.	Accts. Rec. Cr.	Sales Cr.	Sundry Cr.
Jan. 1	Henry Roe Co.		350		350		
2	Cash sales		180			180	
2	Notes payable		1,000				1,000
3	M. Billings Co.		490	10	500		
Jan. 31	Monthly totals		17,210	110	10,200	4,620	2,500

Example 6-3 illustrates the sort of transactions that might occur. The first entry recorded in the cash receipts journal involves a cash receipt on account; therefore, the cash debit and accounts receivable credit columns are used. The second transaction is a cash sale, so the cash debit and sales credit columns are used. The third transaction involves the receipt of cash on a note that was given to the bank. This transaction is recorded in the cash debit column and (since there is no special column for notes payable) in the miscellaneous credit column. The fourth transaction is a receipt on account in which the customer took advantage of credit terms and deducted a sales discount from his payment.

Cash Payments Journal. The cash payments journal is similar in many respects to the cash receipts journal. Columns are established for common transactions that involve cash payments. A journal with a few transactions is illustrated in Example 6-4. Note that the monthly totals indicate that equal debits and credits have been entered.

EXAMPLE 6-4

Cash Payments Journal

Page 15

Date	Account Debited	PR	Accts. Pay. Dr.	Sundry Dr.	Sundry Cr.	Purch. Disct. Cr.	Cash Cr.
Jan. 1	Repairs expense			48			48
2	Brown Supply Co.		1,100				1,100
2	Sales salaries			450			450
3	Acme Company		800			16	784
Jan. 31	Monthly totals		10,400	1,985	20	70	12,295

The format of the cash payments journal could vary considerably depending on the type of business and the types of transactions that take place. In a particular business situation, a column could easily be set up for other repetitive transactions, such as cash purchases or payments of salaries. The only limitation is the size of the page on which the journal is printed and the ability of the accountant to handle a large number of columns.

Posting Journals

The time saved in using specialized journals is not limited to the time saved in recording the transactions in the journal itself. Time is also saved in posting the transactions from the journal into specific ledger accounts. Postings are generally made from specialized journals at the end of the accounting period or at the end of the month, rather than during the

Part II   Processing Accounting Data

Posting totals

period. Instead of posting each individual transaction, such as the sale to John Doe, the accountant totals all similar transactions at the end of the period and posts the totals to the specific accounts involved. For example, the accountant adds up all of the sales recorded in the sales journal during the period and posts the total as a debit to accounts receivable and a credit to sales revenue. Thus, even if 300 or 400 sales on account are made during a period, the work of posting to the ledger involves only one debit to accounts receivable and one credit to sales.

The same procedure is followed in the other specialized journals. From the purchases journal, for example, there is one entry to the ledger each period involving a debit to purchases and a credit to accounts payable. From the cash receipts journal at the end of the period, there is one entry involving a debit to cash for the total of the cash receipts during the period, a credit to accounts receivable for the total of the accounts collected during the period, and a credit to sales revenue for the total cash sales during the accounting period. The miscellaneous column is handled a little differently, since it consists of a series of unusual and less frequent cash receipts. Because a variety of items is included in the miscellaneous credit column it is impossible to post one total to any particular account at the end of the accounting period. Thus, each miscellaneous transaction is posted to the particular accounts specified in the journal. These postings are made daily as transactions occur, periodically during the accounting period, or at the end of the accounting period.

The posting process for an abbreviated cash receipts journal is shown in Example 6-5. Note that four of the column totals are posted at the end of the month. The Sundry Cr. column is posted during the month (as is the note payable item); therefore the accountant makes the notation that the total has already been posted.

Note that the total amounts posted from this journal involve equal debits and credits. The total debits to cash and sales discounts amount to $17,320 ($17,210 + $110), as do the credits to accounts receivable, sales, and sundry credits ($10,200 + $4,620 + $2,500 = $17,320). Thus, equality of debits and credits is maintained, just as it was in the general journal.

Advantages of Specialized Journals

Using specialized journals saves time and energy in recording transactions and in posting the transactions to the ledger. The system of specialized journals also allows for a division of labor and the use of less skilled personnel, with a consequent saving on labor costs. For example, one bookkeeper can work on the sales journal and another on the purchases journal. Since the work is repetitive, clerical personnel can generally handle the bookkeeping. The general journal is an exception in this respect. Because it involves less common and more complicated transactions, it re-

EXAMPLE 6-5   Illustration of Posting Process

Cash Receipts Journal

Page 17

Date	Account Credited	P.R.	Cash Dr.	Sales Discount Dr.	Acct. Rec. Cr.	Sales Cr.	Sundry Cr.
Jan. 1	Henry Roe Co.		350		350		
2	Cash Sale		180			180	
2	Notes payable	204	1,000				1,000
Jan. 31	Monthly totals		17,210 #100	110 #401	10,200 #110	4,620 #400	2,500 (Posted)

Cash
#100

	Bal.				8,000
Jan. 31		CR17	17,210		25,210

Accounts Receivable
#110

	Bal.				12,300
Jan. 31		CR17		10,200	2,100

Notes Payable
#204

Jan. 31		CR17		1,000	1,000

Sales
#400

Jan. 31		CR17		4,620	4,620

Sales Discounts
#401

Jan. 31		CR17	110		110

177

quires a person with greater knowledge of the accounting system and more ability.

Cross-Referencing

Cross referencing between the general ledger and the various journals can be accomplished by using the number of the ledger accounts in the various journals whenever a posting is made. This procedure was illustrated in Example 6-5. In that example the accounts receivable account is numbered 110. Therefore, after posting a journal column to the accounts receivable account, the bookkeeper writes the number 110 under the posted column. The number 400 under the sales credit column in Example 6-5 indicates that the credit has been posted to sales, account 400.

The ledger must also be cross-referenced to the journals, because each of the many journals involved is a potential source for each debit and credit in the ledger. The cross-referencing is accomplished by listing in the ledger account the page number and the journal from which the items originated. For instance, in the accounts receivable account in Example 6-6, the debit is indicated as coming from S23. This means page 23 of the sales journal. The credit is indicated as being from CR17. This indicates that it came from page 17 of the cash receipts journal. By similar notations, the cross-referencing of all accounts is facilitated.

EXAMPLE 6-6

		Accounts Receivable			Acct. No. 110
Jan. 31		S23	12,300		12,300
31		CR17		10,200	2,100

SUBSIDIARY LEDGERS

The general ledger is made up of individual asset, liability, and owners' equity accounts. Normally, these accounts do not include detailed information about the particular asset, liability, or owners' equity item. For example, a store may have a general ledger account for merchandise inventory that simply shows the cost of all the merchandise inventory owned by the store. The one account may represent thousands of different items stocked by the store. Detailed information on the individual items must be found in other records. Frequently, the records that give the details of general ledger accounts are called *subsidiary ledgers*. The general ledger

Control account

account that summarizes a detailed subsidiary ledger is called a *control account.* The general ledger account gives a *control balance*, the details of which are found in the subsidiary ledger.

The subsidiary ledger for accounts receivable is singularly important in credit-granting businesses. An account is maintained for each customer, showing name and address, credit rating and limit, special billing instructions, amounts purchased, amounts paid on account, and balance owed. The form in Example 6-7 is the type used in many businesses. The customer's account provides all the information that will appear on the monthly statement sent to the customer.

EXAMPLE 6-7

Name B. C. Burton   No.   109-10
      12 Circle Street   Rating 01
      Boulder, Colorado 80303 Limit $500

Date	Reference	Charges	Credits	Balance	Previous Balance
Jan. 5	8451	155.00		155.00	.00
Jan. 19	9550	210.00		365.00	155.00
Feb. 8	Cash		155.00	210.00	365.00

The physical form of the customers' ledger will vary. Very large businesses employing computers use magnetic tape, magnetic disk files, or punched cards. The differences do not change the basic purpose of the customer's account, which is to provide a continuing record of the customer's transactions with the company.

Subsidiary ledgers are essential in many areas of operations. The following list indicates the variety of subsidiary ledgers that exists in business firms.

1. Customers' ledger
2. Accounts payable ledger
3. Raw materials ledger
4. Plant and equipment ledger
5. Notes receivable ledger
6. Selling expense ledger
7. Administration expense ledger
8. Capital stock ledger

Examples of subsidiary ledgers

The above list is not exhaustive but merely indicative of the areas in which subsidiary ledgers would be useful. In brief, a subsidiary ledger may be desirable wherever it is necessary to have detailed information about an asset, liability, or owners' equity item.

The relationships that exist among journals, subsidiary ledgers, and general ledger accounts can be illustrated by looking at sales and cash receipt transactions.

Credit sales and cash receipts transactions for January are recorded in the sales journal and the cash receipt journal in Example 6-8. Check marks in the P.R. column indicate that the amount has been posted to the appropriate subsidiary ledger account. The related general ledger accounts are found in Example 6-9, and the individual customer accounts are in Example 6-10.

EXAMPLE 6-8

CLANECO, INC.
Sales Journal

Page 1

Date	Explanation	Invoice	P.R.	Accts. Rec. Dr. Sales Cr.
Jan. 5	C. D. Adams	1823	✓	4,000
23	J. C. Belski	2425	✓	8,200
Various	All other customers	Various	✓	91,000
Jan. 31	Total			103,200
				(102/601)

CLANECO, INC.
Cash Receipts Journal

Page 1

Date	Explanation	P.R.	Cash Dr.	Accts. Rec. Cr.	Other Credits
Jan. 12	C. D. Adams	✓	1,000	1,000	
13	J. C. Belski	✓	4,200	4,200	
Various	All other customers		52,100	52,100	
Various	Other cash receipts		3,000		Various Accounts 3,000
Jan. 31	Totals		60,300	57,300	3,000
			(101)	(102)	

EXAMPLE 6-9

CLANECO, INC.
General Ledger Accounts
Cash

Acct. No. 101

Date		Ref.	Dr.	Cr.	Balance
	Balance Forward				59,000
Jan. 31		CR1	60,300		119,300

Accounts Receivable

Acct. No. 102

Date		Ref.	Dr.	Cr.	Balance
	Balance Forward				80,000
Jan. 31		S1	103,200		183,200
31		CR1		57,300	125,900

Sales

Acct. No. 601

Date		Ref.	Dr.	Cr.	Balance
Jan. 31		S1		103,200	103,200

EXAMPLE 6-10

Customers' Ledger Accounts

C. D. Adams

Date	Explanation or Invoice Number	Ref.	Sales	Payments Received	Balance Owed
Jan. 1	Balance owed				1,000
5	1823	S1	4,000		5,000
12		CR1		1,000	4,000

J. C. Belski

Jan. 1	Balance owed				4,200
13		CR1		4,200	–0–
23	2425	S1	8,200		8,200

All Other Customers

Jan. 1	Balance owed				74,800
—	Various	S1	91,000		165,800
—		CR1		52,100	113,700

Trial Balance of Customers' Accounts January 31

C. D. Adams	$ 4,000
J. C. Belski	8,200
All other customers	113,700
Total (equals the balance in Accounts Receivable)	$125,900

January began with a balance of $80,000 in accounts receivable. The Customers' Ledger in Example 6-10 shows that C. D. Adams owed $1,000, J. C. Belski owed $4,200, and all other customers owed $74,800. Looking at Adams's account we note the following: a sale of $4,000 recorded on January 5 (sales journal) increased his balance owed to $5,000. On January 12, Adams made a cash payment of $1,000 (cash receipts journal), reducing his balance to $4,000. The student will be helped by tracing through the other sales and cash receipts transactions. The net effect of January accounting is revealed in the trial balance of customers' accounts in Example 6-10. The sum of the balances owed by individual customers equals the balance in the accounts receivable account in the general ledger. This equality gives assurance that all transactions affecting customers have been recorded both in the general ledger account and in the customers' ledger.

LIMITATIONS OF MANUAL DATA PROCESSING

Human data processors, while highly versatile, are severely limited in their ability to process data at high speeds and with great accuracy. Speed is a function of mental and physical processes. A human's top speed in writing legibly is perhaps 40 to 50 words per minute. When copying material from a source document, a human is slowed somewhat by the mental process of reading the data. Arithmetic operations are notoriously slow when carried out "in one's head." Human beings' record in accuracy is extremely bad. They cannot remember data or instructions stored in their brains beyond a very short time. Even in short time spans they may mix up the sequence of numbers. They lack ability to concentrate on their work and to follow directions explicitly and unvaryingly. In short, human beings unaided are ineffective and inefficient in data processing.

Humans have been successful, however, in developing data processing aids that greatly amplify their limited abilities. The journals and ledgers discussed above are examples of effective tools. Ingenious arrangements of several documents separated by carbon paper have been accomplished on a device called the *pegboard*. On the pegboard, an accounting transaction need be written only *once* to accomplish two or three separate accounting operations. Mechanical and electronic accounting machines combine the capabilities of a typewriter and printing electronic calculators to give business an effective means for handling medium volumes of transactions. But the big data processing leap forward has come with the electronic computer and electronic data processing (EDP).

ELECTRONIC DATA PROCESSING (EDP)

Advantages of computer

EDP can help accountants accomplish much of the routine accounting work of an organization with speed and great accuracy. Substituting the computer for human effort has brought about substantial savings in time for many organizations, giving accountants more opportunity to improve the reports they give to managers, and to consider new approaches to accounting data analysis that may develop new useful information.

The heart of the EDP system is the digital electronic computer. Physically, the computer consists of large numbers of electronic circuits designed and organized to provide for the storage, movement, and computation of data under the direction of a program of instructions. The term *digital* refers to the representation of all data and instructions within the computer by numbers.

Computer defined

Computers come in all sizes—large, medium, small, mini, and micro. There is a computer or combination of computers to fit virtually any enterprise. Large companies with heavy demands for data processing probably require large computers. The small business may well find that the mini computer with appropriate printing devices can serve its accounting needs. The mini computer and the small computer are now economically feasible for many small businesses.

Computer Organization and Operation

The computer is organized into several functional parts. The central processing unit (CPU) has two sections: (1) a *control section* that interprets and executes (or causes some other part to execute) instructions and directs the movement of data and (2) an *arithmetic/logic section* that performs arithmetic and logical functions. The *memory* unit holds the instructions and data during processing. We need to communicate with the computer, and we want the computer to communicate with us. Communication is accomplished by input/output devices such as a card reader for inputting data and instructions into the computer and a printer for printing out the results of computer processing. A schematic showing the input/output units and the parts of the computer is given in Figure 6-3.

Input/output

The arrows in Figure 6-3 indicate the flows that occur from input to final output. First, a program of instructions on punched cards or magnetic tape must be inputted into the computer, because the computer can do only what it is programmed to do. Computers understand only *machine language,* codes given in zeros and ones. Because programming in machine language is difficult, most programs today are written in a *programming language.* A programming language is oriented to the user, not to the computer. FORTRAN (an acronym for FORmula TRANslation) is a language using mathematical notation. COBOL (an acronym for COmmon Business Oriented Language) is a language designed for accounting and other business applications. A program in a programming language, say COBOL, is converted by another program, called a compiler, into machine language. Programming languages have proved to be a

Program

Programming languages

Part II   Processing Accounting Data

FIGURE 6-3   Schematic of Computer and Input/Output

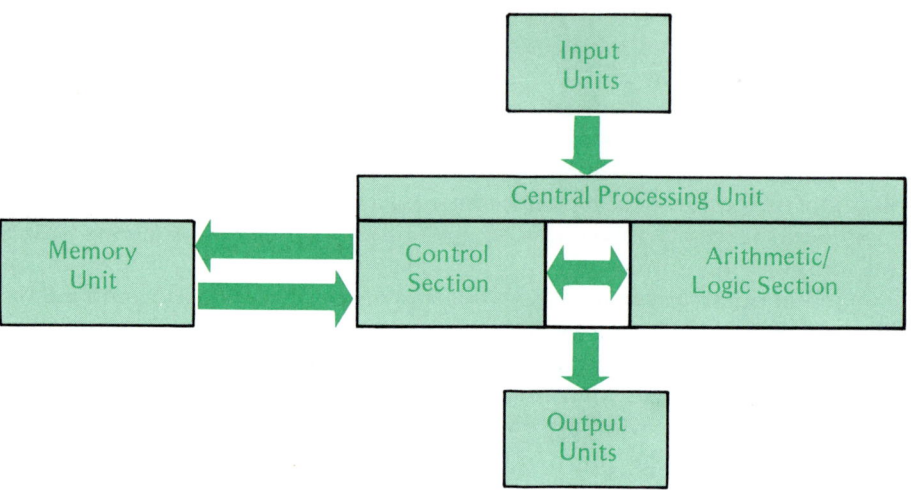

great boon to computer users, since they can be written without a knowledge of the machine language.

Data records from input

Processing results to output

The control section moves the program to locations in memory, then proceeds to interpret and execute each instruction, one at a time. For typical accounting applications, the control section (under the direction of the program) moves a *record* from an input unit into memory locations; moves data from the record in memory to the arithmetic/logic section, where required operations are performed; and moves the results of the operations back into memory. When all operations called for have been performed, the program instructs the control section to move the results from memory to an appropriate output unit. For many applications, the output unit is a printer for producing documents such as an invoice, a paycheck, or a report for management. The program then instructs the control section to bring in the second data record for a repeat of all operations called for by the program.

Typical Applications

Master file

In typical accounting applications of EDP, *master files* are *updated* using data in *"transaction files."* A master file is analogous to a ledger. The general ledger of a company contains a record of each balance sheet account and income statement account used by the company. The inventory ledger contains a record of each item kept in the inventory. Similarly a master file contains records, one record for each subject. Each record in the master file includes the more or less permanent characteristics of the subject and the current status of the subject. For example, the accounts receivable master file contains a record of each credit customer. Each customer record may show the customer's name and address, special identification number, credit limit, balance owed at the beginning of the period, purchase transactions of the period, payment transactions of the period, and resulting balance owed.

The transaction file is analogous to a special journal. A transaction file contains one record for each transaction of a particular type. For example, the credit sale transaction file contains a record of each credit sale made during a certain time period, perhaps one day. The data in transaction files are used to update the master files. The term *update* means to bring the records in the master file up-to-date. In accounting parlance, updating means to post the transactions in the transaction file to the records in the master file. *Transaction file*

Before a file can be used by the computer, it must be in a form recognizable by the computer, such as punched cards or magnetic tape. In accounting applications, transaction files are frequently on punched cards, while master files are on magnetic tape. The records in a master file are kept in a specific order; for example, customer records might be organized according to customer account number. To facilitate processing, transaction file records should be in the same order as the records in the master file. Thus, a sorting operation may be called for to put the transaction file in the same order as the master file before updating of master files can begin.

To get an idea of how an EDP system works, consider the accounting problem of updating the inventory master file with the purchases made yesterday. For this illustration, the purchase transaction file is on punched cards and the inventory master file is on magnetic tape. Thus, two input units are used: a card reader and a magnetic tape drive. We assume that the purchase invoices of yesterday have been sorted so that the inventory items are in the same order as the inventory records in the inventory master file. The desired output in this illustration is (1) an updated inventory master file on magnetic tape and (2) a printed (hard-copy) purchase journal. Thus, two output units are needed: a printer and a magnetic tape drive. *Illustration*

The purchase transaction file is created by keypunching the data from the purchase invoices, which have been carefully edited to detect any errors in the data. After punching, the cards are verified to detect and correct any keypunch errors. After correcting any errors, data processing proceeds as follows:

The program for updating the inventory master file is inputted to the computer in order to store it in computer memory. The purchase transaction file is loaded on the card reader, and the inventory master file is mounted on the input tape drive. Under the direction of the program, the computer reads the first record in the transaction file and moves the data therein to memory, then reads the first record in the inventory file and moves that record to memory. Then the program has the computer compare the two records. If there is no transaction for the first inventory record, the computer is instructed to copy the inventory record on a magnetic tape mounted on an output tape drive. This output tape then becomes the updated inventory master file. If there is a purchase transaction for the first inventory item, the computer is instructed to add the amount of the purchase to the inventory balance. At this point, the program directs the computer to copy the updated inventory record on the updated inventory master file, which is on the output magnetic tape drive, and to print the first transaction in the purchase journal, which is located in the printer. We have gone through one cycle of the program and have completed processing the first transaction. The program then directs the computer to repeat the cycle with the second transaction record. This process is continued until all transactions are processed.

The above illustration is limited to the bare bones of inventory updating. The program may also provide for various listings from the master file. For example, the purchasing manager may want a listing of all inventory items that are equal to or below a certain inventory balance so that these items can be ordered.

On-Line Data Processing

Batch

On-line

Most computer processing is *batch* processing. Similar transaction data are accumulated in groups, or batches, and processed as a unit. In *on-line* processing, the user is in direct contact with the computer via a terminal employing a teletypewriter or a typewriter combined with a cathode ray tube display. This type of data processing is invaluable in situations requiring continuous or near continuous updating of files and in situations requiring a quick feedback of information. Several examples will illustrate.

Examples of on-line systems

Most airlines employ on-line systems that give the airline representative immediate information on reservation requests. The system continuously updates the inventory balance of seats on specific airline flights.

In the banking industry, automatic tellers accept deposits, give withdrawals, and continuously update the customers' accounts. The systems may also handle loan payments.

In the retail industry, *point of sale* terminals with optical scanning devices are being introduced. As the customer goes through a check stand, the optical scanner reads product codes from packages. The computer, on-line with the scanner and cash register, looks up the product code and its price and causes the cash register to record the price. The customer sees what the price is and receives a cash register tape. This point of sale system is expected to speed up the check-out function and to provide a continuous update of sales, inventory, and cash records.

Implications of the Computer for Accounting

Traditionally, the company accountant has been concerned with the development of accounting policies and with the means to accumulate the accounting data and to translate data into accounting reports and business documents. The accountant also has been involved with paperwork essential to the safeguarding of assets against wrongful conversion, such as theft, and the safeguarding of the accuracy of accounting data. The work of the accountant in carrying out these responsibilities consists chiefly of supervising and advising subordinates.

Accountant's responsibility

The introduction of data processing equipment does not change the accountant's responsibilities; they remain the same and continue to determine the accountant's work. However, the computer's capabilities show promise of changing the emphasis of that work. Less attention will be paid to supervising bookkeeping clerks, because their functions can largely be taken over by the computer. Some manual checking will be essential, but it will not require the number of clerks once considered necessary. The accountant can place more emphasis on helping computer specialists devise more efficient computer systems and programs for accomplishing the routine aspects of accounting. In addition, the accountant can use the computer to develop new kinds of information from accounting data.

The computer enables the firm to analyze data to a depth of detail not formerly possible. Mathematical models such as linear programming provide the methods for analyzing data, much of which represent physical quantities rather than financial. Accounting data can be used as inputs to inventory models and to financial planning models that provide information to managers for gaining better control over the enterprise.

Mathematical models

What does the computer imply for accountants? First, accountants must learn how to use the computer in carrying out their responsibilities. They should be able to work closely with computer specialists in devising systems and programs that will do routine accounting work efficiently. Second, they should learn how analytical techniques such as statistics and linear programming can be used to solve management problems. This should enable accountants to identify the data requirements of these techniques and to devise systems for collecting the appropriate data. Third, accountants and system analysts should advise managers on the broad range of information—from routine reports to quantitative analyses —they should expect from the computer.

SUMMARY

Accounting data can be processed in a variety of ways. Manual processing makes use of the multi-columnar journal or an array of special journals (such as sales, purchases, cash receipts, and cash payments journals), combined with subsidiary ledgers. Manual data processing has strict limitations because of the low speed and inaccuracy of the human data processor. In recent years, humans have overcome their inherent deficiencies in data processing by employing electronic data processing (EDP).

In the typical EDP system, raw data from source documents are converted to punched card form for computer input. The punched cards constitute a transaction file. Under the direction of a computer program, data from the transaction file are combined with data in master files to update master files. After the master file is updated, the computer is instructed to print out a variety of usable outputs, including a listing of all the transactions (a journal) and pertinent reports for managers.

The accountant's responsibility in connection with EDP includes analyzing the firm's needs for accounting information and working with computer specialists to determine the most effective and economical way to satisfy management's need for information. This is one of the most challenging and interesting aspects of accounting.

IMPORTANT TERMS

Data processing
Data inputs
Data manipulation
Information outputs
Multi-columnar journal
Specialized journals
Sales journal
Purchases journal
Cash receipts journal
Cash payments journal

Subsidiary ledger
Control account
Electronic data processing
Computers
Computer program
Batch processing
On-line processing
Master files
Transaction files

QUESTIONS

6-1. Why do large companies require so many written reports?

6-2. What is *relevant information?* Give an example.

6-3. What is *timely information?* Give an example.

6-4. What is a *source document?* What function does a source document perform? What determines the kinds of data recorded on source documents?

6-5. The Ranwell Retail Company operates a large store with two sales departments in a large city. About 80% of its sales are made on open account and 20% are cash sales. All of its merchandise purchases are on account from about 30 different suppliers. The store has about 2,000 credit customers whom it serves each month. What journals would you recommend for this firm? What money columns would you provide in each of these journals? Be sure to indicate debit or credit designation of the columns.

6-6. What advantages does a computerized system have over the manual processing of data? Do you see any disadvantages?

6-7. "The use of computers has eliminated concern for accuracy, since computers don't make mistakes." Comment on this statement.

6-8. Distinguish batch processing from on-line processing.

6-9. "The computer will probably replace accountants in the not-too-distant future." Comment on this statement.

6-10. Are the problems connected with establishing a computer system different from those involved in a less sophisticated system? Discuss.

EXERCISES

6-11. *Specialized journals—choosing the journal to use.* Handy Dandy Company uses a one-column sales journal, a one-column purchases journal, a cash receipts journal, a cash disbursements journal, and a general journal in recording its transactions. Indicate in which journal (or journals) each of the following transactions would be recorded.
   a. Sold merchandise on credit.
   b. Sold merchandise for cash.
   c. Purchased merchandise for cash.
   d. Purchased merchandise on account.
   e. Customer returned merchandise previously sold to him on credit.
   f. Purchased store supplies on account.
   g. Received cash on account.
   h. Paid cash on account.
   i. Paid the sales salaries.
   j. Recorded the end-of-the-period adjusting entries.

6-12. *Control account and subsidiary ledger.* Wells, Inc., posts its customers' accounts directly from sales invoices. Each day's total credit sales are entered in the sales journal on one line. Cash collections on account are handled similarly. The customers' accounts are posted directly from cash receipt forms, while the day's total collections on account are recorded on one line in the cash receipts journal.

   Required:
   Assuming manual bookkeeping procedures, give your recommendations for procedures that would assure Wells, Inc., that the customers' ledger is always in agreement with the accounts receivable control account.

6-13. *Cash payments journal.* Below are some of the transactions of the Folwell Company for January.

Jan. 1   Paid $6,000 to the Dibble Company on account.
Jan. 12   Paid the bank $8,320 in payment of a note payable due today. The principal amount of the note was $8,000.
Jan. 13   Paid Realtors' Service, Inc., $3,000 for the current month's rent.
Jan. 19   Paid $2,000 for a shipment of merchandise from the Wallspot Company.
Jan. 20   Paid the Magazine Subscribers' Service $200 for three-year subscriptions to several trade and business magazines.
Jan. 22   Paid $6,860 to Frank Co. on a $7,000 purchase made Jan. 12, which had terms of 2/10, n/30.
Jan. 29   Paid $9,000 to the Getchell Company on account.

Required:

a. Set up a cash payments journal with money columns for Cash (Credit), Purchase Discounts (Credit), Accounts Payable (Debit), Purchases (Debit), and Sundry (Debit). Also set up general ledger T accounts for Cash, Accounts Payable, Purchases, Purchase Discounts, Notes Payable, Interest Expense, Subscriptions Expense, Rent Expense.

b. Enter the above transactions in the cash payments journal; post from the journal to the general ledger accounts.

6-14. *Cash receipts journal.* Below are some of the transactions of the Drebbin Company for March.

March 1   Issued capital stock for cash, $25,000.
March 2   Sold merchandise for cash, $5,000.
March 3   Collected cash of $12,000 from J. Edwards, a customer, on account.
March 4   Borrowed $5,000 from the bank. The bank accepted Drebbin's 6-month, 8% note.
March 16   Sold marketable securities for cash of $6,000. The securities had cost $6,200 4 months ago.
March 20   Collected $1,960 on account from S. Weiscoff on a $2,000 sale made March 5, with terms of 2/10, n/30.
March 27   Collected cash from B. Jones, a customer, on account, $8,000.

Required:

a. Set up a cash receipts journal that provides money columns for Cash (Debit), Sales Discounts (Debit), Accounts Receivable (Credit), Sales (Credit), and Sundry (Debit and Credit). Also set up general ledger T accounts for Cash, Accounts Receivable, Sales, Sales Discounts, Capital Stock, Notes Payable, Marketable Securities, and Loss on Sale of Assets.

b. Enter the above transactions in the cash receipts journal.

c. Post from the journal to the general ledger accounts.

6-15. *Purchases journal.* Below are some of the transactions of the Durrel Company for February.

Feb. 1   Purchased merchandise on account from Merritt Co., $3,000, terms n/30.
Feb. 3   Ordered merchandise from Waters & Co., cost $5,000.
Feb. 4   Received the merchandise from Waters & Co.

Feb. 5   Purchased office supplies on account from Ajax Co., $800.
Feb. 16   Purchased merchandise on account from Samuels, Inc., $8,000, terms 2/10, n/30.
Feb. 22   Returned merchandise to Samuels, Inc. The merchandise, which cost $600, was defective and could not be sold.
Feb. 27   Purchased office equipment on account from Ajax Co., $3,000.
Feb. 28   All other cash purchases total $23,000.
Feb. 28   All other purchases on account total $61,000.

Required:

a. Draft a purchases journal with one money column and general ledger T accounts for Purchases and Accounts Payable.

b. Which of the above transactions would *not* be entered in the purchases journal? In which journals would these transactions be recorded?

c. Enter all remaining transactions in the purchases journal.

d. Post from the purchases journal to the two general ledger accounts.

6-16. *Sales journal.* Following are some of the transactions of the Criswell Corporation for May.

May 1   Sold merchandise for cash, $300.
May 2   Sold merchandise to I. Fagger on account, $500, terms n/30.
May 3   Sold marketable securities to Belski & Co., a brokerage firm. The securities, which cost $2,120, were sold for $2,500. Belski & Co. will pay for them in June.
May 4   Sold merchandise on account to B. Well, $800, terms 2/10, n/30.
May 5   M. Crabbe, a customer, purchased merchandise for $700 on account.
May 6   Sold an old typewriter to an employee for cash, $50.
May 9-31   All other credit sales of the month totaled $15,000.
May 9-31   All other cash sales of the month totaled $1,200.

Required:

a. Draft a sales journal with one money column, and general ledger T accounts for Accounts Receivable and Sales.

b. Indicate which of the above transactions would *not* be recorded in the sales journal. In which journal would these transactions be recorded?

c. Enter all remaining transactions in the sales journal.

d. Post from the sales journal to the two general ledger accounts.

6-17. *Control account and subsidiary ledger.* Upon completing the manual posting of customers' accounts directly from the sales invoices, Wilma, the bookkeeper, discovers that the total amount of the sales invoices entered in the sales journal does not agree with the total of the debits made to individual customer accounts. You have been asked to assist her to find and correct any errors. The adding machine tapes of the sales invoices in random order and the debits made to customers' accounts in customer alphabetical order are given below.

    Upon checking the sales invoice tape against the sales invoices, you discover that it is correct except that the invoice of Nemitz is actually $505.00 instead of $550.00. All other items on that tape are correct.

Part II   Processing Accounting Data

	Sales Invoices		Debits to Customers' Accounts
Famwell	2 2 3 . 2 2	Adams	2 3 . 4 5
Skagg	2 4 5 . 0 0	Alrik	5 6 . 2 0
Alrik	5 6 . 2 0	Famwell	2 3 2 . 2 2
Tripp	1 2 . 3 8	Herring	4 0 0 . 1 5
Lovett	3 4 5 . 6 8	Lovett	3 4 5 . 6 8
Nemitz	5 5 0 . 0 0	Nemitz	5 0 5 . 0 0
Adams	2 3 . 4 5	Newell	6 5 . 7 8
Newell	5 6 . 7 8	Skagg	2 4 5 . 0 0
Jackson	9 2 . 7 5	Tripp	1 2 . 3 8
Wells	1 2 4 . 5 6	Wells	1 2 4 . 5 6
Herring	4 0 0 . 1 5		2 0 1 0 . 4 2*
	2 1 3 0 . 1 7*		

Required:

a. Identify any errors you can find by comparing the two adding machine tapes.

b. How would you correct the errors that you have discovered? Include any journal entries to be made.

6-18. *Special journal design.* The Evans Company uses a cash payments journal to record its cash payments. Cash payments are primarily payments on account to creditors (70% of all payment transactions) with no discounts available. A number of payments are also made to employees for both sales salaries and office salaries. Income tax and social security taxes are withheld from employees. A number of checks are also written each month for various expenses, such as rent, office supplies, and repairs. It is convenient to provide column totals for as many as 10 columns. Columns must be totaled each day. Approximately 100 checks are written each day.

Required:

a. What columns should be set up in the cash payments journal?
b. How should postings to individual creditor accounts be handled?
c. If columns are totaled every day, how should postings to accounts such as accounts payable and cash be handled?

6-19. *Computer.* Refer to exercise 6-18 and assume that Evans Company uses an electronic computer.

Required:

a. How would cash payments data be inputted into the computer?
b. What uses would be made of computer memory in connection with cash payments?
c. What output would be printed by the computer in connection with cash payments?

6-20. *On-line computers.* A local department store has a cash register that is connected directly with its computer. Sales clerks punch data into the cash register that indicate not only the sales price but also (1) the customer account number in the case of charge sales and (2) a code that describes the items sold and their cost (read from the sales tags). The data on items sold is used not only to compute cost of goods sold but also to keep inventory up to date and to trigger reorders when stock gets low.

What possibilities for error exist in this system? How can errors be minimized?

PROBLEMS

6-21. *Specialized journals, sales and cash receipts—subsidiary ledgers.* The following sales, cash receipts, and other transactions were completed by The Tracy Supply Company during March of the current year:

March 1	Sold merchandise on credit to Alvin, Invoice No. 801, $850, terms 2/10, n/30.
March 3	Sold merchandise on credit to Baker, Invoice No. 802, $1,100, terms 2/10, n/30.
March 5	Baker returned for credit $125 of the merchandise purchased on March 3 because it did not meet specifications.
March 7	Tod Tracy, the principal owner of The Tracy Supply Company, invested an additional $8,500 in the business and received capital stock.
March 10	Received a check from Alvin in full of Invoice No. 801.
March 12	Sold merchandise on credit to Conrad, Invoice No. 803, $720, terms n/30.
March 14	Sold merchandise on credit to Baker, Invoice No. 804, $875, terms n/30.
March 15	Cash sales for the first half of the month were $5,482. (Cash sales are commonly recorded daily from the cash register reading. They are recorded only twice in this problem in order to shorten the problem.)
March 15	(Make the individual postings from the journals. Normally, items that are posted as individual amounts from the journals are posted daily; but since the number of such items in this problem is small, you are asked to post them only on two occasions.)
March 17	Sold merchandise on credit to Damcan, Invoice No. 805, $1,900, terms 2/10, n/30.
March 18	Gave Flatirons National Bank a 60-day, 6% promissory note in order to borrow $1,500.
March 22	Received a check from Conrad in full of Invoice No. 803.
March 24	Sold merchandise on credit to Conrad, Invoice No. 806, $700, terms 2/10, n/30.
March 24	Received a check from Baker in full of Invoice No. 804.
March 25	Issued a credit memorandum to Damcan for $200 of merchandise purchased on March 17 and returned.
March 27	Received a check from Damcan in full of Invoice No. 805, less the return.
March 29	Received a check from Baker in full of Invoice No. 802, less the return.
March 29	Sold merchandise on credit to Damcan, Invoice No. 807, $175.

March 30   Cash sales for the last half of the month were $4,268.
March 31   (Make the individual postings from the journals.)
March 31   (Make the month-end postings from the journals.)

Required:

a. Open general ledger accounts: Cash (1); Accounts Receivable (2); Notes Payable, (3); Capital Stock (4); Sales (5); Sales Returns and Allowances, (6); Sales Discounts (7).

b. Open accounts for customers: Alvin, Baker, Conrad, Damcan.

c. Prepare a sales journal, a cash receipts journal, and a general journal similar to the ones illustrated in this chapter. Enter the transactions in the journals and post to the accounts at the points where you are instructed to do so in the narrative of the transactions.

d. Prepare a month-end trial balance and a schedule of accounts receivable. (Ignore the fact that you have not entered all the transactions of the firm.)

6-22. *Specialized journals, purchases and cash disbursements—subsidiary ledgers.* CB, Inc., completed the following purchases, cash disbursements, and miscellaneous transactions during January of the current year:

Jan. 1   Received merchandise and an invoice dated December 27, from Moore Mfg. Co., $2,050.

Jan. 1   Issued a check in payment of the January rent, $350.

Jan. 3   Received merchandise and an invoice dated January 2, from Sara Wholesale Company, $2,600, terms 2/10, n/30.

Jan. 6   Mailed Moore Mfg. Co. a check in full payment of the invoice dated December 27.

Jan. 9   Received merchandise and an invoice dated January 6 from Bell Sales Company, $3,125.

Jan. 10 Mailed a check to Sara Wholesale Company in full of the invoice dated January 2.

Jan. 11 Received a credit memorandum from Bell Sales Company for $105 of merchandise from the invoice dated January 6 returned for credit.

Jan. 13 Purchased a new office typewriter from Nolan Office Supply, $250.

Jan. 15 Paid the office salaries for the first half of the month, $900.

Jan. 15 (Make the individual posting from the journals. Normally, items posted individually from the journals are posted daily; but since the number of such items is small in this problem, you are asked to post them on only two occasions.)

Jan. 16 Sent Bell Sales Company a check in payment of its invoice of January 6, less the return.

Jan. 17 Issued a check in payment of $200 of advertising expense.

Jan. 19 Received merchandise and an invoice dated January 18 from Sara Wholesale Company, $2,000, terms 2/10, n/30.

Jan. 24 Received merchandise and an invoice dated January 22 from Moore Mfg. Co., $1,500.

Jan. 27 Sent a check to Sara Wholesale Company in full of its invoice of January 18.

Jan. 28 Received a credit memorandum from Moore Mfg. Co. for $310 of the merchandise of their invoice of January 22 returned.

Jan. 31   Paid the office salaries for the last half of the month, $900.
Jan. 31   (Make the individual postings from the journals.)
Jan. 31   (Make the month-end postings from the journals.)

Required:
a. Open general ledger accounts: Cash (1); Office Equipment (2); Accounts Payable (3); Purchases (4); Purchase Returns and Allowances (5); Purchase Discounts (6); Advertising Expense (7); Rent Expense (8); Office Salaries (9).
b. Open accounts payable ledger accounts: Sara Wholesale Company; Nolan Office Supply; Moore Mfg. Co.; Bell Sales Company.
c. Prepare a purchases journal, a cash disbursements journal, and a 2-column general journal similar to the ones illustrated in this chapter. Enter transactions in the journals and post to the accounts at the points where you are instructed to do so in the narrative of the transactions.
d. Prepare a month-end trial balance and a schedule of accounts payable. (Ignore the fact that you have not entered all the transactions of the firm.) (Solution in Appendix B.)

6-23. *Specialized journals.* Debby's Drug Store makes sales on account and for cash. Sales and purchases are classified by department (drugs and sundries), and a periodic inventory system is used. All disbursements are made by check, and all receipts are deposited daily. Merchandise is purchased daily, employees are paid weekly, and rent is paid monthly. The company uses the following specialized journals: cash receipts journal, cash disbursements journal, sales journal, purchases journal. The store had the following transactions in July:

July 1	Sales on account (all drug sales), $300
	Cash sales, $200 (drug sales $50, sundries $150)
	Collections on accounts receivable, $125
	Payments on accounts payable, $180
	Purchases on account, $600 (drugs $400, sundries $200)
	July's rent, $200, paid in cash
July 2	Sales on account, $450 (drugs, $425, sundries $25)
	Cash sales, $600 (drugs $195, sundries $405)
	Collections on accounts receivable, $58
	Payments on accounts payable, $60
	Purchases on account, $400 (drugs $300, sundries $100)
	Supplies purchased for cash, $65
July 3-4-5	Store closed for holiday
July 6	Sales on account, $600 (drugs $250, sundries $350)
	Cash sales, $1,000 (drugs $300, sundries $700)
	Collections on accounts receivable, $55
	Payments on accounts payable, $105
	Cash purchases, $425 (drugs $125; sundries, $300)
	Purchases on account, $700 (all drugs)
	Interest paid, $27 (previously recorded as a liability)
July 7	Sales on account, $345 (all drugs)
	Cash sales, $700 (drugs, $175; sundries, $525)
	Collections on accounts receivable, $400

Payments on accounts payable, $50
Cash purchases, $100 (all sundries)
Equipment purchased for cash, $1,075

Required:

a. Set up the required journals, indicating the money columns required (and whether each column is a debit or credit column) and the information columns required. Use 3-column sales and purchases journals.
b. Record the transactions in the appropriate journals.
c. Add the columns of each of the journals (except the general journal). Assure yourself that the sum of the debit columns equals the sum of the credit columns in each special journal.

6-24. *Specialized journals—recording and posting transactions.* The following transactions were completed by Flatirons Sales Company during the month of February of the current year:

Feb. 2	Paid the rent for the month of February, $500.
Feb. 3	Received merchandise and an invoice dated February 1, from Bowen Manufacturing Company, $3,950.
Feb. 4	Sold merchandise to Fusilier on credit, $2,900. Number all sales invoices beginning with 209.
Feb. 7	Cash sales for first week of February, $2,859.
Feb. 9	Sold merchandise on credit to Rosin, $1,250.
Feb. 10	Sent a check to Bowen Manufacturing Company in full of the invoice of February 1.
Feb. 11	Received merchandise and an invoice dated February 7 from Wasley Mfg. Co., $980.
Feb. 14	Received a check from Fusilier in full of the invoice of February 4.
Feb. 14	Cash sales for the week ended February 14, $2,185.
Feb. 14	(Make the individual postings from the journals. Normally items posted as individual amounts are posted daily, but in order to shorten the problem you are asked to post these items only twice during the month.)
Feb. 16	Sold merchandise on credit to Rosin, $1,850.
Feb. 16	Paid the sales salaries for the first half of February, $842.
Feb. 18	Received merchandise and an invoice dated February 15 from Curry Company, $3,742.
Feb. 19	Received office equipment and an invoice dated February 18, from Frascona Office Supply Company, $284.
Feb. 21	Cash sales for the week ended February 21, $1,943.
Feb. 22	Received merchandise and an invoice dated February 18 from Bowen Mfg. Co., $1,524.
Feb. 23	Received a credit memorandum from Curry Company for merchandise of its invoice of February 15 returned because it did not meet specifications, $295.
Feb. 24	Sent a check to Curry Company in full of the invoice of February 15, less the return.
Feb. 25	Sold merchandise on credit to Fusilier, $2,480.

Feb. 27   Borrowed $5,000 from Boulder National Bank by giving a 60-day, 6% promissory note.
Feb. 27   Issued a credit memorandum to Fusilier for defective merchandise purchased on February 25 and returned, $480.
Feb. 28   Paid the sales salaries for the last half of the month, $840.
Feb. 28   Cash sales for the week ended February 28, $2,482.
Feb. 28   (Make the individual postings from the journals.)
Feb. 28   (Total and make the month-end postings from the journals.)

Required:
a. Open the following general ledger accounts: Cash (1); Accounts Receivable (2); Office Equipment (3); Notes Payable (4); Accounts Payable (5); Sales (6); Sales Returns and Allowances (7); Purchases (8); Rent Expense (9); Sales Salaries Expense (10); Purchase Returns and Allowances (11).
b. Open the following accounts receivable subsidiary ledger accounts: Fusilier; Rosin.
c. Open the following accounts payable subsidiary ledger accounts: Frascona Office Supply Company; Wasley Manufacturing Company; Bowen Manufacturing Company; Curry Company.
d. Set up forms for a sales journal, purchases journal, cash receipts journal, cash disbursements journal, and general journal.
e. Enter the transactions in the journals and post from the journals to the general and subsidiary ledgers as indicated in the narrative of transactions.
f. Prepare a trial balance of the general ledger and schedules of the accounts receivable ledger and the accounts payable ledger.

6-25. *Posting special journals.* Below are the special journals of the Welldrop Retailing Company.

Sales Journal
p.101

Account	PR	Amount
Customer A		2,000
Customer B		3,200
Customer C		2,500
		7,700

Purchases Journal
p.105

Account	PR	Amount
Company X		1,200
Company Y		1,100
Company Z		2,200
		4,500

General Journal
p.243

Accounts	PR	Debit	Credit
Accounts payable—Co. Z		200	
Purchases returns			200

Cash Receipts Journal

p.642

Accounts	PR	Sundry	Accts. rec.	Sales	Cash
Notes payable		5,000			5,000
Customer A			2,000		2,000
Capital stock		3,000			3,000
Customer C			1,000		1,000
Cash sales				2,500	2,500
		8,000	3,000	2,500	13,500

Cash Disbursements Journal

p.973

Accounts	PR	Sundry	Accts. Pay.	Cash
Company X			1,200	1,200
Supplies expense		150		150
Company Y			1,100	1,100
Salaries expense		600		600
		750	2,300	3,050

Required:

a. Draw T accounts for the following general ledger accounts:

Number	Account Title	Number	Account Title
1	Cash	35	Purchases
2	Accounts Receivable	37	Purchase Returns
11	Notes Payable	40	Salaries Expense
12	Accounts Payable	48	Supplies Expense
20	Capital Stock		
30	Sales		

b. Post from the journals to the general ledger accounts you have drawn in *a* above.

c. Draw T accounts for the accounts receivable ledger and for the accounts payable ledger. There are three customers: Customer A, Customer B, and Customer C. There are three creditors: Company X, Company Y, and Company Z.

d. Post from the journals (as required) to the subsidiary ledger accounts which you have drawn in *c* above.

(Solution in Appendix B.)

6-26. *Comprehensive problem — accounting cycle with worksheet.* The Argus Appliance Shop sells and services various appliances. Sales are made on account and for cash. Sales are classified into two categories: Sales of Merchandise and Services Revenue. The cost of goods sold is computed following a periodic inventory taken monthly. Purchases are made on account as merchandise and supplies are needed (several times a week). There are six employees, and they are paid weekly. All disbursements of cash are by check. All cash receipts are deposited intact daily. Rent is paid monthly. The company uses the following journals:

Purchases journal (columns: Accounts Payable, Supplies on Hand, Purchases)
Sales journal (three columns)
Cash receipts journal (columns: Cash, Accounts Receivable, Merchandise Sales, Service Revenue)
Cash disbursements journal (columns: Cash, Accounts Payable, Supplies on Hand, Wages)
General journal

The July 1 trial balance was as follows:

	Debit	Credit
Cash in bank	$ 3,000	
Accounts receivable	9,000	
Merchandise inventory	18,000	
Supplies on hand	3,600	
Prepaid rent	900	
Accounts payable		$ 2,200
Capital stock		25,000
Retained earnings		7,300
	$34,500	$34,500

Transactions for July (summarized by weeks) were as follows:

first week:
Sales, merchandise $3,500 (all on account)
Service revenue, $1,000 (all for cash)
Merchandise purchased on account, $5,000
Wages paid, $600

second week:
Sales, merchandise, $4,500 (all on account)
Service revenue, $1,250 (all for cash)
Supplies purchased, $1,000 (for cash)
Collection of accounts receivable, $2,500
Wages paid, $750

third week:
Service revenue, $1,750 (all on account)
Sales, merchandise, $4,000 ($2,500 on account, $1,500 for cash)
Payment of accounts payable, $2,000
Purchase of supplies, $750 (on account)
Payment of wages, $600

fourth week:
Sales, merchandise, $3,800 ($2,000 on account, $1,800 for cash)
Service revenue, $1,500 ($1,275 on account, $225 for cash)
Purchase of merchandise, $2,100 (all on account)
Purchase of supplies, $200 (all for cash)
Collection of accounts receivable, $3,000
Payment of accounts payable, $1,500
Payment of wages, $1,000

Data for Adjustments:
- Accrued wages, July 31, $900
- Merchandise inventory, $19,600
- Supplies inventory, $3,000
- Prepaid rent, $400

Required:
a. Set up general ledger accounts with the beginning balances obtained from the July 1 trial balance.
b. Record the transactions for July in the journals.
c. Total and prove each journal and post to the ledger.
d. Prepare a worksheet (8 columns are sufficient).
e. Prepare financial statements.
f. Journalize and post adjusting and closing entries.
g. Prepare a post-closing trial balance.

PART III

Measurement of Assets, Liabilities, and Income

7

Asset Valuation Concepts, Cash and Short-Term Receivables, and Revenues

In this and the following three chapters we discuss assets and their valuation and the revenues and expenses related to assets. This chapter begins with a brief discussion of valuation concepts and then concentrates on cash and short-term receivables and their related revenues.

ASSET VALUATION CONCEPTS

Asset valuation is vitally important in accounting. If assets are valued poorly, the balance sheet is not useful. The income statement also suffers, because the amounts of many revenues and expenses are related to the valuation placed on assets. At this point we will discuss some aspects of valuation of assets in accordance with present accounting principles, which are based to a large extent on historical cost. Chapter 15 broadens this discussion, dealing with the problems posed by changing prices and alternative valuation systems that have been suggested. Although the next few chapters emphasize traditional asset valuation, questions will be raised from time to time about the ability of the traditional approaches to reflect economic realities.

Part III   Measurement of Assets, Liabilities, and Income

Assets are those economic resources of an entity that can be measured in dollars, are expected to have future benefits, and are recognized in accordance with accounting principles. The basis for recognition is generally a transaction of the entity together with expectation of some future economic benefit or service potential to the entity. Some economic resources are not recognized because no transaction has occurred or because it is difficult to measure the value of the resource.

Initial valuation

Once an economic resource has been recognized as an asset, the question of valuation becomes important. When assets are initially recognized in a transaction, the transaction price is the basis for initial measurement, or valuation, of the asset. This is relatively straightforward and, as a matter of fact, initial valuation is not usually a problem. In some cases there is a question about whether a transaction has taken place; for example, when the item involved in the transaction can be returned within a period of time without any penalty. In other cases there is a question about the transaction price; for example, when a building is sold in exchange for a piece of land or when merchandise is sold for a note that does not bear the usual market rate of interest. But these types of problems are uncommon, and the initial price can usually be determined relatively easily.

Later valuation

Should the original price continue to be used to value the asset? In general, the answer is yes. But asset valuations should always be examined when statements are prepared at subsequent dates to see whether the valuations still have validity. In particular, the accountant should determine whether the asset has declined in value, whether some of the asset has been used up, or, indeed, whether an asset still exists. If any of these things have happened, the asset valuation should be reduced or eliminated. The chapters that follow deal with a variety of assets and discuss problems of valuation for particular assets.

In chapter 3, we saw that asset valuation was closely related to income determination. To use a simple illustration, the amount at which inventory is recorded will become an expense when that inventory is sold. Similarly, when a sale is made, the amount at which the receivable asset is recorded will also be the amount of sales revenue that is recognized. Thus, errors in asset valuation will lead to errors in revenues and expenses.

TYPES OF ASSETS

Assets can be conveniently divided into two main groups: monetary assets and unexpired costs.

Monetary assets are assets of an enterprise held for their general usefulness.

They consist primarily of cash and claims that will be converted directly into cash (accounts receivable and notes receivable, for example). These assets are held, not for their own sake, but because they are useful in acquiring other assets for production or sale, or because they are useful in meeting obligations of the enterprise as the obligations come due, or because they are a convenient place to invest idle funds.

Monetary assets defined

One of our primary concerns with any asset is valuation. What is the appropriate valuation for monetary assets? To answer this question, we must look at the function of these assets, which is to provide general purchasing power in an enterprise. This implies that monetary assets should be valued at the amount of purchasing power they represent. For cash, which is purchasing power in a pure form, valuation is not difficult; but in the case of most other monetary assets, valuation can present a problem. The valuation problem of each asset is solved in a different way, but in each case the valuation approach can be understood if the general objective is kept in mind: to value the asset at the amount of purchasing power it represents.

Purchasing power

Monetary assets arise from many sources. In the course of normal business operations, there is an inflow of cash and receivables into the enterprise. This inflow is the primary source of monetary assets. A company also may obtain cash and other monetary assets through activities such as borrowing or issuing new shares of stock. Monetary assets are used to finance operations, to pay liabilities, and to acquire other assets. Thus, a study of the sources and uses of monetary assets covers many operations of a company. Some of these operations will be discussed here, and others will be dealt with in a more specific context; for example, chapter 12, "Stockholders' Equity," considers issuance of stock.

Unexpired costs are those assets that will become expenses in future accounting periods. They are assets acquired because of their usefulness to a particular enterprise. Unexpired costs are shown as assets until the time comes to transfer them to the expense category. The successful operation of an enterprise requires a combination of unexpired costs with different characteristics and functions. Some of these assets have usefulness over the short run; others are useful over a long period of time. Enterprises strive for an optimum combination of productive assets of varying characteristics. This optimum combination varies from enterprise to enterprise and is difficult to attain. Regardless of the combination, all unexpired costs are acquired because of their usefulness.

Unexpired costs defined

This chapter is concerned with cash and short-term receivables, which are monetary assets. Chapter 8 considers investments, including both bond investments, which are monetary assets, and investments in other companies, which are indirect investments in productive assets of other enterprises. Chapters 9 and 10 concentrate on two important types of unexpired costs: inventories and plant and equipment.

Part III   Measurement of Assets, Liabilities, and Income

CASH

Cash is the most liquid resource of a business enterprise; that is, it is readily usable in transactions. It consists of coin and currency on hand, amounts on deposit in banks, and checks and money orders received from customers. The checks and money orders are included because they generally will be deposited or cashed in the near future. Any item that cannot be cashed for some time, such as a postdated check, should be excluded from the cash total.

Cash is generally divided into two categories: cash on hand and cash in banks. Most businesses deposit their receipts in a bank and make their disbursements by check; therefore, the amount of cash on hand is nominal, being limited to cash register change or perhaps undeposited receipts for a day's transactions. Even the cash on hand generally consists primarily of checks, rather than coins and currency, since much of the business in this country is carried on through use of checks. In retail establishments, the extensive use of credit cards also tends to reduce the amount of coins and currency on hand.

Control of Cash

Because cash is a liquid asset, it must be carefully controlled. What steps can a business take to make sure that it receives all the cash it should, that only proper disbursements are made, and that cash balances cannot be embezzled?

Control of cash, though more critical than control of other assets because of the liquidity of cash, is based on general concepts of control that apply to all assets. The most obvious general concept is that there should be adequate physical safeguards. Applied to cash, this means that a cash register should be used for retail sales, that access to the register should be limited, that cash received through the mail should be recorded promptly, that cash should be deposited in the bank daily, that disbursements should be made by checks, and that blank checks (and signature plates, if used) should be carefully controlled. Physical safeguards, however, are only one general control device, and they are not adequate in themselves.

The general characteristics of a satisfactory system of internal control include

Internal control characteristics

1. A plan of organization that provides appropriate segregation of functional responsibilities
2. A system of authorization and record procedures that provides reasonable accounting control over assets, liabilities, revenues and expenses

3. Sound practices to be followed in the performance of duties and functions of each of the organizational departments
4. Personnel of a quality commensurate with responsibilities[1]

Let us see how each part of the system applies to control of cash. The first characteristic listed involves appropriate segregation of duties. This means that the person who handles the cash should not keep the accounting records of cash receipts and disbursements. In general, physical custodianship of assets should be separated from record keeping in connection with the assets. Also, insofar as possible, the activities of one person should complement and check the activities of others.

For example:

- Person A checks computations on an invoice (bill) received by the company.
- Person B compares the receiving report with the invoice.
- Person C reviews the previous work and approves the invoice for payment.
- Person D prepares the check.
- Person E signs the check (after reviewing previous work).
- Person F records the payment in the cash disbursements journal.
- Person G posts the entry to the appropriate account in the accounts payable subsidiary ledger.

In a large organization, such a division of duties can be easily accomplished. In a smaller organization, some of the functions may have to be combined in the duties of one person. In such a case, care must be exercised to avoid having one person control the physical handling of an asset or process, the recording of it, and the authorization procedures connected with it. Thus, functions exercised by A, B, and G may be combined, but those of E and F should not be combined.

The second characteristic is an adequate system of authorization and record procedures. Such a system can be implemented as follows: The receiving department makes a report of items received by the company. Before payment is made, an accounts payable clerk compares a copy of this report to invoices received. The manager of the accounts payable department authorizes payment, reviewing all invoices for reasonableness (for example, invoices should represent items that the enterprise would reasonably purchase, and the price should be appropriate).

The sound practices referred to in the third general characteristic include physical safeguards as well as the establishment of routine procedures such as limiting access to cash registers, making sure that cash

---

1. *Auditing Standards and Procedures* (New York: American Institute of Certified Public Accountants 1963), pp. 28–29. See also the discussion of internal control in Statements on Auditing Standards No. 1, AICPA, 1973.

registers stay closed unless change is being made, and asking customers not to send cash through the mail. It is easy to frustrate the workings of a basically sound system by becoming lax in the performance of duties and functions. Two sound practices with respect to people are the rotation of duties and a requirement that vacations be taken. It is also appropriate to have a periodic audit of records and procedures so that there will be added assurance that the system is operating as planned.

Finally, the effectiveness of an internal control system depends on competent personnel. People must operate the system, and if they are not competent the system will break down, no matter how well it is designed. There is no need to hire an Einstein to compare receiving reports to invoices, but the person who does that job must be alert and aware of the possibilities for discrepancies.

An effective control system like the one we have discussed should be used in all areas of business enterprise. Cash control is particularly important because of the liquidity of cash, but other aspects of the business also must be carefully controlled. We need not always examine control systems for particular aspects of a business in detail, because the general characteristics of all control systems are similar. Of course, individual control systems tend to vary according to type of operation, number and training of personnel, and sensitivity of the assets or other items involved.

To summarize, we outline the types of procedures for controlling cash:

Cash control procedures

1. *Cash Receipts*
   a. Record is made of all incoming receipts.
   b. Cash goes to the cashier for deposit.
   c. Record of receipts is used to prepare receipts journal and post to the customers' subsidiary accounts.
   d. All receipts are deposited intact daily.
2. *Cash Balances*
   a. Bank statements are reconciled monthly with cash records.
   b. Change and petty cash funds are counted periodically.
3. *Cash Disbursements*
   a. All disbursements except minor items are made by prenumbered checks.
   b. Minor disbursements are made from a petty cash fund.
   c. Checks are issued only for approved invoices and upon authorization of a responsible official.
   d. Record keeping is separated from the authorization and check-signing functions.
4. *General*
   a. Personnel are of sufficient caliber to perform their tasks competently.
   b. All employees are required to take yearly vacations.
   c. Duties are rotated from time to time.

d. Employees who handle cash or who control disbursements should be bonded. This means the company is insured against defalcation by the employee.

We must emphasize that the above is only a bare outline, and its implementation in a particular enterprise would involve careful study and planning. Some phases of the above outline have not yet been discussed, notably bank reconciliations and petty cash funds. If money is kept on deposit in a bank, the bank will send a monthly statement of the depositor's account and also will return the cancelled checks from the month's transactions. It usually is necessary to examine the bank statement carefully and reconcile the balance shown by the bank with the balance shown on the book records. This reconciliation should be done by someone other than the person who handles cash or writes the checks. A detailed consideration of the techniques of bank reconciliations will be found in the appendix to this chapter.

Petty Cash

A *petty cash fund* is a fund of cash used for making minor disbursements. The purpose of such a fund is to avoid writing checks for small, insignificant expenditures. The fund is entrusted to a particular employee. It is that employee's responsibility to see that all expenditures are properly accounted for, usually by means of slips signed by the person receiving the cash. At any one time the total of cash on hand plus signed receipts should be equal to the fund balance. The fund is established by issuing a check to the petty cashier; the journal entry might be as follows:

		Debit	Credit
Jan. 1	Petty cash fund	100	
	Cash		100
	Check to Mary Sharp to establish petty cash fund.		

No entries are made on the books when disbursements are made from the fund; instead, the petty cashier keeps informal records. When the need arises to replenish the fund, an entry is made to record the various expenses and a check is issued. Following is a sample entry:

		Debit	Credit
Jan. 31	Postage	23.00	
	Office supplies expense	18.00	
	Miscellaneous office expense	14.20	
	Cash		55.20
	To record petty cash expenditures for January, and issuance of check to Mary Sharp to replenish fund.		

Note that the cash account is credited, rather than the petty cash fund account. This is done because the fund itself is to remain at $100, and therefore the petty cash account need not be changed. What the replenishment entry accomplishes is the recording of a whole series of minor transactions in one entry and also the recording of the net outflow of cash that was involved in all those transactions.

ACCOUNTS RECEIVABLE

Accounts receivable appear on the records of a company as a result of sales of goods and services. Receivables are recorded when goods are sent to customers and they are billed for them or when a service has been rendered and the customer is billed for the service. Technically, the receivable should be recorded when title to the goods passes or when the service is rendered. Title to goods usually passes when they are delivered into the hands of the buyer or the buyer's agent; thus, delivery determines title passage. The actual billing and recording procedures of an enterprise should be established in such a way that the accounting entries correspond as closely as possible to the legal technicalities of title passage.

The terms under which goods are shipped, designated **FOB** (free on board), indicate the responsibility for payment of freight and the time at which title passes. Generally, the person who pays the freight has title to goods that are in transit. There are two basic types of **FOB** terms, described as follows:

FOB terms

FOB Shipping Point: Seller pays freight only to the shipping point. This means that any freight cost must be borne by the purchaser, who has title to the goods as soon as they are shipped.

FOB Destination: Seller pays freight to the destination. This means the seller bears the freight cost and will incur a freight out expense. The purchaser will not obtain title to the goods until they arrive at the purchaser's place of business.

Valuation and Bad-debt Provisions

Accounts receivable are valuable assets to an enterprise although they are not useful in themselves. Their value lies in the general purchasing power they provide to the company when they are collected. We value receivables on the basis of the purchasing power that they represent. Unlike the asset cash, of which the entire amount on hand or in the bank is itself purchasing power, the receivables on the records might not all become available as purchasing power. The receivables might be collected in full, but there also might be bad debts, sales returns, sales allowances, and discounts. If any of these items are of significant size, and if there is a reasonably accurate way of estimating them, appropriate provision should be made in the accounts.

The bad debts provision, discussed to some extent in chapter 5, will now be explored further. Most businesses provide for possible bad debt losses, but fewer companies provide for estimated returns, discounts, and allowances. There is no theoretical reason for treating these items differently; the same principles apply. In general, therefore, the following discussion of allowances for doubtful accounts also applies to provisions for returns and allowances.

A provision for estimated bad debts is needed to state the receivables at their purchasing power and also to match expenses and revenues for the period properly. The purposes coincide, and the typical entry for a bad debt provision has a dual effect:

Purpose of bad debts provision

	Debit	Credit
Bad debts expense	XXX	
Allowance for doubtful accounts		XXX

The debit part of the entry accomplishes the proper matching of expenses and revenues, and the credit, made to an account that is deducted from the receivables on the balance sheet, states the accounts receivable at the purchasing power they represent. (It is unlikely that either of the two purposes of the provision will be accomplished in precise terms, for the estimates involved are subject to considerable error.)

Bad debts can be estimated in several different ways. If the primary emphasis is on matching of expenses and revenues, a specific percentage of sales (often net sales made on account) will be determined for the period, with the percentage based on past experience. The resulting figure will be charged (debited) to bad debts expense and credited to the allowance account. If the primary emphasis is on asset valuation, the accounts receivable balance will be analyzed and the allowance for doubtful accounts will be adjusted to the total amount needed. Often a percentage derived from past experience is applied to the outstanding accounts receivable. Sometimes the accounts are analyzed in detail according to the time they have been outstanding, and judgments are made on the collectibility of each age category of accounts. That method is called *aging the accounts*. Regardless of which method is used, the results should be about the same, differing only in the usual variations found in a series of estimates.

Aging

Example 7-1 illustrates the estimating procedure that takes place at

Part III   Measurement of Assets, Liabilities, and Income

the end of an accounting period. Notice the difference between method *a* and methods *b* and *c*.

EXAMPLE 7-1

Bad Debts Estimation

	Debit	Credit
Account balances at end of year:		
Accounts receivable	40,000	
Allowance for doubtful accounts		300
Sales on account	200,000	
Cash sales	100,000	
Total sales		300,000
Sales returns and allowances (on credit sales)	4,000	
Bad debts expense	—0—	

Bad debt estimates:
  a. On the basis of net sales on account
    Percent based on past experience: 1%
    Computation:
      Net sales on account:
        $200,000 - $4,000 = $196,000
      Bad debts expense:
        1% × $196,000 = $1,960

  Entry:

		Debit	Credit
Dec. 31	Bad debts expense	1,960	
	Allowance for doubtful accounts		1,960

  b. On the basis of percent of receivables balance
    Percent based on past experience: 5%
    Computation:
      Total allowance needed:
        5% × $40,000 = $ 2,000
      Bad debts expense:
        Total allowance needed $ 2,000
        Less balance in allowance
          account   300
        Additional amount needed $ 1,700

  Entry:

		Debit	Credit
Dec. 31	Bad debts expense	1,700	
	Allowance for doubtful accounts		1,700

  c. On the basis of aging of accounts
    Age analysis of accounts:

	Amount	Bad Debt Percent	Allowance Needed
Over 90 days	$ 2,000	40	$ 800
60–90 days	3,000	25	750
30–60 days	5,000	5	250
Current	30,000	1	300
Total allowance needed			$ 2,100
Less balance in allowance account			300
Additional amount needed			$ 1,800

Entry:

		Debit	Credit
Dec. 31	Bad debts expense	1,800	
	Allowance for doubtful accounts		1,800

Write-off of Bad Accounts

When an account actually becomes uncollectible, it is written off against the allowance. The allowance is set up to take care of just this type of situation. The following entry is required:

		Debit	Credit
May 3	Allowance for doubtful accounts	200	
	Accounts receivable		200
	To write off account of J. Bird, who is bankrupt		

Presumably, entries of this nature gradually will exhaust the balance in the allowance account. Nobody expects the actual write-offs to equal the allowance exactly, but the amounts should be fairly close. If the bad debt provision is inadequate or too high, the estimating procedure should be revised to take care of the discrepancy.

If an account that has been written off is subsequently collected, the usual entry involves a credit to the allowance account. The customer's account is often put back on the books to indicate the reestablishment of credit. The following entries are made:

Subsequent recovery

		Debit	Credit
July 5	Accounts receivable	200	
	Allowance for doubtful accounts		200
July 5	Cash	200	
	Accounts receivable		200
	To record collection of J. Bird's account, previously written off as uncollectible.		

To be assured that accounts are written off only after appropriate efforts have been made to collect them and to avoid embezzlement, businesses should require that accountants write off receivables only on written authorization by a responsible official of the company.

Credit Terms

As indicated in chapter 4, credit terms are often specified in connection with sales. Terms vary considerably, with credit terms of a particular company tending to follow the general patterns in the industry. At times, discount terms allow purchasers to pay less than the invoice price if they pay cash within a certain period of time. Also, the terms of sale often indicate a date after which the entire amount becomes overdue. The stringency of enforcement of credit terms varies from industry to industry. Definitions of typical credit terms are listed below:

2/10, n/30:	Two percent of invoice price may be deducted if paid within 10 days; total amount is due in 30 days.
2/10, 1/30, n/60:	Two percent of invoice price may be deducted if paid within 10 days; 1% deducted if paid between the eleventh day and the thirtieth day; total amount is due in 60 days.
2/10, E.O.M.:	Two percent of invoice price may be deducted if paid within 10 days after the end of the month.
Net:	Total amount must be paid; no discounts are allowed. The total time allowed for payment will depend on the industry practices if no time is specified.

In most cases, discounts offered are large enough to make prompt payment worthwhile. For example, a 2% discount on purchases of $1,000,000 amounts to $20,000. This saving could make quite a change in the profit picture for a company. Therefore, many businesses make it a matter of policy to take advantage of any discounts. Of course, if you are the selling company, you will generally not be able to predict your customers' behavior; thus you wait until a customer takes a discount before you record it. Discounts are usually given only for cash payments. If there is any other form of settlement—a note, for example—no discount is given. Sales discounts are recorded in a separate account, and total sales discounts are deducted from sales on the income statements. Entries for sales discounts are illustrated in Example 7.2.

Returns and Allowances

Customers occasionally return goods for credit or receive allowances because of damaged or unsatisfactory goods. Instead of reducing sales directly when this occurs, accountants use a separate account for sales returns and allowances. This procedure is followed so that management is provided with specific information about returns and allowances. This information is important, for each return or allowance indicates a sale that has gone awry. Thus, trends in amounts of returns and allowances are usually studied carefully by management. The sales returns and allowances account is deducted from total sales (along with sales discounts) on the income statement in arriving at a figure for net sales.

Example 7-2 illustrates credit terms and allowances.

EXAMPLE 7-2

Burns Company has the following transactions:

June 1 Sells merchandise to Allen Co. for $6,000 on account. Terms 2/10, n/30, FOB destination.
June 2 Pays $300 freight on shipment to Allen.
June 5 Allen Co. returns $400 of goods that are defective.
June 10 Allen Co. pays $2,000 of the account by sending a check for $1,960.
June 28 Receives Allen Co. note for the balance owed.

Entries to record the above transactions follow:

		Debit	Credit
June 1	Accounts receivable (Allen)	6,000	
	Sales		6,000
June 2	Freight out expense	300	
	Cash		300
June 5	Sales returns and allowances	400	
	Accounts receivable (Allen)		400
June 10	Cash	1,960	
	Sales discounts	40	
	Accounts receivable (Allen)		2,000
June 28	Notes receivable	3,600	
	Accounts receivable (Allen)		3,600
	$6,000 - 400 - 2,000 = $3,600		

NOTES RECEIVABLE

Definition

A note is a written promise to pay a definite sum of money on demand or at some fixed or determinable future date. A note differs from an open account in that a note is a more formal debtor-creditor arrangement. A note is a negotiable legal instrument and can be transferred between parties more easily

Part III   Measurement of Assets, Liabilities, and Income

FIGURE 7-1

Note

$ _1200.00_   Fergus Falls, Minnesota, _____July 1_____, 19 _____

Sixty Days

after date, for value received, I promise to pay to the order of FERGUSON MERCHANDISE COMPANY of Fergus Falls, Minnesota

_____Twelve Hundred and 00/100_____ DOLLARS,

payable at this office, with interest at the rate of ___10___ percent a year

from ___July 1___ until ___Aug. 30___, interest payable _at maturity_

Secured by ___100 shares Apex Co. common stock___

                                                        Francis Frame
                                                        55 First Ave.
                                                        Fergus Falls

---

than an account can.[2] Notes receivable arise from a variety of transactions. Sometimes notes are used to settle an open account. At other times, a note is given when money is lent. Banks and other financial institutions deal extensively in notes. Notes can be complicated, sometimes involving more than two parties. We are interested, however, in the simpler, more general, two-party notes. The form of a note is shown in Figure 7-1.

Notes often bear interest. Unless otherwise indicated, this interest is expressed as a yearly percentage of the face amount of the note. Thus, if A gives B a $1,000, 2-month, 9% note, this means that interest is at a yearly rate of 9% on the $1,000. Since two months is 1/6 of a year, the interest is $15 for the period of the note. The general computation of interest is:

Interest formula

$$\text{Principal} \times \text{Rate} \times \text{Time} = \text{Interest}$$

In using this formula for calculation, the rate is expressed in hundredths (e.g., 9% is 9/100), and time is expressed as a fraction of the year or as the number of days over 365 (e.g., 45 days is 45/365).[3]

---

2. Accounts receivable can be sold for cash, however, and some businesses specialize in this sort of financing arrangement.
3. Three hundred sixty days is sometimes used in computing interest as a matter of convenience, even though 365 days is more precise. Banks use 365 days consistently and com-

Asset Valuation Concepts, Cash and Short-Term Receivables, and Revenues Chapter 7

Two-party notes may take several forms. The simplest type is the non-interest-bearing note. In this case, entries in the notes receivable account are simple; they are made for the face of the note[4]—the amount for which the note is written. Example 7-3 illustrates a non-interest-bearing note.

Non-interest bearing note

EXAMPLE 7-3

On September 1, A receives a 2-month, non-interest bearing note for $1,000 on account from B. A makes the following entry:

		Debit	Credit
Sept. 1	Notes receivable	1,000	
	Accounts receivable		1,000
	Two-month note on account from B.		

When the note is paid two months later, the entry is as follows:

		Debit	Credit
Nov. 1	Cash	1,000	
	Notes receivable		1,000
	Payment of note by B.		

Needless to say, most lenders insist on interest on notes that they hold. The interest may be explicit, as in the case of an interest-bearing note, or it may be implicit, as in the case of a non-interest-bearing note that is taken at a discount. The rate of discount must, of course, be agreed upon by the parties involved. Example 7-4 illustrates the non-interest-bearing note taken at a discount.

Discount

EXAMPLE 7-4

C gives D a non-interest-bearing, 2-month note for $1,000 to apply toward C's account receivable on D's books. D accepts the note at a 9% discount, giving C credit for $985. The entry on D's books is as follows:

	Debit	Credit
Notes receivable	1,000	
Accounts receivable—C		985
Interest revenue		15
C's 2-month note accepted on account at a 9% discount.		

In this example, the parties agreed to a 9% rate of discount. The amount is the same as it would be if the note bore interest at a 9% rate.

---

pute a term such as two months as an exact number of days. We use a fraction of a year for simplicity in computation and because businesses often use a fraction of a year when note terms are expressed as a number of months.

4. This is true only if the term of the note is relatively short. For a longer term, note interest must be imputed if no interest rate is stated.

217

The difference is that for the discounted note, the interest is deducted in advance, rather than being paid at the maturity of the note. Two months after giving D the note, C will pay D exactly $1,000. The entry on D's books will be as follows:

Cash	1,000	
Notes receivable		1,000
Received payment on C's note.		

Interest bearing note

In contrast to Example 7-4, Example 7-5 illustrates entries for an interest-bearing note, using a similar 9% rate of interest.

EXAMPLE 7-5

E gives F a 9%, 2-month note for $1,000 to apply toward E's account receivable on F's books. F accepts the note, giving E credit for $1,000. Entry on F's books is as follows:

	Debit	Credit
Notes receivable	1,000	
Accounts receivable-E		1,000
Received E's 2-month 9% note on account.		

When E makes payment at maturity, the following entry is made:

	Debit	Credit
Cash	1,015	
Notes receivable		1,000
Interest revenue		15
Collected principal and interest on E's note due today.		

In examples 7-4 and 7-5 the timing gives rise to a difference in the entries. In the case of an *interest-bearing* note, the interest is paid or collected at maturity and is recorded at that time. In the case of a *discounted note*, the interest is deducted at the time of issuance of the note and is recorded at that time. The effective rate of interest on a discounted note exceeds the stated rate of interest. That is, the interest amount is the same in both examples, but the maker of the note in Example 7-4 pays the $15 interest on a smaller amount of money ($985) because the note is discounted. The effective rate is the rate on the actual amount of money borrowed on credit received.

In making the appropriate entries, it is helpful to recognize *that the notes receivable account is always debited or credited for the face amount of the notes.* Any interest amounts are always put in separate accounts. Only one notes receivable account is used in most businesses. Subsidiary records of individual notes are also maintained so that relationships with various parties can be kept straight.

Maturity Dates and Terms of Notes

Recall that the formula for interest is:

$$\text{Principal} \times \text{Rate} \times \text{Time} = \text{Interest}$$

In order to compute interest, therefore, three factors must be known. The principal of the note and the rate of interest are usually stated in the note itself. The time also may be stated (for example, 2 months, or 60 days), but sometimes it must be computed, as when a note dated May 3 is due on June 20. Parties to notes typically want to know both the number of days of interest and the day the note is due, so that the note can be paid at the appropriate time.

If a note is due in a specified number of months from the date of the note, the due date will be the same date of the month, the specified number of months later. A note dated May 14 with a 3-month term will be due on August 14. For a note due in a specific number of days, the exact number of days must be counted. In counting, either the first day or the last day of the period is not counted. For example, the maturity date of a 90-day note dated May 14 would be computed as follows:

Days remaining in May:	
(31 total days less 14 days to date)	17
Days in June	30
Days in July	31
Sub-total	78
Total days needed	90
Additional days needed in August	12

Maturity date therefore is August 12. (Note that in figuring the remaining days in May, only 17 are counted, from May 15 to May 31 inclusive. May 14 is not counted.) In the procedure illustrated, whole months were added until the last month was reached. The day in the month of maturity was then determined by subtracting the days accumulated from the total needed.

In computing the number of days' interest on a note, it is easy to deal with a note expressed in months by using the fraction of a year. Thus, 5 months would involve 5/12 of a year's interest.[5] When a note is due on a particular day, the exact number of days until maturity must be counted. A note dated May 22 that is due on September 19 has a term of 120 days, computed as follows:

---

5. Banks use the exact numbers of days in computing interest for notes with terms expressed in months.

Days remaining in May:
 (31 total days less 22 days to date) — 9
Days in June — 30
Days in July — 31
Days in August — 31
Days in September — 19
Total days — 120

When all factors (principal, rate, and time) are known, it is easy to compute interest by means of the formula ($PRT = i$). The ways in which these factors are combined in journal entries have already been illustrated.

Accruals

Interest on notes accumulates day by day. When notes originate in one accounting period and mature in another, the daily accrual of interest becomes a factor that must be considered in statement preparation. To reflect revenue earned or expense incurred during a period, adjusting entries for interest must be made. Example 7-6 illustrates the adjusting entries necessary for interest-bearing notes; Example 7-7 shows the entries necessary for non-interest-bearing notes taken (or given) at a discount.

EXAMPLE 7-6

A 60-day, 9% note for $2,000 is received from a customer on November 20 to apply toward the customer's account. The entry on that date is as follows:

		Debit	Credit
Nov. 20	Notes receivable	2,000	
	Accounts receivable		2,000
	Received 60-day 9% note on account.		

If the fiscal year ends on December 31, an adjusting entry must be made to record interest earned on the note since November 20, even though no interest will be collected until the note becomes due on January 19. Since the note has been held for 41 days (10 days in November and 31 days in December), the company has earned interest for 41 days. The accumulated interest is recorded as follows:

		Debit	Credit
Dec. 31	Interest receivable	20.22	
	Interest revenue		20.22
	41 days' interest accrued on note of November 20.		

Compute the interest to see if you arrive at the same figure. When the note is finally collected on January 19, the following entry will be made:

		Debit	Credit
Jan. 19	Cash	2,029.59	
	Interest receivable		20.22
	Interest revenue		9.37
	Notes receivable		2,000.00
	Collection of November 20 note. Interest is $2000 × 9% × 60/365.		

In this entry, only $9.37 of interest is recorded as revenue. This amount covers the period of January 1 to January 19 and represents interest earned in the new fiscal period. Interest for the preceding 41 days already has been recorded as a receivable. When it is collected in January, there is no reason to record it as interest revenue again.

EXAMPLE 7-7

A 60-day, non-interest-bearing note is received from a customer on November 20, at a 9% discount. The entry on November 20 is as follows:

		Debit	Credit
Nov. 20	Notes receivable	2,000.00	
	Accounts receivable		1,970.41
	Interest revenue		29.59
	Received note at a 9% discount.		

The customer is given credit for only $1,970.41 (the face of the note less 9% for 60 days). On December 31, the end of the fiscal year, the company must recognize that not all of the $29.59 recorded as interest revenue has been earned. Only 41 days have passed, so only $20.22 has been earned. The other $9.37, applicable to the remaining 19 days, must be deferred until the next period, since it is in the next year that this portion of interest actually will be earned. The following adjusting entry is needed on December 31:

		Debit	Credit
Dec. 31	Interest revenue	9.37	
	Unearned interest		9.37
	To record 19 days' interest unearned.		

The unearned interest, which is a current liability, will be recorded when earned in the next year, perhaps when the note is collected. The entries on January 19 will then be:

		Debit	Credit
Jan. 19	Cash	2,000	
	Notes receivable		2,000
	Collection of note.		
Jan. 19	Unearned interest	9.37	
	Interest revenue		9.37
	To record 19 days' interest earned in the year.		

The entries on January 19 are somewhat awkward. The awkwardness can be partially avoided by crediting unearned interest, instead of interest revenue, for the $29.59 in the original entry on November 20. The adjusting entry on December 31 then becomes:

Dec. 31	Unearned interest	20.22	
	Interest revenue		20.22
	To record 41 days' interest earned.		

In the next period, the company must again make sure that the remaining interest revenue is recorded, but this procedure will be automatic, since all unearned interest amounts must be adjusted in order to reflect interest earned.

Discounting of an Interest-Bearing Note

At times, the holder of an interest-bearing note will use it to obtain funds. In this case, the holder endorses the note to a bank or other party in return for cash (or possibly credit on account). If the other party is satisfied with the rate of interest on the note, he or she will take the note over at its face amount and pay the holder for interest earned during the time the note was held. Example 7–8 illustrates this situation.

EXAMPLE 7-8

H holds G's 60-day, 6%, $3,000 note dated November 20. On December 10, H endorses the note to the bank, receiving cash for the face amount of the note plus interest earned from November 20 to December 10 ($9.86). The entry on H's book is as follows:

		Debit	Credit
Dec. 10	Cash	3,009.86	
	Notes receivable		3,000.00
	Interest revenue		9.86
	Discounted G's note at the bank.		

The bank will collect the note from G at maturity, plus total interest of $29.59 ($3,000 at 6% for 60 days). The interest collected, less the $9.86 paid to H, determines the amount that the bank earns ($19.73 for the 40 days it held the note).

At times, the third party will apply a different rate of interest from that stated on the note and take the note at a discount. For example, the bank in Example 7-8 may require 10% interest instead of 6%. Thus, the bank takes the note at a 10% discount. The complicated computation of the proceeds of such a transaction can be simplified by following a definite procedure. The salient points of the computation are that *the discount rate is always applied to the maturity value of the note* (face of the note plus interest to maturity) and that *the discount covers the period from date of discount to maturity date.* Consider Example 7-9.

EXAMPLE 7-9

K holds J's 60-day, 6%, $3,000 note dated November 20. On December 10, K discounts the note at the bank at 10%, receiving cash for the proceeds. The computation is as follows (with each step numbered):

1. Maturity value:
   $3,000 face + 29.59 interest (60 days at 6%) = $3,029.59
2. Maturity date:
   Days remaining in November:
       (30 total days less 20 days to date)   10
   Days in December   31
     Subtotal   41
   Total days needed   60
   Additional days needed in January   19
       Maturity date is January 19.
3. Days to run (discount period):
   Days in December:
       (31 total days less 10 days to date
         of discount)   21
   Days in January   19
       Total days   40
4. Discount:
   (Maturity value × Discount period ×
     Discount rate)
   $3,029.59 × 40/365 × 10/100   =   33.20
5. Proceeds:
   (Maturity value − Discount)
   $3,029.59 − 33.20   = $2,996.39

The necessary entry on K's books is as follows:

		Debit	Credit
Dec. 10	Cash	2,996.39	
	Interest expense	3.61	
	Notes receivable		3,000.00
	J's note discounted at 10%.		

An entry like the one in Example 7-9 is formed by debiting cash for the proceeds, crediting notes receivable for the face amount of the note, and debiting interest expense or crediting interest revenue for the amount needed to balance the entry. In the illustration, there was a debit to interest expense because the discount taken by the bank exceeded the total interest on the note to maturity; thus K was unable to keep any of the interest earned by holding the note for the first 20 days. K actually came out short on the entire arrangement and thus recorded some interest expense.

When K endorses a note to another party, K retains some liability on the note. If the maker of the note, J, does not pay at maturity, K must do so. This liability is thus contingent on the actions of the maker (in this case, J). It is not an actual liability until J refuses to pay. This type of liability is expressed on the financial statements in a note explaining the nature and amount (if known) of the contingent liability. The following is an example of such a note, using the note described in Example 7-9.

K COMPANY
December 31
Notes to Financial Statements

The Company is contingently liable on $3,000 of notes receivable discounted with banks.

REVENUE REALIZATION

The inflow of cash or receivables to an enterprise is often the result of sale of goods or services to the customers. Sales of goods are recorded when title passes to customers. This event meets the criteria of the realization principle, which requires (a) that a transaction take place and (b) that the earning process be complete or virtually complete. When goods are delivered, the earning process is virtually complete and there is strong evidence that a transaction has been consummated.

A sale that has been recorded as revenue may subsequently go awry because of returns or allowances or an uncollectible account. These events are somewhat unusual, and the change in revenue can easily be handled by deducting returns and allowances from the sales and recognizing uncollectibles as an expense (or even as a direct reduction of sales revenue). Sales discounts, which are an adjustment of the original sales price, are also deducted from sales revenue to arrive at net sales on the income statement as follows:

X COMPANY
Partial Income Statement

Sales			$360,000
Less: Sales returns and allowances		$11,000	
Sales discounts		5,200	16,200
Net sales			$343,800

When an enterprise sells services to customers, it is generally agreed that revenue ought to be recognized when the service is rendered. At this point the earning process is completed (at least to the extent of the portion of services rendered), and a transaction has taken place in that service has been rendered and accepted by the customer. Thus, an electric utility company will bill a customer at the end of a month or other convenient time interval for service rendered and will also recognize revenue at that time by making the following entry:

		Debit	Credit
May 31	Accounts receivable	30	
	Revenue from electricity sales		30
	Service to Jones for May.		

The telephone company, which bills for basic service one month in advance, should not recognize revenue at the time it is billed because revenue has not been earned.

Some types of revenue are earned with the passage of time. This is true of interest, which accumulates day by day. Interest is only recorded when it is collected, unless financial statements are prepared at an earlier date. If statements must be prepared before interest is collected, an adjusting entry is made to record accrued (accumulated) interest up to the date of the statements.

SALES CONTROLS

Before we leave the subject of revenues, some aspects of control deserve our attention. We will discuss sales controls, as an example. The control principles and ideas for sales can be adapted to other areas, for the principles of control are the same in all areas; only the applications differ.

Organizations, both public and private, find it necessary not only to record their sales correctly, but also to have effective controls of the sales function. Effective controls usually involve a system of authorizations and procedures that assure the following:

1. Sales orders are processed promptly.
2. All goods shipped are billed to customers.
3. Customers are billed promptly for goods shipped.
4. Credit ratings of customers and credit terms are checked carefully.

The control system can be simple in a small organization, but it may be very complex indeed in a large company. When the owner or manager is separated from the day-to-day operations, elaborate controls and checks must be substituted for his or her personal supervision. Elaborate control systems for sales can be constructed. A fairly elaborate internal control system for sales might include the following steps:

1. Sales orders arrive from customers.
   a. Sales department checks prices and credit terms, gives preliminary approval, and prepares prenumbered sales invoices in five copies.

b. Credit department reviews invoice and approves credit for customer.
c. Shipping department prepares and sends shipment after credit is approved. Shipping report is sent to accounting and sales.
d. Accounting department checks multiplication and totals and records sale in sales journal on basis of copy of sales invoice and shipping report.
e. Accounts receivable clerk posts to subsidiary ledger on basis of copy of sales invoice.

2. Cash is received from customers.
    a. Receipts are recorded by customer and amount as mail is opened. Checks are routed to cashier's department. Copy of remittance list is sent to accounting. Cash is deposited intact daily.
    b. Accounting department records cash receipts after checking for discount terms.
    c. Receivables clerk posts to subsidiary ledger.
3. Other events.
    a. Returns and allowances are recorded only after approval by a responsible official. Returned goods must be received by receiving department before return is recorded.
    b. Monthly statements are sent to customers.
    c. Credit department reviews status of accounts periodically and initiates appropriate collection efforts when necessary.

This system is designed to give assurance that sales are made only to customers who are likely to pay, that cash collections are properly recorded and deposited, and that appropriate efforts are made to collect receivables. The critical area is cash collections, which was also discussed earlier in the chapter.

The system discussed above must be adapted to the needs and personnel of the enterprise in each actual business situation. The system design should be governed by the features of a good system of internal control that were listed earlier in the chapter.

SUMMARY

Cash and short-term receivables have been the primary topics of discussion in this chapter. Cash is a critical element in enterprise operations, and control of cash resources is particularly important. For this reason, procedures in dealing with cash were emphasized.

Accounting for receivables involves several aspects. Valuation of accounts receivable usually calls for an allowance for uncollectibles. The allowance can be computed in several ways—by relating the allowance to the accounts receivable balance, by aging the accounts, or by establishing a relationship between sales and bad debts expense. An appropriate valuation will yield realistic balance sheet figures and also appropriate expenses on the income statement.

Notes receivable can present some complicated accounting problems. Interest computations, accruals, and discounting were all discussed.

Controls of cash and sales were also discussed in this chapter. The general features of a good control system are division of functions, check of one person's duties by another, separation of record keeping from physical handling of goods or cash, and a system of authorizations and approvals. Knowledge of these general features can be used in the design of any system of internal control.

Consideration of cash and receivables goes hand in hand with consideration of revenue and revenue realization. Revenue is realized in the sale of goods when title passes to the customer. Revenue is realized in the rendering of services when the service is performed for the customer. These general rules must be applied with caution when unusual circumstances exist.

IMPORTANT TERMS

Asset valuation
Monetary assets
Unexpired costs
Control of cash
Internal control
Cash
Petty cash
FOB (Free on Board)
Bad debts expense
Allowance for uncollectibles or
Allowance for doubtful accounts

Aging
Returns and allowances
Sales Discounts
Notes receivable
Contingent liability
Revenue realization
Sales controls
Bank reconciliation
Deposits in transit
Outstanding checks
NSF checks

APPENDIX 7-1: BANK RECONCILIATIONS

The use of checking accounts helps in the control of cash. When disbursements are made by check, the endorsements on the check constitute good evidence that the payment has been made. Prompt deposit of cash helps avoid misappropriations. Furthermore, cash is safer in the vaults of a bank than it is in a company's cash register or safe.

Banks usually give checking account customers a monthly statement indicating the deposits, checks cashed, other items handled, and balance in the account. The cancelled checks are returned with the bank statement. The bank statement coincides roughly with the company's account for cash in the bank. There are usually some differences, however, between the company's records and the bank statement. Because of these differences, a bank reconciliation statement should be prepared. A typical bank reconciliation statement appears in Example 7–10, followed by the corresponding journal entries.

The bank reconciliation starts with the bank balance on one hand and the balance per books on the other. A series of adjustments are made of each balance, and finally a correct total is arrived at for each balance. The corrected balances should be equal in order to have a complete reconciliation. These balances are what would have appeared on both sets of records if everything had been recorded and had been recorded correctly. The journal entries are made to bring the book balance into agreement with the corrected balance in the reconciliation statement.

Let us discuss each of the items on the reconciliation and then review the steps in its preparation.

EXAMPLE 7-10

HUSTED COMPANY
Bank Reconciliation Statement

July 31

Balance per Bank, 7/31		$7,218.12
Add:		
Deposit in transit, 7/31	$1,284.81	
Check of Hested Corp.		
charged erroneously	120.00	
Total additions		1,404.81
		8,622.93
Deduct:		
Outstanding checks, 7/31:		
#1722	300.00	
#1728	135.00	
#1729	28.17	
#1732	1,620.00	
#1734	417.30	
#1735	89.20	
Total deductions		2,589.67
Corrected balance, 7/31		$6,033.26
Balance per Books, 7/31		$5,094.41
Add:		
Note collected by bank	$1,000.00	
Interest on note	20.00	
Total additions		1,020.00
		6,114.41

(Continued)

Example 7-10 (Cont.)

Deduct:		
Bank charges	7.15	
Error on check #1708,		
written as $87.00		
recorded as 78.00	9.00	
Customers' NSF checks		
returned by bank	65.00	
Total deductions		81.15
Corrected balance, 7/31		$6,033.26

Journal Entries:

			Debit	Credit
July 31	Cash in bank		1,020.00	
	Notes receivable			1,000.00
	Interest earned			20.00
	To record note collected by bank.			
July 31	Miscellaneous expense		7.15	
	Cash in bank			7.15
	To record bank charges for July.			
July 31	Accounts payable		9.00	
	Cash in bank			9.00
	To correct recording of check #1708, written as $87.00, but recorded as only $78.00. Check was in payment of an account payable.			
July 31	Accounts receivable		65.00	
	Cash in bank			65.00
	Customers' NSF checks returned by bank on July 31, recorded as receivables.			

Items on the Reconciliation

Deposit in transit. The *deposit in transit* is a deposit recorded by the company, but not yet recorded by the bank. This delay could occur because the amount was put in the bank's night depository after business hours, or because it was deposited on a Saturday and will not be recorded by the bank until the next Monday. There is only a timing difference here, but the bank's balance is out of date because of this item.

Check of Hested Corp. charged erroneously to Husted Company's account by the bank. This type of mistake will be corrected by the bank when it is brought to its attention. Of course, the Husted Company learns about the error only when it examines the cancelled checks that are returned with the bank statement.

Outstanding checks. Outstanding checks are those checks that the company has written, but that have not yet reached the bank. A certain amount of delay is inevitable at times, especially if the checks are sent through the mail. A check is identified as outstanding by comparing the cancelled checks returned by the bank with the checks written according to company records. Consecutive numbering of checks aids in this comparison.

Note collected by bank, plus interest. Sometimes a company will leave a note receivable in the hands of its bank, and the bank will collect the note when it becomes due. Usually the bank notifies the company quickly, and an entry is made. It can happen, however, that the company finds out about the collection of the note when it receives the bank statement. If this is the case, the collection of the note must appear in the bank reconciliation statement.

Bank charges. The bank charges a company for its services in handling the company's deposits, checks, and other items. The company does not know the amount of this charge until it receives the monthly bank statement. Since the charge has not been recorded before, it appears on the reconciliation statement as a correction of the book balance.

Error on check written as one amount but recorded as another. This is an instance of a mistake by the company. The bank, of course, cashes the check for the amount for which it is written. The company, therefore, should correct its records to agree with the actual situation. An error such as this could be in the opposite direction, of course, and require an addition to the cash balance instead of a subtraction.

Customer's NSF checks returned by bank. The initials NSF stand for "not sufficient funds." When a customer's check is received, it is endorsed and sent to the company's bank. The bank accepts the check and credits Husted's account. Then, Husted's bank endorses the check to whichever bank it is written on. If the customer's account does not contain enough funds to cover the check, it will be returned, marked NSF. The Husted Company's bank will charge Husted's account and return the bad check to Husted Company. Some checks of this type may be returned with the bank statement at the end of the month. The company must correct its records for these items. Usually they are recorded as accounts receivable, and further efforts are made to collect the amounts from the customers involved.

The above items are only samples of the kinds of items that appear in these statements. Often, other items also appear.

Procedure in Preparing Bank Reconciliations

Preparation of a bank reconciliation statement is fairly simple. When the bank statement for the month is received, the cancelled checks are put in numerical order, and other items returned by the bank are separated.

Through an item-by-item comparison of items in the bank statement with items in the company's records (the cash receipts journal and cash disbursements journal, for example), certain differences between the two sets of records are disclosed. These differences appear on the bank reconciliation statement. The reconciliation statement starts with the bank balance and the book balance. The bank balance appears on the bank statement; the book balance can be obtained from the cash account in the company's ledger. Differences between the bank and book records are classified as additions to, or deductions from, these balances. If a difference arises because of a mistake or omission on the company's books, it is classified as a change in the book balance. If a difference arises because of a mistake by the bank or because the bank has not yet recorded an item (deposits in transit or outstanding checks), it is classified as a change in the bank balance. Each side is added algebraically to obtain a corrected balance.

The bank will enclose debit or credit memoranda with the statements to indicate some of the differences between the bank and the company's books. The memoranda may include a charge slip for bank charges and a credit memorandum for notes collected. But differences such as outstanding checks, deposits in transit, and errors by the bank or the company will be disclosed only by a detailed item-by-item comparison of the items recorded by the bank with those recorded on the books.

The reconciliation statement may not balance for any of several reasons. There may be an error in addition or subtraction on the reconciliation. This should be checked first. An item may have been added when it should have been subtracted, or vice versa. An error of this kind will show up as a difference in the corrected balances of *twice* the amount involved. Another possibility is that some reconciling item may have been omitted from the reconciliation. Discovering such an item may entail retracing all the steps taken before, including item-by-item comparisons. This is a time-consuming process, and other possibilities should be exhausted first. The amount of the missing item can sometimes be discovered by taking the difference between the two "corrected balances." The difference between the totals always should be obtained, and an accountant should look for an item equal to the amount of the difference or equal to one-half of the difference.

In addition, when comparing cancelled checks to the cash disbursements records, it is wise to examine endorsements. Even a cursory examination can sometimes disclose improper items. An actual example of such an inproper item involved a check made out to "Minnesota Mining and Mfg. Co." and endorsed in longhand. Since almost all companies use rubber stamps for endorsements, this check looked suspicious. It turned out that embezzlement was involved; an employee was intercepting the checks, cashing them, and keeping the money for himself. This embezzlement could have been discovered by an alert person in preparing a bank reconciliation.

Bank reconciliations should be prepared monthly. They should be prepared by someone other than the person who writes the checks or prepares deposits. This provides an internal check on the functions of these people. Finally, when preparing a bank reconciliation it is a good idea to check that all items in the previous bank reconciliation have been taken care of—previous deposits in transit have arrived at the bank, outstanding checks have cleared, etc.

QUESTIONS

7-1. What are *monetary assets?* How are they distinguished from unexpired costs?

7-2. Short-term monetary assets are generally valued at the purchasing power they represent. Explain what this means and explain the logic behind this method of valuation in the case of monetary assets.

7-3. What are some of the basic ideas, or rules, of *internal control?*

7-4. After the owner of a retail clothing store complained about cash shortages, a CPA recommended that a cash register be installed. Later the CPA observed that several employees were ringing up sales on it. Why would the CPA object to this procedure?

7-5. Why is it desirable to have disbursements made by check? Why should cash receipts be deposited intact daily?

7-6. Why should credits to customers' accounts for returns, allowances, and write-offs be approved by an appropriate executive?

7-7. What is the purpose of setting up estimated uncollectible receivables?

7-8. Most department stores make a provision for estimated returns and allowances on accounts receivables as well as for estimated uncollectibles. Most other companies do not make a provision for estimated returns and allowances. Explain why department stores find this provision desirable.

7-9. When is revenue realized in a sale of merchandise? If there is substantial doubt about collectibility of the receivable, should the point of revenue recognition be changed?

7-10. When is revenue realized in the rendering of services to a customer?

EXERCISES

7-11. *Petty cash.* Give the entry in general journal form for the replenishment of a $100 petty cash fund, when the petty cashier reports the following authorized disbursements:

Postage	$12
Miscellaneous office expense	30
Freight-in	13
Store supplies	20
Delivery expense	8

The cash balance in the fund at this point is $15.

7-12. *Petty cash.* John Stewart uses the title First National Bank for his cash in bank account. On October 1, he set up a petty cash fund in the amount of $50. The fund was replenished on October 10, at which time the disbursements from the fund had been as follows:

Miscellaneous selling expense	$21.46
Miscellaneous general expense	22.02
Postage	2.42

On October 23, the petty cash fund was increased to $100.

Give the required journal entries in general journal form.

7-13. *Cash control.* The Wramis Company has three employees in its office. Duties are divided as follows:

- Jane Doe keeps cash receipts book, deposits daily cash collections, and keeps accounts receivable subsidiary ledger.
- John Roe keeps cash disbursements book, writes and signs checks, and reconciles bank account monthly.
- David Sloe keeps other journals, posts to general ledger, and keeps accounts payable subsidiary ledger.

Required:

a. Criticize the internal control of the Wramis company. What are the bad and good features of its system?

b. Assign the duties listed above to the three persons so that the internal control system is adequate.

7-14. *Bank reconciliation.* From the following information, prepare a bank reconciliation in good form, as of May 31:

Balance per bank, May 31	$2,000
Balance per cash account, May 31	1,740
Checks outstanding	300
NSF checks of customers	50
Bank charges	10
Deposit in transit	180
Note collected by bank that has not been recorded on the books	200

7-15. *Bad debts.* Give entries in general journal form for the following: December 31, Year 1 — Estimated uncollectibles are 1% of net sales on account. Selected account balances are as follows:

	Debit	Credit
Accounts receivable	36,000	
Allowance for uncollectibles	140	
Sales (of which $80,000 are for cash)		248,000
Sales allowances	4,000	

February 28, Year 2 — The account receivable of D. Beet in the amount of $220 is written off as uncollectible.

September 20, Year 2—$100 is collected from Mr. Payer on his account of $100, which had been previously written off.

7-16. *Bad debts.* On December 31, the following account balances appear on the books of A Company:

Sales	$125,000
Accounts receivable	11,500
Allowance for uncollectibles (credit)	150

Prepare the journal entry to recognize possible losses on uncollectible accounts if the company:
  a. Normally experiences 1% loss on credit sales, which are 45% of total sales.
  b. Bases the estimate on an analysis of accounts receivable, which reveals accounts totaling $610 are expected to be uncollectible.

7-17. *Notes.*
  a. Find the maturity date of a note dated February 2, term 90 days.
  b. Find the maturity date of a note dated November 30, term 6 months.
  c. Find the number of days on a note that is dated March 14 and is due on June 2.
  d. Find the interest on a $1,800 note, term 60 days, 9%.
  e. Find the interest on a $1,500 note, term 43 days, 8%.

7-18. *Notes receivable.* On April 6, N. T. Ruck gave Carter Brothers his note for $840. The note had a term of 3 months at 8% interest. On the date the note came due, however, he could not pay the full amount and remitted only $350 cash. Carter Brothers accepted the $350 and took a new note from Mr. Ruck for the unpaid principal and interest. The new note was for 90 days at 9% interest.
  a. What is the due date of the first note?
  b. What is the maturity value of the first note?
  c. What is the due date of the second note?
  d. What is the face value of the second note?
  e. What is the maturity value of the second note?
  f. Show the journal entry that Carter Brothers should make when they receive the second note.

7-19. *Notes, interest.* During Year 1, the X Company received notes from two customers in settlement of their open accounts. The first note was a 6%, 8-month note for $6,000 dated March 1, Year 1. The second note was a 1-year, 6% note dated November 1, Year 1, for $3,000.
  a. Give all journal entries required in Year 1 by above facts. Be sure to include the adjusting entry required on December 31, Year 1.
  b. What interest revenue will be reported on the income statement for Year 1?
  c. What assets (other than cash) will be reported on the financial position statement of December 31, Year 1, because of the above transactions and adjustments?
  d. Give the journal entry to record collection of the November 1 note in Year 2.

7-20. *Notes, accruals.* Make entries for the following selected transactions of the Carlton Company:

Oct. 26   Receive a 90-day, 8% note on account from a customer, J. Morgan, in the amount of $3,000.

Nov. 21   Receive a $2,100, 60-day note on account from P. Rose, a customer. The note is taken at a 9% discount and Rose is given credit for the proceeds.

Dec. 31   Give adjusting entries for the above two notes.

January   Give entries for collection of the notes at maturity. Be sure to indicate date collected.

(Solution in Appendix B.)

PROBLEMS

7-21. *Fraud cases.* Indicate how an effective system of internal control would lead to discovery of each of the following embezzlements:

a. A clerk lists cash received from customers as receipts but pockets the money.

b. A clerk puts currency received from customers in his pocket and does not list the amount collected on receivables.

c. The clerk authorized to sign checks makes checks out to himself but does not record the item in the cash disbursements journal.

d. The clerk authorized to sign checks makes checks out to himself, records the checks as payments to suppliers, and removes the checks from the cancelled checks returned by the bank.

e. The petty cashier takes $12 out of the fund and records a $12 fictitious disbursement for postage.

f. A clerk pockets $300 of cash received after the receipt has been recorded and covers the defalcation by recording a fictitious disbursement of $300 for advertising.

g. A clerk steals securities and sells them. He pockets the money and does not record the sale of the temporary investments.

7-22. *Bank reconciliation.* From the following information, prepare a bank reconciliation statement in good form for the Atlas Company on June 30.

Balance per books, June 30: $4,309.70

Checks outstanding:

#611	$ 380.20	#633	$ 13.12
614	119.16	634	194.50
621	1,048.20	638	200.00
632	61.27		

(#621 is a certified check)

On June 30, the company made a night deposit of $1,411.25.

Bank charges for the month of June amount to $3.60.

Balances per bank statement: May 31—$3,481.50; June 30—$4,063.10.

The bank had deducted a $300 check written by the Atlast Corporation from the Atlas Company's account during June. This error is discovered when the cancelled checks are examined.

A note of $500 was collected by the bank, but had not been recorded on the books.

(Solution in Appendix B.)

7-23. *Bank reconciliation.* Given the following information, prepare a reconciliation statement and the adjusting entries required on the books of B. O. Blanchfield.

The checkbook of B. O. Blanchfield, distributor of Bateman batteries, has a balance of $1,299.50 on October 31. It reveals the following checks issued in October:

#47	$69.50	#52	$ 75.30	#57	$29.75
48	50.25	53	49.95	58	46.00
49	25.60	54	72.55	59	45.50
50	37.15	55	151.20	60	52.35
51	void	56	15.00		

The balance as shown by the bank statement on October 31 is $1,099.71. Enclosed with the statement are debit memos for (a) check dishonored, October 30 (NSF) $32.50; (b) bank charges, $3.24; and (c) the following cancelled checks:

#48	$50.25	#53	$ 49.95	#58	$64.00
49	25.60	55	151.20	59	45.50
52	75.30	56	15.00	60	52.35

The amounts on the cancelled checks may be assumed to be correct. On examining the statement, Mr. Blanchfield discovers that a deposit of $355 made on October 30 has not been included in the bank statement.

7-24. *Sales discounts and notes and bad debts.* Prepare entries in general journal form for the following miscellaneous transactions on our books. Show calculations. Assume that controlling accounts are in use for customers and creditors.

May 2	We sell merchandise on account to John Mills for $1,200, terms, 1/10, n/30, invoice dated May 2.
May 2	We pay a $50 freight bill on the goods sold Mills today.
May 4	Mills returns part of the merchandise, which was damaged in transit. We allow him $40 credit on account (see May 2 above).
May 6	We receive a check of $200 from Mills to apply on account (see May 2 above). A discount is allowed.
May 20	We receive a check from Mills in full payment of the account (see above).
May 29	L. Carver, a customer, transfers to us to apply on account a 60-day, 6% note for $300, dated May 19, signed by R. Matthews. We allow Carver credit for the face value plus accrued interest to date.
June 18	D. Pickle, a customer who owes us $300, has declared bankruptcy. We receive $120 in full settlement of his account.

June 19   We discount at the bank our $600, 60-day, non-interest-bearing note dated today and receive cash for the proceeds. Discount rate is 6 percent.

(Solution in Appendix B.)

7-25. *Sales notes.* Give entries for the following.

Jan. 5	Sell merchandise to B. Bright on account, $8,000. Terms 2/10, EOM.
Jan. 27	B. Bright returns $400 of merchandise sold to him on January 5.
Feb. 4	Bright pays us the balance due.
Mar. 5	Sell merchandise to Fillmore on account, $800. Terms 2/10, n/30.
Mar. 10	Receive a 2-month, 6% note from Fillmore on account for amount owed.
May 10	Fillmore pays the note due today.
May 15	Sell merchandise to Ackley on account, $300.
Nov. 20	Write off Ackley's account (May 15) as uncollectible.
Dec. 31	Record bad debts expense for the year. Bad debts are estimated at 1% of net sales. Account balances are Sales, $200,000; Sales Discounts, $3,000; Allowance for Uncollectibles, $600 debit.

CASE PROBLEM

7-26. *Revenue Realization.* The Desert Wells Land Development Company develops and sells lots in its Desert Rancho Estates subdivision. Lots are sold for $6,000, with terms of $300 down and payments of $300 per year plus interest for the next 19 years. Buyers of lots can rescind their purchase and get their money back any time during the first six months after sale. A default after the first year results in repossession of the lot by the company and no refund to the customer. Past experience of the company is as follows:

Per 100 lots sold

	Lots
Sales rescinded and money refunded	40
No payments after first year by customers	15
No payments after second year by customers	10
Customers who continue payments	35
Total	100

How do you suggest that Desert Wells handle the realization of revenue in this development? How should amounts forfeited by customers because of default be handled?

I. Temp Invst
   A - Acquis'tn - Cost
   B - Subsequt - Lower of Cost or Mkt value
        (Loss appears on Income Statemt)

II. Long Term
   A) Stock
      1) Acquis'tn - Cost
         a) Small (Less tht 20%) Lower of Cost or mkt
            (Loss appears in Equity Section)
         B) Large (20% or more) Equity method

   B) Bonds
      Acquis'n - Cost - (present value)
      Subsequt - Cost (adj for amortization)

8

Investments

A business enterprise may invest in securities and other assets not used in business operations for various reasons. *Temporary investments* in marketable securities are made primarily to earn income on otherwise idle cash within the year. *Long-term investments* in securities may be made to earn income over a longer term, because they are an attractive speculation, or because the investment may be the means of gaining control or exerting some influence over another company. Occasionally, a company will invest in tangible assets such as land that will not be used in operations for several years. In this chapter, both temporary investments and long-term security investments will be examined. Long-term investments present some complicated accounting problems and will receive the major portion of our attention.

TEMPORARY INVESTMENTS

An enterprise sometimes finds that it has more cash than it can effectively use in the near future. The excess cash is often invested in marketable securities that are safe and easily converted to cash. The company can earn income on the securities and can convert the securities to cash when the need arises. If the securities are to be converted within the year, they are referred to as temporary investments and are classified as current assets on the balance sheet. If management intends to hold the securities for a longer period of time, they are long-term investments and should not be listed among current assets, since the purchasing power will not be available for current use. Note that it is management's intention that makes the difference in classification. Identical securities held by two different companies might be classified as a current asset in one case and as a long-term investment in the other, because the intentions of management differ in the two companies.

Types of Marketable Securities

Marketable securities held for the short term should possess liquidity. This means that the security can easily be converted to cash with a minimum risk of loss. The securities that best meet the liquidity requirement are short-term debt instruments of the United States Treasury, high-grade (prime) corporation commercial paper, and negotiable certificates of deposit (CDs) issued by large commercial banks. Occasionally an enterprise will include high-quality corporate stocks and bonds in its temporary investments. Generally, this is not considered to be sound financial management because stocks and bonds are not nearly as liquid as the short-term debt instruments. Securities frequently used for temporary investments are discussed below.

United States Treasury Bills. These are non-interest-bearing obligations of the U.S. Treasury with maturities of one year or less. The Treasury agrees to pay the bearer of the bill its face value at maturity. Investors can buy the bills from commercial banks or dealers or directly from the Treasury at a discount (a price below the maturity value). The interest earned by the investor is the difference between the price paid and the maturity value (or the resale price if the bill is sold before maturity). Treasury bills, being the most highly liquid short-term investment, do not yield as high a return as alternative securities.

The most popular bills are the 3-month and 6-month maturities. These are issued weekly. The enterprise can acquire the maturities that accord most closely with its investment needs. For example, a company wants a 7-week investment. It buys 3-month Treasury bills of $100,000 that are due in 7 weeks at a total price of $99,300. The company will earn $700 over the 7-week period. This is equivalent to an annual interest rate of approximately 5.25%. The computation for the equivalent annual rate is as follows:

$$\frac{\$\ 700}{\$99,300} = .0070493, \text{ or } .70493\% \text{ for 7 weeks or 49 days}$$

$$.70493\% \times \frac{365 \text{ days}}{49 \text{ days}} = 5.25\% \text{ annual rate}$$

Tax-anticipation Bills. These are U.S. Treasury bills with maturities that make them ideal for quarterly income tax payments. Maturity dates are set a week after the quarterly tax payments are due. The bills are accepted by the Treasury for tax payments at the full maturity value. The taxpayer receives the maturity value one week before it is due. This feature provides a strong incentive to use the bills for tax payments rather than hold them to maturity.

Commercial Paper. Most of the commercial paper used for temporary investments is in the form of short-term, non-interest-bearing promissory notes issued by large, well-known corporations. The corporation promises to pay the bearer of the note the face value at maturity. The notes can be acquired through a commercial bank at a discount. Because the notes cannot easily be sold, the investor selects the maturities that closely match the investor's needs. Interest is earned because the price paid for the note is less than the maturity value.

Negotiable Certificates of Deposit (CDs). CDs are time certificates of deposit issued by large commercial banks. They are bought and sold by some commercial banks and other dealers. The issuing bank agrees to pay the bearer the amount on the certificate plus a specified rate of interest on the maturity date given on the certificate. The investor pays the maturity value less a discount. For example, a one-year CD for $10,000 that pays 6.0% interest has a maturity value of $10,600. Suppose that an investor buys this certificate 73 days before maturity at a price of $10,483. The investor earns $117 on an investment of $10,483 over 73 days. This is equivalent to an annual interest rate of approximately 5.58%. The computation is:

$$\frac{\$117}{\$10{,}483} \times \frac{365 \text{ days}}{73 \text{ days}} = .0558 \text{ or } 5.58\%$$

Accounting for Temporary Investments

Several aspects of accounting for temporary investments must be considered: accounting at acquisition and accounting for investments subsequent to acquisition.

Acquisition of Temporary Investments. Temporary investments are recorded originally at their cost. Example 8-1 illustrates.

Record at cost

EXAMPLE 8-1

On July 1, The Humphrey Speaker Company has excess cash to invest in U.S. Treasury bills and negotiable CDs. The company acquires $200,000 in Treasury bills that mature on August 19 at a price of $198,600, and $100,000 in 12-month CDs that mature on September 12th. The CDs bear interest of 6.0% and are acquired at a price of $104,834, which provides an annual return at 5.56%. The accounting entry is as follows:

(Continued)

Example 8-1 (Cont.)

		Debit	Credit
July 1	Temporary investments	303,434	
	Cash		303,434

Purchased temporary investments:
U.S. Treasury bills	$198,600
Negotiable CD's	104,834
	$303,434

Note that the securities are recorded at their cost, not at their face amount or value at maturity.

Accounting Subsequent to Acquisition. Accounting entries will be required when temporary investments are disposed of through sale or redemption, and at the close of the accounting period. Example 8-2 illustrates.

EXAMPLE 8-2

On August 19, the Humphrey Speaker Company redeems the Treasury bills.

		Debit	Credit
Aug. 19	Cash	200,000	
	Temporary investments		198,600
	Interest revenue		1,400

Received $200,000 from the U.S. Treasury in payment of the maturity value of the Treasury bills. Interest revenue earned:

Cash received	$200,000
Cost of bills	198,600
Interest revenue	$ 1,400

The company's fiscal year ends on August 31. It is necessary to accrue interest revenue earned on the CDs.

		Debit	Credit
Aug. 31	Temporary investments	974	
	Interest revenue		974

To accrue 61 days of interest earned on investment in CDs as follows:

Maturity value of the 12-month CDs on September 12:
Amount of certificate	$100,000
6% interest for 12 months	6,000
	106,000
Cost of CDs on July 1	104,834
Interest revenue for 73 days	1,166

Interest revenue for 61 days:

$$\$1{,}166 \times \frac{61 \text{ days}}{73 \text{ days}} = \$974$$

or: $\$104{,}834 \times .0556 \times \frac{61 \text{ days}}{365 \text{ days}} = \$974$

Note that the accrued interest was added to the temporary investments rather than debited to an account for interest receivable. This was done because the investment actually grows from its cost of $104,834 on July 1 to $106,000 on September 12. The adjusting entry on August 31 recognizes the growth to that date.

Valuation of Temporary Investments on the Balance Sheet

Companies hold temporary investments because they want to earn a return on otherwise idle cash, and because the securities have a cash value that can easily be realized. It would seem reasonable that temporary investments would be reported on the balance sheet at their cash value, or market value. However, this is not the case. The general rule is that temporary investments are valued at the "lower of cost or market." Cost is used if the market value exceeds cost; market is used if the market value is below cost. In practice, this means that market is used if it is "significantly" below cost.

The rule does not present a problem for the short-term debt securities that most companies hold for temporary investment. Normally, these are held for short periods of time. The cost, adjusted for accrued interest, will tend to approximate market value unless there has been a substantial change in market interest rates.

The method of lower of cost or market is not particularly logical, since market fluctuations are recognized in only one direction. It is justified primarily on the basis of conservatism in accounting. Assets cannot be overstated, although they can be stated at a low figure. Unrealized losses are recognized, but not unrealized gains.[1]

Conservatism

Conservatism is such an important force in accounting that a reduction to the lower of cost or market is now required by the accounting profession in valuing temporary investments in marketable equity securities (stocks of other companies).[2] Cost is generally used for other short-term investments. Example 8-3 illustrates the lower of cost or market method.

EXAMPLE 8-3

Our company held the following stocks on December 31:

Stocks	Acquisition Cost	Market Price on Dec. 31
ABC Company	$ 3,200	$ 2,500
GH Company	12,700	9,000
MN Company	15,000	16,400
Totals	$30,900	$27,900

(Continued)

---

1. Except to the extent of previously recognized unrealized losses.
2. See Financial Accounting Standards Board, "Accounting for Certain Marketable Securities," *Statement of Financial Accounting Standards No. 12*, December, 1975.

Example 8-3 (Cont.)

The accounting entry to record the loss of $3,000 is as follows:

		Debit	Credit
Dec. 31	Loss on market decline in temporary investments	3,000	
	Allowance to reduce temporary investments to market		3,000

LONG-TERM INVESTMENTS

Cash surrender value

Long-term investments are those that management intends to retain for an extended period of time. They are usually classified in a separate section of the balance sheet called investments. Most of these investments are in the form of securities, such as stocks or bonds. Other items also may appear in this category. The cash-surrender value of life insurance policies held by the company is an example. This investment arises when a company insures the lives of officers and key personnel. Some life insurance policies accumulate a cash value as time goes by. The holder of such policies may turn the policies in to the insurance company and receive this cash value at any time. It is obvious that there is an asset in such a case, and a very liquid asset at that. The company that invests in these policies, however, generally has no intention of converting the policies into cash. Therefore, the cash values of the policies are classified as long-term investments. Similarly, a company may hold a piece of land for potential market price increase, rather than for use as a factory site. In such a case, the land would be classified as a long-term investment.

Valuation of Long-Term Investments

Valuation problems

Because long-term investments are held for a variety of purposes, appropriate valuation is not as clear-cut as in the case of short-term investments. That is, long-term investments are not necessarily clear examples of monetary assets. Sometimes they are held as eventual sources of cash, and valuation at the purchasing power they represent is appropriate. When investments are held for possible market appreciation, the market price has appeal as a basis of valuation. When long-term investments are held for purposes of control, purchasing power as indicated by market price is not as important.

Initial recording

Long-term investments, like other assets, are recorded initially at cost and are often maintained at this amount. This procedure is followed because current accounting principles emphasize historical cost valuation, not necessarily because the current market value is irrelevant. It is true that market value is not particularly helpful when control is the objective, but neither is historical cost. A case can be made for market valuation because it does give an indication of the current value of the investment on the market, whereas cost does not give any indication of current valuation, just of dollars originally invested. The present situation is that lower of cost or market is used for certain investments in stock of other companies. For other investments market values are usually not recognized, although current market values are often indicated parenthetically on the balance sheet. An exception to cost valuation occurs in the case of a marked or significant decline in market value. Suppose, for example, that securities purchased for $100,000 are now worth only $40,000 on the market. The asset should be written down to $40,000, and the decline of $60,000 should be recognized as a loss in the income statement. Such a decline in market value should be recognized in order to avoid showing inflated values among the assets. An increase in value of the same amount would not be shown, however, since it is the general practice not to recognize such gains until the assets are sold. Nevertheless, value increases can, and should, be shown parenthetically on the balance sheet.

Market values

Long-term Investments in Stocks

Long-term stock investments may range from small proportions of stock of companies held as speculations, to fairly significant proportions of stock that allow the investing company to exert influence on the other company, to high proportions that allow absolute control over the company whose stock is owned.

When a company owns enough stock of another company to exercise control (usually more than 50% of stock available), the company owned is called a *subsidiary*. The financial statements of subsidiaries are often combined with those of the owner, or "parent," company and *consolidated statements* result. Consolidated financial statements are discussed in chapter 13.

When a company owns a small proportion of stock, the investment is carried at the lower of cost or market. An allowance account is set up just as in the case of temporary investments, but the loss is not carried to the income statement; instead, it is shown as a deduction in the stockholders' equity section.[3] Dividends received are recorded as dividend income.

Investments that are substantial but that fall short of a controlling interest pose special accounting problems. A substantial investment, defined as ownership of 20% to 50% of the voting stock of another company, implies that the investor can exercise substantial influence on the company

---

3. Financial Accounting Standards Board, "Accounting for Certain Marketable Securities," paragraph 11.

Part III   Measurement of Assets, Liabilities, and Income

Equity method

owned. In this situation, the *equity method* of accounting is required. Under the equity method, the investor's share of the owned company's profits and losses are taken up as they are earned. Thus, if a 30% owned company reports a $60,000 profit, $18,000 of income (30%) will be recognized as income by the investor. The income is credited to investment income. The debit is to the investment asset. The idea is that income earned by the owned company increases the value of the investment and represents income to the owner. The payment of dividends by the owned company is simply a matter of remitting cash to the investor and does not represent income to the owner. In fact, the remitting of dividends, which is a transfer of funds, reduces the amount invested and is recorded as a credit to the investment. The entries are shown in Example 8-4.

EXAMPLE 8-4

Blue Company has a 30% interest in Black Company. Black reports income of $70,000 for the year. Entry by Blue:

		Debit	Credit
Dec. 31	Investment in Black stock	21,000	
	Investment income		21,000

On January 20 Black pays a dividend of $30,000 to stockholders. Entry by Blue:

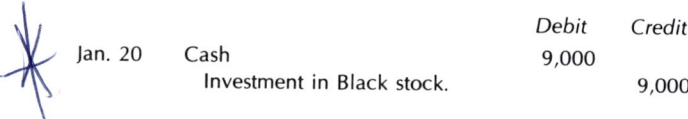

		Debit	Credit
Jan. 20	Cash	9,000	
	Investment in Black stock.		9,000

Long-term Investments in Bonds

Premium and discount

Long-term investments in bonds are recorded originally at cost. However, some adjustments of cost are necessary if the bonds are purchased at an amount other than the face value of the bonds. Because of market conditions, a company may purchase bonds at more than their face amount, thus paying a *premium;* or a company may purchase bonds at less than their face amount, thus purchasing them at a *discount*. If the bonds are held to maturity, however, the *face amount* (the amount printed on the bonds) will be received. Therefore, any difference between the purchase price and the face amount of the bonds (any premium or discount) should be eliminated by the time the bonds mature. Premium or discount generally is written off, or *amortized,* over the life of the bonds.

Before illustrating the amortization procedure, let us find out why a bond would sell at something other than its face value. For example, if people know that a Z Company bond will pay $1,000 at maturity 10 years from now, why should they pay anything other than $1,000 for it? The answer lies in the market conditions at the time of purchase, particularly the current rate of interest on investments of similar quality and risk. If the bonds carry a 7% contract rate of interest, and the market rate for similar securities at that time is 8%, no one will be willing to purchase the Z Company bonds at $1,000. The price of the bonds will be depressed by the market until the bonds yield 8%. Similarly, if the bonds carry a 10% rate of interest, and the current market rate is 8%, buyers will be eager to purchase the Z Company bonds. In fact, the buyers will bid the price up until the bonds return 8%. Thus, *the premium or discount is inextricably related to the market rate of interest on bonds.* As a result, when the premium or discount is amortized, the income statement account used is "interest earned" or "interest revenue."

Straight-Line Amortization. One method of amortizing premium or discount is to write off equal amounts in each period during which the bonds are held. Since bond investments are recorded at cost, any premium or discount will be listed in the investment account as an amount above or below the face value of the bonds. Thus a $1,000 bond bought at a premium of $60 would be recorded at a cost of $1,060. The same bond bought at a discount of $20 might be recorded at a cost of $980. The way in which the amortization is handled is illustrated in Example 8-5.

EXAMPLE 8-5

On January 1, Year 1, the company purchases $100,000 of Z Company 9% bonds at 104 (bonds are quoted at percents of face value). The bonds will mature in five years. Interest is paid semiannually, on June 30 and December 31.
Entries:

Year 1		Debit	Credit
Jan. 1	Investment in Z Co. bonds	104,000	
	Cash		104,000
	Purchase $100,000 of Z Co. 9% bonds at 104. Maturity date is January 1, Year 6.		
June 30	Cash	4,500	
	Interest revenue		4,500
	Collect semiannual interest on Z Co. bonds.		
Dec. 31	Cash	4,500	
	Interest revenue		4,500
	Collect semiannual interest on Z Co. bonds.		
Dec. 31	Interest revenue	800	
	Investment in Z Co. bonds		800
	Amortize 1/5 of premium on Z Co. bonds.		

(Continued)

Example 8-5 (Cont.)

The same entries as shown above will be made in Years 2 through 5. In Year 6 the following entry will be made at maturity:

		Debit	Credit
Jan. 1	Cash	100,000	
	Investment in Z Co. bonds		100,000
	Z Co. bonds redeemed at maturity.		

Several points should be noted about Example 8-5. First, the 9% interest is an annual rate on the face amount, and only $4\frac{1}{2}\%$ is collected each six months. Second, the last entry each year *amortizes*, or writes off, the difference between cost and the face amount of the bonds, and adjusts the interest earned. The investment account gradually is written down (or up, when there is a discount) to the face amount. The investment account for the five years would appear as follows:

Investment in Z Co. Bonds

Jan. 1, Year 1	104,000	Dec. 31, Year 1	800
		Dec. 31, Year 2	800
		Dec. 31, Year 3	800
		Dec. 31, Year 4	800
		Dec. 31, Year 5	800
		Jan. 1, Year 6	100,000

The bond investment would appear on the balance sheet on December 31, Year 1, as follows:

Investment in Z Company 9% bonds $103,200

This figure gradually would be reduced (by $800 a year) until on December 31, Year 5, just before the bonds were redeemed, they would be shown as follows:

Investment in Z Company 9% bonds $100,000

It is appropriate that the interest revenue be reduced, because the premium at date of issue is related to the interest rate on the bonds. Because of the premium, the cash received each year as interest is greater than the interest earned. It is for this reason that the interest revenue account is reduced by the amortization of premium.

The entries and reasoning in the case of a discount are analagous to the foregoing. Interest revenue is increased, of course, rather than decreased; and the investment account gradually is increased from the cost figure to the face amount of the bonds.

A final point: adjusting entries to accrue interest may be necessary if bond interest is unpaid at the end of the company's fiscal year. Also, one yearly adjusting entry to record amortization of premium or discount is usually sufficient. Of course, if statements are prepared each quarter, amortization must also be recorded each quarter.

Effective-Interest Method (Scientific Method) of Amortization. Bonds, being a type of long-term receivable, are valued in the market at the present value of the cash flows expected from the bond. The market price is computed by discounting the future cash flows at the current rate of interest. Bond investments yield two types of cash flows: (1) the periodic interest each year until maturity and (2) the payment of the principal at maturity. The interest payments are a series of equal amounts paid at regular intervals; thus, they fit the definition of an annuity. The present value can be computed by using a present value of annuities table for the interest payment and a table of present values for the principal amount. (See Appendix 8-1 for a discussion of present values and compound interest. Present value tables are in Appendix C at the end of this book.)

If a $1,000, 8%, 10-year bond (interest payable annually) is offered on the market at a time when the market interest rate is 8%, the bond will sell at $1,000, computed as follows:

Present value of cash flows:

```
Yearly interest $80 × 6.710 (Appendix C, Table III) = $  536.80
Principal $1,000 × .4632 (Appendix C, Table II)    =    463.20
                Total present value                   $1,000.00
```

The interest each year will be $80, which is 8% of the investment.

Suppose, however, that the above bond is offered at a time when the market interest rate is 10%. The present value is computed as follows, using the 10% rate from the tables:

Present value of cash flows:

```
Yearly interest $80 × 6.145 (Table III)   = $491.60
Principal $1,000 × .3855 (Table II)       =  385.50
                Total present value         $877.10
```

This computation illustrates the way in which bonds are actually priced in the market. Daily quotations are based on computations similar to the above. How would this investment be recorded? The initial investment entry, assuming a January 1, Year 1, purchase date, is as follows:

			Debit	Credit
Jan. 1	Bond investment		877.10	
	Cash			877.10

Earlier in the chapter, we explained that the difference between the face amount of bonds and the cost could be amortized over the life of the bonds on a *straight-line* basis. Under that basis, the $122.90 discount in the example above would be amortized at the rate of $12.29 per year. To

249

be consistent with present value computations, however, effective-interest rather than straight-line amortization is appropriate. Entries for the first two years follow:

Year 1		Debit	Credit
Dec. 31	Cash	80.00	
	Bond investment	7.71	
	Interest earned		87.71
	$80 interest received; interest earned is 10% of the investment of $877.10.		

Notice that the interest rate is applied to the balance of the bond investment and not to the face amount of the bond.

Year 2		Debit	Credit
Dec. 31	Cash	80.00	
	Bond investment	8.48	
	Interest earned		88.48
	$80 interest received; interest earned is 10% of investment of $877.10 + 7.71.		

Notice that the interest increases in the second year because the total investment has grown in value and the 10% rate thus yields a larger amount. The increase in the bond investment also grows year by year. The total discount of $122.90 will be absorbed exactly over the 10 years (although some small difference may appear because of rounding). The method of amortization used in the example is called the effective interest method (or the *scientific method*) of amortization. It is more accurate than straight-line amortization, because the interest is always the initial market rate times the investment balance. Differences between the two methods tend to be small in most years if the term of the bonds is short but may be large for long-term issues.

A bond investment that carries an interest rate more than the market rate of interest would have a price in excess of the face amount of the bond. Suppose a 9%, $1,000 bond is bought on January 1, Year 1, when the market rate of interest is 8%. The bond matures in 5 years. (Note: the bonds are very likely to be more than 5-year bonds originally.) Interest is payable semiannually. The market price is computed as follows:

Present value of cash flows:
  Semiannual interest $45 × 8.111 (Appendix C, Table III) $ 365.00
  Principal $1,000 × .6756 (Table II)   675.60
    Total present value $1,040.60

Note that an interest rate of 4% for 10 periods is used (5 years times 2 payments per year).

The entries in Year 1 are as follows:

			Debit	Credit
Jan. 1	Bond investment		1,040.60	
	Cash			1,040.60
July 30	Cash		45.00	
	Bond investment			3.38
	Interest earned			41.62
	4% × $1,040.60 = $41.62 interest			
Dec. 31	Cash		45.00	
	Bond investment			3.51
	Interest earned			41.49
	4% × ($1,040.60 − 3.38)			

Computations in later periods are similar. A schedule of amounts of interest and amortization each period, called an amortization schedule, is presented in Table 8-1.

This schedule indicates that, as a result of interest and amortization each period, the bond investment will be carried at $1,000 just prior to receipt of the principal of the bonds at maturity. Note that the interest earned goes down each period and the amortization increases. The decline in interest is caused by a smaller investment each period. Note the contrast with straight-line amortization, where the semiannual amortization would be $4.06 each period. Both methods arrive at $1,000 at maturity, but there is a difference in interest earned each period.

The effective-interest method of amortization provides added accuracy in determining interest earned each period and the valuation of the investment asset. Interest should change if the amount of the investment changes. The amount of the investment at any one time should be

TABLE 8-1. Amortization Schedule
(9%, $1,000 bond. Market rate: 8%, with interest paid semiannually.)

Date	Interest Earned (4% of Principal)	Cash Received	Amortization	Principal Balance
Jan. 1, Year 1				1,040.60
June 30, Year 1	41.62	45.00	3.38	1,037.22
Dec. 31, Year 1	41.49	45.00	3.51	1,033.71
June 30, Year 2	41.35	45.00	3.65	1,030.06
Dec. 31, Year 2	41.20	45.00	3.80	1,026.26
June 30, Year 3	41.05	45.00	3.95	1,022.31
Dec. 31, Year 3	40.89	45.00	4.11	1,018.20
June 30, Year 4	40.73	45.00	4.27	1,013.93
Dec. 31, Year 4	40.56	45.00	4.44	1,009.49
June 30, Year 5	40.38	45.00	4.62	1,004.87
Dec. 31, Year 5	40.13*	45.00	4.87	1,000.00

* Adjusted for rounding error.

equal to the present value of the future amounts of cash to be received. This will only be true if the effective-interest method is used.

Differences between straight-line and effective-interest methods will often be minor, but differences can be large when the discount or premium on the bonds is substantial. In these cases, the effective-interest method is the only accurate and acceptable method.

Valuation of Bond Investments—Further Considerations

Interest rates change, sometimes rather drastically. Rates on high-quality corporate bonds were as low as 2½% in 1950. Rates have climbed rapidly in recent years, reaching 9% for high-quality bonds in 1974. Every time the interest rate changes, the market quotations for bonds also change. To illustrate, suppose a 5%, $1,000, 20-year bond is purchased when the market rate is 5%. The bond will have a market price of $1,000. Five years later, the interest rate climbs to 8%. The market value of the bond will be computed as follows:

Present value of cash flows:
Annual interest $50 × 8.559 (Appendix C, Table III) $427.95
Principal $1000 × .3152 (Table II)   315.20
Total present value $743.15

(Factors from the tables were for 15 periods at 8%)

The change in interest rates reduces the market price of the bonds more than 25%.

Once an investment is made and recorded at cost, the subsequent market quotations are usually ignored under generally accepted accounting principles. This approach is debatable, since it means that substantial changes in market value may be ignored.

Those who favor retention of cost (adjusted for amortization) claim that market values are not relevant because the company presumably has no intention of selling long-term investments before maturity. No matter what happens to market prices, the bonds will be redeemed at face value at maturity (unless there is a default). Those who favor market valuation claim that assets with a readily ascertainable market price should be valued at that price. If the price increases or decreases, the investor has had a gain or loss. The gain or loss exists in real terms whether or not it is recognized in accounting. They claim the current market value should be recognized so that users of financial statements have a clearer idea of where the company stands at any particular time. They also claim that current market price is an important factor in the decision to either hold or sell the investment, and that this decision must be made each period.

Controversy in this area continues. It is our opinion that current market valuations are the most appropriate valuation basis. The student is cautioned that this view is not the accepted view at present.

SUMMARY

This chapter dealt with the accounting problems connected with investments. Temporary investments are those that are intended to be held only for a relatively short time. These investments are recorded at cost and are often maintained at cost except for marketable equity securities, which are carried at lower of cost or market. In applying lower of cost or market, the accountant records a loss and uses an allowance account to record the market decline in the balance sheet. Market valuation is favored by the authors as a valuation method because it accords better with the objectives of valuation of this type of asset.

Long-term investments include a variety of items. This chapter concentrated on investments in stocks and bonds. Long-term investments in stocks are valued by the equity method if they constitute a 20% to 50% interest in the company owned. Smaller investments are carried at the lower of cost or market, although losses on market declines do not appear in the income statement. When a controlling interest is held in another company, results of that company are usually consolidated with the owner company's results.

Long-term investments in bonds are initially recorded at cost. Any differences between cost and the face value of the bonds are amortized over the remaining term of the bonds. Two methods of amortization were illustrated, the straight-line method and the effective-interest method. The effective-interest method uses the market rate of interest to compute the amortization of premium or discount.

Issues are not as clear in valuation of long-term investments as in valuation of temporary investments. Valuation at current market price is not as important for long-term investments because there is often no intention of engaging in market transactions. We suggested, however, that market values are often the most relevant values for investors and creditors.

IMPORTANT TERMS

Temporary investments
Long-term investments
Certificates of deposit
Treasury bills
Commercial paper
Lower of cost or market
Cash surrender value
Equity method
Premium
Discount
Amortization
Straight-line amortization
Effective-interest method of amortization
Present value
Annuities
Amortization schedule

APPENDIX 8-1: PRESENT VALUE

The present value of something is its cash value now. The concept of present value is important because money or cash on hand today is worth more today than the promise of an equal amount of money to be received in the future. This statement is true even in the absence of inflation. Money on hand today can be invested to earn interest; consequently, today's money (if invested) will grow in value over time.

For example, a dollar on hand today is worth more today than a dollar to be received two years from now. The dollar you have today can be invested to earn interest so that at the end of two years you will have an amount greater than the dollar you started with. Suppose that 10% interest can be earned each year. A dollar invested for two years would grow to $1.21 by the end of the two years, as follows:

Investment today	$ 1.00
Interest for the first year at 10%	.10
Total value of investment at the end of the first year	$ 1.10
Interest for the second year at 10%	.11
Value of investment at the end of the second year	$ 1.21

Note that the amount of interest in the second year is higher than that in the first year because interest is earned on both the principal and the first year's interest. This is called compounding, which simply means that interest is earned on both the principal and any accumulated interest. Thus, $1.00 will grow to $1.21 in two years at compound interest of 10% (compounded annually). The formula for finding a future amount at compound interest is as follows:

$$\text{Future Amount} = p(1+i)^n$$

where p = the amount at the present
i = rate of interest per period and
n = number of periods

For the illustration above, the formula could be used as follows:

$$\begin{aligned}\text{Future Amount} &= \$1(1+.10)^2 \\ &= \$1(1.10)^2 \\ &= \$1.21\end{aligned}$$

Appendix C, Table I, gives the compound future amount, or value, of $1.00 for a number of different interest rates and for a series of different periods. The table can be used to compute future amounts for any present value. For example, how much would $1,000 accumulate to at the end of 10 years if invested at the rate of 8% compounded annually? First, find the column for the rate of 8% (.08 in the table). Next, locate the table value in this column for 10 periods. The table value of 2.159 is based on an investment of $1.00, so it must be multiplied by 1,000 to derive $2,159, the amount to which $1,000 will accumulate at the end of 10 years.

The computation illustrated above can be turned around and looked at from the other direction. The $1.21 two years from now is equivalent to the $1.00 now invested at a 10% rate of interest, compounded annually, and the $1.10 one year from now is equivalent to the $1.00 now, invested at a 10% rate of interest. The present value, which means simply the value today, of the $1.21 to be received two years in the future is $1.00 at an interest rate of 10% compounded annually.

Suppose that you are promised $1,000 two years from now and your rate of interest is 10%. What is the present value of the $1,000? Obviously, it is less than $1,000 because of interest. The question is, how much would have to be invested now at 10%, compounded annually, to accumulate to $1,000 at the end of two years, or how much would you be willing to pay now for the promise of $1,000 two years from now? Using the formula above—$1,000 = Present value $\times$ $(1.10)^2$—we can solve for the unknown present value.

$$\text{Present Value} = \frac{1,000}{1.21} = \$826.45.$$

Proof: $\$826.45 + .10(\$826.45) = \$909.09$ Value at end of first year
$\$909.09 + .10(\$909.09) = \$1,000$ Value at end of second year

Thus, $826.45 invested now at 10% rate of interest compounded annually would grow to $1,000 by the end of two years.

The formal expression for finding the present value of an amount is as follows:

$$\text{Present Value} = \frac{\text{Future Amount}}{(1+i)^n}$$

where i = rate of interest and n = number of periods.
This formula is simply an algebraic variation of the formula for a future amount.

For the illustration above, the computation using this formula would be:

$$\frac{\$1,000}{(1+.1)^2} = \frac{\$1,000}{(1.10)^2} = \frac{\$1,000}{1.21} = \$826.45$$

Fortunately, present value tables are available to speed calculations. These tables can be found in Appendix C. Table II gives the present value of $1.00 for a number of different interest rates and for a series of different periods. To use the table, find the factor for the number of periods and the interest rate desired. Then multiply this factor by the future amount given. Thus, under the column labeled .10 opposite the row labeled 2 periods, we read .8264. Multiply this by $1,000 to arrive at $826.40. To take another example, the promise of $5,000 six years from now at 8% per year is worth $5,000 × .6302 = $3,151. This figure can be checked by compounding the $3,151 at 8% for six years.

Tables I and II are reciprocals, because the formula for the compound future amount of 1 multiplies 1 by $(1+i)^n$, whereas the formula for the present value of 1 divides 1 by $(1+i)^n$.

Fractional Period Compounding

The illustrations so far have been based on yearly compounding. If you are faced with semiannual or quarterly compounding, Tables I and II (or similar, more detailed tables) can still be used. $1,000 due in 3 years and discounted[4] at 8%, compounded annually, has a present value of $1,000 × .7938 (Table II) = $793.80. Interest is usually quoted as an annual rate, but compounding may occur more frequently. If the same note is discounted at 8%, compounded semiannually, the present value cannot be determined by using 8% in the table. Eight percent compounded semiannually means that 4% interest is computed each half-year on the instrument. Since there are 6 half-year periods in 3 years, the factor can be found by looking up 6 periods under 4% in the table. The present value then is $1,000 × .7903 = $790.30, slightly less than if the interest is compounded annually because the accumulation process under compounding is multiplicative rather than additive. The interest in the first year would be $64.49, computed as follows:

```
First half-year: $790.30 × .04              = $31.61
Second half-year: (790.30 + 31.61) × .04 =    32.88
   Total interest for first year             $64.49
```

If the same $1,000 is discounted at 8%, compounded quarterly for 3 years, the procedure is to find 4 times the number of periods in the table and to use one-fourth of the annual interest rate. Thus, we would use 12 periods at 2% to determine the discount factor. The present value is $1,000 × .7885 = $788.50. This is again slightly less than the previously computed amounts because a greater amount of interest is earned when interest is compounded more often.

Annuities

Some investments are of the type where an investment is made now (a present value) and there is one yield a few years later (a future amount).

---

4. The term *discounted* means the process of converting a future amount, or value, to its present value.

In such cases, Tables I and II in Appendix C are applicable. It is common, however, for an investment to yield a series, or stream, of future amounts. Let us consider this possibility. Because most accounting applications involve finding of present values, only the present value of a future amount or stream of payments will be considered.

Suppose you are promised $100 in one year and $300 at the end of two years. What is the present value of this promise if the interest rate is 10%, compounded annually? The present value will be the sum of the present values of the two amounts, as follows:

a. Present value of $100 to be received in first year at 10% plus
b. Present value of $300 to be received in second year at 10%.

These amounts are:

a. P.V. = $100 × .9091 (Table II) = $ 90.91
b. P.V. = $300 × .8264 (Table II) = $\underline{247.92}$
    Total present value = $338.83

The mathematical formula is:

$$\text{P.V.} = \frac{F_1}{(1+i)^1} + \frac{F_2}{(1+i)^2} + \cdots + \frac{F_n}{(1+i)^n}$$

where $F_1 \ldots n$ = future amount in periods 1 to n
i = the rate of interest

Note that the present value computed above is less than the total of $400 that is to be received. This is due to the effect of interest. A deposit now of $338.83 at 10% interest compounded annually is enough to yield $100 in one year and $300 more in two years.

An annuity is a special case of the type just discussed. In an annuity the payments or receipts each period are equal in amount. Thus, if $200 is promised at the end of each of two periods and the compound interest rate is 10% per period, the present value would be as follows:

a. P.V. of $200 in first period = $200 × .9091 = $181.82
b. P.V. of $200 in second period = $200 × .8264 = $\underline{165.28}$
    Total $347.10

Proof:
Initial investment	$347.10
10% interest in first period	$\underline{34.71}$
Total	381.81
Less withdrawal at end of first period	$\underline{200.00}$
Balance	181.81
10% interest in second period	$\underline{18.18}$
Total	199.99
Less withdrawal at end of second period	$\underline{200.00}$
Balance	−.01*

*Not exact because table is rounded to 4 places.

Mathematically, the formula for the present value of an annuity is as follows:

$$\text{Present Value for } n \text{ Periods} = \frac{R}{(1+i)^1} + \frac{R}{(1+i)^2} + \frac{R}{(1+i)^3} + \cdots \frac{R}{(1+i)^n}$$

where R = the periodic payment or receipt
or, algebraically summed:

$$\text{Present Value} = \frac{R\left(1 - \frac{1}{(1+i)^n}\right)}{i}$$

Tables can easily be constructed for annuities. The $347.10 present value derived above is the amount that, if invested now, would yield $200 a period for two periods. To look at it somewhat differently, the $200 a period yield provides for recovery of the original amount ($347.10) plus a 10% return. Table III in Appendix C is a table of the present values of annuities of $1 (where $1 is the periodic amount, or receipt) for various interest rates and various periods. It gives the present value of an annuity of $1 per period for a given number of periods at a given interest rate per period. Thus, the present value of an annuity of $1 a year for two years at 10% compounded annually is $1.736. The present value of an annuity of $200 a year for two years at 10% compounded annually is 1.736 multiplied by 200, or $347.20 — essentially the figure we obtained above. Thus, Table III can be used to find the present value of a stream of equal amounts of money. The table can be used directly only if the stream is constant in amount. If the receipts or payments are unequal, the present value is found by summing the present values of each separate receipt. Table II would be used for this type of problem.

Applications

Ideal asset valuation

Many accounting theorists assert that the value of an asset to its owner is fundamentally based on the present value of the estimated future net cash receipts (cash receipts less cash expenditures) from the asset. This theoretically ideal valuation involves a compound interest calculation, using either Table II or Table III in Appendix C, or both. Examples 8-7, 8-8, and 8-9 indicate how the tables can be used if future cash flows or net cash receipts are known.

EXAMPLE 8-7

A security investment is expected to yield $4,000 of cash when it is sold 3 years from now. The market interest rate is 12% per year, compounded annually. The value of the asset today is $4,000 × .7118 (Table II) = $2,847.20.

EXAMPLE 8-8

A note receivable is expected to yield $2,000 of cash per year at the end of each year for 6 years. The interest rate is 14% compounded annually. The value of the note today is $2,000 × 3.889 (Table III) = $7,778.

EXAMPLE 8-9

A piece of land is expected to yield $1,000 rent per year for 8 years and is to be sold at the end of the eighth year for $6,000. The market interest rate is 10% compounded annually. The value of the land today is

$1,000 × 5.335 (Table III) = $5,335
$6,000 × .4665 (Table II) = 2,799
Total present value $8,134

In most situations, however, the timing and amount of future cash flows are not known, and the appropriate interest rate cannot be determined. As a result, assets in accounting are generally recorded at a market price established in a transaction, and this price, called historical cost, remains the basis for future valuations in accounting. The market price, incidentally, presumably measures the discounted cash flow valuation of the parties operating in the market at that time.

Present value calculations are useful in a number of situations. The most important application is for long-term receivables and payables. The timing and amount of the cash flows of these particular assets and liabilities are reasonably certain. Under present generally accepted accounting principles these items should be carried at the present value of the net future cash amounts associated with them. This valuation conforms to the theoretical ideal mentioned above.

For most accounts receivable from customers and accounts payable to creditors the requirement that the amounts be valued at net present value is not burdensome. A receivable due in 30 to 60 days has a present value that is fairly close to the stated amount of the receivable. No material misstatement is believed to result if interest is ignored on short-term receivables and payables.[5]

The impact of the present value requirement becomes apparent when long-term receivables and payables are considered. As long as the receivable or payable carries an interest rate that approximates the market rate of interest for similar securities, the present value will be well represented by the face amount of the receivable or payable. However, if a sale is made for a $1,000, non-interest-bearing receivable due in two years, the sale cannot be recorded at $1,000 because the $1,000 includes implicit interest. There is implicit interest on the note because the seller gives up the opportunity of investing $1,000 and earning interest at the market

---

5. "Interest on Receivables and Payables," *APB Opinion No. 21*, August, 1971.

rate for the two years. An opportunity cost is involved. In business there is no such thing as a true non-interest-bearing note. Instead, the present value of the receivable must be determined and the sale recorded accordingly.[6] Assuming an interest rate of 10%, the entries for a sale on January 1, Year 1, with 2-year terms, would be as follows:

			Debit	Credit
Jan. 1	Long-term receivable		826.40	
	Sales			826.40
	$1,000 \times .8264$ (Table II) = $826.40			

An adjusting entry would be necessary at the end of the year:

Year 1			Debit	Credit
Dec. 31	Long-term receivable		82.64	
	Interest earned			82.64
	10% interest on $826.40 for one year.			

Finally, the receivable would be collected at the end of Year 2 and interest for the second year would be recorded:

Year 2			Debit	Credit
Dec. 31	Long-term receivable		90.96	
	Interest earned			90.96
	10% interest on ($826.40 + 82.64, plus .06 adjustment for rounding)			
Dec. 31	Cash		1,000.00	
	Long-term receivable			1,000.00
	Collection of account.			

What is the end result of the required treatment? Note first that the original sale is recorded at a lower amount. Second, interest is recorded in each period in which the receivable remains in effect. The total revenue from the illustrated transaction is $1,000, but instead of the total being recorded at the date of sale, a lesser amount is recorded at that date and the balance is recorded as interest over the term of the receivable. This difference in timing is crucial to determination of the correct income in each period, which is the most important objective of financial accounting.

The present value requirement also becomes important if a note bears interest but the rate of interest is well below the market rate. The market rate should be used to determine the present value and the subsequent interest on the note. Suppose a January 1 sale is made for a $1,000, 3% note, due in two years, with the interest collectible annually.

---

6. Ibid.

If the market rate varies widely from 3%, all parties will know that 3% is not the real interest rate in the transaction. The present value of this note is computed as follows, using an assumed current market rate of 10%:

Principal of note $1,000 × .8264 (Table II) = $826.40
Yearly interest $30 × 1.736 (Table III) =   52.08
Total present value   = $878.48

The following entries are made to record the transaction:[7]

			Debit	Credit
Year 1				
Jan. 1		Notes receivable	878.48	
		Sales		878.48
		Record sale at present value.		
Dec. 31		Cash	30.00	
		Notes receivable	57.85	
		Interest earned		87.85
		Record interest earned: 10% of $878.48; and $30 collected.		
Year 2				
Dec. 31		Cash	30.00	
		Notes receivable	63.67	
		Interest earned		93.67
		Record interest earned: 10% of $878.48 + 57.85 = $93.63 + .04 rounding error; and $30 collected.		
Dec. 31		Cash	1,000	
		Notes receivable		1,000
		Collection of principal.		

Note that the 10% interest each year exceeds the 3% interest collected. The balance is added to the note. The note grows to $1,000 by the time it is collected ($878 + 58 + 64 = $1,000).

Bonds

Bonds are a particular type of long-term receivable or payable. The two types of cash flows from bonds are (1) the periodic interest each year until maturity, which is an annuity, and (2) the payment of the principal at maturity. These amounts are discounted to their present value using a table of annuities and a table of the present value of $1. Bond investments are discussed in chapter 8, and bond liabilities are discussed in chapter 11.

---

7. Some prefer to record the note initially at $1,000 and credit an unamortized discount account for $121.52. In the later entries the accountant would debit the unamortized discount account rather than notes receivable.

Recording of interest earned or interest expense on a present value basis is also discussed in those chapters.

Leased Assets

Leases may be used as a means of purchasing. When a lease is used in this fashion, the asset and the obligation under the lease should be recorded at the present value of the payments to be made. Since the periodic payments are an annuity, the approach and the tables of this appendix should be applied. Leases are discussed more fully in chapter 11, where the use of present value computations is discussed. The basic procedure is to compute the present value of the future payments and to record this amount as the cost of the asset and as the lease obligation. A lessor who sells property by means of a long-term lease should record the sale at the present value of the lease payments to be received. The interest rate to be used in these calculations is often set by the terms of the lease contract. If it is not, the rate in the economy that is used for similar transactions would be the correct rate to use.

Further Uses of Present Value Tables

Present value problems can be somewhat less straightforward than those illustrated so far. A slightly more complicated problem is illustrated in Example 8-10.

EXAMPLE 8-10

A building is bought for $50,000. The building is expected to last for 20 years and have no salvage value. How much net proceeds (rent less costs) must be collected at the end of each year to provide a 16% return, assuming rents and costs are stable?

Proceeds × Factor (Table III) = Present Value
Proceeds × 5.929 = $50,000
Proceeds = $50,000 ÷ 5.929
Yearly Proceeds = $8,433

In this example the interest rate and years are known but instead of computing the present value, we must determine the periodic payments.

Three elements are involved in present value tables: an interest rate, a number of periods, and a present value factor. If any two of these elements are known, the third can be determined. In all previous illustrations an interest rate and a number of periods were given and the factor was then located in the appropriate table. One can also solve problems in which two other factors are known. Examples 8-11 and 8-12 illustrate.

EXAMPLE 8-11

A property yields rents of $5,000 per year for 15 years and has no salvage value. The cost of the property is $30,700. What interest rate does this investment yield?

$$\text{Rent} \times \text{Factor (Table III)} = \text{Present Value}$$
$$\$5,000 \times \text{Factor} = \$30,700$$
$$\text{Factor} = \$30,700 \div \$5,000 = 6.140$$

Looking in Table III under 15 years and reading across, the factor 6.140 is found to correspond to an interest rate of approximately 14%. Thus, the answer is 14%. (It is possible to interpolate in the tables, but an approximation usually suffices in most cases.)

EXAMPLE 8-12

How long would it take for an investment of $10,000 to grow to $20,000 if the interest rate is 12% compounded annually?

$$\text{Future Amount} \times \text{Factor (Table II)} = \text{Present Value}$$
$$\$20,000 \times \text{Factor} = \$10,000$$
$$\text{Factor} = \$10,000 \div \$20,000 = .500$$

Looking in Table II under 12% and reading down, a factor approximating .500 is found at 6 years. Thus, the answer is 6 years.

Many other types of problems could be illustrated, but examples 8-11 and 8-12 perhaps give a sufficient insight into the possibilities.

Annuities Due

Table III is constructed under the assumption that all payments are made at the end of the period. This type of annuity is called an *ordinary annuity*. If the payments are made at the beginning of the period rather than the end, we have what is called an *annuity due*. With an appropriate modification, Table II can be used for annuities due. Suppose $1 is paid at the end of each of 3 years with an interest rate of 10%. The present value is $1 × 2.487 (Table III) = $2.487. Table III can be used directly for this annuity. The situation is pictured in Figure 8-1.

FIGURE 8-1

Ordinary Annuity, 3 Periods, 10%

	1/1/77	12/31/77	12/31/78	12/31/79
Payments	0	$1.00	$1.00	$1.00
Interest Periods	Present	1	2	3

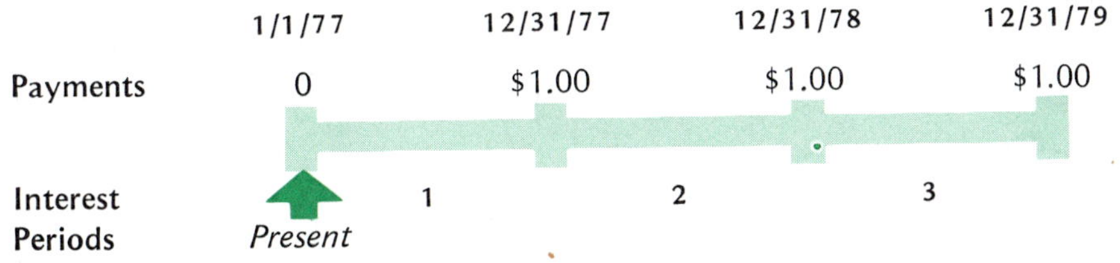

The present value of this annuity is:

$$\frac{1.00}{(1.10)^1} + \frac{1.00}{(1.10)^2} + \frac{1.00}{(1.10)^3} = 2.487$$

Note that there are three interest periods. The $1 at the end of the third year must be discounted for three periods in arriving at the present value.

Now suppose that the $1 is received at the beginning of each of the three years. This situation is pictured in Figure 8-2.

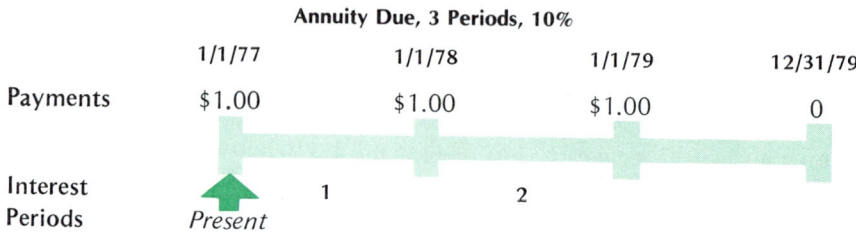

FIGURE 8-2

The present value of this annuity is:

$$1.00 + \frac{1.00}{(1.10)^1} + \frac{1.00}{(1.10)^2} = 2.736$$

This amount is higher than the ordinary annuity because all payments are received one period earlier. The first payment comes at the present and has a present value of $1, by definition. The other two amounts must be discounted for one and two periods, respectively (Year 1 and Year 2). If you used three periods in Table III, you would have three interest periods, as indicated in the first graph and computation. To find just two interest periods in the table, you would have to look under two periods in the table. The factor under two periods is 1.736, which is the present value of the amounts to be received at the beginning of the second and third years. Adding to this the present value of the $1 received at the start yields the present value of the annuity due, $2.736. To use Table III for the present value of an annuity due, the general rule is as follows: Look up one fewer period in the table and add $1.00 to the factor. Multiply the periodic payment by this total. The $1.00 is added to take care of the present value of the first payment.

QUESTIONS

8-1. What are the advantages and disadvantages of investing idle cash in temporary investments?

8-2. How are short-term investments distinguished from more permanent investments?

8-3. How should temporary investments be valued on the books?

8-4. Discuss the advisability of valuing temporary investments at current market prices.

8-5. If a bond carries an 8% interest rate and the investor pays more than par for the bond, is the yield more or less than 8%? Explain.

8-6. Is a bond that sells at a premium a better buy than a bond that sells at a discount? Explain.

8-7. Discuss the appropriateness of using current market prices to value long-term investments.

8-8. How would the market price of a 6%, $1,000 bond due in 8 years be determined?

8-9. Under the equity method of accounting for investments in stock, a dividend is considered to be a reduction of the investment. Explain the reasoning behind this treatment.

8-10. What are the arguments in favor of valuing long-term investments in stocks (less than 20% ownership) at cost? What are the arguments in favor of valuing them at lower of cost or market?

EXERCISES

8-11. *Temporary investments, accrual.* Give entries in general journal form for the following transactions of the Dunker Company:

Aug. 1   Purchase $100,000 (maturity value) in U.S. Treasury bills at a price of $97,400. The bills have a maturity date of January 28.

Nov. 2   Sold $60,000 (maturity value) of the bills for $59,246.

Dec. 31   Make the adjusting entry on the remaining Treasury bills.

8-12. *Temporary investments.* Give journal entries for the following transactions and the year-end adjustments for the High Products Co. At year-end, the company values the stock investments at the lower of cost or market. The method is applied to the aggregate of the stock investments; an allowance account is used.

Year 1

Jan. 25   Purchase 100 shares of Bowser Company stock at $45 per share.

Mar. 30   Purchase a $10,000 negotiable, 12-month CD that carries an interest rate of 6.0% at a price of $10,295. The maturity date of the certificate is September 26.

Apr. 30   Purchase 200 shares of General Rotors stock at $95 per share.

June 6   Receive a $1.20 per share dividend on the General Rotors stock and $2.00 per share on Bowser stock.

Sept. 26   Receive $10,600 cash for the CD acquired on March 30.

Dec. 31   This is the close of the company's fiscal year. Stocks owned are quoted at the following prices: Bowser Co., $47; General Rotors, $91. Prepare the appropriate adjusting entry.

8-13. *Temporary investments.* Give the entry that the High Products Company of Exercise 8-12 would make for the following transaction in Year 2:

Feb. 3   Sell the Bowser Company shares for $5,100, less a commission of $150 to the broker for handling the sale.

8-14. *Equity method.* Give entries for the following transactions of Keller Co., which uses the equity method to account for substantial investments in stock.

Jan. 5   Purchase 25% of the stock of DeCoster Co. stock for $540,000 cash.
May 15   Receive $10,000 of cash dividends from DeCoster.
Oct. 15   Receive $8,000 of cash dividends from DeCoster.
Dec. 30   DeCoster reports earning net income of $220,000 for the year.

(Solution in Appendix B.)

8-15. *Bond investment, price determination.* What is the market price of a $1,000, 7% bond due in exactly 8 years? Assume that interest is payable annually. The market interest rate is 10%.

8-16. *Long-term investments, straight-line amortization.* The Handly Company purchases Exeter Co. bonds of $10,000 face value on January 1, Year 1, at 98. The bonds are to be held as a long-term investment. The bonds bear interest at 6%, payable semiannually. Discount is to be amortized once each year. The bonds are due on January 1, Year 5. Give entries for the following:

a. Collection of interest on June 30, Year 1, $300.
b. Collection of interest on December 31, Year 1.
c. Amortization of discount on December 31, Year 1, using straight-line amortization.
d. Collection of the principal amount of the bonds on January 1, Year 5, assuming that the company made correct entries in the intervening years.

8-17. *Bond investment, price determination.* What is the market price of a $1,000, 10% bond due in exactly 9 years if the market rate of interest is 8%? Assume that interest is payable semiannually.

8-18. *Bond investment, effective-interest amortization.* A $1,000, 6% bond of the Steen Co. is purchased as a long-term investment for $727.44 on January 1 of the current year. The bond is due in 12 years and interest is payable each December 31. The bonds are valued so that they yield 10% interest.

a. Give entries for the first year, including effective-interest amortization of discount.
b. Give the entries for the second year, including the amortization entry.

PROBLEMS

8-19. *Investments.* Give entries for the following transactions of the Newton Co. in the current year. All investments are temporary investments.

Feb. 25   Purchase 300 shares of AT&T stock at $55 per share. Broker's fees are $147.
May 1   Purchase $10,000 face amount of Ling 6% bonds for $8,300 plus $150 accrued interest since last interest date. Interest is payable on February 1 and August 1.

May 20	Buy 1,000 shares of Honeywell at $75 per share. Broker's fees are $640.
Aug. 1	Collect 6 months' interest on Ling bonds.
Aug. 15	Receive a $450 dividend on AT&T stock.
Aug. 20	Receive a $500 dividend on Honeywell stock.
Nov. 20	Sell the AT&T stock for $60 per share. Broker's fees are $152.
Dec. 31	Record accrued interest on Ling bonds.
Dec. 31	The Ling bonds are quoted at $8,100 on December 31. Honeywell stock is quoted at $74. Make any necessary adjustment to the lower of cost or market basis (treat all investments as a group and use an allowance account).

(Solution in Appendix B.)

8-20. *Temporary investments.* The Smiley Company has the following portfolio of temporary investments on December 31:

Common stocks:

	Number of Shares	Cost
Heaven Scent Co.	100	$ 3,200
Mord Foto Co.	200	12,600
Dividends receivable as of December 31:		
Heaven Scent Co.		$ 80
Mord Foto Co.		200

Note: Dividends Receivable is an account separate from Temporary Investments

U.S. Treasury bills:

Maturity Date	Days to Maturity	Maturity Value	Cost plus Interest Earned through Dec. 31
May 6	126	$ 60,000	$ 58,950
June 24	175	150,000	146,208
July 29	210	200,000	193,700

Give journal entries for the following:

Jan. 16	Collected the dividends that were receivable on December 31.
Feb. 19	Purchased negotiable 12-month CDs issued by the Greater Mercantile Bank. The certificates are for $50,000, are dated February 19, and carry an interest rate of 6.5%. The total cost to Smiley Company is $50,236, to yield an annual interest rate of 6.0%.
May 6	Redeemed the May 6 Treasury bills.
May 24	Sold 50 shares of the Heaven Scent stock for a net price of $38 per share.
June 24	Redeemed the June 24 Treasury bills.
June 26	Received notice of dividends declared on June 24 and payable on July 21: Mord Foto, $1.20 per share; Heaven Scent, $.90 per share.
June 30	Prepared adjusting entries as required on temporary investments owned on June 30. The market price of the common

stock owned (after deducting the dividends declared): Heaven Scent, $30 per share; Mord Foto, $65 per share.

8-21. *Bond investment, effective-interest amortization.* On January 1 of the current year the Welsh Company decides it will buy $10,000 face amount of White Company 8% bonds. The bonds are due in exactly 11 years and pay interest annually on December 31. The current market rate on similar bonds is 10%. The bonds will be held as a long-term investment.
  a. Compute the price to be paid for the bonds.
  b. Give entries for the current year, including effective-interest amortization of interest.
  c. Give entries for the second year, including amortization.
  d. Give the entry for sale of the bonds on January 1 of the third year for $9,725.

(Solution in Appendix B.)

8-22. *Bond investment, straight-line amortization.* On April 1 of the current year the Larson Company decides it will buy $10,000 face amount of Zlatko 7% bonds. The bonds are due in exactly 10 years and pay interest annually on March 31. The current market price, based on a 10% market interest rate, is $8,156.00.
  a. Give the entry for the purchase on April 1.
  b. Give the entries on December 31 for accrued interest and amortization for the first year. Use straight-line amortization.
  c. Give the entry for receipt of interest on March 31 of the second year.
  d. Give the entries on December 31 of the second year.
  e. Give the entry for sale of the bonds on January 1 of the third year for $9,120 plus accrued interest.

(Solution in Appendix B.)

8-23. *Bond investment, effective-interest amortization.* Refer to problem 8-22 and solve the problem using effective-interest amortization.

8-24. *Classification of investments.* Analyze each situation below and determine the amount of the investment and whether the investment is short-term or long-term.
  a. Company X buys 5½%, 91-day bills of the U.S. Treasury. The total price is $20,850.
  b. We lend $30,000 cash to one of our suppliers, Smalch Company. The Smalch president gives us the company's 6%, 5-year note in face amount of $32,000.
  c. We sell a machine to the X-Y Company for $20,000. The X-Y Company gives us a 4-year, non-interest-bearing note in face amount of $26,000.
  d. One of our highly valued raw materials suppliers is experiencing financial difficulty. In order to insure a continuing source of raw materials, we lend him $300,000 on a 7%, 6-month note. We have agreed to renew the note at the end of each 6-month period for up to 4 years. However, accrued interest will be paid to us at the end of each 6-month period.
  e. We are planning to expand our plant facilities. We will break ground for the new plant in 3 years, but the cash is available now. We invest this

cash in 6%, 10-year bonds of face value $500,000 at a total price of $480,000.

8-25. *Classification of investments.* Careless Company has one general ledger account labeled Investments. As the CPA auditor, you discover this account includes the following as of December 31:

	Debit	Credit	Balance
20,000 shares of Caremore Company stock. These shares represent 12% of Caremore outstanding stock; they were acquired several years ago for $60,000.	60,000		60,000
Dividend received from Caremore this year		2,000	58,000
U.S. Treasury bills purchased this year, at cost	213,500		271,500
Redemption of Treasury bills this year for cash of $219,375		219,375	52,125

Required:
a. What amount should be reported as investments on the December 31 balance sheet? Should this be shown as a temporary investment or long-term investment?
b. What adjusting entries should be made to reflect the investments of Careless Company correctly?

8-26. *Long-term investments.* The Manning Company had the following transactions in its long-term investments during the year. Give appropriate entries.

Mar. 1 — Purchase Baughn bonds of $20,000 par value for $20,600, including broker's fees. The bonds bear interest of 6%, payable semiannually on February 28 and August 31. The bonds mature on February 28, 6 years hence.

Apr. 15 — Purchase 2,000 shares of stock of Clark Company at $34 per share. This is less than 1% of Clark's stock.

May 1 — A dividend of $.20 per share is received on Clark Company stock.

Aug. 31 — Record interest received on Baughn bonds.

Dec. 31 — Record accrued interest and premium amortization on the Baughn bonds. Use straight-line amortization.

Dec. 31 — Because of a disastrous and uninsured earthquake at its main plant, Clark Company stock has dropped to $20 per share at the end of the year.

CASE PROBLEM

8-27. *Investment valuation.* Several years ago Owens Illinois Corporation had the following amounts under the long-term investments category in its balance sheet in 2 successive years:

	(in thousands)	
	Year 2	Year 1
Investments in Owens Corning Fiberglas stock, at cost	$2,092	$2,296

The market value of the investments was $162 million in Year 1 and $145 million in Year 2. These amounts were shown parenthetically in the balance sheet. The reduction in cost occurred because Owens Illinois sold $204,000 of Owens Corning stock for $13,700,000, resulting in a gain before tax of $13,500,000. Analysis indicates that the market value of the stock in Year 1 was 70.5 times the cost. In Year 2 it was 69.3 times the cost.

Required:

a. Was Owens Illinois's accounting proper from the standpoint of generally accepted accounting principles? Is the disclosure adequate?

b. Discuss the accounting treatment from the standpoint of the usefulness of the information provided to investors.

9

Inventories and Cost of Goods Sold Expense

Unexpired costs are assets that will become expenses in future accounting periods. They are shown as assets until the time comes to transfer them to the expense category. This important category of assets includes items such as plant and equipment, inventories, intangibles, and prepaid assets. Two main aspects of unexpired costs are emphasized in this text:

1. Determination of the expense that arises when a cost "expires," or is used up
2. Determination of the asset balance that remains to be charged to later accounting periods

These two aspects are closely interrelated, since determination of the appropriate expense almost automatically determines the asset balance that remains. Some of the knottiest conceptual and practical problems of accounting are involved in these two aspects of unexpired costs.

The common characteristic of short-term unexpired costs is that they will become expenses in the near future—usually in the next accounting period of the enterprise. The occasion for transferring unexpired costs to expense may be a physical event, such as sale of inventory or use of office supplies. In other cases the occasion for transfer to expense may be the passage of time. For example, prepaid insurance becomes insurance expense as time passes.

Types

Short-term unexpired costs are of two main types: inventories and prepaid expenses. *Inventories* consist of items that lead directly to revenues (such as sales). *Prepaid expenses* are items that will become expenses, but do not directly produce revenues. This distinction is not perfect, for in essence all items of expense should be incurred only if they will contribute to the total revenues of the firm and to the profit of the company. But the

Part III Measurement of Assets, Liabilities, and Income

relationship of prepaid expenses to revenues is less direct than that of inventories. This chapter discusses inventories, the most important short-term unexpired cost. Chapter 10 discusses long-term unexpired costs.

DEFINITIONS AND OBJECTIVES

Inventory defined

Inventory refers to items of tangible personal property that are being held for sale in the ordinary course of business, are being produced for sale, or are to be consumed in the near future in producing goods or services for sale. Inventories include the following:

Merchandise inventory	Found in trading concerns
Finished goods inventory }	
Goods in process inventory }	Found in manufacturing
Raw materials inventory }	concerns
Supplies inventory (supplies on hand)	Found in all types of companies

Classes of goods held for sale include merchandise inventory in a trading concern and finished goods inventory in a manufacturing concern. Goods being produced in a manufacturing concern are called *goods in process inventory.* Items that are not yet even in the stage of production are called *raw materials inventories.* Supplies on hand are often classified as inventory, but this category of inventory differs from others in that supplies are used up in activities and do not become part of the products that are offered for sale.[1]

Accounting for inventories has the following objectives:

Objectives

1. To measure the periodic income of a business
2. To determine the financial position of the business
3. To assist in managing assets efficiently and profitably

The first step in fulfilling these objectives is to define and measure the items that constitute inventory. Thus we want the answers to two questions:

1. What items are included in inventory?
2. What is the cost of these items?

ITEMS INCLUDED IN INVENTORY

Rule on items included

In general, a company will inventory all items that it owns. Ownership usually, though not always, involves holding title to goods. In deciding

---

1. This is also true of "indirect materials" in a manufacturing operation.

which goods a company owns, therefore, we generally look at who holds title. In transactions between companies, we similarly focus our attention on passage of title. Passage of title brings in a legal concept and therefore some complications. Generally, title passes when goods are delivered, either to the buyer or to the buyer's agent. If delivery is made directly to the buyer by the seller, there is no problem. If there is an intermediary, however, such as a delivery agent or railroad, the situation is less clear. If the terms of sale provide that the seller pay the freight (FOB destination), the intermediary acts as the seller's agent, and title does not pass until the goods reach the destination. If the terms provide that the buyer pay the freight (FOB shipping point), the railroad or delivery agent acts as the agent of the buyer, and title passes as soon as the intermediary obtains possession of the goods. These rules usually hold, but sometimes common trade practices take precedence over the rules in determining when title passes.

Another aspect of the problem deserves mention. At times, a company has items on its premises that it does not own. It may hold these goods on consignment from someone else. The supplier (consignor) retains ownership of the items, even though they are held by the party who will sell them (consignee).[2] The items should be excluded from the consignee's inventory, since the consignee does not own them. The items should be included in the consignor's inventory, even though they are at someone else's place of business.

COST OF INVENTORY

Cost rule

The cost of an inventory item to a company is the net cash cost of obtaining the item and getting it ready for use or sale. This definition needs some explanation.

Net cash cost refers particularly to trade or cash discount terms sometimes offered to a purchaser. Cash discount terms of 2/10, n/30, for example, allow purchasers to reduce their payments by 2% if they pay within 10 days from the date of purchase. Is this 2% an added revenue to the buyer, or should it be considered a reduction of cost? Accountants favor the latter view, which is based on the idea that a company makes a profit by selling goods, not by buying them. Accountants look on the real price of a purchase with terms of 2/10, n/30 as being 98% of the list price, with a 2% penalty if payment is not made within 10 days.

Transport cost

The phrase "getting it ready for use or sale" refers to the fact that the cost of goods often includes costs other than invoice price. It is obvious that goods purchased from a supplier in Chicago by a buyer in Los Angeles

---

2. The party with goods on consignment from others will sell these goods and earn a commission on items sold.

do no good if they remain on the loading dock in Chicago. The goods must be transported, and the transportation must be paid for. If the buyer pays the freight, this cost should be added to the invoice price itself in determining the total cost of the goods. Freight is an important cost element in many situations and may be the deciding factor in choosing between two different suppliers. In the above example, freight costs may dictate purchasing from a supplier in Long Beach rather than one in Chicago. Any other necessary costs involved in getting the goods to the display counters or warehouses or stockrooms are also integral parts of the cost of the items. Thus, technically, transportation, handling, and storage costs; excise and sales taxes; import duties; and other costs directly associated with obtaining an item should be added to the cost of the item.

Materiality

When actually costing items in the inventory, some of the costs mentioned above can be ignored on the basis of materiality or expediency. *Materiality* refers to relative size and importance, and when these costs are minor in amount, they often can be safely ignored. Expediency enters in when it is too difficult to determine these costs and assign them to units in inventory. Any departure from a theoretically correct approach should be recognized as such; and, of course, such departures should be justified in some way. Justification on the basis of expediency is not appealing, but it may be necessary when a company faces the practical difficulties of assigning costs.

DETERMINATION OF INVENTORY COSTS AND COST OF GOODS SOLD

We have indicated that an enterprise should include in inventory all goods that it owns, and that the costs of the inventory should include all net cash costs involved in getting it to the place of business and ready for use or sale. Let us now consider what happens to costs after they appear in the enterprise. This aspect of inventory leads to a consideration of measurement of periodic income and determination of financial position.

Measuring periodic income

In measuring the periodic income of a business, costs are associated with related revenues. Economic, rather than physical, association of cost with related revenues is basic in the matching process.[3] Economic significance concerns us because we consistently try to report on the conditions and operations of a company in relationship to the economy. Therefore, we are not as concerned with what management does as we are with the economic significance of what management does. This distinction means

---

3. Some accountants disagree with this view and criticize the phrase "economic association of cost" as being meaningless. Most accountants find the concept helpful in dealing with inventories.

that we are concerned with dollars rather than with physical units, insofar as the dollars reflect the economic significance of items. This statement implies that the actual, physical movement of goods and the assumed movement of goods through the enterprise for periodic income determination and asset valuation do not necessarily have to correspond.

The process of associating costs and revenues (matching) is facilitated by tracing costs to items of inventory, as described above. The next step in the process is to transfer the costs to expense in the period in which the goods are sold. The cost of the inventory items can be matched against revenues directly by means of the perpetual inventory approach or indirectly by means of the periodic inventory approach.

Periodic Inventory Method

The periodic inventory method assumes that the cost of goods no longer on hand belongs in cost of goods sold. Purchases, returns and allowances, discounts, and freight-in are all recorded in separate accounts. The inventory at the end of the period is counted and recorded and cost of goods sold is then computed. This approach has been illustrated in chapters 4 and 5.

Perpetual Inventory Method

Under a perpetual inventory method, the cost of all merchandise acquired is debited to the inventory account at the time of purchase. Any freight cost incurred in getting purchased merchandise to the place of business is also considered to be a part of the inventory. For example, suppose a company purchases nine pianos on account at a cost of $500 each.

	Debit	*Credit*
Inventory	4,500	
Accounts payable		4,500

If the company pays freight of $72 for delivery of the pianos to the store, the entry is as follows:

	Debit	*Credit*
Inventory	72	
Cash		72

The pianos thus are reflected in the inventory account at a per unit cost of $508 each ($500 invoice price plus $8 freight).

As pianos are sold, two entries are necessary: one to record the sales revenue and one to record the costs of the goods sold. If seven of the pianos are sold for $5,600 cash, the following entries would be made:

	Debit	Credit
Cash	5,600	
Sales		5,600
Cost of goods sold	3,556	
Inventory		3,556
Seven pianos at $508 each.		

The inventory account appears as follows after all entries for the purchase, freight, and sale have been posted:

Inventory

Original purchase	4,500	Cost of goods sold	3,556
Freight	72		
Balance 1,016			

The balance of $1,016 represents the cost of the two unsold pianos (2 × $508). This balance is an unexpired cost that will be matched against revenue in later periods. The $3,556 cost of merchandise sold appears in the income statement as the cost of goods sold. This cost is associated with the sales revenue during the current period.

As a result of using the perpetual inventory method, the dollar amount of inventory that should be on hand is known at all times. No separate purchases, allowances, discount, or freight accounts are used. Instead, all amounts flow into the inventory account. There is no need to record ending inventory because the inventory account should be up to date. Physical counts of inventory should be made periodically under the perpetual inventory method to see whether actual amounts on hand agree with the bookkeeping records. Correcting entries should be made if there are any discrepancies.

COSTING METHODS

Problems

Both of the systems of relating inventory costs to revenues involve considerable problems. In the periodic inventory system, for example, there is the problem of counting and pricing the goods that are on hand so that a company can determine the cost of the goods that must have been sold. In the perpetual inventory system, on the other hand, there is the problem of pricing the units that are removed from the inventory throughout the accounting period. These problems are minimized when there are no price changes during an accounting period; but whenever movements in prices occur—and such movements are common—there is considerable difficulty in determining the cost of the items that are left in the inventory and the cost of the items that have been sold.

Specific Identification Method

One way of solving the problems connected with determining inventory cost and cost of goods sold is to keep track of the cost of each individual item. Determining the cost of inventory in such a situation consists of adding up the costs of the specific unsold items.

This method, while satisfactory at times, is not an adequate method for most accounting situations. It is impractical when there is a large number of items with small unit costs. Even when the number of items is small enough so that counting them is practical, the specific identification method has serious shortcomings. The measurements produced by the specific identification method may be erratic rather than orderly; that is, management may be able to influence the amount of its income and assets arbitrarily by selecting an item for sale solely on the basis of its specific cost, even though the item is otherwise identical with other items in a group. Remember that accountants emphasize the economic rather than the physical relationship of cost and revenue. At times, the physical identification of the item might not truly reflect the economic significance of the item. For example, a company may have on hand at a particular point of time two items that have the same economic service potential but different costs. Two cans of coffee may have been purchased at different times and at different prices, but this does not mean they have different economic significance. The specific identification method allows management to choose either one of these items and thus influence the amount of cost to be matched against revenue.

Automobile dealers find that the specific identification method is satisfactory for use in their business, since the cars that they sell can often be differentiated from one another, and the unit costs involved are high. For most business situations, however, the specific identification method is both impractical and arbitrary and thus must be rejected. A method that assumes a logical economic flow of cost from asset to expense is more objective and more practical than the specific identification method. Let us now turn to a discussion of assumed economic cost flows in a periodic inventory system. Perpetual inventory records are discussed in the appendix.

Assumed Cost Flows

There are three common methods involving assumed flows of cost. *First-in, first-out* (FIFO) assumes that the costs of the first units acquired are the first costs disposed of, and that the costs left in the inventory are the costs of the units from the most recent purchases. *Last-in, first-out* (**LIFO**) assumes that the costs of the last units acquired are the first costs disposed of. In this system, the ending inventory of a period is composed of costs of units from the earliest acquisitions, usually the beginning inventory plus current acquisitions to the extent applicable. The later costs (last ones in) are matched against the revenues of the accounting period. The third method is the *weighted average-cost method*, which assumes that the costs of units acquired flow into a pool where the cost of one unit cannot be distinguished from that of another. Items withdrawn for sale or use have a cost that is an average of the cost of all acquisitions *weighted by the quantities acquired* at each acquisition date. Naturally, the items left in the inventory also will be at an average cost.

The data in Table 9-1 are assumed for purposes of illustrating each of these three cost methods. (Note that prices rise gradually throughout the period.)

TABLE 9-1

	Units	Unit Cost	Total Cost
January 1 Inventory	100	$1.00	$100
Purchases:			
March 28	50	$1.10	$ 55
April 30	100	1.20	120
June 25	100	1.30	130
September 8	50	1.40	70
November 20	100	1.50	150
Total purchases	400		$525
Goods available for sale	500		$625
Sales during the year: 100 units on April 15			
100 units on July 20			
100 units on Sept. 30			
Units left in inventory: 500 available minus 300 sold equals 200			

First-In, First-Out (FIFO). The company's inventory on December 31 under the first-in, first-out assumption as to flow of cost would be composed of the cost of the last 200 units bought, determined as follows:

	Units	Unit Cost	Total Cost
Nov. 20	100	$1.50	$150
Sept. 8	50	1.40	70
June 25	50	1.30	65
	200		$285

Notice that the costs of only 50 of the units bought on June 25 are included in the inventory, since 50 of this lot are all that are needed to make up a total of 200 units. The items not listed in the ending inventory, of course, are assumed to be in cost of goods sold expense under the assumption of first-in, first-out. Observe also that the costs have been rising for the period under consideration. With this situation the first-in, first-out method will give

Features of FIFO

1. An ending inventory balance closely in line with current acquisition costs (since latest costs are in inventory)
2. A cost of goods sold that is out of date, since it consists of the earliest costs of the period

To amplify the second point, note that price changes in goods purchased are not reflected immediately in the cost of goods sold under FIFO. Instead, such costs remain in inventory until all goods purchased previously have been sold. Thus, there is a time lag in application of latest costs to cost of goods sold. Many accountants believe that this feature of FIFO results in a poor matching of current costs against current revenue.

On the other hand, FIFO is objective, since it results in an orderly, chronological procession of costs in which the oldest costs are matched against revenue, or expire, first. It is reasonable that businesses should attempt to move and sell the old items first, and thus FIFO is often in accordance with the normal physical flow of costs. Also, FIFO is a suitable inventory method whenever turnover is rapid and there is only a short time lag between the acquisition of goods and the sale (between the purchase of the goods and the transfer of the cost of goods from inventory into cost of goods sold expense). This method is inadequate in times of rapidly changing prices because it tends to leave the most recent costs in inventory and to place the older costs, which are somewhat out of date, in cost of goods sold expense. Although sales are recorded in terms of up-to-date, current figures at all times, current costs take some time to get into costs of goods sold under FIFO. Therefore, somewhat old and out-of-date costs are matched against revenues.

Matching

Under FIFO, cost of goods sold expense would be computed by subtracting the ending inventory cost from the cost of goods available for sale, as follows:

Cost of goods available for sale	$625
Less inventory cost	285
Cost of goods sold expense	340

This figure represents the cost of the first 300 units on hand during the year, which, in accordance with the first-in, first-out assumption, would be the first ones sold. The cost can be computed directly by counting costs of units sold, starting with the beginning inventory, as follows:

	Units	Unit Cost	Total Cost
Jan. 1	100	$1.00	$100
Mar. 28	50	1.10	55
April 30	100	1.20	120
June 25	50	1.30	65
	300		340

Last-In, First-Out (LIFO). The ending inventory of the company under the last-in, first-out method would be composed of the cost of the first 200 units on hand or purchased during the period, as follows:

	Units	Unit Cost	Total Cost
Jan. 1	100	$1.00	$100
Mar. 28	50	1.10	55
April 30	50	1.20	60
	200		215

In the computation, notice that the costs of only 50 of the items from April 30 are included, since that is all that is required to make a total of 200 units.

Cost of goods sold expense would be computed by subtracting the ending inventory from the cost of goods available for sale, as follows:

Cost of goods available for sale	$625
Less inventory cost	215
Cost of goods sold expense	410

This figure represents the cost of the last 300 units acquired during the year, which, in accordance with the last-in, first-out assumption, would be the first units sold. The cost can be computed directly by counting costs of units sold, starting with the most recent purchase, as follows:

	Units	Unit Cost	Total Cost
Nov. 20	100	$1.50	$150
Sept. 8	50	1.40	70
June 25	100	1.30	130
April 30	50	1.20	60
	300		410

The costs left in inventory under this method are the costs of the oldest items. Since the costs of the last items in are the first ones out, the cost of the first items in are left in inventory. This seems like a paradoxical inventory method, since it is certainly not in accordance with the normal physical flow of goods through an enterprise. Actual flows on a LIFO basis are rare. An example is the flow from a keg or bin of nails that is filled from the top. Items are drawn off the top as sales are made; the nails left at the bottom may have been there for years.

Since this sort of flow is unusual, isn't LIFO unrealistic? In answer to this question, we can repeat that the flow of costs through the enterprise does not necessarily have to correspond to the physical movement of goods through the enterprise; in fact, it is economic rather than physical relationships with which we are concerned. The principal argument in favor of LIFO is that it does a better job of matching current purchase prices (the last ones in) against current sales prices than do the other methods of inventory pricing. The basis for stating that LIFO does accomplish a better matching is the likelihood that sales prices and cost prices will move together. If they do move together, it is logical to match against the revenues of an accounting period the costs which are most nearly related to them—that is, the latest costs. The argument also might be put in terms of economic relevance. The costs that have the most relevance or impact on current decisions are current costs. The LIFO method shows these current costs in cost of goods sold expense, thus giving a sound measurement of income.

Matching

LIFO, however, can result in an asset balance that is substantially out of line with current costs if the quantity in the inventory remains stable or increases. For example, the January 1 inventory costs in the illustration would be included in the inventory on December 31. These costs could continue to stay in the inventory for years, regardless of movements of prices. In fact, the only way to eliminate these old costs would be to reduce the inventory quantity almost to zero, which is impractical in most companies. Therefore, a company that carries its inventory at LIFO and that has experienced steadily rising prices will tend to have an inventory in its statement of financial position that is out of date and therefore unrepresentative of current costs.

Effect on assets

Finally, it should be noted that a company can use the LIFO method for tax purposes only if it also uses LIFO for financial reporting purposes. This is not true of other inventory methods. Some accountants would consider this provision of the tax law to be a serious drawback.

Weighted Average Cost. A weighted average cost can be computed in different ways.[4] One common way of computing it is illustrated below:

Average cost of goods available:

$$\frac{\text{Cost of All Units}}{\text{Number of Units}} = \text{Unit Cost}$$

$$\frac{\$625}{500} = \$1.25$$

---

4. A weighted average gives more weight to items that occur more frequently. A simple average would take the six prices, add them together, and divide the total by six.

$$\text{Units in inventory} \times \text{Unit Cost} = \text{Cost of Inventory}$$
$$200 \times \$1.25 = \$250$$

The cost of goods sold is computed by subtracting the cost of the inventory from the cost of goods available for sale, as follows:

Cost of goods available for sale	$625.00
Less inventory cost	250.00
Cost of goods sold expense	$375.00

The cost of goods sold can also be computed by multiplying the number of units sold (300) by the unit price ($1.25), but one must beware of rounding errors.

The *weighted average method* tends to give an inventory cost that lies between those resulting from FIFO and LIFO. By its nature, the weighted average method tends to be a compromise between the extremes of FIFO and LIFO. It avoids pronounced distortion in the inventory in a time of changing prices, because it cannot get too far out of date. It also matches average costs against the revenues of the period, rather than using either the latest costs (LIFO) or the earliest costs (FIFO). As a method, the weighted average approach is generally objective, orderly, and free from manipulation. However, when there are many types of articles in the inventory, or when acquisition costs change frequently, the method requires a large number of computations and can become burdensome.

Comparison of Results of the Assumed Cost Flow Methods. The results of the three assumed cost flow methods are summarized in Table 9-2. From the summary, it is obvious that in a time of rising prices, first-in, first-out gives the highest inventory figure ($285), weighted average is in between ($250), and last-in, first-out gives the lowest ending inventory ($215). The situations are reversed in regard to cost of goods sold, with LIFO giving the highest cost of goods sold in the time of rising prices ($410), weighted average being in the middle ($375), and FIFO giving the lowest cost of goods sold ($340).

Note that the total is the same with all three methods. This will only be true if beginning inventories and purchases are the same, as they are in this example. In subsequent periods the beginning inventories will differ, and therefore the total will also be different.

TABLE 9-2. Comparison of Results of Inventory Methods

	Ending Inventory Value	Cost of Goods Sold Expense	Total
FIFO	$285.00	$340.00	$625.00
LIFO	215.00	410.00	625.00
Weighted average	250.00	375.00	625.00

Inventories and Cost of Goods Sold Expense   **Chapter 9**

LIFO and taxes

If the business objective is to minimize income taxes in an accounting period, it is advantageous to the business to use LIFO in a time of rising prices. The higher amount for cost of goods sold will reduce net income and reduce income taxes. This tax effect will persist as long as prices continue to rise. On the other hand, it is advantageous from an income tax standpoint to use FIFO when prices are dropping. Since the United States has had a steady inflationary rise for more than two decades, many businessmen have found LIFO to be a method that suits their desires exactly. Unfortunately, the tax minimization aspect of LIFO is allowed to outweigh most of the other considerations regarding its use. There are serious disadvantages of the LIFO method that businessmen often have disregarded solely because of its tax advantages.

LIFO disadvantages

One obvious disadvantage of using LIFO is that in a time of rising prices income will tend to be lower than it would be if other inventory methods were used. This lower level of income can have adverse effects on stockholder relations and may make it more difficult to obtain funds in the market (by issuing capital stock or borrowing). A company using FIFO generally will show a relatively higher income and may appear more attractive in a time of rising prices, though the firm also will pay higher income taxes. Because LIFO inventories usually will be carried at old costs, which will be lower than current costs in a time of inflation, a company that uses FIFO also will look better from the standpoint of the amount of assets owned.

Income manipulation

The LIFO method has another disturbing feature. LIFO permits manipulation of income. As mentioned above, LIFO inventories can easily include old and out-of-date costs. The depletion of a company's inventories (that is, reducing the number of units below the number in the beginning inventory, either accidentally or intentionally) will have the effect of throwing old costs into cost of goods sold and may cause significant distortions in net income. This situation cannot occur with FIFO or average costing. As a result of the possibility of distorted income, accountants usually recommend that LIFO not be used in a company that has large fluctuations in inventory quantities.

Economic policy

Finally, let us look at the different inventory methods from the standpoint of broad economic policy. Most governments are committed to a policy of trying to reduce business cycle fluctuations. LIFO is the inventory method that is most consistent with this policy. Business cycle theorists generally agree that the psychology of businessmen is an important force in business cycles, having especially strong effects on capital investment decisions and on purchasing, production, and pricing policies. Because LIFO shows lower profits during inflation and higher profits during deflation, it dampens business enthusiasm during inflation and encourages businessmen during a period of deflation. LIFO's effects on business psychology should produce economic effects that are in accordance with countercyclical policies in general.

283

The preceding discussion of the advantages and disadvantages of the various inventory methods is by no means exhaustive. It does, however, give some indication of the complex issues involved.

Inventory Methods and Reality

Inventory is an important factor in determining cost of goods sold and income for a period. Inventories are often one of the most important assets of a merchandising or producing company. Their valuation has a considerable effect on balance sheet representations. The summary of results in Table 9-2 revealed that both the income statement results and the balance sheet presentation can vary considerably, depending on the inventory method adopted. Two companies with an identical physical situation would show very different financial statements in a time of changing prices if one used FIFO and the other used LIFO.

Any statement that is prepared is to some extent an interpretation of the underlying reality on which it reports. We do not expect financial statements prepared by different people to be exactly the same, since people differ and their interpretations therefore differ. But it is proper to ask whether accurate interpretations can vary significantly from one another. Consider Example 9-1.

EXAMPLE 9-1

Facts: Companies A and B are similar in all respects. A uses FIFO; B uses LIFO. Cash on January 1, Year 1, is $500.
Beginning inventory Year 1 100 at $20
Purchases (for cash) Year 1 100 at $22
　　　　　　　　　　　Year 2 100 at $25
　　　　　　　　　　　Year 3 100 at $30
Sales (for cash) Year 1 100 at $30
　　　　　　　　　Year 2 100 at $33
　　　　　　　　　Year 3 100 at $36
Expenses of $500 each year are paid in cash.
Income tax rate: 50%. No dividends are paid.

Income Statements

	Company A (FIFO)			Company B (LIFO)		
	Year 1	Year 2	Year 3	Year 1	Year 2	Year 3
Sales	$3,000	$3,300	$3,600	$3,000	$3,300	$3,600
Cost of goods sold	2,000	2,200	2,500	2,200	2,500	3,000
Gross profit	1,000	1,100	1,100	800	800	600
Expenses	500	500	500	500	500	500
Income before tax	500	600	600	300	300	100
Income tax	250	300	300	150	150	50
Net income	$ 250	$ 300	$ 300	$ 150	$ 150	$ 50

Statements of Financial Position
End of year

	Company A			Company B		
	Year 1	Year 2	Year 3	Year 1	Year 2	Year 3
Assets:						
Cash	$ 550	$ 550	$ 350	$ 650	$ 800	$ 850
Inventories	2,200	2,500	3,000	2,000	2,000	2,000
Total assets	$2,750	$3,050	$3,350	$2,650	$2,800	$2,850
Equities:						
Capital stock	$2,500	$2,500	$2,500	$2,500	$2,500	$2,500
Retained earnings	250	550	850	150	300	350
Total equities	$2,750	$3,050	$3,350	$2,650	$2,800	$2,850

Real and apparent differences

In this abbreviated example, the choice of inventory method has a considerable effect on the net income and the current assets of the companies. In a comparison, Company A looks like a more profitable firm with more assets *each year* during a time of rising prices. Of course, there is no real difference in the inventory quantities of the two enterprises. The apparent difference in the inventories is caused only by different accounting methods. The only real difference between the two companies appears when income taxes are computed. Company A pays a larger tax than Company B, and thus ends up with less actual cash, even though it shows higher profits.

A naive investor looking at the income results of the two companies probably would conclude that Company A was managing its resources better than Company B. A more sophisticated investor could be expected to look beyond the inventory figures for the basis of inventory valuation. Most companies provide this information, often showing it parenthetically on the balance sheet, and at times putting the information in the notes to the statements. Therefore, the educated investor often can find it. Some readers of the statements will not recognize the importance of tne information, even if they do find it, for they will not understand what it means or the effects it might have on the financial statements. The sophisticated investor will come to the following conclusions:

1. A knowledge of inventory methods used is vital to comparisons between companies.
2. LIFO provides tax advantages during inflation.
3. Two companies cannot be directly compared if their inventory methods differ.
4. Investment decisions cannot be made solely on the basis of the apparent content of the financial statements.

This means that even a sophisticated investor is unable to use statements effectively in making comparisons when accounting methods differ. A less sophisticated investor may make comparisons that are largely meaningless.

Conclusions such as the above are disturbing to many accountants and to many users of financial statements. Many accountants believe that different accounting methods should not be used unless they are justified by differences in circumstances. The accounting profession in the United States is moving toward the goal of narrowing areas of differences through the Financial Accounting Standards Board. This body has the authority to indicate acceptable accounting practices, and its activities may well decrease diversity in methods in the future.

Inventory Methods and Changing Prices

Many countries have experienced fairly severe inflation in recent years. Price fluctuations, mostly in an upward direction, have been common phenomena. The previous discussion indicates that all inventory methods have shortcomings under these conditions. FIFO provides fairly current balance sheet figures but older figures for cost of goods sold. LIFO cost of goods sold is fairly current, but the balance sheet amount for inventory is unsatisfactory. Average cost approaches have some drawbacks in both areas.

As long as accounting is restricted to the use of historical dollars, there is no effective way of dealing with the problems posed by price fluctuations. Techniques of adjusting for general price-level changes have been developed. These techniques involve restating historical costs for changes in the purchasing power of the dollar since the costs were incurred. For example, an item bought for $1.20 when the price level is 100 is sold when the price level is 110. The cost is restated to $1.32 ($1.20 × 110/100) if general price-level accounting is used. The $1.32 does not indicate the current cost price of the item unless its price moved exactly with the price level. Restatement for general price-level changes restates for changes in the measuring unit (the dollar) but retains a cost valuation approach.

Techniques have also been developed for use of replacement cost or other types of current costs *instead* of historical costs. For example, if an item with a cost of $2.00 is held in inventory and is then sold for $3.50 when its replacement cost is $2.40, a replacement cost system will charge $2.40 as cost of goods sold. If the item is held in inventory at the end of the period instead of being sold, it will still be valued at replacement cost of $2.40 rather than historical cost. A replacement cost system involves a radical departure from traditional accounting. A departure may be necessary if prices fluctuate rapidly. Slavish adherence to a historical cost system that is not relevant to current needs is not appropriate. This topic is discussed further in chapter 15.

SEC action

In 1976 the SEC took a step toward replacement cost accounting for inventories by requiring large companies to disclose (in footnotes to statements filed with the SEC) the replacement cost of their ending inventories and also what cost of goods sold would have been if replacement costs had been used. This is an important departure from the previous position of the SEC.

ADJUSTMENTS OF INVENTORY COST

The preceding discussion has dealt with flow of costs through the enterprise and the cost valuation of an inventory on the balance sheet. We must now ask whether a cost figure, determined by any of the methods discussed previously, is appropriate as an asset figure. At times, the price paid for an item (its cost) no longer indicates the value or usefulness of the item to the enterprise. For example, in the case of obsolete, damaged, spoiled, or shopworn items, the original cost of the items is no longer appropriate. This fact is recognized in accounting. In such cases, accountants recommend that items be written down to their realizable value (selling price less the costs to complete and sell the item). In this way, the balance sheet valuation is more realistic, and the loss from spoilage or obsolescence is recorded in the period in which it occurs.

Obsolescence and spoilage

At first, it might look as if losses from these causes have nothing to do with normal operations and should therefore be clearly indicated as separate losses (from obsolescence or spoilage) on the income statement. But on further consideration, it is apparent that certain losses of these types are almost inevitable in many business situations. Spoilage losses will be a regular, recurring feature of all produce departments in supermarkets. If a market stocks enough tomatoes, for example, to maximize total sales of tomatoes, spoilage is almost inevitable. Obsolescence is bound to occur in selling fashion clothing, for if the store stocks enough merchandise to attract customers and to offer sufficient choice of styles and sizes, some clothes will be left over at the end of the season and there is nothing as obsolete as last year's dress. Thus, in many cases, losses from spoilage and obsolescence are necessary in order to obtain sales. Therefore, in many cases the losses should be treated as part of cost of goods sold instead of being shown separately. This can be done by subtracting the ending inventory at its net amount (after subtracting losses from spoilage and obsolescence) from the cost of goods available for sale. Losses from obsolescence and spoilage then appear automatically in cost of goods sold.

Some losses of these types, however, have little to do with sales. Some obsolescence arises because management fails to perform its functions correctly. Some damaged goods may be inevitable in the production process, but at times, damage may arise from improper methods or improper supervision. If these losses are due to error and are not a necessary element, they should be shown separately and disclosed fully (assuming that they are significant in size, of course). Choosing between the alternative treatments puts a considerable burden on accountants. They must apply their best judgment in each case. There will often be room for disagreement, so treatment of these types of losses can cause difficulties in practice.

MARKET VALUATIONS

Lower of cost or market

Accountants usually compare the cost of the ending inventory to the current replacement price of the goods at the end of the period. If the current replacement price is lower than the cost figure, the inventory is usually written down; if it is higher, the cost valuation is retained. This practice, known as *lower-of-cost-or-market valuation,* has a long tradition in financial statements. The method is favored by creditors, since it avoids showing an inventory figure in the balance sheet that is higher than current costs. A reduction of ending inventory to market also reduces the net income for the period. The ending inventory (which is deducted from goods available for sale in arriving at cost of goods sold) is lower, which makes the cost of goods sold higher and thus reduces the profit.

The lower-of-cost-or-market method can be applied in a number of different ways. At times, cost is compared to market on an item-by-item basis, the lower of the two figures being chosen in each case. Another method is to evaluate a division or department as a whole, obtaining total cost and total market and taking the lower of the two totals in each department. A third approach is to obtain cost and market totals for the company as a whole and use the lower of the two figures. All these methods are acceptable and can be found in practice. Table 9-3 compares the different methods of market valuation.

In Table 9-3, the cost figures are arrived at by use of one of the inventory methods discussed earlier in the chapter. The market figures are obtained from current price lists and invoices for the items involved. In Table 9-3, all three lower-of-cost-or-market methods give a figure that is lower than cost. This will not always happen, of course, since in a time of rising prices the actual cost of items often will be less than current market prices.

If market is less than cost at the end of the period, as in Table 9-3, the inventory is often recorded at the lower figure. The difference between cost and the lower of cost or market ($7,055 − $6,905 = $150 in the item-by-item case) automatically appears in the cost of goods sold figure, since the ending inventory is deducted from the goods available for sale in arriving at the cost of goods sold. At times, an alternative treatment is used, with cost of goods sold being determined on a cost basis and the loss on market declines being shown separately in the income statement.

TABLE 9-3

	Cost	Market	Lower of Cost or Market, Applied to:		
			Each Item	Each Department	Whole Company
Drug department:					
Aspirin	$ 860	$ 880	$ 860		
Cough Syrup	1,220	1,100	1,100		
Cough Drops	430	420	420		
Sub totals	$2,510	$2,400		$2,400	
Cosmetics:					
Perfume	$2,375	$2,475	2,375		
Cologne	830	810	810		
Lipstick	1,340	1,360	1,340		
Sub totals	$4,545	$4,645		$4,545	
Totals	$7,055	$7,045			$7,045
Inventory value			$6,905	$6,945	$7,045

Figures to be used on balance sheet:
A. If item-by-item method is used $6,905
B. If department totals are used   6,945
C. If company-wide totals are used   7,045

The lower-of-cost-or-market method should be clearly recognized as a departure from cost, which is the usual basis of accounting for assets. Some accountants argue that this type of departure from cost is not justified, and that a loss on market declines should be recognized in the period when the goods are sold, rather than at the time the market decline takes place. The lower-of-cost-or-market method is defended primarily on the ground that it avoids overstating assets on the balance sheet. Dispute as to the validity of the method has persisted for the last 40 years. Despite the disputes, the method continues to be very widely used.

Departure from cost

A final point: lower of cost or market cannot legally be used with LIFO because LIFO is a cost method and deviations from cost are not allowed when LIFO is used for tax purposes.

INVENTORY ERRORS

Errors in inventory, whether accidental or intentional, have a direct effect on net income because inventory is used in determining cost of goods sold. An error in the ending inventory of a particular year affects not only the net income of that year, but also the income of the following year, because the ending inventory of one year is the beginning inventory of the next year. The errors in the two years will counterbalance each other, as shown in Example 9-2.

EXAMPLE 9-2

The December 31, Year 1, inventory of Ace Co. is recorded at $30,000. The correct figure is $36,000. Other income statement amounts are given below. The inventories at the beginning of Year 1 and the end of Year 2 are correct.

Income Statements of Ace Co. for Year One

	Wrong Inventory		Correct	
Sales		$300,000		$300,000
Beginning inventory	$ 40,000		$ 40,000	
Purchases	150,000		150,000	
	190,000		$190,000	
Less ending inventory	30,000		36,000	
Cost of goods sold		160,000		154,000
Gross margin		$140,000		$146,000
Operating expenses		120,000		120,000
Net income		$ 20,000		$ 26,000

Income Statements of Ace Co. for Year Two

	Wrong Inventory		Correct	
Sales		$400,000		$400,000
Beginning inventory	$ 30,000		$ 36,000	
Purchases	210,000		210,000	
	$240,000		$246,000	
Less ending inventory	28,000		28,000	
Cost of goods sold		212,000		218,000
Gross margin		$188,000		$182,000
Operating expenses		160,000		160,000
Income		$ 28,000		$ 22,000

The example indicates that because the ending inventory in Year 1 is understated, the income for Year 1 is also *understated*. The balance sheet effects are an understatement of the asset inventory and a corresponding understatement of retained earnings. The effect in Year 2 is that the understatement of the beginning inventory results in an *overstatement* of the income for the second year. Because the correct inventory appears on the Year 2 balance sheet, the assets are stated correctly at the end of Year 2. The retained earnings are also correct at the end of Year 2 because the understatement of Year 1 income is counterbalanced by the overstatement of Year 2 income.

An overstatement of inventory would have effects opposite to those illustrated in Example 9-2. The effects of inventory errors on financial statement items are summarized in Table 9-4.

TABLE 9-4. Effects of Inventory Errors

Error	Cost of Goods Sold	Net Income	Assets—End of Year	Retained Earnings End of Year
Beginning inventory				
Understated	Understated	Overstated	No effect	No effect
Overstated	Overstated	Understated	No effect	No effect
Ending inventory				
Understated	Overstated	Understated	Understated	Understated
Overstated	Understated	Overstated	Overstated	Overstated

CONTROL AND SAFEGUARDING OF INVENTORY

Our concern with inventory should extend beyond the proper treatment of the costs associated with inventory to the ways in which this asset is controlled and safeguarded, because after cash, it is probably the easiest asset to misappropriate, or embezzle.

Management does not want to spend a lot of time worrying about inventory. Therefore, a system should be set up to assure positive answers to questions such as the following:

- Have goods ordered and paid for actually been received?
- Are opportunities for theft and misuse minimized?
- Are inventory records as accurate as possible?
- Are stocks maintained at appropriate levels?
- Are additional quantities ordered when necessary?

Providing positive answers to these and similar questions involves many problems for the specialist who designs the system and for the auditors who examine the subsequent operation of the system. We cannot cover the subject in detail, but we can indicate briefly some of the general ideas involved.

One basic idea in control, as we noted in the discussion of cash, is separation of duties, particularly custodial and record-keeping duties. Applying this idea to inventories results in a system such as the following: A purchasing department is set up to receive requests from the operating departments and is made responsible for purchasing goods at the best possible price from a reliable supplier. When the purchased goods are received, a separate receiving department counts and inspects the items; the accounting department records the obligation; and, at a later time, payment is made through the treasurer's department. In a manufacturing concern, the goods themselves are turned over to a storekeeper, who issues the goods only upon approved requests. The perpetual inventory records of quantities on hand are kept by parties who have no physical contact with the goods. At intervals, actual physical counts are made, using carefully prescribed procedures. These counts are made under the supervision of persons who do not perform other inventory functions. Payments for purchases also are clearly separated from the record keeping in connection with accounts payable. The accuracy of records and the operation of the system are periodically checked by the company's internal audit staff or by independent auditors (CPAs).

Responsibilities of the people involved in the system should be clearly defined and stated. This is particularly important in connection with the physical control of the inventory. Adequate physical safeguards, such as a locked, limited-access storeroom, are an important factor in enabling storekeepers to discharge their responsibility.

Designing a system that will use the available staff effectively, provide maximum control, and serve the information needs of management is a difficult task. In one respect, the use of computers in industry makes this task somewhat easier. It is logical to centralize the record keeping in the computer, thus making separation of duties easier. On the other hand, the proper utilization of the computer offers a challenge to the systems designer. Because the computer can do so many things and provide such diversified information, the systems specialist must be imaginative in incorporating the computer into the system.

In addition to incorporating the controls and safeguards necessary for inventories, the system often is constructed to help management keep the inventory investment at a minimum and order appropriate replacement quantities at appropriate intervals.

SUMMARY

Short-term unexpired costs are significant factors in most companies' operations. The most important problem with these unexpired costs is in distinguishing between costs that have expired and will appear in the income statement and costs that will benefit future periods and will be shown among the current assets in the balance sheet.

Although the discussion of inventories pointed out only a few of the problems that can be involved, it did indicate how complex the accounting problems can become. First, there is the problem of what items should be included in inventory. Generally, a company will include all goods to which it has title. Second, there is the problem of what should be included in the costs of inventory. Inventory costs should include the net cash cost of obtaining the item and getting it ready for use or sale. Finally, there are several possible assumptions as to the flow of costs through the enterprise. FIFO, LIFO, and weighted average cost allocation methods were discussed. These methods may result in significant differences in cost of goods sold amounts and in inventory amounts on balance sheets and may have interesting economic repercussions. Advantages and disadvantages of the various allocation methods were discussed, and results of cost flow assumptions were evaluated.

After a discussion of the allocation of costs between goods sold and goods on hand, obsolescence and market declines were explained. Finally, some control features of an accounting system for inventories were discussed.

IMPORTANT TERMS

Unexpired costs
Inventory
Materiality
Periodic inventory
Perpetual inventory
Specific identification
First-in, first-out
Last-in, first-out
Weighted average method
Replacement cost
Obsolescence
Spoilage
Lower of cost or market

APPENDIX 9-1: PERPETUAL INVENTORY RECORDS

The perpetual inventory method requires that records be kept of increases, decreases, and balances on hand for each inventory item. Example 9-3 illustrates perpetual inventory record keeping using the FIFO and LIFO methods. For this example, we use the data from Table 9-1, which we used earlier to illustrate the periodic inventory method.

EXAMPLE 9-3

Data on purchases and sales:

	Units	Unit Cost	Total Cost
Jan. 1 Beginning inventory	100	$1.00	$100
Purchases			
March 28	50	1.10	55
April 30	100	1.20	120
June 25	100	1.30	130
Sept. 8	50	1.40	70
November 20	100	1.50	150
Sales			
April 15	100		
July 20	100		
September 30	100		

(Continued)

Example 9-3 (Cont.)

FIFO Perpetual Inventory Record

Date	Purchases Units	Price	Total	Issues Units	Price	Total	Balance Units	Price	Total
Jan. 1							100	1.00	100
Mar. 28	50	1.10	55				[100	1.00	100
							50	1.10	55
									155
April 15				100	1.00	100	50	1.10	55
April 30	100	1.20	120				[50	1.10	55
							100	1.20	120
									175
June 25	100	1.30	130				[50	1.10	55
							100	1.20	120
							100	1.30	130
									305
July 20				50	1.10	55	[50	1.20	60
				50	1.20	60	100	1.30	130
						115			190
Sept. 8	50	1.40	70				[50	1.20	60
							100	1.30	130
							50	1.40	70
									260
Sept. 30				50	1.20	60	[50	1.30	65
				50	1.30	65	50	1.40	70
						125			135
Nov. 20	100	1.50	150				[50	1.30	65
							50	1.40	70
							100	1.50	150
									285

LIFO Perpetual Inventory Record

Date	Purchases Units	Price	Total	Issues Units	Price	Total	Balances Units	Price	Total
Jan. 1							100	1.00	100
Mar. 28	50	1.10	55				[100	1.00	100
							50	1.10	55
									155
April 15				50	1.10	55			
				50	1.00	50	50	1.00	50
						105			
April 30	100	1.20	120				[50	1.00	50
							100	1.20	120
									170

Date	Qty	Price	Total	Qty	Price	Total	Qty	Price	Total
June 25	100	1.30	130				50 100 100	1.00 1.20 1.30	50 120 130 300
July 20				100	1.30	130	50 100	1.00 1.20	50 120 170
Sept. 8	50	1.40	70				50 100 50	1.00 1.20 1.40	50 120 70 240
Sept. 30				50 50	1.40 1.20	70 60 130	50 50	1.00 1.20	50 60 110
Nov. 20	100	1.50	150				50 50 100	1.00 1.20 1.50	50 60 150 260

The records in Example 9-3 should be studied carefully to see how issues and balances are handled. An average cost record would be kept in a similar manner, with a new average cost computed after each purchase.

The FIFO record yields the same result as the FIFO periodic inventory method illustrated in the chapter—ending inventory is $285 and cost of sales is $340 (found by adding the Total Issues column). The LIFO record, on the other hand, differs from the periodic inventory illustrated in the chapter. The ending inventory is $260 rather than $215, and cost of goods sold is $365 ($105 + $130 + $130) instead of $410. The reason for these differences is that the sales on April 15 and July 20 require that some of the lower cost units be removed from inventory under the perpetual inventory method. Under the periodic inventory method the units left at the end of the period are priced at the earliest prices of the period, regardless of what has happened during the period.

QUESTIONS

9-1. There is considerable difference between the objectives in accounting for *monetary* assets and the objectives for *unexpired costs*. Contrast the objectives for these two classes of assets, and explain the reasons for the differences in these objectives.

9-2. Discuss the advantages and disadvantages of the FIFO method of pricing inventory.

9-3. What are some of the advantages and shortcomings of the LIFO inventory method?

9-4. Company B uses the periodic inventory method. Its inventory of December 31, Year 1, was understated by $12,000. What effect will this error have on the net income reported for Year 1? Year 2? Year 3?

9-5. A retailer was overheard to say, "I can't use LIFO because I have to be sure that my merchandise is sold in the order in which it is purchased. If I used LIFO, I would soon suffer heavy losses from deterioration." Do you agree? Explain.

9-6. An appliance business has a television set in the December 31, Year 1, inventory that cost the firm $100. Because of damage it has received from careless handling, its expected selling price is only $60. Explain how you would deal with these facts in determining the inventory cost and the cost of goods for Year 1.

9-7. What is the reason for writing inventory down to the lower of cost or market?

9-8. Indicate clearly how the basic ideas of internal check and control can be applied to the control of inventories.

9-9. During the inflation of 1973 and 1974 many companies changed from FIFO to LIFO for inventory valuation. What was the probable effect of the change on income in the year of change and in subsequent years? What effects were likely on the market price of the stock of the companies?

9-10. Valuing inventory at cost is consistent with the usual practice in accounting of carrying assets at their original purchase price. A number of accounting theorists have argued that inventory should be carried at some current price rather than at historical cost, which may be out of date. Discuss this proposal from the standpoint of the relevance, comparability, understandability, and neutrality of current price information. How would you recommend the proposal be handled?

EXERCISES

9-11. *Inventory cost.* The Flowsy Co. purchases some goods with an invoice price of $4,000 from the Supreme Fashion Co. on February 15. Terms of the purchase are 2/10, n/30, and Flowsy Co. is to pay the freight. The invoice is paid on February 22, and freight of $86 is paid on February 20 when the goods are delivered. Through study, the Flowsy Co. determines that the following costs apply to this purchase:

Purchasing department	$54
Receiving department	24
Warehousing costs	80
Insurance costs	28

All of these goods remain in the inventory on February 28.
Required:
a. What is the theoretical cost of the inventory of these goods on February 28?
b. What is the amount at which these goods would probably be carried as a practical matter? Explain.

9-12. *Cost of goods sold.* During the current year, the College Men's store received merchandise invoiced at $225,000, terms 2/10, n/30. The discounts taken were $6,500. Transportation charges were $4,500. Goods costing $44,650 (including transportation costs less discounts) were on hand at the end of the year, December 31. On January 1, the inventory was $42,560. Merchandise was sold during the year for $350,000. Invoices are recorded at gross price. Prepare a partial income statement to the point of gross profit.

9-13. *Inventory methods.* Following are data for the inventory and purchase and sales transactions of Mr. Rhee. Find the value of the ending inventory (showing computations) by (a) FIFO method, (b) average cost method, and (c) LIFO method.

	Number	Price
Beginning inventory	300	$12
First purchase	190	15
Second purchase	110	17
Third purchase	80	18
Fourth purchase	220	17
Sales in units	580	

9-14. *Inventory methods.* From the following data concerning the inventory of the Brown Kandy Co., compute the ending inventory of 20 units using (a) LIFO and (b) FIFO.

	Units	Unit Cost	Total
Beginning inventory	15	$1.00	$15.00
First purchase	10	1.10	11.00
Second purchase	10	1.20	12.00
Third purchase	10	1.30	13.00
Fourth purchase	16	1.25	20.00

9-15. *LIFO versus FIFO.* The purpose of this problem is to contrast LIFO with FIFO as they affect the stated net income in a time of rising prices. The Imaginary Store has been in business for several years. The inventory December 31, Year 1, consists of 20,000 units of product X. On a FIFO basis all 20,000 units have a cost price of $4.25—the last invoice price in Year 1. On a LIFO basis 10,000 units cost $2, 5,000 cost $3, and 5,000 cost $4. During Year 2, 80,000 units are purchased at $4.50, and 78,000 units are sold. Calculate the difference in Year 2 income caused by the different methods of pricing the inventory. Explain why the difference occurs.

(Solution in Appendix B.)

9-16. *Lower of cost or market.* From the data below, prepare an adjusting journal entry to record the ending merchandise inventory of the Jerrybilt Furniture Co. Use cost or market, whichever is lower, on an item by item basis.

	Number	Cost per Unit	Replacement Price
chairs	40	$ 32	$ 29
tables	148	11	13
sofas	107	168	163
end tables	84	38	35
coffee tables	125	20	18

297

9-17. *Lower of cost or market.* Give the entry to record the correct inventory at the end of the year under the periodic inventory method assuming (a) lower of cost or market is applied on an item-by-item basis, (b) lower of cost on market is applied to the inventory as a whole.

	Number	Cost	Replacement Cost	Estimated Selling Price
Stern winches	30	$110	$ 95	$130
Uphand gears	60	70	72	79
Franigassets	200	60	58	79
Digglewidgets	35	200	205	210

9-18. *Inventory errors.* An examination of the books and records of a certain company discloses that the inventory of December 31, Year 1, was overstated by $3,000 and that the inventory of December 31, Year 2, was understated by $5,000.

Required:
a. What is the dollar effect of these inventory errors on the Year 1 net profit?
b. What is the dollar effect of these inventory errors on the Year 2 net profit?
c. What is the dollar effect of these inventory errors on the Year 3 net profit?
d. What effect did the two inventory errors have on the total net profit of the three years ending Dec. 31, Year 3?

9-19. *Inventory control.* We have reason to believe that Miss Thrall, a saleslady in the housewares department, is financing her monthly flights to Europe by stealing pots and pans. On April 15, we take a surprise count of the inventory in her department. Our count totals $23,000 at cost. From the following information, determine the estimated amount of stolen goods in Miss Thrall's department. Show all computations.

Inventory, January 1	$ 42,000
Purchases, January 1 to April 15	60,000
Sales, January 1 to April 15	101,000
Usual rate of gross profit	36% of sales

PROBLEMS

9-20. *Inventory methods.* The Bitter Pill Company had an inventory of 3,000 units of D at a cost of $6.00 per unit on December 31 of the previous year. During the current year, sales amounted to 18,000 units for a total sales price of $165,000, and the following purchases were made:

Feb. 12	5,000 units at $6.10 each
Apr. 4	2,000 units at 6.25 each
June 19	4,000 units at 6.75 each
Oct. 12	6,000 units at 7.00 each
Dec. 14	3,000 units at 6.50 each

Required:
a. Compute the ending inventory using FIFO.
b. Compute the ending inventory using LIFO.
c. Compute the gross margin on sales using FIFO.
d. Compute the gross margin on sales using LIFO.
For *c* and *d*, present a partial income statement in good form.

9-21. *Inventory Methods LIFO.* C. Senor uses the last-in, first-out method of pricing goods. He has an inventory of 200 units of A and 450 units of B at the end of the year. Compute the ending inventory valuation from the data given below. Show all computations, clearly labeled.

	Goods	Units	Unit Price	Total Cost
Beginning inventory	A	180	$10	$1800
	B	200	5	1000
Purchases, in chronological order	A	120	11	1320
	A	200	12	2400
	B	60	4	240
	A	80	15	1200
	B	100	3.50	350
	B	400	3	1200

9-22. *Change in inventory method.* A business that has used the FIFO method in previous years decides to change to the LIFO method. Information for the current year is below. There are 500 units in the ending inventory. Market value on December 31 is $10.50.

Beginning inventory (FIFO)	300 units at $10.00	$ 3,000
Purchases: Mar. 3	1500 units at 10.10	15,150
June 10	1500 units at 10.25	15,375
Oct. 1	1500 units at 10.40	15,600

Required:
a. Report all information relative to inventory that would appear on the statement of financial position of December 31.
b. How should expired product cost be reported, and what other information is needed on the income statement?
c. Under the circumstances, does choice of LIFO result in a tax saving?

9-23. *Lower of cost or market.* The X Clothing Store, which sells a limited line of women's suits, coats, and shoes, had an inventory on January 31 composed of the following items:

Part III Measurement of Assets, Liabilities, and Income

	Quantity	Actual unit cost	Unit market price
Suits:			
Style 157	10	$ 50	$40
Style 213	15	40	42
Style 214	27	60	50
Style C 5	40	25	30
Coats:			
Style F13	60	50	43
Style A 2	50	50	70
Style Q 6	11	100	90

Required:
a. Compute the inventory on January 31 at the lower of cost or market, applying the method to each item in the inventory.
b. Compute the inventory on a departmental basis.
c. Compute the inventory on a storewide basis.

(Solution in Appendix B.)

9-24. *LIFO perpetual inventory.* Compute the ending inventory for the Agnew Spear Company on December 31, using (a) LIFO perpetual inventory and (b) LIFO periodic inventory. The company had the following purchases and sales during the year:

Beginning inventory	400 spears at $11 each
Purchase Jan. 24	600 spears at $12 each
Sale Feb. 3	700 spears at $20 each
Purchase Mar. 10	500 spears at $13 each
Sale Apr. 29	400 spears at $20 each
Purchase Aug. 3	600 spears at $14 each
Sale Oct. 7	300 spears at $21 each

9-25. *Perpetual inventory transactions.* The Sadat Salad Company uses the FIFO perpetual inventory method. On January of the current year, their inventory of salad oil tanks is 10 at $120 each. Give entries for the following transactions during the year:

Jan. 12 Sell 4 tanks for $200 each.
Jan. 20 Buy 18 tanks for $122 each.
Jan. 21 Pay $36 freight on tanks purchased on January 20.
Jan. 27 Sell 12 tanks for $205 each.
Feb. 4   Buy 20 tanks for $123 cash, delivered.
Feb. 7   Return 2 of the tanks purchased on Feb. 4 because they are defective.
Feb. 20 Sell 15 tanks for $206 each.
Feb. 28 One tank has rusted out and is sold for junk for $20.

(Solution in Appendix B.)

9-26. *Inventory errors.* Compute the correct current income and correct balance sheet amount for inventory at the end of the year for each of the following cases:

	Case			
	(1)	(2)	(3)	(4)
Sales	$100,000	$100,000	$200,000	$200,000
Cost of sales				
Beg. Inventory	10,000	10,000	25,000	25,000
Purchases	60,000	60,000	115,000	115,000
	70,000	70,000	140,000	140,000
Ending inventory	12,000	12,000	30,000	30,000
Cost of sales	58,000	58,000	110,000	110,000
Gross margin	42,000	42,000	90,000	90,000
Expenses	30,000	30,000	70,000	70,000
Net income	$ 12,000	$ 12,000	$ 20,000	$ 20,000
Errors				
Beginning inventory overstated	3,000			5,000
Beginning inventory understated		5,000		
Ending inventory overstated		3,000		6,000
Ending inventory understated			5,000	
Purchases overstated			4,000	
Sales overstated				8,000

(Solution in Appendix B.)

9-27. *Inventory methods and cycle.* The Branden Concerto Burger Company has an inventory of 10 units at a cost of $10 each on January 1 of Year 1. Purchases and sales are as follows:

Year	Purchases	Sales
1	10 at $12	10 at $15
2	10 at 14	10 at 17
3	10 at 16	10 at 20
4	10 at 15	10 at 18
5	10 at 13	10 at 16
6	10 at 10	10 at 14

Required:
Compute the gross margin for each year using (a) FIFO and (b) LIFO. Also compute total income over the 6 years. Comment on your results.

9-28. *LIFO Peculiarities.* The Francisco Company has the following purchases and sales during a 4-year period:

Year	Purchases	Sales
1	12 at $11	10 at $15
2	12 at $12	10 at $16
3	10 at $13	10 at $17
4	4 at $14	10 at $18

Inventory at the beginning of Year 1 was 10 units at $10 each.

Required:

Compute cost of sales and gross margin for each year using (a) FIFO and (b) LIFO. Comment on your results.

CASE PROBLEM

9-29. *Effects of inventory costing method on financial statements.* The Swenson Company, a wholesaler of one product, began operations in January of Year 1, with the following balance sheet.

SWENSON COMPANY
Balance Sheet
January 2, Year 1

Cash	$ 40,000	Accounts payable	$ 20,000
Inventory (10,000 units)	80,000	Capital stock	100,000
	$120,000		$120,000

The company rents its facilities and equipment. All sales are for cash, and all expenses and purchases are paid in such a way that the accounts payable balance remains at $20,000. The income tax rate is 40% (taxes are paid in cash), and the company pays out 50% of its net income after taxes in dividends. Sales, purchases, and expense figures for the first 3 years of operations are as follows:

	Year 1	Year 2	Year 3
Sales (in units)	38,000	47,000	59,000
Sales price	$13.50	$15.00	$16.50
Purchases (in units)	40,000	50,000	62,000
Purchase cost price	$9.00	$10.00	$11.00
Inventory, end of year (in units)	12,000	15,000	18,000
Operating expenses	$100,000	$120,000	$140,000

Required:

a. Prepare income statements for each of the 3 years and a balance sheet at the close of each year under FIFO costing.
b. Same as requirement *a* above, except assume LIFO costing.
c. Comment on the differences you note between *a* and *b*.

10

Property, Plant, and Equipment and Other Long-lived Assets; Depreciation

Business assets are acquired because of their usefulness to the enterprise. Cash and other *monetary assets* provide the company with immediate or virtual purchasing power. Product inventories can be sold, and material inventories can be used in manufacturing processes. Prepaid expenses have specific uses, depending upon the kind. Thus, the enterprise has monetary assets and *short-term unexpired costs* (inventories and prepaid expenses) for specific, short-term uses. Other assets are acquired because they will have long-term usefulness to the enterprise. These assets are called *long-term unexpired costs*.

    This chapter is concerned with the long-term unexpired costs. Three primary problems will be considered. First, what is the appropriate measure of the cost of acquiring these assets? Second, how should the cost of the asset be allocated over the asset's life? In the second problem, we distinguish between (a) the portion of the asset that has been used up in a period and appears as an expense on the income statement or has been incorporated through cost transformation into other assets (as in manufacturing) and (b) the portion of the asset that will benefit future periods and thus should appear on the balance sheet. Third, what is the appropriate accounting for the disposition of long-term unexpired costs?

TYPES OF LONG-TERM UNEXPIRED COSTS

Long-term unexpired costs can be divided into two main classes: tangible assets and intangibles. *Tangible assets have physical substance; intangibles usually involve rights or ideas and cannot be perceived by the senses.*

Tangible Assets

Tangible assets can be divided into natural resources and property, plant, and equipment.

Natural Resources. Natural resources include items such as land, mineral deposits, and timber tracts. Land is the most permanent of assets. Some land is acquired as a site for a building or other facility. This type of land is classified as a property, plant, and equipment asset. Generally, such land has continued, undiminished usefulness to the enterprise. Therefore, after the land has been recorded at its cost, no further accounting treatment is required.

Depletion

Land may be acquired for its mineral deposits or for farming purposes. In the case of land used in the extractive industries or in farming, some accounting may be required after acquisition. Mineral deposits are removed or worked out. Timber is removed from the land. The fertility of land may be exhausted. In these cases, the costs of the natural resources that are exhausted or used up are customarily allocated over their useful lives. This process of allocation is called *depletion accounting.*

In some situations, steps can be taken to maintain the natural resource. For example, forests and orchards can be replanted, and farmland can be fertilized. Generally, depletion accounting is still required for timberlands, but the maintenance cost for orchards and farmlands may be assumed to replace the depletion and thus may be treated as an expense in lieu of depletion. However, there should be clear evidence that the asset is in fact being maintained.

Property, Plant, and Equipment and Other Depreciable Assets. *Property, plant, and equipment includes all land used or planned for use as building sites and all buildings, machinery, equipment, and other tangible, long-lived assets used by a business in business operations.* It is also referred to as simply "plant and equipment" or "fixed assets." (Assets of this type held for speculation or held for sale are excluded from this category and are shown in other sections of the balance sheet.) These assets (excluding land) have limited useful lives and hence are subject to depreciation.

Depreciation

Depreciation accounting is the process of allocating the cost of an asset over its service life. Depreciation accounting is used most often for tangible, inanimate objects such as buildings and machines. However, some types of livestock are also subject to depreciation. Breeding stock on a cattle ranch would be an example. The lives of these animals are limited, and the costs of the animals can be allocated over their useful lives.

Intangibles

Some long-lived assets do not have physical characteristics. Instead, they involve ideas, rights, and relationships, all of which are intangible factors. When a company has an exclusive right to these intangible factors, they may be recorded as assets. These intangibles can be divided into two groups: those with an unlimited term of existence and those with a limited useful life. The first group includes such items as perpetual franchises, trade names, goodwill (generally), and secret processes. The second group includes such items as patents, copyrights, leases, and franchises for a limited term. Theoretically, the first group should be retained on an enterprise's records as long as the individual items have value. Items in the second group, on the other hand, should be recorded as expenses over their useful lives. *The process of allocating the cost of intangibles over their useful lives as an expense is known as amortization accounting*, which will be discussed at a later point.

Amortization

Intangibles, despite their nonphysical nature, are often important assets in business enterprises. In industries where technological changes are common and research activities are widespread, the development of intangibles such as patents and new processes may be of crucial importance to a company.

MEASURING COST

Plant and equipment and other long-term unexpired costs generally are recorded at their cost. Cost includes all necessary expenditures made to obtain or develop the asset, get it to the place of business, and get it ready for use. Four examples follow.

Cost

EXAMPLE 10-1

A piece of machinery is purchased on account for $4,000. Terms of purchase are 2/10,n/30. Freight of $70 and installation costs of $105 are paid.

Cost Computation:
Invoice price	$4,000
Less purchase discount (2%)	80
Net invoice price	$3,920
Freight	70
Installation	105
Total cost of machine	$4,095

305

Note that a net cash price is used in this example. If discounts are offered, the net price after deducting discounts should be used. Freight and installation charges are added because they are necessary in getting the asset to the place of business and ready for use.

EXAMPLE 10-2

A team of 9 machinists spends 4 months in constructing a new machine. Salaries of the men for the 4 months amount to $41,000. Their supervisor (who also supervises 21 other machinists) is paid $30,000 per year. Materials used in building the machine cost $28,000. Installation costs are $1,000. Testing of the machine takes 100 hours of labor (cost of $500) and uses up $1,000 of material:

Cost Computation:	
Labor of machinists	$41,000
Supervision 9/30 × $30,000 × 1/3	3,000
Materials	28,000
Installation costs	1,100
Testing labor	500
Testing materials	1,000
Total	$74,600

Example 10-2 gives a partial insight into some of the complications possible in determining the cost of assets developed by a company. The example is simplified, for no consideration is given to the facilities used by the men in developing the machine. It can be argued that the cost of space, material, supplies, and power and even the light and heat of the area used by the men should be added to the cost of the machine. Deciding just what elements to add to the machine and where to stop in making cost allocations is an interesting accounting problem.

EXAMPLE 10-3

A plot of land is purchased for use as a plant site. $60,000 is paid for the land. Title fees are $700. Legal fees amount to $300. After the land is acquired, an old building on it is removed at a cost of $3,000. $700 is obtained from sale of materials from the old building. $1,500 is spent on grading and leveling the site. $2,000 is paid to excavate for a new building.

Cost Computation:		
Basic price		$60,000
Title fees		700
Legal fees		300
Demolition of old building	$3,000	
Less sale of materials	700	2,300
Grading and leveling		1,500
Total cost of land		$64,800

Several points in Example 10-3 require explanation. The land was acquired for use as a site for a new building. The old building, therefore, is only an obstruction, and the net cost of removing it is part of the cost of getting the land ready for its intended use. Grading and leveling are costs of the land for the same reason. The excavation cost results in an asset, but the asset involved is the new building, not land. Excavation is a necessary cost of constructing a building; it is not a necessary cost of the land itself.

EXAMPLE 10-4

Burgey Company buys a piece of land with a warehouse on it for $160,000. The land has an estimated value of $130,000; and the warehouse, $40,000. Cost is allocated to the land and warehouse as follows:

$$\text{Land } \frac{\$130,000}{\$170,000} \times \$160,000 = \$122,350$$

$$\text{Warehouse } \frac{\$40,000}{\$170,000} \times \$160,000 = \underline{37,650}$$

$$\text{Total cost} = \$160,000$$

The cost is allocated to the various components purchased in Example 10-4 on the basis of their relative market values. This is a common method of allocating costs in a purchase of several assets in a package.

Cost and market value

Assets are recorded at cost because cost is an objective figure arrived at through transactions. The cost of an asset may not always clearly indicate what the asset is worth. In Example 10-2, for example, the cost of the machine is $74,600. The machine may be extremely valuable to the company and perhaps could be sold to outside parties for $120,000. The company, however, would record the asset at its cost and would not attempt to record its value on the records. On the other hand, accountants are reluctant to record an asset at a cost that exceeds the asset's market value. If the machine were worth only $50,000, the balance of the cost, $24,600, should be written off as an expense or loss.

In a situation where market value or value in use far exceeds cost, the difference tends to appear in the income statement. If the machine (or other asset) does indeed have a value higher than cost, it will result in higher revenues or lower expenses than a company would otherwise have. At the same time, the expenses of the machine (as we shall see later) will be based on the lower cost figure, not on value. These revenues and expenses should result in a higher income than would be reported without the machine. This indirect indication of the value of the asset does not solve all of the problems, for the asset will be shown on the balance sheet at a cost figure that gives little indication of what it is worth. This is in contrast to the more usual situation in which the cost of assets is a good approximation of their value at the time they are acquired.

Part III   Measurement of Assets, Liabilities, and Income

Acquisition by issuing stock

At times, corporations acquire assets by issuing capital stock. In this situation the question of appropriate asset valuation is troublesome. If the asset acquired has a readily determinable market value, this amount should be recorded as the "cost" of the asset. The credit to the capital stock accounts will then equal the debit to the asset account. If the market value of the asset cannot be determined, the market value (not the par value) of the stock may be used to determine the asset cost. The accounting rule is as follows: Use market value of the asset or of the stock issued, whichever is more readily determinable. Because the corporation gives none of its resources in issuing stock for assets, no true cost is involved. However, once an asset has been recorded, the recorded amount is thereafter treated just like the cost of any other asset.

The acquisition costs of a long-lived tangible asset typically are incurred with the purchase and installation of the asset. During the asset's life, other expenditures related to the asset are made. The accountant must determine whether the expenditure results in an asset or an expense.

Capital and revenue expenditures

Expenditures that result in assets are called *capital* expenditures. Expenditures that result in expenses are called *revenue* expenditures. Generally, no difficulties arise in making this distinction. For example, cash paid for a truck is a capital expenditure, and gas for the truck is a revenue expenditure. Sometimes, however, difficult decisions are involved. Suppose, for instance, that $200 is spent on new tires for the truck. Is this an asset (to be depreciated over the life of the tires) or an expense of the period? Unfortunately, no hard-and-fast rules can be established in this area. The

General rule

accountant has to be guided by the general rule that expenditures resulting in benefits that are expected to last for several accounting periods should be set up as assets. Expenditures having no future benefits should be charged to expense. Practical considerations dictate, however, that minor items often are charged to expense even if they benefit several future periods.

Repairs

Repairs to assets may cause some problems. *Extraordinary repairs* extend an asset's life or capacity and should be capitalized. *Ordinary repairs* and maintenance are needed to keep the asset operating and are expenses. Ordinary repairs and maintenance are usually required on a recurring basis. Generally, expenditures that recur year in and year out just to keep assets in good operational condition are treated as expense. The more technical features of repair expenditures are treated in more advanced financial accounting courses.

SUBSEQUENT TREATMENT OF UNEXPIRED COSTS

The treatment of each of the main types of long-term unexpired costs will be discussed separately. All of the treatments are basically similar, however, since the objective in each case is to allocate the cost of the asset over its useful life in a reasonable and systematic manner. The charges in particular years or other periods should be related to the service benefits yielded by the asset. Because benefits can flow from assets in different ways, there are different methods of allocating asset cost, just as there are different methods of inventory pricing, as discussed in chapter 9.

Service benefits

The useful life of an asset is an estimate, often based on previous experience with similar assets, or perhaps based on engineering studies or manufacturers' representations.[1] Two types of factors influence useful life: physical and economic. The *physical factors* involve such things as wear and tear and the action of the elements. The primary *economic factor* is obsolescence, which is considerably important in a dynamic economy. In many industries, plant and equipment assets often become obsolete long before their physical life comes to an end.

Wear and tear

Obsolescence

The service benefits yielded by an asset are also a matter of estimate. The different views as to the flow of benefits are the basis for the different depreciation and amortization methods, which will be discussed later.

NATURAL RESOURCES

Some natural resources have undiminished usefulness for the life of an enterprise and therefore require no *depletion accounting*. The costs of natural resources that do wear out or become exhausted are subject to depletion accounting. The costs are allocated to depletion over the accounting periods that make up the life of the asset. The periodic depletion becomes a cost of the quantity of the resource removed and thus becomes a part of the inventory cost of the resource. As the resource is sold, the inventory cost (including the depletion portion) becomes an expense. Because the complications of inventory cost accounting, we shall assume that all minerals extracted are sold.

Periodic depletion is computed by (1) estimating the total quantity of mineral or other resource acquired and (2) assigning a proportionate amount of the total resource cost to the quantity extracted in the accounting period. Example 10-5 illustrates this procedure.

Computing depletion

EXAMPLE 10-5

A company invests $60,000 in an oil well that contains an estimated 100,000 barrels of oil. The residual value of the land containing the oil is estimated to be $5,000. In the first year, 12,000 barrels of oil are extracted and sold. The depletion for the first year will be

(Continued)

---

1. The Internal Revenue Service publishes depreciation guidelines that are often used in estimating useful lives for both financial accounting and tax purposes.

Example 10-5 (Cont.)

$$\frac{12{,}000}{100{,}000} \times (\$60{,}000 - 5{,}000) = \$6{,}600.$$

The journal entry to record the depletion is as follows:

	Debit	Credit
Depletion expense	6,600	
Accumulated depletion—oil well		6,600

The same result can be obtained by arriving at a cost per barrel for the entire number of barrels estimated to be contained in the well and then multiplying the units produced by the cost per barrel. The depletion cost per barrel is ($60,000 − 5,000)/100,000 barrels = $.55 per barrel. The first year's depletion is 12,000 barrels × $.55 = $6,600. The accumulated depletion account is credited, rather than the asset account, so that a figure for original cost is retained in the accounts. The accumulated depletion is subtracted from the asset cost on the balance sheet, as follows:

Property, Plant and Equipment:		
Oil well	$60,000	
Less acumulated depletion	6,600	
Unexpired cost		$53,400

For tax purposes the Internal Revenue Code allows businesses to deduct the larger of cost depletion or percentage depletion in computing taxable income. *Percentage depletion is computed as a percentage of revenue.* Rates allowed vary widely, from 22% for oil and certain minerals to 5% for sand and gravel. Percentage depletion is often greater than cost depletion. Only cost depletion appears on the financial statements.

PROPERTY, PLANT, AND EQUIPMENT

An important tangible asset in this category is land used as a building site. Land used for this purpose does not depreciate. Sometimes economic events will drastically alter the value of the land. For example, the value of plant sites in a region of the country may decline because manufacturing activity has declined in that region. Changes of this kind are usually dealt with on an individual basis. Generally, the cost of land is not systematically depreciated.

The costs of plant and equipment and other, similar long-term unexpired costs are allocated to the periods of the assets' lives on the basis of the service benefits obtained from the assets. The periodic charge is called *depreciation expense.* Several different methods of computing depreciation are available. Each method results in a different pattern of depreciation charges over the life of the asset. Theoretically, a depreciation method should be chosen on the basis of the pattern of benefits that is associated with the asset under consideration. If benefits flow evenly over the life of the asset, one method is chosen (straight-line); if the benefits are higher in the early years, a method that provides diminishing charges would be appropriate (sum-of-the-years'-digits or declining-balance). At times, income tax and other practical considerations will dictate use of a method that is not theoretically correct. It is unfortunate when such considerations result in the use of a method that does not accurately reflect the flow of benefits for an asset, but income tax is such an important factor in most business enterprises that good accounting practices often are sacrificed on the altar of tax minimization.

Choosing a depreciation method

In the discussion and examples that follow, depreciation of a single asset is the focus of attention. In practice, depreciation is often computed for groups of assets rather than single assets. The principles involved are the same, however, and the computational aspects of group depreciation are left for other accounting courses.

Straight-Line Method

Straight-line is the simplest depreciation method. It allocates the cost (less salvage) of an asset over its life in equal amounts. Expressed in a formula, it is

$$\frac{C - S}{n} = D,$$

where C = cost, S = salvage, n = years or periods of life, and D = depreciation per year or period. To illustrate the application of this method, consider Example 10-6:

EXAMPLE 10-6 STRAIGHT-LINE METHOD

The Quep Company acquires a truck on January 1 for $6,600. The truck is expected to last 6 years and to have a salvage value of $300 at the end of that time.

$$\text{Depreciation per year: } \frac{\$6,600 - \$300}{6} = \$1,050$$

This amount would be recorded each year of the asset's life. The annual entry is:

	Debit	Credit
Depreciation expense	1,050	
Accumulated depreciation — truck		1,050

The depreciation expense is shown as an operating expense on the income statement, and the accumulated depreciation is deducted from the

311

asset on the balance sheet. The truck in Example 10-6 would appear on the balance sheet at the end of the *second* year as follows:

Plant and Equipment:		
Truck	$6,600	
Less accumulated depreciation	2,100	
Unexpired cost		$4,500

Note that the accumulated depreciation is the accumulated amount for two years ($1,050 + 1,050).

Sum-of-the-Years'-Digits Method

The *sum-of-the-years'-digits method* is a depreciation method that charges larger amounts of asset cost to expense in the early years of life and lesser amounts in later years. The method is somewhat arbitrary, but the computation is fairly easy. To compute the depreciation, first list numerically the years of an asset's life and sum this arithmetic progression.[2] Then use the highest number in the series as the numerator and the sum of the series as the denominator of a fraction that is multiplied by the cost (less salvage) of the asset. Each subsequent year, use the next lower number in the series; in this way, the fraction decreases each year. Example 10-7 clarifies this computation. Consider the truck used in the discussion of straight-line depreciation.

EXAMPLE 10-7 SUM-OF-THE-YEARS'-DIGITS METHOD

Sum-of-the-years'-digits (6-year life): $1 + 2 + 3 + 4 + 5 + 6 = 21$

First year's depreciation: $\frac{6}{21} \times (\$6,600 - 300) = \$1,800$

Second year's depreciation: $\frac{5}{21} \times (\$6,600 - 300) = \$1,500$

The depreciation expense on the income statement is higher in the early years than with straight-line depreciation. On the other hand, the sixth year's depreciation by the straight-line method would still be $1,050, but the depreciation would be only $1/21 \times (\$6,600 - 300)$, or $300, using sum-of-the-years'-digits depreciation. The truck would be shown on the balance sheet at the end of the second year as follows:

---

2. For longer lives the formula for the sum of an arithmetic progression can be used: sum of digits $= n \left(\frac{n+1}{2}\right)$, where $n =$ number of years of asset's life.

Plant and Equipment:
Truck $6,600
Less accumulated depreciation   3,300
Unexpired cost $3,300

The accumulated depreciation is, as before, the sum of the amounts recorded in the first two years ($1,800 + 1,500). Note that a smaller asset balance is left with sum-of-the-years'-digits depreciation than with straight-line. This smaller asset balance is caused by writing off larger amounts to expense in these years. Both methods will arrive at a $300 balance (the salvage) at the end of the 6-year life.

Declining-Balance Method

The *declining-balance method* (often referred to as the double-declining-balance method) is similar to the sum-of-the-years'-digits method in charging larger amounts of depreciation to the early years of an asset's life. In this method, a constant rate is applied to the asset balance, that is, to the cost less accumulated depreciation. The rate that usually is used for new assets is twice the straight-line rate, since this is the maximum allowed by the Internal Revenue Code.[3] The truck used in the previous examples is used in Example 10-8.

EXAMPLE 10-8 DOUBLE-DECLINING-BALANCE METHOD

Rate: Straight-line rate $= \dfrac{1}{\text{No. of years}} = \dfrac{1}{6}$

Declining-balance rate $= \dfrac{1}{6} \times 2 = \dfrac{2}{6}$ or $\dfrac{1}{3}$

First year's depreciation: $\dfrac{1}{3} \times \$6{,}600 = \$2{,}200$

Second year's depreciation: $\dfrac{1}{3} \times (\$6{,}600 - \$2{,}200) = \$1{,}466.67$

Table 10-1 (see page 314) lists the depreciation for the six years.

---

3. Mathematically, the rate should be 1 less the nth root of the salvage divided by the cost:

$$1 - \sqrt[n]{\dfrac{S}{C}}$$

The rate allowed for tax purposes is close enough to this mathematical ideal in most cases so that there is little difference in amounts.

Part III Measurement of Assets, Liabilities, and Income

TABLE 10-1. Depreciation for Entire Six Years

Year	Cost	Rate	Depreciation Expense	Asset Book Value End of Year
1	$6,600.00	1/3	$2,200.00	$4,400.00
2		1/3	1,466.67	2,933.33
3		1/3	977.78	1,955.55
4		1/3	651.85	1,303.70
5		1/3	434.57	869.13
6		1/3	289.71	579.42*

* Obviously, the balance will never reach zero. Tax laws allow you to switch to straight-line depreciation at any point in the life of an asset in order to write the asset down to salvage.

Two points should be noted:

Distinctive features

1. The rate is applied to the net asset balance at the end of the previous year (this balance goes down each year and is a *declining balance*).
2. No salvage is deducted as in other methods; the rate is applied to the original asset balance instead.

These are distinctive features of the declining-balance method. In no other method is a constant rate applied to a declining balance. All other methods deduct salvage. But in the declining-balance method, a salvage value is, in effect, built into the method itself. This is so because a balance of undepreciated cost will always remain, no matter how often a rate is applied.

How is the desired salvage value reached under the declining balance method? It is acceptable for a company to change to the straight-line method at some point in an asset's life to bring the book value of the asset down to the desired salvage value. To illustrate, in Example 10-8, if the company were to change to straight-line in Year 5, the result would be the figures shown in Table 10-2.

TABLE 10-2

Year	Depreciation Expense	Asset Balance End of Year
4	as in Example 10-8	$1,303.70
5	501.85*	801.85
6	501.85*	300.00

* Book value, end of Year 4	$1,303.70
Desired salvage value	300.00
Total Depreciation over Years 5 & 6	$1,003.70
Depreciation each year	$ 501.85

Units-of-Production Method and Service-Hours Method

At times, depreciation is computed on the basis of the usage or activity of the particular asset. This type of depreciation involves an estimate of service life in terms of units of production, hours of service, or miles of travel, rather than in terms of years of life. The computation is basically similar to the computation of depletion in the case of natural resources. A machine might be depreciated on the basis of units produced each period. The truck in our examples might be depreciated on the basis of the number of miles driven. (See computation in Example 10-9.)

EXAMPLE 10-9

Cost of truck	$6,600
Salvage	$ 300
Estimated total mileage	210,000 miles
Usage:	
First year	30,000 miles
Second year	41,000 miles

Depreciation in first year: $\frac{30,000}{210,000} \times (\$6,600 - 300) = \$\ \ 900.00$

Depreciation in second year: $\frac{41,000}{210,000} \times (\$6,600 - 300) = \$1,230.00$

Depreciation computed in this way depends on activity instead of lapse of time. There often is some difficulty in estimating the service life, and it is often difficult to keep track of units of production for each period of the asset's life. Therefore, these methods are not used extensively. Of course, other depreciation methods, such as straight-line, also involve difficult estimates. The methods that base depreciation on output are particularly appropriate when an asset's usefulness is closely related to production or usage rather than to time factors.

Comparison of Depreciation Methods

In order to compare the various depreciation methods that have been discussed above, let us look at a comprehensive illustration.

EXAMPLE 10-10

Equipment is purchased at a cost of $7,600, with estimated life of 8 years and estimated salvage of $400 at the end of that time. Total production hours are expected to be 18,000 over the 8-year life. Table 10-3 (see page 316) gives depreciation figures resulting from each of the methods described above.

TABLE 10-3. Comparison of Depreciation Methods (By Years)

Year	Straight-Line Depr. Rate: 1/8 = 12½%	Sum-of-Digits Fraction (sum = 36)	Depr.	Declining-Balance Depr. (25% rate)	Asset Bal.	Production-Hours Hours in Year	Depr.
1	$900	8/36	$1,600	$1,900	$5,700	2,800	$1,120
2	900	7/36	1,400	1,425	4,275	1,500	600
3	900	6/36	1,200	1,069	3,206	3,000	1,200
4	900	5/36	1,000	802	2,404	2,100	840
5	900	4/36	800	601	1,803	1,700	680
6	900	3/36	600	451*	1,352	2,200	880
7	900	2/36	400	338	1,014	1,600	640
8	900	1/36	200	254	760	3,100	1,240
Total Depr.	$7,200		$7,200	$6,840			$7,200

* The company could shift to straight-line in Year 6 in order to arrive at the $400 salvage value.

The student should understand the computation of each of the amounts in Table 10-3. Note that all of the methods except declining-balance automatically arrive at a $400 salvage value. This does not mean that some methods are more accurate than others. We must remember that estimates are involved in any method. There is no guarantee that the asset will last exactly 8 years (or will run for 18,000 hours), or that the salvage value will be exactly $400. Estimates are more often wrong than right. The whole problem of what is done when estimates prove inaccurate will be discussed later. At this point, it is sufficient to note that depreciation accounting involves a number of difficult estimates. Therefore, no depreciation method can be expected to yield perfect results.

Many enterprises rent or lease plant assets instead of purchasing them. In these companies, rent expense will appear in their income statements in place of depreciation expense or in addition to depreciation expense. (Leasing is discussed in chapter 11.) A business that rents a sizable proportion of its assets will not have as large a figure for plant assets on its balance sheet as it would have if it owned the assets instead. This should be kept in mind in comparing enterprises.

Why does a company rent instead of buy assets? Many factors could be listed, but basically, a business should decide between renting and buying on the basis of an analysis of the relative advantages of each alternative.

When assets are leased under contracts that are in effect simply long-term financing arrangements for purchase of the assets, the assets should be recorded in the accounts of the lessee company (with a corresponding long-term liability), and depreciation (and interest expense) should be recorded instead of rent.

INTANGIBLES

The amortization of intangibles has a purpose similar to that of depreciation—namely, to spread the cost of the assets over their useful lives in a systematic and reasonable manner. Those intangibles with a limited life, such as patents and copyrights, should be written off (amortized) to expense over their useful life. The life of this type of intangible may be limited by law or agreement or by economic conditions. If the economic life of these assets is less than their legal life, the shorter period should be used as the basis for amortization.

Basis for amortization

Some intangibles, such as trademarks and organization costs, are recognized to have an essentially unlimited term of life. Formerly the accepted treatment of these assets was to carry them at their cost until evidence appeared of loss in value or worthlessness. In 1970, the Accounting Principles Board of the American Institute of CPAs issued APB Opinion 17, which requires that all intangibles be amortized over a period not to exceed 40 years. This opinion, issued to correct some abuses in treatment of intangibles (especially goodwill), is now followed by all U.S. companies.

APB Opinion 17

A straight-line method of amortization is followed for most intangibles. There is no compelling reason why other methods, such as sum-of-the-years'-digits, could not be used when circumstances warrant.

Goodwill

Goodwill is an asset that arises in the purchase of a company when the purchase price exceeds the net assets (assets minus liabilities) of the purchased company. Usually, the payment exceeds net assets because the earning capacity of the purchased company exceeds normal earnings for that type of company. The payment for goodwill represents the estimated excess future earnings of the purchased company.

Nature of goodwill

Suppose that you are purchasing a local supermarket. The store has been in existence for many years and has established such excellent relations with customers that it earns $180,000 per year on average. The net assets of the store are carried at $1,200,000, which is also the market value of the assets, and the normal return is 10% on net assets. It seems clear that the purchase price of the net assets ought to exceed $1,200,000. The previous owners will want to be paid for the excess earning capacity of their business. You, on the other hand, will not be willing to pay for

Part III   *Measurement of Assets, Liabilities, and Income*

Goodwill illustration

this excess earnings capacity unless there is reasonable assurance that it will continue in future periods when you are the owner. Thus, any payment for goodwill usually will rest upon the existence of reasonably assured future earnings that exceed normal.

The payment for goodwill in a particular case is a matter of negotiation between the parties involved. Suppose, in buying the supermarket, you and the owners finally decide on a price of $1,500,000. Presumably, the amount of goodwill is $300,000, which is the amount by which the agreed price exceeded the net assets of the supermarket. The journal entry on your books would be as follows (assuming liabilities are $500,000):

	Debit	Credit
Inventory, building, and other specific assets	1,700,000	
Goodwill	300,000	
Specific liabilities assumed		500,000
Cash		1,500,000

The goodwill should be amortized over the number of years the excess earning capacity is expected to last. Let us say that you estimate that the supermarket earning capacity advantage will last 10 years. You would make the following entry each year for 10 years:

	Debit	Credit
Amortization of goodwill	30,000	
Goodwill		30,000

Amortization of goodwill is an expense account and would be reported on the income statement. Goodwill, an asset account, would be reported on the balance sheet. At the end of the first year, the balance sheet would show the following:

Intangible assets:
    Goodwill (net of amortization) $270,000

A company's expectations about the value of goodwill may change. When it becomes evident that the excess earning capacity will last for a shorter time than originally expected, or that the goodwill has simply disappeared, the asset goodwill should be adjusted to reflect the reality. For example, suppose that after 6 years of supermarket operations, you conclude that the goodwill you purchased has disappeared mainly because of competition that came upon the scene. The following entry would be appropriate:

	Debit	Credit
Unusual losses—goodwill write-off	120,000	
Goodwill		120,000

This entry recognizes that after 6 years of periodic amortization of $30,000 per year, the remaining goodwill of $120,000 has disappeared. The loss would be reported on the income statement as an expense, shown separately if it is a material amount. This treatment of goodwill also applies to other intangibles when it is determined that their value has disappeared.

The determination of goodwill is usually more complicated than in our simple illustration. Usually, the individual assets of the purchased company must be appraised so that proper values can be assigned them. The rule is that various assets should be recorded on the buyer's books at their *current* values. If the agreed purchase price of the business exceeds the current value of the net assets, the excess is recorded as goodwill.

A further complication appears when the business is purchased by issuing capital stock. The total purchase price, which sets the amount of the goodwill, may then be hard to determine, especially if the amount of stock issued is large or if there is not an active market in the stock. Under these circumstances, it may be impossible to determine the cost of the goodwill.

Goodwill has been discussed thus far in the context of a purchase of a business. Suppose that a company, through operating for a period of years, builds up good customer relations and thus earns profits in excess of normal returns on the assets employed. Should such a company record goodwill? Goodwill does exist, but accountants have generally held that it should not be recorded, since the cost of the asset has not been objectively determined by an enterprise transaction. Thus, the only time goodwill appears on a balance sheet is when the company has purchased it in connection with the acquisition of another company. The presence of goodwill can sometimes be detected in companies that have made no purchases when the earnings are higher than could be expected on the basis of the net assets of the company.

Internally generated goodwill

Patents

Patents are granted for a period of 17 years and give the holders exclusive rights to processes or inventions. The cost of a patent is amortized over its useful life by an entry such as the following:

	Debit	Credit
Patent amortization expense	xxx	
Accumulated amortization—patents		xxx

Straight-line amortization is generally used, unless one of the diminishing-charge methods of amortization can be demonstrated to be more appropriate. The useful life of a patent frequently may be shorter than its legal life because of limited markets or rapid technological change. In these circumstances the amortization should reflect the shorter life. Sometimes accountants credit amortization directly to the patents account rather than using an accumulated amortization account, as in our example above.

Copyrights

Copyrights are granted to authors and composers for life plus 50 years after death. The copyright costs of books, for example, are usually written off by the publisher as an expense over the first printing.

Research and Development Costs

Many companies spend large amounts on research and development. The purpose of such expenditures is to ultimately develop new products and/or new manufacturing processes. A Financial Accounting Standards Board ruling states that virtually all research and development costs incurred after January 1, 1975, are to be "charged to expense when incurred." The FASB so ruled in FASB Statement No. 2. The statement means that no research and development expenditures after January 1, 1975, can appear as assets. The position of the statement is not theoretically sound, but it is justified as a practical accounting approach in an area where asset values are difficult to determine and the asset itself may be difficult to distinguish.

Organization Costs

Organization costs are the costs incurred in organizing a corporation. They include items such as incorporation fees paid to the state, legal fees paid in organizing the corporation, accounting fees, promotional costs incurred in selling securities, and costs of printing stock certificates. Because these costs are necessary to the formation of the enterprise, they constitute, at least theoretically, an intangible that has value as long as the corporation continues to exist. Organization costs, like other intangibles, must be amortized over a maximum life of 40 years according to APB Opinion No. 17. For tax purposes most organization costs may be written off over a 5-year period. Many companies write these costs off to expense either as they are incurred or in the first few years, because they are minor in amount.

Other Intangibles

The costs of intangible assets are written off over their useful (not legal) lives in a systematic and rational manner. The charges to individual periods are properly based on the benefits yielded to each period. There are many different types of intangibles, and it is not feasible to discuss each type. The accountant, instead, must rely on the general approach indicated above when new types of intangible assets are encountered.

Intangibles are often carried on corporate balance sheets at a nominal amount, such as $1. This type of treatment represents a surrender to the uncertainties of intangible asset valuation. As techniques for handling uncertainty are perfected (as in some areas of modern statistics), this kind of treatment should gradually disappear.

DISPOSITION OF LONG-TERM UNEXPIRED COSTS

Disposals of long-term unexpired costs take three forms: the asset may be scrapped, sold, or traded in on a new asset. The accounting treatments of these possibilities vary somewhat. Let us look first at asset sales and other outright disposals of fixed assets.

Sales and Scrapping of Assets

When a long-term asset is sold, the cost of the asset and any related accumulated depreciation or amortization must be removed from the books. Suppose that a piece of equipment that cost $10,000 and has accumulated depreciation of $6,000 is sold for $4,000 cash. The entry to record the sale would be as follows:

	Debit	Credit
Cash	4,000	
Accumulated depreciation—equipment	6,000	
Equipment		10,000

Note that no gain or loss occurs in this situation, since the selling price is the same as the book value of the asset ($10,000 cost less $6,000 accumulated depreciation). If the asset is sold for something other than $4,000, then a gain or loss will occur on the sale. If the sale is for $3,500, for example, the entry will be as follows:

	Debit	Credit
Cash	3,500	
Accumulated depreciation—equipment	6,000	
Loss on sale of equipment	500	
Equipment		10,000

The loss (or gain) on the sale is the difference between the selling price and the book value of the asset sold. The loss (or gain) also can be com-

Gain or loss

puted as the amount needed to balance the entry for the sale, with a loss recorded if a debit is needed, and a gain recorded if a credit is required. The latter approach must be used carefully, since all the other accounts and amounts must be correct if the forced figure for the loss or gain is to be correct.

To take another example, suppose Company A's patent, which cost the company $60,000 early in Year 1 and had an estimated life of 10 years, is found to be worthless early in Year 5. In such a case the patent should be written off as follows:

	Debit	Credit
Accumulated amortization of patents	24,000	
Loss on patents	36,000	
Patents		60,000

Treatment of loss or gain

In the last two cases, a loss is recorded, and a logical question to ask is how such a loss should be treated in the financial statements. A nominal loss, such as the $500 in the first example, would be shown in the income statement as a miscellaneous expense or revenue. A more substantial loss, such as the $36,000 loss on patents, must also be shown on the income statement. A sizable loss (or gain) should always be clearly disclosed, preferably as a separate item among the revenues and expenses of the period. The Accounting Principles Board has decreed that losses or gains on sale or disposal of plant and equipment assets should not be treated as extraordinary items.

Trades of Plant Assets

At times, assets are traded in on other assets, instead of being sold outright. Then the cost of the old asset and the related accumulated depreciation again must be removed from the books. The important issues are the amount at which the new asset should be recorded and whether a gain or loss should be recognized. It can be argued that a gain or loss should be recognized because a transaction takes place and the old asset is, in effect, sold. However, the APB, in its Opinion No. 29, ruled that no gain should be recorded on a trade of like (similar) assets unless cash is received—an unusual occurrence when a company trades an old asset for a newer one. The basis for the opinion is that a trade is not part of the earning process of a company and a mere change in composition of productive assets should not result in a gain. The new asset acquired should be recorded at an amount equal to the book value (cost less accumulated depreciation) of the old asset plus any additional amounts paid. See Example 10-11. Recognizing a loss on a trade of similar assets avoids showing the new asset at more than its fair market value. The loss is the difference between the book value of the asset traded in and its fair value at the trade date.

Basis of new asset

EXAMPLE 10-11 TRADE OF PLANT AND EQUIPMENT

A truck purchased for $6,000 on January 1, Year 1, with an estimated life of 5 years and estimated salvage of $500 is traded in on January 1, Year 5, for a new truck that has a list price of $7,500. A trade-in allowance of $2,100 is received on the old truck, even though it is worth only $1,800 (the $300 overallowance is in effect a discount on the new truck). Straight-line depreciation has been used on the old truck.

Entry for trade:

	Debit	Credit
Trucks	7,000	
Accumulated depreciation—trucks	4,400	
Trucks		6,000
Cash		5,400

To record trade-in of old truck:

Cost of old truck		$6,000
Accumulated depreciation:		
$\dfrac{\$6{,}000 - 500}{5} \times 4 \text{ years} =$		4,400
Book value		$1,600
Cash payment:		
List price	$7,500	
Less trade-in	2,100	
Net cash paid		5,400
Cost of new truck		$7,000

The cost of the new asset is not necessarily the list price of the item. Instead, the cost is determined by the cash paid and the book value of the asset traded.

For income tax purposes no gain or loss can be recognized on an asset trade. Thus the tax treatment and the basic accounting treatment are often similar. The tax treatment has the effect of submerging the gain or loss in the new asset balance. The gain or loss, instead of appearing on the date of the trade, will appear in higher or lower depreciation charges over the life of the *new* asset.

Where the trade does not involve similar productive assets, a gain or loss will generally be recognized. The new asset acquired will be recorded on the basis of the fair value of the assets used in its acquisition. This type of trade is not a very common business transaction.

Dispositions of Assets during the Year

From an accounting standpoint, it is desirable that all assets be acquired and disposed of at either the beginning or the end of the fiscal year. In such cases, there is no problem as to the correct amount of depreciation or amortization to record. Unfortunately, however, little attention is paid

Depreciation to nearest month

to bookkeeping convenience in the timing of transactions. As a result, the accountant often must deal with sales or trades during an accounting period, rather than at its beginning or end.

If an asset is acquired on March 18, it should be depreciated from that date to the end of the fiscal year (let us assume December 31). Depreciation is usually taken only to the nearest month; so 9 months' depreciation (April through December) would be taken in this case. If an asset is sold or traded at some interim date, let us say September 6, it is necessary to record the appropriate depreciation expense up to the date of sale or trade before the entry for the sale or trade itself is made. In this case, 8 months of depreciation expense (January through August) would be recorded on the asset disposed of.

LONG-TERM ASSET PROBLEMS

We will now explore briefly a few of the problems that arise in connection with long-term assets.

Depreciation and Matching

We have emphasized that depreciation is the spreading of the cost of a long-term unexpired cost over its useful life in a systematic manner. This approach has more logical appeal than has a system in which the cost (less salvage) of an asset is written off at the time of purchase. Depreciation accounting attempts to relate the costs of a fixed asset with the benefits that the asset renders to each period. Accordingly, each period of use will be charged with some depreciation. It is possible that there may be depreciation expense even though an asset is not actually used during a period, since obsolescence and deterioration caused by the elements often will occur regardless of usage. In such a case, the depreciation will appear as an expense in an accounting period solely because it occurs in the period. This is recognition of an expense on the basis of occurrence in a time period, rather than on the basis of relation to specific productive use. Of course, depreciation must be taken in this case for the additional reason that the asset cannot be stated at an amount greater than the benefits that can reasonably be expected in future periods. Deterioration and obsolescence impair the ability of an asset to render future benefits, and this fact must be recorded.

It is interesting to note that the *expenditure* for a fixed asset often comes at the beginning of its life at the time of purchase, while the *expense* of the asset is spread over its whole life. This difference in timing is much greater for long-term assets than it is for other assets. Inventory, for example, is often bought and used up (as cost of goods sold) in the same accounting period. Note also that the entry to record depreciation does not involve any expenditure:

	Debit	Credit
Depreciation expense	xxx	
Accumulated depreciation		xxx

For this reason, some people refer to it as "just a book entry." They mean that the amount of the entry can be changed without affecting the amount of cash or current resources on hand (except through the effect on income taxes). Of course, they are incorrect to the extent that they believe or imply that the depreciation entry is not necessary. Depreciation is an expense of doing business and should be recorded each period in order to determine income.

Depreciation and Reality

Depreciation in financial accounting is an allocation process. The allocation is supposed to be reasonable and systematic. Unfortunately, while it is obvious that most depreciation methods provide a *systematic* allocation, criteria of *reasonableness* have not been clearly established in accounting. In practice, depreciation methods are often adopted because they are easy to compute or affect net income in the desired fashion. These may be sufficient reasons for management, but they hardly qualify as good reasons in an accounting sense.

Allocation problems

The reasonableness of allocations in accounting is difficult to establish. Accountants often speak of relating depreciation to the service benefit provided by an asset. However, the service benefit concept in accounting is itself rather hazy, and tracing the benefits that flow from particular assets or groups of assets is difficult. In fact, it is difficult to refute the view that allocations such as depreciation are essentially arbitrary. Accountants have generally been unwilling to use declines in market values (which are not arbitrary) from year to year to compute the depreciation because market prices are not necessarily relevant when an asset continues to be used instead of sold.

Accountants recognize that depreciation poses some knotty problems. As yet, however, they have been unable to agree on how these problems are to be solved. They will probably continue to rely on vague notions of "reasonable and systematic allocation" for the foreseeable future.

On the basis of the illustrations of depreciation methods earlier in this chapter, it is clear that depreciation charges can vary considerably, depending on the method of depreciation chosen. For a single asset,

Effects of different methods

Expansion

methods such as sum-of-the-years'-digits and double-declining-balance will give larger charges in the early years than will straight-line. Most companies operate with numerous plant assets, adding new ones and disposing of old ones each year. What effect do the different depreciation methods have in a case like this? If the proportion of new and older assets remains the same, depreciation charges will be similar under all methods. Higher double-declining depreciation charges on new assets will be balanced by lower charges on old assets. When a company is expanding, the higher depreciation charges on new assets under the double-declining-balance method will outweigh the lower charges on old assets; therefore, the total depreciation charge will be higher than with straight-line depreciation. If a company is getting smaller, there will be an opposite effect. Many American companies are committed to a policy of expansion at a rate at least equal to the expansion in the economy. As a result, the adoption of one of the diminishing-charge depreciation methods (sum-of-the-years'-digits or declining-balance) is likely to lead to consistently higher depreciation charges than would be the case with straight-line depreciation.

If diminishing-charge depreciation methods are adopted because they clearly reflect the flow of benefits from the assets, the resulting income statements will clearly reflect the earning power of the company. If these methods are adopted primarily because they yield a desired income figure, however, it is possible that the reported new income may give a distorted picture of earnings capacity. This in turn might have unfortunate influences on investor decisions.

Tax advantage

Tax and financial reporting

Many companies have adopted accelerated depreciation methods for tax return purposes because of the tax advantage that they entail. Higher depreciation charges mean lower income and lower taxes. This advantage continues as long as a company continues to expand. If accelerated methods are used for tax purposes they do not have to be used for financial reporting purposes. Thus many companies use straight-line depreciation for financial statements and accelerated methods for their tax returns.

The accelerated depreciation methods are popular for another reason. They allow a business to recover more of the investment in a fixed asset in the first few years of the asset's life. This is an important factor in any situation in which there is a high rate of technological change. It also is important when inflation is a factor (and it has been a part of the American experience since 1945) and depreciation is limited to the original cost of a long-term asset. This factor of inflation deserves a closer look.

Depreciation and Inflation

The rapid inflation of the past several years has led the accounting profession to consider requiring supplementary statements that reflect inflation. These supplementary statements are stated in *units of general purchasing power* (*GPP*). Suppose a building costing $400,000 was acquired in Year 1 when the general price index[4] was 117.6 (Base year = 100). Assuming a 40-year life with no salvage, the historical cost depreciation would be $10,000 per year (straight-line method). The depreciation for Year 15 (when the year-end general price index was 178.0) would be $15,140 in GPP units ($10,000 × 178/117.6). The idea is to state revenues and expenses at year-end general prices.

The Securities and Exchange Commission has also required that certain current replacement values be reported as supplementary information in annual reports filed by large companies with the SEC. With respect to plant assets, the SEC requires that companies state the "current cost of replacing the productive capacity together with the current net replacement cost represented by the depreciable, depletable and amortizable assets." Also, companies must report the depreciation or depletion or amortization as if it had been figured on the current replacement cost. The purpose of this requirement is to permit the reader to see the impact of specific price movements. This is different from GPP statements, which are aimed at showing the effects of general inflation.

The issues and techniques of presenting GPP statements and current values are discussed in chapter 15 of this text.

Depreciation and Amortization Corrections

Depreciation, depletion, and amortization computations are based on estimates, the most important of which is the estimated life in years or in units. Actually, nobody expects the estimates to come out exactly. Most accountants are happy if the estimates turn out to be reasonably close to the actual events. A problem arises, however, when the estimates turn out to be unrealistic. Perhaps a machine with an estimated life of 15 years turns out to have a total life of 10 years. Or perhaps a mineral deposit estimated at 40,000 tons turns out to consist of 70,000 tons after the deposit is partially mined. In either of these cases, the rate of amortization is so incorrect that something should be done about it. The problem can be approached in either of two ways:

1. Spread the remaining cost (less salvage) at the time of discovery of the mistake over the remaining useful life of the asset.
2. Compute the correct periodic charge, and revise and correct the amortization already recorded.

Example 10-12 illustrates the two possibilities.

---

[4]. The index usually recommended is the Gross National Product Implicit Deflator. This price index represents the average price of a wide range of goods and services.

Part III   Measurement of Assets, Liabilities, and Income

EXAMPLE 10-12

A machine was purchased for $15,000 on January 1, Year 1. The estimated life was 15 years, and there was no estimated salvage value. Straight-line depreciation is used. On January 1, Year 6, it is discovered that the machine will last only 10 years in total. On this date the machine is carried on the books as follows:

Machine	$15,000
Less accumulated depreciation	5,000
Net unexpired cost	10,000

Corrections:
  Method 1 — spread remaining cost over remaining life.

Remaining cost	$10,000
Remaining life	5 years
Depreciation expense	$ 2,000

This expense will be recorded in each of the years, Year 6 to Year 10.
  Method 2 — revise prior depreciation.

Cost of machine	$15,000	
Correct estimated life	10 years	
Depreciation charge per year	$ 1,500	
Correct depreciation for Years 1 to 5		$7,500
Actual depreciation taken		5,000
Correction of prior depreciation		$2,500

The expense for each of Years 6 to 10 will be $1,500.
The entry for correction of past depreciation is

	Debit	Credit
Corrections of prior years' expense	2,500	
Accumulated depreciation		2,500

Questions as to the validity of the two methods are complicated and are not discussed in this text. The first method is the one commonly used in practice.

PRESENTATION IN FINANCIAL STATEMENTS

Since long-term unexpired costs are an important factor in most businesses, facts relating to them should be prominently disclosed in the financial statements. On the income statement, this means that depreciation, depletion, and amortization generally should be shown separately and that the method of write-off should be indicated. On the balance sheet, the amount of each major class of long-lived assets should be shown, and the accumulated depreciation, depletion, and amortization to date should be indicated. Significant acquisitions and disposals also should be indicated in the statements, particularly in the statement of changes in financial position.

SUMMARY

The two major classes of long-term unexpired costs are tangible assets and intangibles. Tangible assets are acquired for the economic values inherent in their physical characteristics and include natural resources; property, plant and equipment; and other depreciable assets. Intangibles are acquired because of the economic values inherent in the ideas they represent, the rights they convey to their owners, or the relationships they may have to the business.

At acquisition, the costs of a long-term asset include all expenditures necessary to obtain the asset and get it in location and ready for use. Expenditures on long-term assets made after acquisition are capitalized (capital expenditures) if they result in significant future long-range benefits and expensed (revenue expenditures) if they are required to keep the asset in normal operating condition.

After acquisition, the acquisition cost of an asset is allocated over the asset's useful life in a systematic and reasonable manner. Cost allocation should be related to the time pattern of benefits expected to flow from the asset. In the case of natural resources, depletion expense should reflect the acquisition cost of the quantity of natural resource extracted in a period. The cost of land acquired as a building site is not allocated because land is a permanent asset.

Depreciation expense of a period should reflect the benefits received from the asset in that period. Straight-line depreciation, which allocates an equal amount of acquisition cost to each period, is appropriate if the asset tends to produce equal periodic benefits. Accelerated or diminishing-charge depreciation methods (declining-balance or sum-of-the-years'-digits) allocate a higher portion of acquisition cost to the early years of life and a lower portion to the later years of life. These methods are appropriate for assets that produce a gradually diminishing stream of benefits.

Amortization of the cost of intangibles should also be reasonable and systematic. The APB (in APB Opinion No. 17) has ruled that in any case the maximum amortization period for intangibles should be 40 years.

When a long-term asset is disposed of, the balances of the asset account and the related accumulated depreciation, depletion, or amortization account are written off, and a gain or loss is recognized. In the case of trades of similar assets, no gain or loss is generally recognized.

Depreciation is a phenomenon that poses challenging problems for the accountant. While all methods of measuring depreciation are arbitrary, the method selected does make a difference in the measurement of income. Therefore, the method should tend to reflect the benefits derived from the asset. If accelerated methods are chosen solely because of the desirable income results they produce, reported income may be distorted. The rapid inflation of the past several years has led the accounting profession to consider disclosing effects of inflation in supplementary statements and has led the SEC to require accountants to show current replacement costs and replacement cost depreciation in the notes to the annual reports filed with the SEC. These requirements have raised a number of problems that are discussed in chapter 15.

IMPORTANT TERMS

Natural resources
Depletion
Property, plant, and equipment
Depreciation
Intangibles
Amortization
Capital expenditure
Revenue expenditure
Repairs
Extraordinary repairs
Service benefits
Wear and tear
Obsolescence
Percentage depletion

Straight-line depreciation
Sum-of-the-years'-digits depreciation
Declining-balance depreciation
Units-of-production depreciation
Goodwill
Patents
Copyrights
Research and development costs
Organization costs
Allocation
General purchasing power unit of measure (GPP)

QUESTIONS

10-1. What is the basis for measuring:
    a. Monetary assets?
    b. Unexpired costs?
    And what is the reason for the basis used?

10-2. What are some of the problems in connection with unexpired costs? In your discussion cover:
    a. Problems of measuring and recording acquisition costs.
    b. Problems of measuring and recording cost expirations.

10-3. Discuss the reasons for using acquisition cost in valuing fixed assets in the statement of financial position.

10-4. Distinguish between *capital expenditures* and *revenue expenditures*.

10-5. Classify each of the following as capital or revenue expenditures:
   a. Replacement of the tires on a delivery truck.
   b. The expense of tearing down an old building located on land acquired for the purpose of erecting a new factory.
   c. The wages of a maintenance man who lubricates factory machinery and makes minor repairs.
   d. The salary of the director of research.

10-6. What is *depreciation?* How is the depreciation expense that is assigned to a particular accounting period determined? Answer the latter question in general terms, dealing with the basis used for allocating cost to periods.

10-7. What is an *intangible asset?* Name several intangible assets, and describe their presentation on the balance sheet.

10-8. How would you define *goodwill?* Under what circumstances does goodwill appear on the books of a company as an asset? Under what circumstances should goodwill be amortized?

10-9. Inflation and changing prices cause particular difficulties in connection with depreciation. Why is this so? How do you suggest that these difficulties be handled?

10-10. Is depreciation based on the current replacement costs of plant assets relevant to the decisions of users of financial statements? Explain your answer.

EXERCISES

10-11. *Plant and equipment asset cost.* Equipment is purchased for $8,000 on account. The terms of the purchase are 2/10, n/30, FOB shipping point. The freight bill on the machine is $800. A local contractor is paid $1,500 to prepare a special foundation and supports for the machine and to install the machine. Give journal entries for all of the above.

10-12. *Plant and equipment asset cost.* Prepare journal entries in general journal form for the following transactions involving the purchase, installation, and operation of a new machine.
   a. Purchased a machine, paying cash of $22,000.
   b. The freight bill for shipping costs on the machine was paid, $1,600.
   c. A part that was supposed to be on the machine when shipped from the seller was missing. This part was acquired from a local dealer for cash, $500. The machine seller is to reimburse us for this part.
   d. Paid a local firm $1,400 for installation of the machine.
   e. During the first year of operating the machine, minor repairs costing $75 were made to the machine.

10-13. *Cost allocation.* Assume that land and a building are purchased at a lump-sum price of $50,000. What portion of this cost is applicable to the building if an appraisal of the property immediately after the purchase indicates a value of $15,000 applicable to the land and $45,000 applicable to the building?

10-14. *Depreciation methods.* A machine estimated to have a useful life of 8 years was purchased at a cost of $41,000. Salvage value is estimated to be $1,000.
   a. How much depreciation should be charged on the machine each year under the straight-line method of depreciation?
   b. Assuming double-declining-balance method, what is the second year's depreciation?

10-15. *Depreciation methods.* A delivery truck was acquired on January 1, at a total cost of $4,000. Its useful life is estimated to be 4 years, at the end of which its trade-in value is estimated at $400. During the 4 years, it is expected that the truck will run 80,000 miles.
   Required:
   a. Compute the depreciation expense for the year, using the straight-line method of depreciation.
   b. Compute the depreciation expense for the year, using the units-of-production method. The truck was operated 32,000 miles in the first year.

10-16. *Depreciation methods.* Using the following data, set up a table comparing annual depreciation and annual unexpired cost balances for motor 426 under:
   a. Straight-line
   b. Sum-of-the-years'-digits
   c. Production hours

Cost	$15,000
Estimated salvage value	$5,000
Estimated production hours	1,200
Average production hours/year	400

(Solution in Appendix B.)

10-17. *Depreciation expense.* A tool shop is built at a cost of $15,000 on January 1, Year 1. On January 1, Year 3, an addition to the shop is made at a cost of $2,000. During Year 5, the ordinary repairs made on the tool shop amount to $150. Assuming that the life of the tool shop is not expected to extend beyond December 31, Year 10, what is the total cost of using the tool shop in Year 5? Assume straight-line depreciation.

10-18. *Depreciation methods.* The Talbot Company purchased new manufacturing equipment on December 31, Year 1, for $58,000. The equipment had an estimated life of 6 years or 500,000 units of manufacture and a salvage value of $4,000. The equipment produced 125,000 units in Year 2. Compute the depreciation expense for Year 2, using the following methods:
   a. Straight-line
   b. Sum-of-the-years'-digits
   c. Units-of-production
   d. Declining-balance (use double the straight-line rate).

10-19. *Depreciation expense.* The Fischer Company completed the following transactions affecting delivery equipment during Year 1. Depreciation is computed to the nearest month and recorded at the time an asset is sold or traded; otherwise it is recorded on December 31. The company uses straight-line depreciation. Record the transactions in general journal form, including depreciation entries at the time of sale or trade and on December 31.

Jan. 18	Purchased a delivery truck costing $8,000, with an estimated life of 8 years and a salvage value of $400.
Mar. 14	Purchased a motor scooter to be used in small deliveries. Cost is $500; estimated life, 4 years; and salvage value, $50.
June 20	Traded the delivery truck and paid $2,600 cash for a larger truck with a value of $12,000. The new truck has an estimated 10-year life and $2,000 salvage value.
Sept. 10	Sold the motor scooter purchased on March 14 for $300 cash.

10-20. *Depletion.* The Dry Hole Petroleum Company acquires for $50,000 an oil well estimated to contain reserves of 300,000 barrels of oil. The company extracts 40,000 barrels of oil during the year. Make the journal entry to record the depletion cost for the year.

(Solution in Appendix B.)

10-21. *Depletion.* A lumber company has acquired a timber tract for $20,000 and has incurred costs of $2,000 in developing the tract. The tract is estimated to contain 100,000 board feet of timber and will have a residual value of $5,000 after the timber has been cut. If 40,000 board feet of timber will be cut during the year, what will be the entry for depletion?

10-22. *Patents.* On December 31, Year 1, the balance in the patent account of the Willard Manufacturing Company was $350,000. An investigation determined that the fair value of the patent was only $100,000 on January 10, Year 2, and the patent would have an expected life of 4 years. How should the above estimates be reflected in the Year 2 financial statements?

10-23. *Patent amortization.* On January 1, Year 1, the Fay Company purchased two new patents on articles to be manufactured. Patent A, costing $18,500, was associated with a product expected to be in demand indefinitely. Patent B, costing $15,000, was associated with a novelty item expected to be in demand only a few months or a year. Make the entries necessary to reflect patent amortization in Year 1.

(Solution in Appendix B.)

10-24. *Patent amortization.* The Barret Company acquired a patent on January 1, Year 1, at a cost of $10,000. A 5-year useful life was selected for amortization purposes. On January 1, Year 3, the patent was written off as worthless. Make journal entries for the following transactions:
   a. Purchase of the patent on January 1, Year 1.
   b. Amortization on December 31, Year 1, and December 31, Year 2.
   c. Write-off of patent on January 1, **Year 3.**

10-25. *Copyright.* A copyright for a book was acquired from the copyright owner on December 31, Year 1, at a cost of $14,350. The publisher estimated the book would remain popular for 4 years and that the copyright should be written off as follows: 50% the first year, 35% the second year, 10% the third year, and 5% the fourth year. On December 31, Year 4, at the end of the third year, there appeared to be no future market for the book, and the remaining copyright costs were written off. Prepare entries for the purchase of the copyright and the write-off for each of the three years.

PROBLEMS

10-26. *Plant asset cost, depreciation.* On July 1, Smith Cleaners purchased a delivery truck for cash. The invoice read:

List price	$8,700
Cash discount	800
Net price	$7,900
State sales tax	395
Truck license	125
Gasoline	8
Anti-freeze in radiator	6
Total due	$8,434

Required:
a. Entry on July 1.
b. The life of the truck is estimated at 3 years with a trade-in value of $500 at the end of that time. Give the entry for depreciation at December 31, using straight-line.
c. How would the truck be shown on the financial position statement dated December 31? Show classification and amounts.

10-27. *Asset cost and depreciation.* On December 17 a factory buys a machine with an invoice price of $12,000. Terms are 2/10, n/60. The invoice is paid within the discount period on December 23. Freight costs are $800, and $900 is spent to prepare a special foundation on December 27. Costs of $800 are incurred to complete the installation on December 30. The machine has an estimated life of 10 years and a salvage value of $500. Freight and installation costs are paid in cash. The machine is ready for use on December 31, Year 1.

Required:
a. Prepare entries in journal form for the above transactions.
b. Prepare the entry for the Year 2 depreciation (use double-declining-balance method).
c. State account titles and amounts that would appear on the Year 2 income statement and the December 31, Year 2, balance sheet as a result of the purchase and use of the machine.

10-28. *Asset cost.* Early in September, the Calco Company purchased an old building for $750,000, including $75,000 for the land. Extensive repairs made to the building cost $500,000. In February of the next year, after all the extensive repairs had been made and paid for, the company president changed his mind about the building. He decided to use the building for a completely different purpose from what he had originally planned.

Rather than sell this building ($800,000 present market value, including $75,000 for the land) and buy another building at a cost of $1,300,000 (including $75,000 for land), the president decided to spend another $350,000 to remodel the present building so that it would serve its new intended purpose. The $350,000 was expended, and the building was ready for occupancy and use in May. The company's fiscal year ends June 30.

Required:
a. Prepare journal entries for all of the above events, except depreciation.
b. Defend your treatment of the costs incurred.

10-29. *Plant asset sale; depreciation.* A machine having a book value on January 1, Year 3, of $3,000 was sold on April 1, Year 3, for $3,300. The original cost of the machine was $5,000, acquired on January 1, Year 1. At that time, estimated life of the machine was 5 years, with no salvage value. The last adjusting entry for depreciation (straight-line method) was made on December 31, Year 2. Prepare the journal entries required on April 1, Year 3.

10-30. *Sale or trade.* Record in general journal form the following transactions for the sale or trade of assets. Depreciation is computed to the nearest month and is recorded at the time an asset is sold or traded; depreciation is computed annually on December 31 for remaining assets.

a. A building bought on May 30, Year 1, for $236,000 was sold on May 30, Year 11, for $230,000. Straight-line depreciation had been used, and the building had an estimated life of 50 years and a $10,000 salvage value when purchased.

b. Machinery bought on July 31, Year 1, had a cost of $24,000 and was estimated at that time to have a life of 30 years and no salvage value. The sum-of-the-years'-digits method was used. On July 30, Year 9, the machine was traded for a similar asset with a value of $20,000, and a $5,000 cash difference was paid. (Hint: there is no need to calculate depreciation for each individual year).

c. Office equipment costing $10,000 was bought on January 2, Year 5. The equipment was estimated to have a life of 10 years and salvage value of $500. A constant percentage of 20% on the declining balance was used to depreciate the asset. The equipment was traded on March 31, Year 10, for a similar asset with a cost of $15,000. A cash difference of $8,500 was paid. Record no gain or loss on the trade.

10-31. *Sale and trade.* The Blerb Company has two machines that were acquired on October 1, Year 1, at a cost of $6,500 each. At that time, their estimated life was 10 years, with salvage estimated at $500 each. The company uses straight-line depreciation. Assume that the correct depreciation was recorded on December 31 of Year 1, Year 2, Year 3, and Year 4. You are asked to give the journal entries for the following, which occurred on April 26, Year 5: one machine is sold for $3,900, and the other machine is traded in on a new machine. The list price on the new machine is $9,000, while the trade-in allowance on the old is $4,600. The balance owed is to be paid in cash. The company's year ends on December 31.

(Solution in Appendix B.)

Part III Measurement of Assets, Liabilities, and Income

10-32. *Trade.* On April 1, Year 1, the Freeb Co. purchased a truck for $11,000. Estimated life was 10 years, estimated salvage value was $600, and straight-line depreciation was used. Correct depreciation entries were made in Years 1 through 5. On September 25, Year 6, the Freeb Co. traded in the truck on a new one with a list price of $18,000. Freeb Co. was given a trade-in allowance of $5,400 on the old truck and paid the balance in cash. The old truck had a second-hand market value on September 25 of $5,100. Give the entries for the trade on September 25. The company's year ends on December 31.

10-33. *Depreciation correction.* A building costing $350,000 on January 1, Year 10, has been depreciated on the basis of a 40-year life. On December 31, Year 24, before adjusting the books, it is decided that the life used for depreciating the building should have been 30 years instead of 40. The salvage value used was $50,000. Use straight-line basis.
   a. Assume the accumulated depreciation account will be corrected, and
      (1) Calculate the amount of annual depreciation based on a 30-year life.
      (2) Calculate the balance of the accumulated depreciation account before the Year 24 adjusting entry, based on the initial estimated life.
      (3) Calculate the amount of the error in the balance of the accumulated depreciation account.
      (4) Prepare the journal entry to correct the error.
      (5) Prepare the journal entry for Year 24 depreciation.
   b. Assume the accumulated depreciation account will not be corrected and calculate the depreciation for Year 24.

10-34. *Depletion.* The Unger Mining Company purchased a tract of land on July 1, Year 1, for $56,000. Legal fees connected with the purchase were $3,000, paid on August 1, Year 1. During the next few months, Unger did exploratory work to locate commercial deposits, paying $15,000 for supplies and labor. On the basis of this work, it was estimated that 150,000 tons of ore could be mined and that the land could be disposed of for $2,000 when operations ended. Actual tons mined were 5,000 in Year 1 and 50,000 in Year 2. There were production costs of $6,000 in Year 1 and $14,000 in Year 2. There were no sales in Year 1, but 50,000 tons were sold in Year 2.

   Required:
   a. Calculate the cost of production for Year 1.
   b. Calculate the cost of production for Year 2.
   c. Calculate the cost of goods sold in Year 2, using FIFO.

10-35. *Intangibles.* The Waterstone Rubber Company balance sheet on January 1, Year 30, discloses the following assets:

Patents	$ 20,000
Goodwill	100,000
Trade names	5,000

The patent will have value to the company for approximately 10 years from January 1, Year 30. The goodwill was acquired several years ago when the company purchased another business. Goodwill has been amortized gradually to the $100,000 balance, and now management wishes to write off the remaining goodwill over 10 years, beginning with Year 30. The trade names account contains the cost of a trade name purchased in Year 5 from a company no longer in business. The remaining cost is to be written off as a loss, because there is no evidence that it has value. Record the write-offs and adjustments in general journal form for Year 30.

10-36. *Goodwill.* The H Company is negotiating to buy the net assets of the M Manufacturing Company. A summary of financial position statement is given as of October 31, Year 1.

M MANUFACTURING COMPANY
Financial Position
October 31, Year 1

Assets:		
Cash and receivables (net)		$ 25,000
Inventories (at LIFO cost)		75,000
Plant and equipment (net)		150,000
		$250,000
Equities:		
Liabilities		$ 30,000
Owners' investment		50,000
Retained income		170,000
		$250,000

The H Company and the M Manufacturing Company agree that the current value of the inventories is $100,000, the current value of plant and equipment is $185,000, and the price of the net assets to be paid by the H Company is $300,000. What is the amount of goodwill implied by the purchase price?

(Solution in Appendix B.)

10-37. *Goodwill.* The Burton Company is in the process of purchasing the Sanders Company. Sanders's financial statements for the previous year are as follows:

SANDERS COMPANY
Income Statement
Year 3

Sales		$350,000
Cost of Sales	$200,000	
Depreciation (10%)	20,000	
Management salaries	25,000	
Other operating costs	55,000	300,000
Net income		$ 50,000

Part III   Measurement of Assets, Liabilities, and Income

SANDERS COMPANY
Balance Sheet
December 31, Year 3

Assets:	
Cash and receivables	$ 40,000
Inventories (at FIFO cost)	70,000
Land	20,000
Building and equipment	200,000
Less accumulated depreciation	(60,000)
Total assets	$270,000
Equities:	
Liabilities	$ 40,000
Capital stock	100,000
Retained earnings	130,000
Total equities	$270,000

Burton's analysis indicates that the land is worth $42,000 and the buildings and equipment are worth $240,000 new (the 10-year life Sanders has been using is appropriate). Also, management salaries in the future would have to be $30,000 per year. Similar businesses are usually able to earn an 8% return on tangible net investment. Burton is to pay Sanders an amount based on the value of the net tangible assets plus 5 times the estimated excess earnings.

Required:
a. Prepare an adjusted income statement.
b. Compute the amount of the net tangible assets.
c. Compute the excess earnings and the goodwill.
d. What will next year's income statement look like if goodwill is to be amortized over 10 years?

CASE PROBLEM

10-38. *Effects of depreciation methods on financial statements.* Wells Delivery Service began operations in January, Year 1, with the following balance sheet:

WELLS DELIVERY SERVICE
Balance Sheet, January 2, Year 1

Assets		Equities	
Cash	$11,000	Accounts payable	$ 5,000
Delivery trucks—used	9,000	Capital stock	15,000
Total assets	$20,000	Total equities	$20,000

Wells began business with 3 used trucks, each costing $3,000. The company plans to acquire new trucks and dispose of the used trucks as business expands. Each used truck is expected to last 3 years with no salvage value.

New trucks are expected to cost $6,000 each and to last 5 years with no salvage. The company plans to pay dividends equal to 50% of net income each year. For simplicity, assume that all revenues and expenses (except depreciation) are received or paid in cash, and the income tax rate is 30%. Assume also that the net accounts payable does not change. The revenues, expenses, and other information for the first three years of the firm's existence are detailed below:

	Year 1	Year 2	Year 3
Sales	$31,000	$36,000	$50,000
Cash expenses—wages, rent, salaries, etc.	$25,000	$27,000	$33,000
Sale of used trucks at beginning of year	0	0	1 at $1,000
Purchase of new trucks at beginning of year ($6,000 each)	0	1	2

Required:
a. Prepare income statements for each of the three years and a balance sheet at the end of Year 3, using straight-line depreciation.
b. Prepare income statements for each of the three years and a balance sheet at the end of Year 3, using sum-of-the-years'-digits depreciation.
c. Comment on the differences you note between *a* and *b*.

11

Liabilities

Almost all liabilities will be paid by using monetary assets, particularly cash. As a result, liabilities are generally carried at the amount of cash to be paid. Discounted present values, which allow for interest, are often used if the obligations require payments at dates that are relatively far in the future. Liabilities fall into two broad classes: short-term liabilities and long-term liabilities.

SHORT-TERM LIABILITIES

Short-term liabilities are obligations of a company that must be satisfied in the near future. They usually are satisfied by payment, but they also can be settled by providing goods or services (as in the case of deferred rent revenue, which is earned by providing rental premises to the lessor). Most short-term liabilities do not present a valuation problem, since they are listed at the amount that will have to be paid when the liability comes due. On the other hand, problems of control are important, since an enterprise must be sure that it is paying legitimate obligations.

Many short-term liabilities parallel monetary assets; accounts payable and accounts receivable, and notes payable and notes receivable, are typical examples. As a result, some of the discussion in earlier chapters is applicable to current liabilities.

Accounts Payable

Accounts payable are the current obligations for purchases of goods and services on credit terms. In effect, they are the mirror image of accounts receivable. Accounts payable should be listed in the accounts at the net amount of the obligation they represent; that is, at the amount of purchasing power that will have to be expended to pay the accounts. The only difference between receivables and payables lies in the greater certainty that a company has with respect to the disposition of accounts payable. A company can make definite plans to take advantage of all discounts offered, for example, whereas there is no assurance concerning the discounts that will be taken by customers. Also, there usually is little question about payment of accounts payable, whereas collection of accounts receivable sometimes is doubtful.

The accounting for payables is generally similar to the accounting for receivables. There is, of course, nothing comparable to allowances for doubtful accounts, but purchase returns and allowances are recorded in a separate account for purposes of management information and control, just as are sales returns and allowances.

A difference may appear between receivables and payables accounting in the area of cash discounts. Since the selling company has little control over the actions of its customers, it can do nothing but record discounts as they are taken. On the other hand, a company has control over payments on its own obligations. With this control, the accounting for discounts can be set up to give maximum information to management.

Discounts

Since there are considerable advantages to taking discounts, many companies follow a policy of taking all discounts offered. They view the purchase as being for a net amount, with a penalty for late payment. In their opinion, there is no reason why a discount should not be taken. Therefore, they are interested in an accounting approach that discloses any discounts that have been lost—that is the important information.

Despite these considerations, many companies continue to follow the approach of recording discounts on purchases as they are taken. Thus, the accounts payable liability is recorded at the total, or gross, amount of the invoice. Later, if payment is made within the discount period, the discount is recorded. If payment is made after the discount period is over, no discount is recorded. But more important, no record is made of the lost opportunity.

An alternative system of recording purchases, which emphasizes the reporting of lost opportunities, is sometimes used. Under this system, the purchases and accounts payable are recorded at a net price, after deducting available discounts. Thus, a purchase of $100 with discount terms of 2/10, n/30 would be recorded at $98. If payment is made within the discount period, no discount is recorded. If payment is made after the discount period expires, the loss of the discount is recorded. This procedure is illustrated in Example 11-1.

Recording at net price

EXAMPLE 11-1

	Debit	Credit
a. Purchase of $100, terms 2/10, n/30:		
Purchases	98	
Accounts payable		98
b. Payment after end of discount period:		
Accounts payable	98	
Purchase discounts lost	2	
Cash		100

The advantage of this system is that lost opportunities are clearly disclosed. Management is interested in lost opportunities, because corrective action can be taken, costs can be reduced, and profit can be enhanced. A system in which one knows approximately what has been done correctly, but has no way of identifying specific mistakes, gives little indication of where corrective action should be taken. Management should be more concerned with mistakes than with areas where all is going well. In this respect, the system in which purchases are recorded at net amounts has definite advantages.

To clarify the procedures that have been discussed, Example 11-2 illustrates transactions involving accounts payable. The first part of Example 11-2 shows accounts payable transactions recorded at the gross, or full, amount; the second part shows recording at the net amount.

EXAMPLE 11-2: ACCOUNTS PAYABLE TRANSACTIONS

Transactions

June 1: Y Co. buys $5,000 of goods from X Co. on account, terms 2/10, n/30.

June 2: Y Co. buys $3,000 of goods from Z Co. on account, terms 2/10, n/30.

June 5: Y Co. returns $200 of goods to X Co. because they are unsatisfactory.

June 10: Y Co. pays the balance owed to X Co. by sending a check for $4,704.

June 23: Y Co. sends Z Co. a check for the balance owed.

Recording at Gross Amount

		Debit	Credit
June 1	Purchases	5,000	
	Accounts payable (X)		5,000
June 2	Purchases	3,000	
	Accounts payable (Z)		3,000
June 5	Accounts payable (X)	200	
	Purchase returns and allowances		200
June 10	Accounts payable (X)	4,800	
	Purchase discounts		96
	Cash		4,704
June 23	Accounts payable (Z)	3,000	
	Cash		3,000

If Y Company recorded its purchases at the net amount, the entries would be somewhat different:

Recording at Net Amount

		Debit	Credit
June 1	Purchases	4,900	
	Accounts payable (X)		4,900
	($5,000 − 2% = $4,900)		
June 2	Purchases	2,940	
	Accounts payable (Z)		2,940
	($3,000 − 2% = $2,940)		
June 5	Accounts payable (X)	196	
	Purchase returns and allowances		196
	(returned a net of $200 − 2% = $196)		
June 10	Accounts payable (X)	4,704	
	Cash		4,704
	($4,900 − 196 = $4,704)		
June 23	Accounts payable (Z)	2,940	
	Purchase discounts lost	60	
	Cash		3,000

Because most companies record purchases at the gross amount, that is the approach that will be used in this text, unless otherwise noted.

Purchase Controls

Organizations need to control their purchases carefully so they can be assured that

1. Only those goods that are needed are purchased.
2. The goods ordered have been received.
3. Invoices are paid when due.
4. Quality of goods received is acceptable.

Control is exercised through a control system. The system will vary in complexity, depending on the size and complexity of the organization involved. A fairly elaborate internal control system for purchases might include the following steps:

1. *Stores* department notes that stock is low on an item and initiates a request for purchases (a requisition) in triplicate.
   Copy 1 goes to *accounts payable*.
   Copy 2 goes to the *purchasing department*.
   Copy 3 is retained by *stores*.
2. *Purchasing* reviews the request and prepares a purchase order in sextuplicate.
   Copies 1 and 2 are sent to the *supplier*. *Supplier* keeps one copy,

> acknowledges order on second copy, and sends it back to *purchasing*.
> Copy 3 goes to *accounts payable*.
> Copy 4 goes to *receiving department*.
> Copy 5 goes to *inventory storeroom*, where it is compared to the requisition.
> Copy 6 is retained by *purchasing*.
> 3. *Supplier* sends invoice to company. Invoice is routed to *purchasing*.
> 4. Goods are sent by *supplier*.
> 5. Goods are received by *receiving* department. A receiving report is prepared in 4 copies.
> Copies 1 and 2 go to *inventory storeroom* along with goods.
> Copy 3 goes to *purchasing*.
> Copy 4 is kept by *receiving*.
> 6. *Storeroom* checks quantity of goods against purchase order. Sends approved copy of receiving report to *accounts payable*.
> 7. *Purchasing* compares receiving report to invoice and purchase order, okays invoice for payment, and sends it to *accounts payable*.
> 8. *Accounts payable* compares invoice to purchase order, requisition, and receiving report, determines proper accounts to debit and credit, makes entries, and sends approved invoice to *cash disbursements*.
> 9. *Cash disbursements* reviews invoice for approval and prepares a check when the account is due.

This control system is designed to give assurance that only needed goods are purchased, that goods are received, that the goods are correct in quantity and quality, and that payments are made only for proper invoices.

People and control systems

Several control systems have now been discussed in this text. The systems illustrated would not be applicable to every organization, of course. A system must be adapted to the needs of the particular enterprise involved. Also, no matter how carefully a system is designed, it will not operate effectively unless the people involved know what functions they are supposed to perform and perform those functions carefully. People are central in any control system. Goods do not walk off by themselves; people misappropriate goods and perform embezzlements. Therefore, people must be controlled. But why not trust a person's honesty? Why must an elaborate system be constructed? Unfortunately, not everyone is completely honest. Many employees can be trusted to be completely honest. Another group of employees are basically honest, but might give in to temptation. Some employees look for ways to cut corners. The last two groups require internal control systems by which opportunities for embezzlement and misappropriation are minimized and the work of one employee is checked by that of another. It is unfair to place too many temptations before those who may yield to them. Also, for the company's benefit, the corner-cutters should not be given any opportunities to exercise their peculiar brand of cunning.

There is a danger in constructing an elaborate system to inhibit embezzlements, however. People may find themselves small cogs in a vast machine, doing the same small task day after day in endless repetition, with no opportunity to approach their work creatively. A system that asks people to perform like machines does not reflect favorably upon its designers. Accountants designing a system of internal control must keep this fact in mind. Also, a system that allows and encourages creativity is likely to be an asset to a company. The design of such systems is a challenge to accountants.

Human costs

Notes Payable

Notes payable are a mirror image of notes receivable. It is not necessary to repeat all the discussion in chapter 8 dealing with notes, but a few examples of accounting for notes payable may be helpful. A December 31 year end is assumed in the examples.

EXAMPLE 11-3

On November 21, Baker Co. gives a 60-day, 9% note for $1,200 to a creditor, C Co., on account. Entries on Baker's books:

		Debit	Credit
Nov. 21	Accounts payable (C)	1,200.00	
	Notes payable		1,200.00
Dec. 31	Interest expense	11.84	
	Interest payable		11.84
	Adjustment for accrued interest for 40 days.		
	$1,200 \times 9\% \times 40/365$		
Jan. 20	Notes payable	1,200.00	
	Interest payable	11.84	
	Interest expense	5.91	
	Cash		1,217.75
	Payment of note at maturity.		

Example 11-3 illustrates the adjusting entry necessary for accrued interest at the end of a period when notes are outstanding. The entry for payment in the next accounting period involves payment of the note and of the previously recorded interest liability. In addition, interest expense is recorded for the first few days of January.

EXAMPLE 11-4

On December 16, Baker Co. borrows cash from the bank by giving the bank a 90-day, non-interest-bearing note for $6,000. The bank accepts the note at an 8% discount, giving Baker cash for the proceeds.

		Debit	Credit
Dec. 16	Cash	5,881.64	
	Discount on notes payable	118.36	
	Notes payable		6,000.00
	Note issued at 8% discount. The discount is:		
	$6,000 × .08 × 90/365 = $118.36		
Dec. 31	Interest expense	19.73	
	Discount on notes payable		19.73
	Interest for 15 days:		
	$6,000 × .08 × 15/365 = $19.73		
Mar. 16	Notes payable	6,000.00	
	Cash		6,000.00
Mar. 16	Interest expense	98.63	
	Discount on notes payable		98.63
	Record 75 days of interest expense:		
	$6,000 × .08 × 75/365 = $98.63		

The bank takes the note at a discount and gives credit to Baker for less than the face of the note. The discount is debited to a discount on notes payable account in Example 11-4. The amount borrowed is actually a smaller amount than the face of the note, and interest accumulates on the amount borrowed as the note approaches maturity. This implies that the proper treatment of the discount is to show it as a deduction from the notes payable account on the balance sheet.

Another feature of the discounted note is important. The stated interest rate in Example 11-4 is 8%. The actual interest rate is somewhat higher, because the amount borrowed is $5,881.64, not $6,000. The actual interest rate is 8.16% computed as follows:

$$PRT = i$$
$$5881.64 \times R \times 90/365 = 118.36$$
$$1450.27 \times R = 118.36$$
$$R = .0816$$

Thus 8.16% is the actual rate of interest, even though the stated rate is 8%.

LONG-TERM LIABILITIES

The long-term needs of enterprises are financed in a number of ways. Ownership equity is often the primary source of financing. Financing by means of long-term debt also is widely used. Some enterprises find that debt financing is particularly appropriate. In public utilities, for example, debt financing is used to enhance the rate of return to owners. For example, suppose that funds received from sale of bonds issued at 5% are used to earn a 7% return. The difference (7% − 5%) increases the owners' rate of return.[1] Extensive debt financing is made feasible in the utility field by the relatively stable conditions in that sector of the economy. Enterprises operating in unstable industries find long-term debt a heavy burden and often find lenders reluctant to risk funds in an unstable situation. The feasibility of financing by means of long-term debt thus depends on such factors as stability of the industry, stability of the company within the industry, size of the company, and market conditions at the time of financing. Decisions to borrow on long-term debt, which have an important influence on a company's future operations, are usually made by the highest level of executive personnel and the board of directors.

Long-term debt takes many forms, including pension obligations, long-term liabilities under warranties, and long-term lease obligations, mortgage obligations, and bonded indebtedness. Each of these is discussed in this chapter.

Long-term Notes

Long-term notes are generally handled like short-term notes. A problem can arise if a long-term note is issued with either no interest or an interest rate that is less than the market rate. The note should be discounted at the current market rate of interest so that the liability is shown at its net present value. A few examples will illustrate.

EXAMPLE 11-5

Present value

On January 1, Year 1, the Bacon Company buys a parcel of land by issuing a 2-year, non-interest-bearing note for $20,000. The current market rate of interest is 10%. The company's year ends on December 31.

The present value of the note is $20,000 × .8264 (Appendix C, Table II) = $16,528

			Debit	Credit
Entries:				
Jan. 1, Year 1	Land		16,528	
	Notes payable			16,528
Dec. 31, Year 1	Interest expense		1,653	
	Notes payable			1,653
	10% interest for the year on $16,528.			
Dec. 31, Year 2	Interest expense		1,819	
	Notes payable			1,819
	($16,528 + 1,653) × .10			
Jan. 1, Year 3	Notes payable		20,000	
	Cash			20,000
	Note has grown to $20,000:			
	$16,528 + 1,653 + 1,819 = $20,000			

---

1. This technique is covered more fully in chapter 18, in the discussion of *Leverage*.

In Example 11-5 the note was recorded at its present value, not the face amount. The 10% interest rate is applied to the present value of the note. Interest increases each period because the note payable increases in size as it approaches maturity. Some accountants prefer to record the original transaction as follows:

		Debit	Credit
Jan. 1, Year 1	Land	16,528	
	Discount on notes	3,472	
	Notes payable		20,000

Recording the transaction in this fashion does not change the interest amounts. The credit is to the discount on notes account rather than to notes payable. The authors prefer recording the note at the net amount because it gives the balance sheet amount directly and also minimizes opportunities for error. For example, if the note were recorded at the face amount of $20,000, it would be easy to apply the 10% rate to the $20,000 rather than to the $20,000 less discount.

EXAMPLE 11-6

On June 30, Year 1, the Ham Company issues a 2-year, $40,000 note for purchase of machinery. The note bears 2% interest. Interest is payable each half year. The market interest rate is 8% (4% each half year).

The present value of the note is

Face amount: $40,000 × .8548 (Appendix C, Table II) = $34,192
Interest each ½ year: $400 × 3.630 (Appendix C, Table III) = 1,452
Total present value = $35,644

Entries:

		Debit	Credit
June 30, Year 1	Machinery	35,644	
	Notes payable		35,644
Dec. 31, Year 1	Interest expense	1,426	
	Cash		400
	Notes payable		1,026
	Interest is 4% × $35,644		
June 30, Year 2	Interest expense	1,467	
	Cash		400
	Notes payable		1,067
	Interest is 4% × ($35,644 + 1,026)		
Dec. 31, Year 2	Interest expense	1,509	
	Cash		400
	Notes payable		1,109
	Interest is 4% × ($35,644 + 1,026 + 1,067)		
June 30, Year 3	Interest expense	1,554	
	Notes payable	38,846	
	Cash		40,400
	Interest is 4% × ($35,644 + 1,026 + 1,067 + 1,109)		

The note is discounted by using a 4% rate for four periods, since the interest is paid semiannually. Again, note that the asset acquired is recorded at the net present value of the obligation incurred. The $40,000 face amount of the note is not the proper amount to use in recording the asset because it overstates the cost to the acquiring company.

The procedures illustrated in Example 11-6 would not be used in situations where the stated rate of interest is fairly close to the market rate. For example, if a long-term note bears 8% interest and the market rate is $8\frac{1}{2}$%, the note could simply be recorded at its face amount.

Mortgage Liabilities

Purchases of land and buildings are often financed by mortgages. *A mortgage is a conditional conveyance of property to a creditor as security for a loan.* *Defined* If the loan is not paid, the holder of the mortgage forecloses and takes over the property in question. The intention is for the loan to be repaid in accordance with its terms. A mortgage loan is essentially a long-term note payable and is treated as such in the accounts. Payments on a mortgage are made at regular intervals. Each payment includes both interest and principal. Example 11-7 illustrates.

EXAMPLE 11-7

On March 1, B Co. buys a building for $80,000, assuming an 8%, $50,000 mortgage, and paying the balance in cash. The monthly payments on the mortgage are $600.

		Debit	Credit
Entries:			
March 1	Buildings	80,000.00	
	Cash		30,000.00
	Mortgage payable		50,000.00
	Purchase of building, subject to 8% mortgage loan.		
March 31	Interest expense	333.33	
	Mortgage payable	266.67	
	Cash		600.00
	First payment on mortgage loan. Interest for one month is 8% × $50,000 × $\frac{1}{12}$.		

		Debit	Credit
April 30	Interest expense	331.56	
	Mortgage payable	268.44	
	Cash		600.00
	Second payment on mortgage loan. Interest for one month is 8% × $49,733.33 × $\frac{1}{12}$.		

Subsequent loan payments will involve progressively lower interest amounts and larger amounts applied on principal, until the loan is fully paid. If any of the periodic payments are unpaid at the end of a fiscal period, an entry must be made to record accrued interest payable on the mortgage loan.

The mortgage payable is shown in the balance sheet as a long-term liability. Amounts of the mortgage that will be paid in the next year should be separated and shown among the current liabilities, since they represent current demands on a company's funds.

Pension Obligations

Many companies have pension plans for their employees. These plans impose an obligation on the company to pay pensions to employees after the employees have met certain requirements, such as having worked for the company for a stipulated number of years and having reached a specified age. In effect, a pension plan means that there is some pension expense for every dollar of wages. Each period, companies should record the pension expense and the corresponding pension obligation. The entry might be as follows:

		Debit	Credit
Dec. 31	Pension expense	xxx	
	Accumulated pension obligation		xxx
	To record pension expense for the year.		

The pension obligation is shown on the balance sheet as a long-term liability. As in the case of mortgage obligations, the estimated amount that is to be paid in the next year should be shown among the current liabilities. If the pension plan is financed through an insurance company, or by company contributions to a separate pension fund, it is possible that no pension liability will appear on the books, since the insurance company or fund trustee assumes the obligation to pay pensions in return for certain payments by the company.

Accounting for pensions is complicated because pension plans themselves are complicated. Detailed rules for accounting for pension plans are indicated in Accounting Principles Board Opinion No. 8 (November 1966).

Rental and Lease Obligations

If rents are owed at the end of an accounting period, the liability for these rents must be recorded and shown on the balance sheet as a current liability. In an ordinary lease situation, a company usually is obligated for several months in the future. For example, with a one-year lease dated September 1, a company still has to pay eight months' rent at the end of its fiscal year on December 31. Although it is true that there is an obligation to pay rent, the obligation usually is not recorded, since the lessor of the property also is under an obligation to provide the facilities for the next eight months. When this sort of mutual future obligation exists, a liability usually is not recorded.

At times, enterprises use leases as a way of purchasing property. For instance, a company may build a factory, sell it to a financial institution such as a bank or insurance company, and immediately lease it back on a long-term lease. The financial institution legally owns the factory but is acting only in a financial capacity. In effect, it is lending money over a long term to the company. When a lease situation is, in effect, an installment purchase of property, the asset and the corresponding lease liability should be recorded in the books and shown on the financial statements. Since the lease liability extends over a long period of time, it will be shown as a long-term liability at the present value of the amount to be paid. The amount due for the next year, however, should be separated and shown among the current liabilities.

Long-term Leases as means of purchasing

The periodic payments on the lease in this type of situation are considered payments on a long-term note. Each payment is recorded in two parts: first, interest expense is recorded for the period covered by the payment, then the balance of the payment is recorded as a reduction of the principal of the note. Example 11-8 will help to illustrate.

EXAMPLE 11-8

On January 1, Year 1, the Herd Co. enters into a 30-year lease on a building built to the company's own specifications. The yearly payments on the lease are $50,000. The building has a value of $562,900, and the interest rate used in the financing is 8%. The first payment on the lease is made on December 31, Year 1. Entries for the first two years follow:

		Debit	Credit
Jan. 1, Year 1	Building	562,900	
	Long-term lease payable		562,900
	To record leased building.		
Dec. 31, Year 1	Interest expense	45,032	
	Long-term lease payable	4,968	
	Cash		50,000
	Interest is 8% of $562,900.		
Dec. 31, Year 2	Interest expense	44,635	
	Long-term lease payable	5,365	
	Cash		50,000
	Interest is 8% × ($562,900 − 4,968).		

The Herd Co. would also record depreciation expense on the building each year just as if it owned the building instead of leasing it. In subsequent periods the interest expense decreases as the principal of the lease liability goes down. The interest expense in Year 2, for example, is lower than in Year 1. At the end of 30 years the lease obligation should be reduced to a zero balance. The lease obligation, incidentally, can be computed by multiplying the periodic payment ($50,000) by the present value of an annuity of $1 for 30 periods at 8% (11.258).

Form and substance

The above treatment of leased assets is recommended by the Financial Accounting Standards Board. The Board believes that the form of lease transactions is not as important as their economic substance, and that many leases are in substance a means of long-term financing. Leases must be disclosed carefully in financial statements. Those leases that are means of long-term financing, called *capital* leases, have their present values included among the liabilities on the balance sheet. Those leases that are not clearly a means of long-term financing, called *operating* leases, are disclosed in notes to the financial statements. These notes indicate the present value of operating leases and also the dollar amounts that the company must pay on leases in succeeding years. More comprehensive discussions of leases can be found in intermediate accounting texts.

Capital and operating leases

Bond Obligations

Bonds are used by business and government as a means of borrowing substantial sums of money for an extended period of time. When a company decides to issue bonds, the board of directors authorizes the issuance of a certain number of bonds with a given denomination (usually $1,000) and a specified rate of interest. Those bonds are sold on the market to investors, each of whom purchases whatever quantity of bonds is desired. This procedure is in contrast to the usual mortgage loan, where only one investor is involved. When a corporation or a governmental body wishes to borrow large sums, it is usually easier to obtain the money if bonds can be sold to many parties.

Types of Bonds. If all the bonds in an issue mature on the same date, they are called *term bonds*. Bonds that mature in installments are called *serial bonds*.

Bonds may be secured or unsecured. Bonds that are secured by a mortgage on certain property are *mortgage bonds*. Unsecured bonds are known as debentures. *Debenture bonds* are secured only by the general credit of the enterprise. Bonds that are secured by other securities (stocks and bonds of other companies) are *collateral trust bonds*. If another company guarantees payment in case of default by the issuing company, the bonds are *guaranteed bonds*.

Bonds that can be converted into capital stock of the issuing corporation are *convertible bonds*. *Callable bonds* can be called in and paid at the option of the issuing corporation. *Registered bonds* require the recording of the owner's name on the books of the company. If registered bonds are sold by their first owner to another party, the company must be notified and the bonds registered in the name of the new owner. By contrast, the title to *bearer bonds*, or *coupon bonds*, passes on delivery, and any holder of such bonds collects interest by clipping the interest coupons and sending them to the company or by leaving the coupons with a bank for deposit or collection.

The variety of bonds should not obscure the fact that the value of a bond depends more on the quality of the security or company behind it and the rate of interest that is offered than on the provisions of the bond. With debenture bonds, and indeed in the case of most bonds, the value of the long-term obligation to an investor depends on the long-run prospects of the company involved. If Zilch Co. is in severe financial straits it might have difficulty selling bonds, even if the bonds bear a high rate of interest and have many attractive provisions.

Issuance of Bonds. When bonds are offered for sale, the market classifies them according to quality and values them on the basis of this quality and the rate of interest they bear. The forces of supply and demand work effectively in the bond market. If C Company offers bonds with an interest rate of 6% when the bond market demands 8% for securities of comparable quality, the price will inevitably drop below the face amount of the bonds. If 10% is offered when the usual market rate is 9%, the price of the bonds will be bid up by the market. Only when the rate offered equals the market rate will the bonds sell at their face, or par, amount. The *par amount* is the amount printed on the bonds themselves.

Value of a bond

If bonds are sold at par, the entry is as follows:

		Debit	Credit
Jan. 1	Cash	1,000,000	
	Bonds payable		1,000,000
	Sold 9%, 20-year bonds at par.		

Example 11-9 shows what the entries would be if there was a premium on the bonds.

EXAMPLE 11-9

The Banzer Company sells bonds at a premium.

		Debit	Credit
Jan. 1	Cash	1,040,000	
	Bonds payable		1,000,000
	Premium on bonds		40,000
	Sold 10%, 20-year bonds at 104. Interest dates are June 30 and December 31.		

The "104" means 104% of the par, or face, value of the bonds. Bonds are always quoted as a percentage of par. The premium on bonds account is added to the bonds payable in the long-term liability section of the balance sheet, as follows:

BANZER COMPANY
Partial Balance Sheet
January 1

Long-term liability:
    10% bonds payable, 20 year term $1,000,000
    Premium on bonds   40,000
    Total $1,040,000

The premium on bonds account is part of the total long-term liability; it is connected with the interest over the life of the bonds. It is not a gain in the period the bonds are issued.

If the bonds were sold at a discount, the entries in Example 11-10 would be used.

EXAMPLE 11-10

The Collic Company sells bonds at a discount.

		Debit	Credit
Jan. 1	Cash	970,000	
	Discount on bonds	30,000	
	Bonds payable		1,000,000
	Sold 8%, 20-year bonds at 97. Interest dates are June 30 and December 31.		

The discount on bonds account is subtracted from the bonds payable in the balance sheet. It is part of the long-term liability, although it is sometimes shown among the assets as a deferred charge. It should be noted that bonds payable are handled somewhat differently than long-term investments in bonds (see chapter 8). Investments in bonds are recorded at cost, and any premium or discount is not separated. For bonds payable, on the other hand, the bond liability is recorded at the face amount of the bonds, and discount or premium is put into a separate account. The difference is one of form, however, not of substance.

Straight-line Amortization of Premium or Discount. Both premium on bonds and discount on bonds are related to the interest rate offered on the bonds. *Premium* appears when the interest rate on the bonds exceeds the rate demanded by the market for securities of similar quality. If the interest rate on the bonds is lower than the market demands, a discount will appear. When the bonds reach maturity, the bondholders will receive the *par*, or face, amount of the bonds—no more and no less. Therefore, any premium or discount is written off by the company over the term of the bonds. The write-off is related to the interest expense recorded by the company. Using straight-line amortization, the write-off of premium or discount is made in equal portions over the term of the bonds. To illustrate, consider the entries that would be made by the Banzer Company for the $1,000,000 of 10% bonds sold on January 1 for $1,040,000 (see Example 11-9).

		Debit	Credit
June 30	Interest expense	50,000	
	Cash		50,000
	Paid semiannual bond interest.		
	10% × $1,000,000 × 1/2 year		
Dec. 31	Interest expense	50,000	
	Cash		50,000
	Paid semiannual bond interest.		
Dec. 31	Premium on bonds	2,000	
	Interest expense		2,000
	Amortize premium for the year:		
	1/20 × $40,000		

The last entry reduces the interest expense of the company—part of the excess paid by the bondholders is applied to each year's interest. It also reduces the balance in the premium on bonds account. This balance is reduced by $2,000 each year (in this case) until at maturity the premium account has a zero balance. The total liability at maturity will then be $1,000,000, the amount the company is obligated to pay.

Annual interest on the bonds is $100,000 less $2,000, or $98,000. *Annual Interest* This amount can be proven as follows:

Total payments:	
Interest: 20 years at $100,000 per year	$2,000,000
Face amount of bonds at maturity	1,000,000
Total payment	$3,000,000
Less amount received when bonds were issued	
($1,000,000 × 104%)	1,040,000
Net cost of bonds for 20 years	$1,960,000

Annual cost: $\frac{\$1,960,000}{20 \text{ years}} = \$98,000$

It can be seen from this example that a premium on bonds reduces the net interest expense to a company. In similar fashion, a discount on bonds increases the interest expense. The year-end entry for amortization of the Collic Company bond discount (see Example 11-10) would be as follows:

355

		Debit	Credit
Dec. 31	Interest expense	1,500	
	Discount on bonds		1,500
	1/20 of $30,000 discount		

This entry increases the interest expense for the period and also reduces the balance in the discount on bonds account.

Issuance after Authorization

Discount or premium should be amortized over the time bonds are outstanding. Sometimes bonds are issued after the date of authorization. In this situation the buyer pays for interest accrued to date as well as for the bonds. Suppose $10,000 of 5-year, 9% bonds dated January 1 are issued on March 1. The buyer would pay the issue price and also pay for interest accrued from January 1 to March ($150). If the issue price is $10,290 plus accrued interest, the entry for issuance is as follows:

		Debit	Credit
March 1	Cash	10,440	
	Bonds payable		10,000
	Premium on bonds		290
	Interest payable		150

The interest will be paid the next interest date—let us say December 31. At the end of the period the premium would also have to be amortized. The entries would be as follows:

		Debit	Credit
Dec. 31	Interest payable	150	
	Interest expense	750	
	Cash		900
	Payment of bond interest.		
Dec. 31	Premium on bonds	50	
	Interest expense:		50
	$290 \div 58$ months $= \$5$		
	$\$5 \times 10$ months $= \$50$		

Note that the interest expense is only for 10 months. Also, the $290 premium is amortized over the time the bonds are outstanding, which is 4 years and 10 months, not 5 years.

Adjusting entries may be necessary if interest has accrued at the end of the company's fiscal year. In any case, only one entry need be made each fiscal period for amortization of premium or discount.

Effective-interest Amortization of Premium or Discount. The effective-interest method of amortization, a more accurate approach to amortization of premium or discount than straight-line, utilizes the concept of present value and bases interest computations on the market rate of interest. This approach to amortization is basically similar to that discussed in chapter 8. Suppose the Baker Company issues $1,000,000 of 30 year, 9% bonds (annual interest) when the market rate of interest is 10%. The issue price of the bonds would be $905,730, computed as follows:

Present value of cash amounts:
Principal: $1,000,000 × .0573 (Appendix C, Table II) $ 57,300
Interest: $90,000 × 9.427 (Table III)   848,430
Total present value $905,730

Entries for these bonds are given in example 11-11.

EXAMPLE 11-11

Baker Company issues 9%, 30-year bonds on July 1, Year 1, for $905,730. Interest is payable each June 30. Baker's year ends on December 31.

		Debit	Credit
July 1, Year 1	Cash	905,730	
	Discount on bonds	94,270	
	Bonds payable		1,000,000
Dec. 31, Year 1	Interest expense	45,287	
	Interest payable		45,000
	Discount on bonds		287
	10% interest for 1/2 year on ($1,000,000 − 94,270). Interest payable is 1/2 of 9% of $1,000,000. Difference is credited to discount.		
June 30, Year 2	Interest expense	45,287	
	Interest payable	45,000	
	Cash		90,000
	Discount on bonds		287
	Payment of interest for one year and recording of interest expense for 1/2 year.		
Dec. 31, Year 2	Interest expense	45,315	
	Interest payable		45,000
	Discount on bonds		315
	Expense is 10% × ($1,000,000 − 93,696). $93,696 is balance in discount account.		

From Example 11-11 it can be seen that the interest will increase each year and the amortization of bond discount will grow each year. Contrast the straight-line amortization, which would be $3,142.00 each year ($94,270 ÷ 30). This is in contrast to amortization of $574 the first year in the example ($287 + 287).

After amortization of premium or discount each year, the bonds payable on the balance sheet are carried at an amount that equals the present value of remaining future payments, using the market rate when the bonds were originally issued as a discount factor. Changes in market rates of interest after issuance of bonds are usually ignored by the issuing company. Of course, changing rates do affect the price at which these bonds will be quoted on the market. Computations were illustrated in chapter 8.

Retirement of Bonds. When bonds are retired at maturity, the procedure is very simple. Cash is paid to bondholders equal to the face amount of the bonds, and the liability is eliminated. Any premium or discount on the bonds will have been completely amortized by the maturity date.

Bonds can, of course, be retired before the maturity date. In this case, a gain or loss might occur because of changes in interest rates or particular bond provisions.

EXAMPLE 11-12

On May 1, Year 1, Harris Company purchases $100,000 of its 9%, 30-year bonds in the market for $102,300 and retires them. Accrued interest of $2,250 is also paid on this date. Unamortized premium on May 1 amounts to $1,100.

		Debit	Credit
May 1	Bonds payable	100,000	
	Premium on bonds	1,100	
	Interest expense	2,250	
	Loss on retirement	1,200	
	Cash		104,550

Cash paid is $102,300 + 2,250.
Loss is $102,300 − 101,100.

The amount of gain or loss depends on the premium or discount remaining on the books and the amount paid to retire the bonds.

OTHER LIABILITIES

In addition to the liabilities discussed previously, a number of other liabilities appear on balance sheets. A few of these liabilities are discussed in this section.

The discussion of other liabilities that follows is not meant to be all-inclusive. Instead, it is intended to give a general idea of some types of items that might appear on a balance sheet. The assets and liabilities that actually appear on a company's balance sheet depend on the company's particular business and industry situation. Sometimes balance sheets are difficult to understand unless one has a fairly good knowledge of the industry involved. In most cases, however, anyone with some basic accounting knowledge can interpret the meaning of asset and liability items, especially if they can be related to corresponding items on the income statement. For example, an item among the liabilities called *reserve for guarantees* can be understood to be an estimated liability after an estimated guarantee expense is located on the income statement.

Finally, it is important to note that the interrelationships of assets and liabilities with the revenues and expenses on the income statement means that a misstatement of assets or liabilities often involves a misstatement of revenues and expenses. Thus, if the balance sheet is incorrect, the income statement will often be in error also.

Accrued Salaries and Wages

This item represents amounts earned by employees at the end of the period, but not yet paid to them. Presumably, this liability will be paid early in the next period, on the next payday.

Withholding Taxes and Social Security Taxes Payable

An enterprise is required by law to withhold income taxes from its employees' paychecks. These taxes are remitted periodically (usually by the fifteenth of each month) to the federal and state (if applicable) governments involved.

The government also requires a company to withhold social security taxes from its employees' paychecks. The company has to match the social security tax withheld with contributions of its own. The FICA (Federal Insurance Contributions Act) tax withheld from employees' paychecks thus is matched dollar for dollar by employers. In addition, the employers must pay unemployment compensation taxes to both state and federal governments. These taxes are remitted in accordance with legal requirements, usually quarterly for state unemployment taxes and yearly (by January 31) for the federal unemployment tax. The FICA taxes are usually paid each month with the federal withholding taxes. State withholding tax payments vary, but they often are made quarterly. Any unpaid taxes are shown as a liability on the balance sheet at the end of a period. Example 11-3 illustrates.

The first entry in Example 11-13 records the wages and withholdings from the wages. The second entry records the employer's tax expense on these wages. Note that the FICA tax withheld from employees' paychecks is matched by an equal amount from the employer. The employer is the only one who pays unemployment compensation taxes.

EXAMPLE 11-13

Assume that the Apex Co. pays salaries of $1,000 per week. These salaries are subject to a 6% FICA tax,[2] a 2.7% state unemployment compensation tax, and a .5% federal unemployment tax. Each week, $210 is withheld for federal income taxes. There is no state income tax. The regular weekly entries would be as follows:

	Debit	Credit
Wages expense	1,000	
FICA tax payable		60
Withholding taxes payable		210
Cash		730
To record wage payments for the week.		
Social security taxes expense	92	
FICA tax payable		60
Federal unemployment tax payable		5
State unemployment tax payable		27
To record employer's tax expense on above wages.		

When taxes are remitted, the entry is similar to any other payment of a liability. Suppose, for example, that on November 15 the Apex Co. remits its FICA and income tax withheld for October to the *federal* government. The entry is

		Debit	Credit
Nov. 15	FICA tax payable	480	
	Withholding taxes payable	840	
	Cash		1,320
	Payment of FICA and income tax withheld for October.		

The amounts in the above entry are based on four weeks' withholdings on salaries. In an actual situation, of course, the amounts will vary from week to week because of overtime, days off, hiring of new employees, and other situations.

Because payment requirements and percentage rates of taxes and withholdings tend to vary considerably, there has been no attempt to cover these aspects in detail. In actual business situations, various forms and tables are used to determine the correct taxes and withholdings. With a little practice, the mechanics of payroll calculations become relatively easy. The difficulty in connection with payroll occurs primarily because of the immense volume of work involved when the work force is even moderately large. Many calculations must be made, and there is an immense amount of record keeping. These features make payroll an obvious function to handle with data processing equipment. The steps in the payroll

---

2. The actual rate in 1977 was 5.85%. We have used a 6% rate to simplify the illustration.

process can be programmed into a computer, and the machine can be used to perform the necessary detailed work. Payroll is an area in which computers can eliminate a great deal of human drudgery.

Dividends Payable

A corporation is not required by law to declare dividends out of its profits. Once the dividends are declared by the board of directors, however, the corporation is legally obligated to pay them; that is, the declared dividends become a liability of the company. There may be a lag between the time the dividends are declared by the board of directors and the time they are paid. This time interval is necessary so that the corporation can bring its stockholder records up to date, and so that the dividend checks can be prepared. During this interval, the dividends payable account is carried as a current liability, and it appears as such on any financial statements prepared during the interval. Dividends are discussed more fully in chapter 12.

Estimated Liability for Income Taxes

This liability represents the unpaid portion of corporate income taxes for the current year. Since most large companies have to pay quarterly amounts on their estimated federal income tax, the liability at the end of the year is smaller than the total income tax expense for the year. For smaller corporations, the tax expense on the income statement usually is equal to the tax liability on the balance sheet.

Partnerships and single proprietorships are not taxed as such; instead, each partner or the owner is taxed individually. Each owner's share of the business profit or loss must be reported on his or her personal income tax return. Therefore, an income tax liability appears only on corporate balance sheets. The liability is usually labeled *estimated* because it may be subsequently revised by the Internal Revenue Service.

Deferred Taxes—Allocation of Income Tax Expense

In computing income taxes, differences may arise between financial accounting and tax accounting in the timing of the recognition of revenues and expenses. For example, revenue may be recognized at the point of sale for financial accounting purposes and at the time of cash collection for income tax; depreciation expense computed by the straight-line method may be used on the income statement whereas double-declining-balance depreciation is used on the tax return. Whenever timing differ-

TABLE 11-1. Effects of Tax Allocation

	Without Tax Allocation	With Tax Allocation
Income before tax	$ 50,000	$50,000
Income tax	60,000	20,000
Net income (loss)	$(10,000)	$30,000

ences exist between the books and the tax return there is a potential mismatching of costs and revenues. Income tax paid for a period will be based on a taxable income amount that differs from the income before taxes shown on the financial statements. If the income tax paid is deducted as the expense for the period, a mismatching occurs.

Interperiod income tax allocation

Accountants have agreed (APB Opinion No. 11) that the income tax expense reported in the income statement should be related to the income before tax shown in the statement, not to the income reported in the tax return. The procedure for recognizing the tax expense in the same period as the related book income is known as *interperiod income tax allocation*.

To take a simple illustration, suppose that a $100,000 expense is recorded on the Year 1 income statement but that it cannot be deducted on the tax return until Year 2. Suppose that income before the item is $150,000 in Year 1 and that the tax rate is 40%. Without tax allocation the income tax reported in Year 1 will be based on the $150,000 taxable income. With tax allocation the tax will be based on the $50,000 income reported on the income statement. The results, shown in Table 11-1, are quite different. The result without tax allocation is a distortion of the actual results, since the tax next year will be reduced by the item that could not be deducted in Year 1.

Example 11-14, using depreciation, is more complicated.

EXAMPLE 11-14

Equipment with a 4-year life is acquired at the beginning of Year 1 at a cost of $100,000, with no salvage value. Sum-of-digits depreciation is used for taxes and straight-line for books. Depreciation is shown in Table 11-2.

TABLE 11-2

Year	Tax Return	Depreciation	Books
1	4/10	$ 40,000	$ 25,000
2	3/10	30,000	25,000
3	2/10	20,000	25,000
4	1/10	10,000	25,000
Total depreciation		$100,000	$100,000

We also assume that, for each year, income before depreciation and taxes is $60,000 and the tax rate is 40%. The tax to be paid can be calculated as shown in Table 11-3.

If the company were to deduct the income tax computed for tax purposes on its financial statements, the results would be those shown in Table 11-4. The result in Table 11-4 is a palpable mismatching, with taxes very low the first year (23%) and very high the last year (57%).

Table 11-5 shows the results when the tax is related to the accounting income, using tax allocation.

It should be noted that the total tax is the same in either set of statements, $56,000, even though the tax in each year is different. The

TABLE 11-3. Tax Calculation

	\multicolumn{4}{c}{Year}			
	1	2	3	4
Income before depreciation and taxes	$60,000	$60,000	$60,000	$60,000
Depreciation (sum-of-digits)	40,000	30,000	20,000	10,000
Taxable income	20,000	30,000	40,000	50,000
Income tax (40%)	$ 8,000	$12,000	$16,000	$20,000

TABLE 11-4. Income without Tax Allocation—Using Actual Tax Paid

	Year			
	1	2	3	4
Income before depreciation and taxes	$60,000	$60,000	$60,000	$60,000
Depreciation	25,000	25,000	25,000	25,000
Income before taxes	35,000	35,000	35,000	35,000
Income tax expense	8,000	12,000	16,000	20,000
Net income	$27,000	$23,000	$19,000	$15,000

TABLE 11-5. Income with Tax Allocation—Using Taxes Related to Accounting Income

	Year			
	1	2	3	4
Income before depreciation and taxes	$60,000	$60,000	$60,000	$60,000
Depreciation	25,000	25,000	25,000	25,000
Income before taxes	35,000	35,000	35,000	35,000
Income tax expense (40%)	14,000	14,000	14,000	14,000
Net income	$21,000	$21,000	$21,000	$21,000

only difference is in the way the tax is allocated between years. Most accountants prefer the procedure in Table 11-5, because they believe that tax allocation procedures yield a better matching and a more understandable income statement.

The idea of income tax allocation is well accepted in accounting today. But how should the difference between the income tax expense shown on the income statement (based on the accounting income) and the income tax payable (the amount owed to the government for income taxes based on taxable income) shown on the balance sheet be handled?

Deferred income taxes payable

If income is recognized for accounting purposes before it is recognized for income tax purposes, the difference is treated as a type of liability—*deferred income taxes payable*. This liability measures the income tax that will be paid in the future on income that has already been recognized on the income statement. If, on the other hand, the income is taxed in an earlier period than it is recognized on the income statement, the difference is viewed as a prepayment of income taxes—income taxes that have been paid on income that is not yet recognized as earned.

To illustrate, assume the data from Table 11-5, and assume that each year's taxes are paid in full on March 15 of the following year. The entries to record the tax expense at the end of each year and the payment of the liability the following year are as follows:

		Debit	Credit
Dec. 31, Year 1	Income tax expense	14,000	
	Income taxes payable		8,000
	Deferred income tax		6,000
Mar. 15, Year 2	Income taxes payable	8,000	
	Cash		8,000
Dec. 31, Year 2	Income tax expense	14,000	
	Income taxes payable		12,000
	Deferred income tax		2,000
Mar. 15, Year 3	Income taxes payable	12,000	
	Cash		12,000
Dec. 31, Year 3	Income tax expense	14,000	
	Deferred income tax	2,000	
	Income taxes payable		16,000
Mar. 15, Year 4	Income taxes payable	16,000	
	Cash		16,000
Dec. 31, Year 4	Income tax expense	14,000	
	Deferred income tax	6,000	
	Income taxes payable		20,000
Mar. 15, Year 5	Income taxes payable	20,000	
	Cash		20,000

As a result of the above entries, the deferred income tax account appears as follows:

Deferred Income Taxes

Year	Dr.	Cr.	Balance
1		6,000	6,000
2		2,000	8,000
3	2,000		6,000
4	6,000		–0–

In this example, the difference between taxable income and accounting income was fully offset in a period of 4 years. In an actual situation, differences between accounting and taxable income may extend over lengthy periods of time, and significant amounts of deferred tax liabilities may accumulate. The deferred income taxes account is shown as a liability on the balance sheet. It should be divided into net current and net noncurrent amounts. If the deferred taxes relate to plant and equipment assets, as in Example 11-14, the amount will be a noncurrent (long-term) liability.

Estimated Liability under Warranties or Guarantees

Many companies guarantee their products and will repair or replace them if they are not satisfactory. The guarantee or warranty expense connected with these products should be recorded in the period of sale so that there will be a proper matching of costs against revenues. Since most guarantees cover a short period of time, they will appear among the current liabilities. In the case of warranties that cover a longer period of time, such as two-year or 20,000-mile warranties on new cars, a substantial portion of the liability may appear under the category long-term liabilities.

The fact that this type of liability must be estimated does not affect its status as a liability. This liability is as much an obligation of the company as are the accounts payable. Any inaccuracy in the estimation of the liability can be adjusted as more knowledge and experience in connection with claims under guarantees and warranties becomes available.

SUMMARY

Liabilities can be divided into short-term and long-term liabilities. Short-term liabilities are those that will be satisfied, usually by payment, in the near future. Accounts payable are almost a mirror image of accounts receivable. Because payment of accounts payable can be controlled and because it is good business policy to take all discounts offered, a system of recording accounts payable net of discounts is appropriate. Purchase controls were briefly reviewed in this chapter.

Notes payable are handled like notes receivable. The discounting of notes with a bank or other party was discussed. The rate of interest is slightly higher than the rate of discount used when notes are discounted.

Long-term liabilities include mortgages, notes, pension obligations, leases, and bonds. The accounting problems connected with some of these items are quite complicated, so the discussion in this chapter was not comprehensive. The use of a market rate of interest to discount a long-term note with no interest rate stated or with an artificially low rate was illustrated. Long-term liabilities should always be carried at the present value of the future cash payments, and the discounting process illustrates the application of this principle. Pension obligations are becoming more and more important in our society. If the companies pay pension amounts to a fund currently, no liability need appear on their books. Lease obligations may be recorded at the present value of the cash amounts to be paid if the lease is a capital lease — that is, if it is in effect a purchase of the item being leased. Bond obligations were discussed at some length, and amortization of premium or discount by both the straight-line method and the effective-interest amortization method was illustrated. The chapter concluded with a brief discussion of other liabilities, including tax allocation procedures and deferred income taxes.

IMPORTANT TERMS

Accounts payable	*Guaranteed bonds*
Purchase discounts	*Convertible bonds*
Purchase discounts lost	*Callable bonds*
Financing	*Registered bonds*
Present value	*Bearer bonds*
Mortgage	*Coupon bonds*
Pension	*Bond premium*
Lease	*Bond discount*
Capital lease	*Effective-interest amortization*
Operating lease	*Withholding tax*
Bonds	*FICA*
Term bonds	*Social security tax*
Serial bonds	*Unemployment tax*
Mortgage bonds	*Income tax allocation*
Debentures	*Deferred income taxes*
Collateral trust bonds	*Warranty or guarantees*

QUESTIONS

11-1. What are the advantages and disadvantages of recording accounts payable net of discounts?

11-2. What is the function of receiving reports in a purchase control system?

11-3. What constitutes an optimal control system (use purchase controls as an example)?

11-4. Why is the true interest higher on a note discounted at 8% than on an 8% interest-bearing note?

11-5. A company acquires a tract of land by giving a 5-year non-interest-bearing note for $100,000. The company proposes that it record the land at $100,000. Do you agree? Discuss.

11-6. What are the effects on the balance sheet of recording long-term leases as long-term liabilities?

11-7. How would you react if you were the president of a company that had large amounts of long-term leases and it was suggested that the leased assets be recorded as plant and equipment and the lease obligations be recorded as a liability?

11-8. An employee is hired at a salary of $250 per week. List the additional expenses that the company is likely to incur over and above the $250 per week.

11-9. Distinguish between
    a. Term bonds and serial bonds
    b. Mortgage bonds and debentures
    c. Registered bonds and bearer bonds

11-10. Why might convertible bonds bear a lower interest rate than nonconvertible bonds?

EXERCISES

11-11. *Purchases.* Give entries in general journal form for the following transactions. The company records purchases at the gross price.
    Jan. 3   Purchase merchandise from Acme Company, terms 2/10, n/30, amount $1,800.
    Jan. 4   Purchase goods from Bleeker Company on account. Terms 2/10, n/30, amount $3,000.
    Jan. 10   Pay Bleeker Company in full.
    Jan. 20   Pay the Acme Company for the purchase of January 3.

11-12. *Purchases.* Refer to exercise 11-11 and give entries to record the purchases at the net amount.

11-13. *Purchases.* Give the entries for the following purchases:
    a. You buy 30 cases of soap on account. The price is $20 per case. Terms are 2/10, n/30. (Record purchases at net amount.)

Part III   Measurement of Assets, Liabilities, and Income

    b. You buy 100 cases of canned fruit, giving a promissory note for $1,030, due in 6 months. If you had paid cash, the price would have been $1,000.

11-14. *Notes payable.* Give entries for the following:
- Nov. 16   We issue a 60-day, 8% note for $4,000 on account to Bascom Company.
- Dec. 1   We discount our 60-day note for $6,000 at the bank. The bank takes the note at 10% discount.
- Dec. 31   Record adjusting entries for the 2 notes.
- Jan.   Record payment of the 2 notes.

11-15. *Note—present value.* What is the present value of a non-interest-bearing, 2-year note for $6,000? Assume that 10% is an appropriate interest rate.

11-16. *Notes—present value.* Land is acquired by giving two non-interest-bearing notes. The first note is for $18,000 and is due in 3 years. The other note is for $22,000 and is due in 5 years. Twelve percent is an appropriate interest rate. Give the entry to record the acquisition of the land. Also give the entry to record interest expense for the first year.
(Solution in Appendix B.)

11-17. *Mortgage.* The Curry Comb Company purchases a building for $150,000 on March 1, Year 1, paying $50,000 in cash and signing a mortgage for $100,000. The mortgage is for 20 years and bears interest at 8%. Monthly payments are $850 for principal and interest. Give the entry for the first monthly payment on the mortgage on April 1, Year 1. Give the entry for the second payment on May 1, Year 1.
(Hint: interest will be lower the second month.)

11-18. *Long-term lease obligation.* On January 1, The Mountain View Creamery Company enters into a long-term lease with the Acme Finance Company. The lease provides for rentals of $20,000 per year for 10 years on a new plant that the finance company has constructed to Mountain View's specifications. The finance company pays $147,000 for the building, and sets the rental at a figure that will yield 6% compound interest on its investment. Both parties realize that the lease is, in effect, a purchase.

Required:
a. How should Mountain View Creamery record the situation when it first enters into the lease? Why?
b. What entry should be made by Mountain View for payment of the first year's rental of $20,000? (Hint: some of the $20,000 is interest.)
c. What expenses would Mountain View show in the first year other than interest?

11-19. *Bonds payable.* Give entries in general journal form for the following (use straight-line amortization):
- Mar. 1   Issue $1,000,000 of 6%, 10-year bonds at 98. Interest dates are March 1 and September 1.
- Sept. 1   Pay the semiannual interest on the above bonds. Include proper amortization.

11-20. *Bonds payable.* Make all necessary entries (use straight-line amortization):
a. On July 1, a corporation sells twenty $1,000, 9% bonds at 103. Interest

is payable semiannually, on June 30 and December 31. The bonds mature in 20 years.

    b. The first interest payment on the bonds is made on December 31. Make all entries necessary to record the interest expense.

    c. The bonds are paid in full at maturity date. (All interest entries have been made.)

11-21. *Bonds, effective interest.* The Atkins Company issues $1,000,000 of 11%, 20-year bonds on January 1 at a price that yields 10%. Interest is payable annually on December 31.

    a. Give the entry for issuance of the bonds on January 1.

    b. Give the entry for payment of interest and amortization of premium at the end of the first year, using effective-interest amortization.

11-22. *Payroll.* Henry Steel worked 47 hours for the week ending June 27. His rate is $3.20 per hour, with time and a half for hours over 40. He has a bond deduction of $3.50. Income tax withheld is $17.10. Tax rates: FICA: 6% on employees, 6% on employers. State unemployment compensation rate is 2.7%. Federal unemployment compensation is 0.5%.

Required:

    a. Determine the following and show computations: total earnings, total deductions, cash paid.

    b. Determine each of the employer's payroll tax expenses related to the earnings of Henry Steel for the week ended June 27.

11-23. *Tax allocation.* The data below relate to Ricardo's Appliance. The difference in timing of income occurs because the company uses accelerated depreciation for tax purposes only. Present the relevant sections of the financial statements for each of the two years, assuming (a) tax allocation procedures are not followed, (b) tax allocation procedures are followed.

	Year 1	Year 2	Total
Taxable income	$ 50,000	$200,000	$250,000
Income tax (40%)	20,000	80,000	100,000
Accounting income (before tax)	150,000	100,000	250,000

PROBLEMS

11-24. *Purchases and notes.* The Strauss Company records its purchases at net price. Give entries for the following transactions that take place during the current year.

May 3	Purchase merchandise from B. Sharp for $4,000, terms 2/10, n/30.
May 4	Pay freight of $60 on purchases from Sharp.
May 10	Send Sharp check for amount owed.
June 5	Purchase office supplies from Acme Supply for $300, terms 2/10, n/30.
June 12	Pay Acme amount owed.

Part III Measurement of Assets, Liabilities, and Income

July 10   Purchase merchandise from D. Light Co. for $6,000, terms 2/10, n/30.
July 30   Issue a 60-day, 9% note to Light Co. for amount due.
Sept. ?   Pay note to Light Co.
Dec. 12   Purchase merchandise from C. Clearly Co. for $5,000, terms 2/10, n/30.
Dec. 16   Discount our $6,000, 3-month note at the bank at 8%.
Dec. 31   Prepare any adjusting entries necessary.

11-25. *Bonds payable.* Rodeo Corporation issued $800,000 par value of bonds on September 30. The bonds have a 10-year life and carry 9% interest. The bonds are dated August 31 and are sold for $823,800 plus accrued interest. Interest is payable semiannually on August 31 and February 28. Give entries for the following:
  a. Sale of the bonds on September 30.
  b. Accrual of interest on December 31, the end of the company's fiscal year, and amortization of the premium or discount to date, using straight-line amortization.
  c. Interest payment on February 28. Also record amortization to February 28.

(Solution in Appendix B.)

11-26. *Bonds payable.* Prepare journal entries for the following transactions:
  a. Record on the books of C Corp. the sale of ten $1,000, 8%, 10-year bonds on May 1. The bonds are dated March 1, and interest is payable on September 1 and March 1. The bonds are sold for $9,646 plus accrued interest.
  b. C Corp. pays the first semiannual interest on the above bonds on September 1 (no entry for amortization).
  c. Record the amortization of discount or premium on the above bonds for the year ending December 31, and the accrual of interest at December 31. Use straight-line amortization.
  d. What will be the total interest expense for the fifth year of the above issue? Just state the amount, no entry is necessary. (Hint: this is not an involved computation if you take the year as a unit.)

11-27. *Bonds, effective-interest amortization.* The Hermanson Co. issues $10,000,000 of 9%, 15-year bonds on April 1 at a price that yields 10% interest. Interest is payable annually on March 31.
  a. Give the entry for issuance on April 1 of the current year. Include a schedule to compute the issue price.
  b. Give adjusting entries for interest and amortization at December 31, the end of the first year. Use effective-interest method of amortization.
  c. Give the entry for payment of interest on March 31 of the second year.
  d. Give adjusting entries on December 31 of the second year.

(Solution in Appendix B.)

11-28. *Lease.* Broward Co. enters into a long-term lease with Ajax Computer Co. to acquire a computer. Terms of the lease are $100,000 down on July 1 and $100,000 each 6 months for the next 5 years, a total of 11 payments. The computer has a life of 8 years, and title will be conveyed to Broward

Company as soon as the last payment is made. The parties consider the lease to be, in effect, a purchase. 12% is the agreed on annual rate of interest.

Required:
a. Compute the present value of the leased computer.
b. What is the interest expense for the first 6-month period?
c. What is the amount of other expenses that would be recorded at the end of the first year?
d. What is the interest expense in the second 6-month period?
e. What is the balance of the liability at the end of the second 6-month period?

(Solution in Appendix B.)

11-29. *Payroll.* The Baymore Company hires eight sales and office clerks on June 1. Following are data for the week of June 1–7:

Name	Hours Worked	Rate	Withholding
A. B. Colson	40	$1.90	$ 12.00
D. E. Folson	44	2.40	15.00
G. H. Inverness	48	2.00	23.00
J. K. Lincoln	36	2.80	18.00
M. N. Ogilvy	40	2.25	15.00
P. Q. Ritchie	40	2.60	27.00
S. T. Unger	46	3.20	37.00
V. W. Xerxes	40	2.50	22.00
			$169.00

a. Figure the total pay, FICA, and net pay for each office clerk listed above. Assume a 6% FICA rate and time and a half for overtime (over 40 hours).
b. Give the entry or entries to record the payment of wages.
c. Give the entry to record the employer's tax expense, assuming a 2.7% state unemployment compensation rate and a 0.5% federal rate.
d. Assuming that exactly the same amounts are recorded in entries on June 14, 21, and 28, and that accrued salaries on June 30 amount to $305, what is the wage expense for June?

11-30. *Controls.* Indicate how an effective system of internal control would stop, or lead to the discovery of, each of the following.
a. A supplier sends 100 fewer units than he bills us for.
b. A clerk in the receiving department takes 5 items out of a shipment of 55 items received, but records 55 items received on the receiving report.
c. The requisition clerk in a department orders some goods that are not needed and takes them home for personal use when they are delivered to the department in which he works.
d. The supplier sends an invoice but inadvertently fails to send the goods ordered. The invoice is paid.
e. Discounts on accounts payable are missed because invoices are not paid promptly.

f. The manager of the storeroom takes goods home in his lunch pail at the end of each day.

11-31. *Tax allocation.* On January 1 the Howard Company leased some property to the Pat Corporation for three years beginning on January 1 of this year, and collected $75,000 for the entire three years. All of the rent collection was taxed this year at a rate of 40%. Other taxable income was $30,000 for each of the three years. Record all entries related to rent and income tax for each year covered by the lease. Also show how the relevant items would appear in the classified financial statements for each year. You are to work the problem assuming

a. income tax allocation procedures are not used,
b. income tax allocation procedures are used.

(Solution in Appendix B.)

PART IV

Owners' Equity

12

Stockholders' Equity

A corporation is a creature of the state. Persons desiring to form a corporation submit an application to a designated state official. The application includes the *articles of incorporation*, which must conform to the state's corporation laws. Usually the articles are simple and include the name and address of the corporation, the purpose of the company, the duration (usually stated as perpetual), the kinds of stock and the number of shares authorized of each kind, the designation of the stock (whether par value or no-par value), the names of the incorporators, the number of shares of stock subscribed to by each, and the initial number of directors. If the articles of incorporation conform to the state laws, the state official approves them and the articles become the *charter* of the corporation.

Articles of incorporation

Corporate charter

Ownership in corporations is in the form of shares of capital stock. The ownership shares are evidence of the shareholders' claim against the net assets (assets less liabilities) of the corporation. As is true of all ownership claims, the stockholders' interest is an *undivided, residual* claim against the net assets. It is *undivided* because there are no specific assets that can be claimed by the stockholders. It is *residual* because the stockholders bear the ultimate risk in the business, and if the enterprise should fail, all creditor claims must be satisfied before the owners receive repayment of their investment.

Ownership an undivided, residual claim

RIGHTS OF STOCKHOLDERS

A stockholder receives a stock certificate, similar to the one illustrated in Figure 12-1, which evidences ownership interest in the corporation. As an owner, the stockholder has certain basic rights, the most important being the right to receive dividends when they are declared by the board of

FIGURE 12-1   Stock Certificate (Courtesy of Allyn and Bacon, Inc.)

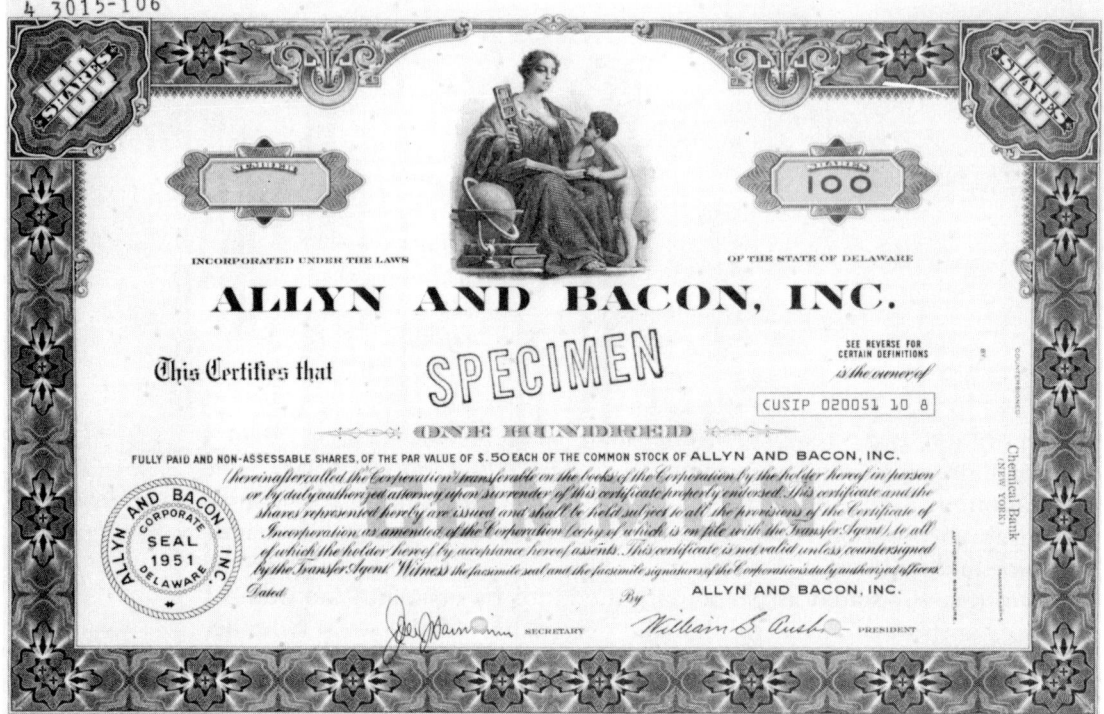

directors. The board of directors, elected by the stockholders for the purpose of governing the affairs of the corporation, decides if and when dividends are to be distributed to the owners.

A stockholder normally has one vote[1] for each share of stock owned and may vote on corporation matters specified in the articles of incorporation, such as the election of directors and the election of the CPA auditor. The stockholder will share pro rata in the net residual assets in the event of dissolution and liquidation. The right to sell or otherwise dispose of one's stock is usually present. In some small corporations, this right may be voided in order to restrict ownership control of the company to the original stockholders or their heirs. A stockholder may have the *preemptive right*, which is the right to maintain a proportionate interest in the stock by purchasing a pro rata share of such additional shares of stock as may be issued by the corporation. The preemptive right is frequently voided by the corporation, since it is a time consuming and costly pro-

---

1. The voting right frequently is withheld from some classes of stock. However, there must be at least one class of stock that has the voting right.

cedure to made additional shares of stock available to present stockholders.

CLASSES OF CAPITAL STOCK

The two main divisions of stockholders' equity in a corporation are contributed capital (or paid-in capital) and retained earnings. Contributed capital consists of amounts paid for original issues of shares, plus any other amounts of capital invested in, or contributed to, the corporation. We begin our consideration of contributed capital by looking at the various classes of capital stock. The two basic classes are *preferred* and *common*.

Preferred Stock

Preferred stock has prior claim to earnings and often prior claim to net assets in the event of liquidation. "Preferred as to dividends" means that the preferred stockholders receive a stipulated dividend, frequently expressed as dollars per share or as a percentage of the par value of the stock, before dividends can be distributed to common stockholders. Usually the dividend preference is also *cumulative*. Thus, if a dividend on preferred is not paid in a year, the unpaid dividend or fractional unpaid dividend accumulates, or carries forward. Any accumulated unpaid dividends and the current year's dividend must be paid to preferred stockholders before any common dividends can be paid. Occasionally, the preferred stock is *participating*, in that preferred stockholders would share (participate) with common stockholders in dividends that exceed a certain amount.

Dividend preference

Cumulative

Preferred stock is often *preferred as to assets in liquidation*. If the corporation dissolves and liquidates assets, the liabilities are paid off first. Then the remaining assets are distributed. First, preferred stockholders receive an amount equal to a specified liquidating value (specified on the stock certificate). Any remaining assets are then paid to the common stockholders.

Asset preference

Preferred stock may have full voting rights, no voting rights, or limited voting rights. In many states, the corporation can withhold the voting right. In some cases, the charter may provide for voting rights in the event that dividends on preferred are not paid. Such voting rights will usually terminate when dividend payments are resumed.

Preferred voting rights

Some preferred stocks are *convertible:* they can be exchanged for shares of common at a specified ratio. Convertibility is attractive to some investors who desire the relative security of preferred stock and yet want the opportunity to benefit should the market price of common stock rise.

Convertible preferred

Typically, the market price of convertible preferred stock will rise along with common. The fixed dividend feature of convertible preferred may prevent its market price from falling as much as common when prices decline. Because of the close tie with common, convertible preferred is sometimes treated as a *common stock equivalent* in figuring common earnings per share. This feature is considered later in the chapter.

Callable preferred

Callable preferred stock may be "called" at the option of the corporation at specified terms covering the call price and time period. This feature enables the corporation to refinance when the market dividend rate on similar preferred shares falls below the original dividend rate. It may be advantageous for the corporation to pay the call price (which is usually more than the original issue price), retire the stock, and issue new preferred stock with a lower dividend rate. The callable feature also enables the company to eliminate the fixed dividend costs should it be financially advantageous to do so in the future.

Common Stock

When stock carries no preferences or there is just one class of stock, it is called *common stock*. When preferred stock exists, the common stock has the residual (last) claim to earnings and, frequently, the last claim to net assets in the event of corporate liquidation. Usually, the voting control in a corporation rests with the common stockholders because the preferred stockholders do not have voting rights or they have fewer total votes than common stockholders.

PAR VALUE AND NO-PAR VALUE STOCK

Par value

Par value is an arbitrary dollar value printed on the stock certificate. A no-par value stock has no such dollar amount indicated. Par value is a concept that goes back to the early days of the corporation when the overriding concern of state lawmakers was to protect the creditors of the corporation. Par value originally was supposed to be the amount actually paid in to the corporation by the stockholder. To prevent corporations from issuing stock at a price below par, many state laws have a *discount liability* feature, which provides that if stock is issued below par (at a discount), the stockholders can become liable in the future to the creditors for the amount of such discount. If the corporation is unable to pay creditors' claims, the creditors can obtain judgments against the stockholders for the amount of the discount. Today, par value cannot be taken as the amount paid in to the corporation. Often, the par value selected for stock (particularly common stock) is relatively low compared to the issue price of the stock. For example, one large company issued stock of $1.00 par value for over $13.00 per share. Thus, par value today has virtually no economic significance.

What then is the significance of par value? It has legal significance in that par value of the stock outstanding (or stated value in the case of no-par stock) is the *legal capital* of the company. Legal capital, a holdover in state laws from the early days of corporations, is supposed to protect the creditor, because the corporation cannot pay dividends that would reduce stockholders' equity below the amount of legal capital. Of course, today's low par value stocks defeat that purpose. From an *accounting standpoint*, the par value is usually the amount credited to the capital stock account when the stock is issued. The accounting entries will be illustrated later in this chapter.

No-par stock was introduced in the state of New York in 1912 to correct abuses associated with par value stock. One persistent problem with par value stock was the inclination of some investors to equate par value with real economic value. Unscrupulous promoters would prey on the gullible investor with the pitch that stock offered at a discount (below its par) was a bargain. For example, a $100 par stock available at $60 was surely a bargain. Stock with no par value printed on the certificate would avoid giving the investor the wrong impression about its value.

No-par stock is usually assigned a *stated value*, an arbitrary value much like par value, to conform with state laws defining legal capital. From an accounting standpoint, the stated value of no-par stock is the amount usually credited to the capital stock account when the stock is issued. The amount received in excess of the stated value is credited to "paid-in capital in excess of stated value."

Legal significance of par

Accounting significance

No-par stock

Stated value

ACCOUNTING FOR THE ISSUANCE OF CAPITAL STOCK

A corporation is authorized by its charter to issue up to a certain number of shares for each class of capital stock. Usually the incorporators provide for enough authorized shares to take care of the anticipated future sales of stock. The number of authorized shares can be changed by the appropriate majority vote of the stockholders to amend the articles of incorporation. Shares that have been sold are referred to as *issued* stock. As long as shares remain in the hands of shareholders the shares are referred to as *outstanding* shares.

A corporation may sell stock for cash or exchange stock for noncash assets or services. When noncash assets or services are received in exchange for shares, the accounting rule is to record the shares at the cash value of the assets or services received. If no market value can be established for the resources received, the recent cash price of the shares should be used. Stock issued at a price in excess of its par value is said to be

Authorized shares

Part IV   Owners' Equity

issued at a *premium*. A more descriptive term for premium is "paid-in capital in excess of par." We shall use that term in this chapter. The following are typical accounting entries made for the issuance of stock:

Typical issuance entries

Par Value Stock

	Debit	Credit
Cash (or other assets)	XX	
Capital stock (at par value)		XX
Paid-in capital in excess of par		XX

No-par Stock

	Debit	Credit
Cash (or other assets)	XX	
Capital stock (at stated value)		XX
Paid-in capital in excess of stated value		XX

Example 12-1 illustrates a variety of stock issue transactions.

EXAMPLE 12-1

Early in year 1, the Bellows Corporation receives its charter, which authorizes it to issue 15,000 shares of $5 cumulative preferred stock having a par value of $60 per share and 180,000 shares of $2.50 par value common stock. The dividend rate on the preferred is $5 per share. The company will operate on a calendar-year basis. No accounting entry is required for stock authorization, but an appropriate notation should be made in the capital stock accounts in the general ledger, and, of course, the authorization should be shown in the official bylaws of the corporation.

Jan. 15, Year 1   Bellows issues 6,000 shares of preferred stock for cash at a price of $60 per share.

	Debit	Credit
Cash	360,000	
Preferred stock, $60 par		360,000

Jan. 25   Bellows issues 40,000 shares of common stock at a cash price of $50 per share.

	Debit	Credit
Cash	2,000,000	
Common stock, par $2.50		100,000
Paid-in capital in excess of par		1,900,000

Exchange for noncash asset

Jan. 28   Bellows exchanges 600 shares of common for 1,000 shares of the common stock of the Smallfry Company. There is no mar-

...ket in the Smallfry stock, so the recent price of the Bellows common is used to record the exchange.

	Debit	Credit
Investment in Smallfry common stock	30,000	
Common stock, par $2.50		1,500
Paid-in capital in excess of par		28,500

Feb. 2   Bellows gives 1,000 shares of common stock in exchange for land having an appraised value of $52,000. *Exchange for land*

	Debit	Credit
Land	52,000	
Common stock, par $2.50		2,500
Paid-in capital in excess of par		49,500

The appraised value is used (if it is relatively dependable) as an indicator of how much was received for the stock. There might be a variety of reasons for accepting stock that has a market value of only $50,000 (see price on Jan. 25), such as the fact that no real estate commission would be involved in this transfer.

Feb. 20   Bellows gives 200 shares of common stock to a lawyer for services received in connection with the organization of the corporation. The lawyer's normal fee for this service would be $11,000. *Exchange for services*

	Debit	Credit
Organization costs	11,000	
Common stock, par $2.50		500
Paid-in capital in excess of par		10,500

Note the debit to the intangible asset organization costs.

Feb. 28   The board of directors wants a balance sheet that reflects all transactions to date.

Early balance sheet

BELLOWS CORPORATION
Balance Sheet, February 28, Year 1

Assets		Stockholders' Equity		
Cash	$2,360,000	Preferred stock, $5 cumulative, $60 par:		
Investment in Small-		Authorized 15,000 shares; issued		
fry common stock	30,000	6,000 shares		$ 360,000
Land	52,000	Common stock, $2.50 par value:		
Organization costs	11,000	Authorized 180,000 shares; issued		
		41,800 shares		104,500
		Paid-in capital in excess of par		1,988,500
Total assets	$2,453,000	Total stockholders' equity		$2,453,000

The different features of capital stock can complicate the owners' equity section of the balance sheet, as the balance sheet for the Bellows Corporation illustrates. In published reports, many companies will show

Stock subscriptions

only the bare bones of the different stock issues in the balance sheet proper, putting the details in notes to the balance sheet.

Some small corporations sell stock by taking *subscriptions* to the stock and then collecting the price over several installments. When the subscriptions are paid in full, the stock is issued. Example 12-2 illustrates the accounting for subscriptions and for no-par stock.

EXAMPLE 12-2

On April 1, the Semple Corporation receives subscriptions to 5,000 shares of common stock, no-par with a stated value of $5 per share. The subscription price is $20 per share. Twenty percent is to be paid immediately, and the balance is to be paid in 2 equal installments: on June 1 and August 1.

Apr. 1, Year 1

	Debit	Credit
Cash	20,000	
Subscriptions receivable	80,000	
Common stock subscribed (at stated value)		25,000
Paid-in capital in excess of stated value		75,000

June 1 The first installment payment is received.

	Debit	Credit
Cash	40,000	
Subscriptions receivable		40,000

Subscriptions on balance sheet

June 30 If a balance sheet is prepared on June 30, the subscriptions receivable balance of $40,000 will be shown as a current asset; common stock subscribed will be reported in stockholders' equity along with any common stock that has been issued, as follows:

Common stock, issued XXXX shares	$XX
Common stock subscribed	25,000
Paid-in capital in excess of stated value	75,000

Aug. 1 The August 1 installment is received and the stock is issued.

Issuance of fully paid subscribed stock

	Debit	Credit
Cash	40,000	
Subscriptions receivable		40,000
Common stock subscribed	25,000	
Common stock, stated value $5		25,000

Defaults on subscriptions are covered in more advanced accounting courses.

SUBSEQUENT OPERATIONS OF CORPORATIONS

Following the issuance of its stock, a corporation engages in many activities. As a result, a profit is earned or a loss incurred, cash and stock dividends are declared and distributed, and other actions are taken that affect stockholders' equity.

Corporate Income and Earnings Per Share

The measurement of corporate income has been covered in earlier chapters, particularly in chapter 3. Here we discuss an important measure of corporate income performance, the *earnings per share*.

Earnings per share is perhaps the most widely used single measure of income performance. The idea is to relate a company's income to the number of shares outstanding to get income per share. The shareholder can then compare this figure with the dividends paid per share and with the current market price per share. The shareholder may find this information useful in deciding whether to keep or sell the stock. Investors may also find the information useful in deciding whether to invest in the stock.

Earnings per share

The concept of earnings per share is simple. Divide the income belonging to the common shareholders by the average number of common shares outstanding during the period. The average is weighted by the length of time (within the period) the shares were outstanding. The term *outstanding* refers to the shares held by stockholders. For example, Galway Company, with only one class of stock, has earnings of $10 million in year 4 and weighted average shares outstanding of 2.5 million shares. The earnings per share in Year 4 are $4.00.

Weighted average shares

In cases where both preferred and common stock are outstanding, the computation is more complex. Consider the Hedri Company, in Example 12-3.

EXAMPLE 12-3

The Hedri Company has 80,000 shares of $5 preferred outstanding at the end of the year. The company had 500,000 shares of common stock outstanding at the beginning of the year and issued 100,000 additional shares on October 1. Net income for the year is $2,080,000. The computation of earnings per share proceeds as follows:

Income calculation

	Income to Common	
Net income		$2,080,000
Less dividends to preferred stock		400,000
Net income to common shareholders		$1,680,000

(Continued)

383

Example 12-3 (Cont.)

Shares of stock calculation

Weighted Average Common Shares Outstanding

Date	Shares Outstanding	Fraction of Year Outstanding	Weighted Average Shares
Jan. 1	500,000 shares	1.0 year	500,000
Oct. 1	100,000 shares	.25 year	25,000
	Weighted average shares outstanding		525,000

Earnings per share of common stock: $1,680,000/525,000 = $3.20

If an income statement includes extraordinary items (gains or losses net of income taxes), an additional analysis is made to show earnings per share before the extraordinary item, the effect of the item on earnings per share, and the final earnings per share. Example 12-4 illustrates.

EXAMPLE 12-4

Last year the Willow Company had an extraordinary loss that affected its income. The company had 400,000 shares outstanding for the entire year.

Extraordinary items

Income before extraordinary item	$1,600,000
Extraordinary loss (net of income tax)	400,000
Net income	$1,200,000
Earnings per share of common stock:	
Income before extraordinary item	$ 4.00
Extraordinary loss	(1.00)
Net income	$ 3.00

Primary Earnings Per Share. The existence of *convertible preferred stock, convertible bonds,* and stock options and rights further complicate the computation of earnings per share. Remember that convertible securities can be exchanged for shares of common stock at some specified ratio. Stock options and rights (to be covered later) permit the holder to buy common stock at some set price and over some set period of time. Stock options and rights are considered to be *common stock equivalents.* In many cases, convertible securities are also common stock equivalents. Generally, a convertible security is a common stock equivalent if the market value of the security is based primarily on its convertibility feature. That is, the security's value "is derived in large part from the value of the common stock to which it is related...."[2] The weighted average common shares must include common stock equivalents to derive what is called *primary earnings per share.*

Common stock equivalents

Fully Diluted Earnings Per Share. Convertible securities that are not considered common stock equivalents do not enter into the computation of

---

[2] See "Earnings per Share," *Accounting Principles Board Opinion No. 15,* p. 226. The student should consult this opinion for further explanation.

primary earnings per share, but are used to compute what is called *fully diluted earnings per share*.

Diluted earnings

The purpose of these adjustments of earnings per share is to recognize the threat of dilution to common share earnings. Earnings per share will be diluted (lessened because of more shares) if convertible securities are exchanged for common shares and/or if stock options and rights are exercised. The adjusted earnings per share figures give the common shareholder a conservative measure of his or her share of earnings.

Dividends

If a company has earned a profit, it may decide to distribute cash dividends to its owners. Even in the case of losses, companies may pay dividends. The declaration and payment of dividends requires

1. Sufficient retained earnings
2. Sufficient cash
3. Action by the board of directors.

Cash dividend requirements

In most states, it is illegal to declare dividends if there is a *deficit* (debit balance) in retained earnings. The company must also have enough cash to pay the dividends. A company can have a large income for the year but may be short of cash. The inflow of net assets, indicated by a net income, may increase cash, but it may also be used to reduce liabilities, invest in new plant and equipment, or expand inventories. If cash is short, a company may use the stock dividend (to be discussed later). Finally, the board of directors must declare a dividend. No dividend can be paid unless the board of directors takes action. Most companies attempt to follow a set dividend policy so that shareholders can rely upon receiving a certain amount every year.

Cash availability

Three dates are important in connection with dividends:

Dividend dates

1. The declaration date
2. The date of record
3. The payment date

The declaration date is the date on which the board of directors meets and declares the dividend. This declaration establishes the *legal obligation* of the company to pay the dividend. The dividend will be paid to "holders of record" as of a certain date, the date of record. The time between the declaration date and the date of record allows stockholders to complete their transactions in the stock and to get their names on the corporation's records as owners. (After the record date, the stock sells "ex-dividends.") The payment date falls sometime after the record date so that checks can be prepared and mailed to the right owners. Usually all of the mechanics of stock ownership records and dividend payments are put in the hands of banks who act as *transfer agents* and *registrars*. The transfer agent is

Liability established

Record date

Payment date

385

responsible for the transfer of stock certificates to the rightful owners, and the registrar is responsible for keeping an up-to-date record of all stockholders and handling dividend payments. The accounting for dividends is illustrated in Example 12-5 for the Bellows Corporation (continued from Example 12-1). Dividends may be debited directly to retained earnings, or a dividends account may be used.

EXAMPLE 12-5

The Bellows Corporation board of directors, being assured by the controller that income is sufficient, by resolution on December 15, Year 1, declare cash dividends payable on January 15, Year 2, to holders of record of December 31, Year 1: $5 per share to preferred and $1.30 per share to common.

Dividend declaration

		Debit	Credit
Dec. 15, Year 1	Retained earnings	84,340	
	Dividend payable—preferred		30,000
	Dividend payable—common		54,340
	Preferred: 6,000 shares × $5 = $30,000		
	Common: 41,800 shares × $1.30 = $54,340		

Balance sheet effects

On the December 31, Year 1, balance sheet, the dividends payable, $84,340 in total, are reported among current liabilities. The retained earnings are the net income for the year less the dividends of $84,340.

Let us assume that after completing the accounting for Year 1, the credit balance in the income summary account is $137,240. The income summary is closed to retained earnings:

		Debit	Credit
Dec. 31, Year 1	Income summary	137,240	
	Retained earnings		137,240
	To close the income summary account.		

In January of Year 2 the cash dividends declared in December are paid:

		Debit	Credit
Jan. 15, Year 2	Dividend payable—preferred	30,000	
	Dividend payable—common	54,340	
	Cash		84,340

Dividends in arrears

Dividends are paid at the option of the board of directors. This is true of all dividends, even those on cumulative preferred stock. When the board of directors elects to pass the preferred dividend or to pay only a fraction of the dividend, the preferred dividends are said to be *in arrears*. Dividend arrearages are indicated in the notes to the balance sheet. Dividend arrearages are not liabilities. Dividends do not become legal obligations of the corporation until declared by the board of directors.

Stock Dividends

Stock dividends are dividends in the form of additional shares of the corporation's stock. A company may distribute stock dividends in order to conserve cash. A stock dividend does not affect cash, it involves only a transfer within stockholders' equity from retained earnings to contributed, or paid-in, capital. A stock dividend is usually expressed as a percentage of the outstanding shares. A 5% stock dividend entitles a person who holds 100 shares to receive 5 additional shares of stock when the dividend is distributed. When the number of shares for a stockholder does not come out to an even number, the person usually can pay for the additional fraction needed for a full share, or else can receive the market value of the fractional share in cash. Thus, a person holding 36 shares is entitled to receive 1.80 additional shares of a 5% stock dividend. The person can usually elect to receive the cash equivalent of .80 shares or purchase another .20 shares at a specified price to make 2 full shares. *Fractional shares*

    The stock dividend helps mollify the stockholders, while enabling the corporation to keep its cash for other purposes. Having more shares, the stockholder may think that he or she is better off than before. However, a common stock dividend given to the common stockholder leaves that person in relatively the same position as before. Each stockholder continues to hold the same percentage of outstanding stock as that held before the stock dividend. Stockholders cannot sell their dividend shares without decreasing their percentage interest in the company. Thus, the stock dividend is not income to the stockholder recipient. No accounting entry need be made by the recipient. Of course, a record should be kept of the shares received. *Effect on recipient*

    From the recipient's standpoint, a cost must be allocated to the dividend shares. The cost of the shares owned that entitled the stockholder to receive the stock dividend is allocated to the original shares plus the dividend shares. For example, a holder of 1,000 shares that originally cost $8.40 per share receives a 5% stock dividend, or 50 shares. The $8,400 cost of the original 1,000 shares is allocated to the 1,050 shares to give a new cost of $8.00 per share.

    Despite the fact that a stock dividend is not a distribution of income to the stockholder, the issuing corporation must make an accounting entry that reduces retained earnings and increases capital stock. Because stockholders may believe that they receive income equal to the value of the shares received, the AICPA requires that retained earnings be "capitalized" to the extent of the *fair value* of the shares distributed. Example 12-6 illustrates this situation for Zebra Corporation. *Retained earnings capitalized at fair value of shares*

EXAMPLE 12-6 STOCK DIVIDEND ILLUSTRATION

The Zebra Corporation has 10,000 shares of common stock outstanding. Par value is $50, and market value is $80. On June 15 the company declares a stock dividend of 4%, or 400 shares, to be distributed on July 15. Following the AICPA requirements, the entries on the corporation books would be as follows:

Declaration of dividend

		Debit	Credit
June 15	Retained earnings	32,000	
	Stock dividend to be issued		20,000
	Paid-in capital from stock dividend		12,000
	Declared a 4% stock dividend on 10,000 shares outstanding at $80 per share.		

Balance sheet treatment

The account *stock dividend to be issued*, a stockholders' equity account, would be shown in the common stock section of the June 30 balance sheet:

Stockholders' equity:
  Common stock, par $50:
    Issued 10,000 shares $500,000
    Stock dividend to be
      issued, 400 shares   20,000

		Debit	Credit
July 15	Stock dividend to be issued	20,000	
	Common stock, par $50		20,000
	Issued the stock dividend of 400 shares.		

Restrictions of Retained Earnings

Generally, a company must have retained earnings before dividends can be paid. A corporation's borrowing agreements frequently will include a restriction on the corporation's payment of dividends by restricting the amount of retained earnings available for dividends. Such restriction is intended to protect the lenders against imprudent dividend payments that could threaten the security of the loan. This restriction must be reported in the financial statements, usually in a footnote. For example, the 1976 financial statements of the Caterpillar Tractor Company included this footnote:

Borrowing agreement restriction

> As of December 31, 1976, under the terms of the most restrictive indenture, approximately $695 million of "Profit employed in the business" was not available for the payment of dividends.

Treasury stock restriction

Further restrictions of retained earnings may come about because of a company's repurchase of its own stock. If the company intends to reissue such stock, the stock is called *treasury stock*. The accounting for treasury stock will be considered later. State law usually requires a company to restrict its retained earnings to the extent of the cost of treasury shares. In such a case, the company indicates the restriction in a footnote or parenthetically in the balance sheet as follows:

> Retained earnings (of which $35,000
> is restricted because of the purchase
> of treasury stock) $165,000

In the example, the company holds shares of its own stock (treasury stock) for which it paid $35,000. Accordingly, only $130,000 of retained earnings is available for dividends.

Stock Splits and Recapitalization

Corporations sometimes effect *stock splits* in order to increase the number of shares of stock in the hands of stockholders and thus reduce the market price per share of their stock. This action may be intended to widen the market for the stock. A *stock split* is the issuance by a corporation to present stockholders of a larger number of shares in exchange for the smaller number of shares presently held. For example, suppose that B Company's $40 par value stock is now selling for $500 per share. The company declares a *four-for-one split*, in which each stockholder receives 4 new shares in exchange for each share presently held. The par value is reduced to $10 per share. In a stock split, the total paid-in capital is usually unchanged. Hence, no accounting entry is necessary. All that is needed is a notation of the new number of shares and the new par, or stated, value. *Stock split defined*

The stock split has the same effect on the stockholder as a stock dividend, except on a larger scale. The accountant distinguishes a stock dividend from a split by its size.[3] The purpose of the action also helps distinguish the two. A stock dividend is in lieu of, or supplementary to, a cash dividend, whereas a stock split is intended to increase the number of shares sufficiently to affect market price. For example, one would expect that a four-for-one split would reduce the market price to about 25% of the price before the split. *Contrast to stock dividend*

Effect on market price

Sometimes circumstances dictate a *reverse stock split*, where old shares are turned in and fewer new shares are issued. This can occur when a company goes through a reorganization because it has been in financial difficulties or when a company feels that its stock is selling at too low a price. *Reverse split*

Stock Options

Stock options grant the holder the right to buy a specified number of shares of stock at a given price and within a given time span. It is now a fairly *Defined*

---

3. When a stock dividend approaches 20 or 25 percent, accountants consider it to be essentially a stock split and refer to it as a large stock dividend.

common practice among American corporations to grant stock options to key employees. If the company is successful and the stock price rises on the market, the holder of the options can exercise them at the specified price, and thus make substantial gains. For example, the president of Q Company is granted options on 1,000 shares at $80 per share. The options run for 10 years and may be exercised at any time after 2 years have passed. In 5 years, when the stock is selling at $130, the president exercises the options. The president pays only $80 per share, and thus can make substantial gains if the shares are sold. Of course, if the stock price goes down, there is no incentive to exercise the options. The existence of stock options is footnoted on the financial statements so that all parties are aware of this method of giving key employees added compensation.

Stock Rights and Warrants

Defined

Stock rights and warrants are similar to stock options—they give the holder the right to purchase shares of stock at a designated price and within a designated period of time. Rights and warrants are often given to present stockholders as a means of exercising their preemptive right. Rights and warrants can often be traded on the market. Their value depends on the terms at which they can be exercised and the market's assessment of the future prospects of the enterprise involved. These securities are perhaps the extreme residual security because, although they are an ownership interest, they do not share in present dividend distributions. Rights and warrants are usually considered common stock equivalents in computing earnings per share.

Accounting entries

A corporation that issues stock rights and warrants records any cash received at the time of issue. No other entry need be made until the rights or warrants are exercised.

Treasury Stock

Defined

Stock of a company that has been issued once, is repurchased by that company, and is held for later reissue is called *treasury stock*. A company may buy its own stock on the market for various reasons; for instance, it may need stock for employee stock purchase plans and stock option plans. There are two methods of handling treasury stock transactions: (1) the cost method (which is most widely used) and (2) the retirement method.

Cost method. Under the cost method, the treasury stock is recorded at its cost, the amount paid to acquire it. When the stock is resold at a later date, the difference between cost and selling price is credited to paid-in capital from treasury stock transactions if there is a gain, and is debited to the same account in the event of a loss. In the loss case, if there is no balance in the paid-in capital from treasury transactions, then other paid-in capital on the same class of shares is debited. When all paid-in capital is exhausted, the retained earnings account is used. Example 12-7 illustrates.

EXAMPLE 12-7 TREASURY STOCK TRANSACTIONS

Feb. 16   The Beason Company purchases 1,000 shares of its $5 par common stock at $70 per share.

Mar. 13   Five hundred shares are resold at $75 per share.

The journal entries would be as follows:

		Debit	Credit
Feb. 16	Treasury stock	70,000	
	Cash		70,000
Mar. 13	Cash	37,500	
	Treasury stock		35,000
	Paid-in capital from treasury stock transactions		2,500
	Sold 500 of the shares purchased on February 16 for $75 per share.		

Balance sheet treatment

If treasury stock is held by a company at the end of its fiscal year, the cost of the treasury stock is deducted from the total stockholders' equity. Any paid-in capital from treasury stock is added to other sources of paid-in capital for the same class of shares. There may be an inclination to treat treasury shares as an asset, on the grounds that it is like an investment in stock. If this argument is sound, the treasury shares would have a value on the market if the corporation ceased operations. This obviously would not be so. Treasury stock is best viewed as a temporary reduction in owners' equity. It is temporary because the intention is to resell the shares. Note also that if there is treasury stock, the number of shares *outstanding* will be less than the number of shares *issued*.

Retirement method. Under this method, the purchase of treasury stock is viewed as an immediate contraction of the stockholders' equity. Accounting entries are made that treat the transaction as a retirement. When the stock is reissued at a later date, the transaction is viewed as a new expansion of owners' equity. This approach is technically complex and will not be illustrated here.

Book Value per Share of Common Stock

Book value defined

The book value per share of common stock is a measure sometimes used in the analysis of financial statements. The measure and its use are discussed in chapter 18. It will suffice here to define book value as the amount of net assets (according to the books of account) per share of common stock.

Part IV   Owners' Equity

COMPREHENSIVE STOCKHOLDERS' EQUITY ILLUSTRATION

In Example 12-8 we use the Bellows Corporation (see Examples 12-1 and 12-5) to illustrate more fully the accounting for stockholders' equity and to integrate the various points discussed in this chapter.

EXAMPLE 12-8

We recall that the Bellows Corporation was organized early in Year 1. The initial stock issues were illustrated in Example 12-1. We assumed in Example 12-5 that the corporation had operated at a profit in the remainder of Year 1 and had paid some dividends to both classes of stockholders. We now show how all of the corporation's activity in Year 1 affected stockholders' equity. Stockholders' equity as of December 31 is shown below:

BELLOWS CORPORATION
Stockholders' Equity
December 31, Year 1

Contributed Capital		
Preferred stock, $5 cumulative, $60 par value:		
Authorized 15,000 shares; issued 6,000 shares		$ 360,000
Common stock, $2.50 par value:		
Authorized 180,000 shares; issued 41,800 shares		104,500
Additional paid-in capital:		
From issuance of common stock in excess of par		1,988,500
Total contributed capital		2,453,000
Retained earnings*		52,900
Total stockholders' equity		$2,505,900
*Income for Year 1	$137,240	
Less dividends	84,340	
	$ 52,900	

Year 2 Events

Jan. 15   Paid the dividends declared on December 10, Year 1.

	Debit	Credit
Dividend payable—preferred	30,000	
Dividend payable—common	54,340	
Cash		84,340
(This entry is repeated from Example 12-5)		

Mar. 25   The board of directors declare quarterly dividends of $1.25 on preferred and $.75 on common.

Retained earnings	38,850	
Dividend payable—preferred		7,500
Dividend payable—common		31,350
Preferred: 6,000 shares × $1.25 = $7,500		
Common: 41,800 shares × $.75 = $31,350		

Mar. 31 The net income for the first quarter, $78,000, is closed to income summary.

Revenue	XX	
Expenses		XX
Income summary		78,000

Income summary will accumulate quarter earnings and be closed to retained earnings at the annual closing.

Apr. 15 Dividends for the first quarter are paid.

Dividend payable—preferred	7,500	
Dividend payable—common	31,350	
Cash		38,850

June 25 Second quarter dividends are declared in the same amounts as in the first quarter.

Retained earnings	38,850	
Dividend payable—preferred		7,500
Dividend payable—common		31,350

June 30 Net income of the second quarter, $135,000, is closed to income summary.

Revenue	XX	
Expenses		XX
Income summary		135,000

July 15 Dividends for the second quarter are paid.

Dividend payable—preferred	7,500	
Dividend payable—common	31,350	
Cash		38,350

Aug. 3 Land worth $40,000 and a building worth $500,000 are contributed to the corporation by the city.

Land	40,000	
Building	500,000	
Paid-in capital from donations		540,000

Sept. 1 Twenty-one thousand additional shares of common stock are sold for cash at $70 per share.

Cash	1,470,000	
Common stock, par $2.50		52,500
Paid-in capital in excess of par		1,417,500

(*Continued*)

Example 12-8 (Cont.)

Sept. 25   Third-quarter cash dividends are declared in the same per share amounts as in Quarters 1 and 2. In addition, a 2% stock dividend on common is declared to supplement the cash dividend. The AICPA rule on stock dividends is followed in the entry below.

Retained earnings	54,600	
Dividend payable—preferred		7,500
Dividend payable—common		47,100
Cash dividends:		
preferred 6,000 × $1.25 = $7,500;		
common 62,800 × $.75 = $47,100		
Retained earnings	87,920	
Stock dividend to be issued		3,140
Paid-in capital from stock dividend		84,780

Common stock outstanding:	
Issued in Year 1	41,800 shares
Issued in September, Year 2	<u>21,000</u>
	62,800 shares
2% stock dividend	1,256 shares
Current fair value	$70 per share
Total dividend	$87,920

Sept. 30   The net income for the third quarter, $162,000, is closed to income summary.

Revenue	XX	
Expenses		XX
Income summary		162,000

Oct. 15   The third-quarter cash dividends are paid; the 2% stock dividend to common is issued.

Dividend payable—preferred	7,500	
Dividend payable—common	47,100	
Cash		54,600
Payment of cash dividend.		
Stock dividend to be issued	3,140	
Common stock, par $2.50		3,140

Nov. 1   The company repurchases 1,200 shares of common stock at $72 per share; these are to be used in employee stock purchase programs.

Treasury stock—common	86,400	
Cash		86,400

Dec. 18 The fourth quarter dividend is declared in the same amount per share as in the third quarter: $1.25 for preferred and $.75 for common.

Retained earnings	54,642	
Dividend payable—preferred		7,500
Dividend payable—common		47,142
Preferred: 6,000 shares × $1.25 = $7,500		
Common: 62,856 shares × $.75 = $47,142		

Common outstanding before stock dividend	62,800
Stock dividend	1,256
Less treasury stock	(1,200)
Shares outstanding	62,856

Dec. 31 The net income for the fourth quarter, $190,400, is closed to income summary. The income summary account (which now shows the total income for Year 2) is closed to retained earnings.

Dec. 31	Revenue	XX	
	Expenses		XX
	Income summary		190,400
Dec. 31	Income summary	565,400	
	Retained earnings		565,400

The Income Summary account at year end contains the total income for the year of $565,400. Dividends are as follows:

First quarter	$ 38,850
Second quarter	38,850
Third quarter:	
Cash	54,600
Stock	87,920
Fourth quarter	54,642
Total	$274,862

The financial statements for Year 2 are prepared. Below are a partial income statement (to show earnings per share), a statement of retained earnings, and the stockholders' equity section of the balance sheet.

BELLOWS CORPORATION
Partial Income Statement
Year Ended December 31, Year 2

Net income (after income taxes)	$565,400
Earnings per share of common stock	$10.80

(Continued)

Part IV Owners' Equity

Example 12–8 (Cont.)

Earnings per share

Earnings per share was computed as follows:

Net income	$565,400
Less preferred stock dividends	30,000
Net income to common stockholders	$535,400

Average Outstanding Shares in Year 2

Weighted average calculation

Date	Number of Shares	Fraction of Year	Weighted Average
Jan. 1	41,800	1.0	41,800
Stock dividend	836	1.0	836
Sept. 1	21,000	4/12	7,000
Stock dividend	420	4/12	140
Nov. 1 Treasury Stock	(1,200)	2/12	(200)
Average shares outstanding in Year 2			49,576

Earnings per share: $535,400/49,576 shares = $10.80

BELLOWS CORPORATION
Statement of Retained Earnings
Year Ended December 31, Year 2

Statement of retained earnings

Retained earnings, December 31, Year 1	$ 52,900
Add net income for Year 2	565,400
	618,300
Less dividends in Year 2	274,862
Retained earnings, December 31, Year 2	$343,438

BELLOWS CORPORATION
Balance Sheet
December 31, Year 2
Stockholders' Equity

Stockholders' equity

Contributed Capital		
Preferred stock, $5 cumulative, $60 par value:		
Authorized 15,000 shares; issued 6,000 shares		$ 360,000
Common stock, $2.50 par value:		
Authorized 180,000 shares; issued 64,056 shares,		
of which 1,200 shares are in the treasury		160,140
Additional paid-in capital:		
From issuance of common stock in excess of par	$3,406,000	
From common stock dividend	84,780	
From donation of property	540,000	4,030,780
Total contributed capital		4,550,920
Retained earnings (of which $86,400 is restricted because of the purchase of treasury stock)		343,438
		4,894,358
Less: treasury stock, common, 1,200 shares at cost		86,400
Total stockholders' equity		$4,807,958

SUMMARY

A corporation comes into existence when the state of incorporation grants a charter pursuant to an appropriate application by the incorporators. Ownership in a corporation is in the form of shares of capital stock. Stockholders have an undivided residual claim against the net assets of the corporation.

Preferred and common stock are the two basic classes of capital stock. Preferred has preference to earnings and often preference to net assets in liquidation. Common stock has the residual claim to earnings and to net assets in liquidation. Preferred stock may be convertible into common stock under specified terms and/or callable under specified terms at the option of the corporation. These and other features of preferred that may exist are stipulated in the articles of incorporation.

Stock may have a par value or no par value. Par value is an arbitrary value printed on the stock certificate, usually low in relation to the issuing price. Par value signifies legal capital, which is the amount of owners' equity that cannot be diminished by dividends. No-par stock usually has a stated value assigned to it. Stated value is the legal capital for no-par stock. Par value and stated value are normally the bases for crediting capital stock accounts.

Operations of a corporation affect retained earnings in that income is realized or losses are incurred. The corporate income statement must include the amount of earnings per share of common stock. With only one class of stock and no options or warrants, the computation is simple. The computation of earnings per share becomes complicated when convertible preferred or convertible bonds exist or stock options and warrants are present. These other securities give rise to the consideration of common stock equivalents in computing primary earnings per share and must be taken into account when computing fully diluted earnings per share.

Dividends are distributed to stockholders only upon declaration by the board of directors. Cash dividends are based on retained earnings and the availability of cash. Stock dividends may be used to supplement, or to take the place of, cash dividends. Stock dividends are recorded at their fair value in accordance with AICPA rules.

Retained earnings are frequently restricted by corporation borrowing agreements. The restriction reduces the amount of retained earnings available for dividends. Treasury stock purchases also may restrict retained earnings.

A stock split is an exchange wherein a larger number of shares is given to the stockholders in exchange for a smaller number of shares. Paid-in capital usually remains unchanged after the split, so no accounting entry is required. The purpose of a split is to increase the number of shares outstanding so that market price will be reduced per share. With a lower market price, the stock should have a wider market. Stock options and stock rights give the holder the right to purchase capital stock at a certain price and for a certain time. Options have been a popular form of compensation for key executives.

Treasury stock is stock that has been issued once and then reacquired. The treasury stock is held for later reissue. It is not an asset but rather a reduction in owners' equity. Treasury stock is usually carried at cost.

This chapter has introduced most of the significant aspects of stockholders' equity. However, many problems and difficulties have been omitted. Stockholders' equity is an area in which subtleties abound, and fuller coverage can be found in advanced accounting courses.

IMPORTANT TERMS

Articles of incorporation
Charter
Contributed capital
Retained earnings
Pre-emptive right
Preferred stock
Cumulative
Convertible stock
Common stock equivalent
Callable stock
Call price
Common stock
Par value stock
Paid in capital in excess of par (or stated) value
Discount liability
No-par value stock

Legal capital
Stated value
Authorized stock
Issued stock
Outstanding stock
Subscribed stock
Subscriptions receivable
Earnings per share
Primary earnings per share
Common stock equivalents
Fully diluted earnings per share
Stock dividend
Restricted retained earnings
Stock split
Stock option
Stock right or warrant
Treasury stock

QUESTIONS

12-1. Why is the stockholders' equity of a corporation considered a residual claim against net assets?

12-2. What happens when preferred stock is cumulative?

12-3. Are preferred dividends in arrears a liability of the corporation?

12-4. When do dividends become a liability of a corporation? How are dividends payable reported in the balance sheet?

12-5. What is the difference between a cash dividend and a stock dividend? Cover the effect on the balance sheet of each type of dividend from the date of declaration to distribution.

12-6. What is the difference between cash dividends and stock dividends from the viewpoint of the stockholders who receive the dividends?

12-7. What is callable preferred stock? Why might a corporation issue callable preferred?

12-8. What is treasury stock? How does the purchase of treasury stock affect the balance sheet?

12-9. Discuss the concept of earnings per share. In your discussion, include a consideration of common stock equivalents and how these affect earnings per share.

12-10. What is convertible preferred stock? Why might a corporation issue convertible preferred stock?

EXERCISES

12-11. *Corporate entries.* The Bullwink Company is authorized by its charter to issue 10,000 shares of 8% preferred stock, $100 par value, and 100,000 shares of common stock, no-par value. The common has a stated value of $5 per share. You are asked to give journal entries for the following:
  a. Sold 4,000 shares of preferred at $102 per share.
  b. Sold 30,000 shares of common at $35 per share.
  c. Three days later gave James Ellrod 1,000 shares of common in exchange for land. The current market value of the land is not readily obtainable.
  d. The city gave the Bullwink Company land adjoining the Ellrod parcel. This land was recently appraised at $75,000.

(Solution in Appendix B.)

12-12. *Stockholders' equity section.* Prepare the stockholders' equity section of the balance sheet after considering the effects of transactions *a* through *d* in Exercise 12-11.

12-13. *Corporate entries.* Prepare journal entries to record the following transactions of the Blimco Company:
  a. Four thousand shares of $1.50 par value common stock are issued for $110 per share.
  b. One thousand shares of no-par, $5 preferred stock are issued for $60 per share. The stated value of the preferred is $25.
  c. The regular preferred dividend is declared; a $6.50 dividend on common is declared. In your entry distinguish the preferred and the common dividends.

Part IV   Owners' Equity

12-14. *Stock dividend.* Zepler Corporation has 20,000 shares of $2.00 par common stock outstanding. The corporation declares a 5% stock dividend on December 15, payable on January 15 of next year. The fair market value of the stock is $30 per share on December 15. Prepare journal entries to record:
  a. the declaration of the dividend on December 15.
  b. the payment or distribution of the stock on January 15.

12-15. *Earnings per share.* The Dopeler Company had net income of $660,000 in Year 3, including an extraordinary loss (net of income tax) of $198,000. Dopeler has only one class of stock. On January 1, Year 3, there were 150,000 shares outstanding. On October 1, the company issued 60,000 additional shares. Compute the earnings per share that should be reported on the company's income statement for Year 3.

12-16. *Corporate entries, stock dividend, cash dividend.* Give journal entries for the following:

Jan. 1, Year 1	Issued 20,000 shares of $10 par value common stock at $105 per share.
Dec. 15, Year 1	Declared a 4% stock dividend; the market value per share was $120.
Jan. 15, Year 2	Distributed the stock dividend.
July 15, Year 2	Declared a 4% stock dividend; the market value per share was $125.
Aug. 15, Year 2	Distributed the stock dividend.
Dec. 15, Year 2	Declared a cash dividend of $5 per share.

12-17. *Stockholders' equity section.* The following accounts are from the trial balance of the Pipple Company on December 31. You are to prepare the stockholders' equity section of the balance sheet as of December 31.

Premium on preferred stock	$ 64,000
Common stock—stated value $50	600,000
Preferred—8% cumulative, $100 par	1,600,000
Paid-in capital in excess of stated value—common	480,000
Paid-in capital—donation	85,000
Retained earnings	275,000

12-18. *Balance sheet classifications.* By appropriate letter or letters, indicate the balance sheet classification of each item below.

Classifications

  a. Current asset
  b. Current liabilities
  c. Property, plant, and equipment
  d. Paid-in capital or contributed capital
  e. Retained earnings

Items to Be Classified

  1. Par value of stock issued
  2. Subscribed stock
  3. Subscriptions receivable on stock

4. Cash dividend payable
5. Stock dividend to be issued
6. Land received as a donation (two classifications)
7. Dividends
8. Income summary
9. Sale of treasury stock at an amount in excess of its cost

PROBLEMS

12-19. *Corporate entries.* Give journal entries for the following transactions of the Abell Corporation. Show computations.
   a. Sold 10,000 shares of 8%, $100 par value preferred at $110.
   b. Sold 40,000 shares of $5 par common stock at $65.
   c. Issued 5,000 shares of common for land. The value of the land is not readily determinable.
   d. The credit balance in the income summary account is $220,000. (Close the account.)
   e. Declared the stipulated preferred dividend.
   f. Declared a 2% stock dividend on common. The fair value was $75 on this date.
   g. Paid the preferred dividend and issued the common stock dividend.
   h. Bought 1,000 shares of common stock to be held in the treasury. The cost was $80 per share.
   i. Sold 600 shares of the treasury stock for $85 each.

(Solution in Appendix B.)

12-20. *Corporate entries; stockholders' equity.* The Loprin Company stockholders' equity was reported as follows on December 31, Year 1:

Stockholders' equity:

8% preferred stock $100 par: 10,000 shares authorized; 6,000 shares issued		$ 600,000
Common stock $6 par: 100,000 shares authorized; 40,000 shares issued		240,000
Paid-in capital in excess of par—common		2,980,000
Total paid-in capital		3,820,000
Retained earnings*		1,380,000
Total stockholders' equity		$5,200,000

  * Retained earnings of $500,000 are restricted because of long-term borrowing agreements.

   a. Give journal entries for the following transactions that occurred in Year 2.

   Feb. 28   One thousand additional shares of preferred are sold at a premium of $2 per share.
   Mar. 15   The first quarter dividends were passed. (That is, the directors did not declare any dividends.)
   June 15   The second quarter dividends were passed.

Sept. 15	Declared preferred dividends sufficient to bring the company up to date through the first three quarters. No common dividends were declared.
Oct. 15	Paid the preferred dividends.
Dec. 15	Declared the fourth quarter dividends on preferred, and a $1.50-per-share dividend on common. In addition, the directors declared a 5% stock dividend on the common. The fair value of the stock was the same as the price originally received for the common shares (see the stockholders' equity section above).
Dec. 31	The net income for the year was $220,000, as revealed by the closing of revenue and expense accounts to income summary. Close the income summary account.

b. Prepare the stockholders' equity section of the balance sheet as of December 31, Year 2, and a statement of retained earnings for the year ended December 31, Year 2.

12-21. *Dividends.* Using the information below, determine the total dividend and the per share cash dividend for each class of stock for each year and the average per share for each class of stock over the 5-year period.

Capital stock outstanding over the 5-year period: preferred stock, 8% cumulative, $100 par, 2,000 shares issued and outstanding; common stock, par value $10, 20,000 shares issued and outstanding. Total dividends declared in each year: Year 1, no dividends; Year 2, $8,000; Year 3, $20,000; Year 4, $25,000; Year 5, $60,000.

12-22. *Corporate entries; earnings per share.* The Larder Company began the year with 6,000 shares of $4 no-par preferred stock and 150,000 shares of $5 par common stock outstanding. The following occurred during the year (the company's year ends on December 31):

Mar. 1	Issued 60,000 shares of common in exchange for properties worth $1,200,000.
July 1	Issued 4,000 shares of preferred for cash at $52 per share. The preferred stock is no-par and has no stated value.
Sept. 1	The board of directors split the common stock two-for-one. The par value was changed to $2.50 per share.
Dec. 15	Declared cash dividends at the regular dividend rate on preferred and $.80 per share on common.
Dec. 31	The income summary account, credit balance of $712,000, was closed.

Required:

a. Prepare journal entries for each of the above, as required. Show all necessary computations as explanations in the entries.

b. Prepare the bottom part of the income statement for the year, showing net income and earnings per share for the year. Show computations for earnings per share.

(Solution in Appendix B.)

12-23. *Stockholders' equity section.* Using the information below, prepare the stockholders' equity section of the balance sheet as of December 31 for the Brake Company.

8% preferred stock, $25 par: Forty thousand shares were authorized. Ten thousand shares were issued originally at par; another 10,000 shares were issued on July 1 of the past year at $27 per share.

Common stock, $1.50 par: One hundred thousand shares were authorized. Fifty thousand shares were issued originally at $20 per share; a 5% stock dividend was distributed 3 years ago when the market value was $17 per share; an 8% stock dividend was distributed on July 1 of this year when the market value was again $17 per share; 5,000 shares of stock were repurchased for holding in the treasury at a cost of $19 per share on September 1 of this year.

Retained earnings: The retained earnings at the beginning of this year amounted to $2,730,000. Quarterly dividends of $.50 per share on preferred and $.40 per share on common were declared on March 15, June, 15, September 15, and December 15 of this year. The net income for this year was $240,000. The state of incorporation provides that retained earnings must be restricted to the extent of treasury stock holdings.

12-24. *Corporate entries, stockholders' equity section.* The Calisher Company was organized 2 years ago with the following authorized stock: $5 cumulative preferred, $60 par value, 40,000 shares; common, no-par with a stated value of $3 per share, 300,000 shares. The following occurred during the company's first 2 years:

Year 1   Issued for cash 20,000 shares of preferred at par and 100,000 shares of common at $15 per share. Net income for the year was $30,000, so no dividends were declared.

Year 2   Issued 10,000 additional shares of preferred at $62 per share. Net income for the year was $600,000. The board of directors declared sufficient cash dividends to pay the current year's preferred plus arrearages, and a $1.50 per share dividend on common.

Required:

a. Prepare all journal entries required for the two years.
b. Prepare a comparative statement of retained earnings showing Year 2 compared with Year 1.
c. Prepare the stockholders' equity section of the balance sheet as of December 31 of Year 2.

12-25. *Corporate entries, comprehensive.* The Belcher Manufacturing Company was organized early in Year 4. Authorized capital stock was 15,000 shares of $20 par, 8% cumulative preferred stock and 250,000 shares of $5 par value common stock. The following occurred in Year 4 and Year 5:

Jan. 20, Year 4   Sold 12,000 shares of preferred at par and 110,000 shares of common at $28 per share.

March 6, Year 4   The city of Stockwell donated land worth $75,000 to the company.

Dec. 31, Year 4   After the revenue and expense accounts were closed, the debit balance in the income summary account was $45,000. No dividends were declared in Year 4.

Jan. 20, Year 5   50,000 shares of common were sold for cash at $35 per share.

Jan. 31, Year 5	Forty thousand shares of common were exchanged for the plant and equipment of another company. No market value for these assets could be ascertained.
March 1, Year 5	Purchased 2,000 shares of common to be held in the treasury at a cost of $36 per share.
April 8, Year 5	Sold 1,000 shares of the treasury stock at $40.
Sept. 15, Year 5	The stockholders approved an increase in authorized common shares to 500,000 and a reduction in the par value to $2.50. The board of directors then approved a two-for-one split of common stock.
Dec. 15, Year 5	The board of directors declared cash dividends sufficient to pay current and arrears dividends on preferred, and a $1.50-per-share dividend on common. In addition, the board declared a 2% stock dividend on common at a time when the shares had a market value of $20 per share.
Dec. 31, Year 5	After closing revenue and expense accounts for the year, the credit balance in income summary was $1,300,000.

Required:

a. Prepare journal entries as required for the above.
b. Prepare a statement of retained earnings comparing Year 4 with Year 5.
c. Prepare the stockholders' equity section of the balance sheet as of December 31, Year 5.

13

Consolidated Financial Statements and Business Combinations

In earlier chapters, we discussed the concept of the business entity. The business entity is an entity separate and apart from the owners, creditors, and others with whom it deals, and financial statements are prepared from the point of view of that entity. Accounting recognizes a corporation as a legal entity separate from the owners, but in some instances it is useful to recognize something other than the corporation as the accounting entity. A corporation, a separate *legal* entity, may be part of a larger *economic* entity that is composed of several corporations.

Economic entity

A single economic entity may be composed of two or more separate corporations rather than one single corporate entity. This occurs when one corporation controls one or more other corporations by owning a controlling interest in the stock of the other corporations. Why would an entity be made up of several separate corporations? There are several reasons:

1. One corporation may acquire stock of another in order to expand with a minimum of additional capital investment.
2. Separate companies may reduce financial or legal risks.
3. Separate companies may be needed to comply with state corporation legislation.
4. There may be tax advantages.

Ownership of one corporation by another is a fairly common phenomenon in our economy.

405

PARENT-SUBSIDIARY RELATIONSHIP

Parent subsidiary defined

When a single economic operating entity is made up of several corporations, we often have what is called a *parent-subsidiary relationship.* In a parent-subsidiary relationship two or more legally separate corporations exist, but the affiliation of the companies is so close that they represent only one economic entity. The corporation that owns a majority of the capital stock of another is called a *parent company,* and the corporation a majority of whose capital stock is owned by another is called a *subsidiary company.* The capital stock held by a parent company in a subsidiary is referred to as the *majority interest* or *controlling interest;* the remainder of the capital stock, owned outside the "family" group, is called the *minority interest.* The parent company may engage in operations itself or it may be purely a holding company, which engages in no operating activities but instead owns the capital stock of one or more subsidiaries whose activities it supervises.[1] The relationship is further complicated if a parent company controls several subsidiaries that, in turn, control several sub-subsidiaries. Subsidiaries may also hold stock in other subsidiaries and in the parent company. Some exceedingly complicated relationships can exist.

Accounting recognition of the complete, or unified, economic entity is accomplished by combining the financial statements of the separate corporations. The resulting consolidated financial statements disregard the lines between the separate legal entities and present the financial position and operating results of the *economic* entity.

CRITERIA FOR CONSOLIDATED STATEMENTS

When one corporation has a controlling financial interest (defined as over 50% ownership) in other corporations and has administrative control over the activities and resources of the subsidiary, consolidated statements are usually considered necessary for a fair presentation. The balance sheet of the parent company, with the investment in the stock of the subsidiary company shown as an asset, presents an incomplete picture of the operating entity. A more realistic picture of the economic entity is presented by combining the individual assets and liabilities of the two legal entities into a consolidated balance sheet.

Similarly, the income statement of the parent company presents an incomplete analysis of the operations of the entity. It shows the

---

1. The term *holding company* is applied to a parent company whose principal assets consist of stocks of other corporations held for purposes of control. An *investment trust,* on the other hand, holds securities of the other corporations for investment purposes rather than for control.

earnings of the parent company and reflects only the net earnings of the subsidiary or the dividends declared by the subsidiary. An income statement showing the total sales to outside interests, the cost of the goods sold, and the operating expenses of the combined companies offers a more meaningful analysis of the operations of the economic entity.

Thus, the purpose of the consolidated statements is to present the results of operations and the financial condition of separate legal entities substantially as they would appear if the entire economic entity had been operated as one corporation. The figures on the statements do not correspond to those on any one set of books. Rather, they are a combination of the figures on the financial statements of the separate independent legal entities.

Purpose

Occasionally, even in the presence of a controlling financial interest and administrative control, consolidated statements are not appropriate because they would be more misleading than helpful. For example, if it appears that the parent's control is likely to be temporary or the subsidiary is about to be disposed of or if the subsidiary is in bankruptcy or legal reorganization, consolidation would not be desirable.

In the cases where consolidated financial statements are desirable, there are many complicated problems in the construction of the statements that are beyond the scope of this discussion. We believe, however, that anyone who uses corporate financial information will find it useful to know something about the basic principles of consolidation as an aid in interpreting the data contained in consolidated statements. These basic principles of consolidation are described and illustrated in this chapter.

CONSOLIDATED BALANCE SHEET

Corporations keep complete records and prepare financial statements of their own. The separate financial statements of affiliated companies do not, however, give a picture of the economic unit as a whole. A consolidated balance sheet is based on information contained in the separate company balance sheets. It is prepared by combining the elements that appear in the individual statements of the parent and subsidiary companies. In the combining process certain adjustments are made to eliminate duplication and to reflect the assets, liabilities, and stockholders' equity from the viewpoint of a single economic entity.

We begin our consideration of consolidated balance sheets by looking at the acquisition of all the stock of a company by another and by considering consolidated statements prepared at date of acquisition. In the discussion that follows, you should note that duplicated items and items that represent interrelationships between companies are eliminated.

The goal is a single statement that indicates the economic entity's relationships with outside parties.

Ownership Acquired at Book Value

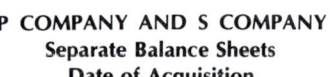

Assume P Company purchases 100% of the capital stock of S Company at the beginning of this year for $100,000 cash, which is equal to the book value of the stock of S Company. Assume also that S's assets have a market value equal to their book value. The separate balance sheets of P Company and S Company, immediately after the acquisition of S Company stock, appear in Example 13-1. The figures in the consolidated balance

EXAMPLE 13-1

P COMPANY AND S COMPANY
Separate Balance Sheets
Date of Acquisition

	P Company	S Company
Current assets	$100,000	$ 50,000
Investment in S Company	100,000	
Plant assets (net)	400,000	70,000
	$600,000	$120,000
Liabilities	$150,000	$ 20,000
Capital stock	300,000	70,000
Retained earnings	150,000	30,000
	$600,000	$120,000

sheet cannot be determined simply by adding each of the items in the separate balance sheets because this would result in a double counting of both assets and equities. The $100,000 investment in S Company stock, which appears as an asset on P Company's balance sheet, represents an interest in S Company's net assets. To include as an asset of the consolidated entity both this stock investment and the underlying net assets of S Company is to count the same economic resources twice. Similarly, there is double counting in the owners' equity. From a consolidated viewpoint, the $100,000 owners' equity of S Company is represented by the capital stock and retained earnings of P Company, since P Company's stockholders own all the outstanding shares of S Company. In this example, the only outside ownership interest in the entity is the interest owned by the stockholders of P Company.

The double counting of assets and equities necessitates an adjustment in preparing a consolidated balance sheet. If we eliminate the ownership equity accounts of S Company against the investment account of P, we will have eliminated the double counting. The remaining account balances can simply be added together and we will have a consolidated balance sheet that portrays the financial position of the economic entity.

It is common practice to use a worksheet to facilitate the preparation of consolidated statements. The worksheet brings together the basic data from the individual companies' statements plus the adjustments, eliminations, and combinations necessary in the consolidation process. The basic procedure in the worksheet used for preparation of a consolidated balance sheet at date of acquisition is to eliminate the owners' equity accounts on the subsidiary's balance sheet against the investment account on the parent's balance sheet[2] and combine the remaining assets and liabilities of the parent and subsidiary. The result is a replacement of the investment account of the parent with the specific assets and liabilities of the subsidiary company. The procedure is illustrated in Example 13-2. The amounts that appear in the last column, headed Consolidated Balance Sheet, would be used for the preparation of the formal consolidated balance sheet. Note that the elimination made on the worksheet is in effect a journal entry in which the equality of the debits and credits is a control feature assuring that equality of the basic accounting equation (Assets = Liabilities + Owners' Equity) will be maintained. Also note that the entries appearing on the worksheet are *not* entered on the books of either company. None of the assets, liabilities, or owners' equity of the individual companies are altered in any way by the consolidation.

Basic worksheet procedure

EXAMPLE 13-2

P COMPANY AND SUBSIDIARY
Worksheet for Consolidated Balance Sheet
Date of Acquisition

	P Company	S Company	Adj. and Elim. Dr.	Adj. and Elim. Cr.	Consolidated Balance Sheet
Current assets	$100,000	$ 50,000			$150,000
Investment in S	100,000			(a) 100,000	
Plant assets (net)	400,000	70,000			470,000
	$600,000	$120,000			$620,000
Liabilities	$150,000	$ 20,000			$170,000
Capital stock—P	300,000				300,000
Retained earnings—P	150,000				150,000
Capital stock—S		70,000	(a) 70,000		
Retained earnings—S		30,000	(a) 30,000		
	$600,000	$120,000			$620,000

(a) Eliminate stock and retained earnings against investment.

---

2. Other adjustments and eliminations may also be required. These are discussed later in the chapter.

Ownership Acquired at More than Book Value

If, in the above example, P Company had acquired all of the capital stock of S Company for $110,000, P would have an investment cost that is $10,000 in excess of the book value of S Company stock. In this situation, the reason for the excess of the investment cost over book value must be ascertained. The cost may differ from the book value because of various factors.

Asset understatement First, inflation or specific price changes may cause the book value (the accounting values, properly recorded) of the subsidiary's assets to be less than the fair market value of those assets. If it can be determined that the price paid for the stock of the subsidiary was greater than the book value of the stock because particular assets were understated, an adjustment of these assets should be made in preparing the consolidated balance sheet.

Example 13-3 illustrates the consolidated workpapers if the extra $10,000 is paid because S Company's plant and equipment assets have a market value of $80,000 rather than $70,000.

EXAMPLE 13-3

P COMPANY AND SUBSIDIARY
Worksheet for Consolidated Balance Sheet
Date of Acquisition

	P Company	S Company	Adj. and Elim. Dr.	Cr.	Consolidated Balance Sheet
Current assets	$ 90,000	$ 50,000			$140,000
Investment in S	110,000			(b) 110,000	
Plant assets (net)	400,000	70,000	(a) 10,000		480,000
	$600,000	$120,000			$620,000
Liabilities	$150,000	$ 20,000			$170,000
Capital stock—P	300,000				300,000
Retained earnings—P	150,000				150,000
Capital stock—S		70,000	(b) 70,000		
Retained earnings—S		30,000	(b) 40,000	(a) 10,000	
	$600,000	$120,000			$620,000

(a) Increase plant assets to market value.
(b) Eliminate stock and retained earnings against investment.

Note that the extra $10,000 appears in the plant assets in the consolidated balance sheet column.

Goodwill A second reason for an excess is that the subsidiary may have a superior earning power that is evidence of unrecorded goodwill or other intangible assets. The parent may be willing to pay for this superior earning power, and this is reflected in the investment cost. Example 13-4 illustrates the excess earning power situation. The excess balance is recorded as "Excess of cost of investment in subsidiary over book value at

EXAMPLE 13-4

P COMPANY AND SUBSIDIARY
Worksheet for Consolidated Balance Sheet
Date of Acquisition

	P Company	S Company	Adj. and Elim. Dr.	Adj. and Elim. Cr.	Consolidated Balance Sheet
Current assets	$ 90,000	$ 50,000			$140,000
Investment in S	110,000			(a) 110,000	
Excess of cost over book value			(a) 10,000		10,000
Plant assets (net)	400,000	70,000			470,000
	$600,000	$120,000			$620,000
Liabilities	$150,000	$ 20,000			$170,000
Capital stock—P	300,000				300,000
Retained earnings—P	150,000				150,000
Capital stock—S		70,000	(a) 70,000		
Retained earnings—S		30,000	(a) 30,000		
	$600,000	$120,000			$620,000

(a) Eliminate stock and retained earnings against investment and set up excess as an asset.

acquisition." It is also often called "Goodwill arising from consolidation," or simply "Goodwill." If the parent paid more than book value for stock in the subsidiary because of the unrecorded intangible assets of the subsidiary, the intangible assets should be recognized in the consolidation process.

Third, the subsidiary may have omissions or errors on its books, or it may have been using excessively conservative accounting practices. Any errors on the subsidiary's books should be corrected before consolidation; if this is not done, any corrections or valuation adjustments may be made on the worksheet and made a part of the process of consolidation.

Omissions or errors

Fourth, the parent company may have been willing to pay more than the fair market value of the subsidiary because the parent recognized the advantages that might arise from the combination of the two firms. The parent may feel that the two firms together will be greater than the sum of the two separately. This part of the excess cost over book value is treated like the $10,000 in Example 13-4 and is part of "Goodwill arising from consolidation" or "Consolidated goodwill."

Whenever an excess of cost over book value of the subsidiary stock appears in consolidation, an effort should be made to determine the cause, which then should provide the basis for allocating the excess to the proper account or accounts in the consolidated balance sheet.

Ownership Acquired at Less than Book Value

If Company P had acquired all the capital stock of S Company for $85,000, it would have an investment cost that is $15,000 less than the book value of the S Company stock. The AICPA's Committee on Accounting Procedure indicates in *Accounting Research Bulletin No. 51*, that "where the cost to the parent is less than its equity in the net assets of the purchased subsidiary, as shown by the books of the subsidiary at the date of acquisition, the amount at which such net assets are carried in the consolidated statements should not exceed the parent's cost."[3] This pronouncement clearly recommends that acquisition cost rather than book value should be the basis of valuation for consolidated balance sheet purposes. Thus, when the cost of a parent's interest in a subsidiary is less than the book value acquired, the accounting treatment of the difference is the reverse of the treatment accorded an excess of cost over book value.

If the difference arises because some asset on the subsidiary's books is overstated or a liability is understated, the credit should be distributed to those accounts as accurately as possible. However, in some circumstances there may be a difference that cannot be completely allocated to specific accounts—this is commonly regarded as a kind of "negative goodwill." If any positive goodwill exists on the statement being consolidated or if any positive goodwill results from consolidation of other subsidiaries, negative goodwill should be deducted from it to the extent possible. If no positive goodwill exists, the unallocated excess of book value over cost might be reported on the consolidated balance sheet as a general valuation account deducted from total assets under a title such as "excess of subsidiary book value over cost."

In Example 13-5, the cost of Company P's investment is $15,000 less than the book value of Company S stock. Assuming that $3,000 of the difference is attributable to understatement of Company S's liabilities, $4,000 is due to overstatement of Company S's plant and equipment assets, and the remaining $8,000 cannot be allocated to specific amounts of the subsidiary, these accounts would be adjusted as indicated in Example 13-5.

Consolidation at Date of Acquisition— Partly Owned Subsidiary

Minority interest

If the parent company does not own all the stock of a subsidiary (but still has control), the equity of the other stockholders in the subsidiary is known as the *minority interest* and appears under this label on the consolidated balance sheet.

To illustrate, assume that P Company acquires an 80% interest in S Company (whose book and market value at the date of acquisition is $100,000) for $80,000 (the book value of the 80% interest P Company is acquiring). The consolidation procedure is illustrated in Example 13-6.

---

3. "Consolidated Financial Statements," *Accounting Research Bulletin No. 51*, paragraph 8.

EXAMPLE 13-5

P COMPANY AND SUBSIDIARY
Worksheet for Consolidated Balance Sheet
Date of Acquisition

	P Company	S Company	Adj. and Elim. Dr.	Adj. and Elim. Cr.	Consolidated Balance Sheet
Current assets	$115,000	$ 50,000			$165,000
Investment in S	85,000			(c) 85,000	
Plant assets (net)	400,000	70,000		(b) 4,000	466,000
	$600,000	$120,000			$631,000
Liabilities	$150,000	$ 20,000		(a) 3,000	$173,000
Capital stock—P	300,000				300,000
Retained earnings—P	150,000				150,000
Capital stock—S		70,000	(c) 70,000		
Retained earnings—S		30,000	(a) 3,000		
			(b) 4,000		
			(c) 23,000		
Excess of book value over cost				(c) 8,000	8,000
	$600,000	$120,000			$631,000

(a) Restate liabilities.
(b) Restate plant assets.
(c) Eliminate stock and retained earnings against investment and set up excess of book value over cost.

EXAMPLE 13-6

P COMPANY AND SUBSIDIARY
Worksheet for Consolidated Balance Sheet
Date of Acquisition

	P Company	S Company	Adj. and Elim. Dr.	Adj. and Elim. Cr.	Consolidated Balance Sheet
Current assets	$120,000	$ 50,000			$170,000
Investment in S	80,000			(a) 80,000	
Plant assets (net)	400,000	70,000			470,000
	$600,000	$120,000			$640,000
Liabilities	$150,000	$ 20,000			$170,000
Capital stock—P	300,000				300,000
Retained earnings—P	150,000				150,000
Capital stock—S		70,000	(a) 56,000		14,000 M
Retained earnings—S		30,000	(a) 24,000		6,000 M
	$600,000	$120,000			$640,000

(a) Eliminate 80% of stock and retained earnings against investment.

The two elements in the Consolidation Balance Sheet column marked *M* represent the 20% interest of the minority stockholders in the

S Company. Since S Company has a stockholders' equity of $100,000, the minority interest's claim against it is $20,000 (20% of $100,000), which is composed of two elements—$14,000 equity in capital stock (20% of $70,000) and $6,000 equity in retained earnings (20% of $30,000). Notice that in the elimination entry the parent's share of the retained earnings of Company S (80% of $30,000) is eliminated against the parent's investment account.

Classification of minority interest

In the formal consolidated balance sheet, the minority interest is commonly presented in, or just above, the parent company's stockholders' equity section. Classification between liabilities and stockholders' equity really avoids any classification at all. Since all the assets and liabilities are consolidated as belonging to the affiliated group as a whole, it appears consistent to treat the minority interest as a specifically designated portion of the ownership equity. From the viewpoint of the entity, the minority interest is like the majority interest—a stockholders' equity interest. In published financial statements the minority interest is usually shown as one account. An example of the stockholders' equity section of a consolidated balance sheet with a minority interest appears in Example 13-7.

EXAMPLE 13-7

Stockholders' Equity:		
Minority interest in stock of Company S		$ 20,000
Majority stockholders' equity		
Capital stock	$300,000	
Retained earnings	150,000	
Majority interest in consolidated stockholders' equity		450,000
Total Stockholders' Equity		$470,000

Accounting for Investment in Subsidiary

After acquisition, the parent company may account for its investment in a subsidiary company by either the *cost* method or the *equity* method.

Cost method. Under the cost method, the investment account is kept at the cost at which the shares of the subsidiary were originally acquired (adjusted, of course, for any additional shares acquired at a later date). As dividends are declared by the subsidiary, the parent's share of those dividends is recognized by the parent as earnings (i.e., dividend income).

Dividends as income

For example, assume P Company acquires an 80% interest in S Company for $80,000 when the net assets of S Company amount to $100,000 (see Example 13-6). During the first year after acquisition, S has earnings amounting to $12,000 and declares and pays dividends of $10,000. Under the cost method, the parent recognizes $8,000 earnings (80% of $10,000) from the subsidiary as follows:

	Debit	Credit
Cash	8,000	
Dividend income		8,000

Thus, at the end of the first year (and at any later time) the investment in S account on the books of the parent has a balance of $80,000 (the original amount of the investment). On the books of the subsidiary, the net assets now amount to $102,000 (the balance at the beginning of the year, $100,000; plus earnings for the year, $12,000; less dividends declared, $10,000).

Equity method. Under the equity method, on the other hand, the parent recognizes its share of the subsidiary earnings as they are earned by the subsidiary. When the subsidiary declares a dividend, the parent treats its share of the dividend as being a return of its investment in the subsidiary. Using the equity method in the above example, P recognizes its share of the subsidiary earnings (80% of $12,000) as follows:

Share of earnings

	Debit	Credit
Investment in S	9,600	
Earnings of subsidiary		9,600

When the subsidiary declares and pays a dividend, the parent treats its share of the dividend (80% of $10,000) as a return of investment:

	Debit	Credit
Cash	8,000	
Investment in S		8,000

Thus, at the end of the first year the balance in the parent's investment account is $81,600 ($80,000 plus $9,600 less $8,000), which is equal to the parent's share of the subsidiary's net assets (80% of $102,000) on that date. The equity method must be used in reporting the investment in an unconsolidated subsidiary in financial statements.

Consolidation after Date of Acquisition

On the individual statements of the parent, the investment in the subsidiary, the earnings of the subsidiary recognized by the parent, and the parent's retained earnings will differ, depending on whether the parent uses the cost method or the equity method in accounting for its investment in the subsidiary. The adjustments and eliminations required in the consolidation process are also different depending on the method the parent uses in accounting for its investment. The consolidated statements, however, are the same in either case. In order to simplify the consolidation process as much as possible, we will illustrate the consolidation process where the parent is maintaining its investment in the subsidiary under the equity method.

The individual balance sheets of P Company and S Company at the end of the first year after acquisition appear in the first two columns of Example 13-8. It is assumed that the earnings of P (including its share of the earnings of S) amount to $60,000 and that P has declared no dividends. The parent's share (80%) of the subsidiary's net worth as of the date of the consolidation is eliminated (leaving the minority interest's share of the subsidiary) against the investment account. Just as there was no excess of cost of investment over book value on the date of acquisition (see Example 13-6), there is none on this date. If there had been a difference between the cost of the investment and the parent's share of the subsidiary's net worth (as in Examples 13-3, 4, and 5) *the same amount* would appear on consolidations at any later date, reduced by any appropriate amortization.

EXAMPLE 13-8

P COMPANY AND SUBSIDIARY
Worksheet for Consolidated Balance Sheet
One Year after Acquisition

	P Company	S Company	Adj. and Elim. Dr.	Adj. and Elim. Cr.	Consolidated Balance Sheet
Current assets	$188,400	$ 57,000			$245,400
Investment in S	81,600			(a)81,600	
Plant assets (net)	390,000	65,000			455,000
	$660,000	$122,000			$700,400
Liabilities	$150,000	$ 20,000			$170,000
Capital stock—P	300,000				300,000
Retained earnings—P	210,000				210,000
Capital stock—S		70,000	(a)56,000		14,000M
Retained earnings—S		32,000	(a)25,600		6,400M
	$660,000	$122,000			$700,400

(a) Eliminate 80% of stock and retained earnings against investment.

Other Adjustments

Up to this point, the only elimination required in the consolidation process has been the elimination of the parent's share of the subsidiary net worth against the investment account of the parent.

Other adjustments are necessary when there are intercompany

obligations. The subsidiary may have declared dividends that have not been paid at the consolidation date; the subsidiary then has a liability, *dividends payable* (part of which is payable to the parent), and the parent has an asset, *dividends receivable*. A parent company may sell goods or buy goods from a subsidiary and treat the resulting obligation as an account receivable or account payable. Intercompany loans are often made between parent and subsidiary. Or one company may invest in bonds issued by the other company. When the financial statements of the two companies are consolidated and intercompany obligations exist, the asset on the books of one and the liability on the books of the other should be eliminated against each other. From the viewpoint of the consolidated entity, neither an asset nor a liability exists—nothing is owed to, or due from anyone outside the economic entity.

Intercompany items

To illustrate the elimination of intercompany obligations, let us assume that P has borrowed $6,000 from S on a note and that the note is unpaid on the balance sheet date. S shows a corresponding receivable for the $6,000 note. The following elimination entry would be made on the consolidated worksheet:

	Debit	Credit
Note payable to S	6,000	
Note receivable from P		6,000

CONSOLIDATED INCOME STATEMENT

A consolidated income statement is prepared by combining the revenues and expenses of the parent and the subsidiary. Revenues and expenses resulting from intercompany transactions are eliminated, and the consolidated net income figure shows the results of operations of the group of companies as though it were a single corporation. Finally, the consolidated net income is divided to show the portion pertaining to the minority interest and the portion pertaining to the majority interest.

To illustrate, we have entered the individual revenues and expenses of P Company and S Company in the first two columns of Example 13-9 (see page 418). Notice that the items have been arranged in a balancing form by adding net income to expenses. Note also that P's 80% interest in S's income is shown among P's revenues.

Assume that during the year, S borrowed money from P. The interest on this loan amounted to $1,800. From a consolidated viewpoint, this $1,800 (which is included in P's interest revenue and in S's interest expense) represents neither revenue nor expense. Hence, the $1,800 (revenue and expense) is eliminated in adjustment (a). Similarly, assume that Company S sold goods (costing $1,500) to Company P for $2,100.

EXAMPLE 13-9

P COMPANY AND SUBSIDIARY
Worksheet for Consolidated Income Statement
for the First Year after Acquisition

	P Company	S Company	Adj. and Elim. Dr.	Adj. and Elim. Cr.	Consolidated Income Statement
Credits:					
Sales	$200,000	$80,000	(b)2,100		$277,900
Interest revenue	2,000		(a)1,800		200
Subsidiary's earnings	9,600		(c)9,600		
	$211,600	$80,000			$278,100
Debits:					
Cost of goods sold	$107,000	$40,000		(b)2,100	$144,900
Operating expenses	44,600	25,500			70,100
Interest expense		2,500		(a)1,800	700
Net income – P	60,000				60,000
Net income – S		12,000		(c)12,000	
	$211,600	$80,000			
Minority interest in income			(c)2,400		2,400M
					$278,100

(a) Eliminate intercompany interest.
(b) Eliminate intercompany sales.
(c) Eliminate parent's share of S's income and set up minority interest.

These goods were in turn sold by P to someone outside the affiliated group for $2,400. From the viewpoint of the economic entity, only one sale (for $2,400) was made—thus, $2,100 should be eliminated from the sales of Company S. Also, the cost to the economic entity of the goods sold outside the entity was $1,500. Hence, $2,100 needs to be eliminated from Company P's cost of goods sold. This elimination is accomplished by entry (b).[4]

Last, in entry (c), the earnings of S are allocated between P and the minority interest. Since P's share of the earnings of S is already included in P's income, the debit for P's share is made to the earnings of subsidiary account. To include both the earnings of the subsidiary and the individual revenues and expenses of S in consolidated income would be double counting of these earnings.

---

4. If the goods had not been sold by P, but remained in the inventory at the date of consolidation, a more complex elimination would be required. From a consolidated viewpoint, profits are made only by sales to outsiders. Hence, any intercompany profit on goods remaining in inventory must be eliminated. The elimination affects the balance sheet valuation of inventory and the sales and cost of goods sold in the income statement.

LIMITATIONS OF CONSOLIDATED STATEMENTS

The objective of consolidated statements is to give interested parties an overall view of the financial position and operating results of a group of affiliated companies. They should not, however, replace the financial statements prepared by each individual company. Creditors must rely on the resources of the debtor corporation—they could be misled if they relied on a consolidated statement that combined the figures of a debtor corporation on the brink of insolvency with those of a company in good financial position. Dividends legally can be declared by a company only from its own retained earnings. Thus the minority interest in a subsidiary can best judge the earning power of the subsidiary and the dividend possibilities of the subsidiary by an analysis of the subsidiary's own statements. These are only a few of the instances in which separate statements of each company are needed. The consolidated statements are useful primarily to the management and owners of the parent company—the majority interest in the affiliated group.

The discussion of consolidations in this text is limited; we have only scratched the surface of this complicated area of accounting. Further discussion is found in advanced accounting texts.

BUSINESS COMBINATIONS—PURCHASE VERSUS POOLING

In recent years many corporations have been combined to obtain various advantages, including economies of large-scale operations, financial stability arising from diversification of operations, and tax savings. There are two ways of handling combinations in financial accounting—as a *purchase* or as a *pooling of interests*. The accounting differences between these methods are in the valuation of assets and the amount of retained earnings for the emerging corporation.

The accounting treatment for the combination depends on whether a significant part of the old ownership interests is eliminated in the combination (a purchase) or whether the ownership interests of the old corporations continue substantially unchanged in the new business entity (a pooling of interests). A purchase is the acquisition of one company by another company—the acquired company is thus eliminated. A pooling of interests, on the other hand, is the merging of two companies—both merge into the new company and thus retain some continuity of existence.

Purchase

Under the purchase concept, the total assets of the company *bought out* (acquired) are valued at the cost to the acquiring company, measured by the cash given or (if consideration other than cash is given) by the fair market value of other consideration given. Individual assets are usually measured at the fair market value of the assets acquired. Retained earnings of the acquired company disappear and are not part of the retained earnings of the emerging corporation.

Accountants agree that the acquisition of the stock of a company solely for cash or other assets is properly classified as a purchase. In each of the parent-subsidiary illustrations earlier in the chapter we assumed that the stock of the subsidiary was acquired by the parent in exchange for cash. Accordingly, in each instance the acquisition was handled as a purchase. Any difference between the cost of the stock and the book value (net assets) of the parent's interest was treated as an adjustment of individual assets or liabilities or assets as a whole.

Effects of pooling

Under the pooling-of-interests concept, on the other hand, the book values of the assets of *both* combining companies (if stated in accordance with generally accepted accounting principles) are carried forward and used as the accounting basis of the assets of the emerging company. The retained earnings of the constituent corporations are combined and carried forward to the surviving corporation. Thus, in a pooling of interests amounts on the records of the pooling companies are combined and no revaluation takes place.

If one company acquires another company through an exchange of shares (stock for stock), the transaction is sometimes interpreted as a purchase and sometimes as a pooling of interests, depending mainly on the desires of management. In *Accounting Research Bulletin No. 48*, issued in 1957, the AICPA stated that the accounting treatment of a business combination should depend on the circumstances. If the combination is in effect a selling out, in which owners of one company are disposing of their interests to another company, it is a purchase. If, on the other hand, there is in reality a combining of interests, the combination should be treated as a pooling of interests. The circumstances to be considered in deciding whether a given business combination should be treated as a purchase or a pooling included (1) relative size of the combining companies, (2) continuity of ownership, and (3) continuity of management.

Because of pressures exerted by businessmen and accountants, accounting practice gradually moved away from the guidelines that were established in *Bulletin No. 48*. The criteria gradually faded away, and in the 1960s most business combinations effected through the exchange of stock were classified according to the desires of management. This was a sad chapter in the story of financial accounting in the United States.

Pooling of interests

Because of inflation and other factors, the original cost of assets is often lower than the fair market value of those assets at the time of the business combination. Under the pooling-of-interests concept, the assets are valued at original cost (adjusted for depreciation). Hence, in later years the cost of those assets charged against revenue (for example, depreciation expense) tends to be less, and net income more, under the pooling-of-interest treatment than it would be under the purchase treatment. Pooling-of-interests accounting has therefore been a popular way for expansion-minded companies to account for their acquisitions. Example 13-10 will clarify the point. Note especially the sizable differences in income and earnings per share between the two methods.

EXAMPLE 13-10

Expando Company acquires Absorbo Company by issuing 10,000 shares of its $100 par stock, presently worth $250 per share in the market. Absorbo's net assets on the date of acquisition have a book value of $1,400,000, but they are worth $2,300,000 on the market. The difference is primarily in the plant and equipment assets. Depreciation based on the fair value of Absorbo's assets is $200,000 per year. Income statements of Expando and Absorbo before the acquisition are as follows:

	Expando	Absorbo
Sales	$5,000,000	$1,000,000
Expenses:		
Depreciation	400,000	100,000
Other expenses	4,000,000	700,000
	4,400,000	800,000
Net income	$ 600,000	$ 200,000
Shares outstanding	50,000	
Earnings per share	$12.00	

After the acquisition, only one income statement will be prepared for the enlarged Expando Company. Assume that operations in the next period duplicate the results before the acquisition. Below is an income statement on a pooling-of-interests basis contrasted with the statement that would have occurred if purchase accounting had been followed:

	Pooling Basis	Purchase Basis
Sales	$6,000,000	$6,000,000
Expenses:		
Amortization of goodwill		5,000*
Depreciation	500,000	600,000
Other expenses	4,700,000	4,700,000
	5,200,000	5,305,000
Net income	$ 800,000	$ 695,000
Shares outstanding	60,000	60,000
Earnings per share	$13.33	$11.58

* $2,500,000 − $2,300,000 = $200,000 goodwill.
$200,000/40 years = $5,000 per year amortization

During the sixties, the entire subject of purchase vs. pooling was a matter of controversy. In 1970, in an effort to settle the disagreement and to correct abuses, the Accounting Principles Board of the AICPA issued Opinion No. 16, "Business Combinations." This opinion was quite controversial. As finally issued, it represented a compromise between op-

APB opinion on business combinations

posing factions. The compromise, however, was much more satisfying to those who support pooling than to those who see no basis in theory for the pooling idea. In the opinion, the APB concluded that

> the purchase method and the pooling of interests method are both acceptable in accounting for business combinations, although not as alternatives in accounting for the same business combination. A business combination that meets specified conditions requires accounting by the pooling of interests method. A new basis of accounting is not permitted for a combination that meets the specified conditions, and the assets and liabilities of the combining companies are combined at their recorded amounts. All other business combinations should be accounted for as an acquisition of one or more companies by a corporation. The cost of an acquiring corporation should be determined by the principles of accounting for the acquisition of an asset. That cost should then be allocated to the identified individual assets acquired and liabilities assumed based on their fair values; the unallocated cost should be recorded as goodwill.[5]

The APB stated that the purchase method must be used in those "business combinations effected by paying cash, distributing other assets, or incurring liabilities."[6] Further, in a business combination involving an exchange of stock for stock, combinations which meet *all* of certain conditions *must* be accounted for under the pooling of interests method. The conditions required in order to have a pooling of interests have to do with the autonomy and independence of the combining companies, the manner of effecting the combination, and the absence of planned transactions that are "inconsistent with the combining of entire existing interests of common stockholders."[7] All other combinations, according to the APB, should be accounted for under the purchase method.

Opinion No. 16 was the result of compromises between the various factions in the controversy about business combinations. The opinion cooled the heated debate that had been raging, and it eliminated some of the accounting abuses that had been occurring. The successor to the APB, the Financial Accounting Standards Board, because of shortcomings in the opinion, has found it necessary to explore the issues in business combinations again. Hammering out a completely satisfactory approach to this problem area will take years.

---

5. "Business Combinations," *Accounting Principles Board Opinion No. 16*, August 1970, paragraph 8.
6. Ibid., paragraph 15.
7. Ibid., paragraphs 46 to 48. The specific requirements for meeting the conditions are detailed and complex.

SUMMARY

This chapter discussed some of the basic principles of consolidated financial statements. When one corporation (a parent) owns another (a subsidiary), the two legally separate entities are treated as one economic entity. If the subsidiary is not fully owned but is still effectively controlled, consolidation is still appropriate. If the ownership interest of the parent is acquired at book value, subsidiary capital accounts are eliminated in the consolidation process against the investment account on the books of the parent. A minority interest remains if there is less than 100% ownership. If the ownership interest was acquired at more or less than book value, the elimination of subsidiary capital accounts leaves a balance that may be the result of overvaluing or undervaluing specific assets, that may be the result of errors or omissions, or that may be goodwill (a payment for excess earnings capacity).

Investments in subsidiaries may be carried at cost, in which case the only recorded income is dividends received, or they may be carried on the equity basis, in which case the parent recognizes its share of subsidiary earnings as they are earned by the subsidiary and treats dividends as a return of its investment. Consolidation after the year of acquisition was illustrated for a company using the equity method.

In a consolidation, intercompany profits and losses, intercompany revenues and expenses, and intercompany assets and obligations must be eliminated so that the financial statements indicate only transactions with parties outside the economic entity.

Business combinations and the controversy involving purchase versus pooling of interests were also briefly discussed. In a purchase, assets acquired are recorded at their current value and no retained earnings of the acquired company are carried forward. In a pooling of interests, assets are carried forward at the book values at which they appeared on the records of the acquired company, and retained earnings of the acquired company are merged with amounts on the books of the surviving company.

IMPORTANT TERMS

Legal entity
Economic entity
Parent-subsidiary
Minority interest
Consolidated statements
Cost method
Equity method
Intercompany items
Business combinations
Purchase
Pooling of interests

Part IV   Owners' Equity

QUESTIONS

13-1. What is the difference between a *legal entity* and an *economic entity*?

13-2. What is meant by each of the following terms:
- **a.** Parent company
- **b.** Subsidiary company
- **c.** Holding company
- **d.** Majority interest
- **e.** Minority interest

13-3. List and briefly discuss reasons why a company might wish to acquire control of another company.

13-4. Why are consolidated statements prepared?

13-5. What are the limitations of consolidated financial statements?

13-6. In a parent-subsidiary relationship where the parent owns less than 100% of a subsidiary's stock, the consolidated balance sheet includes all of the subsidiary's assets. Explain why.

13-7. Why may a parent's cost of an investment in a subsidiary be greater than, or less than, its interest in the book value of the subsidiary's stock?

13-8. How is the minority interest in a subsidiary reported on a consolidated balance sheet?

13-9. In accounting for business combinations, what is the distinction between a purchase and a pooling of interests?

13-10. Why might management be anxious to report a particular business combination as a pooling of interests rather than a purchase?

EXERCISES

13-11. *When to consolidate.* For each of the following situations indicate whether the preparation of consolidated statements would be desirable. Give reasons.
- **a.** National Dry Goods, Inc., a large retail chain, owns 45% of the Local Dry Goods Co., a small retail store.
- **b.** The Rocky Railroad owns 70% of the stock of the Shakey Railroad Corporation, which is currently being operated by a receiver until a final reorganization is approved by the courts.
- **c.** The Madonna Flour Mill, Inc., a large national company with assets of $20 million, owns 90% of the stock of Better Bakeries, Inc., a local concern with assets of $300,000.

13-12. *Consolidated goodwill and minority interest.* On September 30 of the current year, the owners' equity section of the balance sheet of Dodds Company showed the following balances:

Capital stock	$100,000
Retained earnings	60,000
Total	$160,000

On this date the Carlton Corporation purchased 100% of the stock of the Dodds Company for $160,000. What would be the amount (if any) of consolidated goodwill and of the minority interest on a consolidated balance sheet immediately after the acquisition?

13-13. *Consolidated goodwill and minority interest.* Refer to Exercise 13-12. What would be your answer if the Carlton Corporation had purchased 100% of the stock of Dodds Company for $185,000?

13-14. *Consolidated goodwill and minority interest.* Refer to Exercise 13-12. What would be your answer if the Carlton Corporation had purchased 100% of the stock of Dodds Company for $155,000?

13-15. *Consolidated goodwill and minority interest.* Refer to Exercise 13-12. What would be your answer if the Carlton Corporation had purchased 90% of the stock of Dodds Company for $144,000?

13-16. *Consolidated goodwill and minority interest.* Refer to Exercise 13-12. What would be your answer if the Carlton Corporation had purchased 90% of the stock of the Dodds Company for $165,000?
(Solution in Appendix B.)

13-17. *Consolidated goodwill and minority interest.* Refer to Exercise 13-12. What would be your answer if the Carlton Corporation had purchased 90% of the stock of Dodds Company for $170,000, and it was recognized that plant and equipment assets of Dodds were undervalued by $12,000?
(Solution in Appendix B.)

13-18. *Entry for consolidation.* On December 31 of the current year, the Angus Company acquired 100% of the stock of Joyce Corporation for $1,500,000. Net worth of the Joyce Corporation on that date was

Capital stock	$1,000,000
Retained earnings	600,000
	$1,600,000

Prepare (in general journal form) the elimination entry that would be made on the consolidated working papers.

13-19. *Entry for consolidation.* Refer to the information in Exercise 13-18. If Angus had acquired 90% of the stock of Joyce Corporation for $1,500,000, what would the elimination entry be?

13-20. *Computation of minority interest and consolidated goodwill.* On November 30 of the current year, K Corp. acquired 80% of the stock of the L Corp. for $11,000,000. The book value of the L Corp. stock on that date was $12,000,000. Plant and equipment assets of L were undervalued by $600,000 on November 30.

Required:
a. What is the amount of the minority interest that would appear on the

consolidated balance sheet on the date of acquisition? Where on the statement would it appear?

b. What is the amount of consolidation goodwill that would appear on the consolidated balance sheet on the date of acquisition?

PROBLEMS

13-21. *Goodwill and minority interest.* On December 31 of the current year the Greek Corporation purchases 70% of the Alpha Company for $455,000; 80% of the Beta Company for $425,000; and 90% of the Gamma Company for $500,000. The condensed balance sheets of the three acquired companies on the date of acquisition are as follows:

	Alpha	Beta	Gamma
Assets	$800,000	$600,000	$700,000
Liabilities	$150,000	$100,000	$120,000
Capital stock	360,000	475,000	390,000
Retained earnings	290,000	25,000	190,000
	$800,000	$600,000	$700,000

Required:

a. What is the amount of goodwill involved in the acquisition of the Alpha Company?

b. What elimination entry would appear on the consolidation work-sheet for consolidation of Beta Company with the Greek Corporation?

c. What amount would appear on the consolidated balance sheet for the minority interest in the Gamma Company? For goodwill?

13-22. *Consolidated balance sheet.* Assuming that Adam Co. acquired 100% of the stock of Box Co. for cash on December 31 of the current year, prepare a consolidated balance sheet on that date. The condensed balance sheets of Adam and Box on December 31 of the current year appear as follows:

	Adam Co.	Box Co.
Current assets	$ 200,000	$ 50,000
Investment in Box Co.	220,000	
Plant assets (net)	600,000	230,000
	$1,020,000	$280,000
Liabilities	$ 280,000	$ 70,000
Capital stock	600,000	150,000
Retained earnings	140,000	60,000
	$1,020,000	$280,000

13-23. *Consolidated balance sheet.* Refer to the information in Problem 13-22. Assuming that Adam Co. acquired 90% of the stock of Box Co. (for $220,000 cash) on December 31 of the current year, prepare a consolidated balance sheet on that date.

13-24. *Consolidated income statement.* Company P uses the equity method in accounting for its investment in its wholly owned subsidiary, Company S. From the following selected data, prepare a consolidated income statement for the parent company and subsidiary S.

	Company P	Company S
Service revenue		$ 60,000
Sales	$520,000	190,000
Cost of goods sold	310,000	160,000
Operating expenses	175,000	65,000
Dividends declared	20,000	5,000
Earnings of Co. S	25,000	

$30,000 of P's sales were to S. None of the goods sold by the parent to the subsidiary remained in the subsidiary's inventory at the end of the period. The service revenue of S includes $20,000 charged to P for computer services. P records these services as an operating expense.
(Solution in Appendix B.)

13-25. *Consolidated income statement.* Company W uses the cost method in accounting for its investment in its 90% owned subsidiary, Company X. During the year, X made a loan to W Company. The interest on the loan was $18,000. None of the goods sold by W to X remained in X's inventory at the end of the year. From the following selected data, prepare a consolidated income statement.

	W	X
Sales to outsiders	$900,000	$300,000
Sales to subsidiary	100,000	
Cost of goods sold	500,000	180,000
Operating expenses	300,000	60,000
Interest revenue		18,000
Interest expense	24,000	
Dividend income	4,500	
Dividends declared	20,000	5,000

13-26. *Business combination—pooling of interests.* The Rocky Road Company and the Smooth Trail Company entered into a business combination on December 31. Immediately before the combination, their individual balance sheets were as follows:

	Rocky Road	Smooth Trail
Current assets	$ 5,000,000	$150,000
Property, plant, and equipment	8,000,000	350,000
Total assets	$13,000,000	$500,000
Liabilities	$ 3,000,000	$100,000
Capital stock	6,000,000	200,000
Retained earnings	4,000,000	200,000
Total equities	$13,000,000	$500,000

Both parties agreed that the accounts of Smooth Trail were stated in conformity with generally accepted accounting principles, but the fair market

value of the plant assets was $600,000. Accordingly, 2,600 shares of Rocky Road Company $100 par value ($250 market value) stock was given to the shareholders of Smooth Trail in exchange for their stock. Smooth Trail Company will be dissolved as a separate corporation and will be operated as a division of Rocky Road Company. Assuming that the combination is viewed as a pooling of interests, prepare a balance sheet for the entity resulting from the business combination.
(Solution in Appendix B.)

13-27. *Business combination—purchase.* Refer to the information in Problem 13-26. Assuming that the combination does not meet the criteria for a pooling of interests and is therefore viewed as a purchase, prepare a balance sheet for the entity resulting from the business combination.
(Solution in Appendix B.)

13-28. *Business combination—pooling of interests.* On October 1 of the current year, Thursday Company and Friday, Inc., agreed on a merger of the two companies. It was agreed that Thursday Company would issue 2,000 shares of its $25 par value ($60 market value) common stock for all of the 1,000 shares outstanding of Friday, Inc. Friday, Inc., will be dissolved and will be operated as a division of Thursday Company. It was agreed by both companies that while the assets of Friday, Inc., are stated in accordance with generally accepted accounting principles, the fair market value of these assets is $35,000 greater than their book value. Just prior to the combination the balance sheets of the two companies appeared as indicated below. Assuming that the combination is deemed to be a pooling of interests, prepare a balance sheet that reflects the merger of the two companies.

	Thursday Company	Friday, Inc.
Current assets	$ 225,000	$ 50,000
Property, plant, and equipment	775,000	75,000
	$1,000,000	$125,000
Liabilities	200,000	40,000
Capital stock	350,000	50,000
Retained earnings	450,000	35,000
	$1,000,000	$125,000

13-29. *Business combination—purchase.* Refer to the information in Problem 13-28. Assuming that the combination does *not* meet the criteria for a pooling of interests and hence is to be viewed as a purchase, prepare a balance sheet that reflects the merger of the two companies. You may assume that the understated assets are part of the property, plant, and equipment.

14

Sole Proprietorships and Partnerships

Although the corporation is the most important form of business organization in the United States, sole proprietorships and partnerships occupy an important place in the economy and, in terms of sheer numbers, are much more common than corporations. Sole proprietorships are usually simple in their organization. Partnerships, on the other hand, can be complicated. In general, however, neither form involves the complex accounting problems often found in corporations. One of the most important accounting problems in sole proprietorships and partnerships involves maintaining the distinction between the enterprise and its owners. In both forms, the owners are more closely involved in enterprise activities than are most stockholders, and the businesses are not legally separate entities.

SOLE PROPRIETORSHIPS

The owners' equity accounts for a sole proprietorship are quite simple. The account that identifies the owner's investment is usually called the capital account. Thus, if J. B. Smith invests $30,000 cash in a business, the entry is as follows:

	Debit	Credit
Cash	30,000	
J. B. Smith, capital		30,000

Part IV   Owners' Equity

Drawing account

A separate account may be used for withdrawals by the owner. Suppose that Smith takes out $200 for personal expenses. The entry is as follows:

	Debit	Credit
J. B. Smith, drawing	200	
Cash		200

The drawing account is closed out at the end of the year to the capital account. Any profits (or losses) for the year are also closed out to the capital account. Usually, any withdrawals of assets from the enterprise are charged to the drawing account. The owner may think of these withdrawals as salary or as interest on the investment. For example, a sole owner might withdraw assets as compensation for time spent working in the business and record the transaction as a salary expense. There is, of course, no reason why the owner should not do this. But it should be recognized that the resulting "expense" is in some respects different from other expenses of the business. Example 14-1 shows the results for the Smith Company for a year.

EXAMPLE 14-1

SMITH COMPANY
Income Statement for the Year

Sales		$100,000
Cost of sales		60,000
Gross margin		40,000
Salary of owner	$12,000	
Operating expenses	17,000	
Interest on Smith's investment	3,000	32,000
Net income		$ 8,000

Taxable income

For tax purposes, Jerry Smith, the owner, will be taxed on an income of $23,000 in the year, which consists of the $8,000 net income, the $12,000 salary, and the $3,000 interest. He will be taxed on this amount regardless of the amount he has withdrawn from the business. That is, it makes no difference whether Smith has withdrawn $12,000 (the salary), $15,000 salary plus interest), $23,000, or nothing at all. It is up to the owner whether he wants to withdraw this income or plow it back into the business. It also is of no concern to the taxing authorities whether the owner wants to call some of these amounts salary or interest instead of just lumping them in one figure called net income.

A more informative income statement for the Smith Company might appear as in Example 14-2.

EXAMPLE 14-2

SMITH COMPANY
Income Statement for the Year

Sales	$100,000
Cost of sales	60,000
Gross margin	40,000
Operating expenses	17,000
Net income	$ 23,000
Allocated as follows:	
Salary	$12,000
Interest on capital	3,000
Balance	8,000
Total	$ 23,000

Comparability

This type of statement would allow Smith (1) to make comparisons with other enterprises and (2) to evaluate the income he is receiving. If Smith is comparing his results with those of a corporation of the same size, he should probably deduct the $12,000 salary to arrive at an income figure suitable for comparison. Another alternative is to add the manager's salary back to the corporation's net income before comparing it to the Smith Company net income. Corporations can and do deduct salaries to owners or managers as expenses. If Smith wishes to evaluate the performance of the company for the year, the net income should be analyzed into its components. If Smith's efforts would have yielded a salary of $12,000 in an alternative job, and if his capital could have earned $3,000 in alternative investments, then these amounts should be deducted in order to arrive at the pure profit from operating the business.

Useful statements

The accountant's responsibility in a sole proprietorship is to provide financial statements that will help the owner to control operations, evaluate results, and make comparisons with other enterprises. Because the level of sophistication of owners varies, the accountant must tailor the statements carefully to fit the needs of the particular owner involved. There is a premium on imagination in financial reporting for many smaller businesses. For example, it is often appropriate to divide the expenses on the income statement into fixed expenses and variable expenses (those that change as sales volume changes). This may aid the owner in seeing the relationship between volume and profit and may be more helpful than the traditional breakdown into cost of goods sold, selling expenses, general expenses, and incidental expenses.

Taxes

Finally, a word about taxes. A sole proprietorship is not taxed as a business entity. Instead, the owner reports any income from the business on his or her personal tax return and must pay a personal income tax. This procedure may yield a tax advantage to a single proprietorship as

Part IV   Owners' Equity

compared to a corporation. A corporation must pay a corporate income tax, and the stockholders must also pay a personal income tax when earning are distributed in the form of dividends.

PARTNERSHIPS

Accounting for partnerships is more complicated than accounting for sole proprietorships because of the need to keep track of each partner's interest in the enterprise. Further difficulties arise when partners withdraw from the partnership or new partners are admitted after the partnership has been in operation for some time.

Partnerships are a fairly common type of business organization. Among the largest partnerships are international CPA firms. A large firm may have hundreds of partners, several thousand of employees, and revenues from services of over $500,000,000 per year.

In accounting for partnerships, a capital account and a drawing account are set up for each partner. The capital accounts are credited for the investments of the respective partners. The drawing accounts are debited for any withdrawals by the partners during the year. The partners' shares of the earnings for the year are credited either to the drawing accounts or to the capital accounts. At the end of the year, the drawing accounts are usually closed to the respective partners' capital accounts.

The distribution of profits or losses is based on the partnership agreement, which should specify the following:

Partnership agreement

1. The nature and purpose of the business
2. The names and capital contributions of the partners
3. The rights, functions, and duties of the partners
4. The allowable drawings of the partners
5. The manner in which profits and losses are to be distributed among the partners (if the agreement is silent about distribution of profits and losses, they are distributed equally)
6. The procedure for settling disputes among the partners

The agreement is vital if the partnership is to continue in operation. Without a carefully drawn agreement, the partnership form of operation may become an effective means of destroying well-established ties of friendship.

Division of profits

The agreement on distribution of earnings may be simple—for example, "equally among the partners" or "sixty percent to A, thirty percent to B, and ten percent to C." Provisions for distribution are sometimes more complicated because of a desire to recognize certain significant features of some partners' contributions to the business. Suppose that A, B, and C are partners. The original capital contributions were as follows:

432

A	$80,000
B	20,000
C	30,000

A and C are not very active in the company, but B devotes full time to the enterprise. In this case, it is inequitable to divide profits equally, yet no other fractional basis suggests itself. The problem might be handled by a provision in the agreement such as the following:

Profits are to be divided as follows:
1. All partners are to be allowed 8% interest on their capital investments.
2. B is to be allowed $10,000 for salary.
3. Remaining profits and losses are to be divided equally.

If the partnership earned a profit of $42,000, the provision would be applied as follows:

	A	B	C	Total
1. Interest at 8%	$ 6,400	$ 1,600	$2,400	$10,400
2. Salary to B		10,000		10,000
Total				20,400
3. Balance divided equally	7,200	7,200	7,200	21,600
Total	$13,600	$18,800	$9,600	$42,000

The balance in item 3 is the remaining amount necessary to make the total equal the income for the period. The entry would be as follows:

	Debit	Credit
Income summary	42,000	
A. Capital		13,600
B. Capital		18,800
C. Capital		9,600

To distribute profit for the year, per schedule.

The provisions of the partnership agreement should always be carried out, regardless of the amount of profit. Suppose that the profit in the above example was only $6,000, instead of $42,000. The distribution would be as follows:

	A	B	C	Total
1. Interest at 8%	$6,400	$ 1,600	$ 2,400	$10,400
2. Salary to B		10,000		10,000
Total				20,400
3. Balance divided equally	(4,800)	(4,800)	(4,800)	(14,400)
Total	$1,600	$ 6,800	$(2,400)	$ 6,000

Notice that the balance in this case is a negative figure. The entry would be as follows:

	Debit	Credit
Income summary	6,000	
C. Capital	2,400	
A. Capital		1,600
B. Capital		6,800

To distribute profit for the year, per schedule.

In this case, one of the partners ends up with a negative amount for the year, and this amount is debited to his account.

Drawings in a partnership are handled like those in a sole proprietorship. When a partner takes assets out of the business the entry is as follows:

	Debit	Credit
B. Drawing	4,500	
Cash		4,500

At the end of the period the drawing accounts are disposed of by closing them out to the partners' capital accounts. Suppose C's drawing account has a debit balance of $14,300 at the end of the period. The entry to close the drawing account is as follows:

	Debit	Credit
C. Capital	14,300	
C. Drawing		14,300

To close C's drawing account.

In a similar manner, all drawing accounts are closed to the respective capital accounts.

Partnership financial statements usually include a schedule of changes in partners' capital. This schedule lists the share of profits and the amount of withdrawals for each partner. It is similar in purpose to the statement of retained earnings for a corporation. Example 14-3 is a sample schedule of changes.

EXAMPLE 14-3

Changes in partners' capital

	M	N	O	Total
Capital, beginning of year	$45,000	$37,000	$25,000	$107,000
Add additional investments			5,000	5,000
Add share of profits for year	20,000	15,000	15,000	50,000
Deduct drawings	(17,000)	(16,000)	(13,000)	(46,000)
Capital, end of year	$48,000	$36,000	$32,000	$116,000

One point should be noted about profit sharing agreements. Even though some amounts given to partners may be called *salaries* or *interest*, they are not expenses. In general, any amounts allocated to partners are distributions of profits rather than expenses. The earlier discussion of amounts allocated to the owner in a sole proprietorship is applicable here as well.

Note also that the partnership does not pay any tax itself. Instead, each partner is taxed personally on his or her share of the profits (whether the share is called salary, interest, or simply net income). The amounts withdrawn by the partners do not affect the amounts on which they pay taxes.

The last point mentioned above brings up an important point that needs some additional emphasis. In partnerships two types of distribution take place—distribution of profits and distribution of assets. These two types of distribution should be clearly distinguished. A distribution of profits, or income, is simply an allocation of amounts earned during the period to the partners' capital accounts. No assets are given to any of the partners in connection with the allocation. The distribution of assets takes place when assets are actually transferred to partners, usually in the form of cash drawings. Income may be more or less than the amount of the drawings, and the amount of income distributed to individual partners may be more or less than the amount of assets distributed to them during a period. These two types of distribution are essentially independent of each other, although distribution of assets may be based on income shares.

Distribution of profits and assets

ADMISSION OF NEW PARTNERS

When a new partner is admitted to a partnership, the partnership agreement has to be revised, and the new partner's interest has to be recorded.

One way for a new partner to enter a partnership is by purchasing part or all of the interest of one or more of the present partners. If Rapp and Serl are partners and have capital balances of $40,000 and $80,000, respectively, and Tage buys one quarter of the interests of each partner by paying them $10,000 and $20,000, respectively, the following entry is needed on the partnership books:

	Debit	Credit
Rapp, capital	10,000	
Serl, capital	20,000	
Tage, capital		30,000

It might well happen that Tage pays more than $30,000 for a quarter interest, particularly if the partnership has been successful. Each partner might be paid a larger amount, but the entry on the partnership books need not change, because a quarter interest would still be transferred. The cost of Tage's investment is the amount actually paid to the other partners, but there is no reason for the partnership books to reflect this amount. This is similar to the situation in which a person buys a share of stock from another. The corporation simply records the transfer of ownership—it does not receive or pay cash.

Technically, any change in membership dissolves the partnership. Most changes in partnership personnel are accomplished without changing the regular operations of the business, however. For example, when a large CPA firm promotes one of its staff to partner, there is usually no significant change in operations, financial condition, or policies. Changes can be more radical, but many personnel changes do not call for any changes in account balances other than to record the new partner (or eliminate the retiring one).

Some changes in partnership personnel involve investments directly into the partnership, as illustrated in Example 14-4.

EXAMPLE 14-4

Coe invests $50,000 cash for a one-third interest in the partnership of Amos and Bocar. The partners have $100,000 of net assets recorded on their books. The entry to admit Coe is as follows:

	Debit	Credit
Cash	50,000	
Coe, capital		50,000

Note in the example that the new partner, Coe, invests an amount that is exactly equal to one third of the new partnership's net assets (which are $100,000 + $50,000).

It is possible, of course, that the investment of a new partner may differ from the percentage interest obtained. If the partnership is anxious to obtain additional capital, the new partner may get the same interest with a smaller contribution. If the partnership has been successful and the new partner is anxious to be admitted, he or she may pay a premium for the interest acquired. The accounting for these situations may involve recording goodwill, as illustrated in the Examples 14-5 and 14-6.

EXAMPLE 14-5

Farrow invests $40,000 cash for a one-third interest in the partnership of Dorn and Edie. The partners have $100,000 of net assets recorded on their books and share profits equally. They agree to recognize goodwill. The entry to admit Farrow is as follows:

	Debit	Credit
Cash	40,000	
Goodwill	10,000	
Farrow, capital		50,000

The old partners have two thirds of the capital, which is "worth" $100,000; therefore, Farrow's one-third interest is worth $50,000. The goodwill is the difference between this $50,000 and the actual cash contributed by Farrow. In Example 14-5, Farrow received an interest worth $50,000 by investing just $40,000 cash. The difference was debited to goodwill.

Goodwill

EXAMPLE 14-6

Inger invests $60,000 cash for a one-third interest in the partnership of Goe and Hoe. The partners have $100,000 of net assets recorded on their books. They share profits equally. They agree to recognize goodwill. The entries to admit Inger are as follows:

	Debit	Credit
Cash	60,000	
Inger, capital		60,000
Goodwill	20,000	
Goe, capital		10,000
Hoe, capital		10,000
To distribute goodwill implied by Inger's investment to partners in profit ratio.		

In Example 14-6, the excess investment by the new partner implies that goodwill exists in the partnership. If a one-third interest is worth $60,000, then the other two thirds must be worth $120,000. $20,000 of goodwill is recorded and credited to the old partners' capital accounts.

The recording of goodwill in Examples 14-5 and 14-6 is based on the ideas that (1) an excess amount credited to a new partner is evidence that the partner is bringing some excess values to the enterprise and (2) an excess amount paid to join a partnership indicates that some excess values exist in the enterprise. These ideas may have little validity in some instances.

Goodwill need not be recorded when new partners are admitted. An inequity in capital balances might be tolerated. Another possibility is that the excess amount might be charged to the old or new partner's capital accounts (in the profit and loss ratio). For example, using the data from Example 14-5, if Farrow is to be credited with a one-third interest but no goodwill is to be recorded, the following entry could be made:

No goodwill recorded

	Debit	Credit
Cash	40,000	
Dorn, capital	3,333	
Edie, capital	3,333	
Farrow, capital		46,666

Part IV Owners' Equity

Farrow is credited with one third of the new total assets of $100,000 + $40,000 cash = $140,000. The extra $6,666 is provided by the old partners in the profit and loss ratio.

Asset revaluations

Another recording method is possible when a new partner pays more or less than the book value for his or her share of the partnership. It may be that the book value of the assets does not indicate their market value. When the differences are substantial, assets should be revalued, instead of goodwill being recorded. For example, if Inger in Example 14-6 is willing to invest $60,000 because buildings are undervalued by $20,000, the following entries could be made:

	Debit	Credit
Building	20,000	
Goe, capital		10,000
Hoe, capital		10,000
To revalue building.		
Cash	60,000	
Inger, capital		60,000

Further discussion of these types of complications can be found in advanced accounting texts.

DISSOLUTION OF A PARTNERSHIP

When it becomes necessary to dissolve a partnership, some interesting accounting problems may present themselves. Examples 14-7 and 14-8 indicate the nature of the problems. In these examples we assume that Abe, Bay, and Coe are partners in the ABC Company, which has the following balance sheet:

ABC COMPANY
Balance Sheet, December 31

Assets		Liabilities	
Cash	$ 60,000	Accounts payable	$ 30,000
Buildings (net)	150,000		
		Owners' Equity	
		Abe, capital	15,000
		Bay, capital	60,000
		Coe, capital	105,000
Total assets	$210,000	Total liabilities and owners' equity	$210,000

The partners share profits equally.

EXAMPLE 14-7

The partners sell the building for $180,000, pay all debts, and dissolve the partnership. The necessary entries are as follows:

	Debit	Credit
Cash	180,000	
Building		150,000
Gain		30,000
Gain	30,000	
Abe, capital		10,000
Bay, capital		10,000
Coe, capital		10,000
Distribute gain in profit and loss ratio.		
Accounts payable	30,000	
Cash		30,000
To pay debts.		
Abe, capital	25,000	
Bay, capital	70,000	
Coe, capital	115,000	
Cash		210,000
Pay partners in amount of their capital balances.		

Note that the gain or loss on sale is distributed to the partners on the basis of the profit and loss ratio. Note also that creditors are paid before the partners and that *partners receive assets in accordance with their capital balances.*

EXAMPLE 14-8

The partners sell the building for $90,000, pay all debts, and dissolve the partnership.

	Debit	Credit
Cash	90,000	
Loss on sale	60,000	
Building		150,000
Sale of building.		
Abe, capital	20,000	
Bay, capital	20,000	
Coe, capital	20,000	
Loss on sale		60,000
Distribute loss in profit and loss ratio.		
Accounts payable	30,000	
Cash		30,000
Pay debts.		
Cash	5,000	
Abe, capital		5,000
Payment by Abe of deficit balance.		
Bay, capital	40,000	
Coe, capital	85,000	
Cash		125,000
Distribute cash in amount of capital balances.		

If Abe is unable to pay his deficit, the other partners will record a loss of $5,000 ($2,500 each) and receive less cash. It should be noted that Abe will then personally owe the other partners the $5,000.

The foregoing examples are rather simple cases. More complex situations, such as installment liquidations, are covered in advanced accounting texts.

CONVERTING A PARTNERSHIP TO A CORPORATION

Partners can convert a partnership into a corporation by filing articles of incorporation with the state and issuing shares of stock to the partners in agreed-upon amounts. The corporation can use the old partnership books or set up a new set of books. Assets may be revalued to current market values at the time of incorporation. Any gains or losses that occur will affect the partners' capital accounts and the number of shares each partner receives. For example, suppose the ABC Company from Example 14-7 decides to incorporate. The Abco Corporation is to issue shares with a $100 par value. The partners agree that the building is worth $180,000. The partners are to receive 1 share of stock for each $100 of capital balance. Examples 14-9 and 14-10 illustrate two ways to record the conversion.

EXAMPLE 14-9

Abco is to use the partnership books:

	Debit	Credit
Building	30,000	
Abe, capital		10,000
Bay, capital		10,000
Coe, capital		10,000
To write up building and distribute gain to partners.		
Abe, capital	25,000	
Bay, capital	70,000	
Coe, capital	115,000	
Capital stock		210,000
To distribute 250 shares to A, 700 to B, and 1,150 to C.		

EXAMPLE 14-10

Abco Corporation is to use a new set of books. ABC partnership entries:

	Debit	Credit
Building	30,000	
Abe, capital		10,000
Bay, capital		10,000
Coe, capital		10,000
To write up building.		

Stock of Abco	210,000	
Accounts payable	30,000	
Cash		60,000
Building		180,000
To record transfer of assets and liabilities to Abco in exchange for stock.		
Abe, capital	25,000	
Bay, capital	70,000	
Coe, capital	115,000	
Stock of Abco		210,000
To record distribution of stock to partners.		

Abco corporation entries:

	Debit	Credit
Cash	60,000	
Building	180,000	
Accounts payable		30,000
Capital stock		210,000
To record assets and liabilities and capital stock issued to A, B, and C.		

THEORETICAL ISSUES

The preceding discussion has been oriented toward mechanics, indicating how to account for various events that take place in partnerships. A few conceptual issues have appeared, and these deserve some further attention. The conceptual issues are triggered by questions such as these:

- When should goodwill be recorded?
- When is it proper to increase the value of assets held?

These questions are related to a more basic question: When is it appropriate and necessary to revalue assets and to record a corresponding gain or loss? Despite its obvious importance, this question is not answered very clearly in present financial accounting theory.

Asset revaluations

There is no question that asset value changes are recognized when the assets themselves are exchanged. But does a change in partners call for new asset valuations? An ownership change in a corporation does not generally call for a change in recorded asset values (if the whole corporation is sold, of course, assets should be revalued). But a change in ownership in a partnership causes a more fundamental change in the nature of the business entity because ownership and operation are not separated in a partnership as they are in a corporation. Assets invested by new partners are recorded at their current values. Furthermore, partners who withdraw should be paid on the basis of current values of assets and the business as a whole. It is only fair to value the ongoing investments of the other partners on the same basis. This may entail revaluing assets from cost to current market values. It may also involve recording goodwill if there is superior earning power.

But revaluation of assets held is difficult and involves estimates. Intangibles such as goodwill are particularly difficult to quantify. As a result, there is a general tendency to avoid revaluations if at all possible. Also, in the case of changes in partners, an exchange transaction does not clearly exist—when a new partner joins the business, the assets are not sold to the newly formed partnership. Accordingly, the consensus in current practice is probably that assets should not be revalued when partners enter or withdraw. A substantial minority of accountants, however, would recommend revaluation when partners are changed. The difference of opinion exists for two reasons: (1) partnership changes are a very ambiguous type of transaction and (2) generally accepted accounting principles do not spell out the situations in which revaluation is appropriate. Note that if assets were consistently valued at current market prices on financial statements, the problem we have been discussing would not exist. It is the cost basis of accounting, with its stringent rules about retaining acquisition price, that leads to the difficulties.

PARTNERSHIP FORM VERSUS CORPORATE FORM

We conclude this chapter by considering the distinguishing features of partnerships as contrasted with corporations. We have already indicated that a partnership does not pay income tax, whereas a corporation does. A list of other distinguishing features follows:

Partnership	*Corporation*
Life limited by life of owners.	Life not limited by life of owners.
Ownership rights not transferable without consent of other partners.	Ownership rights freely transferable.
Not taxed as a separate entity.	Subject to corporate tax.
Unlimited liability.	Liability of owners limited to their capital investments.
Created by contract among individuals and not extensively regulated.	Operated under authority granted by state and regulated extensively. Not a natural person.
Each partner can generally act for partnership and enter into binding contracts.	Stockholders delegate their power to board of directors and corporate management. Stockholders may not enter into contracts for the company.

In the case of a partnership, unlimited liability means that each partner is fully responsible for the business acts of his copartners. This responsibility extends to the personal fortunes of each partner. Thus, if the partnership loses a lawsuit, each partner's personal assets, as well as the partnership's assets, may be in jeopardy. In a corporation, the owners can lose only their investment in the company; their personal fortunes cannot be touched.

Potentially, corporations can raise larger amounts of capital than partnerships. Instead of searching for specific partners who are willing to risk their personal fortunes, the corporations can sell shares of stock to anyone who cares to invest. Large corporations often have 100,000 stockholders or more. It is highly unusual for a partnership to have as many as 1,000 partners.

Because of the feature of unlimited liability, creditors of partnerships have more security than creditors of corporations, other things being equal. Therefore, if a corporation and a partnership have the same total owners' equity, the partnership will probably have an easier time borrowing money.

Because of the differing features of the two types of organizations, in some situations the partnership form will be more desirable, and in others the corporate form will be preferred. The choice of form is limited in some professions, particularly certified public accounting and law, because in many states they may not legally use the corporate form of organization.

SUMMARY

Accounting problems of sole proprietorships are simple. The major difficulties are separating business activities from the proprietor's personal affairs and preparing statements that can be useful in evaluation and decision making.

Partnerships pose some interesting accounting problems. The partnership agreement must be carefully drawn to avoid disputes. Provisions on division of profits in the agreement are always carried out, so the agreement should carefully specify the desires of the partners. Allocating amounts for capital investments and services contributed can make the allocations more equitable. Distribution of profits must be distinguished from distribution of assets to partners. Allowable distributions of assets should be covered by the agreement. When partners are admitted to a partnership and their payment differs from a pro rata share of the partnership's net assets, goodwill may be implied by the transaction. Techniques for recording admissions were discussed. In dissolutions, gains or losses that occur during the dissolution process are distributed to the partners' capital accounts in the agreed profit ratio. Assets are always distributed on the basis of capital balances, not the profit ratio. Gains or losses that occur during the process of converting a partnership to a corporation are distributed to partners in the profit or loss ratio.

The major theoretical issue in partnership accounting is the question whether assets held by partnership should be revalued when there is a change in partners. This issue has not been resolved under present accounting principles.

The chapter concluded with a discussion of the features of a partnership contrasted with those of a corporation. Partners have unlimited liability, whereas stockholders do not. On the other hand, partnerships are not subject to a separate income tax as are corporations.

The sole proprietorship and the partnership are important forms of business organization. We continue to emphasize corporations in this book, however, because of their vastly greater influence on modern economic activity.

IMPORTANT TERMS

Sole proprietorship *Goodwill*
Drawing account *Partnership dissolution*
Partnership *Asset revaluations*
Partnership agreement *Unlimited liability*
Distribution of profit

QUESTIONS

14-1. Define a *partnership*.

14-2. What difficulties are encountered in comparing the operating results of a sole proprietorship or partnership with those of a corporation? How can these difficulties best be overcome?

14-3. What services can the accountant perform in connection with formation of a partnership?

14-4. List some of the important accounting aspects that should be specified in a partnership agreement.

14-5. When the composition of a partnership changes, should assets be revalued? Discuss.

14-6. Distinguish between distribution of profits or income and distribution of assets.

14-7. What are the advantages of the partnership form of organization over the corporate form? List each advantage and discuss briefly.

14-8. What is the rationale for the recording of goodwill when a new partner is admitted upon payment of a disproportionately large investment?

14-9. What are the advantages of the corporate form of enterprise organization over the partnership form? List each advantage and discuss briefly.

14-10. How is a debit balance in a partner's capital account handled in a partnership dissolution?

EXERCISES

14-11. *Sole proprietorship.* The income summary account of the Bill Jones Service Station was debited with total expenses of $40,000 and credited with total revenue of $49,000.

Required:
  a. Give the remaining closing entry (or entries) if the business is a sole proprietorship and the owner has a drawing account with a $8,200 debit balance.
  b. What was the amount of the profit or loss for the year?

14-12. *Partnership profit allocation.* A, B, and C operate a partnership. Their agreement provides that C is to receive a salary of $250 per month. The partners also are to be allowed interest of 10% on their original investment. Original investments were as follows: A, $50,000; B, $40,000; C, $5,000. Give the entries to distribute this year's $16,000 profit. Show all computations and label clearly.

14-13. *Partnership profit allocation.* A, B, C, and D are partners. For the year, their income is $3,200. Make an entry or entries to distribute this profit, considering the following information: A is to be allowed 5% interest on his $180,000 investment; B and C are to be allowed salaries of $6,000 and $8,000 respectively; and remaining profits and losses are to be shared in a 4:2:1:5 ratio.
(Solution in Appendix B.)

14-14. *Admitting partner.* Brown and Friend are partners with investments of $60,000 and $40,000, respectively. They share profits equally. Schultz acquires a one-third interest in the partnership by investing $60,000. Record Schultz's admission, assuming that goodwill is to be recorded.

14-15. *Admitting partner.* Refer to Exercise 14-14. Record Schultz's admission, assuming no goodwill is to be recorded.

14-16. *Admitting partner.* Refer to Exercise 14-14. Record Schultz's admission, assuming that the partnership building is undervalued by $10,000 and that goodwill will be recorded.

14-17. *Admitting partner.* Anderson and Heap are partners with investments of $60,000 and $40,000, respectively. Rogers acquires a one-third interest in the partnership by investing $40,000. Record Rogers's admission, assuming that goodwill is to be recorded.

14-18. *Admitting partner.* Refer to Exercise 14-17. Record Rogers's admission, assuming the partnership receivables are overvalued by $10,000 and that no goodwill is to be recorded.

14-19. *Transfer of interest.* Newman and Oldster are partners with capital balances of $90,000 and $60,000, respectively. They agree to admit Teener to the partnership. Teener will buy part of the interest of each partner by paying them directly. Record Teener's admission on the partnership books if

a. Teener pays Newman $30,000 cash and Oldster $20,000 cash for one third of each of their interests.

b. Teener pays Newman $60,000 cash and Oldster $32,000 cash for half of each of their interests.

14-20. *Partnership dissolution.* Larson and Jenson decide to dissolve their partnership, which has the following trial balance:

	Dr.	Cr.
Cash	5,000	
Receivables	30,000	
Equipment (net)	26,000	
Accounts payable		5,000
Larson, capital		26,000
Jenson, capital		30,000

Give entries for the following transactions:
a. Receivables are sold for $28,000.
b. Equipment is sold for $22,000.
c. Liabilities are paid.
d. Cash is distributed to the partners.

PROBLEMS

14-21. *Sole proprietorship comparisons.* James Ready operates a hardware store. He wants to compare his operating results for the year to those of the hardware trade association's typical store. Ready could earn $12,000 working for someone else. He owns the building in which his store is located, and it is fully depreciated. Its rental value is $8,000 per year. Ready's capital investment is $150,000. His income statement and the typical income statement are below. Compare Ready's operation with the typical hardware store. Support your comparison with appropriate computations.

Income Statements

	James Ready	Typical Store
Sales	$100,000	$150,000
Cost of goods sold	48,000	75,000
Gross margin	52,000	75,000
Salaries of employees	8,000	15,000
Manager's salary	0	15,000
Rent	0	10,000
Interest on capital (8%)	0	16,000
Other operating expenses	17,000	18,000
Net income	$ 27,000	$ 1,000

14-22. *Sole proprietorship comparisons.* Hans Hammer, who operates a drugstore, wishes to compare his results to those of two other drugstores, one a sole proprietorship and the other a corporation. Data for the enterprises are shown below.

	Investment	Net income
Hammer	$ 80,000	$24,000
Jones (sole proprietor)	120,000	11,000
Smith Corporation	100,000	5,000

Hammer works full time in his store. Jones does not work in her store; she pays a manager $16,000 to run the store. Smith Corporation is run by its president, who works full time and is paid $10,000. Smith Corp. also pays corporate taxes of $3,000. The president of Smith could earn $16,000 working for another druggist. Prepare data that will aid Hammer in making appropriate comparisons.

14-23. *Partnership profit allocation.* Andrews and Bailey are partners whose capital accounts are shown below. A profit of $10,000 was earned by the partnership during the year ended December 31.

Andrews Capital		
	Jan. 1	30,000

Bailey Capital			
Oct. 1	4,000	Jan. 1	20,000
		July 1	2,000

For each of the agreements listed below show each partner's share of the profit, including allowances for interest and salaries when they are involved.

a. All profits and losses are distributed on the basis of the investments at the beginning of the year.

b. Andrews is allowed a salary of $10,000 per year and Bailey is allowed $8,000. Partners are allowed interest at 10% on their capital at the beginning of the year, and the remaining profit is to be divided equally. Salaries are not considered expenses, and no entries have been made for them.

c. No provision for the distribution of profits and losses is made in the partnership agreement.

14-24. *Partnership profit.* Stonewall Jackson is a partner in the firm of Lee, Longstreet, and Jackson. The partners have agreed that Lee and Jackson are to receive salary allowances of $18,000 and $12,000, respectively; that no interest is to be allowed; and that remaining amounts of profit or loss are to be shared among Lee, Longstreet, and Jackson in the ratio of 3:1:2. The partners made no drawings during the year; Jackson's statement of partner's capital shows a balance of $29,300 on January 1 and $30,100 on December 31 (after closing out income summary). You ascertain that Jackson invested $2,000 on March 16. Compute the partnership profit for the year showing all computations.

14-25. *Partnership changes.* Doe, Mee, and Noe are partners in the Domino Company. They share profits and losses in the ratio of 3:2:1 and have capital balances of $50,000, $40,000, and $30,000, respectively. Give entries for each of the following separate cases:

a. Poe is admitted, acquiring a quarter interest by investing $34,000 in the company. Record goodwill.

b. Poe is admitted, acquiring a quarter interest by investing $44,000 in the company. Record goodwill.

c. Poe is admitted, acquiring a quarter interest by investing $44,000 in the company. No goodwill is to be recorded.

d. Poe is admitted, acquiring all of Mee's interest by paying him $47,000.

e. Poe is admitted, acquiring a 50% interest in the company by paying each partner for half of his investment. He pays Doe $55,000, Mee $44,000, and Noe $33,000.

(Solution in Appendix B.)

14-26. *Partnership dissolution.* The Bowsprit partnership has the following balances on March 31, at which time the partners decide to dissolve the partnership.

BOWSPRIT
Balance Sheet
as of March 31

Assets		Liabilities and Owners' Equity	
Cash	$ 2,000	Accounts payable	$ 42,000
Receivables	30,000	Bow, capital	12,000
Inventory	80,000	Spry, capital	55,000
Plant and equipment—net	60,000	Ital, capital	63,000
	$172,000		$172,000

The partners share profits in a 2:2:1 ratio.

During the dissolution, the following occurs:

a. Receivables are sold to a factoring concern for $22,000.

b. The inventory is sold for $63,000.

c. Plant and equipment are sold for $50,000 cash.

d. Liabilities are paid, cash is distributed to partners.

Required:

Record the dissolution of the partnership. Partners with deficits can be assumed to pay amounts owed to the partnership.

(Solution in Appendix B.)

14-27. *Partnership to corporation.* The Brown, Brook, and Natif partnership sells its entire business on October 1 to the Trout Company for 1,500 shares of Trout stock worth $100 per share. The partners share profits equally.

BROWN, BROOK, AND NATIF
Balance Sheet
as of September 30

Assets		Liabilities and Owners' Equity	
Cash	$ 1,000	Accounts payable	$ 15,000
Receivables	25,000	Brown, capital	60,000
Inventory	95,000	Brook, capital	40,000
Plant and equipment—net	14,000	Natif, capital	20,000
	$135,000		$135,000

Required:
a. Give entries to close the partnership books, including the entry to distribute the stock to the partners.
b. Give the entry to record the purchase on Trout's books. Assume that inventories are actually worth $125,000. Trout's stock has an $80 par value.

PART V

Accounting Theory and Analysis

15

Accounting and Changing Prices

Accounting has changed and developed over time in response to changes in the economic environment. The changes have been gradual and evolutionary for the most part. In times when the economy operates smoothly and steadily, pressures for change in accounting tend to be minimal. When the economic environment is in a state of upheaval there tend to be more pressures for change in accounting. The last 15 years have not been noteworthy for their stability. The ferment of the times has affected all areas of life, including accounting. This chapter deals with the effects of changing prices (an important product of an unstable economic environment) on accounting.

LIMITATIONS OF HISTORICAL COST VALUATION

Accounting in North America has traditionally been based on historical cost valuations, with little attention being paid to the changing value of the measuring unit. This valuation approach works well when conditions are stable. However, when prices change, some warts and blemishes appear on the face of historical cost accounting.

One important limitation of historical costs is that their relevance to economic decisions is questionable in a time of changing prices. In the early 1970s oil prices quadrupled in a very short time. An oil company that had an inventory of 100,000 barrels at a historical cost of $2 a barrel could not use this cost figure in decisions. The relevant price for decisions was the current market price of the oil. To take another example, the cost of using a machine (expressed through depreciation) bought at a cost of $40,000 some years ago should probably be related to the current cost of the machine or at least to the cost of the machine adjusted for the effects of inflation since it was acquired. Plant and equipment assets are carried at historical costs, and both the assets and the depreciation expense on the assets are expressed in terms of dollars at the time the assets were acquired. The effects are that (1) the balance sheet includes old cost figures for important assets, and (2) the depreciation expense on the income statement is expressed in old dollars but is related to revenues expressed in current dollars. The situation becomes a problem when the original cost is significantly different from current costs because of changing prices.

Objectivity

Historical cost valuations are defended on the ground that they are objective—that is, the amount can be verified by reference to an invoice. This is an important factor, especially when the threat of litigation is a feature of the environment. However, the advantage of objectivity is not as significant when prices move rapidly. There comes a time when it is better to be subjectively relevant rather than objectively irrelevant. Most accountants agree that historical cost loses its usefulness in a time of extreme price changes. The argument tends to center on these questions: (1) How extreme must changes be before historical cost must be abandoned? and (2) What alternative approaches should accountants adopt?

GENERAL AND SPECIFIC PRICE CHANGES

One complication is that not all prices move together. In a time of general inflation the price of a particular item or service may move up more or less than the general price level. In fact, prices of some items may actually decline while prices in general are increasing. Two types of price changes can be distinguished: general and specific price changes.

General price indexes

General price changes are changes in the average price level of the country, measured by indexes such as the Consumer Price Index (CPI) and the Gross National Product Implicit Price Deflators (GNP Deflators). These indexes attempt to measure the average change in prices and, in effect, give a measure of the general change in the value of the dollar. Knowing the price index at two different points of time allows one to restate prices at the two points of time in terms of equivalent amounts of purchasing power. For example, John Anderson, a salesman, makes commissions of $12,000 in Year 1 when the price index is 100. He makes commissions of $20,000 in Year 5 when the index is 150. His earnings can best be compared by restating both amounts in terms of the same price level.

Earnings	In Year 1 Dollars	In Year 5 Dollars
Year 1	$12,000	$18,000†
Year 5	13,333*	20,000

*$20,000 × 100/150 †$12,000 × 150/100

Note that the change in salary can easily be converted from Year 1 to Year 5 dollars. The comparison of earnings in purchasing power units indicates that Anderson's basic earnings have increased only a little over 10% (11.1%) rather than the 67% increase in nominal earnings. To speak in economic terms, Anderson's *real income* increased only 11%.

Specific price changes are changes in prices of individual goods or services. The change in the price of a quart of milk is an example. Specific prices may change more than, the same as, or less than, the general price level. For example, during a period in 1975 the price of copper was decreasing even though the general trend of prices was upward. A copper producer was in a bad situation, with selling prices down and many costs trending upward. Users of copper, on the other hand, found themselves paying less for this material at a time when most goods were costing more.

Arguments are usually lively and protracted about whether general price-level changes or specific price changes should be recognized in accounting. To some extent the arguments are unnecessary. If it is once granted that historical cost valuations have serious shortcomings, it can be argued that both types of price changes should be recognized. Recognition of general price-level changes can be rationalized as an attempt to standardize the unit of measure in accounting in terms of purchasing power. Recognition of changes in specific prices is an attempt to deal with the specific economic context in which operations take place and to reflect the current economic impact of the goods and services with which the entity deals. If only specific prices are considered, some erroneous conclusions can be drawn. Consider Example 15-1.

Rationale for recognition

EXAMPLE 15-1

On January 1 the Burton Company acquires land for $30,000. During the year the general price level moves from 100 to 110. On December 31, the land has a market value of $35,000.

If only the general price level is considered, the land will be carried at $33,000 on December 31 ($30,000 + 10%). No gain or loss will be shown — the restatement to $33,000 is simply a recognition of a change in the value of the dollar.

If only the specific price change is considered the land will be carried at $35,000 on December 31 (current market price). A gain of $5,000 (perhaps classified as unrealized) will be shown.

If both types of price changes are recognized, the land will be carried at $35,000 on December 31. The gain will be only $2,000, the excess of the specific price increase over the increase in the general price level.

In Example 15-1 it can be readily seen that neither general nor specific price changes are sufficient by themselves. Recognition of both is necessary. The general desirability of recognition of both types of price changes is the view we favor. In addition, we believe that price changes have been so radical in recent years that historical cost valuation is inadequate. Many accountants disagree with this conclusion, seeing no need for a radical change in accounting. You are asked to consider the situation carefully and reach your own conclusions.

ALTERNATIVE VALUATION APPROACHES

The problem of specific price changes is difficult to handle within the framework of present generally accepted principles. Suggested solutions to the problem involve alternative valuation approaches that abandon significant elements of current principles. In fact, a number of valuation methods are put forth by their advocates as more appropriate basic approaches even in a time of relative price stability.

We will first address suggested ways of dealing with specific price changes. In a following section we will discuss a suggested approach to handling general price level changes.

Discounted Cash Flow (DCF)

Economists generally agree that the value of an asset is best measured by the expected net future money flow from the asset, discounted by an interest factor. We saw in chapter 8 that this is the basis on which bond investments are valued on the market. Economists hold that all assets derive their value from this same basic valuation procedure.

EXAMPLE 15-2

An apartment building will produce net cash flows from rentals (rentals less outlays) of $6,000 per year for 10 years and can be sold for $50,000 at the end of that time. The value of the building today is computed by discounting these future cash flows at an appropriate interest rate. Assume 10% is an appropriate rate.

Present value of building:
  $6,000 per year × 6.145 (Appendix C, Table III) $36,870
  $50,000 selling price × .3855 (Appendix C, Table II) 19,275
    Present value at 10% $56,145

The income flowing from the asset should, according to economic theory, be 10% of the asset balance. In the first year the income would be 10% ×

56,145, or $5,614. Since $6,000 is collected and only $5,614 is income, the remaining $386 is recovery of investment. Income the second year would be 10% × the net remaining investment ($56,145 − 386) = $5,576.

The valuation of assets on the basis of discounted cash flows involves a number of difficulties. These difficulties revolve around

Difficulties

1. Identification of cash flows
2. Timing of cash flows
3. Determination of an appropriate interest rate

Identification of cash flows is difficult because of the interrelatedness of assets with each other. Cash flows from an apartment building can perhaps be separately identified, but cash flows from a factory building are a different story. In many cases, identification involves trying to determine the results produced by an individual part of a complex whole.

The timing problem is also severe. The cash flows have to be predicted and associated with particular periods. Specific projections for some years in the future are inexact at best. At times the problems of prediction are almost insurmountable, and much guesswork is involved.

Another important problem concerns the interest rate. The interest rate appropriate to various entities varies, depending on alternative opportunities and risk. Other parties evaluating the apartment building in Example 15-2 may use a higher interest rate than 10% and thus arrive at a lower present value. They may also differ in their forecasts of expected cash flows.

Another problem can arise if expectations change after an asset is acquired. Example 15-3 illustrates.

EXAMPLE 15-3

After two years, the present value of the building in Example 15-2 is $55,335, computed as follows:

Cost		$56,145
Year 1 Net cash flow	6,000	
Less 10% income	5,614	
Return of capital		−386
Value at end of Year 1		$55,759
Year 2 Net cash flow	6,000	
Less 10% income	5,576	
Return of capital		424
Value at end of Year 2		$55,335

This can also be computed as follows:

$6,000 per year × 5.335 (Appendix C, Table III) =	$32,010
$50,000 selling price × .4665 (Appendix C, Table II) =	23,325
Total present value	$55,335

(*Continued*)

Example 15-3 (Cont.)

At the end of the second year, the expectations of future rent decline to $5,200 per year and the expected selling price at the end of year 10 declines to $40,000 because of an influx of rowdy pensioners into the area. The new present value at the end of Year 2 is as follows:

Present value
$5,200 per year × 5.335 (Appendix C, Table III) = $27,742
$40,000 selling price × .4665 (Appendix C, Table II) =   18,660
Total present value at 10% $46,402

The decline in present value is $55,335 less 46,402 = $8,993.

Capital gain or loss

An increase or decrease in present value because of changes in interest rates or expected cash flows is called a *capital gain or loss*. It would be an item of income or loss in the period in which it occurs. When considerable uncertainties exist, as they do in our economy, capital gains and losses appear frequently.

The problems of discounted cash flow valuation prevent its adoption as a general valuation method in accounting, except in cases where cash flows are relatively certain, such as bond investments and most liabilities (discounted cash flow is the proper valuation method for liabilities in general). Does this mean that DCF is largely of theoretical interest? To some extent, yes. However, an understanding of DCF valuation is important because it is the means by which parties operating in the market reach decisions on whether or not to invest (or disinvest) in assets. A market price is established by buyers and sellers operating with their own sets of expectations of cash flows and their own interest rates. The market price presumably is established at an amount that reflects the consensus of these expectations. Thus it can be said that there is a tendency for market prices to be set on a DCF basis. The fact that market prices change, and sometimes change quite rapidly, indicates that the valuations at any one point in time are not necessarily valid at other times.

DCF and market price

Discounted cash flow valuation probably could not be generally applied to accounting. It remains as an ideal toward which many theorists believe we should strive. It thus provides a benchmark to which other approaches can be compared.

Net Realizable Value (NRV)

Defined

Net realizable value is defined as the amount of cash that can be obtained from an asset through sale — it is the sales proceeds less costs of disposal, such as selling costs. A valuation system based on NRV would value assets at net selling prices in the market at the time statements are prepared.

EXAMPLE 15-4

A delivery truck is purchased at the beginning of Year 1 for $6,900. Life is estimated at 4 years, with $900 salvage value. Using historical cost with straight-line depreciation, the book value at the end of Year 1 is as follows:

Cost	$6,900
Less accumulated depreciation	1,500
Book value	5,400
Depreciation expense	$1,500

When NRV is used, the selling price of the truck at the end of Year 1 must be determined. Assume it is $4,600.

Selling price end of Year 1	$4,600
Original cost	$6,900
Cost of usage in Year 1 (depreciation)	$2,300

In Example 15-4 the difference between NRV and historical cost valuation can easily be seen. The asset would be carried in the statement at $4,600. Instead of being determined by a depreciation rate, depreciation would be the decline in NRV from the beginning to the end of the year.

Some interesting effects appear in the case of inventories. Inventory value at the end of a period would be determined by taking the estimated selling price and deducting costs of disposition. Suppose that at the end of the period a clothing store has a suit that cost $80. Selling price is estimated at $140 and selling costs are estimated to be 20% of selling price. The suit will be valued in inventory at $140 - 28 = $112. This NRV valuation means that a profit of $32 will be recognized even though the suit has not been sold. Realization is not vital in this type of valuation system. NRV thus represents a significantly different system than historical cost valuation.

The merits of NRV lie in its use of current market prices. Rather than relying on estimates and allocations (as in present depreciation practices) NRV relies on amounts established in markets. NRV accords with the way many people view the costs of using their own assets, such as cars. The shortcomings of NRV relate to the relevancy of selling prices of assets in situations where the assets are to be used rather than sold.

Replacement Cost (RC)

In a replacement cost valuation system assets are valued at what it would cost to replace the assets (or, more accurately, what it would cost to replace the services provided by the assets). Under an RC system the delivery truck in Example 15-4 would be valued at what it would cost to replace it. This could be either the cost of a one-year-old truck in similar condition, perhaps $5,000 (which is higher than the NRV because the cost of the truck exceeds what it can be sold for), or the cost of a new truck less one year's estimated depreciation, perhaps $7,500 less $1,600 (a larger $1,100 salvage, 4-year life) = $5,900. The cost of using the truck one year would be the difference between the RC amount at the beginning of the year and the replacement cost at the end of the year.

Replacement cost would be used in a similar manner for inventories, with the inventory being valued at the end of the period at its RC. If a company has a suit of clothes on hand at the end of the period with a cost of $80, the replacement cost must be determined. If RC is $90, a $10 gain will be recognized. A $75 replacement cost will lead to a $5 loss (just as in the case of lower-of-cost-or-market valuation of inventories). The gain or loss is called a *holding gain* or *loss* in an RC system. This gain or loss can occur without a sale, so in an RC system realization is not the only determinant of income. In fact, one of the major features of an RC system is that two types of income or loss appear: (1) holding gains and losses from movements in prices of goods held and (2) operating gains or losses from sales of goods and services at amounts in excess of, or below, their replacement cost. In Example 15-5 statements on a replacement cost basis are contrasted with statements on a historical cost basis.

Holding gain or loss

EXAMPLE 15-5

LOTT COMPANY
Income Statement
for the Current Year

	R C Basis	Historical Cost
Sales	$100,000	$100,000
Replacement cost of sales	67,000	
Cost of sales		62,000
Gross margin	33,000	38,000
Operating expenses:		
Depreciation of equipment	13,000	10,000
Other	18,000	18,000
Total expenses	31,000	28,000
Operating income	2,000	10,000
Holding gains and losses:		
Replacement cost increases on merchandise during year	4,500	
Increase in replacement cost of equipment	2,500	
Decrease in replacement cost of land	(1,000)	
Total holding gains	6,000	0
Net income	$ 8,000	$ 10,000

LOTT COMPANY
Balance Sheet
December 31 of the Current Year

	R C Basis	Historical Cost
Current assets:		
Cash and receivables	$ 11,000	$ 11,000
Inventory	25,500	24,000
Total current assets	36,500	35,000
Plant and equipment:		
Land	18,000	10,000
Equipment	52,000	40,000
Less accumulated depreciation	(19,500)	(15,000)
Total plant and equipment	50,500	35,000
Total assets	$ 87,000	$ 70,000
Current liabilities	$ 15,000	$ 15,000
Common Stock	30,000	30,000
Retained earnings*	42,000	25,000
Total equities	$ 87,000	$ 70,000

*Some accountants recommend that retained earnings be separated into holding gains that have not yet been realized through sale or use of assets and the remaining balance.

In the income statement both cost of goods sold and depreciation differ from the historical cost figures because of higher replacement costs. The holding gains are increases in cost *during the year* on items held. For merchandise, these gains relate to items held for a time and then sold and also to inventory held at the end of the period. Replacement cost of sales is higher than historical cost because of price increases taking place during the period, and it is also influenced by holding gains in the inventory at the beginning of the period.[1] The increase in the replacement cost of equipment shown as a holding gain is only the amount of increase that took place during the current year. Similarly, even though there was a holding loss on land this year, the replacement cost of the land is still higher than the original cost because of previous holding gains. In this situation the land had a replacement cost of $19,000 last year, which decreased to $18,000 in the current year.

Proponents of RC argue that the cost of using an asset is not the original cost but the current cost of the benefits provided. They also argue that gains that occur because prices of assets rise during the time they are held should be distinguished from gains that occur because of efficient operations. This is illustrated in the income statement in Example 15-5, where holding gains are separated from operating income.

---

1. The $4,500 figure for the year includes the $1,500 increase that appears in the ending inventory ($25,500 less $24,000) plus increases in replacement cost of goods sold during the year. The $5,000 difference between historical cost and RC cost of goods sold is not all holding gain of the current year because the replacement cost of sales is also influenced by the difference between historical cost and RC cost of the inventory at the beginning of the period.

Note that an RC system is a cost system. In this respect it is similar to historical cost but unlike NRV. It uses current costs of items rather than original costs, however, and thus it represents a significant departure from the traditional historical cost system.

Replacement cost can be determined in many ways and this is a short-coming of the system. Where actual current prices are not available, appraisals or specific indexes are suggested as alternatives. Thus a building might be valued by conducting an appraisal or by multiplying its original cost by an index of construction prices for similar structures.

Value of the Business Entity

One objective of the alternative valuation systems discussed above is to arrive at a total on the balance sheet that gives some indication of the value of the enterprise as a whole. With inflation and changing prices it sometimes becomes painfully obvious that historical cost valuation has little relationship to what a company is worth. Unfortunately, the concept of the value of a business entity is hazy and indistinct. As a result, the question of what system best reflects the value of the business is not easily answered.

Stock market price

One approach to valuing the business as a whole is to find out what people would pay for it. In some cases this would be the market price of the business, if it were offered as a whole. For other businesses, the market price of shares of stock has been suggested as a good indicator. Thus you could simply take today's market price for IBM shares, multiply by the number of shares, and arrive at the net value of IBM. But the price fluctuates daily and is influenced by factors other than IBM's particular situation—for example the status of US–Soviet relations, the balance of payments, and the state of inflation. Furthermore, the market price is based on sales of a limited number of shares. Is this a sufficient basis for valuing millions of shares? Many believe that market value is not a reliable indicator, but it is difficult to suggest anything better.

One shortcoming of most valuation systems is that they do not set a value on the intangible factors connected with the enterprise. Coca-Cola Corporation, for example, has an extremely valuable intangible asset in the name it controls. How is this to be valued? Certainly the total value of the physical assets, whether on a cost, net realizable value, or replacement cost basis, would not indicate what the company is worth.

It is possible to use discounted cash flow as an approach to valuing the business as a whole. As far as investors are concerned, the cash flows from the business are in the form of dividends over the life of the enterprise. (An alternative might be to discount reported net income, but from the investors' point of view income must eventually result in cash flows to them, that is, in dividends.)

EXAMPLE 15-6

Burkom Co. presently pays $3.00 per share dividends yearly on its one million shares outstanding. Dividends in future years are expected to be as follows:

Years 1 and 2	$3.00 per share
Years 3 to 6	3.50 per share
Years 7 to 40	4.50 per share

The discounted present value of one share, using a 10% rate of discount, is as follows:

$3.00 × (1.736)(Appendix C, Table III)   = $ 5.208
3.50 × (4.355 − 1.736)(Appendix C, Table III) =   9.167
4.50 × (9.779 − 4.355)(Appendix C, Table III) = 24.408
Total present value of one share $38.783

Value of business: $38.783 × 1,000,000 = $38,800,000

The total value determined in Example 15-6 would presumably be different from the total of the net assets under any valuation approach. Also, because the approach in the example uses a series of estimates, it is unlikely that different individuals would agree on one value. Nevertheless, in theory those who establish stock prices in the market base their actions on computations similar to the above (perhaps made implicitly). Thus the market price may be a fairly good representation of the average discounted cash flow valuation of the firm as computed by investors.

Income Determination and Capital Maintenance

The primary function of accounting is to measure the progress of an entity—to measure the income or loss it generates. Economists define individual income as the amount a person can expect to spend during a period and still be as well off as when he started. For a business, income would presumably be the amount the business could pay out to owners without reducing the net assets. This way of expressing the income concept brings out a very important point—determination of income is dependent on valuation of assets. Different asset valuation systems produce different income amounts. Historical cost valuation systems use original prices for valuation and produce an income figure heavily influenced by these valuations. Net realizable value and replacement cost systems produce income amounts that vary from historical cost basis amounts and from each other. What then is the correct income amount? This is another of those questions that must be discussed but that cannot be satisfactorily answered.

It is helpful to look at the income problem by stressing capital maintenance. Capital maintenance means simply that income is the amount that is left over after maintaining the productive capital of the enterprise. Income is an excess. If a $500 machine is used to produce $900 of cash inflow and the machine is completely worn out in the production process, the income is only $400. The first $500 is needed to recover original capital or to maintain capital intact.

In a historical cost system capital must be maintained in terms of numbers of dollars invested. In an NRV system capital must be maintained in terms of the net selling price of assets. In an RC system capital must be maintained in terms of the current cost of assets. In a discounted cash flow system, capital must be maintained in terms of the present value of assets.

Criteria for Methods

A number of alternative asset valuation methods are available. Each one has advantages and disadvantages. No one method has gained acceptance as an alternative to historical cost, although replacement cost probably has the most adherents. Almost everyone agrees that historical cost is not a valid method when prices change rapidly. This dissatisfaction can be seen in the efforts made by accountants to avoid some of the shortcomings of historical cost by expedients such as LIFO for inventories and accelerated depreciation methods for plant and equipment. Use of these expedients indicates that many accountants are reluctant to simply abandon historical cost and switch to a different system.

Need for criteria

One reason for a reluctance to change is the lack of agreement on an alternative. Is there some way out of this impasse? Perhaps the best approach would be to agree on certain criteria for a good valuation method and then see which method meets the criteria. As might be expected, no set of criteria exists, but some remarks on the subject may be helpful.

Realism

In the first place, any method used should realistically reflect the environment in which accounting operates. That environment is one in which prices move fairly rapidly and amounts relevant at one particular point in time are not necessarily relevant at another. To be relevant, valuations must be useful in current economic decisions. Since these decisions involve future courses of action, the valuations should aid in projections. It should be possible to conduct studies on which method provides the best basis for predictions. Studies to date have not been conclusive, however. Another aspect of reflecting the environment is that any income figure generated must accord with commonsense evaluations of progress, of being better off. A sale of land at a large excess over cost does not necessarily produce income. The person may be no better off because of inflation or the fact that buying similar land would cost as much as was received on the sale.

Predictive ability

Another criterion for valuation methods is that they must provide understandable results. If users cannot understand the statements produced, they will be unable to interpret them accurately and will probably make poor decisions.

Understandability

A related criterion is that the valuation method must not be so expensive to use that the costs involved exceed the benefits. One advantage of the historical cost method is that it is fairly inexpensive to use. Methods that cost more are under a distinct disadvantage. Costs involve not only the specific costs of obtaining data but also other costs, such as effects on competitive position, on market price of shares, and on the economy as a whole. Considerable uncertainty exists about many of these types of effects and thus many enterprises are reluctant to experiment with alternative methods.

Cost vs. benefits

The whole area of criteria for methods needs further exploration and development. It is a promising area of investigation.

Prospects for Change

Changes from traditional historical cost valuation can take several forms. These include the following:

1. Replacement of historical cost by a new system
2. Supplementing of historical cost with added statements on a different basis
3. Amendments of historical cost in certain areas

It is unlikely that a completely new system can be implemented unless the economic system breaks down completely. Radical change is not very likely. The alternative of supplementary statements or disclosures on an NRV or RC basis is somewhat more likely. This approach appeases those who want change but do not want to abandon historical cost. The drawbacks involve added costs and probably confusion among users.

It may be possible to amend historical cost in selected areas. For example, current values might be required for marketable securities but not for other areas. This type of gradual change appeals to many. Whether it presents the possibility of much long-term progress is debatable.

The three alternative approaches listed are another area of debate. It is possible that accountants will be content to debate the various issues and not take any decisive action unless forced to do so by economic conditions or government action. It should also be mentioned that businessmen are generally averse to changes in present valuation approaches unless they can derive some tax advantages from the change.

The prospects for change were enhanced considerably in 1976 by a Securities and Exchange Commission requirement that large companies report certain replacement cost data in annual reports filed with the SEC. The data required are replacement costs of inventory and plant and equipment and of the related cost of goods sold and depreciation expense. This SEC requirement deals with those assets and expenses most affected by price changes. Because presentation of replacement cost data is an SEC requirement, companies have to present the information whether they want to or not. The requirement is likely to lead to further disclosure of replacement cost data in the future.

GENERAL PRICE-LEVEL ACCOUNTING

The current value systems are designed to deal with specific price changes. However, most specific price changes take place in a context of changes in other prices and changes in the general level of prices. Dealing with specific price changes and ignoring the effects of inflation is likely to produce inadequate results. We now discuss general price-level accounting, which attempts to deal with the general problem of inflation but does not deal with specific price changes.

General price-level changes are measured by price indexes. These indexes attempt to arrive at the average change in prices, which should give an indication of general purchasing power and the value of the dollar. The problems of constructing valid indexes are profound, but indexes such as the GNP Deflators and the Consumer Price Index are serviceable for many purposes. The GNP Deflators constitute a broad-based index that is a fairly good indicator of the general value of the dollar and has been recommended by the rule-making body of the accounting profession.

Monetary and Nonmonetary Items

A restatement for general price-level changes requires the division of assets and liabilities into two classes — monetary and nonmonetary items — because of the differing effects of inflation.

Monetary items defined

Monetary items are those whose amounts are fixed in numbers of dollars regardless of changes in the general price level. An example is cash, which remains the same in amount even if the price level doubles. Receivables and most liabilities have similar characteristics. A $1,000,000 bond liability will be paid with $1,000,000 even if the price level increases — the amount to be paid is fixed in number of dollars.

A holder of a monetary asset such as cash loses money during inflation, because the fixed number of dollars are worth less than before. Similarly, being in debt is an advantage during inflation because the debts will be paid with cheaper dollars. In general price-level restatements a gain or a loss is computed on monetary items. This gain or loss is based on the average net balance of monetary items held. It is a distinctive feature of general price-level statements.

Let us illustrate. The Welloff Company has the following monetary items:

	Dec. 31, Year 2	Dec. 31, Year 1
Cash and receivables	$ 54,000	$ 54,000
Accounts and notes payable	(34,000)	(24,000)
Net monetary items	$ 20,000	$ 30,000
General price index	198	180

Since the company's monetary assets exceed its monetary liabilities, and because the general price index has risen during the year, there is a general price-level loss. Why is this so? Because the net monetary items held are a claim against dollars, and the dollars have lost purchasing power during the year. The loss is figured as follows:

Average monetary items held for a year:

$$(\$30,000 + 20,000)/2 = \$25,000$$

That is, the company held an average of $25,000 in monetary items for a full year, assuming that the change in monetary items took place gradually over the year.

Price level increase factor: $198/180 = 1.10$

Monetary items expressed in December 31, Year 2, prices:
$25,000 \times 1.10 =$ $27,500
Less: actual dollars of monetary items   25,000
General price-level loss $ 2,500

Nonmonetary items defined

Nonmonetary items are all items other than monetary items. They are characterized by the possibility of changes in amounts when inflation occurs. For example, plant and equipment items may change in price when inflation occurs. The prices may go up more than, the same as, or less than, general inflation. As a result, holders of nonmonetary assets may gain, lose, or stay even during a time of inflation, depending on the movement of prices of the assets they hold.

Nonmonetary items in general price-level statements are restated to dollars of current purchasing power by use of price indexes. Each item is multiplied by a factor consisting of the current price level divided by the price level existing at the time the item occurred or was acquired. Consider Examples 15-7, 15-8, and 15-9. The current price level is 200 in each case.

EXAMPLE 15-7

Land was acquired for $60,000 when the price level was 120. Land is restated as follows:

$$\$60,000 \times 200/120 = \$100,000$$

EXAMPLE 15-8

Equipment was purchased for $10,000 4 years ago when the price level was 150. Estimated life is 10 years. Salvage value is zero. Straight-line depreciation is used.

Cost and accumulated depreciation are restated as follows:

Equipment	$10,000 × 200/150 =	$13,333
Accumulated depreciation	$ 4,000 × 200/150 =	$ 5,333

Depreciation expense is restated as follows:

Expense $1,000 × 200/150 = $1,333

EXAMPLE 15-9

Total LIFO inventory is $42,000. Thirty thousand dollars of the inventory was acquired when the index was 150. A layer of $12,000 was added when the index was 180.

Inventory is restated as follows:

	Cost	Factor	Restated
Base	$30,000 ×	200/150 =	$40,000
Layer	$12,000 ×	200/180 =	13,333
Total restated			$53,333

Examples 15-7, 15-8, and 15-9 show how nonmonetary items are restated. Notice that some of the items appear on the income statement — for example, depreciation expense and the inventory amount, which is used in the computation of cost of goods sold. Note also that the plant and equipment items are restated by considerable amounts. The amount of restatement is dependent on movements in the price level since acquisition. Plant and equipment items have a potential for substantial restatements because old costs are often involved.

Restatements are usually made to current dollars, and any statements presented as comparative amounts should also be restated to current dollars. Only in this way will valid comparisons be possible.

Restatement Example

Historical Dollar Statements. To illustrate general price-level restatements we will use the historical dollar statements in Examples 15-10 and 15-11. (all figures in thousands).

EXAMPLE 15-10

CREME COMPANY
Comparative Balance Sheets
December 31, Year 9 and Year 10

Assets

		Year 10		Year 9
Current Assets:				
Cash and receivables		$ 75		$ 45
Inventory (FIFO basis)		40		30
Total current assets		115		75
Plant and equipment:				
Equipment	$200		$200	
Less accumulated depreciation	85	115	70	130
Total assets		$230		$205

Liabilities and Stockholders' Equity

		Year 10		Year 9
Current Liabilities:				
Accounts payable		$ 30		$ 25
Taxes payable		15		10
Total Current Liabilities		45		35
Long-term notes payable		50		50
Stockholders' equity:				
Common stock	$100		$100	
Retained earnings	35	135	20	120
Total liabilities and stockholders' equity		$230		$205

EXAMPLE 15-11

CREME COMPANY
Income Statement
for Year 10

Sales		$200
Cost of sales:		
Beginning inventory	$ 30	
Purchases	120	
	150	
Ending inventory	40	
Cost of sales		110
Gross margin		$ 90
Expenses:		
Depreciation on equipment	15	
Interest expense	4	
Other operating expenses	46	65
Income before tax		$ 25
Income tax		10
Net income		$ 15

Part V   Accounting Theory and Analysis

TABLE 15-1. General Price Indexes and Conversion Factors

Date	General Price Indexes	Conversion factors (December 31, Year 10 ÷ index of period)
Jan. 1, Year 4	100	2.00
Year 4 Average	105	1.90
Year 5 Average	115	1.74
Year 6 Average	125	1.60
Year 9 Average	175	1.14
Year 9 last quarter average	180	1.11
Dec. 31, Year 9	183	1.09
Year 10 average	192	1.04
Year 10 last quarter average	198	1.01
Dec. 31, Year 10	200	1.00

Information for Price-Level Restatement

1. Equipment detail (depreciation is straight-line, no salvage value)

	Cost	Life	Accumulated Depreciation 12/31/Year 9	Accumulated Depreciation 12/31/Year 10
Acquired in Year 4	$100	20 years	30	35
Acquired in Year 6	$100	10 years	40	50

2. Long-term notes are 10-year notes due on January 1, Year 15.
3. Common stock was issued on January 1, Year 4.
4. Sales and expenses are incurred evenly throughout the year.
5. Beginning inventory (FIFO) was aquired in the last quarter of Year 9.
6. Indexes are shown in Table 15-1.

Restatement Procedures. Our objectives in restating the financial statements are to have all nonmonetary items expressed in terms of the year-end price level and to recognize any general price-level gain or loss on the net monetary items held. The general prices are reflected in the General Price Index (which is a hypothetical price index for illustration purposes only). Table 15-1 gives the price indexes needed to restate prices for the Creme Company. To facilitate conversion, the table also gives a conversion factor that is the ratio of the index for the end of Year 10 to the index of the date or period. The conversion factors can be used to convert historical cost data to the general price level at the end of Year 10. Example 15-12 shows a restated income statement for the Creme Company.

Explanation of Restatement of Income Statement

To restate sales, purchases, interest, other expenses, and income taxes, the conversion factor is 1.04. This is the ratio of the index at the end of Year 10 to the average index for all of Year 10. Why? Because it is assumed that sales and the expense items listed were received or incurred evenly throughout the year. Thus, on average, the items were received or paid when the general price index was 192, the average for Year 10. The conversion factor is found as follows:

EXAMPLE 15-12

CREME COMPANY
Restated Income Statement
for Year 10

	Historical	Factor	Restated
Sales	$200	1.04	$208
Cost of sales:			
Beginning inventory	30	1.11	33
Purchases	120	1.04	125
	150		158
Ending inventory	40	1.01	40
Cost of sales	110		118
Gross margin	$ 90		$ 90
Expenses:			
Depreciation	15	below	26
Interest	4	1.04	4
Other expenses	46	1.04	48
Total expenses	65		78
Income before tax and price-level gain	$ 25		$ 12
General price-level gain	—	below	+3
Income tax	10	1.04	10
Net income	$ 15		$ 5

$$200/192 = 1.04$$

Since the inventory turnover is approximately 4 times per year, we can assume that the beginning inventory was acquired in the last quarter of Year 9 when the index was 180. The conversion factor to use is as follows:

$$200/180 = 1.11$$

By the same reasoning, the ending inventory was acquired in the last quarter of Year 10. Hence the conversion factor is as follows:

$$200/198 = 1.01$$

Depreciation is complicated because there were two separate acquisitions of equipment. The computation for historical cost depreciation and restated depreciation is shown in Table 15-2.

TABLE 15-2. Historical Cost Depreciation and Restated Depreciation

Date of Acquisition*	Cost	Depreciation Rate	Historical Cost Depreciation	Conversion Factor	Restated Depreciation
Year 4	$100	5%	$ 5	1.90	$10
Year 6	100	10%	10	1.60	16
Totals			$15		$26

* Both acquisitions are assumed to have occurred at midyear. The conversion factor is found by using the average price index for the year of acquisition: In Year 4, 200/105 = 1.90; in Year 6, 200/125 = 1.60.

TABLE 15-3. Net Monetary Items

	12/31 Year 10	12/31 Year 9
Cash and receivables	75	45
Current liabilities	(45)	(35)
Long-term notes payable	(50)	(50)
Net monetary items	(20)	(40)

The general price-level gain is derived from the monetary items, listed in Table 15-3. The company has greater monetary liabilities than monetary assets; hence a price-level or purchasing power gain is indicated. During Year 10, the average monetary items held for one year was

$$\frac{(40) + (20)}{2} = (30)$$

The price-level gain is figured as follows:

Net monetary items at year-end price level: $(30) \times 1.09 = \$(33)$
Less net monetary items at the actual
   fixed dollar amount   (30)
General price level gain $(3)

Explanation of Restatement of the Balance Sheet

Example 15-13 shows the restated balance sheet for the Creme Company. Monetary items in the current year's balance sheet[2] are not restated because they will be received (in the case of monetary assets) or paid (in the case of monetary liabilities) at a fixed number of dollars regardless of what happens to prices. Monetary items do affect the income statement, as we saw above, in the general price level gain.

The inventory has a conversion factor of 1.01 because of the reasonable assumption that it was acquired in the last quarter of Year 10.

For equipment, we must take into account the two acquisitions made in different years (see Table 15-4).

TABLE 15-4. Equipment Restatement

Date of Acquisition	Cost	Conversion Factor†	Restated Value
Year 4*	$100	200/105 = 1.90	$190
Year 6*	100	200/125 = 1.60	160
Totals	$200		$350

* Equipment is assumed to have been acquired at mid-year. Since equipment is assumed to have been acquired at mid-year, we use the average index for year 4 and the average index for year 6 to figure the conversion factor.

2. If any prior period's balance sheets appear in current reports for comparative purposes, the monetary items of the previous period must be restated to current dollars for comparative purposes.

EXAMPLE 15-13

Creme Company
Restated Balance Sheet
December 31, Year 10

Assets

	Historical	Factor	Restated
Current Assets:			
Cash and receivables	$ 75	—	$ 75
Inventory	40	1.01	40
Total current assets	115		115
Plant and equipment:			
Equipment	200	below	350
Accumulated depreciation	85	below	147
Net	115		203
Total assets	$230		$318

Liabilities and Stockholders' Equity

	Historical	Factor	Restated
Current liabilities:			
Accounts payable	$ 30	—	$ 30
Taxes payable	15	—	15
Total current liabilities	45		45
Long-term notes payable	50	—	50
Total liabilities	95		95
Stockholders' equity:			
Common stock	100	2.00	200
Retained earnings	35	below	23
Total liabilities and stockholders	$230		$318

The accumulated depreciation must also consider the two separate acquisitions (see Table 15-5).

TABLE 15-5. Accumulated Depreciation Restatement

Date of Acquisition*	Cost	Life	Years Owned through Dec. 31, Year 10†	Historical Cost Accumulated Depreciation	Conversion Factor	Restated Accumulated Depreciation
Year 4	$100	20 yrs.	7 yrs. = 35%	$35	1.90	$ 67
Year 6	100	10 yrs.	5 yrs. = 50%	50	1.60	80
Totals				$85		$147

* Acquisition is assumed to be at mid-year.
† This assumes the company takes a full year's depreciation in the year of acquisition.

Common stock was issued on January 1, Year 4; hence the conversion factor is as follows:

$$200/100 = 2.00$$

Retained earnings restated for price-level changes is the residual derived from the other values in the restated column as follows:

		Restated 12/31/Year 10
Total assets		$318
Less: total liabilities	$ 95	
Common stock	200	295
Restated retained earnings		$ 23

When general price-level statements are prepared each year, the retained earnings can be computed by preparing a retained earnings statement, using the price-level restated income and dividends.

Results of Restatement. The results of the restatement are interesting. Income is much lower than on the historical dollar statements. Income is only 2.5% of sales, and income taxes are a much higher proportion of income before tax than on the historical dollar income statement. Comparisons to the historical dollar statements should be limited, because the two sets of statements are prepared with different measuring units. The best comparisons would be with general price-level statements of other years and other companies. Creme Company's income results may be quite good in comparison with other periods and other enterprises, even though they do not compare favorably with historical dollar results.

The restated balance sheet is markedly different from the historical balance sheet. The stockholders' equity is doubled in terms of purchasing power. Plant and equipment is stated at a much higher amount because of the change in the value of the dollar since the acquisition dates. Most other items are changed to a lesser extent, but the total of the balance sheet is quite different from that on the historical dollar statement.

Again, it must be emphasized that the restated asset amounts on the balance sheet are simply restatements of historical costs and not the current values of the assets. The $203,000 figure for net equipment may be more or less than the current value of the equipment, and the inventory figure is not necessarily the same as the net realizable value or replacement cost of the inventory. Monetary assets are stated at their current amounts, just as they are in historical dollar statements.

Techniques of general price-level restatement are well developed and well accepted. The usefulness of price-level statements, on the other hand, is disputed. Certainly price-level restatements do not provide an answer to the problems of changing economic conditions. Price-level statements have a modest purpose and claim. They attempt to use a measuring unit that is stated in terms of purchasing power and thus avoid the problems of the changing measuring unit used in historical dollar accounting.

A final note: while it is true that general price-level statements do not solve all the problems of changing prices, it is equally true that net realizable value and replacement cost approaches that ignore the general problem of inflation are also inadequate answers to these problems. Perhaps the best answer is a combination of some type of current value accounting with an adjustment for the changing value of the dollar.

SUMMARY

Accounting based on historical costs has some severe limitations in a time of changing prices. Specific and general price changes are important aspects of the environment that should not be ignored.

Recognition of specific price changes involves adopting new valuation approaches. Discounted cash flow valuation is based on discounting the predicted cash flows from an asset to the present. DCF is difficult to implement in a practical situation. In the net realizable value approach, assets are valued at their selling price less estimated costs to sell. The relevance of selling prices is questionable in many situations, and this is a major drawback of the NRV system. In a replacement cost approach assets are valued at what it would cost to replace them or, more accurately, the services they provide. In an RC system, holding gains and losses appear when assets are held during a time of price changes. When RC is used, current costs are charged against revenues in computing income from operations.

Should a different valuation system be used? This question cannot be answered in the absence of criteria for valuation methods, and, unfortunately, these criteria are not available. A few criteria were suggested in the chapter.

Change from present generally accepted accounting principles can take several forms. An abandonment of present valuations is unlikely, but supplementary information on other bases is a possibility if the economic system continues to be unstable.

Restating financial statements for general price-level changes is an attempt to adjust for the changing value of our measuring unit, the dollar. Items are divided into monetary and nonmonetary categories. A company gains or loses on monetary items simply because of changes in the price level. Nonmonetary items are restated for changes in the value of the dollar. Restated financial statements do not indicate current values of assets. In fact, the usefulness of general price-level statements is disputed. Perhaps the best approach would be a combination of a current value approach with general price-level restatements.

This chapter only introduces the topic of accounting for changing prices. The accounting literature on this subject is extensive and should be consulted by the interested student. The importance of the topic to intelligent users and preparers of information is the reason for introducing it at this time.

IMPORTANT TERMS

Specific price changes
General price changes
Real income
Unit of measure
Purchasing power
Discounted cash flow
Capital gain or loss
Net realizable value
Replacement cost
Holding gain or loss
Capital maintenance
Predictive ability
Supplementary statements
Monetary items
Nonmonetary items

QUESTIONS

15-1. Point out some specific inadequacies of historical cost valuation in a time of changing prices.

15-2. What is net realizable value? Would a balance sheet prepared by use of NRV indicate what the business is worth?

15-3. What is replacement cost? What inventory method comes close to giving an RC figure in cost of goods sold?

15-4. The text states that the market price of an item is a market estimate of the discounted cash flows from that item. In light of the fact that prices change fairly rapidly, is this statement valid? Discuss.

15-5. Indicate how use of replacement cost valuation for assets would affect income determination.

15-6. The realization principle is not important in the net realizable value approach. Why not?

15-7. Distinguish between monetary and nonmonetary items.

15-8. Why is it suggested that general price-level statements be in terms of current dollars instead of base-year dollars?

15-9. What is the general price-level gain or loss on monetary items?

15-10. Baker Company shows income in its general price-level statement that is 20% lower than income in the historical dollar statement. What is the significance of this difference?

EXERCISES

15-11. *Real income.* Your professor of comparative calisthenics is happy because he has had good salary increases the last few years. Indexes and salary for the last years are as follows:

	Salary	Index
Year 1	$15,000	120
2	16,000	132
3	17,500	150
4	19,000	170

Enlighten the poor fellow. Use Year 4 dollars for your restatement.

15-12. *NRV, RC.* Land is bought for $50,000 at the beginning of the year. By the end of the year, the land has increased in selling price to $60,000. Realtor's commissions on land sales are 6% and must be paid by the seller of property.
  a. What is the replacement cost of the land? What is the holding gain for the year?
  b. What is the net realizable value of the land? What gain or loss would appear on the income statement using NRV?

15-13. *NRV, RC.* An auto dealer buys a car at the beginning of the year for $2,600. At the end of the period he can sell the car for $3,700, but he must pay a 10% commission to his salesman. He could buy a similar car for $2,750.
  a. What is the replacement cost of the car? What is the holding gain or loss?
  b. What is the net realizable value of the car? What gain or loss would appear on the income statement using NRV?
  (Solution in Appendix B.)

15-14. *Monetary items.* The following items appear among the assets and liabilities of Dugong Co.:

	12/31/Year 1	12/31/Year 2
Cash	300	400
Receivables (net)	700	800
Accounts payable	500	500
Long-term notes payable	2,200	2,000

The general price index was 150 at the beginning of the year and 180 at the end. What is the gain or loss on monetary items?
(Solution in Appendix B.)

15-15. *General price level.* Millar Co. purchased $20,000 of equipment with a 10-year life in Year 1 when the price level was 100. At the beginning of Year 7 the index was 140 and at the end it was 150. Indicate historical dollar and restated amounts that would appear on the statements prepared at the end of Year 7. Assume straight-line depreciation and no salvage value.

15-16. *General price level.* Nugent Co. has the following cost of goods sold for the current year (inventory is on a FIFO basis):

Beginning inventory	$ 60,000
Purchases	300,000
	360,000
Ending inventory	80,000
Cost of goods sold	$280,000

The general price index was 120 in the last quarter of the previous year. It rose to an average of 127 during the current year. The index for the last quarter and the end of the current year was 132. Restate the cost of goods sold for general price-level changes. You may assume inventory is acquired in the last quarter of each year. What is the effect on the inventory figure in the year-end balance sheet?

15-17. *RC and general price level.* The Opperman Co. invests $70,000 in common stock of another company on January 1 of Year 1 when the general price index is 100. The stock is held for three years, during which time the following occurs:

	Ending Price	Price Index End of Year
Year 1	$ 73,000	110
2	90,000	115
3	120,000	125

Required:
a. Determine the asset valuation and holding gain for each year if replacement cost valuation is used but general price-level changes are ignored.
b. Determine the asset valuation and holding gain if RC is used and general price-level changes are considered. For income of a year, restate to price levels at the end of that year.

PROBLEMS

15-18. *RC.* The Sellers Company has the following partial income statement for the current year:

Sales		$80,000
Cost of goods sold:		
Beginning inventory		
(1,200 units at $5 each)	$ 6,000	
Purchases		
(10,000 units at $5.20 each)	52,000	
Goods available	58,000	
Ending inventory		
(1,500 units at $5.20)	7,800	
Cost of goods sold (9,700 units)		50,200
Gross margin		$29,800

Restate the partial income statement to a replacement cost basis and indicate the holding gain or loss, using the following replacement costs:

Beginning inventory on January 1	$ 6,200
Beginning inventory at time it was sold	6,300
Goods purchased and sold during the period (8,500 units)	45,900
Ending inventory at end of year	8,300

You may treat all holding gains of the year as part of income for the period. (Solution in Appendix B.)

15-19. *RC and general price level.* During the current year, the DeLouise Company held a piece of equipment that was shown on the balance sheets as follows:

	December 31	
	Current Year	Prior Year
Equipment—at cost	$30,000	$30,000
Accumulated depreciation	12,000	9,000
Net book value	$18,000	$21,000

Depreciation expense for the year was $3,000. The price index rose from 100 at the beginning of the year to 110 at the end. Replacement cost new (before depreciation) of the equipment was $35,000 at the beginning of the year and rose to $40,000 early in the year, remaining at that amount until the year-end.

Required:

a. Prepare balance sheet and income statement information (including holding gains or losses) for the current year's report on a replacement cost basis, ignoring changes in the general price level. Hint: the holding gain is not $5,000 because the equipment is not new.

b. Prepare the balance sheet and income statement information on a replacement cost basis, giving consideration to changes in the general price level. Hint: holding gain is $1,050.

15-20. *DCF.* The Grant Company values its investments on the basis of discounted future cash flows. They use a 12% rate of discount.

Expectations at the beginning of the current year were as follows:

Expected yearly dividends for 10 years	$200
Expected sales price at end of 10 years	$2,000

Expectations at the end of the current year are as follows:

Expected yearly dividends for nine years	$220
Expected sales price at end of nine years	$2,100

Two hundred dollars of dividends were received at the end of the year.

Required:

Compute the asset values on a discounted cash flow basis at the beginning and end of the year. Compute income during the year on a DCF basis. Be careful to separate any capital gain.

(Solution in Appendix B.)

15-21. *NRV.* Restate the following statements of the Lorie Company to a net realizable value basis. You may ignore general price-level changes. Comment on your results.

Part V Accounting Theory and Analysis

Balance Sheets
as of December 31

Assets	Current Year	Prior Year
Cash	$ 1,800	$ 900
Receivables (net)	600	500
Inventory	800	600
Equipment	12,000	12,000
Less accumulated depreciation	(3,600)	(3,000)
Goodwill	3,900	4,000
	$15,500	$15,000
Liabilities and Stockholders' Equity		
Accounts payable	$ 500	$ 400
Bonds payable (at par amount)	5,000	5,000
Capital stock	6,000	6,000
Retained earnings	4,000	3,600
	$15,500	$15,000

Income Statement
for Current Year

Sales		$6,000
Cost of Sales:		
Beginning inventory	$ 600	
Purchases	3,000	
	3,600	
Ending inventory	800	
Cost of sales		2,800
Gross margin		3,200
Expenses:		
Goodwill amortization	100	
Depreciation of equipment	600	
Other operating expenses	1,200	
Interest expense	300	2,200
Net income		$1,000

Dividends paid were $600.
Additional information:
1. Net realizable values of assets are as follows:

	December 31	
	Current Year	Prior Year
Receivables	$ 580	$ 500
Inventory	1,000	850
Equipment, net	7,000	7,800
Goodwill	1,000	1,000

2. The bonds were quoted at 90 on the market last year and at 92 this year. (Show the bonds at the net liquidating value.)
3. Simply force the beginning retained earnings balance. Ending retained earnings can be computed using the income and dividend amounts.

15-22. *RC.* Restate the statements of Lorie Company (see Problem 15-21) to a replacement cost basis. You obtain the following additional information.

1. Replacement costs of assets are as follows:

	December 31	
	Current Year	Prior Year
Receivables	$ 600	$ 500
Inventories	830	620
Equipment (new)	14,400	13,200
Goodwill	2,000	2,000

2. Bonds should be valued at $5,000.
3. Replacement cost of goods sold during the period is $2,950, which includes the $20 holding gain on beginning inventory. (The holding gain on goods purchased and sold during the year is $130.) The cost of goods sold excludes the $30 difference on the ending inventory.
4. Simply force the beginning retained earnings balance.
5. Treat all holding gains as part of income for the year.

15-23. *General price-level restatement.* The Hope Company began business on January 1 of the current year, when the price index was 100. They issued stock, acquired assets, and began operations on January 1. Sales, purchases, and expenses occur evenly throughout the year.

HOPE COMPANY
Income Statement for the Year

Sales		$3,000
Cost of sales:		
Beginning inventory (LIFO)	$ 300	
Purchases	1,700	
Ending inventory (LIFO)	(300)	
Cost of sales		1,700
Gross margin		1,300
Expenses:		
Depreciation	200	
Other expenses	900	1,100
Income from operations		200
Income tax		80
Net income		$ 120

HOPE COMPANY
Balance Sheets
January 1 and December 31 of Current Year

	Dec. 31	Jan. 1
Cash	$ 500	$ 500
Receivables	400	0
Inventory (LIFO)	300	300
Equipment	2,400	2,400
Accumulated depreciation	(200)	0
Total assets	$3,400	$3,200

Accounts payable	$ 200	$ 200
Taxes payable	80	0
Common stock	2,000	2,000
Premium on common stock	1,000	1,000
Retained earnings	120	0
Total liabilities and stockholders' equity	$3,400	$3,200

Required:

Restate the financial statements for general price-level changes, assuming that the price index was as follows:

Beginning of year	100
Average for year	107
End of year	112

All restatements should be to end-of-year dollars. Be sure to include the general price-level gain or loss on monetary items.
(Solution in Appendix B.)

15-24. *General price-level restatement.* You are to restate the balance sheets of the Acme Co. presented below:

ACME COMPANY
Balance Sheets

	Historical	
Assets	12/31/Year 10	12/31/Year 9
Current assets:		
Cash and receivables	$ 600	$ 200
Investment in stocks (Nov. Year 9)	100	100
Inventory (LIFO)	700	600
Prepaid Insurance (last $\frac{1}{4}$ of year)	50	50
	$1,450	$ 950
Plant assets:		
Land (bought in Year 1)	$ 200	$ 200
Building	2,000	2,000
Accumulated depreciation	(450)	(400)
	1,750	1,800
Investment in Byrd Co. (Year 7)	200	200
Total assets	$3,400	$2,950
Liabilities and Stockholders' Equity		
Current liabilities:		
Accounts payable	$ 410	$ 320
Taxes payable	90	80
	500	400
Long-term debt:		
20-year, 6% bonds, issued Year 1	1,000	1,000
Total liabilities	1,500	1,400
Owners' equity:		
Common stock	1,200	1,000
Premium on common	300	200
Retained earnings	500	450
Treasury stock at cost	(100)	(100)
Total owners' equity	1,900	1,550
Total liabilities and stockholders' equity	$3,400	$2,950

Accounting and Changing Prices **Chapter 15**

Added information:

The company was founded in Year 1 and $1,000 of stock was issued at that time. Treasury stock was acquired in Year 7. Additional stock was sold on August 1, Year 10. The building was built in Year 2. The LIFO base was started in Year 1. The only layer (additional quantity of inventory) was added in the first quarter of Year 10.

Year	Price Index	Factor
1	100	1.60
2	103	1.55
7	135	1.19
9	145	1.10
10	155	1.03
9 second ¼	140	1.14
9 third ¼	144	1.11
9 fourth ¼	147	1.09
9 End of year	147	1.09
10 first ¼	150	1.07
10 second ¼	154	1.04
10 third ¼	157	1.02
10 fourth ¼	160	1.00
10 End of year	160	1.00

Required:

Restate the balance sheets of Acme in terms of 12/31/Year 10 dollars. Compute the retained earnings as the balancing figure in each year. Also, by examining the balance sheets, indicate whether Acme probably had a gain or a loss on monetary items.

16

Accounting Theory: Importance, Development, and Prospects

We have dealt at some length with the appropriate accounting procedures in connection with assets, equities, revenues, and expenses. These procedures fall within the scope of "generally accepted accounting principles." But what is the origin of these principles? This chapter will try to trace the development of acceptable accounting, to assess the present situation, and to consider some prospects of financial accounting.

This discussion deals with accounting theory, rather than accounting practice. Particular areas of theory as they relate to specific areas of practice have been considered throughout this book and need not be pursued at this point. Thus the task of this chapter is not to present a theory of financial accounting with all its ramifications but rather to consider the importance of theory, to explain the development of theory in general, and to help the reader understand what accounting theory is and the function it performs.

INTERESTED PARTIES: NEEDS AND PRESSURES

Accounting has grown in response to the needs of parties interested in enterprise progress and position. These parties include management, investors and potential investors, creditors, governmental bodies, employees, and the public. The diversity among these groups implies a diversity in the needs of users of financial accounting information. Accountants are responsible for preparing financial statements to satisfy the diverse needs of a variety of interested parties.

Some parties are in a strategic position when it comes to making their needs felt. Management, for example, employs, directs, and pays the accountant who prepares the statements. Creditors are in an effective position when a company comes to them seeking credit. The government can enforce its needs through legal means. Other parties, such as small investors, employees, and the public, historically have been less able to express their needs effectively.

The previous discussion of assets, liabilities, and equities indicated appropriate treatments of balance sheet and income statement items. Some acceptable variations in accounting procedures were also discussed, including FIFO, LIFO, and average cost methods for inventories and straight-line and accelerated depreciation methods for plant and equipment. These various treatments and acceptable methods were developed in response to needs. The needs that were most effectively expressed and had the most support tended to shape generally accepted accounting procedures.

Management

Management can see its needs more clearly than other groups and can easily convey them to the accountant. Management's needs for information are complex, increasing dramatically as business complexity increases. Many of these needs are answered by the flood of internal reports found in most enterprises. Satisfaction of needs through such internal reports is a prime concern of texts dealing with managerial accounting.

Some of management's needs are expressed in the reports that accountants prepare for parties outside of the enterprise. For example, the officers of a company may want to influence the preparation of income statements so that the report makes them appear in the best possible light. Or unscrupulous management personnel might try to hide unfavorable events instead of disclosing them by asking the accountant to treat them in ways not consistent or proper. But what is proper? A case could be made for the view that if a treatment satisfies the needs of management, it is proper. The difficulty is, of course, that other interested parties have needs that must presumably be given some weight in deciding what is proper and correct in accounting.

The various interested parties can make sure that their needs are expressed and considered in financial accounting by applying pressures of various types.

Economic pressures

One important type of pressure is economic pressure. For example, a creditor can refuse to extend credit without a set of audited statements, or investment bankers might refuse to aid in a new stock issue without revisions of certain accounting procedures that they consider inappropriate. Direct economic pressures of these kinds cannot be brought to bear by all users, but when they can be employed, they are quite effective. Even stockholders can bring some economic pressure to bear by disposing of shares owned. If enough stockholders seek to dispose of their shares, the market price should be reduced.

Legal pressures

Legal pressures are an especially effective type of pressure. Certain disclosures are required by federal securities acts. The tax laws require certain types of financial information. Failure to observe legal requirements can threaten the existence of companies and lead to fines or imprisonment for company officials.

Ethical pressures

Ethical pressures are less direct than either economic or legal pressures but are important influences on accounting practices. Standards of honesty and fairness are important influences on the conduct of most people in business. Furthermore, people with high ethical standards do not like to do business with those who lack those standards. Accountants often pride themselves on their high standards and refuse to give their approval to questionable accounting procedures. Full disclosure of all relevant facts is almost an article of faith to many accountants.

Social pressures

Public opinion is another force that influences accountants and accounting practices. Because the public recognizes that the actions of large corporations affect the lives of everyone, it has demanded more information about these actions. One manifestation of increased public interest is in the extension of conflict-of-interest standards for public officials to the officers of large publicly-held corporations. Because of public pressure, corporations have had to discharge officers who were in conflict-of-interest positions. Recently, there has been a considerable public outcry against payment of bribes in foreign operations of large companies. This outcry has resulted in passage of laws and in resignations of numerous company officials. Public demands are not a direct form of pressure in most cases; instead, they serve to set the tone of the environment in which business operates. In this way, public opinion has a definite effect on accounting.

Pressure from all groups has been increasing in recent years. The accounting profession is being called on by many groups to act more quickly and decisively than ever before in raising standards and seeing that effective mechanisms are established for enforcing standards. Many of the pressures focus on the standards, rules, and procedures that accountants follow in their work. (see Figure 16-1).

Position of the accountant

Thus accountants are, in a sense, arbitrators among all the interested parties. They are under great pressure from various parties. Each party wants a particular type of information presented in a particular way and fights to get it. Because of the importance of information, the pressures on accountants are not casual or intermittent, but intense and continuous.

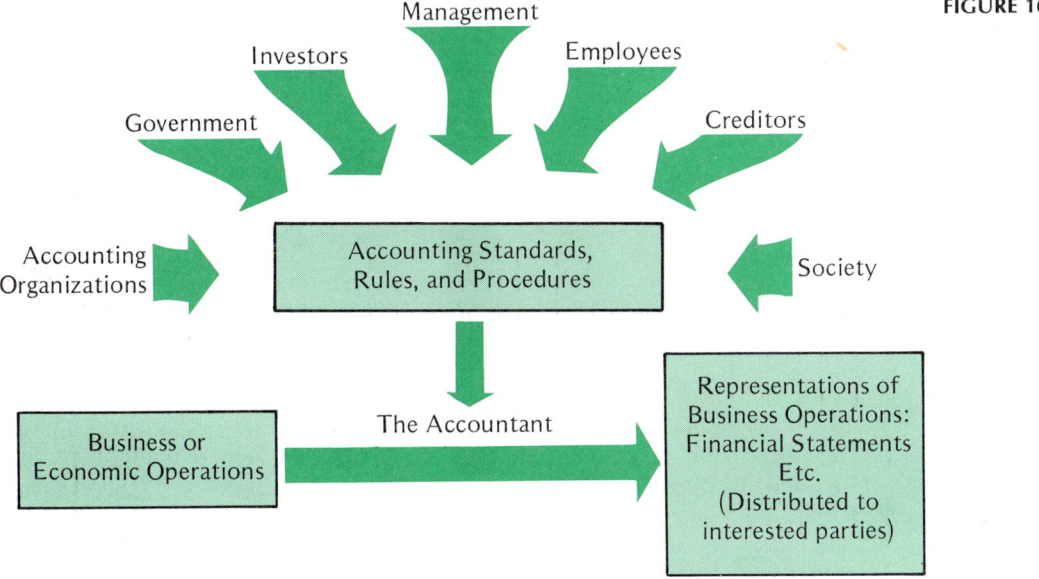
FIGURE 16-1

Unfortunately, there is no settled, authoritative set of broad principles or standards to which accountants can appeal when pressures from any one party become too severe. For many years, the accounting profession relied on a general understanding among accountants as to what constituted proper accounting. This understanding was based on accounting education, on informal exchange of experiences among accountants, and on standards and procedures enumerated by various accounting organizations. Accountants refer to the general understanding derived from these sources as "generally accepted accounting principles." Much of the force behind "good" accounting, or generally accepted accounting principles, has been derived from a general sense of professional solidarity and from a latent threat of legal action by the government if accountants do not keep their house in order. The standards founded on these rather vague bases naturally tend to be vague and inconclusive. As a result, there is considerable variation in practice within the scope of generally accepted accounting principles, and the accountant has considerable room for the exercise of judgment.

GAAP

To see the potential effect of various methods and judgments, compare the two hypothetical companies in Example 16-1. They have the same underlying operations but differ in accounting methods and judgments.

Part V Accounting Theory and Analysis

Effects of differing methods

EXAMPLE 16-1

	Pessi Co.	Opti Co.
Inventory method	LIFO	FIFO
Depreciation method	Declining-balance	Straight-line
Depreciable lives	Short	Long
Patent development costs	Written off as incurred	Capitalized as assets*
Long-term leases	Set up as liabilities	No liabilities recorded†

* This treatment may be in conflict with *FASB Statement No. 2* on research and development costs. However, we believe some discretion still exists.
† The lease agreement can probably be structured to avoid the need to capitalize the lease.

Pertinent operating data:
  This is the first year of operations for each company.
  Sales are 200,000 units for $3,000,000.
  A building worth $800,000 is leased for $75,000 per year for 25 years. The lease involves 8% interest.
  Equipment is purchased for $1,000,000.
  Purchases:

	January	100,000 units at $5
	June	100,000 units at $6
	December	100,000 units at $7

  Expenditures to develop patents (estimated life by Opti Co. is 10 years) are $200,000.
  The companies have sold capital stock, hired and paid employees, and engaged in other activities as might be expected.

Income Statements
First Year of Operation

	Pessi Co.	Opti. Co.
Sales	$3,000,000	$3,000,000
Less expenses:		
Cost of goods sold	$1,300,000	$1,100,000
Patent amortization expense		20,000
Research expenses	200,000	
Depreciation on equipment	250,000*	80,000†
Rent on building		75,000
Depreciation on building	64,000‡	
Interest on lease	64,000§	
Salaries and other expenses	1,000,000	1,000,000
Total expenses	$2,878,000	$2,275,000
Income before taxes	$ 122,000	$ 725,000
Income taxes at 50%	61,000	362,500
Net income	$ 61,000	$ 362,500

* Based on declining balance, 8-year life, no salvage.
† Based on straight-line, 12-year life, $40,000 salvage.
‡ Based on 25-year life, double-declining balance.
§ 8% of $800,000.

Balance Sheets
End of First Year of Operation

	Pessi Co.	Opti. Co.
Assets		
Current Assets:		
Cash	$ 335,000	$ 335,000
Receivables	300,000	300,000
Inventories	500,000	700,000
Total current assets	$1,135,000	$1,335,000
Property, plant, and equipment:		
Land	50,000	50,000
Building	800,000	
Less accumulated depreciation	(64,000)	
Net	736,000	
Equipment	$1,000,000	$1,000,000
Less accumulated depreciation	(250,000)	(80,000)
Net	750,000	920,000
Total plant assets	$1,536,000	$ 970,000
Intangible assets: Patents		$ 180,000
Total assets	$2,671,000	$2,485,000
Liabilities and Stockholders' Equity		
Current liabilities:		
Accounts payable	$ 260,000	$ 260,000
Income taxes payable	61,000	362,500
Total current liabilities	$ 321,000	$ 622,500
Long-term liabilities:		
Lease obligations	789,000*	
Total liabilities	$1,110,000	$ 622,500
Stockholders' equity:		
Capital stock	$1,500,000	$1,500,000
Retained earnings	61,000	362,500
Total stockholders' equity	$1,561,000	$1,862,500
Total liabilities and stockholders' equity	$2,671,000	$2,485,000

* $800,000 beginning obligation less principal payment of $11,000 ($75,000 less interest of $64,000).

The differences on the income statements in example 16-1 are striking. Notice the differences in cost of goods sold, depreciation, research expense, interest expense, and, particularly, net income. Corresponding differences appear on the balance sheets, particularly in inventories, plant assets, intangibles, and long-term liabilities. Some of these differences will become less pronounced in subsequent years of operation, but other differences will continue to be large, especially on the balance sheet. For example, by the tenth year, the expenses shown by Opti Co. for patent amortization expense will be 10% of the costs of each of 10 years. This will approximate the expense shown by Pessi Co. On the balance sheet, however, Pessi Co. will show no intangible asset, whereas Opti Co. will have accumulated patent assets from 10 years (less appropriate amortization).

Long-run effects

Thus, it is clear that two companies with similar operations could display dissimilar results because of different accounting treatments. The different accounting treatments used in Example 16-1 are all acceptable; all of the methods fall within the scope of "generally accepted accounting principles." This is unfortunate, for, to a considerable extent, management can show any results it wants by choosing particular accounting treatments. The only restriction, and it is an important one, is that once a particular treatment is chosen it must be followed consistently.

HISTORICAL DEVELOPMENT OF ACCOUNTING PRINCIPLES AND STANDARDS

We will now trace the historical developments in accounting that have led to the present situation. Besides helping you to understand the present, this summary will help you to see the possible forms that future developments may take.

Early Developments

At about the beginning of this century, the increasing public interest in business affairs, the awakening social conscience of businessmen, the need for large capital investments, and the activities of government combined to bring about an interest in standards of accounting. The growth of accountancy in the United States was accelerated by the income tax provisions of World War I. Accountancy continued to grow during the twenties, when there was increased activity on the part of accounting organizations, principally the American Institute of Certified Public Accountants (AICPA). Other groups, such as banking groups and the New York Stock Exchange, also became active. These groups were interested in full and accurate disclosure in accounting statements, and they worked with the AICPA in developing standards.

The 1930s

The depression of the 1930s, with its widespread economic collapse and its many business failures, brought dramatic changes in the accounting situation. The different groups realized that their previous efforts had been insufficient. There had been too much latitude in accounting procedures and standards. In particular, accountants and businessmen realized that they had allowed the enthusiasm of the twenties to influence them unduly. Accompanying this reassessment by accountants and other interested parties was a considerable intensification of activity on the part of the federal government. This activity involved increased intervention in, and regulation of, business, a trend that has continued to the present. Government activity also involved direct concern with financial statements and accounting standards. The Securities and Exchange Commission (SEC) was established under the Securities Act of 1933 and the Securities Exchange Act of 1934. Companies that issued securities to the public or were listed on the stock exchange were required to file annual audited statements with the SEC. The SEC was given legal power to determine and regulate accounting standards and procedures of companies that fall within its jurisdiction. The SEC acted with remarkable restraint in this area, however. For the most part, it relied on responsible accounting bodies, particularly the AICPA, to regulate the profession and to determine and enforce acceptable accounting principles.

SEC

The AICPA acted with vigor to speak as an authoritative voice in accounting and thus to justify the SEC's reliance. The AICPA's Committee on Accounting Procedure considered accounting problems and, beginning in 1939, issued occasional pronouncements, called Accounting Research Bulletins. Most of these bulletins dealt with specific practical problems, rather than with accounting principles or standards as a whole. The only group that took a more comprehensive approach was the American Accounting Association (composed primarily of professors of accounting), which, beginning in 1936, issued several short summaries of principles, called "Accounting Standards Underlying Corporate Financial Statements." These summaries had some effect on accounting developments, but other emerging forces probably were more influential.

Emerging Forces—Taxes and Inflation

One important factor influencing accounting was the sharp increase in income taxes. With corporate tax rates climbing to 50% and higher, and with individual rates as high as 90% at times, taxes became an important factor in all decisions. For example, if a company was deciding on the appropriate inventory method, the method's effect on income and hence on income taxes became very important. Another factor influencing accounting was the steady inflation that began in 1945 and has continued with varying degrees of severity ever since. Inflation, together with income taxes, influenced accounting profoundly in the post World War II era. We considered the effect of inflation at some length in chapter 15. There it was indicated that the overall effects of inflation on financial statements can be quite significant.

Inflation

The effects of inflation are clouded by the well-accepted accounting principles that state that assets should be carried on the books at their original cost to the enterprise and that changes in the general purchasing power of the dollar are not recognized. These principles have had special force because of the experience of the 1930s, which still has an effect on the thinking of the older generation of accountants. The great depression led accountants to emphasize objective and conservative asset measurements. Unfortunately, such measurements can become out of date and unrealistic in a time of rapid price changes. Nevertheless, accounting bodies such as the AICPA have been unwilling to abandon cost, in spite of the inflation that we have experienced.[1] The minimal steps that have been taken to compensate for inflation were outlined in chapter 15.

Businessmen, economists, and many accountants have argued that statements based on historical cost do not display the economic significance of cost factors. In addition, businessmen have resented paying taxes on "fictitious" income. Authoritative bodies have not been willing to abandon cost, however, and the SEC, for the most part, has supported this position. Therefore, the point of pressure has been shifted to particular practices and procedures in accounting. For example, if the basis of depreciation cannot be changed, the effects of inflation can be mitigated somewhat by writing off the asset more quickly. Therefore, pressure was brought to bear to allow accelerated depreciation methods such as sum-of-the-years'-digits and declining-balance. Similarly, the LIFO method is based on historical cost, but it gives results far different from FIFO (see chapter 9) and results in reduced taxes in a time of inflation. It became an acceptable method because businesses brought a lot of pressure to bear in favor of its adoption. Thus, pressures have led to a variety of acceptable accounting methods.

CPAs and pressure

CPAs have not always resisted this type of pressure effectively. Since CPAs depend on clients for fees, the desires and demands of clients carry a certain amount of weight. The SEC did not react strongly to the proliferation of accounting methods until the 1960s, when it became more sensitive to the effects of varying accounting methods on disclosure and comparability of statements. In recent years, the SEC has pressured the AICPA to reduce the number of acceptable alternatives in accounting practice. The stock exchanges have exerted some pressures toward full disclosure, but generally they have been content to follow the lead of the accounting profession. The forces of inflation and high taxes thus have continued to exert a great influence on accounting, through either the acquiescence or the lack of activity of the various groups that can influence accounting standards and methods.

Another force influencing accounting that often uses tax law as a vehicle is active governmental policy designed to exert some control over the economy. The investment credit provision, which allows a certain proportion of the cost of new depreciable assets to be deducted directly from taxes payable, is an example of a governmental policy designed to stimulate investment that also has accounting implications.

Another policy device of the government was the promulgation in

---

1. In some countries the cost basis has been abandoned in times of severe inflation.

1962 of new, shorter "guideline lives" for depreciable assets. The faster write-offs of assets for tax purposes were designed to increase depreciation expenses and thus to decrease income taxes. Again, the government dealt with an area of accounting policies and procedures and exerted considerable indirect pressure on depreciation accounting—pressure to make financial accounting conform to tax regulations. Even though a business may account for tax purposes on a basis different from that used for financial reporting, the business will generally find it easier and less expensive to keep both sets of records on the same basis. Thus, when a new procedure is suggested for tax purposes, there is a strong temptation for accountants to justify it as a good accounting procedure as well.

Government policy

Recent Developments in the Profession

In 1959, the AICPA responded to increased pressures in the accounting environment by creating the Accounting Principles Board (APB) and a new Accounting Research Division. The research division studied problems and published the results in Accounting Research Studies.[2] The APB considered accounting problems, met and deliberated about them, and from time to time issued APB Opinions and Statements.[3] The APB had more power than its predecessor, the Committee on Accounting Procedure, because departures by companies from recommendations in APB Opinions had to be disclosed and explained on the companies' published financial statements or the accompanying auditor's certificate. The SEC was reluctant to accept financial statements that had any indication of a departure from an APB Opinion.

APB

When the APB and the Accounting Research Division were established, the Director of Accounting Research was asked to make a study of the basic postulates underlying accounting principles and also to study the broad principles of accounting. The results of these studies, after adoption by the APB, were to be the basis for all subsequent pronouncements on financial accounting matters. Thus the AICPA intended to approach accounting problems on a comprehensive basis, in contrast to the piecemeal approach that had been used before.

The Director of Accounting Research, in accordance with his instructions, issued Accounting Research Studies dealing with postulates (ARS No. 1) and principles (ARS No. 3). The APB found these studies "too radically different from present generally accepted accounting principles for acceptance at this time."[4] The board felt that the first attempt to enunciate postulates and principles by the AICPA had turned out badly. After rejecting these two studies, the board reverted to the piecemeal

Postulates and principles

---

2. Fifteen studies were published.
3. Thirty-one Opinions and four Statements were issued.
4. Statement No. 1 of the Accounting Principles Board, April, 1962.

approach to accounting problems that had characterized its predecessor, the Committee on Accounting Procedure.

APB Statement No. 4

The APB did not completely abandon its attempts to set forth the postulates and principles of accounting. In fact, a committee of the board worked for some years on a program to develop a statement of principles. In October, 1970, the board issued *APB Statement No. 4*, entitled "Basic Concepts and Accounting Principles Underlying Financial Statements of Business Enterprises." This statement was a significant step in fulfilling the original purpose of the board. The statement does not purport to solve all the problems of financial accounting. It is limited to (1) setting forth the basic concepts of financial accounting, including objectives, and (2) describing *present* broad accounting principles, with all their faults and inconsistencies. But those two points are important, because the basic concepts had not previously been listed in an official AICPA pronouncement, and an authoritative list of broad accounting principles had never before been presented. The statement does not indicate what accounting principles should be, but it provides a good starting point for developing sound principles.

Despite publication of *Statement No. 4*, the board continued its piecemeal approach to accounting problems, as evidenced by further opinions on specific problem areas in accounting. This approach would not have been bad if the board had used a general frame of reference in dealing with the specific problems. Unfortunately, each problem was approached individually, as if it were essentially separate from the others. The statement on basic concepts and accounting principles had the potential to change the APB's approach considerably and to provide the basis for development of a consistent set of principles. Before its potential could be realized, however, the APB went out of existence. The reason for this was that many were unhappy with the quality of some of the important pronouncements of the APB. The profession concluded that while the APB had shown some promise, it did not fulfill its purposes, and in some areas its performance was very disappointing.

FASB

In 1972, partially in response to the disappointing performance of the APB, the Financial Accounting Standards Board was established. This new board consists of 7 full-time, paid members (in contrast to the 18-member, voluntary APB) and has taken over the function of issuing pronouncements on accounting principles. It has all the power of the APB and is expected to be more independent of pressures and to have more time to devote to issues than the APB. The Financial Accounting Standards Board (FASB) also has a larger basis of support than the APB, and its ties with the American Institute of CPAs are much less strong than were those of the APB. The new FASB has become active and has issued a number of statements of accounting standards. These standards deal primarily with specific problems. The FASB has attempted to deal with the conceptual framework of accounting, but for the most part it continues to deal with problems on a piecemeal basis. This is unfortunate, for the piecemeal approach has a number of drawbacks:

Piecemeal approach

1. It does not provide comprehensive guidelines to what constitutes "generally accepted accounting principles."
2. It leads to inconsistencies in accounting.
3. It leads to proliferation of alternatives.
4. It leads to reliance on practice rather than on theory and thus introduces expediency.
5. It fails to deal with new problems in an effective manner (because there are no precedents in practice).
6. It often perpetuates outmoded alternatives.

Authoritative bodies have a hard time dealing with issues on a consistent conceptual level, perhaps because of the extreme complexity of the environment in which financial accounting operates.

The APB and the FASB have not been the only parties active in the development of accounting principles and practices in recent years. The American Accounting Association, through a series of committees, has made comprehensive pronouncements on a number of basic matters and has issued several brief summaries of theory. In 1966, the AAA issued *A Statement of Basic Accounting Theory*, which emphasizes that accounting is a communication device useful in forming judgments and making decisions. The study differs from present practice primarily in its advocacy of current cost data for both the income statement and the balance sheet (current cost data were discussed at some length in chapter 15). This advocacy of current costs, a considerable departure from accounting tradition, did not receive an enthusiastic reception from the AICPA and the SEC. Essentially, it was the advocacy of current costs that had caused the APB to reject the early Accounting Research Studies on postulates and principles. The American Accounting Association has never been concerned about the immediate adoption of its suggestions, however. It adopts a long-range point of view and attempts to lead current practice by several years rather than simply following it.

AAA statement

Current costs

The SEC has become more active in recent years. In particular, it has put considerable pressure on the APB and the FASB. The chairman and the chief accountant of the SEC have urged greater speed in dealing with the problems of financial statements and the profession.

Other groups have also become more active. The government has established the Cost Accounting Standards Board (CASB) to set standards in the area of accounting for government contracts. Because many companies do business with the government, the CASB has considerable influence. Other groups, such as the Financial Executives Institute, the National Association of Accountants, and the Financial Analysts Federation, have become increasingly concerned with the formulation of ac-

Cost standards board

counting principles. All these groups react to proposed pronouncements and try to influence the FASB, the SEC, and the CASB.

Why is this so? Because accounting deals with important information in our economy, and interested parties want to have a hand in the form and content of the information. To put it differently, the information determined by accounting principles and rules can directly affect the well-being of numerous interested parties, and they are naturally interested in how the principles and rules are shaped.

Litigation

An important result of the strategic position of accountants for the provision of information is their increasing involvement in litigation. As society recognizes the crucial role of information, society begins to hold those who have a part in providing the information responsible for its quality and usefulness. At times, too, we seek a scapegoat when things go badly—hence we sue whoever is involved and whoever might have some degree of responsibility. The courts have shown a tendency to expand the liability of professionals and thus have tended to encourage a climate of litigation. This has been a severe problem in the medical profession, as we are all aware. It has also been a serious problem in the accounting profession.

What effect does increased litigation have? One important effect is an emphasis on safety, on minimizing exposure to risk. Historical cost fits well into this emphasis, because the historical cost amounts are definitely verifiable. Current costs, being based to some extent on estimates or on prices in transactions in which the enterprise is not involved, involve more risks. Another important effect of litigation, pulling in the opposite direction, is a concern that the information provided portray the actual circumstances and be useful in decisions. This tends to lead to current information and current costs. These two crosscurrents present accountants with a problem that has not yet been resolved.

WHERE ARE WE NOW?

At this point, let us look at the present situation in accounting. There are increasing pressures on accounting, but there is also a relatively new structure for dealing with pressures in the form of the Financial Accounting Standards Board. We now have a fairly effective device for enforcing Opinions and Standards. *APB Statement No. 4* provides a list of basic concepts and present principles and may well be the basis for future progress. The FASB has used *APB Statement No. 4* extensively and has attempted to develop a general conceptual framework, but it remains to be seen whether the FASB will abandon a piecemeal approach. There is much pressure to narrow areas of differences in accounting practices. The Financial Accounting Standards Board is highly conscious of this pressure and recognizes that much needs to be done. The board is spurred on by the knowledge that accountants, investors, and others are dissatisfied with the present state of affairs and the present rate of progress. This dissatisfaction indicates that accounting is a fast-moving field of activity and that it shares in the multitudinous problems of a rapidly changing world. If accounting were cut and dried, it would be dull and uninteresting and probably not very significant. The turmoil it is in is a sign of its vitality.

WHERE ARE WE GOING?

Accounting will undergo many changes in the next few years. We can look for continued activity on the part of the FASB, prodded at times by the SEC. It is unlikely that either the board or the SEC will advocate radical innovations in accounting, however. Radical changes in accounting will probably stem from radical changes in our society. Use of current costs in financial statements, for example, will probably become generally accepted only under the impetus of a high degree of inflation.

We can also look for continued and increased pressure on accounting standards and procedures in the future. The groups discussed earlier will probably intensify their interest in the results of the accounting process. One reason is that the effects of changes in accounting standards can often be measured in millions of dollars. But the basic reason is that information is a precious commodity in our world, and since the accounting process is an information process, it is naturally the focus of much attention.

Increased pressures

When a field expands quickly and undergoes rapid change, some basic thought must be given to its functions, its boundaries, its direction, and its effectiveness. Most of the significant work in defining the boundaries of accounting, tracing its relationships to other disciplines, and delineating its purposes and methodology has been done by individuals rather than organizations. Typically, these individuals concentrate on one particular phase of accounting, although sometimes they take a more comprehensive approach and construct a complete system of accounting theory. The efforts of individuals are discussed, mulled over, criticized and reformulated in new ways, and finally they have an overall effect on the development of accounting.

Theory development

One interesting avenue of exploration in recent years has been the study of the fundamental assumptions or postulates of accounting—the basic foundation on which all accounting standards and practices are built. In addition to the study on postulates by the Accounting Research Division, contributions have been made by many individuals.

Another interesting feature of research in accounting theory has been the exploration of interrelationships with other disciplines. The web of interrelationships has been woven by the modern, many-legged spider of complexity and interaction. Accountants are just now beginning to try to untangle the strands of this web. Interesting relationships to logic, communications theory, economics, psychology, mathematics, and other fields are being explored. The results, while beyond the scope of this chapter, suggest some interesting new insights for the field of accounting. Only as accountants attain fuller understanding of their position in the web of interrelationships and reach an understanding of the nature and strength of the pressures that affect them can they become really effective in fulfilling the purposes of accounting.

Accountants are becoming increasingly known as information processing specialists. In the future, therefore, accountants will be expected to become involved in preparing all sorts of information needed by society. For example, if compliance with environmental legislation is questioned, CPAs might be called on to audit compliance; if productivity is being measured, accountants might be involved in the measurement; if success of social programs is being measured, accountants might be called on to do the measuring. These types of activities provide tremendous opportunities to the accountant of the future, as long as he or she does not have too narrow a view of what accountants do.

PURPOSES AND OBJECTIVES OF ACCOUNTING

Basic Purpose

We have suggested throughout this book that accounting is an instrument that yields services to others. The particular area of service is provision of information about economic affairs (usually enterprise-oriented) that is useful in making decisions. Indeed, this is the basic purpose of financial accounting. However, this basic purpose can be interpreted in a variety of ways. The Accounting Principles Board gave its interpretation of the basic purpose by listing objectives of financial statements in *APB Statement No. 4*. These objectives are of two types—general and qualitative. The general objectives are to provide the following:

General Objectives

1. Reliable information about an enterprise's economic resources and obligations
2. Reliable information about economic progress of the enterprise
3. Reliable information about other changes in the enterprise's resources and obligations
4. Information helpful in estimating earnings potential.
5. Other financial information needed by users

These general objectives, which were discussed in chapter 1, relate financial accounting information to the environment in which the enterprise operates, to the underlying economic activities of enterprises, and to the interests and needs of users of the information. The objectives direct our attention to the "real world" and suggest that we should attempt to measure and communicate information about economic resources and obligations and economic progress. Our balance sheet and income statement attempt to do this, but we must not lose sight of what it is we are trying to measure.

The qualitative objectives are as follows:

Qualitative objectives

1. Relevance (the primary objective)
2. Understandability
3. Verifiability
4. Neutrality
5. Timeliness
6. Comparability
7. Completeness

The qualitative objectives specify the qualities accounting information should have. They are ideal standards that we should try to attain. An emphasis on relevance directs our attention to users' needs and users' decision processes. This is an important element in developing useful financial accounting information.

The efforts of the APB to develop objectives were followed by the appointment in 1971 of a study group on objectives of financial statements. This group, which originally was supposed to make the objectives of accounting from *APB Statement No. 4* operational, published its report, *Objectives of Financial Statements,* in 1973. The basic objective developed by the group is to provide information useful for making economic decisions. Further objectives of financial statements, according to the report, are as follows:

- To serve primarily those users who must rely on financial statements as their principal source of information
- To provide information useful to investors and creditors for predicting, comparing, and evaluating potential cash flows
- To provide users with information for predicting, comparing and evaluating enterprise earning power
- To supply information useful in judging management's ability to utilize enterprise resources effectively in maximizing cash return
- To provide information about transactions and other events that is useful in predicting, comparing, and evaluating enterprise earning power
- To provide a statement of financial position, a statement of periodic earnings, and a statement of financial activities useful for predicting, comparing, and evaluating enterprise earning power
- To provide information useful for the predictive process
- To report on those activities of the enterprise affecting society that can be determined and described or measured and that are important to the role of the enterprise in its social environment

Objectives from 1973 report

Cash flows

These objectives are interesting for their emphasis on cash flows and also for their emphasis on predictions. The relationship of cash flows to income flows is dealt with in chapter 17. We believe that cash flows must be used with care as indicators of enterprise progress. The objectives study group relied on the regular financial statements in connection with cash flow prediction, but the relationships were not clearly developed in the study group report. Also, it should be noted that the report did not necessarily contemplate financial statements in their present form. It is quite likely that financial statements useful in predicting and comparing cash flows or cash-flow-oriented earning power might be quite different from traditional statements.

The report on objectives of financial statements also included seven qualitative characteristics of reporting that information should possess. These are

- Relevance
- Form and substance
- Reliability
- Freedom from bias
- Comparability
- Consistency
- Understandability

It can be seen that these characteristics are similar in content to the qualitative objectives listed earlier.

There is some argument about the extent to which the report of the study group advanced the profession in its search for operational objectives. The report is important because it is another indicator of the concern of the profession with the purpose and function of accounting. It is also important because it introduced explicit concern with cash flows into the official literature.

The FASB issued its tentative conclusions on objectives in 1976. The board enunciated three very broad objectives. The first identifies the users of statements—investors and creditors. The second identifies their needs—for information about possible cash flows. The third indicates the information that should aid in meeting user needs—information about economic resources and obligations and changes in resources and obligations. These objectives combined some of the ideas of the objectives in *APB Statement No. 4* and of the objectives study group report. They further emphasized the primary importance of the usefulness of financial statements for economic decisions.

The FASB has now issued its final report on objectives. The conclusions did not differ significantly from those in the tentative report issued in 1976. In future years the implications of the objectives of financial accounting will be developed in accounting practice. The objectives form an important basis for judging accounting standards or principles and are an important determinant of the direction accounting can be expected to take.

The discussion in previous chapters should be reconsidered in light of the basic purpose of providing useful information and the supporting objectives. Many rules and procedures were discussed in previous chapters, and it is easy to begin to emphasize them as ends in themselves. The rules and procedures, however, have developed because of their usefulness to interested parties (or to the accountants themselves, who must, of course, consider their own well-being). These rules and procedures should constantly be examined to see if they are still useful and if they contribute to the overall usefulness of accounting or just to the needs of one particular group.

Using objectives

Accounting has often demonstrated its usefulness to particular groups by providing them with specialized information that fits their particular needs. Some hold that the financial statements are themselves the vehicle for providing information to one special group—investors. Most accountants agree, however, that financial accounting seeks to serve many interested parties by providing basic financial statements that have general usefulness. Does financial accounting successfully serve the many groups to whom it presents information? Or does it, in seeking to serve many diverse parties, end up not being very useful to anyone? This last question is one that strikes at the very roots of financial accounting, but it is typical of the questions that must be asked when basic ideas in accounting are evaluated. It is the type of question that must constantly be asked in a dynamic field of study such as accounting.

FINANCIAL ACCOUNTING THEORY IN PERSPECTIVE

Accounting theory has been emphasized throughout the preceding chapters, but no attempt has been made to present a coordinated picture of financial accounting theory or to place the various concepts and ideas in any framework of theory. That is the task of this section.

The Environment

It is helpful to begin by considering the environment in which financial accounting operates. This environment, pictured in Figure 16-2, consists of the world of economic interactions, with particular emphasis on activities of enterprises. The users of accounting information and accountants themselves are part of the environment. The series of interactions indicated in the diagram reflects the fact that the user's needs and decisions affect accountants and enterprises; the nature of enterprises affects ac-

Part V   Accounting Theory and Analysis

FIGURE 16-2   Environment and Economic Activity

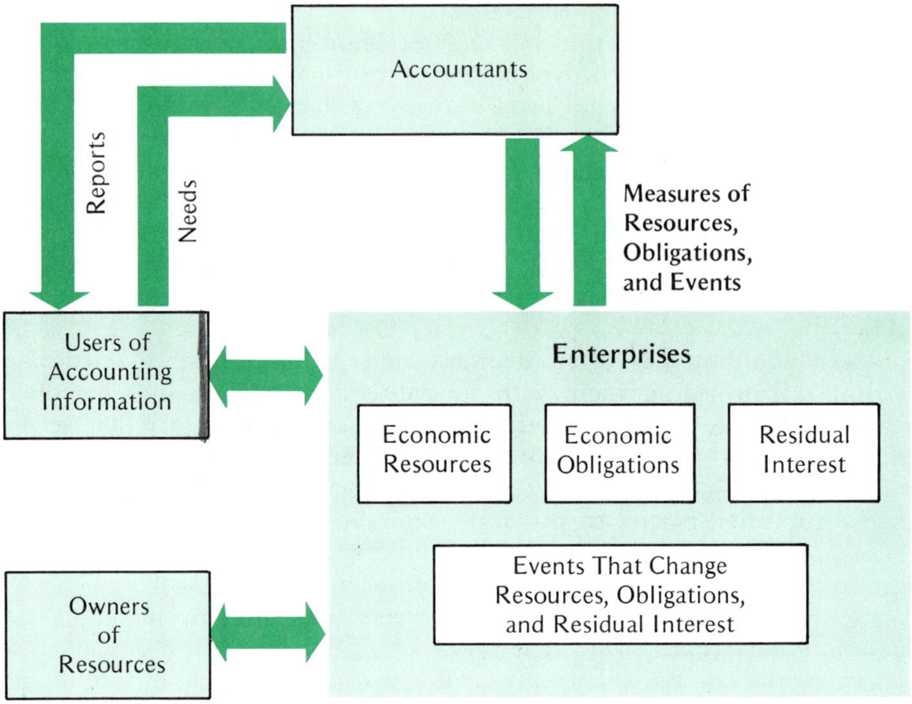

countants and the way they interpret and measure activities; the enterprise activities affect the income, position, and power of users; and so on.

The environment is characterized by immense complexity and by interactions of parties and activities, posing grave difficulties to anyone who tries to isolate and measure events. It is necessary to abstract from environmental complexity and to interpret the environment in order to deal with it successfully. This is one of the purposes of a body of theory. In turn, a theory can be judged by how well it reflects and deals with the environment.

A Theory Framework

In order to bring some of the ideas of previous chapters together and to relate concepts to each other, a brief summary of financial accounting theory is presented below. The framework is pictured in Figure 16-3.

The student should recognize that the framework illustrated would not necessarily be accepted by all accountants. For example, it uses terms

Financial Accounting Theory Framework

FIGURE 16-3

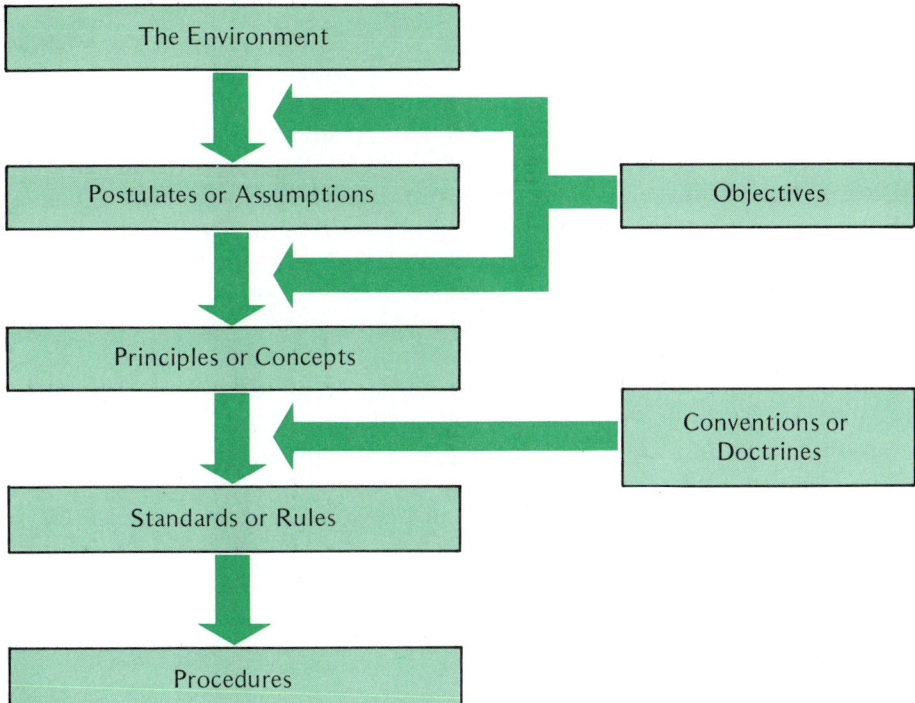

such as objectives, postulates, principles, conventions, rules, and procedures. These terms are not rigorously defined in present accounting thought, and not all accountants would agree with the way the terms are used in the framework.

The framework begins with the environment. This is the source of theory. The postulates, or assumptions, are interpretations and abstractions from the environment and are the starting point for deductively oriented theoretical systems. They serve as the foundation on which the structure of concepts is erected. Every area of study operates on the basis of certain assumptions, or postulates, and accounting is no exception. When investigating theory, it is important to recognize what the assumptions are, since only in this way can real progress be made. Objectives are ideas that shape our interpretation of the environment and the derivation of principles from postulates. Principles, or concepts, presumably should follow from assumptions. Each principle should be derived from, and related to, assumptions and other principles and should be consistent with objectives. The function of principles is to spell out the implications of the assumptions and objectives when they are applied to a particular area of inquiry. The principles also provide a guide as to what constitutes proper accounting. The principles listed in detail below are present principles, which are not necessarily ideal principles. Most theorists believe that present principles have serious defects. The principles are listed because they are the basis for present practice and the starting point for future progress in developing more satisfactory principles. Conventions, or doctrines, in accounting are conceived of as auxiliary concepts that influence the application of principles to practice. They are typical behavior patterns of accountants. Their nature can be seen in the listing below. When the principles are applied to practical situations, a series of rules, or standards, are formulated. The actual application to particular situations involves procedures derived from the standards or rules.

Before stating the various elements of the theory framework, we should mention that the following summary is limited to financial accounting. The theory behind managerial accounting is not included because it is outside the scope of this book and because managerial accounting does not have a well-developed theory structure.

The summary below is based in part on *APB Statement No. 4*. The parenthetical information indicates the previous objectives, assumptions, or principles to which the item is related. The relationships are not spelled out specifically but can be established if the various concepts are studied carefully. The letters and numbers used are for identification only; they do not indicate any standard numbering or listing system that is used in accounting generally.

SUMMARY OF FINANCIAL ACCOUNTING THEORY

Basic Purpose

To provide financial information about individual business enterprises that is useful in making economic decisions.

Objectives

General objectives
To present

G1 Reliable information about enterprise resources and obligations.
G2 Reliable information about economic progress of the enterprise.
G3 Reliable information about other changes in enterprise resources and obligations.
G4 Information helpful in estimating earnings potential.
G5 Other financial information needed by users.

Qualitative objectives

Q1 Relevance (the primary objective).
Q2 Understandability.
√Q3 Verifiability.
Q4 Neutrality.
Q5 Timeliness.
Q6 Comparability.
Q7 Completeness.

Postulates

P1 Accounting entity—Economic activities of entities can be distinguished from those of their owners.

P2 Going concern—Continuation of entity operations can be assumed in the absence of evidence to the contrary.

√ P3 Measurement of economic resources and obligations—Financial accounting is concerned primarily with measurement of economic resources and obligations and changes in them.

P4 Time periods—Financial information is most useful when it is expressed in terms of relatively short time periods.

P5 Measurement in terms of money—The unit of money is an appropriate unit of measure.

P6 Accrual—Determining periodic income and financial position depends on measurement of noncash resources and obligations.

P7 Exchange price—Financial accounting measurements are primarily based on exchange prices.

P8 Approximation and judgment—Approximations are inevitable in the allocations required in financial accounting. Measures of economic events are tentative and require the use of judgment.

P9 General-purpose financial information—General purpose financial information is useful to a variety of interested parties.

P10 Stable unit of measure—The measuring unit is stable. (This assumption is quite controversial and is rejected by many. It is used in present accounting, however.)

Principles or Concepts

C1 Initial recording—Assets and liabilities generally are initially recorded on the basis of events in which the enterprise acquires resources from other entities or incurs obligations to other entities. The assets and liabilities are measured by the exchange prices at which the transfers take place. (P3, P4, P7, Q3)

C2 Realization—Revenue is generally recognized when both of the following conditions are met: (1) the earning process is complete or virtually complete, and (2) an exchange has taken place. (P7, Q3)

C3 Associating cause and effect—Some costs are recognized as expenses on the basis of a presumed direct association with specific revenue. (P3, P6)

C4 Systematic and rational allocation—In the absence of a direct means of association with revenue, some costs are associated with specific accounting periods as expenses on the basis of an attempt to allocate costs in a systematic and rational manner among the periods in which benefits are provided. (P6, P8)

C5 Immediate recognition—Some costs are associated with the current accounting period as expenses because (1) costs incurred during the period provide no discernible future benefits, (2) costs recorded as assets in prior periods no longer provide discernible benefits, or (3) allocating costs either on the basis of direct association with revenue or among several accounting periods is considered to serve no useful purpose. (P6, P8)

C6 Modification to reflect change—Accounting statements and reports should be based on information that has been appropriately modified or adjusted to reflect changes since the original recording date. (P3, P6, P8)

C7 Facilitation of comparisons—Accounting reports should include classifications, summaries, and arrangements of data to facilitate comparisons between periods and among entities and to facilitate decision making. (P9, Q2, Q6)

C8 Full disclosure—Accounting reports should include disclosures of changes in application of accounting rules from period to period and other information of a financial nature that might aid the user in interpreting the basic financial statements. (P9, Q1, Q7)

Conventions or Doctrines

(Conventions or doctrines modify the application of principles.)

M1 Conservatism—Certain rules adopted by the accounting profession as a whole require that possible errors in measurement be in the direction of understatement rather than overstatement of net income and net assets. (Q3, P8)

M2 Emphasis on income—Accounting rules that are deemed to increase the usefulness of the income statement are sometimes adopted by the accounting profession as a whole regardless of their effect on the balance sheet or other financial statements. (P8)

M3 Consistency—Once an accounting method is adopted, it should not be changed. If a change is made, the effects should be clearly disclosed. (Q6)

M4 Substance over form—Financial accounting often emphasizes the economic substance of events even though the legal form may differ from the economic substance and suggest different treatment. (P3)

M5 Smoothing of periodic income—Certain rules have been adopted by the accounting profession that smooth periodic income by spreading gains and losses over several periods instead of recognizing the full effect of the item in one period.

M6 Application of judgment by the accounting profession as a whole—When strict adherence to the basic principles is considered to produce results that are unreasonable in the circumstances or possibly misleading, the applications are modified in accordance with rules adopted by the profession. (P8)

M7 Materiality—Financial reporting is only concerned with significant information. (Q1)

Standards or Rules

From the principles and conventions above, accountants formulate rules, or standards, for application to actual situations. Examples of accounting rules follow:

- The cost of a piece of equipment should be allocated over its useful life in such a way that the cost assigned to each period reflects the benefits rendered to the periods. (Based on C1, C3, C4, C6, C7. Assignment to periods is expected to be useful in decisions [C7]; it probably will involve adjusting entries [C6]; it is related to original cost [C1]; and it facilitates matching and should reflect the flow of benefits [C3 and C4].)

- The recorded cost of an asset should include the net cash cost of the asset plus any expenditures necessary to get the asset to the place of business and ready for use. (Based on C1 and a consideration of the question of what constitutes cost.)

Procedures

The procedures of accounting deal with the application of rules, or standards, in a specific case. Examples of procedures that might be used to apply the above depreciation rule follow:

- Straight-line depreciation—Take the cost less the salvage and divide it by the number of periods of asset life to obtain the periodic charge.
- Declining-balance depreciation—Double the straight-line rate and apply

this percentage to the cost less accumulated depreciation each period to obtain the periodic charge.

When there are several alternatives, the accountant should theoretically choose procedures that best make the data in the specific situation conform to accounting principles and rules and best conform to the objectives.

Comments on Theory

The outline of theory presented above is based on traditional accounting. At present, there is considerable unrest among accounting theorists, and many authors believe the above framework is too restrictive. The first section of this chapter indicated some of the problems that have been raised in this area and also indicated possible directions for accounting theory.

The outline is not perfect and certainly is subject to revision. It is meant to pass the test of internal consistency, fruitfulness, and relevance, however. *Consistency* means that various parts of the theory do not contradict each other. *Fruitfulness* means that the theory has important implications and is not trivial. *Relevance* means that the theory influences a sphere of action. We leave unanswered the question whether a different set of postulates and principles would be more fruitful and relevant. This question must be answered by each person individually. It is a question that the accounting profession is actively exploring at present and one that many thoughtful accountants are concerned about. Many believe that basic changes in the accounting theory structure are necessary. Some possible avenues of approach were indicated in chapter 15.

We hope that the framework presented above not only helps the student to see how the parts hang together, but also stimulates discussion and criticism. At the same time, the reader is cautioned that a critical examination of accounting theory must involve further study of concepts that were only hinted at or at most briefly considered in this text.

SUMMARY

In this chapter we have looked at the historical development of accounting, considered some of the pressures acting on accountants, and tried to indicate the open-endedness of many questions facing accounting today. A simple framework of accounting theory was also presented. The framework began with the environment, and continued with the objectives, postulates, principles, rules, and procedures. The framework, although it is far from perfect, should provide a basis for organizing the conceptual material presented in this text.

The entire discussion emphasized the continuing dynamism in the area of accounting theory and the room for growth and development in both the theory and the practice of accounting.

IMPORTANT TERMS

Generally accepted accounting principles
AICPA
SEC
Committee on Accounting Procedure
American Accounting Association
Accounting Principles Board
Accounting Research Studies
Postulates or assumptions
Principles
Financial Accounting Standards Board
Cost Accounting Standards Board
General objectives
Qualitative objectives
Environment
Conventions or doctrines
Standards or rules
Procedures

QUESTIONS

16-1. How successful is accounting in fulfilling its basic purpose? Be specific in your criticism.

16-2. Is it desirable to narrow areas of differences in accounting practice? Discuss arguments for and against.

16-3. How would you suggest that we narrow differences in the following specific areas: depreciation methods, inventory methods?

16-4. Can the independent accountant (the CPA) be an arbitrator among the various parties in an enterprise in light of the pressures to which he is subjected?

16-5. Why is management in a strategic position for influencing the accounting for an enterprise? What are the implications of this position of influence?

16-6. If management wanted to maximize the amount of net income shown on this year's statement, what possible steps might it take? Discuss accounting approaches, not operating approaches.

16-7. Should the SEC take a more active role in promulgating accounting principles? Why or why not?

16-8. What is the relationship between the going concern assumption as discussed in the text and the valuation placed on those assets described as *unexpired costs*?

16-9. Refer to the brief summary of accounting theory at the end of the chapter.
  a. What postulates or assumptions do you question? State these in a form that is more acceptable to you.
  b. What principles and conventions do you question? Indicate the changes you would recommend.

16-10. If your expanding company were faced with considerable inflation and the possibility of slightly higher income tax rates, which of the alternative accounting methods would you choose from the following sets? State your reasons.
   a. LIFO or FIFO for inventories.
   b. Straight-line or declining-balance depreciation.
   c. Minimum or maximum estimated life for depreciation.
   d. Capitalize or immediately write off patent development costs.

16-11. A friend of yours who is studying economics expresses doubt that there is such a thing as accounting theory. Write a short defense of the position that there is accounting theory.

16-12. Suppose that price levels changed radically and it became desirable to reflect the effects of price-level changes in accounting reports. Could this be done within the theory framework set forth in the chapter? If not, indicate which postulates and principles would have to be changed in order to reflect the effects of price-level changes in accounting reports.

16-13. Why do accountants generally ignore market values in valuing assets? What exceptions are there to disregarding market prices in valuation?

16-14. Explain the concept of realization in accounting. Why do accountants generally ignore the fact that income is earned throughout the process of production?

16-15. What is the going concern assumption? In light of the fact that there is a rather low survival rate for new businesses, is this a valid assumption?

16-16. What is meant by materiality in accounting?

16-17. Describe the three expense recognition principles used in financial accounting. Are these principles unambiguous; that is, could different people apply them to the same data and arrive at essentially similar results? Discuss.

16-18. As the federal income tax is used more and more as an instrument of social and economic policy, what is the relationship between what is good accounting and what is good for taxes? What is the likely effect of tax innovations and changes on accounting practices?

EXERCISES

16-19. *Terminology.*
   a. Earned
   b. Realization
   c. Consistency
   d. Periodicity
   e. Recognition
   f. Accrual accounting
   g. Conservatism
   h. Cash basis accounting
   i. Stable unit of measure assumption

Each of the terms above has special implications in accounting. Match the correct term with the listed definitions and descriptions below.
1. The process of recording in the accounting records some transaction of the enterprise.
2. The occurrence of some event that causes an economic development of the firm (e.g., a revenue) to become certain enough and objective enough to be recorded in the accounting records.
3. The type of accounting that attempts to recognize expenses and revenues at the time of their economic influence on the firm rather than when the expenses and revenues are paid and received.
4. The concept that recognizes the usefulness of analyzing a firm's activity in terms of time periods even though that activity usually occurs on a continuous basis without clear time breaks.
5. The policy that requires that inventory be written down if market values are below cost but that frowns on write-ups when market exceeds cost.
6. The accounting policy that requires that chosen accounting methods be followed by an enterprise without repeated changes from one method to another.

16-20. *Full disclosure.* A company shows the long-term investments in its balance sheet as follows: Investments (market value $300,000) at cost $100,000.
  a. Is this full disclosure? Comment. Does this treatment conform to the concepts of accounting? Explain. What is your overall evaluation of this treatment?
  b. Suppose that the above investments, which cost $100,000, had been held for a number of years, and that last year the market value of the investments was $360,000. Comment on the income statement disclosure in this case.
  c. In part *a*, would it make any difference if the asset was a building instead of an investment? Explain.

16-21. *Matching.* How should the accountant handle each of the following situations in the accounts in order to relate costs properly with revenues? Write brief, but complete, answers.
  a. A company pays $4,000 for advertising this period for a product that will not be offered for sale until next period.
  b. A company collects $20 membership fees in October for one-year memberships that last until the end of next September. The company's year ends December 31.
  c. Ford Motor Company sells a car in the current year with a 2-year, 20,000 mile warranty.
  d. Time-Life, Inc., sells a 3-year subscription to one of its magazines for $27.
  e. Time-Life, Inc., receives a payment in December for advertising to be run in January issues, which will appear in the next fiscal year.
  f. Time-Life, Inc., spends $8,000 in December for layout and other work in connection with the advertising in *e* above.
  (Solution in Appendix B.)

16-22. *Periodicity.* A large toy manufacturer included a $10 million estimated insurance recovery in its income statement. A footnote explained that the amount was the estimated recovery on a business interruption insurance policy that covered operations in a foreign plant that had burned down during the year. The estimated recovery added $.33 a share to earnings, which were $1.11 a share, as compared to earnings of $.92 in the previous year. A critical article in Barron's asked whether it was appropriate to include the $10 million in income for the year, in light of the fact that none of it had been collected and that collection of the full amount was by no means assured. Comment on the appropriate treatment of the estimated insurance recovery.

16-23. *Pressures.* The president of a large construction company realizes that a large construction job that is almost completed at the end of the year will result in a loss of $400,000 rather than a profit. The usual procedure in these circumstances is to reduce the inventory valuation for the job in process by the amount of the loss. The president also knows that there is a lawsuit for $500,000 pending against the company. Income without considering the above two items is $650,000 for the year. The president instructs the chief accountant to ignore both items and not record any effect on net income this year.

Required:

a. If you were the chief accountant, what would you do in this situation?
b. If you were an independent CPA called in to audit the company, what would you do? How might you discover the items?

16-24. *Income concepts.* The Brekker Company manufactures a product that has been phenomenally successful. It has had no difficulty in selling all units it can produce at a price of $12 each. Production costs are $8 per unit. Selling costs amount to $1 per unit. Other expenses are $60,000 per year. During the current year the company produces 60,000 units and sells 50,000 units. The other 10,000 units have just been finished at year-end and are expected to be sold early the next year.

Required:

a. What is the income for the year under generally accepted accounting principles?
b. What is income if the realization principle is ignored and income is recognized when production is completed?
c. What method of income recognition best reflects the economic realities for Brekker? Discuss.

PROBLEMS

16-25. *Alternative procedures.* The LPO Corporation is a large computer manufacturer. The company follows the practice of expensing all research and development costs as they are incurred. R & D expenditures for the last few years have been as follows:

	Millions of dollars	
Year	Research Costs	Net Income
1	$120	$350
2	180	400
3	220	560
4	300	570
5	360	640
6	210	580
7	450	650

Year 6 was a year of general economic downturn.

Research and development has a long-range effect. That is, today's research is often on ideas that become products in 3 to 10 years.

Required:
Comment on the policies of the company and the effects of the expensing of research and development costs.

16-26. *Revenue recognition.* In recent years a number of land development companies have found themselves unable to collect on receivables arising from sales made in earlier years. The customers have surrendered the land they purchased rather than continuing payments. A typical situation might be as follows:

Sale to Jones in Year 1	$10,000
Down payment collected in Year 1	500
Yearly payments	500
Cost of land sold	1,800

Default on payments in Year 3 after $1,300 in total has been collected.

Required:
a. Land development companies typically recorded a $10,000 sale in the year the down payment was received (Year 1). Comment on the results of this procedure.
b. How would you recommend that revenue be recognized? Support your suggested approach by referring to specific objectives, postulates, principles, and conventions.

16-27. *Expense recognition.* An electrical appliance manufacturer guarantees its appliances for 2 years after sale. For each $1,000,000 of sales the experience in the past has been as follows:

Cost of repairs	Amount
First three months after sale	$ 5,000
Fourth to sixth month after sale	10,000
Seventh to twelfth month after sale	12,000
Second year after sale	34,000

How do you suggest that expenses under the guarantees be handled when $1,000,000 of sales are made late in December? Assume that the company's year ends on December 31. Support your answer.

16-28. *Matching.* At the end of November, Reagan Pictures, Inc., completed a film starring that new heartthrob Harry Ford, at a cost of $2,000,000. The expected receipts on the film are as follows:

First month of issue	$ 500,000
Second month of issue	600,000
Total for months 3 to 6	1,700,000
Total for months 7 to 12	1,200,000
Total expected	$4,000,000

Ford will get 5% of total receipts. Advertising of $300,000 is paid on December 1. The advertising will cover the first 6 months on the film, starting in December.

Required:

If receipts in December are $500,000, as expected, what is the income on the film for the year ended December 31? What items should appear on the balance sheet on December 31? Give reasons to support your treatment.

(Solution in Appendix B.)

16-29. *Matching.* Refer to Problem 16-28. If the picture is a flop when released and only brings in $200,000 of receipts in December, what is the income on the film for the year ended December 31? What items should appear on the balance sheet on December 31? Give reasons to support your treatment.

16-30. *Revision of statements.* The Pafko Company has the following financial statements at the end of the first year of operations. Revise the statements of Pafko Company in accordance with generally accepted accounting principles.

PAFKO COMPANY
Income Statement
for the Year

Sales		$204,000
Cost of sales:		
Purchases	$150,000	
Less ending inventory	30,000	
Cost of goods sold		120,000
Gross profit		$ 84,000
Expenses:		
Salaries	$ 30,000	
Depreciation	12,000	
Supplies, taxes, and insurance	17,000	59,000
Total		$ 25,000
Writeup of goodwill created during the year		40,000
Net income		$ 65,000

PAFKO COMPANY
Balance Sheet
as of December 31

Current assets:			Current liabilities:		
Cash		$ 21,000	Accounts payable		$22,000
Receivables		52,000	Accrued liabilities		3,000
Inventory		30,000	Notes payable (due in 4 years)		30,000
Prepaid items		1,000			
Total current assets		$104,000	Total liabilities		$55,000
Plant assets:			Stockholders' equity:		
Buildings	$120,000		Capital stock	$100,000	
Less accumulated depreciation	12,000		Premium on stock	50,000	
Total fixed		108,000	Retained earnings	65,000	
Intangibles:			Total owners' equity		215,000
Goodwill	$ 40,000		Total equities		$270,000
Patents	18,000	58,000			
Total assets		$270,000			

Additional information:

- The inventory consists of 10,000 units valued at selling price of $3 each. Cost price is $2 per unit.
- Receivables and sales include orders of $12,000 that have not yet been shipped.
- The buildings have been written up 20% over cost. A 20-year life is used for depreciation purposes, with double-declining-balance depreciation. The write-up is credited to premium on stock account.
- The patents were acquired for $18,000 before operations began. The patents cover a new process that should provide revenue for 10 years.
- Accounts payable and purchases include a purchase order of $6,000 that was entered into December 28. No goods have been received on this order.
- Goodwill is recorded because of the good acceptance of the company's products during the year.

(Solution in Appendix B.)

CASE PROBLEM

16-31. *Income.* An oil exploration company held leases to potential oil properties in Canada. The cost of the leases was $6,000,000, which covered rights to 2,000,000 acres. Seventeen exploratory wells were drilled. Four of these were promising and the other 13 were dry holes. A mutual fund was interested in acquiring some stock of the oil exploration company. In order to establish a market price for the stock, the mutual fund established a subsidiary company that bought 1/20 of the leases from the oil company for

$2,000,000 cash. On the basis of this sale, the oil company wrote its remaining leases up to $36,000,000. The mutual fund bought a 40% interest in the stock of the oil company for $10,000,000 and valued it in its statements on the basis of the recorded asset values of the oil company. Comment on the appropriateness of the accounting of both the oil company and the mutual fund.

17

The Statement of Changes in Financial Position

The statement of changes in financial position[1] has long been recognized as an important financial statement. Under the impetus of a strong recommendation by the Accounting Principles Board (APB) of the AICPA in 1963,[2] the number of companies including the statement in published annual reports markedly increased. In 1971 the APB (in its *Opinion No. 19* made it mandatory that audited companies include a statement "summarizing changes in financial position" in annual reports.[3]

The statement of changes in financial position (hereafter called the statement of changes) provides information about the financing and investing activities of a business enterprise. This is important to users of financial statements in making decisions because of the information it provides about enterprise actions and policies.

The objectives of the statement are

Objectives

1. To indicate the extent to which the enterprise has generated resources from operations during the period
2. To summarize the other financing and investing activities of the enterprise
3. To provide added information on changes in financial position during the period that is not contained in the income statement and statement of retained earnings.

---

1. The title used for the statement varies considerably. The APB recommends the use of "Statement of Changes in Financial Position." Other titles used include "Statement of Source and Application of Funds," "Statement of Sources and Uses of Working Capital," "Statement of Funds," and "Statement of Resources Provided and Applied."
2. "The Statement of Source and Application of Funds," *APB Opinion No. 3*, October 1963.
3. "Reporting Changes in Financial Position," *APB Opinion No. 19*, March 1971.

Why is the statement of changes in financial position so important that it is now required in financial reports? Briefly, because the statement reports the sources of financing for the enterprise and the investing activities of the enterprise. This information—together with the information given on the income statement, the balance sheet, and the retained earnings statement—gives a relatively complete summary of the financial activities of the enterprise for the period.

In this chapter we shall consider the nature and practical uses of the statement of changes in financial position. We shall also study the content and construction of the statement of changes in financial position and of the closely related cash flow statement.

RESOURCES, OR FUNDS

The statement of changes deals with resources, or funds, provided and applied. It indicates the resources acquired through financing and operating activities and the resources used in investing activities of the enterprise.

The term resources is not well-defined by the APB. It speaks about an "all financial resources" concept but does not make this concept clear. As a result, the term resources is interpreted in various ways in practice. Some companies define financial resources as cash. Most companies define financial resources as the working capital of the enterprise. It is appropriate to explore these ideas a little further.

Resources as cash

Probably to most people, the word *resources* suggests the money resource *cash*. This is not surprising, since cash is the medium of exchange through which all transactions (except barter) eventually pass. The new business firm often receives its capital from owners and creditors in the form of cash. The cash is then exchanged for the specific assets required to run the business. Of course, noncash resources are often acquired by the use of short-term credit. But these short-term obligations are quickly satisfied by cash payments.

Once underway, the business firm uses the assets it has acquired, in combination with its employees and other resources, to create the products (goods and services) it sells to its customers. These income-directed activities create inflows and outflows of cash. The firm receives cash from its customers and pays out cash to employees and other service suppliers. Borrowed funds are paid back, and owners are paid dividends. As the firm grows, additional capital equipment items are acquired. Thus the inflows and outflows of cash become rather complicated.

The importance of cash to the firm seems obvious. If a company knows that the bills due to be paid tomorrow amount to $3,000, then it must make sure that cash of $3,000 is available by tomorrow for paying these obligations. Thus, for immediate bill-paying purposes, the most useful definition of resources is probably in terms of cash. Beyond the immediate present, the cash concept becomes less important and other definitions are more useful.

For periods covering several months to a year, short-term credit assumes importance. The ability to acquire goods and services on credit and to extend credit to customers is valuable. Having a good credit rating is equivalent to possessing immediate purchasing power. Extending credit to customers is an important aid in making sales. Ultimately, of course, credit generates cash receipts and cash payments. Thus, we can consider receivables (credit extended) as a deferred cash receipt, and payables (credit received) as a deferred cash payment.

Resources as net money resources

Under this broader concept, a company's resource balances consist of cash plus other money resources that shortly will be converted to cash less current liabilities (obligations that shortly will require a cash payment). More precisely, resources equal cash plus marketable securities plus receivables minus current liabilities.

Practically speaking, most firms consider that all current assets, including inventories and prepaid expenses, are money resources and that current liabilities reduce the resources available for investing activities. *That is, most companies define resources as working capital: current assets minus current liabilities.* The firm's inventories are included because they are sold so rapidly that they are likely to provide cash resources fairly soon. Furthermore, the prepaid expenses typically are used up rapidly to help the company generate revenue. Because of the rapid turnover of inventories and use of prepaid expenses, most companies believe these assets should be treated the same as the clear-cut money resources. Consequently, for most companies, the most useful definition of resources is working capital. The statement of changes in this chapter will be based on this definition.

Resources as working capital

USES OF THE STATEMENT OF CHANGES

Corporate financial statements are intended to convey financial information to those interested in corporate affairs. The income statement reports on the progress the company has made in its income-directed activities over the accounting period. The balance sheet, or statement of financial position, reports on the status of the company's assets, liabilities, and owners' equity at the close of the accounting period. The retained earnings statement shows the detailed changes in retained earnings during the period. The statement of changes reports the factors that generated the inflows of working capital and the specific purposes for which working capital was used during the accounting period.

The statement of changes complements the other financial statements. It should help the reader gain a more complete knowledge of the financial policies followed by a company. How a company finances plant expansion is answered by the statement. The dividend policy of a firm is disclosed by a comparison of dividends paid with resources provided, particularly those provided by operations. For example, a series of statements of changes that included the following data would be quite revealing:

	Year 1	Year 2	Year 3
		(in thousands)	
Resources provided by operations	$5,000	$6,000	$7,000
Resources applied to dividends	2,000	2,200	2,400

It is apparent in this situation that a smaller proportion of resources provided by operations is being distributed as dividends each year and that more funds are being retained for other purposes.

Information from the statement of changes can be used to provide an interpretive summary of activities during the period. For example:

During the year, the Mason Company generated $3,500,000 of working capital from operations. $1,500,000 of this was used to pay dividends. The remaining $2,000,000, together with $3,000,000 obtained by issuing additional stock, was used to acquire new plant and equipment of $4,500,000 and to increase working capital by $500,000.

Use in comparisons

As noted in chapter 16, differences in accounting methods and in allocations made in accounting make comparisons between companies difficult. Because the statement of changes deals with flows of working capital (or in some cases, cash) and total amounts used in acquisition of resources, some of the major variations in accounting methods and allocations do not affect the statement. Thus statements of changes can be helpful in comparisons. A warning is in order, however. The statement of changes is not a substitute for the income statement. Differences between companies in sales volume, in usage of plant and equipment, and in important classes of expenditures such as those for research and advertising are found only in the income statement.

As with the other financial statements, comparative statements of changes are more valuable than a single statement. A series of statements of changes can show potentially serious trends in specific uses and/or sources of funds. For example, investment in plant assets over a number of years may exceed resources provided by operations. This could be a signal that past growth in assets may not be yielding sufficient profits. A study of the relationship between the changes in sales and the changes in working capital over a number of years may disclose that working capital is not keeping pace with sales, a possible clue to future liquidity problems.

An illustration will help us see how we can use the statement of changes. Example 17-1 gives the statement of changes in financial position

The Statement of Changes in Financial Position   **Chapter 17**

of the Belldon Corporation for Years 1 and 2. Operations provided resources (working capital) of $450,000 in Year 2, a decline of $200,000 from Year 1. Of this $450,000, dividends consumed $110,000, while the remaining $340,000 was combined with long-term capital sources of $110,000 and a reduction in working capital of $245,000 to acquire additional plant and long-term investments of $695,000.

EXAMPLE 17-1

BELLDON CORPORATION
Statement of Changes in Financial Position

	Year Ended December 31	
	Year 2	Year 1
Resources provided by:		
Operations:		
Net income	$ 100,000	$320,000
Add expenses not requiring outlay of working capital in current period:		
Depreciation expense	350,000	330,000
Total provided by operations	$ 450,000	$650,000
Proceeds from long-term borrowing	60,000	180,000
Proceeds from sale of capital stock	50,000	40,000
Total resources provided	$ 560,000	$870,000
Resources used for:		
Additions to plant and equipment	$ 660,000	$430,000
Cash dividends	110,000	110,000
Additions to long-term investments	35,000	115,000
Total uses of resources	$ 805,000	$655,000
Leaving increase (decrease) in working capital	$(245,000)	$215,000

Schedule of Changes in Working Capital

	Year Ended December 31	
	Year 2	Year 1
Increases (decreases) in current assets:		
Cash	$ (10,000)	$ 20,000
Marketable securities	(180,000)	100,000
Accounts receivable (net)	(70,000)	10,000
Inventories	230,000	30,000
Prepaid expenses	10,000	5,000
Total increase (decrease) in current assets	$ (20,000)	$165,000
Less increases (decreases) in current liabilities:		
Accounts payable	$ (10,000)	$ 20,000
Notes payable	360,000	(60,000)
Income taxes payable	(115,000)	(5,000)
Accrued expenses payable	(10,000)	(5,000)
Total increase (decrease) in current liabilities	$ 225,000	$ (50,000)
Increase (decrease) in working capital	$(245,000)	$ 215,000

521

The financial policies indicated by the statement are best seen by looking at both years. Concentrating on Year 2 only may give a distorted view of management's financial policies, as the following comments will show. While Year 2 dividends exceeded net income, dividends for both years were about 50% of the total net income of the two years. While new plant and investment acquisitions in Year 2 weakened the capital structure through a large decrease in working capital and a small increase in long-term debt, the long-term capital asset acquisitions for the two years ($1,240,000) were financed chiefly from operations ($880,000 after dividends) and some capital stock (90,000), requiring only $240,000 of long-term debt and a $30,000 reduction in working capital. About 78% of new capital assets were financed by operations and capital stock and 22% from long-term debt and reduction in working capital. The two-year view of financial policies gives a much more conservative picture than the single Year 2 results.

RESOURCES PROVIDED AND APPLIED

There are two main parts of a statement of changes: resources provided (sources of funds) and uses or application of resources (funds applied). Under *resources provided* are listed all the factors that caused an inflow of working capital into the enterprise. Working capital is provided by income-directed activities of the business, called operations, and by long-term financing and other activities. Under the heading *uses of resources* are listed all the factors that caused an outflow of working capital from the business. Each section of the statement will now be discussed.

Common Sources of Working Capital (Other Than Operations)

Common sources of working capital include

1. Sales of capital stock
2. Borrowing on long-term notes or bonds
3. Sale of plant and equipment assets
4. Sale of intangible assets
5. Sale of long-term investments

Most of these sources are obvious. For example, if common stock is sold, there will be a net inflow of current assets, usually cash, to the enterprise from this transaction. If a company sells plant assets, the amount of plant assets is reduced, but the proceeds from the sales will increase the working capital. Clues to the occurrence of events such as those listed can be derived from a study of account balances at the beginning and end of a period. For example, an increase in bonds payable from one year end to the next would lead one to deduce that bonds had been sold and that working capital had increased from this source. A decrease in the land account would lead one to believe that land had been sold.

At times care must be exercised. For example, an increase in the common stock account might come from either a sale of stock or a stock dividend. A look at the retained earnings statement would identify any stock dividends. But even if there is a sale of stock, the change in the common stock account will not necessarily give all the needed information. If the stock is sold at more than par, the analyst must also look at the premium on stock account or additional paid-in capital account to find out what additional amounts were contributed when the stock was sold.

A further complication exists when a plant asset purchase, say of a building, is financed, either in whole or in part, by the issuance of a mortgage note or other long-term debt securities. Assuming that a $100,000 building is financed by a $100,000 mortgage, the preferred treatment in the statement of changes would be as follows:

Long-term debt used to finance plant acquisition

Under the heading of Resources Provided:

    Resources provided by issuance of mortgage note $100,000
       (see building purchase below)

Under the heading of Resources Applied:

    Resources applied to purchase of building $100,000
       (see mortgage note above)

This treatment has the virtue of fully disclosing this major business transaction of the company. To omit this transaction on the grounds that no working capital was involved would be shirking a reporting responsibility.

Common Uses or Applications of Resources (Other than for expenses)

Common uses of resources include the following:
1. Acquisition of plant and equipment assets (expansion of physical facilities)
2. Payment of cash dividends
3. Payment of long-term debt (notes or bonds) and reclassification of debt from long-term to short-term
4. Purchase of intangible assets
5. Purchase of long-term investments
6. Retirement of capital stock and purchase of treasury stock

Again, most of these uses of working capital are self-explanatory. If plant and equipment assets are purchased, the company will either pay cash or incur a liability. The payment of dividends requires the payment of cash also. (Of course, no working capital will be involved in a stock dividend, since the dividend will be "paid" by issuing additional shares of stock.) Again, as in the case of sources of funds, clues to the occurrence of such events will be uncovered by a study of changes in account balances from year to year. For example, if delivery equipment increases from $28,000 in Year 1 to $34,000 in Year 2, we conclude that $6,000 was expended during the period to acquire equipment.

A change in an account balance can result from several causes. For example, some equipment may have been purchased during a period, and other equipment may have been sold or retired. This type of complication will be considered later in the chapter.

Operations and Resources

Operations is the only other common source or use of funds that has not been discussed thus far. Income has been defined as "an increase in net assets arising out of (a) the excess of revenue compared with related expired cost and (b) other gains and losses to the enterprise from sale, exchanges, or other conversions of assets . . ." Consider the meaning of "increase in net assets." When goods or services are sold, an enterprise acquires either cash or accounts receivable from the customer. Thus, most revenues result in an inflow of assets, usually current assets. On the other hand, most expenses require either the expenditure of assets or the incurrence of liabilities. The *difference between revenues and expenses,* therefore, is a change in net assets. Like revenues, most expenses involve current items: the use of current assets or the creation of current liabilities. For example, salaries are paid in cash, and a bill for advertising may result in the recording of an account payable. Therefore, net income in general is a source of working capital, since the inflow of working capital from revenues exceeds the outlay of working capital in connection with expenses if the operations are successful. (On the other hand, a net loss might yield a decrease in working capital.)

Depreciation

One complication is the problem of depreciation (and similar expenses such as depletion and amortization of intangibles). The entry to record depreciation does not involve the outlay of cash; in fact, it does not involve any current asset or current liability. It consists of a debit to an expense account and a credit to the plant assets:

	Debit	Credit
Depreciation expense	xxx	
Accumulated depreciation		xxx

Even though the above entry does not involve the outlay of current resources, the debit to depreciation expense is used to determine the net income of a period. It follows that the amount of net income in a period is not indicative of the amount of improvement in a company's current position from operations. Depreciation (and similar expenses) must be eliminated from the list of revenues and expenses if an accurate picture is to be drawn of the net improvement in current position from this source. If operations are successful, the working capital of a company tends to increase by the amount of the income plus depreciation and similar expenses.

As an illustration, consider the operations of the Cash Company, which makes all its sales for cash and purchases all merchandise for cash. It also pays all of its expenses for cash with the exception, of course, of depreciation. Example 17-2 shows a comparison of the company's income statement and working capital flow for the current year.

Income and cash flows

EXAMPLE 17-2

INCOME AND CASH FLOW COMPARISON

		Income Statement		Working Capital Flow
Sales		$100		$+100
Cost of goods sold		55		− 55
Gross margin		45		+ 45
Expenses	$15		$−15	
Depreciation	10		0	
Total expenses		25		− 15
Net income		$ 20	Net Cash	+ 30

These figures show that the net cash inflow is greater than the amount of the net income. To arrive at the cash inflow by working from the net income, add the amount of the depreciation to the net income. Using the data in the table, add the $10 depreciation to the $20 net income and thus arrive at the $30 net cash inflow. Other expenses that have the same characteristics as depreciation, such as patent amortization and depletion, are treated in a similar fashion. On a statement of changes, the inflow of working capital from successful operations is shown among the sources (a net outflow in connection with unsuccessful operations is shown among the uses of resources).

The fact that the statement of changes shows working capital provided by operations and not net income is important. Some of the major variations in accounting methods for such expenses as depreciation and amortization are eliminated in the computation of resources provided by operations. For example, let us consider two identical companies that differ in depreciation methods. Summary income statements given in Example 17-3 highlight the effects of the different depreciation methods.

EXAMPLE 17-3

Summary Income Statements
Year Ended December 31

	Cary, Inc.	Ryder Company
Sales	$1,000,000	$1,000,000
Expenses (except for depreciation)	$ 800,000	$ 800,000
Depreciation expense	150,000	60,000
Total expenses	$ 950,000	$ 860,000
Net income	$ 50,000	$ 140,000

Partial Statements of Changes
Year Ended December 31

	Cary, Inc.	Ryder Company
Resources provided by operations:		
Net income	$ 50,000	$ 140,000
Add depreciation	150,000	60,000
Total resources from operations	$ 200,000	$ 200,000

The variation in net income that different depreciation methods cause is eliminated in computing resources provided by operations. This feature has made the statement of changes attractive to analysts. Resources provided by operations should not be considered a replacement for net income, but rather additional information that aids in understanding enterprise operations and policies.

PREPARING THE STATEMENT OF CHANGES

The statement of changes is prepared from two information sources: the financial statements (income statement, statement of retained earnings, and comparative balance sheets), and additional facts about changes in assets and equities not obtainable directly from the statements. The method of preparation will be illustrated using the financial statements of the Wicker Company (Example 17-4) and the additional fact that in Year 2 the company sold land (cost $38,000; selling price, $60,000).

EXAMPLE 17-4

WICKER COMPANY
Income Statement
Year Ended December 31, Year 2
(in thousands)

Sales		$9,000
Cost of goods sold		6,000
Gross margin		$3,000
Operating expenses:		
Salaries and wages	$1,500	
Advertising and promotion	700	
Rents and insurance	80	
Repairs and maintenance	20	
Depreciation	90	
Taxes—property and payroll	35	
Total operating expenses		2,425
Income from operations		$ 575
Less interest expense		(15)
Add gain on sale of land		22
Net income before income taxes		$ 582
Income taxes		282
Net income		$ 300

WICKER COMPANY
Statement of Retained Earnings
Year Ended December 31, Year 2
(in thousands)

Balance, beginning of year		$ 935
Add: net income for year		300
		$1,235
Less: cash dividends	$115	
stock dividend	80	195
Balance, end of year		$1,040

WICKER COMPANY
Balance Sheet
(in thousands)

	December 31		
	Year 2	Year 1	Change
Assets			
Cash	$ 224	$ 194	$ +30
Accounts receivable (net)	3,000	3,300	−300
Merchandise inventory	1,216	1,136	+80
Total current assets	$4,440	$4,630	$−190
Land	$ 100	$ 80	$ +20
Buildings	300	250	+50
Equipment and fixtures	600	520	+80
	$1,000	$ 850	$+150
Less: accumulated depreciation	300	210	+90
Total plant assets	$ 700	$ 640	$ +60
Total assets	$5,140	$5,270	$−130

(Continued)

Example 17-4 (*Cont.*)

Liabilities and Stockholders' Equity

Notes and accounts payable	$1,800	$2,000	$−200
Accrued liabilities	115	100	+15
Federal and state income taxes payable	85	40	+45
Total current liabilities	$2,000	$2,140	$−140
Long-term debt	100	275	−175
Total liabilities	$2,100	$2,415	$−315
Common stock, par $2	$ 500	$ 480	$ +20
Premium on common stock	1,500	1,440	+60
Retained earnings	1,040	935	+105
Total stockholders' equity	$3,040	$2,855	$+185
Total equities	$5,140	$5,270	$−130

The Schedule of Working Capital Changes

The first step in the preparation of the statement of changes is to determine the change in working capital. This is usually done in a schedule of changes in working capital (Example 17-5) that shows the change in each working capital account and its effect on working capital. The example shows that in Year 2, the working capital of the Wicker Company decreased by $50,000. This decrease can be explained by the changes that occurred in the noncurrent assets, the long-term liabilities, and stockholders' equity in Year 2. The analysis of the noncurrent account changes will provide the information that is used in the statement of changes itself.

EXAMPLE 17-5

WICKER COMPANY
Schedule of Changes in Working Capital
Year Ended December 31, Year 2
(in thousands)

Working Capital Item	Balance, Dec. 31		Working Capital	
	Year 2	Year 1	Increase	Decrease
Current assets:				
Cash	$ 224	$ 194	30	
Accounts receivable	3,000	3,300		300
Merchandise inventory	1,216	1,136	80	
Total current assets	$4,440	$4,630		
Current liabilities:				
Notes and accounts payable	$1,800	$2,000	200	
Accrued liabilities	115	100		15
Taxes payable	85	40		45
Total current liabilities	$2,000	$2,140		
Working capital	$2,440	$2,490		
			$310	$360
Net decrease in working capital			50	
			$360	$360

Analysis of Noncurrent Accounts

While we could begin with any of the noncurrent accounts, it is most productive to begin with retained earnings. The analysis of retained earnings yields the figure for net income for the year and the dividends paid during the year. If the retained earnings statement is not available, the information on net income can be found in the income statement, and dividends can usually be determined by the following formula:

Beginning Retained Earnings + Net Income − Ending Retained Earnings = Dividends

Analysis of retained earnings

For the Wicker Company, the retained earnings statement discloses net income of $300,000 and cash dividends of $115,000. The stock dividend of $80,000 did not use up working capital, hence it is not included in the statement of changes. We now have isolated two factors accounting for part of the $50,000 decrease in working capital:

Resources from operations:		Resources applied to pay	
Net income	$300,000	dividends	$115,000

The net income figure leads us naturally to the income statement. We use the income statement to get the full picture of resources from operations. We examine the statement carefully to identify all expenses and losses that do not require an outlay of working capital. These are added back to net income. The revenues and gains that did not provide any working capital during the period or that are more appropriately reported as parts of other items on the statement because they are not part of regular operations are subtracted from net income. If the income statement is not available, the analysis of other noncurrent accounts, such as accumulated depreciation, or the additional facts provided will help us determine the relevant information. These complications are discussed later in the chapter.

Depreciation and gain on sale of land

The Wicker Company income statement discloses depreciation of $90,000 and a gain on sale of land of $22,000. We can now complete the resources from operations:

Resources from operations:		
Net income		$300,000
Add depreciation expense	$90,000	
Less gain on sale of land	22,000	68,000
Total from operations		$368,000

The depreciation expense of $90,000 directs our attention to the balance sheet account accumulated depreciation. We note that this

529

account has changed by exactly the amount of the depreciation expense, and we can therefore conclude that the effects of any changes in accumulated depreciation have been fully explained. The gain on sale of land directs our attention to the land account in the balance sheet and also to the additional information about the sale of land. The effects of the sale of land are as follows:

Resources provided by sale of land:	
Cost of land sold (from additional fact)	$38,000
Add gain on sale of land	22,000
Total from sale of land	$60,000

If the only change in the land account had been the sale, the account would have decreased by $38,000. However, land increased by a net amount of $20,000, as indicated on the balance sheet. The additional analysis is as follows:

Cost of land owned on December 31, Year 1	$ 80,000
Less cost of land sold (from additional fact)	38,000
Cost of land owned on December 31, Year 2, if no additional land had been acquired	$ 42,000
Add cost of land apparently acquired during Year 2	58,000 (forced)
Cost of land owned on December 31, Year 2, per balance sheet	$100,000

Plant assets

Since no additional facts are given for the other plant assets, we can assume that the increase in buildings of $50,000 and the increase in equipment and fixtures of $80,000 represent additional purchases of these assets. Hence, for plant assets we can write

Resources used for plant acquisitions:	
Land (from analysis above)	$ 58,000
Buildings (increase in account per balance sheet)	50,000
Equipment and fixtures (increase in account per balance sheet)	80,000
Total used for plant acquisitions	$188,000

Long-term debt

The only remaining noncurrent account to consider is long-term debt. This account was reduced by $175,000 during the year, suggesting that Wicker Company repaid long-term debt. Of course, there is the possibility that this change was a net difference between additional borrowing and repayment of loans. If this were so, we would report the additional borrowing as resources provided and the repayment as resources applied. Lacking information to the contrary, we assume that the decrease in long-term debt represents the repayment of long-term debt.

Resources used to retire debt $175,000

At this point all of the noncurrent accounts have been analyzed and the statement of changes can be prepared (see Example 17-6). Note that the decrease in working capital of $50,000 is the amount previously computed in the schedule of working capital changes in Example 17-5.

EXAMPLE 17-6

WICKER COMPANY
Statement of Changes in Financial Position
Year Ended December 31, Year 2
(in thousands)

Resources Provided

Operations:		
Net income	$300	
Add expenses not requiring the use of working capital:		
Depreciation	90	
	$390	
Less gain on sale of land	22	
Total from operations		$368
Sale of land		60
Total of resources provided		$428

Resources Applied

Dividends	$115
Retirement of bonds payable	175
Acquisition of plant assets	188
Total resources applied	$478
Decrease in working capital	$ 50

The steps in preparing the statement of changes can be summarized as follows:

Steps in preparation

1. Segregate current assets and current liabilities and prepare a schedule of changes in working capital.
2. Analyze noncurrent accounts to determine resources provided and applied.
   a. Analyze retained earnings to determine the net income and dividends. Analyze the income statement to derive other factors affecting resources from operations. If the income statement is not furnished, this information can be derived from an analysis of accumulated depreciation and other noncurrent accounts that affect the income statement and/or from additional facts provided.
   b. Analyze the noncurrent accounts pointed to in the analysis of the income statement to derive additional resources provided and applied.
   c. Use additional facts provided to determine additional resources provided and applied. Analyze any noncurrent accounts affected by the items described in the additional facts.
   d. Analyse any remaining noncurrent accounts for the remaining changes in resources.

3. Record all effects (resources provided and applied) in a statement of changes. Be sure that the difference between total resources provided and total resources applied is equal to the change in working capital derived in *1*.

COMPLICATIONS IN PREPARING STATEMENTS OF CHANGES

Preparation of a statement of changes can be much more complicated than has been indicated above. This is particularly true when more than one transaction affects a particular account. We now consider a few examples.

EXAMPLE 17-7

The F Company's accounts show the following:

	Balances	
	12/31/Year 2	12/31/Year 1
Machinery	$40,000	$30,000
Accumulated depreciation on machinery	15,000 (Cr.)	12,000 (Cr.)

Additional investigation reveals that machinery with a cost of $6,000 and a book value of $2,000 was sold for $2,000 cash during Year 2. To trace the effect on resources, we must analyze both the machinery account and the related accumulated depreciation in detail. Before doing so, we remember that a cost of $6,000 and a book value of $2,000 means that there must be accumulated depreciation of $4,000 for the piece of machinery that was sold. The entry for the sale must have been

	Debit	Credit
Cash	2,000	
Accumulated depreciation	4,000	
Machinery		6,000

Notice that there was no gain or loss, since the machine was sold for its book value. Analysis of the two accounts is accomplished by tracing through the year's activity in detail, as follows:

Machinery Account

Beginning balance	$30,000 (given)
Cost of machine sold	−6,000 (see entry above)
Balance	$24,000
Apparent purchase of machinery	+16,000 (forced)
Ending balance	$40,000 (given)

Accumulated Depreciation Account

Beginning balance	$12,000 (given)
Less accumulated depreciation on machine sold	−4,000 (see entry above)
Balance	$ 8,000
Apparent depreciation for the year	+7,000 (forced)
Ending balance	$15,000 (given)

The effects of the above items would be detailed as follows on the statement of changes:

Resources provided:	
By operations:	
Net income	xxx
Add: depreciation for year	7,000
Total from operations	xxx
By sale of machinery	2,000
Resources applied:	
To purchase machinery	16,000

The sale of machinery provided $2,000 cash, which is recorded as the amount of working capital provided by the sale.

EXAMPLE 17-8

The G Company accounts show the following:

	Balances	
	12/31/Year 2	12/31/Year 1
Long-term investments	$90,000	$120,000
Net income for the year	60,000	

Additional information: During Year 2, investments costing $50,000 were sold for $43,000 cash. The entry for the sale of investments must have been

	Debit	Credit
Cash	43,000	
Loss on sale of investments	7,000	
Investments		50,000

A loss was incurred because the investments were sold for less than their cost.

    The analysis of the long-term investments accounts reveals the following:

(Continued)

Example 17-8 (Cont.)

Long-Term Investment Account

Beginning balance	$120,000 (given)
Cost of investments sold	50,000
Balance	$ 70,000
Apparent purchase of investments	20,000 (forced)
Ending balance	$ 90,000 (given)

Some of the working capital effects are obvious. The sale provided cash of $43,000. The purchase would involve the use or application of $20,000 of resources. The only remaining problem is the loss of $7,000 on the sale of investments. The loss itself neither provides nor applies resources. The entire effect of the sale is displayed in the $43,000 cash received from the sale. The loss does affect the net income, however, and net income does appear on the statement of changes.

Net income for G Company was $60,000 in Year 2. If there had been no loss on sale of investments, the income would have been $67,000. This $67,000 should be shown on the statement of changes for two reasons:

1. The loss on the investments is not part of ordinary operations and should be excluded in arriving at resources provided by *operations*.
2. The loss does not provide or use working capital and should be added back (a gain should be subtracted) just like other items (such as depreciation) that do not affect working capital.

The effects of the items above would be detailed as follows on the statement of changes:

Resources provided:	
By operations:	
Net income	60,000
Add: depreciation	xxx
loss on sale of investments	7,000
Total from operations	xxx
By sale of long-term investments at a loss	43,000
Resources applied:	
To purchase long-term investments	20,000

Examples 17-7 and 17-8 indicate the complexities that can arise in connection with statements of changes. The technique illustrated for dealing with such complications is usable for even very complicated situations. This technique involves

1. Analyzing complicated noncurrent accounts by detailing the changes in the accounts for the year.
2. Making sample journal entries for complicated transactions in order to see the various effects
3. Looking for evidence of disposals or other important changes in accounts and deducing amounts of acquisitions or other changes

Technical difficulties should not hinder an analyst from seeing the overall objective of the statement of changes, which is to give some idea of the flow of financing in an enterprise. Intelligent use of the statement can give an investor considerable insight into a company's policies and operations.

SUMMARY

The statement of changes in financial position, now required in the certified financial reports of audited companies, complements the other financial statements. It provides information on the financial policies of business firms in such important areas as dividends, plant expansion, and chief sources of financing relied upon by the firm.

The most important definition of resources is working capital. The next most commonly used concept is cash. Whether a company ought to publish a statement of changes based on working capital (accompanied by a schedule of changes in working capital) or a statement of cash flows probably depends upon the relative importance of working capital composition in the company.

The primary emphasis in the chapter was on a statement of changes in which resources are defined as working capital. The most important resources provided and applied that were identified in the chapter are the following:

Resources provided:
1. Operations—net income adjusted for income statement items that do not use up or provide resources
2. Long-term borrowing
3. Issuance of capital stock
4. Sale of noncurrent assets

Resources applied:
1. Purchase of noncurrent assets
2. Retirement of long-term debt or reclassification of debt as a current liability
3. Dividends (excluding stock dividends)

The preparation of the statement of changes consists basically of analyzing the changes in nonworking capital accounts to identify the total changes in working capital. The schedule of changes in working capital provides the details of the total change in working capital reported on the statement of changes.

Part V   Accounting Theory and Analysis

IMPORTANT TERMS

> Resources provided   Resources applied
> Funds   Working capital
> Cash flows

APPENDIX 17-1: THE STATEMENT OF CASH FLOWS

The statement of changes in financial position based on the sources and uses of working capital appears to offer the greatest advantages to most users of the statement. However, many financial analysts believe that cash as a measure of resources is highly significant in companies that have large inventories and receivables. Furthermore, the notion that resources and cash are equivalent is so deeply ingrained that many analysts prefer a *statement of cash flows* to the statement of working capital flows.

The cash flow statement is illustrated in Example 17-9 (see page 537) with data taken from the Wicker Company schedule of changes in working capital and statement of changes (Examples 17-5 and 17-6).

The chief advantage of this form of the statement of cash flows lies in the treatment of working capital elements. The interested reader of the statement of changes must look to the schedule of changes in working capital to find how the total change in working capital was allocated among the various working capital elements. The reader of the cash flow statement is informed directly about the distribution of the working capital change among the various working capital elements. If the composition of the working capital change is important to most financial report readers, then it seems that the cash flow statement would serve a very useful purpose.

The statement of cash flows for the Wicker Company in Example 17-9 is only one possible form that the statement may take. The statement combines the elements of the statement of changes in financial position with the elements of the schedule of changes in working capital. The special feature of the statement is connected with the additions to, and deductions from, the income figure. To explain these, we consider a few examples.

Revenue and receipts

Wicker's sales for the year were $9,000,000. Two steps were probably involved before cash was received: (1) sale on account and (2) collection of the receivable. Any accounts receivable at the end of the year represent sales made during the year but not collected. Receivables at the beginning of the year are probably collected during the year. To compute collections from sales, the following calculation is made:

EXAMPLE 17-9

WICKER COMPANY
Statement of Cash Flows
Year Ended December 31, Year 2
(in thousands)

Sources of Cash

Operations:			
Net income		$300	
Add depreciation expense	$90		
Less gain on sale of land	22	68	
Total			$368
Add: Decrease in current assets:			
Accounts receivable		$300	
Increases in current liabilities:			
Accrued liabilities		$ 15	
Income taxes payable		45	360
Total additions to cash			$728
Less: Increase in current assets:			
Merchandise inventories		$ 80	
Decreases in current liabilities:			
Notes and accounts payable		200	
Total deductions from cash			280
Net increase in cash from operations			$448
Sale of land			60
Total sources of cash			$508

Uses of Cash

Dividends	$115	
Retirement of bonds payable	175	
Acquisition of plant assets	188	
Total uses of cash		$478
Increase in cash		$ 30

Sales during the year	$9,000,000
Less receivables—end of year	3,000,000
Collected on sales	6,000,000
Add receivables—start of year	3,300,000
Cash collected during year	$9,300,000

Notice that the calculation could be shortened by adding the decrease in the receivables balance during the year, just as it was in Example 17-9.

Most expenses involve cash outlays, but the cash *expenditure* need not coincide exactly with the *expense.* Prepaid insurance involves a cash outlay when a policy is paid for, but the insurance expense is recorded over the life of the policy and involves no cash outlay when the expense is recorded. For Wicker Company the salaries and wages of $1,500,000 recorded during the year do not necessarily represent the cash payments made. If we assume that all the accrued liabilities are for wages payable, then $115,000

Expenses and cash payments

of wages remained unpaid at the end of the year. Furthermore, the $100,000 of accrued liabilities at the beginning of the year would be paid during the year. To compute cash paid for salaries the following calculation is made:

Salaries and wages expense	$1,500,000
Less wages payable—end of year	115,000
Paid on salaries	1,385,000
Add wages payable—start of year	100,000
Total cash paid during year	$1,485,000

This calculation could also be shortened by simply deducting the increase in the accrued wages from the salaries expense. An increase in the accrued liabilities indicates that cash paid was less than the expense recorded because more was owed at the end of the year. This increase in liabilities is shown in Example 17-9 as an addition to income, because it represents a lesser amount of cash expended than the amount of expense included in the net income calculation. In a similar manner, the decrease in notes and accounts payable is deducted because cash had to be paid to reduce those liabilities. The cash payment is connected with income because the accounts and notes are probably connected with purchases of merchandise, supplies, and services, which are part of income.

Understanding the relationships between items that affect income and those that affect cash is important. Table 17-1 lists a few transactions and their effects and should aid in clarifying the relationships.

The items in the table show clearly that cash flows differ from working capital flow and income effects. A study of the table in relation to the statement of cash flows should provide a rationale for what appears in the statement.

Some assumptions are made in connection with Example 17-9. It is

TABLE 17-1. Effects of Transactions

	Effect on		
Transaction	Income	Working Capital	Cash
Make sale on account	increase	increase	no effect
Collect account receivable	no effect	no effect	increase
Purchase merchandise on account	no effect (until sold)	no effect	no effect
Record cost of goods sold	decrease	decrease	no effect
Pay accounts payable	no effect	no effect	decrease
Pay wages	decrease	decrease	decrease
Accrue wages at year end	decrease	decrease	no effect
Pay for insurance (prepaid)	no effect	no effect	decrease
Record insurance expense	decrease	decrease	no effect
Record depreciation expense	decrease	no effect	no effect

assumed that (1) the changes in noncash working capital accounts (e.g., accounts receivable) directly affect cash provided or applied in operations, and (2) the other sources and uses of cash affect cash directly without any intermediate steps (e.g., equipment is not bought on account). These assumptions are fairly realistic in most cases. Any significant deviation from the assumptions would probably be fairly obvious and could be treated as an exception. For example, suppose dividends were declared but unpaid at the end of a period. A balance in the dividends payable account would lead the preparer of the statement to deduct the amount unpaid from the dividends amount in the cash flow statement.

On a statement of cash flows, sources of cash other than operations are generally the same as those on the statement prepared on a working capital basis. The specific uses are also generally the same as those on the earlier statement of changes. For example, the retirement of bonds probably involves a cash payment. If care is exercised, the nonoperating items should be easy to deal with. The important and novel elements of a statement of cash flows are those connected with operations, which we have discussed at some length.

Sources other than operations

Some analysts prefer a statement of cash *receipts* and *disbursements* to the statement of cash flows illustrated in Example 17-9. Cash receipts and disbursements reflect the total cash flows of the period more completely. The statement in Example 17-10 illustrates this approach for the Wicker Company. It includes notes that explain the derivation of some specific amounts. Other figures are the same as those in Example 17-9.

EXAMPLE 17-10

WICKER COMPANY
Statement of Cash Receipts and Disbursements
Year Ended December 31, Year 2
(in thousands)

Cash receipts:	
From customers (Note 1)	$9,300
From sale of land	60
Total cash receipts	$9,360
Cash disbursements:	
For merchandise purchases (Note 2)	$6,280
For expenses paid (Note 3)	2,572
For dividends paid	115
For repayment of Long-term debt (Note 4)	175
For acquisition of plant assets	188
Total cash disbursements	$9,330
Increase in cash balances	$ 30

Note 1: Sales of $9,000 plus the decrease in accounts receivable of $300 gives $9,300 collected from customers during the year.

Note 2: Cost of goods sold of $6,000 plus the increase of $80 in merchandise inventories gives $6,080 for purchases made. The purchases of $6,080 plus the decrease

(Continued)

Example 17-10 (Cont.)

of $200 in accounts and notes payable gives $6,280 as the cash paid out for merchandise purchased.

Note 3: Total operating expenses of $2,425 minus depreciation of $90 plus interest expense of $15 plus income taxes of $282 gives a total of $2,632 in expenses subject to payment. This $2,632 minus the increase in accrued expenses of $15 and minus the increase in income taxes payable of $45 gives $2,572 as the expenses paid in cash.

Note 4: It is assumed that the decrease in long-term debt came about because of repayment.

QUESTIONS

17-1. Which definition of resources is most useful, in your opinion? Why?

17-2. Why should the statement of changes in financial position accompany the income statement and balance sheet?

17-3. What is the single most important source of increases in working capital?

17-4. Wilcox, Inc., floated a $5 million first mortgage bond issue this year for the purpose of financing a new plant. The new plant was completed this year at a cost of $6 million. How would these facts be reported in the statement of changes for the year?

17-5. How should a stock dividend issued in shares of common stock to the common stockholders be reported in the statement of changes?

17-6. The Accounting Principles Board of the American Institute of CPAs stated in their *Opinion No. 19* that the statement of changes in financial position should clearly disclose "conversion of long-term debt or preferred stock to common stock." Why do you suppose the APB took this position, since the conversion transaction referred to is a trade of bonds or preferred stock for common stock?

17-7. The Accounting Principles Board stated, "The amount of working capital or cash provided from operations is not a substitute for or an improvement upon properly determined net income as a measure of results of operations and the consequent effect on financial position." Do you agree? Explain.

17-8. Is depreciation a source of working capital? Discuss the relationship of depreciation to working capital flows.

17-9. How does a cash flow statement differ from the statement of changes?

17-10. Y Company pays a current liability of $8,000. How will this affect uses of resources? How will this affect uses of cash? Explain.

EXERCISES

17-11. *Identifying resources provided and applied.* Prepare a table like the one given below. In the appropriate column, write the amount of resources provided or applied by each of the events given. If the event has no effect on resources, write the amount in the column "No Effect." Resources are to be defined as working capital.

The Statement of Changes in Financial Position Chapter 17

	Resources	*Resources*	
Events	*Provided*	*Applied*	*No Effect*

a. Borrowed $5,000 on a 5-year note.
b. Net income for year was $6,000.
c. Issued stock dividend of $4,000.
d. Borrowed $3,000 on a 90-day note.
e. Sold investments costing $2,000 for a gain of $7,000.
f. Issued common stock for cash of $4,000.
g. Recorded the depreciation expense for the year of $7,000.
h. Accepted a customer's note for $500 in payment of his open account.

17-12. *Resources provided from balance sheet figures.* An excerpt from the balance sheet of Q Company is given below. During Year 2, the company retired $25,000 of bonds. Compute the resources provided by the sale of bonds.

	December 31	
	Year 2	Year 1
Bonds payable	$50,000	$60,000

17-13. *Resources provided and applied.* An excerpt from the balance sheet of K Company is given below. Equipment that had cost $10,000 several years ago was sold for $2,000 during Year 2. There was no gain or loss on the sale.

	December 31	
	Year 2	Year 1
Equipment	$50,000	$30,000
Less accumulated depreciation	30,000	20,000
Unexpired cost	$20,000	$10,000

Required:
a. Compute the resources applied to purchase equipment in Year 2.
b. What was the amount provided by sale of equipment?
c. Compute the depreciation expense for Year 2.
(Solution in Appendix B.)

17-14. *Resources provided and applied.* An excerpt from a balance sheet is given below. The net income for Year 2 was $18,000. The Year 2 dividends include a stock dividend of $4,000.

	December 31	
	Year 2	Year 1
Retained earnings	$40,000	$30,000

Required:
a. Compute the total dividends (both stock and cash) in Year 2.
b. Compute the resources applied to pay cash dividends in Year 2.

17-15. *Resources provided and applied.* An excerpt from a balance sheet is given below. The income statement reports that the amortization of patents was $8,000 in Year 2 and the amortization of goodwill was $15,000 for Year 2.

	December 31	
	Year 2	Year 1
Patents (net)	$20,000	$25,000
Goodwill (net)	78,000	60,000

Required:
a. Show how the amortization of patents and goodwill would be reported on the statement of changes for Year 2.
b. Compute the amount of resources applied to patents and goodwill in Year 2.

17-16. *Statement of Changes.* On the basis of the comparative trial balances of Hatcher Corp. presented below, prepare a statement of changes in financial position, including details of changes in working capital. A fully depreciated item of equipment with a cost of $3,000 was discarded during the year. The retained earnings account was credited with net income of $25,000 and charged with cash dividends of $10,000.

	December 31	
	Year 2	Year 1
Cash	$ 24,000	$ 30,000
Accounts receivable (net)	27,000	25,000
Inventories	50,000	45,000
Equipment	62,000	58,000
Land	12,000	—
	$175,000	$158,000
Allowance for depreciation	$ 32,000	$ 30,000
Accounts payable	21,000	21,000
Common stock $25 par	100,000	100,000
Retained earnings	22,000	7,000
	$175,000	$158,000

17-17. *Statement of Changes.* Prepare a statement of changes in financial position for the Wilding Company for Year 2. The net income for the year was $5,500; ⨍ ⏋00 was paid in dividends.

WILDING COMPANY

	December 31	
	Year 2	Year 1
Assets		
Cash	$ 3,000	$ 4,000
Accounts receivable (net)	20,000	12,000
Inventories	25,000	20,000
	$48,000	$36,000

Liabilities and Stockholders' Equity		
Accounts payable	$12,000	$ 7,000
Accrued wages payable	1,000	500
Note payable due December 31, Year 5	6,000	—
Capital stock	10,000	5,000
Retained earnings	19,000	23,500
	$48,000	$36,000

17-18. *Cash inflow from sales.* A balance sheet excerpt for Cable Company is given below. Total sales for Year 2 were $975,000. Compute the cash receipts from customers in Year 2.

	December 31	
	Year 2	Year 1
Accounts receivable	$112,000	$105,000

17-19. *Cash disbursements for merchandise purchases.* A balance sheet excerpt for Flatt Company is given below. The cost of goods sold in Year 2 was $350,000. Compute the cash disbursements for merchandise purchases in Year 2.

	December 31	
	Year 2	Year 1
Merchandise inventory	$33,000	$27,000
Accounts payable (for merchandise)	40,000	35,000

(Solution in Appendix B.)

PROBLEMS

17-20. *Statement of changes.* From the following information, prepare a statement of resources provided and applied. Net income for the year was $8,000; $7,000 was paid in dividends.

	12/31/Year 2	12/31/Year 1
Assets		
Cash	$ 4,000	$ 4,000
Accounts receivable	28,000	30,000
Patents	2,000	3,000
Equipment	30,000	25,000
Less accumulated depreciation	(7,500)	(5,000)
	$56,500	$57,000
Liabilities and Stockholders' Equity		
Accounts payable	$ 7,000	$ 3,000
Accrued wages payable	1,500	2,000
Bonds payable	15,000	20,000
Capital stock	20,000	20,000
Retained earnings	13,000	12,000
	$56,500	$57,000

17-21. *Use of statement of changes.* The total resources applied and provided in the following two companies are the same. However, the operating policies of the two companies are different. Comment on the information disclosed by the statements.

	Company S		Company Y	
Resources provided:				
By operations	$10,000		$10,000	
Issue of long-term notes	40,000			
Sale of capital stock	0		40,000	0
		$50,000		$50,000
Resources applied:				
Purchase of additional plant	$10,000		$35,000	
Payment of dividends	30,000	40,000	5,000	40,000
Increase in working capital		$10,000		$10,000

Working Capital Changes

	Company S		Company Y	
	Increase	Decrease	Increase	Decrease
Current Assets:				
Cash		$ 5,000	$10,000	
Receivables	$35,000		10,000	
Inventories	55,000		15,000	
Current Liabilities:				
Accounts payable		25,000		$ 5,000
Notes payable		50,000		20,000
	$90,000	$80,000	$35,000	$25,000

17-22. *Statement of changes.* Given the following financial statements and supplemental information, prepare a statement of changes in financial position. Also prepare a supporting schedule of working capital changes.

Income Statement for Year 2

Sales		$100,000
Expenses		
Cost of sales	$48,000	
Salaries	21,000	
Insurance expense	4,000	
Depreciation expense	8,000	
Interest expense	4,500	85,500
Net income		$ 14,500

Comparative Balance Sheets
December 31

		Year 2	Year 1
Assets			
Cash		$10,000	$31,500
Accounts receivable		20,000	25,000
Inventories		15,000	11,000
Prepaid insurance		2,500	1,500
Equipment	$80,000		
Accumulated depreciation	8,000	72,000	-0-
Land		-0-	30,000
Total assets		$119,500	$99,000

Liabilities and Stockholders' Equity		
Accounts payable	$ 15,000	$ 10,000
Salaries payable	4,000	5,500
Dividends payable	2,500	-0-
Bonds payable, 10%	60,000	50,000
Common stock	20,000	20,000
Retained income	18,000	13,500
	$119,500	$99,000

Additional information:
Dividends declared were $10,000.
Dividends paid were $7,500.
There was no gain or loss on the land sold during the year.

17-23. *Statement of changes.* Prepare a statement of changes in financial position from the information below. Include a statement of working capital changes. Additional patents were purchased during the year for $800. Goodwill was written off against retained earnings. A long-term loan was obtained from the bank for $1,000. Net income for the year amounted to $3,000.

M. CO.
Comparative Balance Sheets
December 31

	Year 2	Year 1	Changes
Cash	$ 8,420	$ 6,990	1,430
Accounts receivable	10,680	12,600	1,920*
Merchandise	13,600	10,000	3,600
Patents	3,000	2,500	500
Goodwill	-0-	2,000	2,000*
	$35,700	$34,090	
Accounts payable	$ 7,890	$ 9,680	1,790*
Long-term notes payable	4,000	3,000	1,000
Common stock	22,000	20,000	2,000
Retained earnings	1,810	1,410	400
	$35,700	$34,090	

* decrease

17-24. *Cash disbursements for operating expenses.* An excerpt from the balance sheet of Shields Stores, Inc., is given below. The income statement for the fiscal year ended May 31 reports the following: wages and salaries, $160,000; advertising expense, $30,000; utilities expense, $20,000; insurance expense, $6,000; property and payroll taxes, $15,000; other expenses, $8,000. Compute the cash disbursements for operating expenses in the fiscal year ended May 31.

	May 31	
	Current Year	Prior Year
Prepaid insurance	$ 5,000	$3,000
Supplies inventory	2,500	3,100
Accrued property and payroll taxes payable	10,000	8,000
Other accrued expenses payable	2,600	3,000

17-25. *Statement of sources and uses of cash.* From the information below, prepare a statement of sources and uses of cash for the Hollow Company for the fiscal year ended September 30.

HOLLOW COMPANY
Working Capital

	September 30	
	Year 2	Year 1
Current assets:		
Cash	$ 3,000	$ 7,000
Accounts receivable (net)	22,000	20,000
Inventory	28,000	22,000
Prepaid expenses	1,000	1,000
Total current assets	$54,000	$50,000
Current liabilities:		
Accounts payable	$20,000	$18,000
Accrued wages and salaries	2,000	3,000
Income taxes payable	5,000	6,000
Other accrued expenses	3,000	3,000
Total current liabilities	$30,000	$30,000
Working capital	$24,000	$20,000

Statement of Changes in Financial Position
Fiscal Year Ended September 30, Year 2

Resources provided:			Resources applied:	
Operations:			Dividends	$ 7,000
Net income	$15,000		New equipment	30,000
Depreciation	9,000	$24,000	Purchase treasury stock	3,000
Long-term borrowing		20,000	Total uses	$40,000
			Increase in working capital	4,000
Total		$44,000	Total	$44,000

(Solution in Appendix B.)

17-26. *Cash receipts and cash disbursements.* Using the data given for the Hollow Company (Problem 17-25) and the additional facts given below, prepare a statement of cash receipts and disbursements for the fiscal year ended September 30. Sales for Year 2 were $210,000; the cost of goods sold for Year 2 was $125,000; operating expenses (including depreciation expense of $9,000) and income taxes for Year 2 totaled $70,000.

17-27. *Comprehensive statement of changes.* Prepare a statement of changes for Year 2 from the information below. Investments costing $90,000 were sold at a loss (see income statement). Plant assets that cost $400,000 several years ago and had accumulated depreciation of $161,000 were sold at a gain (see income statement). Certain corporation officers exercised their options to buy 300 shares of the company's stock at $20 per share. These shares came from previously unissued shares.

GRANICK COMPANY
Comparative Balance Sheets

	December 31	
	Year 2	Year 1
Assets		
Cash	$ 88,000	$ 91,000
Marketable securities	465,000	600,000
Accounts receivable	1,140,000	950,000
Less estimated uncollectibles	(14,000)	(13,000)
Inventories	480,000	482,000
Prepaid expenses	155,000	156,000
Total current assets	$2,314,000	$2,266,000
Investments	$ 606,000	$ 536,000
Plant and equipment	$9,600,000	$8,640,000
Less accumulated depreciation	(4,530,000)	(4,040,000)
Total plant assets	$5,070,000	$4,600,000
Total assets	$7,990,000	$7,402,000
Liabilities and Stockholders' Equity		
Notes payable	$ 193,000	$ 92,000
Accounts payable	642,000	679,000
Accrued liabilities	181,000	202,000
Income taxes payable	203,000	160,000
Total current liabilities	$1,219,000	$1,133,000
Long-term debt	1,600,000	1,300,000
Total liabilities	$2,819,000	$2,433,000
Capital stock, par $10	$1,883,000	$1,880,000
Capital in excess of par	1,708,000	1,705,000
Retained earnings	1,580,000	1,384,000
Total stockholders' equity	5,171,000	$4,969,000
Total equities	$7,990,000	$7,402,000

Income Statement
Year Ended December 31, Year 2

Sales		$6,310,000
Cost of goods sold		3,900,000
Gross profit		$2,410,000
Selling and administrative expenses	$829,000	
Depreciation expense	651,000	1,480,000
Net operating income		$ 930,000
Other income and (expense):		
Interest expense	$ (87,000)	
Loss on sale of long-term investments	(30,000)	
Gain on sale of plant assets	140,000	23,000
Net income before taxes		$ 953,000
Income taxes		433,000
Net income		$ 520,000

(Solution in Appendix B.)

Part V Accounting Theory and Analysis

CASE PROBLEM

17-28. *Interpretation.* The Libbey-Owens-Ford Company statement of changes is given below.

LIBBEY-OWENS-FORD COMPANY
Statement of Changes in Consolidated Financial Position

	Year Ended December 31	
	1974	1973
Source of Working Capital		
Provided from operations:		
Net earnings for the year	$ 31,704,906	$ 62,210,960
Add (deduct) items not affecting working capital:		
Provision for depreciation	31,365,595	28,286,342
Loss on properties abandoned or sold	325,230	1,670,079
Deferred income taxes—noncurrent	3,441,200	5,450,040
Amortization of tooling, licenses, etc.	1,112,195	1,202,017
Equity in earnings of foreign affiliates	(1,550,437)	(420,564)
Total from operations	66,398,689	98,398,874
Proceeds from sale of plants and properties	3,031,092	3,811,416
Amounts resulting from employee stock option transactions	49,457	1,839,324
Values assigned to common shares issued in acquisitions	1,750,265	
Borrowing on long-term debt	62,427,407	247,590
Other	405,097	2,453,229
	$134,062,007	$106,750,433
Application of Working Capital		
Cash dividends to shareholders	$ 29,484,395	$ 33,122,139
Expenditures for plants and properties:		
New plants, facilities, and equipment	31,155,544	61,904,374
Properties of businesses acquired	6,010,156	
Payments and transfer to current maturities of long-term debt	1,279,508	1,946,081
Cost of capital stock purchased	3,144,967	13,041,662
Other	51,291	1,729,154
	71,925,861	111,743,410
Increase (Decrease) in Working Capital	$ 62,136,146	$ (4,992,977)

Required:
  a. What significant changes took place from 1973 to 1974? Specifically, how did the company deal with the lower amount provided by operations?
  b. L-O-F reduced dividends substantially in 1974. Why?
  c. What peculiarities do you note in the statements?
  d. Are there any advantages in the comparative statements given by Libbey-Owens-Ford?

18

Analysis of Financial Statements

Those outside of a business enterprise, including most investors, creditors, employees, and members of the public, must rely on information provided either by the enterprise (on a voluntary or required basis) or by other sources. Financial statements published in companies' annual reports (and to a lesser extent in their quarterly reports) are a major source of information for these outside parties. The annual report focuses primarily on the needs of investors and potential investors, although the statements presumably are broad enough so that they are useful to other parties as well. The discussion in this chapter also focuses primarily on investors and their decisions, but the discussion is broad enough so that needs and interests of other groups are also mentioned.

INVESTORS' DECISIONS

The investment decision is complicated because it includes such decisions as whether to invest in a company, whether to withdraw an investment in a company, and when to invest or disinvest. It also involves a consideration of the possible future course of events. Investors must predict how the company will do and how the economy in general will perform compared to the company. They also must predict the stock market's reaction to the performance of the company and the economy, particularly if they are interested in short-term market gains.

The stock market is an extremely complicated creature whose behavior cannot be predicted with any assurance, especially in the short run. To indicate the difficulty investors face in evaluating the possible

Stock market

movement of market prices, let us list some of the factors that influence changes in the market price of a company's stock. Among the factors are company performance, political climate, market psychology, financial strength of the company, industry prospects, company prospects, state of United States-Soviet relations, actions of competitors, rumors about the company, comparative "glamor" of other stocks, weather, degree of confidence in company officials, government monetary and fiscal policies, actions of the OPEC[1] countries, and state of the president's health. Many of these factors primarily affect the short run, but some have a considerable influence on long-run trends. Few of these factors are reflected immediately in published financial statements. The facts that can be gleaned from the financial statements are important, of course, for company performance and financial strength are matters that concern investors. But in any one situation it is possible, perhaps even likely, that other factors will be more important. There is no doubt, for example, that

Expectations expectations of future performance have a profound influence on the value of a company's stock. Information about expectations does not appear in the formal financial statements (though it is often referred to in the annual report). The statements may give some clues to future performance, since it is reasonable to assume some continuity in operations. This assumption, however, is too often erroneous to deserve a great deal of trust.

Where, then, do investors stand? They stand in a precarious position indeed. Investors make decisions on the basis of limited information. Furthermore, there is no assurance that the market as a whole will react rationally, even if the investors' own decisions turn out to be reasonable. The rational investor will use the limited information to the fullest extent possible, of course, but the investor may still make errors and mistakes.

Long- and short-term investors We should keep in mind the distinction between the investor who is interested in short-run profits and the investor who intends to commit funds to an investment for a long period of time. For the long-term investor, basic financial and operating strength are relatively more important than other factors. But even the long-run investor must be concerned with many other factors. In many ways, the long-term investor's position is even more uncertain than the short-run investor's because projections must be made much further into the future. Our changing world has often demonstrated the futility of such predictions.

The rest of this chapter discusses analysis of financial statements, but with the knowledge that such analysis has severe shortcomings and should *never* be the sole basis of an investment decision. The income statement and the balance sheet are emphasized in this chapter. The statement of changes in financial position, which provides additional information, was discussed in chapter 17. The information that the statement

---

1. OPEC is the organization of oil producing and exporting countries.

of changes provides about financing and investing activities is an important input to analysis of a company.

Analysis of statements is more helpful than passive acceptance of statement data. Analysis involves subjecting the data to scrutiny, drawing relationships, looking for trends, and ascertaining strengths and weaknesses. But it does not necessarily lead to the "right" decision. With this word of warning, we proceed.

ANALYSIS OF OPERATING RESULTS

In many situations, the most important area of analysis is operations. Operations are analyzed to ascertain the effectiveness of past performance and to form an idea of what might happen in the future. When operations are analyzed, trends are noted and various relationships are drawn. The analysis, which goes beyond the bare statements themselves, gives information that is helpful in reaching decisions.

Some relationships can be drawn by looking at information that appears only on the income statement. Other relationships can be studied by examining both the income statement and the balance sheet. We look first at analysis within the income statement.

Analysis within the Income Statement

One informative type of analysis is percentage analysis of income statement items. The base for percentages should generally be net sales. Some of the most important percentage relationships are gross margin to sales, income from operations to sales, and net income to sales. A detailed percentage analysis provides information about changes in specific operating items and can highlight items that deserve attention.

A sample analysis is given in Example 18-1. Many of the percentages shown are only interesting when compared with figures for other years and with norms for the industry. Industry norms are published by trade associations and companies such as Dun and Bradstreet.

In Example 18-1, sales increased and net income decreased. Some significant factors accounting for this were the following:

- Increase in returns and allowances from 1.5% to 4.1%.
- Increase in cost of goods sold from 60% to 61%.
- Increase in advertising from 5.5% to 7.3%.

Partially offsetting these increases in costs were small decreases in the percentages of officers' salaries, depreciation and taxes. Notice that although officers' salaries and depreciation remained the same in dollar amount, their percentages decreased because the base, sales, went up.

EXAMPLE 18-1

DOLORES COMPANY
Percentage Analysis of Income Statement
Year 6 and Year 7

	Year 7	% of Net Sales	Year 6	% of Net Sales
Gross sales	$2,290,000	104.1	$2,030,000	101.5
Less returns and allowances	90,000	4.1	30,000	1.5
Net sales	$2,200,000	100.0	$2,000,000	100.0
Cost of goods sold	1,342,000	61.0	1,200,000	60.0
Gross profit	$ 858,000	39.0	$ 800,000	40.0
Operating expenses:				
Officers' salaries	$ 130,000	5.9	$ 130,000	6.5
Office salaries	90,000	4.1	80,000	4.0
Depreciation	60,000	2.7	60,000	3.0
Advertising	161,000	7.3	110,000	5.5
Supplies	62,000	2.8	50,000	2.5
Property and employment taxes	42,000	1.9	40,000	2.0
Miscellaneous	25,000	1.1	20,000	1.0
Total operating expenses	570,000	25.9	490,000	24.5
Net operating profit	$ 288,000	13.1	$ 310,000	15.5
Other income and expense – net	12,000	.5	10,000	.5
Income before taxes	$ 300,000	13.6	$ 320,000	16.0
Federal income tax (50%)	150,000	6.8	160,000	8.0
Net income for the year	$ 150,000	6.8	$ 160,000	8.0

The significant features revealed by the percentage analysis can be summarized as follows:

> The Dolores Company increased its sales, possibly through the sizable increase in advertising. There were large increases in returns and allowances. Costs of goods sold went up more than proportionately, resulting in a lower gross profit percentage. Most other factors remained substantially the same. It appears that the advertising program did not yield the benefits expected.

Industry comparison

This summary is tentative, for there is no information about industry trends and percentages. For example, even though the situation of the Dolores Company looks negative, it may have done well in the face of adverse trends in the industry and the economy. An investor always should beware of over-concluding on the basis of inadequate information.

Note that the percentage analysis leads to consideration of trends in the company. To look at trends more closely, consider the figures for the Dolores Company in Table 18-1.

An examination of Table 18-1 yields a fuller picture of the company's operations. Sales have increased steadily over the five years—a percentage increase of 29.4% [($2,200,000 − 1,700,000)/1,700,000]. This increase has not yielded a higher profit; in fact, net income has decreased 7.4% (from $162,000 to $150,000) over the five years. The apparent causes of this decrease include

TABLE 18-1. Dolores Company

Selected Figures and Percentages — 5 Years

	Year 3	Year 4	Year 5	Year 6	Year 7
Net sales	$1,700,000	$1,860,000	$1,900,000	$2,000,000	$2,200,000
Gross profit	$ 714,000	$ 763,000	$ 760,000	$ 800,000	$ 858,000
Gross profit percentage	42.0%	41.0%	40.0%	40.0%	39.0%
Advertising as percent of sales	4.0%	4.2%	5.0%	5.5%	7.3%
Operating expenses	$ 401,000	$ 446,000	$ 460,000	$ 490,000	$ 570,000
Operating expenses as percent of sales	23.6%	24.0%	24.2%	24.5%	25.9%
Income from operations	$ 313,000	$ 317,000	$ 300,000	$ 310,000	$ 288,000
Operating income percentage	18.4%	17.0%	15.8%	15.5%	13.1%
Net income	$ 162,000	$ 162,000	$ 156,000	$ 160,000	$ 150,000
Net income percentage	9.5%	8.7%	8.2%	8.0%	6.8%

1. A decrease in gross profit percentage, indicating that costs are increasing more rapidly than sales
2. An increase in the operating expense percentage, especially in advertising

Operating expenses increased from 23.6% to 25.9% in five years, and advertising increased from 4.0% to 7.3%. Apart from advertising, therefore, the operating expenses went down as a percent of sales. Apparently the company tried to increase sales through additional advertising, but the sales increase did not bring increased profit. Not only has the percent of operating income to sales and net income to sales decreased considerably (from 9.5% to 6.8%), but the actual dollar amount of net income has dropped as well.

Before we condemn the management of the Dolores Company, however, we should compare company results with other companies in the industry. If the industry in general has experienced worse cost squeezes, the management of the Dolores Company has been doing well. If the industry has enjoyed high profit margins, the management of the Dolores Company has been doing poorly.

Trend analysis can help in evaluating an enterprise, but a few words of caution are in order. In the first place, trends do not necessarily continue. A steady increase in sales for 20 years does not mean that sales will go up during the twenty-first year. Normally, some degree of continuity can be assumed, but there are many abnormal situations. In the second place, the causal factors behind trends are important. For example, sales may increase because of the acquisition of other companies, rather than as a result of a real growth of sales in a company's original products. Or growth may be largely illusory, caused by inflation in prices rather than an increase in the number of units sold.

Trend analysis

Another factor to keep in mind is the effects of price-level changes.

Inflation

A 10% rise in sales must be interpreted differently if prices in general rise 12% than if prices do not change. It seems reasonable to expect a company's sales to at least keep pace with inflation. Circumstances may prevent this type of performance, for company prices do not necessarily follow the general price level; but the standard, nevertheless, seems reasonable.

Changing prices and price levels also affect the financial statements, because old costs may be matched with current revenue. Effects of this type were reviewed in chapter 15. These effects are important and should be remembered in a time of instability.

Accounting methods and comparisons

Percentage analysis and trend analysis, if used carefully, can aid in evaluating a company's performance. Generally, trends and percentages of one company can be compared to those of another company, but the analyst must be careful. In chapter 16, we saw that different accounting methods can affect statement results. Comparisons between two companies will yield erroneous conclusions if their accounting methods differ markedly; therefore, comparisons should be made cautiously.

If expenses of the enterprise are divided into fixed and variable expenses on the income statement, some helpful analyses can sometimes be made. Unfortunately, most published income statements do not divide expenses in this way; therefore, the effects of changes in volume on net income are often hard to determine. Sometimes analysis of items on the income statement will reveal which items are fixed and which are variable. For example, in the Dolores Company statements it is apparent that officers' salaries, depreciation, and miscellaneous expense are relatively fixed. Even if fixed costs can be identified, however, care must still be exercised. Fixed costs change over a period of years, and in some instances they can change radically. For example, if a company has a large expansion program, the depreciation expense may change considerably from year to year.

Analysis Utilizing Both Income Statement and Balance Sheet

Effective analysis of performance must go beyond the boundaries of the income statement. Income statement figures should be related to assets and equities on the balance sheet in order to obtain a complete picture of performance.

The focus of attention for most investors is rate of return. The dollar amount of income is important, but not nearly as significant as the relationship between income earned and investment. Information on this can be gleaned from a company's financial statements. Statements of CD Company (Examples 18-2 and 18-3) will be used to illustrate the various ratios used in analysis. Each example in the following pages refers to the figures on CD Company's statements.

EXAMPLE 18-2

CD COMPANY
Income Statements
Year 3 and Year 2
(in thousands)

	Year 3		Year 2	
Sales		$220		$200
Cost of goods sold:				
Beginning inventory	$ 25		$ 25	
Purchases	124		120	
Goods available	$149		$145	
Less ending inventory	21		25	
Cost of goods sold		128		120
Gross profit		$ 92		$ 80
Operating expenses		59		53
Income from operations		$ 33		$ 27
Interest expense		3		3
Income before taxes		$ 30		$ 24
Income taxes		15		12
Net income		$ 15		$ 12

EXAMPLE 18-3

CD COMPANY
Balance Sheets
December 31, Year 3 and Year 2
(in thousands)

	12/31/Year 3		12/31/Year 2	
Assets				
Current assets:				
Cash		$ 10		$ 10
Receivables (net)		24		20
Inventory		21		25
Total current assets		$ 55		$ 55
Plant and equipment—net		120		110
Intangibles		15		15
Total assets		$190		$180
Liabilities and Stockholders' Equity				
Current liabilities:				
Accounts payable		$ 26		$ 22
Accrued liabilities		12		10
Total current liabilities		$ 38		$ 32
Long-term liability—bonds payable		50		50
Total liabilities		$ 88		$ 82
Stockholders' equity:				
Capital stock	$60		$60	
Retained earnings	42		38	
Total stockholders' equity		102		98
Total liabilities and stockholders' equity		$190		$180
Data from Year 1 statements:				
Stockholders' equity 12/31/Year 1		$ 98		
Total assets 12/31/Year 1		$180		
Dividends paid in Year 3		$ 11		

Rate of Return on Owners' Equity. The investments of owners of a business are found in the owners' equity section of the balance sheet. In a corporation, the owners' equity (stockholders' equity) includes the capital stock issued, any other paid-in capital, and amounts of income retained in the business—retained earnings.[2] The rate of return on this equity is determined as follows:

$$\text{Rate of Return on Owner's Equity} = \frac{\text{Net Income}}{\text{Average Owners' Equity}}$$

For CD Company:

$$\text{Year 2} \quad \frac{\$12}{(\$98 + 98)/2} = \frac{\$12}{\$98} = 12.2\%$$

$$\text{Year 3} \quad \frac{\$15}{(\$98 + 102)/2} = \frac{\$15}{\$100} = 15.0\%$$

The average owners' equity is used because the income is earned throughout the year on the average investment by the owners.[3] Ending owners' equity may be used when beginning amounts are not available. The rate is based on net income (income after taxes), because this is the income claimed by the owners. If both preferred and common shares have been issued, the rate of return usually is computed on the common stockholders' equity, as follows:

Return on common

$$\text{Rate of Return on Common Stock} = \frac{\text{Income to Common Stockholders}}{\text{Common Stockholders' Equity}}$$

The income available to common stockholders is the net income less the dividends on preferred stock. The common stockholders' equity is usually the total stockholders' equity less the par value of the preferred stock. Unless there are dividends in arrears on preferred stock, the retained earnings and other paid-in capital are claimed by common stockholders in their position as the residual equity in the corporation.

Rate on Return on Total Assets. Management is responsible for effective use of all assets in the business. These assets come from two sources—owners and creditors. The rate of return on owners' equity focuses on only one aspect of management responsibility. The rate of return on total assets is a broader measurement of effectiveness and is computed as follows:

---

2. Many financial analysts prefer to subtract intangible assets from total assets and owners' equity in computing ratios on the ground that intangibles are too ephemeral. All assets are used in the ratio computations in this chapter.

3. A number of averages in this chapter are computed by using an average of beginning and end of year amounts. Where these amounts are not typical or representative, additional data points should be used to compute an average.

$$\text{Rate of Return on Total Assets} = \frac{\text{Income from Operations}}{\text{Average Total Assets}}$$

For CD Company:

$$\text{Year 2} \quad \frac{\$27}{(\$180 + 180)/2} = \frac{\$27}{\$180} = 15.0\%$$

$$\text{Year 3} \quad \frac{\$33}{(\$180 + 190)/2} = \frac{\$33}{\$185} = 17.8\%$$

Income from operations is used in this ratio instead of net income,[4] thus excluding nonoperating items from the ratio, particularly interest expense. Assets contributed by creditors may involve an interest cost. The interest cost is a return paid to creditors that is analogous to the dividends paid to investors. The rate of return on assets is computed by using the income before deducting any amounts paid as returns to providers of assets. At times, attention is focused on the net return on assets, with the rate being computed (less accurately) as follows:

$$\text{Rate of Return on Total Assets} = \frac{\text{Net Income}}{\text{Average Total Assets}}$$

For CD Company, the Year 3 figures are

$$\frac{\$15}{(\$180 + 190)/2} = 8.1\%$$

We prefer the use of income from operations in this analysis.

Incremental Analysis. A slightly more sophisticated analysis of rate of return may be performed by relating changes in income to changes in investment. This focuses on the effectiveness of additional investment in producing additional profits. The basic formula is

$$\frac{\text{Rate of Return on}}{\text{Added Investment}} = \frac{\text{Change in Income}}{\text{Change in Investment (Owners' Equity at Year-End)}}$$

For CD Company:

$$\text{Year 3} \quad \frac{\$3}{\$4} = 75\%$$

This type of analysis can often be helpful, but it also has its drawbacks. Other factors besides added investment often influence operating results for a period. At times the other factors may swamp any effect of the additional investment. Governmental actions, the state of the econ-

---

4. Some analysts use net income plus interest instead of income from operations. This ignores the fact that interest is tax deductible.

omy, or inflation can outweigh the efforts of the company itself and sometimes provides a smaller net return even though more has been invested, or provides a larger return than would otherwise be expected (as in CD Company). If this type of analysis is used with discretion, however, it can be useful. After all, it makes sense to hold a company responsible for using additional investment to earn additional income.

Leverage. Most companies finance part of their total assets by the use of interest-bearing debt. A company's use of debt is referred to as *leverage*. (It is also frequently called *financial leverage*). Companies using debt intend that the income earned from the assets financed by the debt will be large enough to cover the interest on the debt, income taxes, and a residual for the stockholders. It is a matter of borrowing money at 10%, for example, and using it to earn 15%. The 5% left after interest is subject to income taxes. Assuming a marginal income tax rate of 40%, there is a residual of 3% left over for the stockholders. Leverage is favorable when the assets financed by borrowing earn more than the interest cost on the debt, unfavorable when the reverse occurs. Debt financing therefore must be handled with caution. Borrowing saddles a company with interest expense that must be paid whether or not the company has profits. In addition, the debt must be paid back or arrangements must be made for refunding or refinancing at maturity dates. Financing with stock issues does not entail either of these responsibilities.

How does the CD Company fare with its use of debt? How can we discover whether it has favorable or unfavorable leverage? We can compare what CD's net income would have been without interest-bearing debt with the actual net income. We make this comparison in Table 18-2, using Year 3 figures.

Clearly, the CD Company has favorable leverage. If the company did not have interest-bearing debt of $50, the return on stockholders'

TABLE 18-2. Leverage—CD Company

	Without Interest-Bearing Debt	*With Interest-Bearing Debt*
Income from operations	$ 33	$ 33
Interest expense	0	3
Income before taxes	33	30
Income taxes (at 50% rate)	16.5	15
Net income	$ 16.5	$ 15
Average stockholders' equity	$150*	$100†
Return on stockholders' equity	11.0%	15.0%

* If there were no interest-bearing debt, the average stockholders' equity would be $50 (the amount of the debt) more than the stockholders' equity with the debt.
† ($98 + 102)/2 = $100

equity would have been 11.0%. The use of interest-bearing debt at a cost of $3 per year has raised the return on stockholders' equity to 15.0%.

Earnings Per Share. Earnings per share (EPS) were defined and discussed briefly in chapter 12. Many investors focus on EPS and emphasize it in their decision making. Figures for EPS are included on published income statements, so the information is readily available. If we look at a few annual reports, however, we will notice that in many cases several EPS figures are given for each year. First, if extraordinary gains and losses have occurred during the year, the statements will often give figures for EPS as follows:

	Year 3	Year 2
Earnings per common share:		
Income before extraordinary item	$3.00	$2.60
Extraordinary item	.27	—
Net income	$3.27	$2.60

Second, when the companies have common stock equivalents (warrants, convertible preferred, or convertible debt) outstanding, two figures will be given for EPS, usually labeled "primary earnings per share" and "fully diluted earnings per share." These companies are following the requirements of *APB Opinion No. 15*, "Earnings Per Share." The Opinion requires that if some outstanding securities are in substance equivalent to common stock (common stock equivalents), the primary EPS should be based on those issues as well as the common stock outstanding. The fully diluted EPS reflects the reduction in EPS that would occur if all contingent issues were converted to common stock. Primary EPS represents a substantial likelihood (of conversion, etc.), while fully diluted EPS includes all possibilities, no matter how remote.

Primary and fully diluted EPS

Common stock equivalents

The classification of securities as common stock equivalents and the computation of the EPS are governed by Opinion 15. The opinion is very complicated and is in some respects quite arbitrary.

Earnings per share of CD Company, assuming a par value of $10 per share of stock and 6,000 shares outstanding, are

$$\text{Year 2} \quad \frac{\$12,000}{6,000} = \$2.00 \text{ per share}$$

$$\text{Year 3} \quad \frac{\$15,000}{6,000} = \$2.50 \text{ per share.}$$

Book Value. The book value per share, or the *net asset value per share*, is the amount of corporate assets backing each share. It can be looked upon as the amount of money that would be received for each share if the company were liquidated at its balance sheet values. Of course, bondholders, other creditors, and preferred stockholders would have to be satisfied first, so the amount left for common stockholders is a net amount. For CD Company the book value is computed as follows:

	Year 2	Year 3
Total assets	$180,000	$190,000
Less total liabilities	82,000	88,000
a. Stockholders' equity—net assets available to common	$ 98,000	$102,000
b. Common shares ($10 par)	6,000	6,000
Book value per share (a/b)	$16.33	$17.00

A person buying a share of CD's stock in Year 3 probably would pay more than the book value of $17, because the high rate of return on owners' equity (15%) would make the shares attractive on the market.

Net asset value of securities can be computed for preferred stock or bonds as well as common. In Year 3 the asset value per bond (assuming each bond is $1,000 par amount) can be computed as follows:

	Year 3
Total assets	$190,000
Less current liabilities	38,000
Net assets available to meet bondholders' claims	$152,000

$$\frac{\$152,000}{50} = \$3,040 \text{ net asset value per \$1,000 bond}$$

Book values are helpful in some situations, but in a time of changing prices their usefulness is limited. In fact, book values can be misleading. Profitable companies may have a low book value and very substantial earnings. A high book value, on the other hand, is no guarantee of high earnings, as has been shown repeatedly in the case of railroads.

Rate of Return on Stock Investments. Supply-and-demand conditions determine the market price of shares. Suppose that Joe Doe buys a share of CD Company stock in Year 3 for $25. His return is not the 15% return on owners' equity. He must relate his return to the investment he has in the stock—$25. He can do this by computing the following:

$$\text{Rate of Return on Investment} = \frac{\text{Earnings per Share}}{\text{Investment per Share}}$$

For Joe Doe, the computation would be

$$\frac{\$2.50}{\$25.00} = 10\%$$

Any investor can compute his or her own rate of return in this way. Potential investors characteristically look at earnings per share divided by the current market price in evaluating investment opportunities. Sometimes this fraction is turned upside down to get the price-earnings ratio.

$$\text{Price-Earnings Ratio} = \frac{\text{Market Price per Share}}{\text{Earnings per Share}}$$

Price-earnings ratio

The market prices for stocks differ from their value on the books in most situations. For example:

	Book Value of Common Stock 12/31/76	Market Price 12/31/76
General Motors	$49.81	$78½
IBM Corporation	85.02	279⅛
Avon Products	10.15	49½
U.S. Steel	62.39	49¾

Investors also look at dividend yield per share of stock, which is computed by dividing the dividends per share by the price per share. For CD Company the yield in Year 3 on a $25 investment would be

Dividend yield

$$\text{Dividends per share:} \quad \frac{\$11{,}000}{6{,}000} = \$1.83$$

$$\text{Dividend yield:} \quad \frac{\$1.83}{\$25.00} = 7.32\%$$

Dividend information for listed companies is readily available in publications such as the *Wall Street Journal*.

USE AND QUALITY OF ASSETS

How assets are used in the enterprise is another interesting aspect of performance. A company that uses its assets efficiently will generally be a better investment than a company that does not. The statement of changes in financial position provides information about how assets change during a period. Several ratios aid in determining how effectively the company uses its assets.

Asset Turnover

An idea of the use of total assets can be derived from the asset turnover.

$$\text{Asset Turnover} = \frac{\text{Sales}}{\text{Average Total Assets}}$$

For the CD Company the figures are

$$\text{Year 2} \quad \frac{\$200}{\$180} = 1.11 \text{ times}$$

$$\text{Year 3} \quad \frac{\$220}{\$185} = 1.19 \text{ times}$$

The increase in the asset turnover shows that the assets are being used more efficiently in Year 3 than in Year 2. That is, the assets produce more sales per dollar of assets than in Year 2. The question of profitability of use must be asked, of course; mere dollars of sales in themselves are not important. The profitability of assets is found in the rate of return on total assets and the profitability of sales, as indicated by the rate of profit on sales. Both these ratios were discussed earlier. These ratios are combined with asset turnover in the following way:

Relationship to returns

Rate of Profit on Sales × Asset Turnover = Rate of Return on Total Assets

or breaking each ratio down into its parts:

$$\frac{\text{Income}}{\text{Sales}} \times \frac{\text{Sales}}{\text{Average Total Assets}} = \frac{\text{Income}}{\text{Average Total Assets}}$$

For the CD Company, using net income, the Year 3 figures are as follows:

$$\frac{15}{220} \times \frac{220}{185} = \frac{15}{185}$$

$$6.8\% \times 1.19 = 8.1\%$$

If income from operations is used, the figures are

$$\frac{33}{220} \times \frac{220}{185} = \frac{33}{185}$$

$$15\% \times 1.19 = 17.8\%$$

These relationships yield some interesting information. One business may make a small profit per dollar of sales but turn its assets rapidly to yield a good rate of return on assets. If it also uses leverage, the rate of return on owners' equity can be good. Another company may earn a large return on sales but have a low asset turnover and thus not be any better off than a company with a low return on sales. For example, contrast the following companies:

	Company E	Company F
Rate of return on sales	1%	20%
Asset turnover	10 times	0.5 times
Rate of return on assets	10%	10%

The operations of the two companies are diverse, but they both earn the same return on assets. Company E might be a supermarket, and Company

F a jewelry store. The supermarket makes a small profit on each sale but turns its assets rapidly. The jewelry store makes a high profit on each sale but makes fewer sales in relationship to its assets.

Turnovers

Before discussing various turnover ratios, consider the general meaning of the term turnover. Any turnover involves relating the activity in an item (usually an asset) to its balance, as follows:

$$\text{Turnover} = \frac{\text{Activity of Item}}{\text{Average Balance of Item}}$$

Since the activity covers a period of time, the average balance of the item for the period should be used. Sometimes the ending balance is used, with slightly incorrect figures resulting, but probably no great overall distortion as long as the amount is fairly representative. The asset turnover mentioned in the preceding section uses the sales as the measure of activity of all assets in the enterprise.

The inventory turnover is determined as follows:

$$\text{Inventory Turnover} = \frac{\text{Cost of Goods Sold}}{\text{Average Inventory}}$$

Inventory turnover

The cost of goods sold is the best measure of activity to use in connection with merchandise inventory. The inventory turnovers for the CD Company are

$$\text{Year 2 Turnover} = \frac{\$120}{(\$25 + 25)/2} = \frac{120}{25} = 4.8 \text{ times}$$

$$\text{Year 3 Turnover} = \frac{\$128}{(\$25 + 21)/2} = \frac{128}{23} = 5.6 \text{ times}$$

The inventory figures are derived from the cost of goods sold section of the income statement and from the balance sheet. The increase in turnover means that the company used its inventories well in Year 3. Two words of caution are in order. First, the inventory turnover can get too high, with inventory being kept at such a low level that customer demand is not satisfied. Second, the inventory pricing procedure can affect this ratio. A company using LIFO will have old costs in inventory, which might well be low and out-of-date during inflation. The turnover will therefore look better than it actually is, since the cost of sales will be divided by an unrealistically low figure. A comparison with a company using FIFO will not be valid. Neither will the turnover be the true physical turnover of goods during the period.

Lifo and Fifo

Inventory turnover rates are used extensively; they are a good tool for analyzing the effectiveness of operations and of inventory control.

Percent of Year's Sales Uncollected

Prompt collection of receivables is an important feature of asset control. The percent of year's sales uncollected indicates company progress in this area. It is computed as follows:

$$\text{Percent of Year's Sales Uncollected} = \frac{\text{Receivables at Year End}}{\text{Sales}} \times 100$$

If information about cash and credit sales is available, the credit sales should be used, since only they give rise to receivables. For CD Company the figures are

$$\text{Year 2} \quad \frac{\$\ 20}{\$200} \times 100 = 10.0\%$$

$$\text{Year 3} \quad \frac{\$\ 24}{\$220} \times 100 = 10.9\%$$

These percentages can be translated into the number of days by multiplying the figures by 365:

Year 2 10.0% × 365 = 36.5 days
Year 3 10.9% × 365 = 39.8 days

Both computations indicate that the company did worse in its collections in Year 3.

This ratio can be related to the usual credit terms in an industry. If the credit terms in the CD Company's industry are usually 2/10, n/30, for example, the performance in both years is unsatisfactory.

ANALYSIS WITH A CREDITOR EMPHASIS

Many ratios deal with the financial strength of a company, particularly with its ability to pay its debts. The statement of CD Company in Examples 18-2 and 18-3 will be used to illustrate these ratios also.

Current Ratio

The current ratio, or working capital ratio, is widely used. The ratio is

$$\text{Current Ratio} = \frac{\text{Current Assets}}{\text{Current Liabilities}}$$

The ratios for CD Company are

$$\text{Year 2} \quad \frac{\$55}{\$32} = 1.72 \text{ to } 1$$

$$\text{Year 3} \quad \frac{\$55}{\$38} = 1.45 \text{ to } 1$$

The ratio went down in Year 3, and the trend does not look good. This does not mean that the company will soon become insolvent, but it is a warning to a creditor or investor.

The current ratio is a good measure and should be supplemented by some analysis of the composition of the current assets and current liabilities. Thus if the ratio stays the same but the proportion of inventory climbs, this fact should be noted. Year-to-year changes in the assets and liabilities are often important in financial analysis.

Acid-Test Ratio

The acid-test, or quick asset, ratio focuses on a company's immediate ability to pay debts. The assets that an enterprise has available to pay its current obligations as they come due include cash, temporary investments, and receivables (which should be collected shortly). Inventories are excluded because they must be sold and the resulting receivables collected before they produce assets for paying bills. Prepaid items are excluded because they will be used up, not collected, and thus will provide no money for paying bills. Cash, temporary investments, and receivables are called *quick assets,* because they can be turned into cash quickly. The acid-test ratio is

Quick assets

$$\text{Acid-Test Ratio} = \frac{\text{Quick Assets}}{\text{Current Liabilities}}$$

For the CD Company the ratios are

$$\text{Year 2} \quad \frac{\$30}{\$32} = .94 \text{ to } 1$$

$$\text{Year 3} \quad \frac{\$34}{\$38} = .89 \text{ to } 1$$

If a company is to have resources to pay its bills, a ratio of at least 1 to 1 should be maintained. The CD Company is in a poor position with regard to short-term debt-paying ability, as revealed by both the current ratio and the acid-test ratio. Moreover, the position grew slightly worse in Year 3.

Amount of Working Capital

The working capital of a company is usually defined as its current assets minus its current liabilities.[5] For CD Company, the working capital is as follows:

---

5. Some people refer to this as *net* working capital and define working capital as just total current assets. We prefer defining working capital as current assets minus current liabilities.

$$\text{Year 2} \quad \$55 - 32 = \$23$$
$$\text{Year 3} \quad \$55 - 38 = \$17$$

There is a substantial reduction in the working capital in Year 3. Further information about changes in working capital can be obtained from the statement of changes in financial position.

Ratio of Owners' Equity to Debt

The ratio of owners' equity to debt is designed to give some insight into how a business is financed—whether by owners or by creditors. The ratio is determined as follows:

$$\text{Ratio of Equity to Debt} = \frac{\text{Owners' Equity}}{\text{Total Liabilities}}$$

For the CD Company the figures are

$$\text{Year 2} \quad \frac{\$98}{\$82} = 1.20 \text{ to } 1$$

$$\text{Year 3} \quad \frac{\$102}{\$\ 88} = 1.16 \text{ to } 1$$

This ratio has declined slightly for the CD Company, although the owners' equity is still larger than the debt.

    No desired or normal figure exists for this ratio. In general, a company in a relatively stable industry can afford to maintain a lower ratio than a company in a cyclical industry. A company that uses considerable leverage will have a lower ratio than one that does not. Naturally, companies should beware of large debts when their future is uncertain. Also, in a time of inflation, there is some advantage to being in debt, so a low ratio of equity to debt is not necessarily the wisest management. In addition, in a time of inflation owners' equity tends to be understated in real terms, which in turn understates the ratio of owners' equity to debt.

    Variants of this ratio are the ratio of debt to total assets and of owners' equity to total assets. These ratios also indicate the financing of the enterprise. Many people just look at the ratio of the long-term debt to equity. This emphasizes long-term financing.

Times Interest Earned

Another ratio that focuses on debt-paying ability is the number of times interest is covered by net operating profit. The ratio is computed

$$\text{Times Interest Earned} = \frac{\text{Income from Operations}}{\text{Interest Expense}}$$

For the CD Company the figures are

$$\text{Year 2} \quad \frac{\$27}{\$\ 3} = 9 \text{ times}$$

$$\text{Year 3} \quad \frac{\$33}{\$\ 3} = 11 \text{ times}$$

When the ratio is as high as it is in this case, a change is not particularly significant. When the ratio is low, say 2 times, it can become important, for interest must be paid, and a decline in profits could put the company in a very tight position.

The times interest earned computation can be made more meaningful by including other fixed charges, such as contractual lease payments. Since long-term leases are becoming a popular financing method, a ratio of the income before fixed charges to the fixed operating charges and interest is quite significant.

THE COMPOSITE PICTURE

Other ratios could be discussed and computed, but the primary elements in ratio and percentage analysis of a company have been presented. We now look at the ratios and percentages for the CD Company and attempt to draw some overall conclusions (see Table 18-3). The picture that emerges

TABLE 18-3   CD Company

Ratios and Percentages

	Year 3	Year 2
Rate of return on owners' equity	15.0%	12.2%
Rate of return on total assets— using income from operations	17.8%	15.0%
Rate of return on total assets— using net income	8.1%	6.7%
Asset turnover	1.19 times	1.11 times
Net income on sales	6.8%	6.0%
Inventory turnover	5.6 times	4.8 times
Percent of sales uncollected	10.9%	10.0%
Current ratio	1.45 to 1	1.72 to 1
Acid-test ratio	.89 to 1	.94 to 1
Amount of working capital	$17	$23
Ratio of owners' equity to debt	1.16 to 1	1.20 to 1
Times interest earned	11 times	9 times
Gross profit rate	42%	40%
Percentage increase in sales	10%	
Percentage increase in net income	25%	

from a study of these ratios and percentages is of a company that is increasing its profits but deteriorating in debt-paying ability. The absolute amounts for the two years must also be considered. Sales have increased 10% from Year 2 to Year 3, from $200 to $220. Profits increased from $12 to $15, a 25% increase. Total assets increased from $180 to $190. Total current assets remained at $55, and current liabilities increased from $32 to $38, almost a 20% increase. Some of these changes are good; others are not. Financial statement figures for CD Company as a whole present a mixed picture to the analyst. The company looks like a good investment, but there are some weak spots.

BEYOND FINANCIAL ANALYSIS

The ratios and percentages discussed constitute only a part of the investigation necessary in evaluating a company. Ratios and percentages only sketch in the outlines; the detail must be provided by other sources. The management of the enterprise is a particularly important feature. In fact, quality of management is a factor rated very highly by analysts. Unfortunately, it is hard to quantify. Another important factor is the future of the industry involved. The particular company's place in the industry's future, determined to a large extent by management, is vital. Customer and employee relations should be considered, and governmental relations also are becoming an important factor in many situations. Financial analysis is only a part of the overall evaluation of an enterprise for investment or other purposes.

OVERALL CRITIQUE OF FINANCIAL ANALYSIS

Statement analysis can be helpful, but the astute investor should be aware of the significant limitations that exist in this type of analysis. Without an awareness of these limitations, statement analysis can cause more harm than good. Some of the limitations of statement analysis can be traced to limitations of accounting itself. Accounting measurements of financial position and enterprise progress are necessarily tentative and inexact. Also, the problems in accounting measurement are multiplied in a complex, dynamic economy, particularly when the economy is characterized by changing prices. The variety of accounting alternatives and the unsettled state of accounting principles provide good evidence of these problems.

Ratios and percentages can be no better than the statements on which they are based. If there is a lack of comparability in the statements, then ratios and percentages based on the statements also will lack comparability. If statements are distorted by price-level changes, ratios and percentages based on the statements will also be distorted. Thus, the reader should develop a healthy distrust of elaborate and involved ratio and percentage analysis. The foundation is usually not adequate to support an elaborate superstructure.

SUMMARY

This chapter dealt with financial statement analysis. It began by considering analysis of operations and rate of return analysis—the main focus of investor interest. Discussion of ratios dealing with the use of assets and financial solvency completed the picture of statement analysis. Both trend analysis and ratio analysis were emphasized.

A recurrent theme of the chapter was that statement analysis has definite limitations. Investors and other users of analysis must be aware of these limitations if they are to use these analytical tools properly.

IMPORTANT TERMS

Stock market
Investor
Percentage analysis
Gross profit rate
Trend analysis
Rate of return
Incremental analysis
Leverage
Earnings per share (EPS)
Primary EPS
Fully diluted EPS

Common stock equivalents
Book value
Price-earnings ratio
Dividend yield
Asset turnover
Inventory turnover
Current ratio
Acid-test ratio
Times interest earned
Ratio of owners' equity to debt

QUESTIONS

18-1. How effective is analysis of published financial statements in the process of reaching an investment decision? How effective is such analysis in reaching a decision to extend credit to a company?

18-2. If you had your choice between the advice of a qualified professional analyst and that of a fortune teller who was correct in predictions 50% of the time, which would you choose if you were deciding on common stock investments?

18-3. What ratios and percentages should be used in evaluating operating success of an enterprise?

18-4. What ratios should be used in evaluating financial strength of an enterprise? Suppose you want to evaluate strength for the long run?

18-5. What is the name of each of the three parts of the equation below? What is the significance of each of the three parts to management and investors in the company?

$$\frac{\text{Net Income}}{\text{Investment Base}} = \frac{\text{Sales}}{\text{Investment Base}} \times \frac{\text{Net Income}}{\text{Sales}}$$

18-6. The current ratio is supposed to be related to a company's ability to pay its short-term debts. What further information would you want before concluding a specific current ratio was good or bad?

18-7. A certain store has maintained the same investment in inventory over a period of two years. In addition, its markups and the quality of merchandise have remained approximately the same. During the first year, its turnover was 5, and in the second year its turnover was 6. Estimate the probable effects of this increase in turnover on dollar sales, cost of sales, and gross profit.

18-8. Two companies use different inventory methods—one uses FIFO and the other LIFO. What ratios are likely to be affected? Can valid comparisons be made of the two companies?

18-9. Y Company pays a current liability of $8,000. How will this affect the current ratio? How will this affect the amount of working capital? You may assume that the current ratio is higher than 1 to 1 before the payment takes place.

18-10. Z Company returns some goods to suppliers, receiving credit on account (that is, getting a reduction in accounts payable). The current ratio and acid-test ratio are higher than 1 to 1 before this return.
   a. How will this affect the inventory turnover rate?
   b. How will this affect the acid-test ratio?
   c. How will this affect the rate of net income on sales?

EXERCISES

18-11. *Rate of return.* On December 31, the statement of financial position of Company R showed total assets of $200,000 and total liabilities of $100,000. On the same date, the statement of Company S disclosed total assets of $200,000 and no liabilities. The average interest rate of R's liabilities was 5%. The net income before interest and income taxes (at a rate of 30%) was $14,000 for Company R and $16,000 for Company S.

Required:
a. On the basis of the information given, in which company did the management appear to be more efficient? Why?
b. Which company earned the greater return for its owners? Comment.
(Solution in Appendix B.)

18-12. *Ratios.* Following are a list of ratios and a list of factors about which you are attempting to make conclusions. Indicate which ratios you would compute to help you reach a conclusion. More than one ratio may be appropriate for some factors.

- Current ratio
- Net income to net sales
- Times interest earned
- Net income to total assets
- Number of days' sales uncollected
- Net income to owners' equity
- Acid-test ratio
- Inventory turnover
- Ratio of owners' equity to debt
- Asset turnover

a. You are interested in the efficiency of asset use in the business.
b. You are concerned with the firm's ability to meet its current obligations in the very near future.
c. You are trying to estimate the risk of insolvency over the long run.
d. You suspect that expenses have been increasing at a rate that is faster than the overall business activity of the firm.
e. You suspect that the credit terms offered by your firm have resulted in your losing customers to your competitors.
f. You are questioning the need to be more competitive by expanding the line of merchandise stocked, at the same time recognizing that the items not now handled are rather slow moving.
g. You are contemplating issuing bonds to finance expansion.

18-13. *Ratios.* A company has the following summary balance sheet on a certain date:

Assets	$100,000	Liabilities	$25,000
		Stockholders' Equity	75,000

Required:
a. The company earns an operating income of 10% on its assets. If the interest on liabilities averages 6%, what percentage is earned on stockholders' equity? Ignore taxes.
b. What further information would you need before computing the asset turnover? The current ratio?

18-14. *Ratios.* A certain company carries an average inventory of $20,000. Its inventory turnover the past year was 4½, and its gross profit on sales was 25%.
Required:
a. Compute the net sales for the past year.

b. If this company increased its merchandise turnover to 5 for the coming year, retained the same average inventory amount, and increased the gross profit rate to 30%, what would its gross profit be for the coming year?

18-15. *Turnover.* The Fairfax Company had sales of $3,000,000 and an average inventory of $500,000 for the current year. It is estimated that the sales for next year will be $4,000,000 and that the gross profit percentage of 25% realized for the current year will be maintained next year. What average inventory will be needed to increase the turnover next year to 7 times?

18-16. *Turnover.* Using the following information, compute inventory turnover for each article carried in stock and for the total inventory.

Article	Units in Inventory Last Year	Units in Inventory This Year	Unit Cost	Sales in Year	Gross Profit Rate
A	32	40	$3.00	$ 864	25%
B	57	63	7.00	6,000	30%
C	99	93	9.00	17,280	40%

18-17. *Ratios.* The following data are given for the YZ Company.

Income Statement
Years Ended 12/31/Year 2 and 12/31/Year 1

	Year 2	Year 1
Sales	$120,000	$100,000
Cost of sales	78,000	60,000
Gross margin	42,000	40,000
Operating expenses	20,000	20,000
Operating profit	$ 22,000	$ 20,000
Interest expense	2,000	2,000
Income before taxes	$ 20,000	$ 18,000
Income taxes	5,000	4,500
Net income	$ 15,000	$ 13,500

Required:
a. Compute the rate of return on sales for both years.
b. What factors accounted for the change in rate of return?
c. The YZ Company had average total assets of $100,000 in Year 2. Compute the rate of return on total assets for Year 2.
d. The average accounts receivable for Year 2 amounted to $20,000. All sales made by this company are made on account. What is the approximate collection period?
e. The average inventory for this company was $20,000 in Year 2. What was the inventory turnover in Year 2?

18-18. *EPS, Market values.* The Hobar Company had a net income of $280,000 last year. Stockholders' equity consists of capital stock (50,000 shares) of $1,000,000, premium on stock of $200,000, and retained earnings of $600,000. Market price of the stock is $50.

Required:
a. Compute the book value per share.
b. Compute the earnings per share.
c. Compute the price-earnings ratio.
d. Comment on the discrepancy between book value and market price.

18-19. *Market value.* The earnings per share for Jean Company for the past 5 years have been as follows:

Year 1	$2.50
Year 2	3.00
Year 3	3.50
Year 4	4.00
Year 5	4.50

The past trend in earnings is expected to continue until earnings reach $6.00 per share, when they are expected to stabilize. What do you consider an appropriate price for the shares? Discuss.

PROBLEMS

18-20. *Analysis, EPS, Book value.* Following is the equity section of the Gorge Company's balance sheet and other information.

GORGE COMPANY
Balance Sheet
Liabilities and Stockholders' Equity Section

Current liabilities		$ 200,000
Long-term debt (8% interest)		100,000
Stockholders' equity		
Common stock $10 par	$200,000	
Premium on common	40,000	
Retained earnings	160,000	400,000
Total liabilities and stockholders' equity		$ 700,000

Other information:

Sales during year	$1,050,000
Net income (after taxes of $40,000)	60,000

Required:
a. Compute rate of return on stockholders' equity (before tax).
b. Compute income from operations.
c. Compute rate of return on assets. Does Gorge use leverage effectively?
d. Compute earnings per share.
e. Compute book value per share.
(Solution in Appendix B.)

18-21. *Ratios.* Following are data for three years for two companies engaged in the same type of business. On the basis of the data given, answer the questions below. If computations are needed, be sure to include them in your solution.

(Figures in Thousands)

	Company A			Company B		
	Year 1	Year 2	Year 3	Year 1	Year 2	Year 3
Average stockholders' equity	$1,000	$1,100	$1,200	$2,000	$1,900	$2,200
Average total assets	2,000	2,200	2,300	3,000	3,000	3,400
Net sales	5,000	6,000	7,000	6,000	7,000	8,000
Cost of goods sold	2,900	3,600	4,340	3,300	3,850	4,320
Net income before taxes	300	340	360	720	646	836
Net income after taxes	150	170	180	360	323	418

Required:
a. Which company has the highest percentage of net income to sales in Year 3?
b. Which company has the highest percentage of net income to stockholders' equity in Year 1? In Year 3?
c. Which company shows the greatest improvement in net income?
d. Which company has the greatest percentage increase in sales from Year 1 to Year 3?
e. Which company apparently distributes a higher proportion of its net income as dividends to stockholders each year? Use some supporting figures in your answer. You may assume that neither company sold any stock over the three years.
f. On the basis of the figures given, which company obtains the greater amount of its total capital by borrowing from creditors?
g. Which company has the highest number of asset turnovers in Year 1?
h. Which company has the highest gross margin percentage in Year 2?

18-22. *Ratios.* Using the data below, determine the following (include computations):
a. The current ratio
b. The rate of gross profit per sales dollar
c. The rate of inventory turnover
d. The percent of sales uncollected at the end of the year
e. The ratio of owners' equity to debt
f. The rate of profit earned on total assets
g. The rate of return on owners' *average* capital investment
h. The acid-test ratio

X COMPANY
Balance Sheet
at Year-end

Assets		Liabilities and Stockholders' Equity		
Current assets:		Current liabilities:		
Cash	$ 80,000	Accounts payable		$ 60,000
Accounts receivable	60,000	Accrued liabilities		30,000
Inventory	60,000			$ 90,000
	$200,000	Bonds payable (6%)		100,000
Investments	50,000	Stockholders' equity		
Plant and equipment (net)	150,000	Capital Stock	$100,000	
		Retained earnings*	110,000	210,000
	$400,000			$400,000

* Cash dividends of $18,000 were declared and paid during the year. No changes took place in capital stock.

X COMPANY
Income Statement for the Year

Net sales (including cash sales of $100,000)		$300,000
Cost of goods sold:		
Beginning inventory	$ 44,000	
Purchases	214,000	
	$258,000	
Ending inventory	60,000	198,000
Gross profit on sales		$102,000
Expenses		64,000
Net income		$ 38,000

18-23. *Ratios.* Given below are figures for the Shocking Electric Company.

	Year 1	Year 2
Sales	$4,000	$4,500
Cost of goods sold	2,400	2,610
Gross margin on sales	$1,600	$1,890
Operating expenses	1,200	1,450
Net income before tax	$ 400	$ 440
Federal income tax	200	220
Net income	$ 200	$ 220
Average total assets	$8,000	$8,200
Average stockholders' equity	4,000	4,400

Required:

a. Compute:
  1. Rate of net income (after taxes) on sales for both years
  2. Percent of gross margin on sales for both years
  3. Rate of return on stockholders' equity for both years (after taxes)
  4. Percent increase in sales
  5. Percent increase in net income

b. Briefly comment on significant trends and changes, using computations above to help make your points.

18-24. *Ratios.* Following are the balance sheets at December 31 of Years 1 and 2 and the income statement for the year ended December 31, Year 2, for the Ames Manufacturing Company.

AMES MANUFACTURING COMPANY
Comparative Balance Sheets
December 31 of Years 2 and 1

	Year 2	Year 1
Assets		
Current:		
Cash	$ 30,000	$ 49,000
Accounts receivable	100,000	100,000
Inventories	300,000	150,000
	$430,000	$299,000
Plant and equipment	$180,000	$140,000
less accumulated depreciation	(60,000)	(40,000)
	$120,000	$100,000
Goodwill	$ 50,000	$ 60,000
	$600,000	$459,000
Liabilities and Stockholders' Equity		
Current:		
Accounts payable	$150,000	$ 70,000
Other liabilities	30,000	50,000
	$180,000	$120,000
Long-term:		
Bonds payable	60,000	none
	$240,000	$120,000
Stockholders' equity:		
5% preferred stock	$100,000	$100,000
Common stock	200,000	200,000
Retained income	60,000	39,000
	$360,000	$339,000
	$600,000	$459,000

AMES MANUFACTURING COMPANY
Income Statement
Year Ended December 31, Year 2

Net sales	$600,000
Cost of goods sold expense	450,000
Gross margin	$150,000
Selling and administrative expenses	90,000
Operating income	$ 60,000
Other expenses: Bond interest	3,000
Income before income taxes	$ 57,000
Income taxes	21,000
Net income	$ 36,000

Required:
Using data from the statements, compute the following:
a. Current ratios for December 31 of both years
b. Acid-test ratios for both years
c. Inventory turnover for Year 2
d. Percent of Year 2 sales uncollected
e. Turnover rate for total assets in Year 2
f. Rate of return on total assets in Year 2 (use operating income)
g. Rate of return on common stockholders' equity in Year 2
h. Number of times bond interest was earned in Year 2

18-25. *Ratios.* The following information is given for the Lane Co.

	Dec. 31, Year 2	Dec. 31, Year 1
Cash	$ 8,000	$12,000
Accounts receivable (net)	20,000	25,000
Merchandise inventory	40,000	30,000
Prepaid expenses	3,000	3,000
	$71,000	$70,000
Accounts payable	$28,000	$30,000
Accrued liabilities	5,000	5,000
	33,000	35,000
	$38,000	$35,000

	Year 2
Net sales	$180,000
Cost of goods sold	108,000
Net income for year	10,000

Required:
a. What is the working capital as of December 31, Year 2?
b. Compute the acid-test ratio as of December 31, Year 2.
c. Compute the merchandise turnover for Year 2.
d. Compute the percent of year's sales uncollected at the end of Year 2.
e. The company makes a gross profit of 40% on its net sales. Its accounts payable outstanding as of December 31, Year 2, and its accrued liabilities must be paid within 15 days. Will this company be able to pay its obligations without borrowing from the bank? Explain.

18-26. *Ratios.* Compute the following items from the financial statements of Acme Merchandise Co., which appear below.
a. Rate of return on net sales for Year 2.
b. Turnover of assets for Year 2.
c. Rate of return on total assets for Year 2. Use operating income.
d. Acid-test ratio at December 31, Year 2.
e. Inventory turnover for Year 2.
f. Acme plans to increase its average total assets in Year 3 to $1,200,000. How much must net sales be in Year 3 for Acme to maintain the same rate of return on total assets in Year 3 as it experienced in Year 2?
g. Amount of dividends paid in Year 2.

Income Statement
Year Ended December 31, Year 2

Gross sales		$1,132,000
Less sales returns and allowances	$20,000	
Sales discounts	12,000	32,000
Net sales		$1,100,000
Cost of goods sold		600,000
Gross margin		$ 500,000
Operating expenses (including depreciation of $60,000)		290,000
Income from operations		$ 210,000
Interest expense		15,000
Income before income taxes		$ 195,000
Income taxes		95,000
Net income		$ 100,000

Balance Sheets
As of December 31

	Year 2	Year 1
Cash	$ 50,000	$ 40,000
Accounts receivable (net)	60,000	50,000
Merchandise inventory	120,000	80,000
Plant assets (net)	870,000	730,000
	$1,100,000	$900,000
Accounts payable	$ 80,000	$ 70,000
5-year, 6% notes payable	250,000	100,000
Capital stock, par $5	500,000	500,000
Retained earnings	270,000	230,000
	$1,100,000	$900,000

(Solution in Appendix B.)

CASE PROBLEM

18-27. *Trend analysis.* Analyze the trends revealed by the 5-year summary of Del Monte's operations (see Table 18-4).

TABLE 18-4. Del Monte Corporation and Subsidiary Companies Five-Year Financial Review

	1975	1974	1973	1972	1971
Summary of Operations for the year: (1)					
Sales and operating revenues	$1,279,274	$1,042,608	$946,531	$836,298	$765,824
Cost of products sold and operating expenses	997,678	809,729	726,523	644,821	585,780
Selling, general, and administrative expenses	184,861	154,287	163,357	136,616	126,196
Interest expense	30,804	19,090	17,988	18,684	18,290
Federal, state, and foreign taxes on income	25,108	23,943	16,207	16,476	15,776
Earnings for the year	47,245	39,136	26,014	23,592	21,501
Per share of capital stock (2)	3.94	3.26	2.16	1.92	1.75
Fully diluted earnings per share (3)	3.76	3.12	2.09	1.87	1.71
Cash dividends paid	15,306	14,115	13,179	13,264	13,095
Dividends per share of capital stock	1.28	1.18	1.10	1.10	1.10
Additions to plant and equipment, net	35,957	18,782	34,546	18,802	19,732
Provision for depreciation	18,578	18,037	17,227	15,965	15,934
Percent return on sales	3.69%	3.75%	2.75%	2.82%	2.81%
Percent return on shareholders' equity	17.28%	15.75%	10.79%	10.23%	9.67%
At Year-End:					
Working capital	$ 281,674	$ 225,133	$ 203,989	$ 220,081	$ 217,980
Ratio of current assets to current liabilities	2.10	2.19	2.21	2.32	2.55
Plant and equipment, net	209,031	191,652	190,907	173,588	170,571
Long-term debt	193,431	145,498	150,747	154,301	158,686
Shareholders' equity, per share	25.43	22.76	20.68	19.62	18.78
Shares outstanding (in thousands)	12,003	12,013	12,013	12,285	12,285
Number of shareholders	24,333	24,144	23,460	22,398	22,639

(1) Dollar amounts shown in thousands, except for per share data.
(2) Earnings per share of capital stock based on weighted average number of shares outstanding during the year.
(3) In calculating fully diluted earnings per share, it is assumed that all of the outstanding convertible debentures issued in March 1969 were converted to capital stock at the beginning of the year.

APPENDIX A

Glossary

Account. A continuous record of effects of transactions on an individual asset, liability, stockholders' equity, revenue, or expense item.

Account form. A form of balance sheet in which assets are shown on the left and liabilities and owners' equity on the right.

Accounting. The activity of providing quantitative information, primarily financial in nature, that is intended to be useful in making economic decisions; the process of measuring the assets, liabilities, and owners' equity of an enterprise and the changes in them and communicating the measurements to interested parties.

Accounting conventions. Auxiliary accounting concepts based on typical behavior of accountants; conventions modify principles.

Accounting cycle. The sequence of steps in the accounting process.

Accounting equation. A truism expressed mathematically: Assets equal liabilities plus owners' equity.

Accounting inputs. Source documents showing events, both external and internal, that affect the enterprise.

Accounting outputs. The financial statements and other business documents, such as bills to customers, that are generated by the financial accounting process.

Accounting postulates. Basic broad foundations, or assumptions, that underlie accounting.

Accounting transaction. See *Transaction*.

Accounts payable. Amounts owed to general creditors as a result of purchasing material goods or services on account.

Accounts receivable. Claims to cash usually arising from credit transactions with customers.

Accrual basis of accounting. A method of accounting that recognizes revenue and expenses when they occur rather than when cash is received or paid.

Accumulated amortization. The cumulative amount of amortization taken on an intangible asset; deducted from the asset on the balance sheet.

Accumulated depreciation. The cumulative amount of depreciation taken on owned assets; deducted from the assets on the balance sheet.

Acid-test ratio. The ratio of cash and other quick monetary assets to current liabilities.

Adjusting entries. Journal entries made at the end of an accounting period to bring the accounts up to date.

Administrative expense. Expenses associated with the general administrative activities of the enterprise; a subcategory of operating expense.

Allowance for doubtful accounts. The estimated amount of accounts receivable that will be uncollectible; deducted from receivables on the balance sheet.

American Accounting Association (AAA). National professional organization of accounting teachers; has made several pronouncements on basic accounting theory.

American Institute of CPAs (AICPA). The national professional organization of CPAs; has been instrumental in developing financial accounting principles.

Amortization. Cost of an intangible asset allocated to an accounting period.

Applications (uses) of working capital. Events that require the outflow of working capital.

Articles of incorporation. A statement about a corporation that defines its purpose and duration and includes certain key features of the corporation's capital stock. When approved by the state, the articles become the *charter* of the corporation.

Asset. A resource that has current and future monetary value to an enterprise and that is recognized for accounting purposes.

Asset turnover. The ratio of sales to average total assets.

Auditing. A branch of accounting in which financial statements are reviewed for conformance to generally accepted accounting principles.

Average-cost method. An inventory cost method that assumes that the cost of units acquired flow into a pool where the cost of one unit cannot be distinguished from the cost of another.

Bad debts expense. An estimate of losses on uncollectible accounts.

Balance sheet. See *Statement of financial position.*

Batch processing. Accumulation of data in batches prior to processing in an EDP system.

Board of directors. The governing board of a corporation elected by the voting stockholders.

Bond discount. The amount by which a bond price is below the face value, or par value, of the bond.

Bond discount amortization. The periodic write-off of bond discount; added to the interest on the bond.

Bond premium. The amount by which a bond price is above the face value, or par value, of the bond.

Bond premium amortization. The periodic write-off of bond premium; reduces the interest on the bond.

Bonds payable. A series of long-term notes payable, each having the same principal amount; frequently issued in denominations of $1,000.

Book of original entry. See *Journal.*

Book value, or net book value. The value of an asset per the books of account; frequently refers to assets subject to depreciation, depletion, and amortization and represents original cost less accumulated depreciation, depletion or amortization.

Book value (stock). The net assets per share of stock outstanding.

Business combination. Two or more corporations brought together to obtain various advantages through outright purchase of stock, exchange of stock, or purchase of assets.

Business combination accounting. Combinations may be recognized as a *purchase* of one company by another or, under certain conditions, as a *pooling of interests* in which assets, liabilities, and owners' equity are merged at book values.

Callable bonds. Bonds that can be called in and paid at the option of the issuing company.

Callable preferred. Preferred stock that may be bought back at the option of the corporation at a specified call price.

Capital. The amount of ownership interest of an owner in a single proprietorship or a partnership.

Capital expenditure. An expenditure that results in an asset; the expenditure is *capitalized.*

Capital lease. A lease used as a means of long-term financing.

Capital maintenance. A concept of enterprise income in which income is the amount left after maintaining the productive capital of the enterprise.

Cash. Money, checks, and other negotiable instruments acceptable for direct deposit by a bank, and checking account balances. Cash, the most liquid asset, has general purchasing power.

Cash discount. The reduction in invoice

price if the invoice is paid within a certain period.

Cash flow. A series of periodic cash receipts generated by some asset, group of assets, or enterprise.

Certified public accountant (CPA). A person who is licensed by the state to offer professional accounting service to the public; license is granted upon successful completion of an examination and completion of qualified professional experience.

Charter. See *Articles of incorporation*.

Classified balance sheet. A balance sheet showing the typical classification of assets, liabilities, and owners' equity:

Current assets	Current liabilities
Investments	Long-term liabilities
Property, plant, and equipment	Contributed capital
	Retained earnings
Intangibles	

Classified income statement. Usually refers to the multiple-step income statement, which shows the following classifications:

Revenue	Other revenue and expense
Cost of goods sold	
Operating expense	Income taxes
	Extraordinary item

Closing entries. Journal entries made to close the nominal accounts and transfer net income (or loss) and dividends to retained earnings.

Common stock. The residual ownership claim to income and assets in a corporation. Usually has the voting control.

Common stock equivalent. Convertible bonds, convertible preferred stock, and common stock rights and options that are treated as if they were common stock in computing primary earnings per share.

Comparability. A qualitative objective; accounting information should be comparable from period to period for the same enterprise and comparable between enterprises.

Completeness. A qualitative objective; accounting information should not omit information required to fulfill user needs.

Conservatism. A conventional mode of behavior in accounting in which a method that reduces assets or income is preferred.

Consistency. A convention in accounting that once a method has been adopted it should not be changed (without full disclosure).

Consolidated statements. Financial statements that combine parent company and subsidiary company accounts and show results for the economic entity.

Contributed capital. Amounts invested and donated to a corporation by its owners and others. Also called paid-in capital.

Control account. A general ledger account that summarizes details found in a subsidiary ledger.

Convertible bonds. Bonds that may be exchanged for shares of common stock under specified terms.

Convertible preferred. Preferred stock that may be exchanged for common stock under specified terms.

Copyright. An exclusive right, granted to authors and composers for life plus 50 years, to publish literary or musical works.

Corporation. A legal entity created by the state, with ownership vested in shares of stock.

Cost. The sacrifice incurred in economic activities. In accounting, the amount at which assets are initially recorded, usually based on a transaction price.

Cost accounting. The field of accounting in which a major activity is the determination of product costs.

Cost allocation principle. Costs are recognized as expenses on the basis of a systematic and rational allocation of costs to the period or periods benefitted by the costs.

Cost expiration. The stage at which cost becomes an expense.

Cost incurrence. The initial entry of costs into the enterprise; an asset is acquired.

Cost method. Accounting method in which an investor company keeps its investment in the stock of a subsidiary at the cost of the shares acquired.

Cost of goods sold. An expense measured by the total cost of the goods that were sold during the period.

Cost principle. Assets continue to be stated

at their original cost to the enterprise as established in transactions until another transaction takes place or the assets are used up or become worthless.

Cost transformation. A cost is changed from one form of asset to another form.

Credit. The right side of an account, used to record increases in liability and owners' equity accounts and decreases in asset accounts.

Cumulative preferred. Preferred stock with a fixed dividend that accumulates if dividends are passed; all accumulated dividends are paid before common receives any dividends.

Current assets. Cash and other assets that are reasonably expected to be realized in cash or sold or consumed in the normal operating cycle of the business or a year, whichever is longer.

Current liabilities. Obligations due to be paid or settled within the normal operating cycle of the business or one year, whichever is longer.

Current ratio. The ratio of current assets to current liabilities.

Current value accounting. The measurement of assets and expenses in terms of current market values rather than in historical cost dollars.

Data processing. The collection and manipulation of data to obtain reports and other business documents.

Debit. The left side of an account; debit is used to record increases in assets and decreases in liability and owners' equity accounts.

Declining-balance depreciation. A depreciation method that results in a larger periodic depreciation in the early years and lesser amounts in later years; the diminishing yearly pattern is accomplished by applying a fixed rate to the declining book value of the asset. Practically, the rate used in most cases is twice the straight-line rate, which is the IRS-approved rate. The practical method is called the double-declining-balance method.

Deferred income taxes payable. A liability that is recognized when income tax expense is recognized for accounting purposes before it is recognized for tax purposes.

Depletion accounting. The process of allocating the cost of exhaustible natural resources over their useful lives.

Depreciation. The portion of plant and equipment asset cost allocated to the accounting period.

Direct matching principle. Costs are recognized as expenses on the basis of a direct association, or matching, with revenue.

Discounted cash flow. Present value of expected net future money flows from an asset; present value determined by discounting future money flows by an interest factor.

Dividend arrearage. The amount of accumulated unpaid dividends on cumulated preferred stock. See *Cumulative preferred.*

Dividends. A pro rata distribution of corporate income to stockholders, the amount and time of which is determined by vote of the board of directors.

Donated capital. That part of stockholders' equity that comes from gifts by nonowners.

Double-declining-balance depreciation. See *Declining-balance depreciation.*

Drawing account. An account found in proprietorships and partnerships to accumulate an owner's withdrawals from the firm; one account is established for each owner.

Earned surplus. See *Retained earnings.*

Earnings per share. Basically, the net income belonging to common stockholders divided by the weighted average number of shares of common stock outstanding. Affected by common stock equivalents.

Economic entity. Two or more separate corporations that are associated through one company's majority stock ownership of the other, subsidiary, company or companies.

Economic resources. The scarce means for carrying on economic activities.

Effective-interest method of amortization. A method of figuring interest in which the interest rate is applied to the net investment or obligation so that the interest rate is constant while the amortization changes each period.

Electronic data processing (EDP). A data processing system employing digital computers; consists of programs, input and output units, central computer, internal memory, and magnetic media files.

Enterprise value. The hypothetical present dollar value of the enterprise as a whole, measured by discounting all future estimated cash flows of the enterprise or by reference to some type of market value.

Entity assumption. Assumption that the object of accounting is the business entity, which is separate from its owners.

Equity method. Accounting method in which an investor company records its share of invested company profits or losses.

Estimated liabilities. Liabilities whose amounts must be estimated; estimated liabilities for income taxes and estimated liability under product warranties.

Expense. The outflow of assets or increase in liabilities that takes place in connection with products and services transferred to customers during a period of time and in connection with other income-directed activities of the enterprise.

Expired cost. Another term for expense.

External event. An exchange or other event that involves the enterprise and some other person or organization and that changes assets, liabilities, or owners' equity.

Extraordinary items. A large gain or loss that is unusual in nature and infrequent in occurrence that is shown separately on the income statement.

Extraordinary repairs. Repairs to an asset that prolong its life and therefore are capitalized.

Financial accounting. The area of accounting devoted primarily to the development of the general-purpose financial reports of the enterprise designed for investors, stockholders, and other outsiders; provides a chronological record of the assets, liabilities, and owners' equity of a business enterprise and provides a record of the transactions that change assets, liabilities, and owners' equity.

Financial accounting process. The procedures by which accounting inputs are processed to yield accounting outputs.

Financial Accounting Standards Board (FASB). The principal organization for developing authoritative financial accounting standards in the U.S.A.; succeeded the Accounting Principles Board of the AICPA.

Financial accounting theory. A framework of objectives, assumptions, and principles formulated to improve accounting practice.

Financial position. The assets, liabilities, and owners' equity of an enterprise and the relationship among them as displayed on a statement of financial position.

Finished goods inventory. Goods that have been manufactured and are ready for sale. See *Merchandise inventory.*

First-in, first-out (FIFO). An inventory cost method based on an assumption of a flow of goods: first goods in are the first goods out.

Full disclosure. A standard of financial reporting; all important information should be presented.

Fully diluted earnings per share. Earnings per share computed as if all options, rights, and convertible securities had been exchanged for common shares.

Funds. In financial accounting, current assets less current liabilities.

General journal. The simplest and most general book of original entry, consisting of date, account name and explanation, reference, and two money columns, one for debits and one for credits.

Generally accepted accounting principles (GAAP). General understandings governing accounting measurements derived from the long-range experience of accounting.

General price change. Change in average prices, measured by a price index such as Consumer Price Index (CPI) or Gross National Product Implicit Price Deflator.

General purchasing power (GPP). A measure of current general prices derived by utilizing a general price index such as the Consumer Price Index or the Gross National Product Implicit Price Deflator.

Going concern. The accounting assumption that the enterprise will have an indefinite future life.

Goodwill. An intangible asset usually related to superior earning power of a company; recognized if paid for in the purchase of another company.

Gross margin. Revenue from sales less cost of goods sold expense.

Gross profit. See *Gross margin.*

Holding company. A parent company whose principal assets consist of the stocks of subsidiary companies.

Holding gain or loss. The increase or decrease in replacement cost over the period an asset is held.

Immediate recognition principle. Costs are recognized as expense in the current accounting period because there is no discernible future benefit associated with the costs.

Income-directed activities. Enterprise activities that generate revenues and expense; directed toward increasing net assets.

Income statement. A statement that shows the revenues and expenses of an enterprise over a specified period of time.

Income summary. A temporary account used in the closing process to accumulate all revenue and all expense; income summary is closed to retained earnings.

Income tax allocation. The procedure of relating income tax expense in a period to the income of the period.

Intangibles. Relatively long-lived, non-physical assets conveying rights and/or other benefits to the owner.

Interest. The charge for borrowing money or the income from lending money.

Internal control system. The procedures and records intended to safeguard enterprise assets and assure reliability of accounting outputs.

Internal event. An event or condition within the firm that changes assets, liabilities, or owners' equity.

Inventory. Merchandise, raw materials or supplies, goods in process, and manufactured goods owned.

Inventory turnover. The ratio of cost of goods sold to average inventory.

Investments. Relatively permanent commitments of funds to securities and other assets.

Journal. A record in which transactions are entered in debit and credit form as they occur; a chronological record of transactions.

Last-in, first-out (LIFO). An inventory cost method based on the cost-flow assumption that last costs in are the first costs out.

Lease obligations. A long-term liability reflecting the present value of future rental payments to be made because of long-term lease arrangements.

Ledger. A complete group of accounts.

Ledger account. See *Account.*

Legal capital. The amount of stockholders' equity that cannot be reduced by the payment of dividends. Usually defined by the par value of par-value issued stock or the stated value of no-par issued stock. See *Par-value stock* and *stated value.*

Leverage. The use of borrowed capital at a fixed interest rate with the intent of improving the return on owners' equity.

Liability. A present obligation to convey assets (usually cash) or render service in the future.

Liquid assets. Cash and other short-term assets that are expected to be converted to cash within a short period of time. See *Monetary assets.*

Long-term liabilities. Obligations that come due a year or more hence.

Long-term unexpired costs. Long-lived assets acquired for their usefulness; consist of tangible and intangible assets.

Lower-of-cost-or-market. A conservative rule for valuing temporary investments and inventories for financial statement presentation.

Appendix A   Glossary

Majority interest. The ownership interest held by the parent company.

Management accounting. A major area of accounting concerned with the financial information designed for internal enterprise management.

Manual processing. Data processing done by people with little or no mechanical help.

Matching. See *Direct matching principle.*

Merchandise inventory. Goods held for sale; the term frequently used in retail and wholesale enterprises. See *Finished goods inventory.*

Merger. See *Business combination.*

Minority interest. The ownership interest (less than a majority) held by persons other than the parent company in a parent-subsidiary relationship.

Monetary assets. Assets that are in the form of cash or claims to cash or highly marketable securities; valued for the purchasing power they represent.

Mortgage. A conditional conveyance of property to a creditor as security for a loan.

Mortgage bonds. Bonds secured by a mortgage on specific property.

Mortgage payable. A long-term note payable secured by a mortgage on property of the company.

Multiple-step income statement. See *Classified income statement.*

Natural resources. Tangible assets consisting of land, mineral deposits, timber stands and other exhaustible assets.

Net book value. See *Book value.*

Net income. Revenues of a period minus expenses of a period.

Net realizable value. Selling price less costs to complete and sell. An alternative asset valuation approach.

Net working capital. See *Working capital.*

Neutrality. A qualitative objective; accounting information should be generally useful and not slanted for particular users.

Nominal accounts. Income statement accounts.

Nonmonetary items. In general price-level accounting, items whose amounts may change because of price changes.

No-par stock. Stock that does not have a par value; may be assigned a stated value for legal and accounting purposes.

Notes payable. Obligations evidenced by a promissory note. If due within one year, a current liability; if due a year or more hence, a long-term liability. See *Promissory note.*

Notes receivable. Claims evidenced by a promissory note. If due within one year, a current asset; if due after one year, usually included in other assets. See *Promissory note.*

Objectives of accounting. Statements of goals or ends of accounting intended to guide the development of accounting principles.

Objectivity. In accounting, freedom from personal bias.

Obligation. A present commitment to convey or pay resources or provide services in the future.

Obsolescence. A major factor in depreciation, resulting from technological change or market changes.

On-line data processing. EDP system in which the user has direct access to the EDP system via a terminal and can input data or request outputs.

Operating cycle. The movement from cash to inventory to receivables to cash; usually defined as the time it takes to acquire goods, sell them, and collect the receivable.

Operating expense. All expense of operations other than cost of goods sold.

Operating income. Gross margin less operating expense; the income generated by the main-line activities of the enterprise.

Ordinary repairs. Repairs made on a recurring basis to keep the asset operating; they are expensed.

Organization costs. Costs incurred in organizing a business; an intangible asset to be amortized like other intangibles.

Other assets. A miscellaneous category for assets not classified as current, property, plant and equipment, investments, or intangibles.

Other revenue and expense. Financing revenue and expense and minor, incidental revenue and expense.

Output method of depreciation. See *Units-of-production depreciation*.

Owners' equity. The dollar amount of the owners' interest in a business; assets minus liabilities.

Paid-in capital. See *Contributed capital*.

Paid-in capital in excess of par. Amount paid in by stockholders in excess of arbitrary value printed on stock certificate.

Paid-in capital in excess of stated value. The amount paid-in on no-par stock that exceeds the stated value.

Parent company. A company that owns a majority of the stock of another company.

Partnership. An enterprise formed by an agreement between two or more persons, who contribute capital and/or their services to the enterprise.

Partnership agreement. The contract that details the various important arrangements among the partners including the capital contributions and the distribution of partnership profit and loss.

Par value stock. Stock that has an arbitrary value printed on the stock certificate; usually defines the legal capital of the corporation. Usually is the amount credited to the capital stock account. See *Legal capital*.

Patent. Gives the owner the exclusive right, for seventeen years, to the benefits of a process or an invention.

Pension obligation. A long-term liability reflecting the present value of estimated future payments to be made to employees because of employee pension plans.

Percentage analysis. In financial statement analysis, an approach by which items in statements are shown as percentages of a total; in income statement, each item is shown as a percentage of sales; in balance sheet, each asset is shown as a percentage of total assets.

Percentage depletion. A method of computing depletion for income taxes; not allowed on financial statements.

Percentage of year's sales uncollected. The ratio of year end receivables to sales for the year.

Periodic inventory method. A system in which the quantity in inventory is determined periodically by a physical count of the items, usually at least once a year.

Perpetual inventory method. A system for keeping a continuous record of each item in the inventory.

Physical safeguards. A standard of internal control that specifies reasonable physical security for assets.

Post-closing trial balance. A trial balance of the general ledger taken after closing entries have been posted; should include only balance sheet accounts.

Posting. The process of transferring debits and credits from a journal to the appropriate accounts in a ledger.

Preemptive right. The right of a shareholder to maintain a proportionate share of corporate ownership by purchasing a proportionate number of additional shares that are issued; this right has been voided in many corporations.

Preferred stock. A major class of capital stock that possesses certain preferences over common such as first right to dividends and to assets in liquidation. May be *convertible* and *callable*. Dividend preference is usually cumulative.

Premium on stock. Amount paid in by stockholders in excess of par value.

Prepaid expense. Assets to be used up in a short period of time, such as prepaid insurance and office supplies.

Primary earnings per share. Net income belonging to common stockholders divided by the number of shares represented by common stock and common stock equivalents.

Production method of revenue recognition. Revenue is recognized upon production; method is applicable where production is the most important activity and sale is guaranteed.

Promissory note. An unconditional written promise to pay a definite sum of money on demand or at some fixed or determinable future date.

587

Property, plant, and equipment. Long-lived, tangible assets acquired for use value. Also known as *fixed assets.*

Proprietorship. An enterprise owned by an individual.

Public accounting. Field of accounting in which professionals (usually CPAs) offer accounting services to the public.

Purchases journal. A specialized journal for recording credit purchases of merchandise.

Qualitative objectives. Objectives of accounting that pertain to the desirable properties of accounting information.

Rate-of-return analysis. Financial statement analysis that links the income, or return, to the investment base.

Rate of return on owners' equity. The ratio of net income to average owners' equity.

Rate of return on total assets. The ratio of operating income to average total assets.

Raw materials inventory. Material items held for future production; includes *direct material* that is incorporated in the product and *supplies* that are used to facilitate production.

Real accounts. Balance sheet accounts.

Real income. Income measured in terms of goods and services.

Realizable value. Selling price less costs to complete and sell; a value used for obsolete or shop worn goods.

Realization principle. Revenue is recognized only when the earning process is complete or virtually complete and an exchange has taken place.

Relevance. A qualitative objective; accounting information should bear upon decisions for which it is to be used.

Replacement cost. The present cost to replace an asset or the services provided by the asset. An alternative asset valuation approach.

Research and development costs (R & D). The cost incurred for research in new products and processes and in developing new products and processes; such costs are now expensed as incurred rather than capitalized, according to FASB Statement No. 2.

Reserve for income tax. An obsolete term referring to the estimated liability for income taxes.

Residual interest. The interest in enterprise net resources possessed by enterprise owners. See *Owners' equity.*

Resources. (1) Scarce means available for accomplishing objectives. See *Economic resources.* (2) In the statement of changes in financial position, frequently used in place of the term *funds* or the term *working capital.* See *Funds, Working capital.*

Restricted retained earnings. The amount of retained earnings unavailable for dividends, usually as a result of borrowing agreements or purchase of treasury stock.

Retained earnings. Amounts accumulated from the earnings of a corporation; earnings less dividends and less losses. Also (rarely) called earned surplus.

Revenue. The inflow of assets to an enterprise as a result of products and services transferred to its customers during a period of time.

Revenue expenditure. An expenditure that results in an expense, as contrasted with capital expenditure.

Scientific method of amortization. See *Effective-interest method of amortization.*

Securities and Exchange Commission (SEC). The federal agency charged with developing and enforcing standards and rules for company information to be made available to investors.

Segregation of duties. A standard of internal control that specifies that individuals who control the assets should be separate from those who account for assets.

Selling expense. Expense associated with the sale and distribution of the product; a subcategory of operating expense.

Short-term liabilities. See *Current liabilities.*

Single-step income statement. A simple form of income statement with one section for revenues and one section for expenses and net income.

Social security taxes. The FICA tax and the unemployment compensation tax.

Source document. A record of an accounting input.

Sources of working capital (resources). Factors that provide inflows of working capital.

Specialized journal. A journal dedicated to recording one type of transaction.

Specific identification method. An inventory costing method that keeps track of the specific cost of each item.

Specific price change. A change in the price of individual goods and services.

Stable unit of measure. The accounting assumption that the dollar is a stable measurement standard.

Stages of cost. The different phases or stages of cost: incurrence, transformation, expiration.

Stated value. A per share value assigned to no-par stock by the corporation; usually the amount credited to the no-par capital stock account. See *Legal capital.*

Statement of cash flows. A statement that shows net inflows of cash and outflows of cash.

Statement of cash receipts and disbursements. A statement that shows gross cash receipts and gross cash disbursements.

Statement of changes in financial position. The statement that shows the sources and uses of working capital over a specified period.

Statement of financial position. A statement that shows the assets, liabilities, and owners' equity of a business enterprise at a certain date.

Statements of change. Three statements that show changes in financial position over an accounting period: income statement, showing changes resulting from revenue and expense transactions; statement of retained earnings, showing changes in retained earnings; and statement of changes in financial position, showing *all* changes from inflows and outflows of working capital.

Stock certificate. Piece of paper describing stock; evidence of ownership.

Stock dividend. A pro-rata distribution of stock to stockholders, usually in lieu of, or to supplement, a cash dividend; not considered income to the recipient.

Stockholders' equity. The ownership interest in a corporation.

Stockholders' rights. Usually include right to receive dividends, to vote, and to share in residual net assets upon dissolution and liquidation. Some rights of some classes of stock may be voided by the corporate charter.

Stock options, rights, warrants. The right to acquire a certain number of shares of stock at a specified price.

Stock split. The issuance by a corporation of a larger number of shares in exchange for shares presently held. Differs from a stock dividend in its size and intent, the intent being to reduce the market price of the stock to widen its market.

Straight-line depreciation. A depreciation method that results in equal periodic depreciation on an asset.

$$\frac{\text{Cost} - \text{salvage}}{\text{Useful Life}} = \text{Periodic Straight-Line Depreciation}$$

Straight-line premium or discount amortization. A method of amortizing bond premium or discount in which the write-off each period is the same.

Subsidiary company. A company in which controlling interest in its stock is owned by another company.

Subsidiary ledger. A group of accounts that provide the details of a general ledger account.

Sum-of-the-years' digits depreciation. A depreciation method that results in larger periodic depreciation in the early years and lesser amounts in later years; the diminishing yearly pattern of rates is established by the following sequence, where N is the useful life:

Year 1	Year 2	Year N
$\dfrac{N}{(1+2\ldots+N)}$	$\dfrac{N-1}{(1+2\ldots+N)}$	$\dfrac{1}{(1+2\ldots+N)}$

T account. The simplest form of an account, consisting of account title and spaces for debits and credits.

Taxation accounting. Area of accounting devoted to determination of tax liabilities and to tax planning.

Temporary investments. Investment in highly liquid securities, usually government notes, that can quickly and readily be liquidated; excess cash usually put into temporary investments.

Timeliness. A qualitative objective; accounting information should be communicated early enough to be useful.

Times interest earned. The ratio of operating income to interest expense.

Transaction. An event that changes assets, and/or liabilities and/or owners' equity.

Treasury stock. Shares of stock, once issued, repurchased with the intent of selling them at a later time.

Trial balance. A listing of account balances in the general ledger to see if the total of the debit balances equals the total of the credit balances.

Turnover. A measure of activity in an asset derived by the ratio of activity of the item to the average balance of the item.

Undepreciated cost. See *Book value.*

Understandability. A qualitative objective; accounting information must be clearly understood by users.

Unexpired costs. See *Book value.*

Units-of-production depreciation. A depreciation method in which periodic depreciation is based on the quantity of asset usage or output during the period. The formula to determine depreciation per unit of output is

$$\frac{\text{Cost} - \text{Salvage}}{\text{Life in Units of Output}} = \frac{\text{Depreciation per}}{\text{Unit of Output}}.$$

Unlimited liability. In a proprietorship or a partnership, the liability of owners is not limited to the owners' investment.

Useful life. The estimated time over which an asset will yield benefits; a function of physical and economic factors. See *Wear and tear; Obsolescence.*

Uses of working capital. See *Applications of working capital.*

Verifiability. A qualitative objective; accounting information should be capable of being corroborated by independent accountants.

Wear and tear. A major physical factor in depreciation resulting from use of the asset.

Working capital. The excess of current assets over current liabilities. Sometimes called *Net working capital.*

Work in process. Goods currently in the production process.

Worksheet. A columnar sheet that facilitates the adjusting of accounts and the preparation of financial statements.

APPENDIX B

Solutions to Selected Problems

CHAPTER 1

1-25.   (*30 minutes*)

BEDROCK CLEANING COMPANY
Statement of Financial Position
December 31, Year 1

Assets		Liabilities		
Cash	$ 250	Accounts payable		$1,500
Cleaning supplies	800			
Prepaid rent	150	*Owners' Equity*		
Cleaning equipment	6,500			
Total assets	$7,700	Capital stock	5,000	
		Retained earnings*	1,200	6,200
		Total liabilities & owners' equity		$7,700

* Retained earnings is:

Total assets		$7,700
Less liabilities	$1,500	
Capital stock	5,000	6,500
		$1,200

This is correct because total assets = total liabilities + owners' equity.

Appendix B   Solutions to Selected Problems

CHAPTER 2

2-23. *(30 minutes)*

An Oil Company
Liabilities and Stockholders' Equity
December 31, Year 1
(In millions)

Liabilities

Current liabilities:		
Accounts payable	$51.5	
Notes payable	46.5	
Long-term debt—current maturities	2.6	
Income taxes payable	2.9	
Taxes payable	13.3	
Accrued liabilities	6.8	
Total current liabilities		$123.6
Long-term debt:		
Mortgage notes payable		62.9
Other notes payable		2.6
Other liabilities:		
Deferred federal income taxes*		5.1
Total liabilities		$194.2

Stockholders' equity

Common stock, par value $1	$ 7.1	
Additional paid-in capital	6.5	
Retained earnings	85.5	
Total stockholders' equity		99.1
Total liabilities and stockholders' equity		$293.3

*Could be listed under long-term liabilities.

2-27. *(30 minutes)*

MANN COMPANY
Balance Sheet
December 31, Year 1

Assets

Current assets:			
Cash			$ 8,000
Accounts receivable		$18,000	
Less allowance for uncollectible			
accounts		1,000	17,000
Merchandise inventory			14,000
Office supplies inventory			2,000
Total current assets			
			$41,000

Plant and equipment:
Building	$45,000		
Less accumulated depreciation	19,000		
Net book value		$26,000	
Equipment	24,000		
Less accumulated depreciation	8,000		
Net book value		16,000	
Book value of plant assets			42,000
Total assets			$83,000

Liabilities

Current liabilities:
Accounts payable	$10,000	
Notes payable	4,000	
Total current liabilities		$14,000

Stockholders' Equity

Capital stock, $5 par	$12,000	
Capital in excess of par	39,000	
Total paid-in capital	51,000	
Retained earnings	18,000	
Total stockholders' equity		$69,000
Total liabilities and stockholders' equity		$83,000

CHAPTER 3

3-21. (*30 minutes*)

AMMERSON COMPANY
Statement of Changes in Financial Position
Year Ended December 31, Year 1

Sources of Working Capital

Operations:		
Net income	$ 523,000	
Add depreciation	160,000	
Working capital from operations		$ 683,000
Long-term borrowing		1,200,000
Issuance of capital stock		2,500,000
Total sources of working capital		$4,383,000

Uses of Working Capital

Dividends	$ 450,000	
Purchase of plant	3,600,000	
Purchase of machinery	750,000	
Total uses of working capital		4,800,000
Decrease in working capital		$ 417,000

Appendix B   Solutions to Selected Problems

3-24. *(30 minutes)*

ROPER COMPANY
Income Statement
Year 1

Sales		$138,000
Cost of goods sold expense		84,400
Gross margin		53,600
Operating expense:		
Sales commissions	$ 3,200	
Salaries	20,000	
Depreciation expense	12,000	
Utilities expense	2,400	
Property tax expense	2,100	
Insurance expense	900	
Office supplies used	1,900	
Estimated loss on uncollectible accounts	1,300	
Total operating expense		43,800
Operating income		9,800
Interest expense		800
Income before income taxes		9,000
Income taxes		1,300
Net income before extraordinary item		7,700
Extraordinary item—Flood loss (net of taxes)		6,000
Net income for the year		$ 1,700

CHAPTER 4

4-20. *(20 minutes)*

	Debit	Credit
a. Accounts receivable	12,000	
Commissions earned		12,000
Sale of apartment building		
b. Salesperson's salaries	300	
Cash		300
June salary		
c. Cash	1,500	
Accounts receivable		1,500
Collected from client		
d. Cash	4,000	
Notes payable		4,000
National Bank, due in 3 months		
e. Office equipment	300	
Cash		300
Typewriter		
f. Cash	150	
Rent revenue		150
Rent from dentist		

g.	Notes payable	2,000	
	Interest expense	30	
	Cash		2,030
	Paid note plus interest		
h.	Accounts payable	200	
	Cash		200
	Paid garage amount due		

4-22. *(15 minutes)*

a. $80,000 − 20,000 = $60,000 owners' equity

b. Sales revenue is $36,000

c. Income computation:

Sales		$36,000
Expenses:		
Cost of sales	$22,000	
Operating expenses	4,000	26,000
Income		$10,000

d. $85,000 − $16,000 = $69,000 owners' equity.

e. Increase in owners' equity = $69,000 − $60,000 = $9,000
Apparently $1,000 of dividends were paid.

4-24. *(30 minutes)*

			Debit	Credit
May 2	Accounts receivable		8,000	
	Sales			8,000
	Tuck, 2/10, n/30			
May 5	Purchases		2,200	
	Cash			2,200
	Bayle Co.			
May 7	Cash		300	
	Purchase returns and allowances			300
	Return to Bayle			
May 10	Cash		7,840	
	Sales discounts		160	
	Accounts receivable			8,000
	Collect from Tuck less 2%			
May 12	Purchases		5,000	
	Accounts payable			5,000
	Lynn Co., 2/10, n/30			
May 14	Freight in		300	
	Cash			300
	Freight on Lynn purchase			
May 17	Purchases		200	
	Accounts payable			200
	Correct Lynn error			

Appendix B Solutions to Selected Problems

May 21	Accounts payable	5,200	
	Purchase discounts		104
	Cash		5,096
	Pay Lynn, less 2%		
May 22	Cash	3,000	
	Accounts receivable		3,000
	Petrocelli		
May 23	Office supplies on hand	600	
	Accounts payable		600
	Ford Office Supply		

Note in the last transaction that the purchases account is not used.

4-26. *(40 minutes)*

	Debit	Credit
Accounts receivable	6,000	
Revenue from services		6,000
Total revenue		
Cash	4,900	
Accounts receivable		4,900
Collected 6,000 − 1,100 increase in receivables		
Rent expense	600	
Cash		600
Paid rent		
Taxes expense	300	
Taxes payable		300
Tax expense		
Supplies used	250	
Supplies on hand		250
Supplies expense		
Insurance expense	100	
Unexpired insurance		100
Insurance used up		
Salaries expense	4,000	
Cash		4,000
Salaries paid		
Cash	1,000	
Capital stock		1,000
Issued stock for cash		
Retained earnings	600	
Cash		600
Dividends. Since income added $750 to retained earnings, but the net increase was $150, $600 of dividends must have been paid.		

Reconciliation of cash:

Appendix B Solutions to Selected Problems

```
                    Cash
Beginning Balance   1,400  | Rent        600
Collections         4,900  | Salaries  4,000
Stock               1,000  | Dividends   600
                    -----  |           -----
                    7,300  |           5,200
  Bal. 2,100
```

CHAPTER 5

5-11. (*15 minutes*)

			Debit	Credit
a. Dec. 31	Rent expense		800	
	Prepaid rent			800
	8 months' expense			
b. Dec. 31	Office supplies expense		256	
	Office supplies inventory			256
	$456 − $200 = $256 used			
c. Dec. 31	Subscriptions received in advance		2,000	
	Subscription revenue			2,000
	$3,125 − $1,125 = $2,000 earned			
d. Dec. 31	Interest expense		45	
	Interest payable			45
	Accrued interest			

5-25. (*15 minutes*)

a. Entries:

		Debit	Credit
Dec. 31	Income summary	16,000	
	Inventory		16,000
	Close beginning inventory		
Dec. 31	Inventory	22,000	
	Income summary		22,000
	Set up ending inventory		

b. Cost of Goods Sold

Beginning inventory		$ 16,000
Purchases	104,000	
Less purchase returns	3,000	
Net purchases		101,000
Freight in		2,000
Cost of goods available for sale		119,000
Less ending inventory		22,000
Cost of goods sold		$ 97,000

Appendix B   Solutions to Selected Problems

5-26. *(25 minutes)*

a.

SUDS LAUNDRY
Trial Balance
December 31, Year 1

	Debit	Credit
Accounts payable		$ 2,000
Accounts receivable	$ 5,000	
Accrued salaries		1,000
Accumulated depreciation		15,000
Cash	5,000	
Capital stock		6,000
Depreciation	1,000	
Equipment	25,000	
Insurance expired	200	
Laundry revenue		20,000
Retained earnings		4,000
Salaries	6,000	
Laundry supplies on hand	2,000	
Laundry supplies used	3,000	
Prepaid insurance	800	
Totals	$48,000	$48,000

b.

Date		Debit	Credit
Dec. 31	Laundry revenue	20,000	
	Income summary		20,000
	Close revenue		
Dec. 31	Income summary	10,200	
	Depreciation		1,000
	Insurance expired		200
	Salaries		6,000
	Laundry supplies used		3,000
	Close expenses		
Dec. 31	Income summary	9,800	
	Retained earnings		9,800
	Close net income		

5-30. *(25 minutes)*

	Debit	Credit
a. Interest receivable	25	
Interest revenue		25
$5,000 \times 6\% \times 1/12$		
b. Insurance expense	264	
Unexpired insurance		264
$594 = 2$ years, 3 months of insurance		
$594/27$ months $= \$22$/month		
$\$22 \times 12 = \$264$		

c. Depreciation expense		3,000	
Accumulated depreciation—building			3,000
3% × $100,000			
d. Supplies on hand		135	
Supplies used			135
Set up unused supplies as an asset			
e. Unearned rent income		400	
Rent income			400
4 months earned			
f. Salary expense		680	
Salaries payable			680
Accrued salaries			

CHAPTER 6

6-22. *(60 minutes)*

a.

CB, INC.

Cash (1)

1/31 CD $11,928	

Office Equipment (2)

1/13 GJ $ 250	

Accounts Payable (3)

1/11 GJ	105	1/13 GJ	250
1/28 GJ	310	1/31 PJ	11,275
1/31 CD	9,670		
	10,085		11,525

Purchases (4)

1/31 PJ 11,275	

Purchases Returns & Allowances (5)

	1/11 GJ	105
	1/28 GJ	310
		415

Purchase Discounts (6)

	1/31 CD 92

Advertising Expense (7)

1/17 CD 200	

Rent Expense (8)

1/1 CD 350	

Office Salaries (9)

1/15 CD 900	
1/31 CD 900	

Appendix B   Solutions to Selected Problems

b.

CB, INC.
Accounts Payable Subsidiary Ledger

Sara Wholesale Company

Date	PR	Debit	Credit	Balance
Jan. 3	PJ		$2,600	$2,600
10	CD	2,600		0
19	PJ		2,000	2,000
27	CD	2,000		0

Nolan Office Supply

Date	PR	Debit	Credit	Balance
Jan. 13	GJ		250	250

Moore Manufacturing Co.

Date	PR	Debit	Credit	Balance
Jan. 1	PJ		2,050	2,050
6	CD	2,050		0
24	PJ		1,500	1,500
28	GJ	310		1,190

Bell Sales Company

Date	PR	Debit	Credit	Balance
Jan. 9	PJ		3,125	3,125
11	GJ	105		3,020
16	CD	3,020		0

c.

CB, INC.
Cash Disbursements Journal

Date		Cash Cr.	Purchases Discounts Cr.	PR	Accounts Payable Dr.	Other Debits Account	PR	Amount
Jan. 1	Rent	350				Rent exp.	8	350
6	Moore Mfg. Co.	2,050		✓	2,050			
10	Sara Wholesale	2,548	52	✓	2,600			
15	Salaries	900				Office salaries	9	900
16	Bell Sales	3,020		✓	3,020			
17	Advertising	200				Adv. exp.	7	200
27	Sara Wholesale	1,960	40	✓	2,000			
31	Salaries	900				Office salaries	9	900
	Monthly totals	$11,928	$92		$9,670			$2,350
		(1)	(6)		(3)			(Posted)

CB, INC.
General Journal

Date	Account	PR	Debit	Credit
Jan. 11	Accounts payable—Bell Sales Co.	(3)/✔	105	
	Purchase returns & allowances	(5)		105
13	Office equipment	(2)	250	
	Accounts payable—Nolan Office Sup.	(3)/✔		250
28	Accounts payable—Moore Mfg. Co.	(3)/✔	310	
	Purchase returns & allowances	(5)		310

Purchases Journal

Date		Explanation	PR	Purchases Dr. Accounts Payable Cr.
Jan. 1	Moore Manufacturing Co.	invoice dated 12/27	✔	2,050
3	Sara Wholesale Co.	2/10, n/30, invoice dated 1/2	✔	2,600
9	Bell Sales Co.	invoice dated 1/6	✔	3,125
19	Sara Wholesale Co.	2/10, n/30, invoice dated 1/18	✔	2,000
24	Moore Mfg. Co.	invoice dated 1/22	✔	1,500
Monthly total				$11,275
				(4)/(3)

d.

CB, INC.
Schedule of Accounts Payable
January 31

Sara Wholesale Company	0
Nolan Office Supply	250
Moore Manufacturing Company	1,190
Bell Sales Company	0
Total	$1,440

CB, INC.
Trial Balance
January 31

	Debit	Credit
Cash		11,928
Office equipment	250	
Accounts payable		1,440
Purchases	11,275	
Purchase returns & allowances		415
Purchase discounts		92
Advertising expense	200	
Rent expense	350	
Office salaries	1,800	
	$13,875	$13,875

Appendix B Solutions to Selected Problems

6-25. *(30 minutes)*

a., b.

Cash			(1)
CR642	13,500	CD973	3,050
10,450			

Accounts Receivable			(2)
S101	7,700	CR642	3,000
4,700			

Notes Payable			(11)
		CR642	5,000

Accounts Payable			(12)
J243	200	P105	4,500
CD973	2,300		2,000

Capital Stock			(20)
		CR642	3,000

Sales			(30)
		S101	7,700
		CR642	2,500
			10,200

Purchases			(35)
P105	4,500		

Purchase Returns			(37)
		J243	200

Salaries Expense			(40)
CD973	600		

Supplies Expense			(48)
CD973	150		

c., d.

Customer A			
S101	2,000	CR642	2,000

Customer B			
S101	3,200		

Customer C			
S101	2,500	CR642	1,000
1,500			
(Total: $4,700)			

Company X			
CD973	1,200	P105	1,200

Company Y			
CD973	1,100	P105	1,100

Company Z			
J243	200	P105	2,200
			2,000
(Total: $2,000)			

The Cash Receipts Journal, with posting references included, appears as follows:

Cash Receipts Journal p. 642

Accounts	PR	Sundry	Acct. rec.	Sales	Cash
Notes payable	11	5,000			5,000
Customer A	✔		2,000		2,000
Capital stock	20	3,000			3,000
Customer C	✔		1,000		1,000
Cash sales	✔			2,500	2,500
		8,000	3,000	2,500	13,500
		(Posted)	(2)	(30)	(1)

CHAPTER 7

7-20. (*30 minutes*)

			Debit	Credit
Oct. 26	Notes receivable		3,000	
	Accounts receivable (Morgan)			3,000
	90-day, 8% note			
Nov. 21	Notes receivable		2,100	
	Accounts receivable (Rose)			2,068.93
	Interest revenue			31.07
	60-day note at 9% discount			
Dec. 31	Interest receivable		43.40	
	Interest revenue			43.40
	$3,000 \times 8\% \times 66/365$ on Morgan note			
Dec. 31	Interest revenue		10.36	
	Unearned interest			10.36
	40 days earned, 20 days unearned			
	$2,100 \times 9\% \times 20/365$ interest			
Jan. 20	Cash		2,100.00	
	Unearned interest		10.36	
	Notes receivable			2,100.00
	Interest revenue			10.36
	Record collection and interest			
	earned for 20 days			
Jan. 24	Cash		3,059.18	
	Notes receivable			3,000.00
	Interest receivable			43.40
	Interest revenue			15.78
	Total interest is $3,000 \times 8\%$			
	$\times 90/365 = \$59.18$			

Appendix B Solutions to Selected Problems

7-22. *(30 minutes)*

ATLAS COMPANY
Bank Reconciliation
as of June 30

Balance per books		$4,309.70
Add:		500.00
Note collected		4,809.70
Deduct:		
Bank charges		3.60
Corrected balance		$4,806.10
Balance per bank		$4,063.10
Add:		
Error on Atlast check	300.00	
Deposit in transit	1,411.25	1,711.25
		5,774.35
Deduct		
Outstanding checks		
#611	380.20	
614	119.16	
632	61.27	
633	13.12	
634	194.50	
638	200.00	968.25
Corrected balance		$4,806.10

Note: Check #621 is not listed as outstanding because the bank deducts the amount of the check from Atlas's balance when the check is certified.

7-24. *(40 minutes)*

			Debit	Credit
May	2	Accounts receivable (Mills)	1,200	
		Sales		1,200
		1/10, n/30		
	2	Freight expense	50	
		Cash		50
	4	Sales returns & allowances	40	
		Accounts receivable (Mills)		40
	6	Cash	200.00	
		Sales discount	2.02	
		Accounts receivable (Mills)		202.02
		Credit to receivables is $200 \div .99$		
	20	Cash	957.98	
		Accounts receivable (Mills)		957.98
		$1,200 - 40 - 202.02 = \$957.98$		
	29	Notes receivable	300.00	
		Interest receivable	.49	
		Accounts receivable (Carver)		300.49
		Interest is $\$300 \times 10/365 \times 6\%$		

		Debit	Credit
June 18	Cash	120	
	Allowance for uncollectibles	180	
	Accounts receivable (Pickle)		300
19	Cash	594.08	
	Interest expense	5.92	
	Notes payable		600

CHAPTER 8

8-14. *(5 minutes)*

		Debit	Credit
Jan. 5	Investment in DeCoster	540,000	
	Cash		540,000
May 15	Cash	10,000	
	Investment in DeCoster		10,000
Oct. 15	Cash	8,000	
	Investment in DeCoster		8,000
Dec. 30	Investment in DeCoster	55,000	
	Income on investments		55,000
	25% × $220,000		

8-19. *(30 minutes)*

		Debit	Credit
Feb. 25	Temporary investments	16,647	
	Cash		16,647
May 1	Temporary investments	8,300	
	Interest receivable	150	
	Cash		8,450
May 20	Temporary investments	75,640	
	Cash		75,640
Aug. 1	Cash	300	
	Interest receivable		150
	Interest revenue		150
Aug. 15	Cash	450	
	Dividend income		450
Aug. 20	Cash	500	
	Dividend income		500
Nov. 20	Cash	17,848	
	Temporary investments		16,647
	Gain on sale of investments		1,201
Dec. 31	Interest receivable	250	
	Interest revenue		250
	5/12 × 6% × $10,000		
Dec. 31	Loss on market declines	1,840	
	Allowance to reduce investments to market		1,840

	Cost	Market
Ling	8,300	8,100
Honeywell	75,640	74,000
	83,940	82,100

8-21. *(30 minutes)*

a. $10,000 × .3505 (Appendix C, Table II) = $3,505
$800 × 6.495 (Table III) = $5,196
Total Price $8,701

b. Jan. 1 Investment in White Bonds   8,701.00
              Cash   8,701.00

  Dec. 31 Cash   800.00
           Investment in White Bonds   70.10
              Interest revenue   870.10
           10% × $8,701 = $870 interest

c. Dec. 31 Cash   800.00
                Investment in White Bonds   77.11
                  Interest revenue   877.11
                10% × $8,771.10 = $877.11 interest

d. Jan. 1 Cash   9,725.00
                Gain on sale of investments   876.79
                Investment in White Bonds   8,848.21

8-22. *(40 minutes)*

a. April 1   Investment in Zlatko Bonds   8,156
                 Cash   8,156

b. Dec. 31   Interest receivable   525
                 Interest revenue   525
                 $700 × 9/12

   Dec. 31   Investment in Zlatko Bonds   138.30
             Interest revenue   138.30
             $1,844 discount × 1/10 × 9/12

c. March 31 Cash   700
                 Interest receivable   525
                 Interest revenue   175

d. Dec. 31   Interest receivable   525
                 Interest revenue   525

   Dec. 31   Investment in Zlatko Bonds   184.40
             Interest revenue   184.40
             $1,844 discount × 1/10

e. Jan. 1   Cash (9,120 + 525)   9,645.00
                 Gain on sale of bonds   641.30
                 Interest receivable   525.00
                 Investment in Zlatko Bonds   8,478.70

Appendix B   Solutions to Selected Problems

CHAPTER 9

9-15. *(20 minutes)*

Cost of goods sold on FIFO basis:
Beginning inventory (20,000 × $4.25)	$ 85,000	
Purchases 80,000 × $4.50	360,000	
Goods available	445,000	
Ending inventory (22,000 × $4.50)	99,000	
Cost of goods sold	$346,000	

Cost of goods sold on LIFO basis:
Beginning inventory
  10,000 × $2 = $20,000
  5,000 × 3 = 15,000
  5,000 × 4 = 20,000 $ 55,000
Purchases   360,000
Goods available   415,000
Ending inventory
  Beginning amount   55,000
  + 2,000 × $4.50   9,000   64,000
Cost of goods sold $351,000

Difference in income: FIFO produces an income that is $5,000 higher.
Reason: With FIFO, 20,000 units at $4.25 get into cost of goods sold. With Lifo, all units sold are at $4.50. 20,000 units × $.25 = $5,000.

9-23. *(30 minutes)*

Suits	Q	Unit Cost	Unit Market	Cost	Market	Lower
157	10	$ 50	$40	500	400	400
213	15	40	42	600	630	600
214	27	60	50	1,620	1,350	1,350
C5	40	25	30	1,000	1,200	1,000
				3,720	3,580	
Coats						
F13	60	50	43	3,000	2,580	2,580
A2	50	50	70	2,500	3,500	2,500
Q6	11	100	90	1,100	990	990
				6,600	7,070	
Total				$10,320	$10,650	$9,420

a. Item by item $ 9,420
b. Departmental $3,580 + $6,600 = $10,180
c. Storewide $10,320

Appendix B Solutions to Selected Problems

9-25. *(30 minutes)*

			Debit	Credit
Jan. 12	Cash		800	
	Sales			800
12	Cost of goods sold		480	
	Tank inventory			480
	4 × 120			
20	Tank inventory		2,196	
	Cash			2,196
21	Tank inventory		36	
	Cash			36
	Cost is now $122 + $2 freight			
27	Cash		2,460	
	Sales			2,460
27	Cost of goods sold		1,464	
	Tank inventory			1,464
	6 × $120 = 720			
	6 × $124 = 744			
Feb. 4	Tank inventory		2,460	
	Cash			2,460
7	Cash (or receivables)		246	
	Tank inventory			246
20	Cash		3,090	
	Sales			3,090
20	Cost of goods sold		1,857	
	Tank inventory			1,857
	12 × $124 = $1,488			
	3 × $123 = $ 369			
28	Cash		20	
	Cost of goods sold		103	
	Tank inventory			123
	The amount could also be charged to a loss account.			

The ending inventory is 14 tanks at $123 = $1,722. This is also the balance in the inventory account.

9-26. *(25 minutes)*

Corrected Income	Case			
	(1)	(2)	(3)	(4)
Sales	$100,000	$100,000	$200,000	$192,000
Cost of sales				
Beginning inventory	7,000	15,000	25,000	20,000
Purchases	60,000	60,000	111,000	115,000
	67,000	75,000	136,000	135,000
Ending inventory	12,000	9,000	35,000	24,000
Cost of sales	55,000	66,000	101,000	111,000
Gross margin	45,000	34,000	99,000	81,000
Expenses	30,000	30,000	70,000	70,000
Net income	$ 15,000	$ 4,000	$ 29,000	$ 11,000
Correct inventory on balance sheet	$ 12,000	$ 9,000	$ 35,000	$ 24,000

Appendix B   Solutions to Selected Problems

CHAPTER 10

10-16. *(20 minutes)*

The estimated life is found by using the following formula:

$$\frac{\text{Estimated production hours}}{\text{Yearly average production hours}} = \frac{1{,}200}{400} = 3 \text{ years}$$

	Straight-Line		*Sum-of-the-Years'-Digits*		*Production**	
Year	Annual Depreciation	Unexpired Cost	Annual Depreciation	Unexpired Cost	Annual Depreciation	Unexpired Cost
1	$3,333	$11,667	$5,000	$10,000	$3,333	$11,667
2	3,333	8,334	3,333	6,667	3,333	8,334
3	3,334	5,000	1,667	5,000	3,334	5,000

* This works out the same as straight-line because the average yearly hours are used. Normally, the actual hours used would vary from year to year, causing a variation in the annual depreciation.

10-20. *(5 minutes)*

	Debit	Credit
Depletion expense	6,667	
Accumulated depletion		6,667

$$\frac{\$50{,}000}{300{,}000 \text{ bbls.}} = \$.16 \text{ 2/3 depletion per bbl.}$$

40,000 bbl. × .16 2/3 = $6,667 depletion for year

10-23. *(10 minutes)*

	Debit	Credit
Amortization of patents	16,088	
Patents		16,088

Patent A $\dfrac{\$18{,}500}{17 \text{ yrs.}} = \$1{,}088$

Patent B*   15,000

Total $16,088

*Only expected to last a year or less

609

Appendix B **Solutions to Selected Problems**

10-31. *(60 minutes)*

	Debit	Credit
April 26, Year 5		
Depreciation expense	400	
Accumulated depreciation—machinery		400

$$2 \times \frac{(\$6{,}500 - \$500)}{10 \text{ years}} = \$1{,}200 \text{ annual depreciation on the two machines}$$

$1{,}200 \times 4/12 = \$400$ depreciation for 4 months (even months)

Cash	3,900	
Accumulated depreciation—machinery	2,150	
Loss on sale of machine	450	
Machinery		6,500

To record sale of one machine
  Cost $6,500
  Accumulated depreciation   2,150
  $6000 \times 3 \ 7/12$ yrs. $\times .10$
  Expired life: October Year 1–April 26, Year 5

Year 1	1/4 year
Year 2	1
Year 3	1
Year 4	1
Year 5	1/3
total	3 7/12 years

	Debit	Credit
April 26, Year 5		
Machinery (new)	8,300	
Accumulated depreciation—machinery	2,150	
Loss on trade	450	
Machinery (old)		6,500
Cash		4,440

Cash payment $\$9{,}000 - \$4{,}600 = \$4{,}440$

Loss: Market value		3,900
Less book value (\$6,500 − \$2,150)		4,350
Loss		(450)

Cost of new machine is $4,400 cash plus $3,900 value of old machine.

10-36. *(5 minutes)*

Current value of net assets:		
Cash and receivables	$ 25,000	
Inventories	100,000	
Plant and equipment	185,000	
	310,000	
Less liabilities	30,000	
Book value	280,000	
Purchase price	300,000	
Implied goodwill	$ 20,000	

CHAPTER 11

11-16. (*15 minutes*)

		Debit	Credit
Land		25,295	
Notes payable			25,295
$18,000 × .7118 (Appendix C, Table II) = $12,812
$22,000 × .5674 (Table II)   = 12,483
$25,295
End of year	Interest expense	3,035	
	Notes payable		3,035
	12% × $25,295

11-25. (*30 minutes*)

			Debit	Credit
a. Sept. 30		Cash	829,800	
		Interest payable		6,000
		Premium on bonds		23,800
		Bonds payable		800,000
		Interest payable is
		$800,000 × 9% × 1/12 year.
b. Dec. 31		Interest expense	18,000	
		Interest payable		18,000
		Total interest since Sept. 30.
Dec. 31		Premium on bonds	600	
		Interest expense		600
		$\frac{\$23,800}{119 \text{ mos.}} = 200/\text{mo.}$
c. Feb. 28		Interest expense	12,000	
		Interest payable	24,000	
		Cash		36,000
Feb. 28		Premium on bonds	400	
		Interest expense		400
		Two months.

11-27. (*45 minutes*)

a. Issue price:

    $10,000,000 × .2394 (Appendix C, Table II) = $2,394,000
      $900,000 × 7.606 (Table III)   = 6,845,400

      Total $9,239,400

			Debit	Credit
April 1		Cash	9,239,400	
		Discount on bonds	760,600	
		Bonds payable		10,000,000

Appendix B   Solutions to Selected Problems

b.

Dec. 31	Interest expense		692,955	
	Interest payable			675,000
	Discount on bonds			17,955
	$10,000,000 − 760,600 = $9,239,400			
	Expense is 10% × $9,239,400 × 9/12			
	Payable is 9% × $10,000,000 × 9/12			
	Discount is difference			

c.

Mar. 31	Interest expense		230,985	
	Interest payable		675,000	
	Cash			900,000
	Discount on bonds			5,985
	Expense is 10% × $9,239,400 × 3/12			
	Cash is 9% × $10,000,000			

d.

Dec. 31	Interest expense		694,751	
	Interest payable			675,000
	Discount on bonds			19,751
	Interest is 10% × ($10,000,000 − 736,660) × 9/12			

11-28. *(40 minutes)*

a. Present value:

Initial payment	$100,000
Added payments $100,000 × 7.360 (Appendix C, Table III) (10 periods, 6%)	736,000
Present value	$836,000

b. Interest expense is 6% × ($836,000 − 100,000) = $44,160
c. Depreciation is 1/8 × $836,000 = $104,500 per year
d. Interest expense:
   Balance paid on principal in first 6 months is
      $100,000 − 44,160 = $55,840
      Interest is 6% × ($736,000 − 55,840) = $40,810
e. Liability:
   Balance paid on principal in second 6 months is
      $100,000 − 40,810 = $59,190
      Liability is $736,000 − 55,840 − 59,190 = $620,970

11-31. *(60 minutes)*

			No Tax Allocation (a)		Tax Allocation (b)	
Year 1						
Jan. 1	Cash		75,000		75,000	
	Deferred Rental Income			75,000		75,000
Dec. 31	Deferred Rental Income		25,000		25,000	
	Rental Income			25,000		25,000
Dec. 31	Income Tax Expense		42,000		22,000	
	Deferred Income Taxes				20,000	
	Income Taxes Payable			42,000		42,000
Year 2						
Dec. 31	Deferred Rental Income		25,000		25,000	
	Rental Income			25,000		25,000
Dec. 31	Income Tax Expense		12,000		22,000	
	Deferred Income Taxes					10,000
	Income Taxes Payable			12,000		12,000
Year 3						
Dec. 31	Deferred Rental Income		25,000		25,000	
	Rental Income			25,000		25,000
Dec. 31	Income Tax Expense		12,000		22,000	
	Deferred Income Taxes					10,000
	Income Taxes Payable			12,000		12,000

	(a)			(b)		
	Year Ended 12–31			Year Ended 12–31		
Income Statements	Year 1	Year 2	Year 3	Year 1	Year 2	Year 3
Income from Operations	$30,000	$30,000	$30,000	$30,000	$30,000	$30,000
Rental Income	25,000	25,000	25,000	25,000	25,000	25,000
	$55,000	$55,000	$55,000	$55,000	$55,000	$55,000
Income Tax Expense	42,000	12,000	12,000	22,000*	22,000*	22,000*
	$13,000	$43,000	$43,000	$33,000	$33,000	$33,000
Balance Sheets at Year-end						
Deferred Income taxes— Debit balances	$ —0—	$ —0—	$ —0—	$20,000	$10,000	$ —0—
Income taxes payable (current liability)	42,000	12,000	12,000	42,000	12,000	12,000
*Currently payable				$42,000	$12,000	$12,000
Deferred				(20,000)	10,000	10,000
Total				$22,000	$22,000	$22,000

CHAPTER 12

12-11. (*20 minutes*)

No journal entry is needed to record the *authorized* stock; a notation as to number of authorized shares should be made in the general ledger accounts for preferred and common.

a.

	Debit	Credit
Cash	408,000	
Preferred stock		400,000
Paid-in capital in excess of par—preferred		8,000

b.

Cash	1,050,000	
Common stock		150,000
Paid-in capital in excess of stated value—common		900,000

c.

Land	35,000	
Common stock		5,000
Paid-in capital in excess of stated value—common		30,000
Note that the land was valued at the most recent cash price of the stock.		

d.

Land	75,000	
Paid-in capital from donation		75,000

12-19. (*40 minutes*)

a.

	Debit	Credit
Cash	1,100,000	
Preferred stock		1,000,000
Paid-in capital in excess of par—preferred		100,000

b.

Cash	2,600,000	
Common stock		200,000
Paid-in capital in excess of par—common		2,400,000

c.

Land	325,000	
Common stock		25,000
Paid-in capital in excess of par—common		300,000
Note that the land is valued at the most recent price of stock given for it.		

d.

Income summary	220,000	
Retained earnings		220,000

Appendix B   Solutions to Selected Problems

e.
Retained earnings	80,000	
Dividends payable—preferred		80,000
$100 × .08 × 10,000 shares = $80,000		

f.
Retained earnings	67,500	
Common stock dividend to be issued		4,500
Paid-in capital from stock dividend		63,000
(40,000 + 5,000) × .02 × $75 = 900 shares × $75 = $67,500 fair value of dividend; 900 shares × $5 = $4,500 par value of dividend.		

g.
Dividend payable—preferred	80,000	
Cash		80,000
Common stock dividend to be issued	4,500	
Common stock		4,500

h.
Treasury stock—common	80,000	
Cash		80,000

i.
Cash	51,000	
Treasury stock—common		48,000
Paid-in capital from treasury stock		3,000
600 × $85 = $51,000 price received		
600 × $80 = 48,000 cost of treasury stock		
$ 3,000 Gain on sale		

12-22. *(60 minutes)*

a. Journal entries

			Debit	Credit
Mar. 1	Property		1,200,000	
	Common stock			300,000
	Paid-in capital in excess of par			900,000
July 1	Cash		208,000	
	Preferred stock			208,000
	Note: no-par stock is usually credited with the price received if there is no stated value.			
Sept. 1	No journal entry required. After the split is accomplished, there will be 420,000 shares of common outstanding at a new par of $2.50			
Dec. 15	Retained earnings		376,000	
	Dividend payable—preferred			40,000
	Dividend payable—common			336,000
	Preferred (6,000 + 4,000) × $4 = $40,000			
	Common 420,000 × $.80 = $336,000			
Dec. 31	Income summary		712,000	
	Retained earnings			712,000

615

b. Earnings per share

	Net income	$712,000
	Earnings per share of common stock	$1.68

Computation
Net income	$712,000
Less preferred dividends	40,000
Net income to common	$672,000

Earnings per share:

$$\frac{\$672,000}{400,000 \text{ shares}^*} = \$1.68$$

*Weighted Average Shares

Date	Shares	Fraction of Year	Weighted Average
Jan. 1	150,000		
Add: shares for split	150,000		
	300,000	1.0	300,000
Mar. 1	60,000		
Add: shares for split	60,000		
	120,000	10/12	100,000
Weighted average shares outstanding			400,000

CHAPTER 13

13-16. *(10 minutes)*

Book value of Dodds	$160,000
90%	144,000
Cost of investment	165,000
Goodwill	21,000
Minority interest	
10% × $160,000 =	$ 16,000

13-17. *(10 minutes)*

Book value of Dodds	$160,000
Add adjustment of plant and equipment	12,000
Total	$172,000
90%	$154,800
Cost of investment	170,000
Goodwill	$ 15,200
Minority interest	
10% × $172,000 =	$ 17,200

13-24. *(30 minutes)*

	P	S	Adj. & Elim.		Consol.
Credits					
Service revenue		$ 60,000	(b) 20,000		$ 40,000
Sales	$520,000	190,000	(a) 30,000		680,000
Earnings of Co. S	25,000		(c) 25,000		
	$545,000	$250,000			$720,000
Debits					
Cost of goods sold	$310,000	$160,000		(a) 30,000	$440,000
Operating expenses	175,000	65,000		(b) 20,000	220,000
Net income—P	60,000				60,000
Net income—S		25,000		(c) 25,000	—0—
	$545,000	$250,000			$720,000

(a) Eliminate intercompany sales
(b) Eliminate intercompany service
(c) Net income of S

The income statement would be prepared from the last column in the worksheet, as follows:

COMPANY P & SUBSIDIARY
Consolidated Income Statement
For the Year 19—

Sales	$680,000
Cost of goods sold	440,000
Gross margin on sales	240,000
Service revenue	40,000
Total	280,000
Operating expenses	220,000
Net Income	$ 60,000

13-26. *(20 minutes)*

ROCKY ROAD COMPANY
Balance Sheet
as of December 31

Assets

Current assets	$ 5,150,000
Property, plant, and equipment	8,350,000
Total assets	$13,500,000

Equities

Liabilities	$ 3,100,000
Capital stock	6,260,000
Capital in excess of par	—0—
Retained earnings	4,140,000*
Total equities	$13,500,000

* $4,000,000 + 200,000 − 60,000 that had to be transferred to capital stock because par value of stock was $260,000.

Appendix B   Solutions to Selected Problems

13-27. (*25 minutes*)

ROCKY ROAD COMPANY
Balance Sheet
as of December 31

Assets	
Current assets	$ 5,150,000
Property, plant and equipment	8,600,000
Total assets	$13,750,000

Equities	
Liabilities	$ 3,100,000
Capital stock	6,260,000
Capital in excess of par	390,000*
Retained earnings	4,000,000
Total equities	$13,750,000

* $2,600 × 250 = $650,000 less $260,000 par = $390,000

CHAPTER 14

14-13. (*12 minutes*)

	A	B	C	D	Total
5% interest to A	$9,000				$ 9,000
Salaries		$6,000	$8,000		14,000
					$23,000
Balance	(6,600)	(3,300)	(1,650)	($8,250)	(19,800)
Total	$2,400	$2,700	$6,350	($8,250)	$ 3,200
Shares of balance:	$\frac{4}{12}$	$\frac{2}{12}$	$\frac{1}{12}$	$\frac{5}{12}$	

Entry:

	Debit	Credit
Income summary	3,200	
D, capital	8,250	
A, capital		2,400
B, capital		2,700
C, capital		6,350

14-25. (*25 minutes*)

a.

	Debit	Credit
Cash	34,000	
Goodwill	6,000	
Poe, capital		40,000

b.

Cash	44,000	
Poe, capital		44,000
Goodwill	12,000	
Doe, capital		6,000
Mee, capital		4,000
Noe, capital		2,000

$44,000 \div \frac{1}{4} = \$176,000 \times \frac{3}{4} = \$132,000$

c.

Cash	44,000	
Doe, capital		1,500
Mee, capital		1,000
Noe, capital		500
Poe, capital		41,000

Poe gets $\frac{1}{4}$ of ($120,000 + $44,000)

d.

Mee, capital	40,000	
Poe, capital		40,000

e.

Doe, capital	25,000	
Mee, capital	20,000	
Noe, capital	15,000	
Poe, capital		60,000

14-26. (*20 minutes*)

a.

	Debit	Credit
Cash	22,000	
Gain or loss on dissolution	8,000	
Receivables		30,000

b.

Cash	63,000	
Gain or loss on dissolution	17,000	
Inventory		80,000

c.

Cash	50,000	
Gain or loss on liquidation	10,000	
Plant and equipment		60,000

d.

Accounts payable	42,000	
Cash		42,000
Bow, capital	14,000	
Spry, capital	14,000	
Ital, capital	7,000	
Gain or loss on liquidation		35,000
Cash	2,000	
Bow, capital		2,000
Spry, capital	41,000	
Ital, capital	56,000	
Cash		97,000

Appendix B   Solutions to Selected Problems

CHAPTER 15

15-13. (*10 minutes*)

a. Replacement cost is $2,750. Holding gain is $2,750 − $2,600 = $150.
b. Net realizable value is $3,700 − 370 = $3,330. Gain is $3,330 − 2,600 = $730.

15-14. (*15 minutes*)

Net monetary items 12/31/1 = ($1,700)
Net monetary items 12/31/2 = ($1,300)
Average net monetary items   (1,500)

Gain ($1,500) $\times \dfrac{180}{150}$ = (1,800) − (1,500) = $300 gain.

15-18. (*35 minutes*)

Sales		$80,000
Replacement cost of goods sold:		
From beginning inventory	$ 6,300	
Goods purchased and sold during the period	45,900	52,200
Gross margin		$27,800
Holding gains:		
On beginning inventory		
$ 6,300 − 6,200 =	$100*	
On goods purchased and sold		
$45,900 − (8,500 × 5.20) =	1,700	
On ending inventory		
$8,300 − 7,800 =	500	
Total holding gains		2,300
Total		$30,100

* The other $200 would have been recorded as a holding gain last year.

15-20. (*25 minutes*)

Asset value — Beginning of year
  $ 200 × 5.650   (Appendix C, Table III) = $1,130
  $2,000 ×   .3220   (Table II)   =   644
    Total $1,774
Asset value — end of year
  $ 220 × 5.328   (Appendix C, Table III) = $1,172
  $2,100 ×   .3606   (Table II)   =   757
    Total $1,929

Income		
12% × 1,774	= $ 213	Current income
$1,929 − 1,787*	= 142	Capital gain
Net income	$ 355	

*$1,774 + 12% − 200 = $1,787 asset value under old expectations.

15-23. (*80 minutes*)

Factors 112/107 = 1.047
        112/100 = 1.120

HOPE COMPANY
Restated Income Statement for the Year

Sales $3,000 × 1.047 (1.0467)		$3,140
Cost of sales:		
Beginning inventory $300 × 1.120 =	$ 336	
Purchases $1,700 × 1.047	1,780	
	2,116	
Ending inventory $300 × 1.120	336	
Cost of sales		1,780
Gross margin		1,360
Expenses:		
Depreciation $200 × 1.120	224	
Other expenses $900 × 1.047	942	
Total expenses		1,166
Income from operations		194
Price-level loss on monetary items*		50
Income tax $80 × 1.047		84
Net income		$ 60

*Monetary assets 12/31 $620
Monetary assets 1/1 $300

Because the price-level change is not even throughout the year, the use of the average monetary assets gives a figure that is slightly off, $55. A somewhat more accurate method is as follows:

$$\text{Loss} = 300 \frac{(1.07 - 1.00)}{1.00} + 620 \frac{(1.12 - 1.07)}{1.07}$$

$$\text{Loss} = 50$$

Appendix B   Solutions to Selected Problems

HOPE COMPANY
Restated Balance Sheet
in 12/31 Dollars

	Dec. 31	Jan. 1
Cash	$ 500	$ 560*
Receivables	400	0
Inventory $300 × 1.120	336	336
Equipment $2,400 × 1.120	2,688	2,688
Accumulated depreciation $200 × 1.120	(224)	0
Total assets	$3,700	$3,584
Accounts payable	$ 200	$ 224*
Taxes payable	80	0
Common stock $2,000 × 1.120	2,240	2,240
Premium on common $1,000 × 1.120	1,120	1,120
Retained earnings	60	0
Total equities	$3,700	$3,584

*Cash on January 1 $500 × 1.120 = $560
Accounts payable on January 1 $200 × 1.120 = $224
These are January 1 items restated to December 31 purchasing power. The items must be restated if the entire statement is to be in terms of December 31 dollars.

CHAPTER 16

16-21. (*15 minutes*)

    a. Record the advertising as an asset, prepaid advertising, rather than an expense because benefit comes next period.
    b. Record $5 as revenue and the other $15 as unearned revenue, a liability.
    c. Record the sale in the current year, and also record an estimated expense for warranties together with an estimated liability. When the work is performed, debit the liability rather than an expense.
    d. Record as revenue only the part that relates to the current year. Record balance as unearned revenue.
    e. Record advertising as unearned revenue because ads have not yet appeared.
    f. Record costs as some sort of prepaid asset, to be recorded as expense in the next year when the ads are run.

16-28. (30 minutes)

Income:		
Revenues		$ 500,000
Expenses:		
Cost of movie		250,000
Gross margin		$ 250,000
Advertising*	$53,571	
Royalty to Ford (5%)	25,000	78,571
Income		$ 171,429

* $300,000 × 500/2,800

Balance sheet items:	
Assets:	
Unamortized cost of film	$1,750,000
Prepaid advertising	246,429
Liabilities:	
Payable to Ford	25,000

Also, amounts will appear for cash and retained earnings. The film cost is divided on the basis of the proportion of December receipts to total receipts. Advertising is divided on the basis of the proportion of December receipts to expected receipts for 6 months.

16-30. (50 minutes)

PAFKO COMPANY
Income Statement
for the Year

Sales		$192,000
Cost of sales:		
Purchases	$144,000	
Less ending inventory	20,000	
Cost of goods sold		124,000
		$ 68,000
Expenses		
Salaries	$ 30,000	
Depreciation	10,000	
Supplies, taxes, and insurance	17,000	
Patent amortization expense	1,800	58,800
Net income		$ 9,200

Appendix B   Solutions to Selected Problems

PAFKO COMPANY
Balance Sheet
as of December 31

Current assets:			Current liabilities:		
Cash		$ 21,000	Accounts payable		$ 16,000
Receivables		40,000	Accrued liabilities		3,000
Inventory		20,000	Total current liabilities		$ 19,000
Prepaid items		1,000	Long-term liability		
Total current assets		$ 82,000	Note payable (due in 4 yrs.)		30,000
Plant assets			Total liabilities		$ 49,000
Buildings	$100,000		Stockholders' Equity:		
Less accumulated depreciation	10,000		Capital stock	$100,000	
Total plant assets		90,000	Premium on stock	30,000	
Intangibles:			Retained earnings	9,200	
Patents		16,200	Total owners' equity		139,200
Total assets		$188,200	Total equities		$188,200

CHAPTER 17

17-13.   (*10 minutes*)

    a. Beginning balance $30,000
        Less sale   10,000
              20,000
        Purchases   30,000 (forced)
        Ending balance $50,000

    b. $2,000

    c. Beginning balance $20,000
        Less sale ($10,000 − 2,000)   8,000
              12,000
        Depreciation for year   18,000 (forced)
        Ending balance $30,000

17-19.   (*10 minutes*)

    Cost of goods sold $350,000
    Less increase in accounts payable   5,000
          345,000
    Add increase in inventory   6,000
    Cash paid for purchases $351,000

Check:
Cash paid	$351,000	
+ Ending accounts payable	40,000	
	391,000	
Less Beginning accounts payable	35,000	
Purchases	$356,000	
Beginning inventory	27,000	
+ Purchases	356,000	
	383,000	
Less ending inventory	33,000	
Cost of goods sold	$350,000	

17-25. (*40 minutes*)

HOLLOW COMPANY
Statement of Cash Flows
Year Ended September 30

Sources of Cash

Operations:		
Net income		$15,000
Add depreciation		9,000
Total		24,000
Add: Increases in current liabilities		
Accounts payable		2,000
		26,000
Deduct:		
Increases in current assets		
Accounts receivable	$ 2,000	
Inventory	6,000	
Decreases in current liabilities		
Accrued wages	1,000	
Income taxes payable	1,000	
		10,000
Increase in cash from operations		16,000
Long-term borrowing		20,000
Total sources of cash		$36,000

Uses of Cash

Dividends	$ 7,000	
Equipment	30,000	
Treasury stock purchases	3,000	
Total uses of cash		40,000
Decrease in cash balance		($4,000)

Appendix B   Solutions to Selected Problems

17-27. *(80 minutes)*

GRANICK COMPANY
Statement of Changes in Financial Position
for Year 2

Resources Provided:
By operations
Net income		$ 520,000
Add back expenses not requiring the use of working capital:		
Depreciation		651,000
Loss on sale of investments		30,000
Deduct gain on sale of plant assets		(140,000)
Total provided by operations		1,061,000
By sale of investments		60,000
By sale of plant assets		379,000
By issuing long-term debt		300,000
By issuing stock		6,000
Total resources provided		$1,806,000
Resources Applied:		
To purchase investments	$ 160,000	
To acquire plant assets	1,360,000	
To dividends	324,000	
Total resources applied		$1,844,000
Decrease in working capital		($38,000)

GRANICK COMPANY
Schedule of Working Capital Changes
Year 2

	Balance, Dec. 31		Working Capital	
	Year 2	Year 1	Increase	Decrease
Cash	$ 88,000	$ 91,000		$ 3,000
Marketable securities	465,000	600,000		135,000
Accounts receivable	1,140,000	950,000	$190,000	
Estimated uncollectibles	(14,000)	(13,000)		1,000
Inventories	480,000	482,000		2,000
Prepaid expenses	155,000	156,000		1,000
	2,314,000	2,266,000		
Notes payable	193,000	92,000		101,000
Accounts payable	642,000	679,000	37,000	
Accrued liabilities	181,000	202,000	21,000	
Income taxes payable	203,000	160,000		43,000
	1,219,000	1,133,000		
Net working capital	1,095,000	1,133,000		
Total increases and decreases			248,000	286,000
Decrease in working capital			38,000	
Total			$286,000	$286,000

Plant Assets:
Balance, January 1		$8,640,000
Less sale		400,000
		8,240,000
Purchases (forced)		1,360,000
Balance, December 31		$9,600,000

Accumulated Depreciation (check):
Balance, January 1		$4,040,000
Add depreciation		651,000
		4,691,000
Sale		−161,000
Balance, December 31		$4,530,000

Proceeds from sale of plant assets:
Cost		$ 400,000
less accumulated depreciation		161,000
Book value		239,000
Add gain		140,000
Proceeds		$ 379,000

Investments:
Balance, January 1		$ 536,000
Less sale		90,000
		446,000
Purchases (forced)		160,000
Balance, December 31		$ 606,000

Proceeds from sale of investments:
Book value		$ 90,000
Less loss		30,000
Proceeds		$ 60,000

Proceeds from sale of stock ($6,000) appear in Capital Stock ($3,000) and in Capital in excess of par ($3,000).

Retained earnings
Balance, January 1		$1,384,000
Add income		520,000
		1,904,000
Less dividends (forced)		324,000
Balance, December 31		$1,580,000

CHAPTER 18

18-11. *(20 minutes)*

    a. Rate of return on total assets:

$$\underset{R}{\frac{\$\ 14,000}{\$200,000} = 7\%} \qquad \underset{S}{\frac{\$\ 16,000}{\$200,000} = 8\%}$$

S used its assets more efficiently.

Appendix B   Solutions to Selected Problems

b. Rate of return on owners' equity:

	R	S
Income before interest & taxes	$ 14,000	$ 16,000
Interest	5,000	
Income before tax	9,000	16,000
Income tax (30%)	2,700	4,800
Net income	$ 6,300	$ 11,200
Owners' equity	$100,000	$200,000
Return on owners' equity	6.3%	5.6%

R earns a greater return than S.

There is a conflict between the answers to *a* and *b*. S seems to be managing its assets better, but R uses leverage to increase the return to owners.

18-20. *(30 minutes)*

a. Income before tax: $60,000 + 40,000 = $100,000
Return on equity: $100,000/400,000 = 25%
b. Income from operations: $100,000 + 8,000 interest = $108,000
c. Return on assets: $108,000/700,000 = 15.4%. Gorge uses leverage to boost rate of return on owners' equity to 25%, before tax.
d. EPS: $60,000/20,000 = $3.00 per share.
e. Book value: $400,000/20,000 = $20 per share.

18-26. *(45 minutes)*

a. $100,000/1,100,000 = 9.09%, using net income
or $210,000/1,100,000 = 19.09%, using operating income
b. Average assets = $1,000,000
Turnover $1,100,000/1,000,000 = 1.1 times
c. $210,000/1,000,000 = 21%
$a \times b = c$ $19.09 \times 1.1 = 21\%$
d. $110,000/80,000 = 1.4 to 1
e. $600,000/100,000 = 6 times
f. Income must increase to 21% of $1,200,000 or $252,000. $252,000 will be 19.09% of sales, therefore sales = $252,000/.1909 = $1,320,062 or $1,320,000, an increase of 20%. This is the same as the increase in average assets. The net income could also be used in answering this question. The result is the same.
g. Increase in retained earnings = $40,000
Income − dividends = $40,000
$100,000 − dividends = $40,000
dividends = $60,000

APPENDIX C

Present Value Tables

TABLE I. Compound Amount of One Dollar at the End of N Periods at Specified Rates of Interest

Periods	.02	.03	.04	.06	.08	.10	.12	.14	.16	.18	.20
1	1.020	1.030	1.040	1.060	1.080	1.100	1.120	1.140	1.160	1.180	1.200
2	1.040	1.061	1.082	1.124	1.166	1.210	1.254	1.300	1.346	1.392	1.440
3	1.061	1.093	1.125	1.191	1.260	1.331	1.405	1.482	1.561	1.643	1.728
4	1.082	1.126	1.170	1.262	1.360	1.464	1.574	1.689	1.811	1.939	2.074
5	1.104	1.159	1.217	1.338	1.469	1.611	1.762	1.925	2.100	2.288	2.488
6	1.126	1.194	1.265	1.419	1.587	1.772	1.974	2.195	2.436	2.700	2.986
7	1.149	1.230	1.316	1.504	1.714	1.949	2.211	2.502	2.826	3.185	3.583
8	1.172	1.267	1.369	1.594	1.851	2.144	2.476	2.853	3.278	3.759	4.300
9	1.195	1.305	1.423	1.689	1.999	2.358	2.773	3.252	3.803	4.435	5.160
10	1.219	1.344	1.480	1.791	2.159	2.594	3.106	3.707	4.411	5.234	6.192
11	1.243	1.384	1.539	1.898	2.332	2.853	3.479	4.226	5.117	6.176	7.430
12	1.268	1.426	1.601	2.012	2.518	3.138	3.896	4.818	5.936	7.288	8.916
13	1.294	1.469	1.665	2.133	2.720	3.452	4.363	5.492	6.886	8.599	10.699
14	1.319	1.513	1.732	2.261	2.937	3.797	4.887	6.261	7.988	10.147	12.839
15	1.346	1.558	1.801	2.397	3.172	4.177	5.474	7.138	9.266	11.974	15.407
16	1.373	1.605	1.873	2.540	3.426	4.595	6.130	8.137	10.748	14.129	18.488
17	1.400	1.653	1.948	2.693	3.700	5.054	6.866	9.276	12.468	16.672	22.186
18	1.428	1.702	2.026	2.854	3.996	5.560	7.690	10.575	14.463	19.673	26.623
19	1.457	1.754	2.107	3.026	4.316	6.116	8.613	12.056	16.777	23.214	31.948
20	1.486	1.806	2.191	3.207	4.661	6.727	9.646	13.743	19.461	27.393	38.338
25	1.641	2.094	2.666	4.292	6.848	10.835	17.000	26.462	40.874	62.669	95.396
30	1.811	2.427	3.243	5.743	10.063	17.449	29.960	50.950	85.850	143.371	237.376
35	2.000	2.814	3.946	7.686	14.786	28.102	52.800	98.100	180.314	327.997	590.668
40	2.208	3.262	4.801	10.286	21.725	45.259	93.051	188.883	378.721	750.378	1,469.771

TABLE II. Present Value of a Payment of One Dollar to Be Received at the End of N Periods at Specified Rates of Interest

Periods	.02	.03	.04	.06	.08	.10	.12	.14	.16	.18	.20	.22	.24	.26	.28	.30
1	.9804	.9709	.9615	.9434	.9259	.9091	.8929	.8772	.8621	.8475	.8333	.8197	.8065	.794	.781	.769
2	.9612	.9426	.9246	.8900	.8573	.8264	.7972	.7695	.7432	.7182	.6944	.6719	.6504	.630	.610	.592
3	.9423	.9151	.8890	.8396	.7938	.7513	.7118	.6750	.6407	.6086	.5787	.5507	.5245	.500	.477	.455
4	.9238	.8885	.8548	.7921	.7350	.6830	.6355	.5921	.5523	.5158	.4823	.4514	.4230	.397	.373	.350
5	.9057	.8626	.8219	.7473	.6806	.6209	.5674	.5194	.4761	.4371	.4019	.3700	.3411	.315	.291	.269
6	.8880	.8375	.7903	.7050	.6302	.5645	.5066	.4556	.4104	.3704	.3349	.3033	.2751	.250	.227	.207
7	.8706	.8131	.7599	.6651	.5835	.5132	.4523	.3996	.3538	.3139	.2791	.2486	.2218	.198	.178	.159
8	.8535	.7894	.7307	.6274	.5403	.4665	.4039	.3506	.3050	.2660	.2326	.2038	.1789	.157	.139	.123
9	.8368	.7664	.7026	.5919	.5002	.4241	.3606	.3075	.2630	.2255	.1938	.1670	.1443	.125	.108	.094
10	.8203	.7441	.6756	.5584	.4632	.3855	.3220	.2697	.2267	.1911	.1615	.1369	.1164	.099	.085	.073
11	.8043	.7224	.6496	.5268	.4289	.3505	.2875	.2366	.1954	.1619	.1346	.1122	.0938	.079	.066	.056
12	.7885	.7014	.6246	.4970	.3971	.3186	.2567	.2076	.1685	.1372	.1122	.0920	.0757	.062	.052	.043
13	.7730	.6810	.6005	.4688	.3677	.2897	.2292	.1821	.1452	.1163	.0935	.0754	.0610	.050	.040	.033
14	.7579	.6611	.5775	.4423	.3405	.2633	.2046	.1597	.1252	.0985	.0779	.0618	.0492	.039	.032	.025
15	.7430	.6419	.5553	.4173	.3152	.2394	.1827	.1401	.1079	.0835	.0649	.0507	.0397	.031	.025	.020
16	.7284	.6232	.5339	.3936	.2919	.2176	.1631	.1229	.0930	.0708	.0541	.0415	.0320	.025	.019	.015
17	.7142	.6050	.5134	.3714	.2703	.1978	.1456	.1078	.0802	.0600	.0451	.0340	.0258	.020	.015	.012
18	.7002	.5874	.4936	.3503	.2502	.1799	.1300	.0946	.0691	.0508	.0376	.0279	.0208	.016	.012	.009
19	.6864	.5703	.4746	.3305	.2317	.1635	.1161	.0829	.0596	.0431	.0313	.0229	.0168	.012	.009	.007
20	.6730	.5537	.4564	.3118	.2145	.1486	.1037	.0728	.0514	.0365	.0261	.0187	.0135	.010	.007	.005
21	.6598	.5375	.4388	.2942	.1987	.1351	.0926	.0638	.0443	.0309	.0217	.0154	.0109	.008	.006	.004
22	.6468	.5219	.4220	.2775	.1839	.1228	.0826	.0560	.0382	.0262	.0181	.0126	.0088	.006	.004	.003
23	.6342	.5067	.4057	.2618	.1703	.1117	.0738	.0491	.0329	.0222	.0151	.0103	.0071	.005	.003	.002
24	.6217	.4919	.3901	.2470	.1577	.1015	.0659	.0431	.0284	.0188	.0126	.0085	.0057	.004	.003	.002
25	.6095	.4776	.3751	.2330	.1460	.0923	.0588	.0378	.0245	.0160	.0105	.0069	.0046	.003	.002	.001
30	.5521	.4120	.3083	.1741	.0994	.0573	.0334	.0196	.0116	.0070	.0042	.0026	.0016	.001	.001	.000
35	.5000	.3554	.2534	.1301	.0676	.0356	.0189	.0102	.0055	.0030	.0017	.0009	.0005	.000	.000	.000
40	.4529	.3066	.2083	.0972	.0460	.0221	.0107	.0053	.0026	.0013	.0007	.0004	.0002	.000	.000	.000

TABLE III. Present Value of Annuity of One Dollar Per Period for N Periods at Specified Rates of Interest

Periods	.02	.03	.04	.06	.08	.10	.12	.14	.16	.18	.20	.22	.24	.26	.28	.30	.35	.40
1	.980	.971	.962	.943	.926	.909	.893	.877	.862	.847	.833	.820	.806	.794	.781	.769	.741	.714
2	1.942	1.913	1.886	1.833	1.783	1.736	1.690	1.647	1.605	1.566	1.528	1.492	1.457	1.424	1.392	1.361	1.289	1.224
3	2.884	2.829	2.775	2.673	2.577	2.487	2.402	2.322	2.246	2.174	2.106	2.042	1.981	1.923	1.868	1.816	1.696	1.589
4	3.808	3.717	3.630	3.465	3.312	3.170	3.037	2.914	2.798	2.690	2.589	2.494	2.404	2.320	2.241	2.166	1.997	1.849
5	4.713	4.580	4.452	4.212	3.993	3.791	3.605	3.433	3.274	3.127	2.991	2.864	2.745	2.635	2.532	2.436	2.220	2.035
6	5.601	5.417	5.242	4.917	4.623	4.355	4.111	3.889	3.685	3.498	3.326	3.167	3.020	2.885	2.759	2.643	2.385	2.168
7	6.472	6.230	6.002	5.582	5.206	4.868	4.564	4.288	4.039	3.812	3.605	3.416	3.242	3.083	2.937	2.802	2.508	2.263
8	7.325	7.020	6.733	6.210	5.747	5.335	4.968	4.639	4.344	4.078	3.837	3.619	3.421	3.241	3.076	2.925	2.598	2.331
9	8.162	7.786	7.435	6.802	6.247	5.759	5.328	4.946	4.607	4.303	4.031	3.786	3.566	3.366	3.184	3.019	2.665	2.379
10	8.983	8.530	8.111	7.360	6.710	6.145	5.650	5.216	4.833	4.494	4.192	3.923	3.682	3.465	3.269	3.092	2.715	2.414
11	9.787	9.253	8.760	7.887	7.139	6.495	5.938	5.453	5.029	4.656	4.327	4.035	3.776	3.543	3.335	3.147	2.752	2.438
12	10.575	9.954	9.385	8.384	7.536	6.814	6.194	5.660	5.197	4.793	4.439	4.127	3.851	3.606	3.387	3.190	2.779	2.456
13	11.348	10.635	9.986	8.853	7.904	7.103	6.424	5.842	5.342	4.910	4.533	4.203	3.912	3.656	3.427	3.223	2.799	2.469
14	12.106	11.296	10.563	9.295	8.244	7.367	6.628	6.002	5.468	5.008	4.611	4.265	3.962	3.695	3.459	3.249	2.814	2.478
15	12.849	11.938	11.118	9.712	8.559	7.606	6.811	6.142	5.575	5.092	4.675	4.315	4.001	3.726	3.483	3.268	2.825	2.484
16	13.577	12.561	11.652	10.106	8.851	7.824	6.974	6.265	5.668	5.162	4.730	4.357	4.033	3.751	3.503	3.283	2.834	2.489
17	14.292	13.166	12.166	10.477	9.122	8.022	7.120	6.373	5.749	5.222	4.775	4.391	4.059	3.771	3.518	3.295	2.840	2.492
18	14.992	13.754	12.659	10.828	9.372	8.201	7.250	6.467	5.818	5.273	4.812	4.419	4.080	3.786	3.529	3.304	2.844	2.494
19	15.678	14.324	13.134	11.158	9.604	8.365	7.366	6.550	5.877	5.316	4.843	4.442	4.097	3.799	3.539	3.311	2.848	2.496
20	16.351	14.877	13.590	11.470	9.818	8.514	7.469	6.623	5.929	5.353	4.870	4.460	4.110	3.808	3.546	3.316	2.850	2.497
21	17.011	15.415	14.029	11.764	10.017	8.649	7.562	6.687	5.973	5.384	4.891	4.476	4.121	3.816	3.551	3.320	2.852	2.498
22	17.658	15.937	14.451	12.042	10.201	8.772	7.645	6.743	6.011	5.410	4.909	4.488	4.130	3.822	3.556	3.323	2.853	2.498
23	18.292	16.444	14.857	12.303	10.371	8.883	7.718	6.792	6.044	5.432	4.925	4.499	4.137	3.827	3.559	3.325	2.854	2.499
24	18.914	16.936	15.247	12.550	10.529	8.985	7.784	6.835	6.073	5.451	4.937	4.507	4.143	3.831	3.562	3.327	2.855	2.499
25	19.523	17.413	15.622	12.783	10.675	9.077	7.843	6.873	6.097	5.467	4.948	4.514	4.147	3.834	3.564	3.329	2.856	2.499
30	22.396	19.600	17.292	13.765	11.258	9.427	8.055	7.003	6.177	5.517	4.979	4.534	4.160	3.842	3.569	3.332	2.857	2.500
35	24.999	21.487	18.665	14.498	11.655	9.644	8.176	7.070	6.215	5.539	4.992	4.541	4.164	3.845	3.571	3.333	2.857	2.500
40	27.355	23.115	19.793	15.046	11.925	9.779	8.244	7.105	6.233	5.548	4.997	4.544	4.166	3.846	3.571	3.333	2.857	2.500

Index

Account, ledger, 98, 103–104
Accounting:
  and bookkeeping, 13–14
  and communication, 16–17
  defined, 3
Accounting cycle, 145–146, 154
Accounting equation, 30–33, 96, 101
Accounting principles (*see* Principles of accounting)
Accounting Principles Board, 493–495
Accounting Principles Board Opinions, 493–494
  No. 15, Earnings per Share, 384
  No. 16, Business Combinations, 421–422
  No. 17, Intangibles, 317
  No. 19, Changes in Financial Position, 517–518
  No. 21, Interest on Receivables and Payables, 259
Accounting Principles Board Statement No. 4, Basic Concepts, 494, 496, 498
Accounting Research Bulletins, 491
  No. 51, Consolidated Statements, 412
Accounting Research Division, AICPA, 493
Accounting Research Studies, 493
  No. 1, Basic Postulates, 493
  No. 3, Principles, 493
Accounting theory, 484–509
Accounts payable, 340–345
Accounts receivable, 210–215
  aging, 211–213
  bad debt provisions, 134–135, 210–214
  valuation, 210–211
  write-offs, 213–214
Accrual basis, 68–69
Accrual of interest, 220–222
Accrued expenses, 125–128
Accrued revenues, 128
Acid-test ratio, 565
Adjusting entries, 124–138 (*see also* Accrual of interest; Prepaid expenses; Unearned revenues)
  objectives, 124–125
AICPA (*see* American Institute of Certified Public Accountants)
Allocation of income tax expense, 361–365
Alternatives, effects of, 487–490, 554
American Accounting Association, 495
American Institute of Certified Public Accountants, 6, 490–491, 492–495
Amortization of bond premium or discount, 246–252, 354–358
  effective-interest, 356–358
  straight-line, 354–356
Amortization of intangibles, 317–321
Analysis of operations, 551–561
Analysis of statements, 549–569
Annuities, 256–258
  due, 263–264
APB, 493–495
Approximation, 505
Articles of incorporation, 375
Asset turnover, 561–562
Asset valuation, 34–37, 203–204
  alternative approaches, 456–466
  criteria for methods, 464–465
  and income determination, 50
  market values, 36–37
Assets:
  current, 40
  defined, 33–34
  measurement, 34–37
  revaluation, 441–442
  valuation, 203–204
Assumptions, 80, 505
Auditing, 11

Bad debts (*see* Accounts receivable)
Balance sheet (*see* Financial position, statement of)
Bank reconciliations, 228–232
Basic concepts (*see* Accounting Principles Board Statement No. 4)
Bearer bonds, 353
Bond discount, 353–354
Bond investments, 246–252
Bond obligations, 352–358
  issuance, 353–354
  premium or discount, 353–354
  types of bonds, 352–353
Bond premium, 353–354
Bonds:
  bearer, 353
  callable, 352–353
  convertible, 352
  coupon, 353
  debenture, 352
  guaranteed, 352
  mortgage, 352
  registered, 353
  retirement, 358

Index

Book value, 41, 391, 559–560
Business combinations, 419–422
Business enterprise:
    purpose, 14–15
    forms, 15–16

Callable bonds, 352–353
Capital expenditures, 308
Capital maintenance, 463–464
Capital stock:
    classes of, 377–378
    dividends, 385–388
    issuance of, 379–382
    no par, 378–379
    options, 389–390
    par value, 378–379
    premium, 380
    rights and warrants, 390
    splits, 389
    subscriptions, 382
    treasury, 390–391
Cash, 206–210
    control, 206–209
Cash basis, 63
Cash discounts, 112, 114–115, 214–215
Cash flow statements, 536–540
Cash payments journal, 175
Cash receipts journal, 174–175
Cash surrender value of life insurance, 244
Cause and effect, 64–65
Certificates of deposit, 241
Certified public accountants, 11–12, 492
Changes in financial position, statement of, 517–535
    complications in preparation, 532–535
    objectives, 517
    preparation, 526–532
    uses, 519–522
Changes in resources and obligations, 17
Closing, 140–145
COBOL, 183
Collections in advance, 128–130
Commercial paper, 241
Common stock equivalents, 378, 384
Communication in accounting, 16–17
Comparability, 22–23, 431, 554
Comparative statements, 40
Completeness, 23
Computer, electronic, 183–187
Computer files, 184–186
Computer languages (*see* Machine languages)

Computer programs, 183–184
Computerized data processing, 182–187
Computers, 183–187 (*see also* Data processing)
Concepts of financial accounting, 80–82
Conservatism in accounting, 243, 506
Consigned goods, 273
Consistency, 506
Consolidated statements, 405–419
    balance sheet, 407–417
    criteria, 406–407
    income statement, 417–418
    limitations, 419
Consolidation:
    after date of acquisition, 415–416
    date of acquisition, 407–415
Contingent liability on notes, 224
Contributed capital, 42–43
Control:
    cash, 206–209
    human aspects, 344–345
    inventory, 291–292
    purchases, 343–345
    sales, 226–227
Control account, 178–179
Conventions of accounting, 506–507
Convertible bonds, 352
Convertible preferred, 377–378
Copyrights, 320
Corporate charter, 375
Corporate equities (*see* Stockholders' equity)
Corporate income, 383–385
Corporation versus partnership, 442–443
Corporations, 15–16
    issuance of stock, 379–382
    shareholders' rights, 375–377
    subsequent operations, 383–391
Cost:
    classification, 70–72
    expiration, 67–68
    of goods sold, 70–71
    incurrence, 66
    stages of, 66–68
    transformation, 66–67
    valuation, 34–37
Cost Accounting Standards Board, 495
Cost allocation principle, 64–65
Cost principle, 35, 49
Coupon bonds, 353
CPA, 11–12, 492

Credit, 98
    terms, 214–215
Credit cards, 112
Creditor analysis, 564–567
Cross-referencing, journals, 106–110
Current assets, defined, 40
Current liabilities, defined, 42
Current ratio, 43, 564–565

Data processing, defined, 168–169
Data processing systems:
    electronic, 182–187
    manual, 169–182
    on-line, 186–187
Debenture bonds, 352
Debit, 98
Declaration of dividends, 385
Declining-balance depreciation method, 313–314
Deferred income taxes, 364–365
Depletion, 309–310
Depreciation, 132–134
    accelerated methods, 312–314
    corrections, 327–328
    defined, 304
    guideline lives, 504
    and inflation, 326–327
    and matching, 324–325
    and reality, 325–326
Depreciation methods, 311–317
    comparison of, 315–317
    declining balance, 313–314
    service hours, 396
    straight-line, 311–312
    sum-of-the-years'-digits, 312–313
    units of production, 315
Development of accounting, 4–7
Direct matching principle, 64
Disclosure, 24
Discount on bonds, 354
Discounted cash flows, 36, 456–458
Discounting of notes, 217–218, 222–224, 346, 348
Discounts, cash, 112, 114–115, 214–215, 341–343
Dividend yield, 538
Dividends, 385–388 ✓
Dividends payable, 361 ✓
Doctrines, 506–507
Double entry, 32, 99
Drawing account, 430

Earnings per share, 383–385, 395–396, 559

Index

Economic entity, 405
Economic obligations, 17
Economic resources, 17
Effective-interest amortization, 249–252
Electronic data processing, 182–187
Emphasis on income (convention), 506
Enterprise, 14
Entity concept, 49, 80, 405
Environment and financial accounting, 501–502, 503
Equities, corporate, 38
Equity method, 246, 415
Estimated liabilities, 361, 365
Events, 17
Evolution of accounting, 4–7
Expense classification, 70–72
Expense, operating, 72
Expense recognition, 64–65
Expenses:
 defined, 63
 recognition principles, 64–65
External events, 95
Extraordinary items, 65, 72–73, 384
Extraordinary repairs, 308

Fair value in stock dividends, 387
FICA, 359–360
FIFO, 278–280
Financial accounting:
 defined, 29
 purpose, 19
Financial Accounting Standards Board, 6, 20, 494, 496–497
Financial accounting theory, summary of, 504–508
Financial position, statement of, 29–48
 classifications, 38–43
 content, 44–48
 function, 29
 illustrated, 39–40
 interpretation, 43–44
 preparation, 44–48
Financial reports, 18–19
Financial statement analysis, 549–569
Financial statement preparation, 111, 138–140
Financial statements, 18
Finished goods inventory, 272
First-in, first-out inventory method, 278–280
Fixed assets (*see* Depletion; Depreciation; Plant and equipment)

FOB terms, 210
Footnotes to financial statements, 29–30
FORTRAN, 183
Freight costs, 273–274
Full disclosure, 24
Function of accounting, 19, 498–501
Funds, 518–519
Funds statement (*see* Changes in financial position, statement of)

General journal, 104–106
General price-level changes, 454–455
 accounting for, 466–475
General purpose financial information, 18, 505
Generally accepted accounting principles, 487 (*see also* Principles of accounting)
Going concern, 35–36, 49, 80, 505
Goods in process, 272
Goodwill, 317–319
 from consolidation, 410–411
 partnership, 436–437, 441
Governmental and nonprofit organizations, 10
Gross margin, 73
Guaranteed bonds, 352
Guarantees, 365

Historical cost (*see also* Cost principle)
 limitations, 453–454
Historical influences, 4–7, 490–496
Holding gain or loss, 460–461

Immediate recognition principle, 65
Incidental revenues and expenses, 72
Income, 14, 61
 and capital maintenance, 463–464
Income statement, 61–77
 classified, 69–75
 consolidated, 417–418
 defined, 61
Income tax liability, 361
Incremental analysis, 557–558
Inflation:
 and depreciation, 326–327
 and historical cost, 491–492
 and theory, 491–493

Initial recording, 505
Input/output units, 183
Inputs, 94, 168–169
Installment basis, 63
Intangibles, 41–42, 305, 317–321
Intercompany transactions, 417
Interest computations, 219–222
 accruals, 220–221
Interested parties, 484–490
 creditors, 485
 government, 485
 management, 485
 owners and investors, 486
 public, 486
Internal control, 206–207 (*see also* Control)
Internal events, 95–96
Interperiod income tax allocation, 361–365
Inventory, 135–138, 272–295
 adjustments of cost, 287–288
 assumed cost flows, 277–284
 comparison of methods, 282–284
 control, 291–292
 cost of items, 273–274
 defined, 272
 errors, 289–291
 FIFO, 278–280
 items included in, 272–273
 LIFO, 280–281
 market valuations, 288–289
 methods, 276–284
 methods and changing prices, 286–287
 methods and reality, 284–286
 periodic, 113, 136–138
 perpetual, 275–276, 293–295
 turnover, 563
 types, 272
 weighted average, 281–282
Investment in subsidiary, 414–416
 cost method, 414–415
 equity method, 415
Investments, 41, 239 (*see also* Long-term investments; Temporary investments)
Investments, in affiliated companies, 245–246
Investors' decisions, 549–551
Investors' interest in accounting reports, 9–10

Journal, 104–106, 171–178
Judgment, application of, 507

Language of business, 16–17

635

Index

Last-in, first-out inventory method, 280–281
Lease obligations, 350–352
Ledger, 97–98
   account, 98
   subsidiary, 178–182
Legal capital, 379
Leverage, 558–559
Liabilities:
   current, 42, 340
   defined, 37, 340
   long-term, 42, 346
   other, 358–365
   recognition, 37
   short-term, 340
Life insurance, cash surrender value of, 244
LIFO, 280–281
Litigation, 496
Long-term investments, 244–252
   affiliated companies, 245–246
   bond premium or discount, 246–252
   bonds, 246–252
   stocks, 245–246
   valuation, 244–245, 252
Long-term liabilities, 42
Long-term receivables and payables, 259–261
Long-term unexpired costs, 303–305. (*See also* Plant and equipment)
Losses, 65
Lower of cost or market method:
   inventories, 288–289
   investments, 243–244

Machine languages, 183
   COBOL, 183
   Fortran, 183
Management's interest in accounting reports, 9
Market value, 36–37
Marketable securities (*see* Temporary investments)
Master file, 184–186
Matching, 64, 324–325
Materiality, 507
Measurement, 34–37, 80
Memory, computer, 183–184
Merchandise inventory (*see* Inventory)
Merchandising transactions, 111–115
Mini computer, 183
Minority interest, 406, 412
Monetary assets:
   defined, 204–205
   sources, 205
   valuation, 205
Monetary items, 466–467
Money measurement, 80
Mortgage bonds, 352
Mortgage liabilities, 349–350
Multi-columnar journal, 172

Natural resources, 304, 309–310
Net book value, plant and equipment, 41
Net income, 61
Net realizable value, 458–459
Neutrality, 22
Nominal accounts, 140
Nonmonetary items, 466–468
No-par value stock, 378–379
Normal operating cycle, 40
Notes payable, 345–346
   long-term, 347–349
      discounting, 348
   short-term, 345–346
      discounting, 346
Notes receivable, 215–224
   contingent liability on, 224
   discounting:
      of interest-bearing notes, 222–224
      of non-interest-bearing notes, 217–218
   interest-bearing, 218–220
   maturity dates, 219–220
   terms, 219–220
NSF checks, 231

Objectives of accounting, 19–25, 498–501
Objectives of financial accounting, 19–25
   achievement, 24–25
   FASB conclusions, 500–501
   general, 498–499
   1973 report, 499
   qualitative, 20–23, 499
   summary, 504–505
Objectivity of historical cost, 36, 454
Obligations, 17
On-line processing, 186–187
OPEC, 550
Operating cycle, 40
Operating expenses, 72
Operating gains, 460–461
Operating performance analysis, 551–561
Operations and resources, 524–526
Organization costs, 320
Other revenues and expenses, 72

Outputs, 93–94
Owners' equity, defined, 38
Owners' equity to debt ratio, 566
Owners' interest in accounting reports, 9

Pacioli, Fr. Luca, 5
Paid-in capital (*see* Contributed capital)
Par value stock, 378–379
Parent-subsidiary relationship, 406
Partnerships, 15, 432–443
   admission of new partners, 435–438
   agreement, 432
   converting to corporation, 440–441
   dissolution of, 438–440
   division of profits, 432–434
   schedule of partners' capital, 434
   theoretical issues, 441–442
   versus corporation, 442–443
Patents, 319–320
Pegboard accounting, 182
Pension obligations, 350
People in accounting, 11–13
Percent of sales uncollected, 564
Percentage analysis, 551–554
Performance analysis, 551–561
Periodic inventory method, 113, 136–138
Periodicity, 80
Perpetual inventory method, 275–276, 293–295
Petty cash, 209–210
Plant and equipment, 41, 303–317, 321–330 (*see also* Depletion; Depreciation)
   disposition of, 321–324
   measurement of cost, 305–308
   presentation in statements, 328–329
   problems, 324–328
   subsequent treatment of, 308–317
   trades, 322–323
Pooling of interest, 420–422
Position (*see* Financial position, statement of)
Posting, 106–110, 175–177
Postulates of accounting, 493, 505
Predictive ability, 464
Preferred stock, 377–378
Premium on bonds, 353–354
Prepaid expenses, 130–132
Present value, 254–264
Price-earnings ratio, 561

636

Index

Price-level indexes, 466
Principles of accounting, 80–81, 487, 493
   Accounting Research Study No. 3, 493
   historical development, 490–496
   list of, 505–506
Procedures of accounting, 507–508
Processing, 94–95
Production method, revenue, 63
Programming, 183–184
Property, plant, and equipment (*see* Plant and equipment)
Public accountants, 11–12
Public opinion and accounting principles, 486
Public's interest in accounting reports, 10
Purchase controls, 343–345
Purchase of business, 419–420, 422
Purchases, 113–114
Purchases journal, 174
Purchases, recording at net, 341–343
Purpose of financial accounting, 19, 504
Purposes of accounting, 19, 498–501

Quick assets, 565

Rate of return analysis, 556–559
Real accounts, 140
Realization of revenue, 62–63
Realization principle, 62–63
Real-time data processing (*see* On-line processing)
Recording transactions, 97–102
Relevance of financial statements, 20–21
Rental obligations, 350–352
Repairs, 308
Replacement cost valuation, 459–462
Research and development costs, 320
Residual interest, 17
Resources, economic, 17
Resources (funds), 518–519
Resources provided and applied, 522–526
Restatement procedures, price-level accounting, 466–474
Retained earnings:
   defined, 43, 77
   restrictions, 388–389
   statement of, 77, 396
Return on investment, 560–561
Returns and allowances, 112, 114
Revenue:
   defined, 61
   exceptions to sale basis, 63
   operating, 70
   other, 72
   realization (recognition), 62–63, 224–225
   sources, 61–62
   unearned, 128–130
Revenue expenditures, 308
Rights of stockholders, 375–377
Rights, stock, 390
Role of accounting, 7–10
Rules of accounting, 507

Sales controls, 226–227
Sales journal, 173–174
Sales, percent of uncollected, 564
Securities and Exchange Commission (SEC), 491, 492–493, 495, 497
Serial bonds, 352
Shareholders' rights, 375–376
Short-term unexpired costs, 271–272
Single-step income statement, 69–70
Smoothing of periodic income (convention), 507
Social role of accounting, 10
Social security taxes, 359–361
Sole proprietorships, 15, 429–432
Source documents, 168–169
Sources of working capital, 522–523
Specialized journals, 172–178
Specific identification inventory method, 277
Specific price changes, 454–455
Stable measuring unit, 36, 49, 80
Stages of costs, 66–68
Standards of accounting, 507
   (*see also* Principles of accounting)
Stated value (stock), 379
Statement analysis, 549–569
Statement of Basic Accounting Theory, American Accounting Association, 495
Statement of financial position (*see* Financial position, statement of)
Stock (*see* Capital stock)
Stock dividends, 387–388
Stock market, 549–550

Stock options, 389–390
Stock rights, 390
Stock splits, 389
Stockholders' equity, 42–43, 375–398 (*see also* Capital stock; Retained earnings)
Straight-line depreciation, 311–312
Subscriptions receivable, 382
Subsidiary companies, 406 (*see also* Investment in subsidiary)
Subsidiary ledgers, 178–182
Substance over form (convention), 507
Sum-of-the-years'-digits depreciation, 312–313
Systematic and rational allocation (expense recognition), 64–65

Tax allocation, 361–365
Taxable income of sole proprietorship, 430–432
Taxes and accounting principles, 491–493
Temporary investments, 239–244
  acquisition, 241–242
  disposition of, 242
  types of, 240–241
  valuation of, 243–244
Term bonds, 336
Theory framework, 502–503
Timeliness, 22
Times interest earned, 566–567
Trades of plant and equipment assets, 322–323
Transaction file, 184–186
Transactions, 34
  defined, 95
  external events, 95
  internal events, 95–96
  revenue and expense, 136–138
  types of, 96–97
Treasury bills, 240
Treasury stock, 388–389, 390–391
Trend analysis, 553–554
Trial balance, 110–111, 145
Turnover ratios, 563

Understandability, 21
Unearned revenues, 128–130
Unemployment compensation tax, 359–361
Unexpired costs, 271–272
  long-term, 303–305

637

Index

Unexpired costs (*continued*)
 short-term, 271–272
Unit of measure (principle), 80
Unlimited liability, 442
Uses of working capital, 523–524

Valuation (*see* Asset valuation)

Value of the business entity, 462–463
Verifiability, 21–22
Verifiability of historical cost, 36, 454

Warrants, stock, 390

Warranty obligations, 365
Weighted average inventory method, 281–282
Withholding taxes, 359–361
Working capital, 43, 565–566
Working capital changes, schedule of, 528
Worksheet, 147–154

CHECKLIST OF KEY FIGURES

1-24	Total assets $42,400	7-18	(d) $506.80; (e) $518.05
2-21	Total assets $40,000	7-19	(b) $270
2-22	Total assets $21,200	7-23	Adjusted balance $1,245.76
2-24	Total assets $298.4		
2-25	Stockholders' equity, Year 2, $89.6	8-11	December 31 interest $878
2-26	Working capital $71,500,000	8-12	Loss on market decline $600
2-28	Total assets $210,900	8-13	Gain on sale $450
2-29	Total assets $210,000	8-15	$839.95
2-30	Total assets $8,300	8-17	$1,126.55
2-31	Total assets $126,000; cash $17,000	8-18	(a) Interest earned $72.74; (b) $74.02
2-32	Total assets $98,000	8-20	June 30 interest revenue $6,508
		8-23	(b) Interest earned $611.70; (d) Interest earned $620.37
3-11	Net income $14,000	8-25	(a) $60,000 long-term
3-13	Net income $1,300	8-26	December 31 interest $400 − 83 = $317
3-16	Cost of goods sold $36.1		
3-18	Net income $191,500		
3-19	Total assets $72,200	9-16	Inventory $25,419
3-20	Current assets $104.3	9-17	(a) $25,650; (b) $25,945
3-22	Sources $93.3	9-20	(c) $49,000; (d) $45,700
3-23	Sources $50.0	9-21	$1,860
		9-22	Difference in income $180
4-14	Cash balance $15,300	9-24	(a) Ending balance $8,800; (b) $8,000
4-17	Cash balance $3,840 CR	9-27	Year 3: FIFO $60; LIFO $40
4-18	Total $42,100	9-28	Cost of sales, Year 2: FIFO $110; LIFO $120
4-23	Total assets $31,275	9-29	(a) Year 1 income $48,600, cash $36,300; (b) Year 1 income $42,600; cash $43,300
4-25	Trial balance $54,225; total assets $52,600		
4-28	Trial balance $84,320; cash $10,290; income $2,770		
		10-18	(b) $15,429; (d) $19,333
5-17	Unearned subscriptions $3,250,000	10-19	June 20 new asset $10,204
5-18	(a) $60,000; (c) $49,300	10-26	(a) Truck cost $8,295; (b) $1,299
5-20	(b) $720 (c); allowance $800	10-27	(b) $2,852
5-21	Depreciation $1,700	10-29	Gain on sale $550
5-23	Rent expense $1,350	10-30	(a) Gain $39,200; (b) new machine $18,058; (c) new equipment $11,613
5-24	(b) $1,080	10-32	New truck $5,720
5-28	(a) Expense $2,200; (b) balance $3,800	10-33	(a5) $10,000; (b) $12,188
5-32	Income $17,100; total assets $96,525	10-34	(a) $8,400; (b) $38,000
5-33	Income statement debit $352; credit $381	10-37	(a) Income $41,000; (c) goodwill $93,000
5-34	Total assets $175	10-38	(a) Year 1 income $2,100, cash $15,050; (b) Year 1 income $1,050, cash $16,025
5-36	Income statement debit $209,042; credit $232,619		
5-37	Corrected income $(462,000)		
		11-14	December 31 interest $39.45 + $49.31
6-13	Cash credit $35,380	11-15	$4,958.40
6-14	Cash debit $62,960	11-19	September 1 interest $31,000
6-17	Corrected total $2,085.17	11-20	(b) Expense $885
6-21	Cash Dr. $24,819; receivables $875	11-21	(b) Expense $108,514
6-23	Cash Dr. $3,138; Cr. $2,287	11-22	(a) Net paid $131.30
6-24	Cash Dr. $17,369; Cr. $9,579	11-23	Tax in Year 1: (a) $20,000; (b) $60,000
6-26	Cash Dr. $11,275; Cr. $7,650; income $8,900	11-24	September 28 interest $88.76
7-14	Adjusted balance $1,880		
7-16	(a) $562.50; (b) $460.00		
7-17	(d) $26.63; (e) $14.14		

11-26	December 31 interest expense $291	15-17	(a) Year 3 gain $30,000; (b) Year 3 gain $22,174
11-29	Total net pay $622.48	15-19	(a) Holding gain $3,500
12-12	Total $1,568,000	15-21	Net income $730; total assets $11,380
12-16	July 15 retained earnings debit $104,000	15-22	Total assets $15,310; Net income $1,890
12-17	$3,104,000	15-24	Total assets $4,379
12-20	(b) Retained earnings $1,323,000		
12-21	Year 5 preferred dividends $27,000	16-24	(a) $90,000; (b) $120,000
12-23	Total $4,324,140	16-29	Loss for year $780,000
12-24	(c) Total $3,550,000		
12-25	(b) Retained earnings, Year 5, $459,600; (c) total $7,132,600	17-15	(b) To acquire goodwill $33,000
		17-16	From operations $30,000
13-19	Goodwill $60,000	17-17	Total provided $16,500
13-20	(b) Goodwill $920,000	17-18	$968,000
13-21	(c) Goodwill $(22,000)	17-20	From operations $11,500
13-22	Goodwill $10,000	17-22	From operations $62,500
13-23	Goodwill $31,000	17-23	From operations $3,300
13-25	Net income $246,200	17-24	$239,000
13-28	Total assets $1,125,000	17-26	Disbursements for merchandise $129,000; for expenses $63,000
13-29	Total assets $1,160,000		
14-20	Cash to Larson $23,000	18-13	11.3%
14-21	Restated income $(5,000)	18-14	(b) $42,857
14-22	Adjusted rate of return for Hammer: 10%	18-15	$428,600
		18-16	Total turnover 10.93
14-23	(b) Andrews $6,500	18-17	(d) 61 days
14-24	Loss for year $(9,600)	18-18	(c) 8.9
14-27	Stock to Brown $70,000	18-19	$44.44 at 12%
15-11	Restated Year 1 salary $21,250	18-22	(g) 18.9%
15-12	(b) Gain $6,400	18-24	(e) 1.13; (f) 11.3%; (g) 12.4%
15-15	Depreciation $3,000	18-25	(e) Cash to be borrowed $17,500
15-16	Cost of goods sold $297,811		